AF898575

Urban Composite Development Index for 17 Shandong Cities: Ranking and Simulation Analysis Based on China's Five Development Concepts

NUS National University of Singapore

LKY Lee Kuan Yew School of Public Policy
ASIA COMPETITIVENESS INSTITUTE

In 2016 and 2017, ACI was ranked 13th globally, 2nd in Asia and 1st in Singapore amongst 90 think tanks worldwide under the "Best University Affiliated Think Tank" category by the Think Tanks and Civil Societies Program at the University of Pennsylvania, USA.

About ACI

The Asia Competitiveness Institute (ACI) was established in August 2006 as a research centre at the Lee Kuan Yew School of Public Policy (LKYSPP), National University of Singapore (NUS). It aims to build the intellectual leadership and network for understanding and developing competitiveness in the Asia region. ACI seeks to contribute to the enhancement of inclusive growth, living standards and institutional governance through competitiveness research on sub-national economies in Asia. It identifies mitigating issues and challenges for potential public policy interventions through close collaboration with regional governments, business corporations, policy think-tanks and academics. ACI's three key research pillars include (i) sub-national economies level competitiveness analysis and city-level liveability analysis, (ii) firm-level competitiveness analysis in 16 Asia economies, and (iii) Singapore's long-term growth strategies and public policy analysis.

ACI's value propositions may be encapsulated in its acronym:
Analytical inputs to initiate policies for policy-makers and business leaders in Asia
Capacity building to enable others through improvement in productivity and efficiency
Intellectual leadership to create pragmatic models of competitiveness and inclusive growth

The institute's core research competencies can also be encapsulated in this acronym describing our evidence-based assessments conducted on public policies for **A**SEAN in the context of the rise of **C**hina and **I**ndia.

Vision and Mission

- ACI's over-arching vision is to build up its research credibility with policy impact, contributing as a professional, world-class think-tank.
- ACI's mission is to establish our niche as a leading policy think-tank by identifying competitiveness trends, opportunities and challenges, as well as promoting competition and synergising complementarities amongst Asian economies and business corporations.
- ACI endeavours to articulate sound recommendations, entice discourse, and shape agenda in the arena of public policy amongst Asian governments.
- ACI undertakes evidence-based analysis of public policy issues and decisions, in order to provide assessment of their effectiveness as well as economic and societal impact.

Research Initiatives and Collaborations

I. Identify trends of competitiveness and policy analysis on trade and investment of ASEAN, within the regional context of competition and complementarities with China and India.

II. Identify competitive strengths and conduct policy analysis on Singapore within the context of regional economies with international benchmarking.

III. We are regularly releasing three indices on liveability ranking including 64 Global Cities, 100 Greater China Cities and 17 Shandong Cities.

IV. We have established an Ease of Doing Business Index on Attractiveness to Investors, Business Friendliness and Competitive Policies for 21 sub-national economies of India and 33 sub-national economies of Indonesia.

V. We have signed Memoranda of Understanding with The World Bank (2015), SPRING Singapore (2014) and European Central Bank (2014). The Memorandum of Understanding between The World Bank and National University of Singapore, coordinated through ACI, was signed in 2016.

VI. We have signed Memoranda of Understanding with various institutions in Greater China economies, including Shanghai Academy of Social Sciences (2016), Shandong Academy of Social Sciences (2015), Chongqing Municipal People's Government (2015), China Institute for Reform and Development, Haikou (2015), Counsellors' Office of the People's Government of Guangdong Province (LOI, 2014) and Chung-Hua Institution for Economic Research, Taiwan (2015).

VII. We have signed Memoranda of Understanding with six Chief Ministers' Offices in Andhra Pradesh (2015 & 2017), Bihar (2015), Chhattisgarh (2015), Madhya Pradesh (2015), Odisha (2015) and Punjab (2015).

VIII. We have signed Memoranda of Understanding with Committee for Acceleration of Priority Infrastructure Delivery at Coordinating Ministry for Economic Affairs, Indonesia (2016), Indonesia Investment Coordinating Board (2014), Indonesian Agency for Agricultural Research and Development at Ministry of Agriculture (2014), Indonesian President's Delivery Unit for Developing Monitoring and Oversight (2013) and Employer's Association of Indonesia (2013).

IX. We have signed Memoranda of Understanding with ASEAN think-tanks and institutions, including Vietnam Chamber of Commerce and Industry (2016), Centre for Strategic and International Studies, Indonesia (2015), Institute of Strategic & International Studies, Malaysia (2015), Philippine Institute for Development Studies (2015), Thailand Development Research Institute (2015) and Central Institute for Economic Management, Vietnam (2015).

About ACI's Research Pillars

ACI has consciously engaged in economic research that has significant relevance to Singapore and the Asian region. Over the years, ACI has focused on our expertise in quantitative competitiveness analysis and simulation, spinning off volumes of research output in the applications of our methodology and regional insight. At this stage, ACI has identified three core research pillars that will guide and define its research efforts moving forward. The three research pillars are as follows:

Pillar I. Sub-national Economies Competitiveness Analysis

ACI engages in systematic and methodical competitiveness analyses of the *sub-national economies* by using an evidence-based, empirical approach involving a comprehensive list of relevant indicators, which are categorised under multiple layers called the 'environments'. A number of our projects, including competitiveness analyses of Greater China, ASEAN-10, India, and Indonesia, as well as other thematic research projects, were conducted by adopting this common methodology, with potential variations in the specific environments and indicators. ACI's competitiveness analysis of Asian economies goes beyond the usual ranking to offer constructive policy recommendations on how individual member states can improve their rankings vis-à-vis their sub-national or regional peers through the application of the 'what-if' simulation, which provides the projected improvements of each state's ranking whereby the bottom one-fifth of its indicators are enhanced.

Pillar II. Micro-based Firm Level Competitiveness Analysis

Micro-based firm level competitiveness analysis is ACI's second research pillar that has been developed in view of the intrinsic importance of firm-level competitiveness in terms of productivity, efficiency, and governance. In the context of globalisation, mobility of economic activities, and blurring of borders, an understanding of the determinants and dynamics of firm-level competitiveness is paramount, in order for policy makers to make adjustments and prepare their industries for an increasingly competitive economic landscape. To this end, ACI has partnered with the European Central Bank to carry out research in this area, possessing a solid foundation in firm-level productivity research in the form of European Competitiveness Network database and methodology. ACI envisaged the expansion of CompNet into Asia, thereby pioneering the Asia CompNet research network encompassing 16 economies in Asia.

Pillar III. Singapore's Long-term Economic Growth Strategies and Public Policies Analysis

The third and imminent research pillar focuses on Singapore's long-term economic growth strategies in the context of changing circumstances, future trends, and emerging opportunities for Singapore in the decades ahead. In particular, ACI will take on the task of critically examining Singapore's public policy strengths and areas of improvement by assessing policy successes of the past, identifying new issues to address and the current policy gaps, through a systematic and evidence-based research inquiry using quantitative methodology and empirical data, leveraging on our network of policy experts.

Founding Patron and International Advisory Panel

Founding Patron

Mr George Yeo
Visiting Scholar, Lee Kuan Yew School of Public Policy, National University of Singapore & Former Minister of Foreign Affairs, Singapore

International Advisory Panel

Co-Chairs:

Professor Michael Porter (2006-2010)
Bishop William Lawrence University Professor

Ms Marjorie Yang (2006-2012)
Chairman, Esquel Group

Members:

Professor Kishore Mahbubani
Dean, Lee Kuan Yew School of Public Policy, National University of Singapore

Dr Kuntoro Mangkusubroto
Head, President's Delivery Unit for Developing Monitoring and Oversight (UKP4), Indonesia

Mr Narayana Murthy
Chairman, Infosys Technologies Limited

Mr Philip Yeo
Chairman, SPRING Singapore

Mr Loh Khum Yean
Permanent Secretary, Ministry of Trade and Industry

Ms Yong Ying-I
Permanent Secretary, Public Service Division

Professor Chan Kam Leung Alan
Dean, College of Humanities, Arts and Social Sciences, Nanyang Technological University

Asia Competitiveness Institute

Co-Directors:

Associate Professor Tan Khee Giap (2011 till now)
Professor Tan Kong Yam (2011 till now)

Urban Composite Development Index for 17 Shandong Cities: Ranking and Simulation Analysis Based on China's Five Development Concepts

Tan Khee Giap
Co-Director, Asia Competitiveness Institute
Lee Kuan Yew School of Public Policy, National University of Singapore

Zhang Xuyao
Research Fellow, Asia Competitiveness Institute
Lee Kuan Yew School of Public Policy, National University of Singapore

Lim Tao Oei
Research Assistant, Asia Competitiveness Institute
Lee Kuan Yew School of Public Policy, National University of Singapore

Song Lin
Research Assistant, Asia Competitiveness Institute
Lee Kuan Yew School of Public Policy, National University of Singapore

Reviewers

Yang Jinwei
Vice President, Shandong Academy of Social Sciences,
People's Republic of China

Li Wei
Deputy Director, Institute of Applied Economics,
Shanghai Academy of Social Sciences, People's Republic of China

Wang Kejian
Chairman, Urban Construction Press, People's Republic of China

Lee Kuan Yew School of Public Policy
Asia Competitiveness Institute

NUS National University of Singapore

World Scientific

Published by

World Scientific Publishing Co. Pte. Ltd.
5 Toh Tuck Link, Singapore 596224
USA office: 27 Warren Street, Suite 401-402, Hackensack, NJ 07601
UK office: 57 Shelton Street, Covent Garden, London WC2H 9HE

British Library Cataloguing-in-Publication Data
A catalogue record for this book is available from the British Library.

URBAN COMPOSITE DEVELOPMENT INDEX FOR 17 SHANDONG CITIES
Ranking and Simulation Analysis Based on China's Five Development Concepts

Copyright © 2018 by World Scientific Publishing Co. Pte. Ltd.

All rights reserved. This book, or parts thereof, may not be reproduced in any form or by any means, electronic or mechanical, including photocopying, recording or any information storage and retrieval system now known or to be invented, without written permission from the publisher.

For photocopying of material in this volume, please pay a copying fee through the Copyright Clearance Center, Inc., 222 Rosewood Drive, Danvers, MA 01923, USA. In this case permission to photocopy is not required from the publisher.

ISBN 978-981-3272-33-0

Desk Editor: Jiang Yulin

Typeset by Stallion Press
Email: enquiries@stallionpress.com

Printed in Singapore

Contents

Foreword

The Asia Competitiveness Institute (ACI) at the Lee Kuan Yew School of Public Policy, National University of Singapore, has been expanding its city-liveability series since the inception of the Global Liveable Cities Index project in 2012. The series grew to include 100 Greater China cities in 2015. In this book, ACI does an in-depth analysis of 17 cities in China's Shandong Province.

The developing world is urbanising at a rapid rate because of improved transportation and communication. From slightly over half today, the world will be two thirds urbanised by 2050. The quality of urbanisation is critical. Many factors are involved including physical infrastructure, law and order, social services, education and a sense of equity. All of them turn on good governance, which is inseparable from the history of a community and its politics and culture. Economic policies are only as effective as social and political conditions allow them to be.

China's rapid development in the last 40 years cannot be separated from its urbanisation experience. During that period, China's urbanisation has doubled. The challenges have been enormous. It is a story of remarkable successes and failures. For example, no other major country has tackled urban growth with as much planning and organisation. But heater-shelter economic growth also led to severe social inequality, asset bubbles and frightful pollution of air, land and water. The Chinese Government is determined to restore balance in future development. In the 13th Five Year Plan, President Xi Jinping outlined five development concepts — Innovation, Coordination, Green Development, Opening Up and Sharing — as guiding principles for China's future development.

The Urban Composite Development Index developed by ACI is custom-made for China to facilitate the analysis of its urban development by incorporating the five development concepts. Using Shapley values, which are important in cooperative game theory, ACI's methodology ensures greater objectivity in the distribution of weights for the factors that are captured in the Index. This methodological innovation is evidence-based and conceptually powerful. It helps to overcome the main limitation of many existing indices, which is the subjective weighting of factors. ACI is therefore using it for other indices as well like the Global Liveable Cities Index.

"Urban Composite Development Index for 17 cities of Shandong" is a valuable addition to ACI's Cities Liveability and Urbanisation Series. The book analyses urban liveability as part of overall urban development across time and space. It should be a useful guide for Chinese policymakers grappling with the challenges of sustainable development and for those seeking to learn from China's experience.

George Yeo
Visiting Scholar
Lee Kuan Yew School of Public Policy,
National University of Singapore
and Former Minister of Foreign Affairs,
Republic of Singapore

Preface

Asia Competitiveness Institute (ACI) at Lee Kuan Yew School of Public Policy (LKYSPP, National University of Singapore (NUS) has invested great effort studying the liveability of cities. Prior to this book, ACI published two other books under the Cities Liveability and Urbanisation Series entitled "Ranking the Liveability of the World's Major Cities: The Global Liveable Cities Index" in 2012, and "Greater China Liveable Cities Index: Ranking Analysis, Simulation and Policy Evaluation" in 2015. In addition, four journal articles and two editorial-opinions related to the theme were published.

Urbanisation is a rising global phenomenon. According to the United Nations, more than 50 percent of the global population is currently living in urban areas, and more importantly, the ratio is set to rise to over 65 percent by 2050. With China being one of the most populous and fastest growing economies in the world, where approximately 292 million Chinese people are expected to migrate to urban areas in China by 2050, it is critical to understand the challenges it faces at this high speed of urbanisation. In addition, the focus on Shandong is deliberate as it forms a significant part of China. Shandong is the third largest province by land area in China at 158,000 square kilometres, with the second largest resident population of 98,470,000 and third largest Gross Regional Domestic Product RMB 6.3 trillion in 2015. It is in this context that the ACI's liveability research and publications assumes immense significance and value as it aims to inform policymakers of the various strengths and weaknesses in their respective 17 cities for appropriate planning and policy adjustments.

This research is also coming at a crucial time given the current challenges in urban development in China and Shandong. Rapid rise in incomes and affluence across the country have raised expectations for higher standard of living by the Chinese people. In view of these challenges, President Xi Jinping proposed Five Development Concepts, namely Innovation, Coordination, Green Development, Opening Up and Sharing in the 13th Five Year Plan. In particular, recent emphasis to tackle environmental problems were raised by President Xi to build a beautiful China at the 18th National Congress to further emphasise the importance of Green Development, and hence to tackle the environmental issues associated with rapid urbanisation. As such, ACI is actively working towards helping policymakers address these challenges and exploit opportunities.

To construct the Urban Composite Development Index (UCDI), ACI used Chinese government statistics and survey data from over 5000 ordinary residents across 17 Shandong cities. Importantly, this study deeply integrates insights from President Xi Jinping's Five Development Concepts, which will reflect Shandong's unique urban development with Chinese characteristics. The unique methodology and results were presented and endorsed by distinguished academics and professionals such as the Shandong Academy of Social Sciences at several ACI economic forums and conferences. To this end, ACI provides meaningful and precise policy recommendations that is accessible to policymakers in Shandong in this publication.

I am therefore proud to present this remarkable study on urban development in Shandong province with the confidence that the insights shared in this book will enable cities to realise their fullest development potential. I hope that readers gain a better understanding of the unique urban development perspectives, as well as the assessment of liveability in China after reading this book. Given the immense potential of this book, I look forward to future studies that extends the research to include other provinces and regions in China and beyond.

Professor Ramkishen S. Rajan
Vice-Dean (Research) and Professor
Lee Kuan Yew School of Public Policy,
National University of Singapore

Acknowledgements

The Asia Competitiveness Institute (ACI) at the Lee Kuan Yew School of Public Policy (LKYSPP), National University of Singapore (NUS) has been tracking the urban development of the world's major cities since 2012. Inspired by Xi Jinping's Five Development Concepts, ACI introduced a comprehensive urban development framework that comprises six environments, namely Scale and Quality of Economic Activities, Financial Capacity, Labour Market Flexibility and Economic Vibrancy, Good Governance, Effective Leadership and Social Stability, Technological Advancement and Innovation Capability, Public Service Standards and Quality of Life Improvement, and Resource Conditions and Environmental Protection.

Our related works on urban development of cities include two published books entitled "Ranking the Liveability of the World's Major Cities: The Global Liveable Cities Index (GLCI)", and "Greater China Liveable Cities Index: Ranking Analysis, Simulation and Policy Evaluation", four journal articles which were published in international peer-reviewed journals and two editorial opinions.

With rapid urbanisation continuing unabated on a global scale, cities have become the unit of global competition to attract talent, capital, and business investments. Urban development of cities has emerged as one of the most pertinent agenda for decision makers around the world. As such, ACI has decided to expand urban development studies from global liveability of 200 cities to China liveability of 200 cities. Furthermore, ACI pioneered research beyond China, namely at provincial level of Shandong cities in this book.

For this book, "Urban Composite Development Index for 17 Shandong Cities: Ranking and Simulation Analysis Based on China's Five Development Concepts", ACI constructed an urban composite development index for 17 cities in Shandong province on the basis of the framework of previous liveability studies conducted by ACI, to provide the readers a contextualised and updated analysis of urban development. By focusing our basis of reference on the multiple sensibilities of local residents, this book aims to provoke and facilitate peer-to-peer learning among Shandong cities.

Our research has benefited tremendously from inputs through the discussions undertaken by numerous policymakers and field experts during the 2016 Annual ACI Conference, and the Asia Economic Forum held in August 2017. We are grateful to the discussants for their effort and dedication in evaluating the study and providing constructive suggestions. We would therefore like to express our sincere gratitude to the following discussants:

Professor Yang Jinwei
Vice President, Shandong Academy of Social Sciences, People's Republic of China

Dr Li Guangjie
Director, International Economics Research Institute
Shandong Academy of Social Sciences, People's Republic of China

Dr Li Wei
Deputy Director, Institute of Applied Economics
Shanghai Academy of Social Sciences, People's Republic of China

Dr Yuan Hongying
Vice Dean
Shandong Academy of Social Sciences, People's Republic of China

Mr Wang Kejian
Chairman
Urban Construction Press, People's Republic of China

In particular, we also wish to thank Professor Kishore Mahbubani (Dean) and other colleagues at LKYSPP for their support and encouragement, which helped to make this study possible. This publication would not have been possible without the dedicated assistance by research and administrative staff at ACI. We thus note with great appreciation the espirit de corps demonstrated by the ACI's staff, which includes Sasidaran Gopalan, Luu Nguyen Trieu Duong, Diamanta Vania Lavi, Nguyen Duy, Nursyahida Binte Ahmad, Jigyasa Sharma, Leong Puey Ei, Jeremy Zhou Shida, Qian Yuwei, Tracy Cai Jiao, Yap Xin Yi, Yip Fung Yi Estelle, Nurliyana Binte Yusoff and Dewi Jelina Ayu Binte Johari.

Tan Khee Giap, Zhang Xuyao, Lim Tao Oei & Song Lin
Asia Competitiveness Institute,
Lee Kuan Yew School of Public Policy,
National University of Singapore

About the Authors

Tan Khee Giap is a Co-Director of the Asia Competitiveness Institute (ACI) and Associate Professor at the Lee Kuan Yew School of Public Policy, National University of Singapore. He is also the Chairman of the Singapore National Committee for Pacific Economic Cooperation. Upon graduating with a PhD from University of East Anglia, England, in 1987 under the Overseas Research Scheme awarded by the Committee of Vice-Chancellors and Principals of the Universities of the United Kingdom, he joined the banking sector as a treasury manager and served as secretary to the Assets and Liabilities Committee for three years, thereafter he taught at the Department of Economics and Statistics, National University of Singapore, 1990–1993. Dr Tan joined Nanyang Technological University in 1993 and was Associate Dean, Graduate Studies Office, 2007–2009.

Dr Tan has consulted extensively with the various government ministries, statutory boards and government-linked companies of Singapore government including Ministry of Finance, Ministry of Trade & Industry, Ministry of Manpower, Housing & Development Board, Civil Aviation Authority of Singapore, Singapore Tourism Board, Trade Development Board, Maritime Port Authority, Ministry of Information, Culture & Arts, Economic Development Board, Ministry of National Development, Media Development Authority, Ministry of Environment and Water Resources, Singapore Design Council, Ministry of Community Development, Youth & Sports, Singapore Press Holdings, Yayasan Mendaki, StarHub, CapitaLand and Great Eastern Life. He has also served as a consultant to international agencies such as the Asian Development Bank, Asian Development Bank Institute, United Nations Industrial Development Group, World Bank Group, World Gold Council, ASEAN Secretariat, Central Policy Unit of Hong Kong, Kerzner International, Las Vegas Sands and Marina Bay Sands.

Dr Tan is the lead author for more than 20 books, serving as journals editor and published widely in international refereed journals. He is the associate editor of the journal *Review of Pacific Basin Financial Markets and Policies* (US) and is on the editorial advisory board of the journal *Competitiveness Review* (UK). His current research interests include Cost of Living and Purchasing Power Index for World's 105 Cities, Global Liveable Cities Index, Ease of Doing Business Index and competitiveness analysis on sub-national economies of China, India, Indonesia and Association of South East Asian Nations.

Dr Tan was Deputy President of the Singapore Economic Society, 2004. He served in the 2002 Economic Review Committee (ERC), served as Chairman of the Task Force on Portable Medical Benefits (PMB), served as the Deputy Chairman of the IPS Forum for Economic Restructuring (IFER) in 2003 and served as a member of the Resource Panel of the Government Parliamentary Committee for Transport, Government Parliamentary Committee for Finance and Trade & Industry and Government Parliamentary Committee for Defence and Foreign Affairs since 2007. Dr Tan is currently an Independent Director of the publicly listed BreadTalk Group, Boustead Projects, TEE Land and Chengdu Rural Commercial Bank.

Zhang Xuyao is a Research Fellow at the Asia Competitiveness Institute at the Lee Kuan Yew School of Public Policy, National University of Singapore. Dr Zhang received his Ph.D. in Economics from NUS in 2016 and obtained his Bachelor (Honours) degree in Applied Mathematics from NUS as well in 2012. During the Ph.D. candidature, he worked as teaching assistant in conducting undergraduate tutorials, such as Microeconomics, Macroeconomics and Managerial Economics. His research focuses on Industrial Organizations, Applied Game Theory, and Public Economics. In particular, he is interested in technology transfers and anti-trust policies. He studies the optimal environmental taxation on the pollution problems in the presence of corruption. He also works on the beneficiary of research joint ventures with technology transfer. He also studies the Qualcomm's anti-trust case in China.

At ACI, he is the coordinator for the Shandong Urban Development Index project. He is also the co-coordinator for the project studying the impact of exchange rate on trade at provincial level of Mainland China. Dr Zhang is also working on the methodology of applying the concept of Shapley values to index ranking analysis. This method will subsequently serve as a robustness check to all the competitiveness ranking studies in ACI. Additional projects he is working on include the construction of the Special Economic Development Area index and the Infrastructure index.

Lim Tao Oei is a Research Assistant at the Asia Competitiveness Institute (ACI), Lee Kuan Yew School of Public Policy (LKYSPP), National University of Singapore (NUS). He graduated from NUS with a Bachelor of Social Sciences with Honours (Distinction) in Economics, and specialized in Applied and Policy Economics. At ACI, Tao Oei is the project coordinator for the research projects on Urban Development Composite Index for 17 Shandong Cities: Ranking and Simulation Analysis, as well as the Greater China Liveable Cities Index. In addition, he is currently engaged in the update of the Global Liveable Cities Index. His research interests include ASEAN economics, labour economics and behavioural economics.

Song Lin is a Research Assistant at the Asia Competitiveness Institute (ACI), Lee Kuan Yew School of Public Policy (LKYSPP), National University of Singapore (NUS). He graduated from the Bachelor of Environmental Studies (BES) programme at NUS with Honours (Distinction). In his capacity as a research assistant, Song Lin is coordinating with Shandong Academy of Social Sciences on the Shandong city-level competitiveness project. He is also involved in the Greater China competitiveness project, liveable city project and OUE-ACI Business Case Study project. His personal research interests are sustainable urbanisation, renewable energy and urban mobility.

List of Abbreviations

ACI	Asia Competitiveness Institute
ASCI	Arcadis Sustainable Cities Index
BCE	Before Common Era
BRI	Belt and Road Initiative
CASS	Chinese Academy of Social Sciences
CE	Common Era
CICC	China Institute of City Competitiveness
COD	Chemical Oxygen Demand
CPI	Consumer Price Index
EIU	Economist Intelligence Unit
FCLMFEV	Financial Capacity, Labour Market Flexibility and Economic Vibrancy
GCLCI	Greater China Liveable Cities Index
GDP	Gross Domestic Product
GGELSS	Good Governance, Effective Leadership and Social Stability
GLCI	Global Liveable Cities Index
GPCI	Global Power City Index
GRDP	Gross Regional Domestic Product
IUD	Urban International Institute for Urban Development
LKYSPP	Lee Kuan Yew School of Public Policy
NO-x	Nitrogen Oxides
NUS	National University of Singapore
PPI	Producer Price Index
PSSQLI	Public Service Standards and Quality of Life Improvement
QLCC	Quality of Life in Chinese Cities
R&D	Research and Development
RCEP	Resource Conditions and Environmental Protection
RMB	Renminbi
RPI	Retail Price Index
SCSC	Sustainable City Study in China
SEZ	Special Economic Zone

SO2	Sulphur Dioxide
SQEA	Scale and Quality of Economic Activities
TAIC	Technological Advancement and Innovation Capability
UCDI	Urban Composite Development Index
UN Habitat	United Nations Human Settlements Programme
UNESCO	United Nations Educational, Scientific and Cultural Organisation
US $	United States Dollar

List of Tables and Figures

Chapter 9

Chapter 10

Chapter 11

Chapter 12

Chapter 13

Chapter 14

Chapter 15

Chapter 16

Chapter 17

Chapter 18

Chapter 19

Chapter 20

Part III

Chapter 21

Part I
Overview of the Urban Composite Development Index for 17 Cities in Shandong Province

Chapter 1

Introductory Notes: Urbanisation and Balanced Development

Urban areas are in general locations characterised by high population density, good infrastructure and public amenities. Their attraction is undeniable as they promise higher standards of living and quality of life. On the other hand, surging urban populations may overwhelm the very infrastructure they promise to provide, leading to other related problems including urban crime and poverty. In an increasingly interconnected world, urbanisation via rural to urban migration has progressively captured the attention of policymakers, as it requires effective and careful management in order to exploit opportunities while mitigating its risks.

1.1 Global Urbanisation Trends and Challenges

The global population and urbanisation rate are rising. According to the 2017 revision of the World Population Prospects, the global population currently stands at an estimated 7.6 billion people as of mid-2017 and is expected to grow at a rate of 1.1% annually (United Nations 2017). As shown in Figure 1.1, the global population is growing at a decreasing rate since 2006, from 6.6 billion to 7.5 billion in 2017.

Figure 1.1: World Population Trends

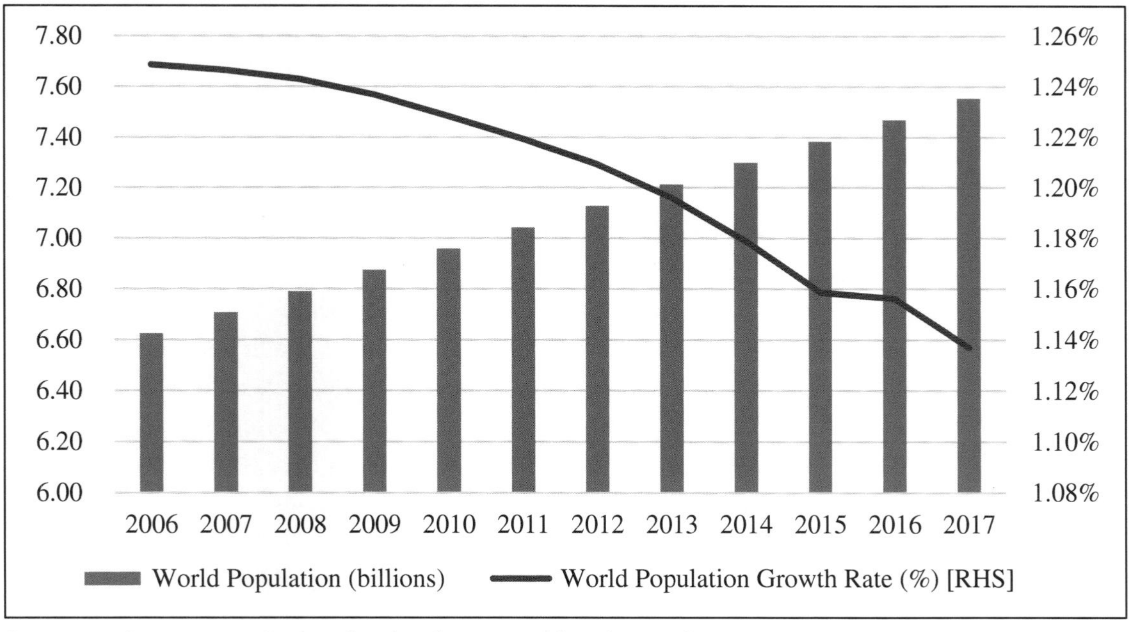

Source: Asia Competitiveness Institute, based on data retrieved from the United Nations.

In line with this trend, the United Nations in their 2014 revision of the World Urbanisation Prospects reports that the global urban population has seen rapid growth, having increased by over three billion people between 1950 and 2014. In addition, the United Nations estimates that this upward trend of the global population is likely to contribute a further 2.5 billion people to the global urban population by 2050, with approximately 90% of this addition coming from Africa and Asia (United Nations 2014). As a result, the absolute number of urban residents is projected to rise to over six billion while the rate of urbanisation[1] at the global level is expected to exceed 65% by 2050 from under 30% in the 1950s (Figure 1.2).

Figure 1.2: Global Population and Urbanisation Rate Projections

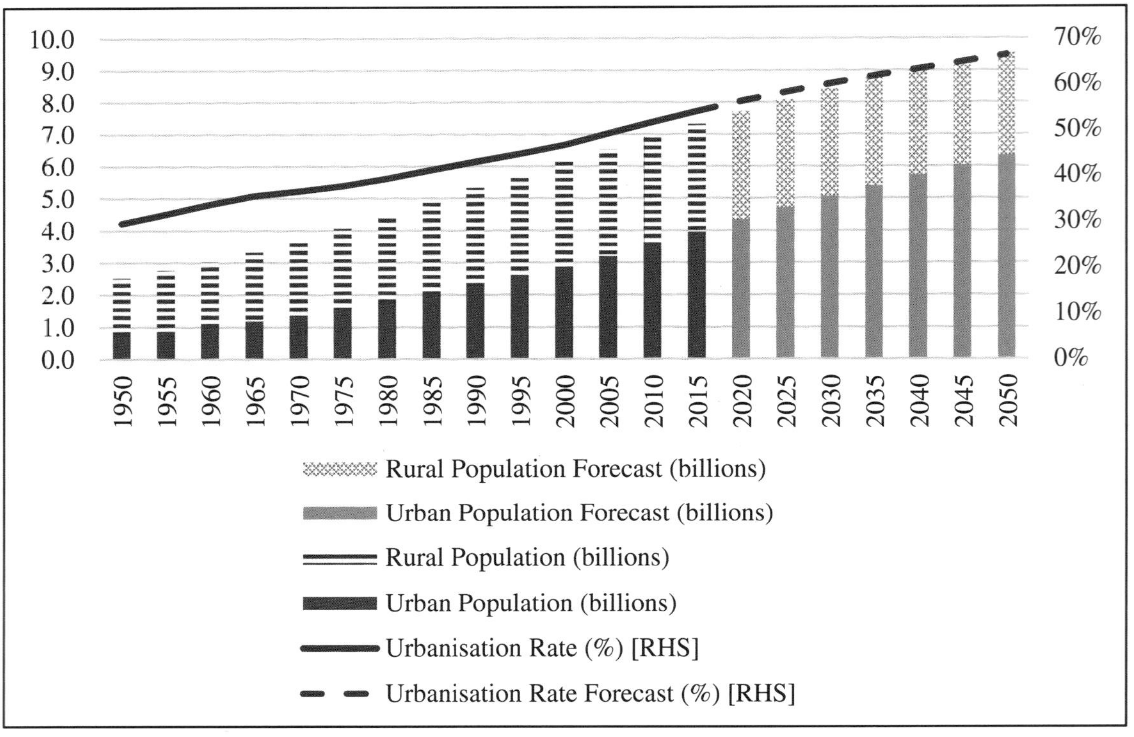

Source: Asia Competitiveness Institute, based on data retrieved from the United Nations.

The rising global urbanisation trend is no surprise given the accelerating pace of globalisation from improving transport and communication technologies, as well as the natural attraction of cities due to the vast economic opportunities available. The presence of good infrastructure and access to services in terms of education, housing, transport and health care in urban areas contribute to the promise of a better life and socioeconomic status. Further, as firms are attracted to regions with good infrastructure and talent, urban areas encourage entrepreneurs to conduct business, and hence providing employment and raising income levels of residents (Zhang and Song 2003). At the national level, urban areas are hubs of innovation and sources of economic growth as they attract foreign investment and promote the exchange of ideas among enterprises (Oort 2004; Henderson 2000). Moreover, with the infrastructure and governance in urban areas,

[1] According to the National Bureau of Statistics of China, urbanisation rate refers to the proportion of a population living in urban areas.

resources such as labour and capital are used more efficiently than in rural areas (Tao and Hao 1999). These factors collectively make urban areas extremely attractive to both residents and policymakers.

Nevertheless, while urbanisation has many benefits and opportunities, it presents a fair share of risks and challenges if it is not properly managed.

Environmental risk from urbanisation is a common negative outcome. Deforestation, for instance, is one of the major concerns since the development of infrastructure including roads and buildings requires significant amounts of land. The loss of forests, and the destruction of ecosystems, natural habitats and biodiversity in the process of making way for such constructions are only some of the damaging consequences to the environment (Foley *et al.* 2005). Another environmental threat of urbanisation is that of pollution from waste generation in urban areas. As economic opportunities expand and income rises, manufacturing activity, industrial waste and household consumption will rise in tandem, leading to increased levels of by-products and unwanted materials released into waterways, landfills and the air (Zurbrügg 2013; Maiti and Agrawal 2005). As such, the continued expansion of urban spaces and populations will bear heavily on the resources from the environment and pose risks to sustainability of such developments.

Another notable challenge of urbanisation is urban poverty and inequality due to the strain on public services and infrastructure. While urban areas and cities have the potential to provide services such as housing, education and health care, it may not be sufficient or distributed equitably throughout the entire urban population. The heavy burden on public finances and weak regulations may result in inadequate provisions to and marginalisation of amenities like housing and sanitation to certain groups, hence resulting in the growth of substandard housing with poor living conditions such as slums (Arimah 2010). Further, the issue of urban poverty can lead to other problems such as increased crime, poor health and education as opportunities narrow for the poor in these urban areas (Montgomery 2009; Ludwig, Duncan, and Hirschfield 2001; Ludwig *et al.* 2001).

Overall, the continued rise in the world's population and urbanisation rate indicates that global discourse of urbanisation looks set to hasten and define the next few decades. Such a trajectory does not just apply to large cities, as the 2016 World Cities Report notes that small and medium sized cities with less than one million inhabitants have the fastest growth rate and account for 59% of the world's urban population (UN Habitat 2016). As such, with the expansion of urban areas continuing against the backdrop of abundant economic opportunities, heightened standards of living and economic growth, there are also the significant challenges of environmental degradation and urban poverty and inequality to manage as well.

1.2 Urbanisation in China and Shandong Province

China is clearly an integral part of this global urbanisation trajectory, being the world's most populous country and comprising 19% of the world's population in 2017, which equates to roughly 1.4 billion people (United Nations 2017). According to the National Bureau of Statistics of China, the urbanisation rate of China has grown rapidly from only 10.64% in 1949 to 26.41% in 1990 and further to 56.1% by 2015 (Figure 1.3). Given that China has approximately 47% of its population (or 635 million people) living in rural areas in 2014 according to estimates by the United Nations, there is a great potential for the rural-to-urban migration of Chinese citizens. Such a development is expected to add 292 million people to urban areas by 2050 (United Nations 2014). Thus, it is worth taking a closer look at China's urban development trends to develop sustainable strategies of growth and improvement.

Figure 1.3: Urbanisation Rate in China

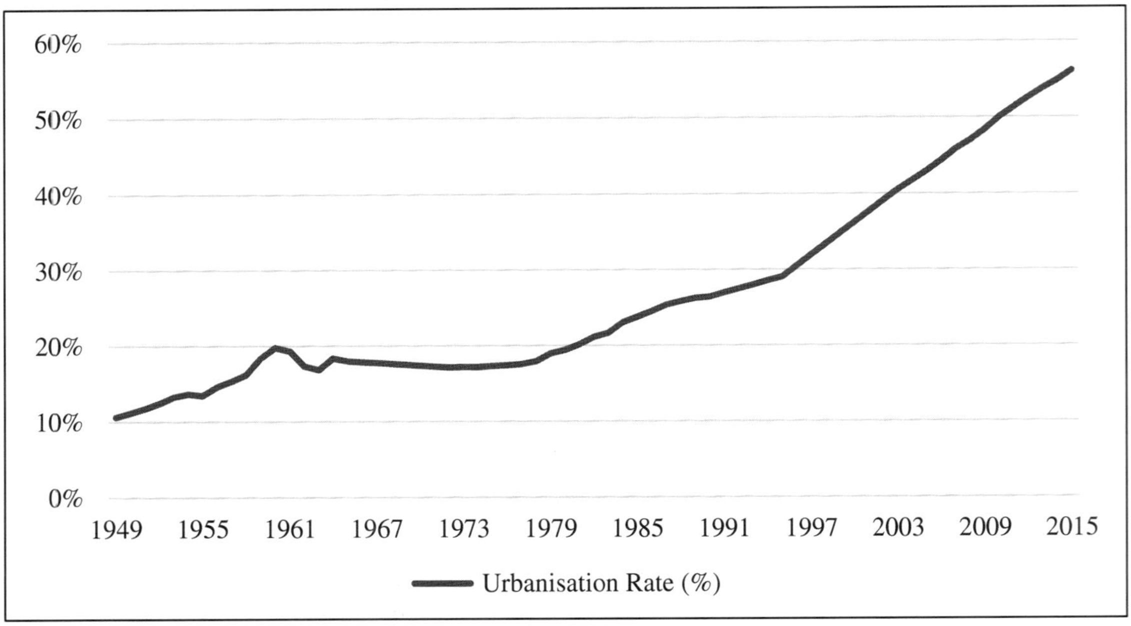

Source: Asia Competitiveness Institute, based on data retrieved from the National Bureau of Statistics of China.

It is worth noting that China's speed and scale of urbanisation are unprecedented in human history. Urbanisation in Europe took 150 years to go from 12% to 51%, while China essentially achieved the same level of urbanisation in less than 70 years, less than half of the time of Europe. As such, the rapid pace has caused disorganised and poorly managed urbanisation in recent years, and has increasingly attracted the attention of the general public on problems such as the depletion of natural resources, traffic congestions in almost all major cities, haze and smog in North China Plain, food safety issues nation-wide and social issues related to migrant workers.

At the same time, with growth and rising prosperity, Chinese citizens cultivate increasingly sophisticated tastes and preferences, which go beyond the bare necessities. Instead of simply pursuing improved economic well-being, citizens now desire better overall quality of life. During the 13th Five Year Plan released on 16 March 2016, China aims to finish building a moderately prosperous society in all respects to fulfil Chinese citizens' increasingly diverse and personalised needs.

At the government level, China has recently charted an ambitious plan to develop the country at the 19th National Congress conducted from 18 to 24 October 2017, underscoring the rapid progress of urbanisation in the country. In his address, President Xi Jinping proposed a two-stage development plan after achieving a "moderately prosperous society" by 2020 (Xi 2017). The first stage is the fundamental realisation of the goal of "socialist modernisation" during the period 2020 to 2035. The second stage, which refers to the period between 2035 and 2050, will see China developing to become a modern socialist country that is prosperous, strong, democratic, culturally advanced, harmonious and beautiful. Many of these concepts of a modern socialist country are enduring value goals outlined at the national level at the 18th National Congress in 2012.

Although China enjoyed high and positive Gross Domestic Product (GDP) growth rates in the past, it has slowed down in recent years towards more moderate levels, as shown in Figure 1.4. This is not surprising as President Xi Jinping mentioned at the 18th Party Congress that GDP growth rates are no longer the sole indicator of the success and health of the economy. It is therefore evident that while China intends to embark on an ambitious development plan to achieve a prosperous society, considerations beyond GDP growth such as environmental protection, social development, welfare improvement and public service standards are beginning to garner greater attention.

Upon closer inspection of the provinces within China, Shandong stands out due to its significant economic impact in the country. Shandong is a thriving economic centre, being the third largest province by land area in China with the second largest resident population of 98,470,000 and third largest Gross Regional Domestic Product (GRDP) of RMB 6.3 trillion in 2015, according to the National Bureau of Statistics of China. However, it is worth noting that while Shandong's economy is still growing at a positive rate, it has been consistent with the national trend of tapering growth rates in recent years, as shown in Figure 1.4.

Figure 1.4: China GDP and Shandong GRDP Growth Rate

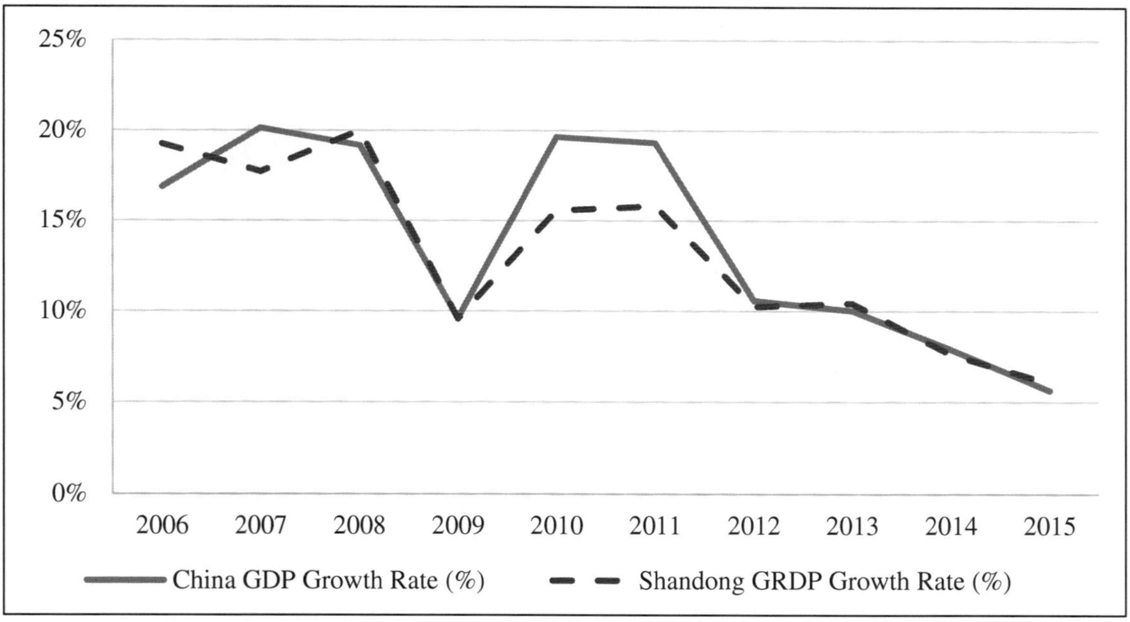

Source: Asia Competitiveness Institute, based on data retrieved from the National Bureau of Statistics of China.

Nevertheless, the steadily increasing value-added of secondary and tertiary industries in Shandong over the past decade suggest a bright prospect for the province as it indicates a move towards higher-value output (Figure 1.5). Moreover, as analysed in Asia Competitiveness Institute's (ACI) 2016 update of the ranking of 34 Greater China Economies, Shandong province ranks eighth overall and is among the top three provincial contributors to China's GDP growth at 9.31% in 2015 (Tan, Wang, and Xie 2017).

Figure 1.5: Value-Added of Secondary and Tertiary Industries in Shandong

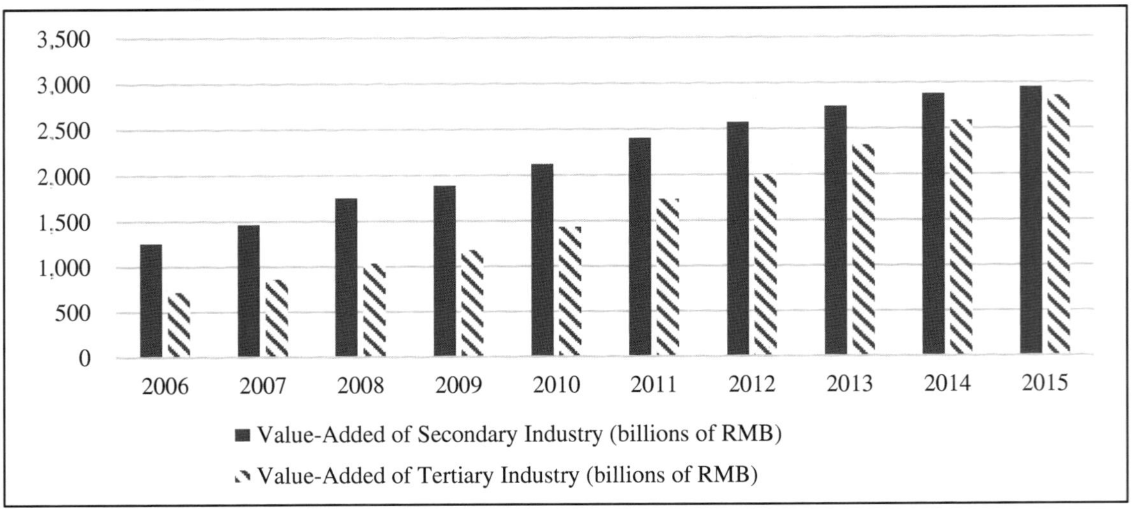

Source: Asia Competitiveness Institute, based on data retrieved from the National Bureau of Statistics of China.

As such, Shandong is evidently an attractive region and its characteristics have promoted a steady increase in its urban population reaching a peak at 56,140,000 as of 2015. In addition, the growing proportion of Shandong residents living in urban areas (i.e. urbanisation rate) is largely in line with that of China as a whole, progressively rising over the past decade and surpassing 50% of the total provincial population since 2011, as shown in Figure 1.6. Through this process, each of the 17 Shandong cities differentiated themselves by building on their unique advantages. Currently, urbanisation in Shandong is going through a transformation and upgrade, with added emphasis on improving urban services and focus on urbanites' needs by closely integrating modern information and communication technology. Such developments prompt a growing imperative to develop effective strategies to manage the mounting needs of an urban population in its cities.

Figure 1.6: Urbanisation Rate in China and Shandong

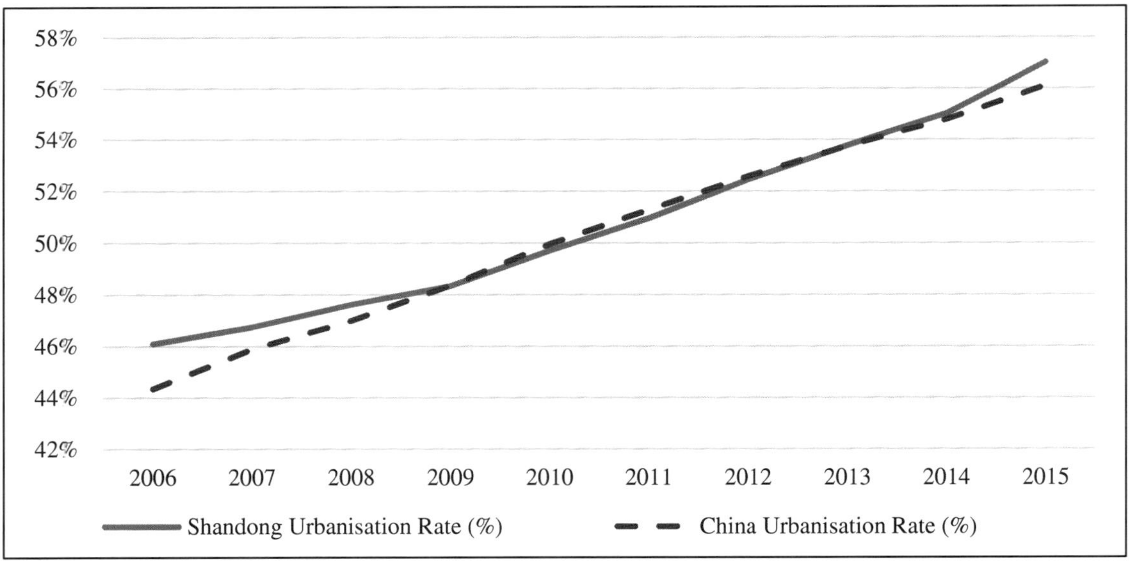

Source: Asia Competitiveness Institute, based on data retrieved from the National Bureau of Statistics of China.

As pointed out in the 19th National Congress by President Xi Jinping, the principal contradiction facing the Chinese society in the new era is that between unbalanced and inadequate development and the people's growing needs for a better life (Xi 2017). In recent years, Shandong has optimised its regional planning and sectorial distribution to reduce regional inequality. In particular, Shandong has accelerated the integration process through the construction of its high-speed railway network and the formation of the Shandong Peninsular City Cluster, Provincial Capital Circle, Western Shandong Economic Emergence Zone and Southern Shandong Economic Zone. In addition, the establishment of the Yellow River Delta High-Efficiency Eco-Development Zone and Shandong Peninsula Oceanic Economic Zone serves as a national strategy to further support growth in the region. While these overlapping regional development strategies offer new opportunities for cities to specialise and differentiate, they also bring intensified competition.

Despite Shandong's success and prosperity, it is also facing substantial challenges and limitations. Firstly, the tertiary sector is underdeveloped, contributing only 45.3% of GRDP in 2015 according to the National Bureau of Statistics of China. Secondly, the regional economy is reliant on energy-consuming and polluting industries, posing a significant threat to the environment. Thirdly, state-owned enterprises play a dominant role in Shandong's economy. Compared to Jiangsu and Zhejiang, the private sector in Shandong is relatively weak and small and medium enterprises are less vibrant. Through stronger financial support and various tax benefits, Shandong is working towards a more innovative and business-friendly economy.

In addition, Shandong's development remains geographically unbalanced, especially between its rural and urban areas and among different regions. Further, given the diversity of economic conditions and development trajectories of cities within the province, the 17 cities in Shandong need to explore alternative development pathways and navigate through the challenges of cooperation and competition. In doing so, local policymakers can achieve improved economic conditions with healthy and sustainable development.

In response to these issues, Shandong has been making improvements to its urban development and is currently at a critical point of economic upgrading and restructuring. Through an innovation-driven development strategy, Shandong is actively implementing its "Made in China 2025" strategy and "Internet Plus" action plan to upgrade its manufacturing sector and promote its service sector. With 3,000 kilometres of coastline, Shandong has a substantial potential of expanding its ocean industries and developing a "blue economy". In particular, the Shandong Peninsula National Innovation Zone was recently established in 2016, signifying its commitment towards a new phase of innovation-led growth.

1.3 Profile of Shandong Province: Geographical, Historical, Cultural and Competitiveness

1.3.1 Geography

Shandong is a coastal province located to the southeast of Beijing and Hebei, to the east of Henan, and to the north of Jiangsu. Shandong covers a land area of 157,900 square kilometres, and its population was recorded as 98,470,000 at the end of 2015 (Government of Shandong Province 2017a). The provincial capital is Jinan, and the territories the province administers notably contain the final stretch of the Yellow River before it empties into the Bohai Sea — which is situated to the north of the province. At the north-eastern edge of the province is located the Shandong peninsula, which stretches east to separate the Bohai Sea from the Yellow Sea, to the south. Shandong is in its entirety located on the expansive North China Plain — a vast, relatively flat alluvial plain which owes its existence to sediments and other material naturally transported and deposited by the waters of the Yellow River, along with other regional waterways, as they flow out towards the coast.

That one of China's two most famous great rivers flows through it has contributed significantly to the region's remarkable agricultural productivity, and the North China Plain's rich, fertile soil allows for the growth of grain crops such as wheat, corn, sorghum and soybeans, as well as cash crops such as cotton and hemp (Government of Shandong Province 2017b). These characteristics have enabled Shandong province to function for much of Chinese history as a hotbed of agricultural development, and a breadbasket for the surrounding regions.

Emerging abruptly from this expanse of mostly flat and undulating terrain at the centre of the province is the Taishan massif, the tallest peak of which stands a towering 1.53 kilometres above the sea level. Mount Taishan and its composite peaks are venerated as some of China's most sacred natural landmarks, and play an important part in Chinese folk religion. They are today still regarded as widely venerated as one of China's "Five Great Mountains". Their significance in the context of China's spiritual landscape has in turn been translated into varying degrees of political and cultural significance as well, and the divine peaks have received visits from Chinese Emperors seeking to legitimise their rule, as well as poets and artists seeking inspiration.

1.3.2 History

Due to these factors, the territories which today comprise Shandong province have played host to sizeable populations since the advent of organised human settlement in China, and numerous archaeological sites attributed to Neolithic civilisations such as the Beixin (5300–4100 BCE), Dawenkou (4100–2600 BCE) and Longshan (3000–1900 BCE) cultures have been discovered (Government of Shandong Province 2017c). Such discoveries serve to hint at the region's attractiveness even during Chinese prehistory, and are indisputable testaments to its integral importance to Chinese civilisation as a whole. Indeed, it is likely due to Shandong's prominence in early Chinese history that several sources have cited the region as the likely birthplace of the mythical Yellow Emperor Xuanyuan, who is credited with the foundation of China as a centralised state (Travel Shandong 2017).

Shandong is also located just adjacent to modern Henan, within which was located the capital cities of China's two earliest dynasties — the earlier, semi-mythical Xia (2070–1600 BCE) and the Shang (1600–1046 BCE). The Shandong region accordingly rose to varying degrees of prominence during these periods. As a space removed from the at times ill-defined territories of both of these early dynasties — while still being located on the peripheries of their dominions — the Shandong region became understood during these early periods as a liminal space in which civilised and barbarian cultures interacted (Government of Shandong Province 2017c). During this period, western Shandong would eventually come to be integrated into the consolidated territories of the Shang dynasty, though eastern Shandong would remain independent until the Qin dynasty (221–206 BCE).

During the Zhou dynasty (1046–249 BCE), which conquered and replaced the Shang dynasty, the Shandong region would play host to two powerful feudal states — Qi and Lu. With the decline of the Zhou dynasty's power and authority during the Spring and Autumn period (771–476 BCE), both Qi and Lu would grow in prominence, and vie for hegemony over each other and their most proximate neighbours. Eventually, however, Lu was annexed by Chu, and while the state of Qi retains the honour having persevered the longest of all of the Qin's rivals, it too would fall, bringing the entirety of the Shandong region under the dominion of China's first imperial dynasty.

China's first emperor, the infamous Qin Shi Huang Di, declared himself emperor of a united China in a ceremony held at the top of Mount Taishan. This ceremony, the "Fengshan sacrifices", were intended as a tribute to the mountain and an announcement to the heavens that the emperor had unified China's disparate kingdoms, setting a precedent that would be adhered to by subsequent emperors and in so doing forging a link — however tenuous — between the legitimacy of imperial rule and a landmark of Shandong's geography (UNESCO World Heritage Centre 2017). Shandong would subsequently become an indivisible component of China's territory throughout much of Chinese imperial dynastic history, only falling out of a given imperial dynasty's direct sphere of influence during periods of tumultuous societal upheaval.

The region would notably grow in economic prominence during the Han dynasty (206 BCE–220 CE), and its position as a fertile crop-producing area conveniently located on the arterial Yellow River meant that it was well positioned to provide for less agriculturally productive regions, such as dynastic China's political centres in the arid Guanzhong region around modern-day Xi'an (Government of Shandong Province 2017c). Shandong would also play host to vital maritime trade and transport networks, and function to facilitate the smooth transport of goods from provinces in the south to provinces in the north, and vice-versa (Boxer 2013). Shandong's importance to inter-regional trade was further reinforced during the Yuan dynasty (1271–1368 CE) with the construction of an extension to the Grand Canal which directly linked the imperial capital of Beijing to the canal's southern terminus in Hangzhou. As this route traversed western Shandong, the region became even more integral to China's economic activities (Boxer 2013).

The rise of the Ming dynasty (1368–1644 CE) brought with it the official definition of Shandong as a distinct administrative entity, and efforts were made by imperial governments to encourage resettlement in areas which had been damaged by war, or simply fallen into disrepair during preceding cycles of societal upheaval. Shandong would subsequently remain a vital cornerstone in the Chinese economy for much of the Ming and Qing dynasties.

The decline of the Qing dynasty (1644–1912 CE) in the 19th century coincided with the rise of Europe's maritime powers, which would, emboldened as they were beyond any initial awe at China's venerable history, seek to gain any advantages they could at the expense of the vulnerable Qing government. As a coastal province with easy access to the Yellow River, Shandong was found to be an attractive proposition for many foreign powers. The Empire of Japan, for example, occupied Shandong for a time after the First Sino-Japanese war (1894–1895 CE). Following this, Germany and Britain would leverage the vulnerability of the Qing government to obtain favourable leases on the cities of Qingdao and Weihai respectively in 1898. These cities in Shandong would accordingly serve as outposts for these foreign powers during this tumultuous period in Chinese history, with German interests in the regions being granted to the Japanese at the conclusion of the First World War (1914–1918 CE) — a situation that would stand until some way into the Second World War (1939–1945 CE).

During the Second World War, Shandong, along with territories in Northeast China and the Korean peninsula, constituted the Empire of Japan's primary beachhead on the East Asian mainland, with Japanese forces gaining control of much of the province during the contiguous and concurrent Second Sino-Japanese War (1937–1945 CE). As the war drew to a close, however, Shandong would also play host to the Battle of Tai'erzhuang — the Empire of Japan's first major defeat at the hands of a Chinese force and a victory that is credited with decisively dispelling the myth of Japanese military invincibility (Government of Shandong Province 2017c). After the Second World War, successful Communist military efforts against Nationalist forces during the ongoing Chinese Civil War (1927–1950 CE) would see them establishing full control over the entirety of Shandong province by 1948 (Boxer 2013).

1.3.3 Culture

Over its long and storied history, Shandong has borne witness to momentous, arguably world-changing events, and played host to luminaries in every field. As a region which saw inhabitation from a very early point in Chinese prehistory, Shandong has been a rich repository of archaeological artefacts dating back millennia. A multitude of archaeological sites identified with the Beixin and Dawenkou cultures have been found in the region, with continuing investigations even unearthing traces of Palaeolithic inhabitation. Moving further along, some of the finest and best preserved examples of the distinctive black pottery for which the ancient Longshan culture is famed have been discovered in Shandong (The Editors of Encyclopædia Britannica 2010). These and other discoveries have made Shandong extremely useful for Chinese archaeologists and historians seeking to better understand the cultural geography of the region, prior to the advent of written records (The Editors of Encyclopædia Britannica 2010).

Despite the significance of these findings, however, Shandong's most momentous contributions to Chinese culture — and perhaps world culture as a whole — arguably came about during the Spring and Autumn period. It was during this period that Confucius was born in an area near present-day Qufu, which was at the time located within the boundaries of the feudal state of Lu. Today widely acknowledged as China's best-known, pre-eminent philosopher, Confucius is credited with authoring, compiling and editing many texts which are regarded as cornerstones of Chinese civilisation, foremost among which are the Five Classics. This particular set of texts is credited with codifying and defining integral aspects of Chinese moral, political and spiritual ideology, and are regarded as the foundational texts of Confucianism (Tu 2017). Confucian ideology and philosophy are in turn regarded as having had an inconceivably significant effect on conceptualisations of morality, political governance and fundamental propriety in the East Asian region as a whole, with neighbouring states such as Korea and Japan notably borrowing over subsequent millennia from Confucian ideology when constructing their own ideas of rulership, statehood and society (Tu 2017). As Confucianism became entrenched as China's core ideology, Shandong inevitably became established as a centre for its study, playing host to academies and houses of learning dedicated to advancing or deliberating on Confucian ideology. The province would accordingly also produce Mencius (Mengzi), who is renowned as Confucianism's second-most authoritative philosopher, among other notable contributors.

Shandong has also over the course of Chinese history produced many other great and notable individuals, including Sun Tzu, author of the world-renowned Art of War, and Zhuge Liang, the legendary sage of the Three Kingdoms period (220–280 CE) (Government of Shandong Province 2017c).

Another of Shandong's many notable scions is the famed calligrapher Wang Xizhi, who was born in Linyi and is regarded by many in the East Asian region as a whole as the greatest practitioner of calligraphy China ever produced (The Editors of Encyclopædia Britannica 2017). Wang is credited with having pioneered and codified many techniques which are today regarded as the hallmarks of excellent calligraphy, and a museum dedicated to documenting his life and career today stands in the city of his birth.

Shandong's impressive contributions to China's arts and culture have furthermore continued to the present day, and the nation's first Nobel Laureate for Literature hails from the small city of Gaomi near Weifang, in eastern Shandong (The Editors of Encyclopædia Britannica 2015). Gaomi and its surrounding territories furthermore play significant parts in many of Mo Yan's novels — many of which were written in the literary tradition of magical realism and duly deploy elements of the magical or supernatural in otherwise realistic depictions of life, with the goal of magnifying or accentuating otherwise submerged aspects of societal interaction. Mo Yan's novels combine a distinctively visceral writing style with a keen awareness and engagement with Chinese history, mythology and contemporary culture, and stand in many ways as a testament to the cultural vibrancy of his province of origin.

When these contributions are furthermore considered in the context of the immense cultural significance of Mount Taishan, it is evident that the immensity of Shandong's contributions to China's intangible cultural heritage is undeniable, and more than commensurate to its long-standing, pivotal role in Chinese history.

1.3.4 Competitiveness

ACI has consistently provided comprehensive competitiveness analysis of 34 Greater China Economies since 2000 (Tan, Wang, and Xie 2017; Tan, Yuan, and Xie 2016; Tan, Yuan, and Yoong 2015; Tan *et al.* 2013). They take into account different factors that collectively shape the ability of an economy to achieve substantial and inclusive economic development over a sustainable period of time. According to four equally weighted environments: (1) Macroeconomic Stability, (2) Government and Institutional Setting, (3) Financial, Businesses and Manpower Conditions and (4) Quality of Life and Infrastructure Development, Shandong consistently ranked 8th among the 34 economies from 2001 to 2013, except in 2000 when it ranked 9th. The studies have also shown that Shandong performs well in physical infrastructure and economic vibrancy (i.e. the development in first, second and third industries), while it lacks development in technological infrastructure, education and standard living, especially related to environment protection.

Over the course of its history, Shandong province has been a centre for agricultural production as well as an important source of artisan goods. The fertility of its fields, derived as it is from the richness of the Yellow River, allows it to produce a veritable cornucopia of both subsistence and cash crops. At the same time, the region's inherent mineral wealth made it a centre for metallurgy from relatively early in its history, with cities such as Laiwu becoming well known as centres for the production of high-quality iron and steel. Shandong was also notable for having been a significant source of gold, along with other rare materials (Government of Shandong Province 2017c).

The province was also known for the excellence of its fabrics, and gained a reputation as an important processing and manufacturing base for silks — a great amount of which would make its way west across the Silk Road (Government of Shandong Province 2017c). These historical advantages have largely carried forward to the present day, and Shandong is still well esteemed for its agricultural and mineral wealth, as well as its excellence as a centre for manufacturing. However, Shandong's economy has benefited particularly significantly from China's increasing engagement with world trade.

As a coastal region, many of Shandong's cities are positioned to take full advantage of increased international trade flows into and out of China. The province is home to several large world-class seaports, namely Yantai, Weihai, Qingdao and Rizhao, which collectively process tens of millions of Twenty-Foot Equivalent Units worth of cargo each year. Furthermore, many of Shandong's cities have maximised their engagement with international trade partners, and are the beneficiaries of large amounts of foreign investment. Prime examples of how this can prove beneficial can be found in the cities of Qingdao and Yantai, which were opened up to foreign investment in 1984 due to the ongoing Chinese Economic Reform. Qingdao and Yantai are now respectively the first and second-largest industrial cities in Shandong, and accordingly lay claim to having the largest and second-largest Gross Regional Domestic Products in the province. Shandong's other cities are following suit, and manufacturing industries have been significant drivers of growth in all of the province's cities.

Another factor that positively augments Shandong's competitiveness as a province is the highly developed nature of its transport infrastructure. Situated as it is between Beijing and China's more southerly coastal regions, many of Shandong's cities are well connected, with high-speed rail and highway linkages being comprehensive and easily accessible. Relatively secure in its advantages as a coastal manufacturing base, however, Shandong's cities are now diversifying into the tertiary sectors, with several cities working to encourage the development of service industries, such as hospitality and tourism.

1.4 Outline of the Book

This book will focus on the close examination of Shandong province over 21 chapters across three parts, namely (I) Overview of the Urban Composite Development Index (UCDI) for 17 Cities in Shandong province, (II) In-Depth Analysis on Patterns of Urban Development for 17 Cities in Shandong province and (III) Tentative Conclusion on the Urban Development of 17 Shandong Cities.

The first part on the overview of the UCDI for 17 Cities in Shandong province consists of three chapters, of which this chapter is its first on the introduction to urbanisation, trends and developments within China and Shandong. Chapter 2 will detail both the theoretical and empirical approaches to the construction of our novel UCDI approach by first providing a comprehensive literature review of other rankings, both global and regional, which attempt to benchmark and evaluate liveable cities. Subsequently, Chapter 2 will describe this project's main research objectives, motivations and expected contributions, followed by the conceptualisation of the UCDI based on China's Five Development Concepts of Innovation, Coordination, Green Development, Opening Up and Sharing. Following which, Chapter 2 will proceed to elaborate on the rigorous methodological framework upon which these principles are employed by providing an account of the six environments, 23 sub-environments and 131 indicators included in the index, as well as important data sources, concerns and methodological innovations, including the Shapely weight approach and *What-if* simulations. Chapter 3 will analyse the main empirical findings from this project with an analysis of the overall ranking results and across the six environments. The six environments included are (a) Scale and Quality of Economic Activities, (b) Financial Capacity, Labour Market Flexibility and Economic Vibrancy, (c) Good Governance, Effective Leadership and Social Stability, (d) Technological Advancement and Innovation Capability, (e) Public Service Standards and Quality of Life Improvement, and (f) Resource Conditions and Environmental Protection.

Part two provides an in-depth city-level analysis for each of the 17 cities in the 17 chapters contained in this part, that is, from Chapters 4 to 20. Each chapter is dedicated to one city in Shandong and will expound on the profile and urban development context of that particular city, beginning with a background on the cultural, historical and economic idiosyncrasies of the city. Subsequently, each chapter will delve into the analysis of the urban development performance and ranking under the UCDI framework, both overall and across the six environments. Further insights will be revealed through the *What-if* simulation analysis as well as various strengths, weaknesses and policy recommendations before concluding each chapter for the corresponding city.

Finally, the last part of the book is the conclusion chapter in Part III (Chapter 21) where it summarises the discussion by first identifying key factors affecting the development of Shandong cities, and subsequently provides an evidence-based evaluation for fresh recommendations for Shandong. Chapter 21 further elaborates on the possible extensions of the UCDI into other sub-national economies of China before closing with the concluding remarks and future research agenda.

References

Arimah, Ben C. 2010. 'The Face of Urban Poverty: Explaining the Prevalence of Slums in Developing Countries'. Working Paper 2010,30. Working paper // World Institute for Development Economics Research. https://www.econstor.eu/handle/10419/54181.

Boxer, Baruch. 2013. 'Shandong Province, China'. Encyclopedia Britannica. 2013. https://www.britannica.com/place/Shandong-province-China.

Foley, Jonathan A., Ruth DeFries, Gregory P. Asner, Carol Barford, Gordon Bonan, Stephen R. Carpenter, F. Stuart Chapin, *et al.* 2005. 'Global Consequences of Land Use'. *Science* 309 (5734): 570–74. https://doi.org/10.1126/science.1111772.

Henderson, J. Vernon. 2000. 'The Effects of Urban Concentration on Economic Growth'. Working Paper 7503. National Bureau of Economic Research. https://doi.org/10.3386/w7503.

Ludwig, Jens, Greg J. Duncan, and Paul Hirschfield. 2001. 'Urban Poverty and Juvenile Crime: Evidence from a Randomized Housing-Mobility Experiment'. *The Quarterly Journal of Economics* 116 (2): 655–79. https://doi.org/10.1162/00335530151144122.

Ludwig, Jens, Helen F. Ladd, Greg J. Duncan, Jeffrey Kling, and Katherine M. O'Regan. 2001. 'Urban Poverty and Educational Outcomes [with Comments]'. *Brookings-Wharton Papers on Urban Affairs*, 147–201.

Maiti, Sutapa, and Praween Agrawal. 2005. 'Environmental Degradation in the Context of Growing Urbanization: A Focus on the Metropolitan Cities of India'. *Journal of Human Ecology* 17 (April): 277–87. https://doi.org/10.1080/09709274.2005.11905793.

Montgomery, Mark R. 2009. 'Urban Poverty and Health in Developing Countries'. *Population Bulletin; Washington* 64 (2): 2–16.

Oort, Frank. 2004. 'Urban Growth and Innovation: Spatially Bounded Externalities in the Netherlands', January.

People's Government of Shandong Province. 2015a. 'Geographical Resources "地理资源"'. 15 February 2015. http://www.shandong.gov.cn/art/2014/5/14/art_2738_124107.html.

———. 2015b. 'Historical Facts "历史简况"'. 15 February 2015. http://www.shandong.gov.cn/art/2014/5/14/art_2737_124108.html.

———. 2017. 'Administrative Divisions of Shandong Province "山东省行政区划"'. 7 May 2017. http://www.shandong.gov.cn/col/col2743/index.html.

Tan, Khee Giap, Peng Wang, and Teleixi Xie. 2017. *Growth Slowdown Analysis by Income Thresholds and Annual Update of Competitiveness Analysis for 34 Greater China Economies*. World Scientific.

Tan, Khee Giap, Randong Yuan, and Teleixi Xie. 2016. *Estimation of Agricultural Productivity and Annual Update of Competitiveness Analysis for Greater China: Optimising Agricultural Productivity and Promoting Innovation Driven Growth*. World Scientific.

Tan, Khee Giap, Randong Yuan, and Wei Cher Sangiita Yoong. 2015. *Annual Provincial and Regional Competitiveness Analysis for Greater China Economies: Development Strategies under the New Normal*. World Scientific.

Tan, Khee Giap, Randong Yuan, Wei Cher Sangiita Yoong, and Mu Yang. 2013. *Annual Analysis of Competitiveness, Simulation Studies and Development Perspective for 34 Greater China Economies: 2000–2010*. World Scientific.

Tao, Yang Dennis, and Zhou Hao. 1999. 'Rural Urban Disparity and Sectoral Labour Allocation in China'. *The Journal of Development Studies* 35 (3): 105–33. https://doi.org/10.1080/00220389908422575.

The Editors of Encyclopedia Britannica. 2010. 'Longshan Culture | Anthropology'. Encyclopedia Britannica. 2010. https://www.britannica.com/topic/Longshan-culture.

———. 2015. 'Mo Yan | Chinese Author'. Encyclopedia Britannica. 12 April 2015. https://www.britannica.com/biography/Mo-Yan.

———. 2017. 'Wang Xizhi | Biography, Style, & Facts'. Encyclopedia Britannica. 2017. https://www.britannica.com/biography/Wang-Xizhi.

Travel Shandong. 2017. 'History | Travel Shandong'. 2017. http://travelshandong.com/about/history/.

Tu, Weiming. 2017. 'Confucianism | Meaning, History, Beliefs, & Facts'. 15 December 2017. https://www.britannica.com/topic/Confucianism.

UN Habitat. 2016. 'World Cities Report 2016: Urbanization and Development: Emerging Futures'. *Nairobi, UN Habitat*. http://wcr.unhabitat.org/wp-content/uploads/2017/02/WCR-2016_-Abridged-version-1.pdf.

UNESCO World Heritage Centre. n.d. 'Mount Taishan'. UNESCO World Heritage Centre. Accessed 16 January 2018. http://whc.unesco.org/en/list/437/.

United Nations. 2014. 'World Urbanization Prospects: The 2014 Revision, Highlights'. Working Paper ST/ESA/SER.A/352. United Nations, Department of Economic and Social Affairs, Population Division. https://esa.un.org/unpd/wpp/publications/Files/WPP2017_KeyFindings.pdf.

———. 2017. 'World Population Prospects: The 2017 Revision, Key Findings and Advance Tables'. Working Paper ESA/P/WP/248. United Nations, Department of Economic and Social Affairs, Population Division. https://esa.un.org/unpd/wpp/publications/Files/WPP2017_KeyFindings.pdf.

Xi, Jinping. 2017. 'Secure a Decisive Victory in Building a Moderately Prosperous Society in All Respects and Strive for the Great Success of Socialism with Chinese Characteristics for a New Era; Delivered at the 19th National Congress of the Communist Party of China'. http://www.xinhuanet.com/english/download/Xi_Jinping's_report_at_19th_CPC_National_Congress.pdf.

Zhang, Kevin Honglin, and Shunfeng Song. 2003. 'Rural–Urban Migration and Urbanization in China: Evidence from Time-Series and Cross-Section Analyses'. *China Economic Review* 14 (4): 386–400. https://doi.org/10.1016/j.chieco.2003.09.018.

Zurbrügg, Christian. 2013. 'Urban Solid Waste Management in Low-Income Countries of Asia — How to Cope with the Garbage Crisis?', July.

Chapter 2
The Theoretical Foundations and Methodological Framework of the Urban Composite Development Index

This chapter is divided into two broad sections. The first half will elaborate on the theoretical approach in the construction of the urban development index by first reviewing the relevant literature across the global, national and sub-national levels, to evaluate and rank urban development among cities. Subsequently, we will expound on the research motivations and objectives of this study, as well as the academic and practical contributions this project has to offer. In addition, this chapter will move on to explain the theoretical foundations of the Urban Composite Development Index (UCDI). In particular, there is a strong emphasis on the theoretical underpinnings of the Five Development Concepts introduced by President Xi Jinping of China.

Building upon the foundations of the Five Development Concepts, the second half of this chapter will elaborate on the technical and methodological details of the framework. Specifically, the chapter will describe the six environments used in the framework, including the data and indicators used in each environment. Further, the novel methodological innovation developed by ACI, namely the Shapley weight method, will be outlined.

2.1 Literature Review: Urbanised, Liveable, Sustainable and Intelligent Cities

2.1.1 Ranking Studies and Indices at the Global Level

Many reputable institutions have released their own global city rankings by assessing various aspects of urban development through diverse sets of indicators and theoretical foundations. The variety of perspectives of these studies provide insights to many different groups of people, which makes each ranking unique and relevant to specific audiences.

A well-known and popular index is Mercer's Quality of Living Survey. This study by Mercer is conducted annually to "help multinational organisations compensate employees fairly when placing them on international assignments" (Mercer 2017). By incorporating 39 indicators across 10 categories including Political and Social, Medical and Health Considerations, School and Education, Public Services and Transport, Recreation, Consumer Goods, Housing, Natural, Socio-cultural, and Economic Environments, Mercer provides a fairly robust analysis of quality of life across 450 cities around the world. Even though categories in Mercer's study are comprehensive approaches to evaluate living standards, the number of indicators is too limited to ensure an accurate result. Further, the study focuses narrowly on the perspective of expatriates as they are their primary target audience for this research.

Another popular study conducted annually is the Economist Intelligence Unit's (EIU) Global Liveability Index, which shares similar perspectives and objectives with Mercer's Quality of Living study. EIU's study aims to "benchmark perceptions of development levels" and "assign a hardship allowance as part of expatriate relocation packages" (EIU 2017). The framework adopted by EIU encompasses 30 indicators across five categories, namely Stability, Health Care, Education, Infrastructure, and Culture and Environment for 140 cities worldwide. In EIU's rankings, both of the categories and indicators are narrowly identified, and many crucial aspects such as politics and economics are not included. Same with Mercer's study, the EIU rankings narrowly target their audience to be expatriates.

Monocle Magazine's Most Liveable Cities Index targets readers who are wealthy, mobile and have an affinity to culture, fashion and design. The index conducted annually since 2007 includes 11 indicators and ranks up to 50 cities worldwide. Monocle Magazine's Most Liveable Cities Index remains fairly well received as they account for a broad range of factors in their rankings including Safety, Crime, Medical Care, Climate, Sunshine, International Connectivity, Public Transportation, Quality of Architecture, Environmental Issues and Access to Nature, Urban Design, Business Conditions, Pro-active Policy Development, and Tolerance. However, quality of living in this study is defined from the perspective of a narrow subset of people, namely well-remunerated expatriates. Furthermore, the number of countries selected in Monocle's study is limited for a global city ranking.

The Global Power City Index (GPCI) generated by Mori Memorial Foundation's Institute is another annual study conducted since 2008 for 44 cities worldwide. The GPCI defines urban power as "comprehensive power to attract creative people and business enterprises from around the world" (The Mori Memorial Foundation 2017). With 70 indicators over six categories including Economy, Research and Development, Cultural Interaction, Liveability, Environment, and Accessibility, GPCI provides comprehensive rankings of major cities worldwide.

Apart from an overall ranking, GPCI also gives actor-specific rankings, which are insights into the urban power performance from the perspectives of five types of actors, namely managers, researchers, artists, visitors, and residents. Respondents from each actor-specific category identify indicators that matter to them from 70 indicators in total to formulate five indices. Subsequently, cities are ranked according to their respective and unique index to produce actor-specific rankings. The actor-specific ranking is indeed a novel way to comprehensively evaluate urban power from different points of view. Nevertheless, the number of cities selected is limited, for a global city rankings.

Another more recent annual ranking is the Arcadis Sustainable Cities Index (ASCI), which began in 2015 and ranks 100 global cities by defining sustainability across three dimensions, namely People (social sustainability), Planet (environmental sustainability) and Profit (economic sustainability). By evaluating each city via 32 indicators across these three dimensions, this research provides a thorough analysis of their sustainability profiles. This study considers significant aspects of urban development, hence making it a relatively comprehensive global city ranking. However, ASCI lacks some crucial aspects of city competitiveness, such as those related to politics and culture.

2.1.2 Ranking Studies and Indices on China

Beyond global rankings, there are also studies solely focused on cities in China.

One notable study is the Annual Report on China's Urban Competitiveness (No.15) by the Chinese Academy of Social Sciences (CASS). The CASS report is an annual report focusing on the urban competitiveness of 289 Chinese cities. They define urban competitiveness across three aspects of (a) Urban General Economic Competitiveness, (b) Urban Liveable Competitiveness and (c) Urban Sustainable Competitiveness. The Urban General Economic Competitiveness aspect focuses on the economic vibrancy of the city and represents the current and short-term features of urban competitiveness. The Urban Liveable Competitiveness aspect considers many crucial aspects for residents to ensure a better living quality in the city, while the Urban Sustainable Competitiveness aspect emphasises government's inputs of establishing a sustainable city and represents the long-term elements of urban competitiveness.

However, the CASS report on China's urban competitiveness does not provide an overall evaluation or score across these three aspects and only publishes competitiveness rankings for each part separately. In addition, some indicators appear repeatedly across the three aspects. For instance, GDP Growth Rate and Dependence on Foreign Trade are indicators in both the aspects of Urban General Economic Competitiveness and Urban Sustainable Competitiveness. Other repeated indicators include Air Quality and Disposable Income per capita, which appear in both the aspects of Urban General Economic Competitiveness and Urban Liveable Competitiveness.

The liveability study on Greater China cities by CASS is actually a supplementary study to their competitiveness study. In the most updated report published in 2017, the definition of liveability has an expanded set of categories, relative to past versions. The environments included in the most recent report are Education, Health Care, Security and Social Environment, Environmental Development, Living Environment, Infrastructure, and Vibrancy of Economic Environment. However, the 21 indicators identified in this study are still limited despite the expanded scope on the elements of liveability.

The Sustainable City Study in China (SCSC) by CASS investigates the sustainability of some China cities in their work published in 2011. In this edition, they expanded the definition of sustainability from considering environmental issues to a broader one that embraces the complex relations among the dimensions of "society, economy, population, resources, environment, science and technology, and education" (Zhao 2011). The 12 indicators identified in this study assess 35 China cities using data from 2008. However, while the SCSC study adopted a more comprehensive definition of sustainability, more than half of the indicators selected remain environment-related.

An interesting study conducted annually by the National Institute for Economic Experimentation since 2011 is the Quality of Life in Chinese Cities (QLCC). The QLCC ranks 35 cities in China and consists of subjective satisfaction and objective rankings, which contain different indicators while they belong to the same five environments, namely Living Standards, Costs of Living, Human Capital, Social Security, and Living Experience. The subjective satisfaction ranking in QLCC evaluates residents' perceptions of cities via survey that consists of eight indicators, whereas the objective part in QLCC ranks cities with 20 indicators according to official data. The QLCC thoroughly analyses city performance based on both subjective perceptions and objective data. However, the QLCC only provides subjective and objective rankings separately, and does not include an overall ranking across these two indices.

The China Institute of City Competitiveness (CICC) from Hong Kong publishes a Yearbook of China City Competitiveness annually since 2002. In its 2015 edition, CICC assessed the composite competitiveness and growth competitiveness for 298 Chinese cities (including Hong Kong, Macau and Taiwan). Its composite city competitive index covers the categories of Economic System, Social System, Environmental System and Cultural System with 216 indicators in total. The growth index framework encompasses the four dimensions of Strength, Potential, Vibrancy and Capability. CICC's city competitiveness index framework is fairly comprehensive, but it relies on the subjective opinions from experts for indicators of which the data is inaccurate or unspecific in certain cities.

The Annual Report on Composite Competitiveness of Chinese Cities released by the Urban International Institute for Urban Development (IUD) of Beijing studies the composite competitiveness of 286 cities at the prefectural level and above. The study is based on the data analysis of cities' composite competitiveness, and even includes the 17 cities in Shandong province. From the five perspectives of Power, Capacity, Vitality, Potentials and Charm of the urban system, this study establishes a system with five environments, 15 sub-environments and 39 indicators. Moreover, the research employs both statistical data and survey data to compare the levels of urban development. However, as the report was published in 2009, updated data for indexing and ranking under this framework needs to be obtained to reflect the current trends. In addition, the indicators identified in this framework are too limited. For instance, indicators used to evaluate Infrastructure are only Number of Internet Users, Electricity Consumption Amount per Capita, and Urban Road Area per Capita.

2.1.3 Ranking Studies and Indices at the Sub-National Level in China

Apart from national-level indices and rankings, many other studies in China perform the analysis of cities at the provincial level.

An important provincial-level ranking is by CASS on Shandong province. CASS has been updating the rankings of 17 Shandong cities in their Annual Report on China's Urban Competitiveness (Shandong) since 2002. In its 2015 edition, CASS ranks Shandong cities based on the categories of Urban General Economic Competitiveness and Urban Sustainable Competitiveness. CASS also classifies the cities in Shandong according to their dominant area of competitiveness, including the titles of a knowledge city, a harmonious city, an eco-city, a cultural city, an integrated city and an information city. As this study adopts the same framework used in the CASS Annual Report on China's Urban Competitiveness, the indicators for the Shandong index also include repeated indicators across the categories.

There are many other smaller-scale studies dedicated to the provincial-level ranking of cities in China. For instance, the Study on Urban Competitive Capacities of Hunan Cities sponsored by the Education Department of Hunan Province designed an index system with 34 indicators covering the aspects of Economics, Infrastructure Conditions, Science and Technology, Culture Development, Openness Situation, and Environmental Development. The study examines 13 Hunan cities and classifies them into four categories according to their competitiveness scores. Another similar study is that by the Empirical Research of Harmonious Urban Competitiveness in Anhui Province conducted for Anhui cities with an index system of 38 indicators. These studies analyse the strength of high-ranking cities, identify development problems of low-ranking cities, and provide appropriate recommendations. However, the ranking results in their research are constrained by the limited number of indicators and the lack of important indicators for city competitiveness, such as social security, governance efficiency and public health Care. In addition, these studies are brief reports, which lack in-depth explanation and analysis.

Unlike many previous studies that research from the perspective of a narrow subset of people (notably on expatriates), the theoretical framework of this study developed by the Asia

Competitiveness Institute (ACI) is that of an ordinary resident in the city. Such a framework is vastly different from one that focuses on members of the elite, since ordinary citizens have greater concern for issues like budgeting, and are interested in matters that directly affect their standard of living, such as the average quality of education, the adequacy of the mass transit system, the cost of health Care, among others. This perspective is consistent with both classic Western and Chinese development theories and is highly relevant for China's development challenges now.

It is of significance for researchers to investigate urban development at the provincial level to understand the rapid development of China cities and reasons for the gaps between them. However, many urban development rankings in China currently lack sufficiently deep analyses with a comprehensive set of indicators. This study therefore has a unique contribution to the literature as it provides a holistic and detailed look at one of the largest and prosperous provinces in China — Shandong province.

Furthermore, most relevant studies mentioned in our literature review are built on frameworks with either limited number of indicators or repeated indicators used in different environments. In contrast, our UCDI framework avoids these issues by meticulously relating each indicator to their representative category. In doing so, the UCDI framework ensures accurate research results. As such, it is clear that this study builds on past research to pursue an improved urban development ranking for China that is able to holistically consider and accurately rank cities in Shandong province.

2.2 Research Motivation, Objectives, and Expected Contributions

ACI's Urban Composite Development Index for 17 Shandong cities is a preliminary yet comprehensive attempt to investigate and evaluate the constituents of urban development, and thereby identify and improve on important policy aspects. Given the rising urbanisation in China and Shandong, there is a great potential for both the national and provincial governments to exploit opportunities for economic growth and citizen welfare. At the same time, the challenges and costs of urbanisation have to be managed as well to mitigate harmful damage that results from the mismanagement of the urbanisation process.

To address such issues in the context of the constant rise in urbanisation across Shandong and China, there is a need for a comprehensive framework to evaluate their urban development performance, while providing practical yet effective insights that can inform policymakers of the necessary steps for improved urban development. As such, this research is strongly motivated by the policy applicability for Shandong. In doing so, lessons may be drawn and applied to other regions of China.

Specifically, the objectives for this research are therefore to:

1. Evaluate the urban development performance of each city in Shandong province via the UCDI.
2. Identify differences and gaps between cities to understand their respective weaknesses and advantages.
3. Provide practical yet effective evidence-based policy recommendations that is relevant to the province and city, to empower policymakers with the knowledge of appropriate actions towards better urban development.

This study contributes to the literature by providing a rigorous framework upon which we can holistically evaluate urban development. By applying methodological innovations such as the *What-if* simulation analysis and Shapley weight methodology, we offer additional empirical rigour to support the evidence-based recommendations we propose. For instance, by simulating the improvement of the weakest indicators of a city to that of the provincial average in the *What-if* simulation analysis, we can obtain the rankings for each city under such a scenario. Such a contribution will provide policymakers with more accurate understandings of the positive outcomes that may accrue due to their actions. Additionally, the objective weights derived from the Shapley weight method provide insights on how to assign appropriate weights across the various environments, sub-environments and indicators.

Beyond the literature, a significant contribution of this study are the vital policy implications for Shandong and the various city-level policymakers. This study helps Shandong cities realise their comparative advantages as well as their gaps and weaknesses, which empower government officials and scholars with the added knowledge to formulate policies to improve the standards of city management. As such, this study allows ACI to contribute towards the sustainable urban development of the various cities in Shandong province and thereby enhance China's aspirations of prosperity and sustainable growth.

2.3 Conceptualising the Urban Composite Development Index Based on China's Five Development Concepts

In this book, we characterise liveable cities as those that are able to achieve vibrant economic growth through deep yet complex connections through the close integration with other cities, regions and the world economy. At the same time, the city must be able to strike a balance in terms of its environmental friendliness and sustainability, cultural diversity, excellent living conditions as well as security through social-political harmony.

As previously mentioned, this study adopts the perspectives of ordinary residents to assess the various aspects of urban development that directly affect their quality of life. This perspective is consistent with both the classic Western and Chinese development theories, which are highly relevant to the developmental challenges that China is currently facing.

This study draws inspirations from many significant Western economic and social theories. Concepts to promote the emphasis on people in society include the social contract and popular sovereignty by Jean-Jacques Rousseau (Rousseau 1918), a "people centric" approach to development by François Perroux (Perroux 1983) and Amartya Sen's call for a more participatory approach to national development (Sen 2002). In addition, other important ideas include "innovative development" driven by technological, institutional and ideological innovations by Joseph Schumpeter (Schumpeter 1934), Joseph Stiglitz's exposé of inequality and social discrimination being exacerbated by globalisation (Stiglitz 2003), and Herman Daly's attempt to balance environmental conservation and economic growth through sustainable development (Daly 1996).

In China, the "People Oriented" governing philosophy has deep intellectual roots in the traditional Chinese culture. As early as 220 BC, the idea of "people are the foundation of the state; the state enjoys peace when its people are content" was recorded in Shang Shu (a collection of ancient Chinese documents before Qin Dynasty). Around the same period, Confucius proposed that the state must sustain, enrich and educate its people. Later, another prominent Confucian thought leader Mencius (Mengzi) theorised the relationship between the state, the ruler and the people by suggesting that "people's needs should take precedence before that of the state or the ruler". Based on these philosophies, throughout China's history, generations of Confucian scholars have championed the "Policy of Benevolence" as a fundamental principle of good governance, advising the rulers to adopt economic, social and cultural policies to promote welfare and ensure a decent life for everyone. Furthermore, traditional Chinese philosophers also value equity, balance and harmony. In Analects, Confucius argued that the rulers should "worry not about scarcity, but inequality; worry not about poverty, but instability", emphasising the importance of an equitable allocation of resources across geographical regions and social classes. Zhuang Zhou, another prominent Taoism philosopher, pointed out that "the nature is the origin of all things", reflecting the constant pursuit of a harmony between human and nature in Taoism philosophy.

The "People Oriented" philosophy was valued beyond ancient China, as it also guides the governance strategies of modern Chinese leaders. Since the Chinese Communist Party's 18th National Congress, the new Chinese leadership continues to emphasise the importance of being "people oriented". Wrestling with the challenges of an imbalanced economy, a severely degraded environment and a growing social inequality, the Chinese leadership put forward the Five Development Concepts as the guiding principles for the 13th Five Year Plan to better "serve the people" and to guide policymakers in their effort to tackle the diverse and complex challenges that China currently faces. The Five Development Concepts are Innovation, Coordination, Green Development, Opening Up and Sharing as illustrated in Figure 2.1.

Figure 2.1: Theoretical Framework Based on China's Five Development Concepts

Xi Jinping
7th President of the People's Republic of China

- **I. The focus of innovative development is to address the issue of growth drivers.**
- **II. The focus of coordinated development is to address the issue of unbalanced development.**
- **III. The focus of green development is to address the issue of harmony between humankind and nature.**
- **IV. The focus of open development is to address the issue of internal and external coordination in development.**
- **V. The focus of shared development is to address the issue of social equity and justice.**

Interconnected and mutually reinforcing, these five major concepts form a whole that requires unified implementation. None of the concepts can be emphasized over, or in place of, any of the others. If our implementation of any one of these concepts falls short, our entire process of development will be adversely affected.

— Excerpts from President Xi's speech at the Fifth Plenary Session of the Eighteenth Communist Party of China Central Committee, 29 October 2015

Source: Asia Competitiveness Institute.

Notably, Marxist ideologies are embedded in the Sharing, Innovation and Green Development concepts. Income inequality and social disparity have become increasingly severe in recent years. According to the Global Wealth Report 2013, more than 50% of wealth is concentrated in the top 1% of people (Crédit Suisse, 2013). Karl Marx argued that as long as the factors of production (i.e. resources, factories and technology) continue to be owned by a tiny group of individuals, and as long as the needs of society are not prioritised over capital accumulation of capital owners, poverty will remain and ultimately grow. As mentioned in his Economic Manuscripts of 1857–1858, Karl Marx believed that the purpose of all production is to the benefit all people

The concept of Sharing Development is precisely to tackle this issue of inequality. As of 2017, there are approximately 30 million rural residents still living below the poverty line.[1] By 2020, China has aims to build a moderately prosperous society in all respects, where all rural poverty must be eliminated and all impoverished counties rehabilitated.

Karl Marx believed that social relations are intricately linked to "productive forces" (i.e. the combination of labour and capital). In particular, he notes that "In acquiring new productive forces men change their mode of production; and in changing their mode of production, in changing the way of earning their living, they change all their social relations" (Marx 2008).[2] The complete set of relationships that all human beings must be engaged in order to produce and survive are also referred to by Karl Marx as "relations of production". In addition, the state of these relations of production depends on the different stages of productive forces that currently exist, thereby forming the foundation for social development. The totality of these relations of production are the foundations of economic structure of the society.

In summary, productive forces affects how people interact with one other (i.e. social relationships), which underlie the constituent of relations of production and in turn affect the economic activities of the society. As such, the notion of Innovation Development from the Five Development Concepts is related to these ideas from Karl Marx as this development concept is focused on creating new productive forces that leads to further economic growth. Considering the industrial revolutions the world has undergone since 1765, from the invention of the steam engine and electricity to newer productive forces such as computerisation and digitalisation, which have led to enormous growth in economic activities as well as the economy.

In his manuscript entitled *Estranged Labour*, Karl Marx noted the close relationship between humans and nature. In his words, "Man lives on nature — means that nature is his body… That man's physical and spiritual life is linked to nature means simply that nature is linked to itself, for man is a part of nature". Karl Marx highlighted how nature provides resources not only for humans' livelihoods, but also for their production. Therefore, it is the people's responsibility to protect nature in their daily activities given the intricate relationship and interdependencies between them.

Frederick Engels pointed out that in the short-run, humans may secure a victory against nature, but would eventually lose out in the long-run. Specifically, Engels noted that "For each victory nature takes its revenge on us. Each victory, it is true, in the first place brings about the

---

[1]According to the State Council of People's Republic of China, China's poverty line is RMB 2,300 rural net income per person per year in 2010 constant prices (People's Daily 2011).

[2]Karl Marx first published the book entitled *The Poverty of Philosophy* in Paris and Brussels in 1847.

results we expected, but in the second and third places it has quite different, unforeseen effects which only too often cancel out the first." To illustrate his point, Engels mentioned an example where "the people who, in Mesopotamia, Greece, Asia Minor and elsewhere, destroyed forests to obtain cultivable land, never dreamed that by removing along with the forests the collecting centres and reservoirs of moisture they were laying the basis for the present forlorn state of those countries" (Engels 1974).[3] The concept of Green Development precisely captures this interplay between humans and nature. In the 19th National Congress, President Xi Jinping further emphasised the importance of preserving the environment and ecological civilisation by reiterating that "lucid waters and lush mountains are invaluable assets".

Supported by these development theories from different schools of thought on the centrality of people in the definition of urban development, the UCDI Framework also draws on the insights and principles of the Five Development Concepts. We link them to each of the six environments, which collectively encompass 23 sub-environments, as shown in Figure 2.2. The six environments are (1) Scale and Quality of Economic Activities, (2) Financial Capacity, Labour Market Flexibility and Economic Vibrancy, (3) Good Governance, Effective Leadership and Social Stability, (4) Technological Advancement and Innovation Capability, (5) Public Service Standards and Quality of Life Improvement, and (6) Resource Conditions and Environmental Protection.[4]

The theoretical framework based on China's Five Development Concepts can be elaborated further, as follows:

I. *The focus of innovative development is to address the issue of growth drivers.*

Innovation is the primary driving force of economic and social development. In order to adhere to innovative development, we must put this concept at the core of development. Its main connotation includes the constant promotion of theoretical innovation, institutional innovation, technological innovation and cultural innovation. The more critical goal is to allow the majority of urban residents understand the theory of innovation, to adapt to the innovation system,to obtain the innovative technology and to accept innovative culture, so that they can fully enjoy the fruits of innovation in life.

The UCDI framework embodies the concept of innovative development in the environments of Financial Capacity, Labour Market Flexibility and Economic Vibrancy as well as Technological Advancement and Innovation Capability.

II. *The focus of coordinated development is to address the issue of unbalanced development.*

Coordinated development places a strong emphasis on the balanced growth across different geographical regions and among different aspects of society. Geographically, coordinated development will lead to a balance between urban and rural areas and across Eastern, Central, Western and Southern Shandong. It also aims to achieve a balance among economic growth, socio-cultural development and environmental conservation.

---

[3] Friedrich Engels first produced the book entitled *The Part Played by Labour in the Transition from Ape to Man* in 1876.

[4] A detailed discussion for each environment is featured in Section 2.4 of Chapter 2.

Figure 2.2: Theoretical Framework for the Urban Composite Development Index for 17 Shandong Cities

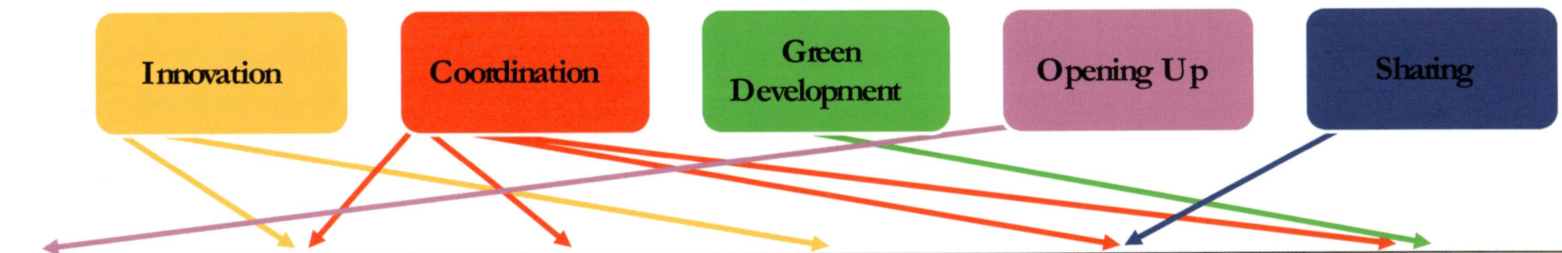

1. Scale and Quality of Economic Activities	2. Financial Capacity, Labour Market Flexibility and Economic Vibrancy	3. Good Governance, Effective Leadership and Social Stability	4. Technological Advancement and Innovation Capability	5. Public Service Standards and Quality of Life Improvement	6. Resource Conditions and Environmental Protection
1.1 Economic Capacity	2.1 Financial Deepening and Business Efficiency	3.1 Fiscal Sustainability	4.1 Research and Development Input	5.1 Social Security and Standard of Living	6.1 Environmental Quality
1.2 Openness to Trade and Services	2.2 Productivity Performance	3.2 Transparency and Accountability	4.2 Technological Innovation Capability	5.2 Public Health Care System	6.2 Natural Resources
1.3 Inflationary Pressure	2.3 Labour Market Flexibility	3.3 Public Governance	4.3 Research and Development Output	5.3 Public Education	6.3 Environmental Management
1.4 Market Development	2.4 Economic Vibrancy and Tripartite Relationship (Government, Employee and Employer)	3.4 Public Security and Social Stability		5.4 Public Transport Infrastructure	
				5.5 Public Culture and Information Services	

Source: Asia Competitiveness Institute.

The UCDI framework embodies the concept of coordinated development in the environments of (a) Financial Capacity, Labour Market Flexibility and Economic Vibrancy, (b) Good Governance, Effective Leadership and Social Stability, (c) Public Service Standards and Quality of Life Improvement, (d) Resource Conditions and Environmental Protection.

III. *The focus of open development is to address the issue of internal and external coordination in development.*

Openness will help China to transcend national and regional limitations and seek cooperation with the world. It requires China to actively participate in globalisation and develop mutually beneficial partnerships. China will also play a more active role in governing the global economy and providing public goods to gain a bigger role in global institutions and guard against a resurgence of protectionism. Meanwhile, to mitigate the downsides of globalisation such as rising inequality, China needs to adopt policy measures to ensure that their benefits of globalisation are distributed equitably within a more inclusive society.

The UCDI framework embodies the concept of open development in the environment of Scale and Quality of Economic Activities.

IV. *The focus of shared development is to address the issue of social equity and justice.*

Sharing emphasises the use of effective public policies and governance innovations to provide extensive public services and tangible benefits for all citizens. By sharing, China will develop a more equitable society and reduce the income gaps across social classes, between urban and rural areas and across different geographical regions. Policy changes and institutional reforms are necessary to ensure basic social security and employment. An equitable sharing of wealth and social benefits is the ultimate goal and result of the other four development concepts.

The UCDI framework embodies the concept of shared development in the environment of Public Service Standards and Quality of Life Improvement.

The Five Development Concepts are a coherently interconnected collection.

Innovation, as the driving force of development, focuses on quality and efficiency. Coordinated development highlights the importance of a balanced development to facilitate environmental conservation and equitable sharing. Green development ensures an enjoyable living condition for all citizens, which is only achievable through constant technological and institutional innovations. Openness leads to a China that is more integrated with the international community where it has to innovate to stay competitive. Meanwhile, with a higher level of participation in global governance, China will likely shoulder more environmental responsibilities. Lastly, sharing will help China to build a more equitable and just society, providing moral grounds and motivations for the other four development concepts.

With the comprehensive integration of the guiding principles from the Chinese leadership, the urban development index constructed is therefore relevant in the context of China in the 21st century, where unique and emerging issues such as inequality and sustainable development are critical. Further, by aligning the assessment of the urban development performance with the principles advocated by the Chinese leadership, the 17 cities of Shandong can accurately evaluate their development standards and make the necessary improvements and contributions to

ordinary residents of cities must be the top priority of the Chinese Communist Party. As eloquently put by President Xi Jinping: "The aspirations of the people to live a better life must always be the focus of our efforts" (Xi 2017).

2.4 Methodological Framework for the Urban Composite Development Index

It is worth noting that the framework adopted by the UCDI follows a similar framework adopted by ACI's previous liveability studies, namely the Global Liveable Cities Index (GLCI) and Greater China Liveable Cities Index (GCLCI). In that framework, ACI assess liveability across five environments, 18 sub-environments and 86 indicators in the GLCI and 96 indicators in the GCLCI. The environments are (a) Economic Vibrancy and Competitiveness, (b) Environmental Friendliness and Sustainability, (c) Domestic Security and Stability, (d) Socio-Cultural Conditions, and (e) Political Governance.[5]

To construct a theoretically sound and empirically robust framework, ACI improved on its past framework and designed the UCDI based on China's Five Development Concepts, as described in the earlier sections. Specifically, ACI has attempted to capture the complex and diverse aspects of urban development in six environments, comprising 23 sub-environments and 131 indicators. The six environments in the UCDI are (a) Scale and Quality of Economic Activities, (b) Financial Capacity, Labour Market Flexibility and Economic Vibrancy, (c) Good Governance, Effective Leadership and Social Stability, (d) Technological Advancement and Innovation Capability, (e) Public Service Standards and Quality of Life Improvement, and (f) Resource Conditions and Environmental Protection. The subsequent sections will describe each environment in detail.

2.4.1 Scale and Quality of Economic Activities

The environment 1 on Scale and Quality of Economic Activities examines the macroeconomic conditions of a city. The four sub-environments are (1) Economic Capacity, (2) Openness to Trade and Services, (3) Inflationary Pressure and (4) Market Development.

The sub-environment of Economic Capacity includes data on the city's Gross Regional Domestic Product (GRDP) and measures on urbanisation. The sub-environment of Openness to Trade and Services comprises indicators describing trade, foreign direct investment inflows, domestic presence of foreign enterprises, ease of doing businesses and tourism. The sub-environment of Inflationary Pressure includes Consumer Price Index (CPI), Producer Price Index (PPI), Retail Price Index, urban residents' income and their satisfaction with the price level. The last sub-environment of Market Development includes indicators describing the contribution of non-state-owned enterprises in different aspects, number of professionals, regulations on businesses and classification of enterprises.

2.4.2 Financial Capacity, Labour Market Flexibility and Economic Vibrancy

The environment 2 on Financial Capacity, Labour Market Flexibility and Economic Vibrancy examines the financial strength and important factors related to productivity in a city. There are

[5] ACI's GLCI and GCLCI research projects produced two books (Tan, Nie, and Baek 2015; Tan, Woo, and Tan 2012) and four journal articles (Tan and Kaur 2016; Tan, Nie, and Baek 2016; Tan, Woo, and Aw 2014; Tan, Woo, and Tan 2014).

four sub-environments under this environment, namely (1) Financial Deepening and Business Efficiency, (2) Productivity Performance, (3) Labour Market Flexibility and (4) Economic Vibrancy & Tripartite Relationship (Government, Employee and Employer).

The sub-environment of Financial Deepening and Business Efficiency includes description on the development of financial institutions and financing conditions of a city. The sub-environment of Productivity Performance describes the productivity and education level of a city. The sub-environment of Labour Market Flexibility mainly comprises measures on employment and salaries. The sub-environment of Economic Vibrancy & Tripartite Relationship (Government, Employee and Employer) includes measures on harmonic working environment of labour, electricity usage, passengers transported and cargo transported.

2.4.3 Good Governance, Effective Leadership and Social Stability

The environment 3 on Good Governance, Effective Leadership and Social Stability describes the fiscal state of a city. This environment comprises four sub-environments, namely (1) Fiscal Sustainability, (2) Transparency and Accountability, (3) Public Governance and Public Security and (4) Social Stability.

The sub-environment of Fiscal Sustainability describes the state of fiscal revenue and expenditure of a city. The sub-environment of Transparency and Accountability includes information on public trust, public satisfaction on judiciary system and bureaucratic corruption. The sub-environment of Public Governance examines the income of residents, the quality and openness of government system, number of civil servants and the number of administration cases. The sub-environment of Public Security and Social Stability includes data on crime rate, degree of harmony in the society, social security, satisfaction with police and urban management personnel.

2.4.4 Technological Advancement and Innovation Capability

The environment 4 on Technological Advancement and Innovation Capability examines the innovative development of a city. There are three sub-environments under this environment, namely (1) Research and Development Input, (2) Technological Innovation Capability and (3) Research and Development Output.

The sub-environment of Research and Development Input considers physical and human capital investment in Research and Development (R&D). The sub-environment of Technological Innovation Capability includes data on the number of innovation platforms and technological specialist, and the degree of satisfaction with innovation environment. The sub-environment of Research and Development Output describes the value-added of high-tech industry using different metrics.

2.4.5 Public Service Standards and Quality of Life Improvement

The environment 5 on Public Service Standards and Quality of Life Improvement describes the quality of household's life from income, health care, education and transportation aspects. The five sub-environments under this environment are (1) Social Security and Standard of Living, (2) Public Health Care System, (3) Public Education, (4) Public Transport Infrastructure and (5) Public Culture and Information Services.

The sub-environment of Social Security and Standard of Living contains measures on housing, insurance, social welfare and poverty. The sub-environment of Public Health Care System comprises data on the expenditure and development of health care in the city. The sub-environment of Public Education consists of measures on the education resources and government expenditure in public education. The sub-environment of Public Transport Infrastructure describes the number of public transport vehicles and the traffic condition. The sub-environment of Public Culture and Information Services considers the cultural facility and infrastructure in the city.

2.4.6 Resource Conditions and Environmental Protection

The environment 6 on Resource Conditions and Environmental Protection focused on the green development of a city, which includes three sub-environments, namely (1) Environmental Quality, (2) Natural Resources and (3) Environmental Management.

The sub-environment of Environmental Quality considers the emissions of chemicals. The sub-environment of Natural Resources includes data on the consumption of energies and the condition of natural resources. The last sub-environment of Environmental Management pertains to the management of water, disposal and green spaces, as well as the environmental expenditure.

It is worth noting that the inclusion of the environment of Resource Conditions and Environmental Protection is an important dimension of city liveability. This captures not only the desire to preserve the environment for the welfare of future generations but also the aesthetic appeal and appreciation of nature as well. Furthermore, this understanding is because people must recognise that sustainability for future generations must mean that they cannot allow their consumption to go unchecked as they can generate irreversible consequences.

2.5 Selection of Ideal Indicators versus Practical Indicators, Data Sources, Constraints, and Proxies

The proposed ideal indicators denote a quantitative attempt to identify and rank cities according to a set of defined concepts which would best reflect urban development and liveability of a city. Thus, the search for ideal indicators usually gives rise to a large number of potential candidates. However, due to data non-availability and cost constrains, it would be reduced to a set of practical indicators devised to reduce large quantity of data down to its simplest form, retaining essential meaning for the questions being asked for the data.

Nevertheless, the selection of relevant indicators remains a subject of intense debate, and their inclusion and appropriateness are subjected to review and being questioned from time to time whenever suggestions for new indicators may become important due to changes in conditions and trends. While we have identified 269 ideal indicators and 131 practical indicators, as listed below, a detailed list of indicators is available in Appendices A and B.

Ideal *Indicators for Six Environments*

1. 55 Ideal Indicators of Scale and Quality of Economic Activities
2. 45 Ideal Indicators of Financial Capacity, Labour Market Flexibility and Economic Vibrancy

3. 49 Ideal Indicators of Good Governance, Effective Leadership and Social Stability
4. 36 Ideal Indicators of Technological Advancement and Innovation Capability
5. 50 Ideal Indicators of Public Service Standards and Quality of Life Improvement
6. 34 Ideal Indicators of Resource Conditions and Environmental Protection

Practical *Indicators for Six Environments*

1. 21 Practical Indicators of Scale and Quality of Economic Activities
2. 26 Practical Indicators of Financial Capacity, Labour Market Flexibility and Economic Vibrancy
3. 23 Practical Indicators of Good Governance, Effective Leadership and Social Stability
4. 11 Practical Indicators of Technological Advancement and Innovation Capability
5. 33 Practical Indicators of Public Service Standards and Quality of Life Improvement
6. 17 Practical Indicators of Resource Conditions and Environmental Protection

With regard to the data used, this study employs data for the year 2016, and has a coverage of all the 17 prefectural-level cities in Shandong province, as shown in Table 2.1.

Table 2.1: List of 17 Shandong Cities Covered in the Study

	City
1	Jinan
2	Qingdao
3	Zibo
4	Zaozhuang
5	Dongying
6	Yantai
7	Weifang
8	Jining
9	Tai'an
10	Weihai
11	Rizhao
12	Laiwu
13	Linyi
14	Dezhou
15	Liaocheng
16	Binzhou
17	Heze

Source: Asia Competitiveness Institute.
Note: The sequence of the cities is based on the Division Code by the Ministry of Civil Affairs of People's Republic of China.

The data sources used in this project includes both hard data (i.e. statistics) and survey data. Hard data was gathered from publicly available sources including the 2017 Shandong Statistical

Yearbook, China City Statistical Yearbooks, Shandong Urban Construction Statistical Yearbook and Regional Development Statistics. On the other hand, survey data was gathered using a survey questionnaire carefully designed by ACI. The random telephone surveys of 5,140 Shandong residents was conducted through a professional data-collection vendor in China. Approximately, 300 valid survey responses were obtained for each city from our data collection efforts. A sample of the survey questionnaire is available in Appendix C.

It should be noted that constructing ranking indices for sub-national economies like cities is far more challenging than that at the national level due to acute difficulties in terms of data availability, quality and accuracy. As such, the main constraint faced in this study was the inability to obtain comprehensive sets of data for every indicator. For instance, as mentioned about the ideal and practical indicators, 269 ideal indicators were identified while less than half (131 indicators) were feasible to collect and use. In addition, some cities had incomplete data in 2016 for the practical indicators identified. As a result, this project's investigation in terms of its extensiveness was less than optimal. Nevertheless, 131 practical indicators is a large number and contributes significantly to the robustness of our result.

To avoid losing relevant indicators due to gaps in the data, this project employs the use of proxies. In particular, for each indicator and city where 2016 data was not available, the latest year's data was used as its proxy. While this is not ideal, it provides a reasonable estimate for the absent data. For the indicators where this remains a problem, such as the Average Years of Education Received and the Workforce Participation Rate, such a practice may have to persist until new data becomes available.

2.6 Equal versus Shapley Weight for Six Environments of the Urban Composite Development Index

2.6.1 Equal Weight

The following section deals with the question of how we process our data by putting them into a format that may be systematically analysed. The 131 indicators used in this research not only have different definitions but also have different units of measurement. For instance, GRDP is measured in RMB 100 million whereas the population size is measured in terms of the number of people. In the remainder of this section, we will explain how to resolve issues caused by differences in definitions and units of measurement for each indicator.

ACI uses the "standardised score" or the z-score statistical method. The standardised score measures the performance difference between a specific city and the average city. There is no need to consider the use of different units of measurement for different indicators because the standardised score itself involves no unit of measurement as it simply measures the relative performance of various cities. In statistical terms, the standardised score measures how many standard deviations each city is away from the average city.

We first compute the average and standard deviation of all cities for each indicator by which the standardised value is calculated as follows:

$$\text{Standardised Value} = \frac{\text{Original Value} - \text{Mean}}{\text{Standard Deviation}},$$

0 (zero) = same as the average of all cities
– (negative) = below the average of all cities
+ (positive) = above the average of all cities

If the standardised score for a city is zero, this means that the city is an average performer in Shandong province. A negative standardised score indicates that the city is performing more poorly than the others, while a positive standardised score indicates that the city is performing better than the others. The farther away the score is from zero, the farther away is the performance of the said city from the average of the 17 cities. In this sense, a negative score with a large magnitude indicates very weak urban development, while a positive score with a large magnitude indicates very strong urban development.

The standardised scores for each indicator are first aggregated at the sub-environment level, subsequently reaggregated at the environment level, and finally aggregated again at the overall level. This enables us to examine the performance of each of the 17 cities at various levels, from the overall performance to specific indicators.

For our conventional study, we assume all the environments carry the same weight, i.e. 1/6. The sub-environments encompassed under each of the environments are also assigned the same weight. A similar weighting scheme is assumed at the indicator level.

Going forward, in order to verify the robustness of our results from the subjective assumption in the equal weight method, we would like to introduce an objective weighting method, namely the Shapley weight method, which will be discussed in detail in the next subsection.

2.6.2 Shapley Value

The Shapley value is the most commonly used solution concept in cooperative game theory. Formally, a coalition game (N, v) in cooperative game theory is defined by a set of players N and a characteristic function $v(S)$: $2^N \to R$, where it maps coalition S (or subset of players) to a real number. The function describes the expected payoffs the S players can obtain by cooperation. The Shapley value of the coalition game is an n-vector, denoted by $\Phi(v)$, satisfying a set of axioms, i.e. Individual Rationality, Efficiency, Symmetry, Additivity and Null Player.

The i-th component of $\Phi(v)$ can be determined by

$$\Phi(v) = \sum_{S \subseteq N \setminus \{i\}} \frac{|S|!\,(N - |S| - 1)!}{N!}(v(S \cup i) - v(S)).$$

In our context, the players will be the indicators used for the construction of the index. The coalition will be the sub-environments and environments, which the indicators belong to. The desirable properties, i.e. the axioms, are meaningful for general index ranking. Individual Rationality ensures that each indicator has a positive contribution to the index score. An indicator must satisfy the Null Player axiom, so that it is economically meaningful for that indicator to be considered relevant to the index. Symmetry guarantees that if two indicators carry the same value, they are equally important in the index scoring. Efficiency and Additivity are also important mathematical properties for the construction of the index.

The application of Shapley value has been well studied in various strands of literature. The concept has been used to solve the taxation and redistribution problem, as described by Aumann and Kurz (1977). It is also used in voting for public goods problems. Aumann and Myerson (2003) for instance have studied the link or coalition formation among players using the Shapley value. Moulin (1992) studied the application of the Shapley value in fair division of unproduced goods under monetary transfer and quasi-linear utilities. Petrosjan and Zaccour (2003) studied to the best of the Shapley value cost allocation in a pollution reduction setting. More recently, Hougaard *et al.* (2017) have applied the Shapley value concept to licensing under FRAND terms.[6] However, our knowledge, the Shapley value has not been applied to index ranking analysis before.

As a robustness check to the equal weight approach, we would like to propose an objective weighting method based on Shapley value — the "Bottom-Up" approach.

2.6.3 Shapley Weight — The "Bottom-Up" Approach

We first compute the Shapley value of each indicator based on the standardised value of the indicator for every city. By our definition, it measures the aggregate dispersion of the indicator, thus reflecting the inequality among the cities. More weights are assigned to those indicators with a higher Shapley value. The weights of sub-environments are computed based on both the absolute performance (standardised score) and the relative performance (weights) of indicators under that particular sub-environment. The weights of environments are computed in a similar way by considering the relevant absolute performance and the relative performance of sub-environments. The detailed description of the methodology can be found in the appendix.

2.6.4 Comparison between the Shapley Weight Method and the Entropy Weight Method

Yet another objective weight assignment method, commonly applied in the area of decision science, is entropy (Zeleny 1982). The entropy for the indicator i is defined as

$$\text{Entropy}_i = -\frac{1}{\ln(E)}\sum_{e=1}^{E} p_{ei}\ln(p_{ei}),$$

where E is the number of economies, $p_{ei} = \frac{v_{ei}}{\sum_{e=1}^{E} v_{ei}}$ and v_{ei} is the characteristic of the raw data x_{ei}. And the weight of indicator i is, then, defined by

$$w_i = 1 - \text{Entropy}_i.$$

The interpretation of the entropy of an indicator concerns the information that the particular indicator transmits. The higher the entropy, the less the information carried, implying a lower weight assigned to that indicator.

While this method appears to be an improvement over a subjective weighting scheme, one of the important reasons why we cannot apply the entropy weight method for our analysis is its inability to handle negative values due to the use of the logarithm operator. Thus, the alternative standardisation method, other than z-score, is required.

---

[6] FRAND is a short notation for Fair Reasonable and Non-Discriminatory.

In the report *Assessing Provincial Development under the Five Development Concepts*, the Institute of Applied Economics Shanghai Academy of Social Sciences has applied the entropy weight method to assign weights to indicators. To avoid negative values, they deploy the *max-min standardisation* method, where

$$v_{ei} = \frac{x_{ei} - \min(x_i)}{\max(x_i) - \min(x_i)}.$$

There is an important drawback to the max-min standardisation. If an economy performs the worst under an indicator, i.e. $x_{ei} = \min(x_i)$, then $v_{ei} = 0$, which cannot be computed by natural log either. Additional assumptions must be made in the computation, i.e. ln(0) must be assigned to 0.

Another reason that the entropy weight method is less appropriate than the Shapley method is that, when applied to the field of index construction, the former method is very sensitive to indicators containing outliers.

Consider the example as illustrated in Table 2.2. There are 11 economies and three indicators with different measurement units. Indicator 1 contains an outlier. All the economies perform equally in Indicator 2. There is a clear divergence of performance among all the economies in Indicator 3. We will use *z*-score standardisation for the Shapley method, while max–min standardisation for the entropy weight method.

Table 2.2: Example to Compare the Shapley and Entropy Weight Methods

Economy	Indicator 1	Indicator 2	Indicator 3
A	10	2	1
B	1	3	2
C	1	2	3
D	1	2	4
E	1	2	5
F	1	2	6
G	1	2	7
H	1	1	8
I	1	2	9
J	1	2	10
K	1	2	11

Source: Asia Competitiveness Institute.

Under the entropy weight method, the weights of indicators are

$$w_1^{\text{Entropy}} = 0.866, \quad w_2^{\text{Entropy}} = 0.045, \quad w_3^{\text{Entropy}} = 0.089.$$

Due to the presence of an outlier under Indicator 1, i.e. Economy A, the entropy weight method predicts that Indicator 1 carries the most information, thus assigning it a much higher weight relative to the rest.

Under the Shapley method, the weights of indicators are

$$w_1^{\text{Shapley}} = 0.308, \quad w_2^{\text{Shapley}} = 0.229, \quad w_3^{\text{Shapley}} = 0.463.$$

As we can observe, similar to the entropy weight method, the Shapley weights assign a relatively higher weight to Indicator 1 than Indicator 2 because of the presence of the outlier. However, the highest weight is assigned to Indicator 3 because of the dispersion observed, overcoming the bias that the entropy weight method generates due to its inability to handle outliers.

To summarise the foregoing discussion between the Shapley and entropy weight methods, the derivation of the final index score must be done with the help of aggregation of all relevant information, implying that all the indicators are the determinants. We should reflect on the importance of indicators which show that the economies are unequally developed (e.g. Indicator 3). However, as noted earlier, the entropy weight method fails to capture this feature, due to the fact that such indicators convey less information than those with an outlier (e.g. Indicator 1). The Shapley method, on the other hand, offers a better alternative as it captures both the fact that economies are most unequally developed under Indicator 3 as well as the existence of the outlier in Indicator 1.

2.7 Beauty Contest versus *What-if* Simulations and Its Shortcomings

Yet another important methodological technique adopted by ACI is the *What-if* simulation. Urban development rankings are like beauty pageants because they only show a list of those that perform well and those that face challenges, without providing constructive recommendations that can help improve urban development. ACI takes a step further by tackling the "so what" question. What impact do urban development rankings have on the policy of a specific city? The data used by ACI enables us to examine the indicators, sub-environments and environments of each city in a targeted manner. By analysing this data, not only we are able to provide an overall performance, we are also able to assess which indicators are weak and which are strong. This then allows us to provide policy suggestions that are specific to each city.

ACI's *What-if* Urban Development Simulation looks at how to improve the top 20% weakest indicators for a city, then recalculate the standardised score based on this improvement. First, we put all of the indicators for a specific city in order from lowest to highest based on their score. We are then able to identify the 26 weakest indicators for that city (20% of the total 131 indicators is 26).

Under most situations, the scores of the 26 weakest indicators are raised to the average scores for all 17 cities. This means that the raw data value of these 26 indicators will be changed to the provincial average. There are special cases for some cities in which some of the 20% weakest indicators are in fact above the provincial average value. For these specific indicators, the value remains at the original value so that the score of the city is not discounted. After increasing the standardised score for the 20% weakest indicators, we recalculate rankings by assuming that the score for other cities remains unchanged. Only one city is analysed during each simulation analysis. After completing simulation analysis of each of the 17 cities in Shandong province, each is given a new standardised score based on the simulated model. This can help us answer the question of how a particular city's overall performance in urban development would change if its weakest indicators improved while other cities' scores stayed the same. Even though this analysis is static, it provides a preliminary yet comprehensive guide for the policymakers to improve the city's urban development.

Overall, this chapter has shown that the UCDI is a carefully constructed index that incorporates China's Five Development Concepts as a sound theoretical basis for the assessment of urban development. Relative to other literature that have attempted to evaluate the urban development of cities, the UCDI is significantly more comprehensive and robust with 131 indicators across six environments that show development. Specifically, the six environments include the (1) Scale and Quality of Economic Activities, (2) Financial Capacity, Labour Market Flexibility and Economic Vibrancy, (3) Good Governance, Effective Leadership and Social Stability, (4) Technological Advancement and Innovation Capability, (5) Public Service Standards and Quality of Life Improvement, and (6) Resource Conditions and Environmental Protection.

To investigate the theoretical understanding of urban development rigorously, this chapter further outlined the ranking and simulation techniques as well as methodological innovations such as the Shapley weight method. As a result, the UCDI is able to translate the Five Development Concepts into an empirically robust framework that is quantifiable. With the theoretical framework and empirical techniques established, Chapter 3 will proceed to present the ranking results for the 17 cities in Shandong province.

References

Arcadis. 2016. 'Sustainable Cities Index 2016'.

Aumann, Robert J., and Mordecai Kurz. 1977. 'Power and Taxes'. *Econometrica: Journal of the Econometric Society* 45 (5): 1137–61. https://doi.org/10.2307/1914063.

Aumann, Robert J., and Roger B. Myerson. 2003. 'Endogenous Formation of Links Between Players and of Coalitions: An Application of the Shapley Value'. In *Networks and Groups*, 207–20. Studies in Economic Design. Springer, Berlin, Heidelberg. https://doi.org/10.1007/978-3-540-24790-6_9.

China Institute of City Competitiveness. 2015. *Yearbook of China City Competitiveness 2015*. 1st ed. China City.

Chinese Academy of Social Sciences (CASS). 2017. 中国城市竞争力报告*(NO.15) Annual Report on China's Urban Competitiveness (No.15) (in Chinese)*. Beijing, China: Social Science Academic Press.

Daly, Herman E. 1996. *Beyond Growth: The Economics of Sustainable Development*. Book, Whole. Boston: Beacon Press.

Economist Intelligence Unit (EIU). 2017. 'The Global Liveability Report 2017: A Free Overview'. 2017. http://www.eiu.com/public/thankyou_download.aspx?activity=download&campaignid=Liveability17.

Hougaard, Jens Leth, Chiu Yu Ko, and Xuyao Zhang. 2017. 'A Welfare Economic Interpretation of FRAND'. SSRN Scholarly Paper ID 2958212. Rochester, NY: Social Science Research Network. https://papers.ssrn.com/abstract=2958212.

Institute of Applied Economics Shanghai Academy of Social Sciences. 2016. '五大发展理念指标体系及省级区域评估报告 Assessing Provincial Development under the Five Development Concepts (in Chinese)'. Shanghai Academy of Social Sciences.

International Institute for Urban Development (IUD). 2009. 中国城市综合竞争力报告 *Annual Report on Composite Competitiveness of Chinese Cities (in Chinese)*. 1st ed. Beijing, China: China Economic Publishing House.

Mercer. 2017. 'Quality of Living Reports'. 14 March 2017. https://www.imercer.com/products/quality-of-living.aspx.

Monocle Magazine. 2017. 'Where to Live Well'. *Monocle* 11 (105): 46–69.

Moulin, Hervé. 1992. 'An Application of the Shapley Value to Fair Division with Money'. *Econometrica: Journal of the Econometric Society* 60 (6): 1331–49. https://doi.org/10.2307/2951524.

National Institute for Economic Experimentation (NIEE). 2015. *Report on the Quality of Life in Chinese Cities*. Beijing, China: Social Science Academic Press.

Perroux, Francois. 1983. *New Concept of Development: Basic Tenets*. Book, Whole. London: Croom Helm.

Petrosjan, Leon, and Georges Zaccour. 2003. 'Time-Consistent Shapley Value Allocation of Pollution Cost Reduction'. *Journal of Economic Dynamics and Control* 27 (3): 381–98. https://doi.org/10.1016/S0165-1889(01)00053-7.

Rousseau, Jean-Jacques. 1918. *Du Contrat Social Ou Principes Du Droit Politique*. Book, Whole. Manchester: Manchester University Press.

Schumpeter, Joseph Alois. 1934. *The Theory of Economic Development: An Inquiry into Profits, Capital, Credit, Interest, and the Business Cycle*. Vol. 46. Book, Whole. Cambridge, Mass: Harvard University Press.

Sen, Amartya Kumar. 2002. *Rationality and Freedom*. Book, Whole. Cambridge, Mass: Belknap Press.

Stiglitz, Joseph E. 2003. *Globalization and Its Discontents*. Book, Whole. New York; London; W.W. Norton.

Tan, Khee Giap, and Sujata Kaur. 2016. 'Measuring Abu Dhabi's Liveability Using the Global Liveable City Index (GLCI)'. *World Journal of Science, Technology and Sustainable Development* 13 (3): 205–23. https://doi.org/10.1108/WJSTSD-11-2015-0054.

Tan, Khee Giap, Tongxin Nie, and Shinae Baek. 2015. *Greater China Liveable Cities Index: Ranking Analysis, Simulation and Policy Evaluation*. Singapore: Whioce Publishing.

———. 2016. 'Empirical Assessment on the Liveability of Cities in the Greater China Region'. *Competitiveness Review* 26 (1): 2–24. https://doi.org/10.1108/CR-11-2015-0087.

Tan, Khee Giap, Wing Thye Woo, and Grace Aw. 2014. 'A New Approach to Measuring the Liveability of Cities: The Global Liveable Cities Index'. *World Review of Science, Technology and Sustainable Development* 11 (2): 176–96. https://doi.org/10.1504/WRSTSD.2014.065677.

Tan, Khee Giap, Wing Thye Woo, and Boon Seng Tan. 2014. 'A New Instrument to Promote Knowledge-Led Growth: The Global Liveable Cities Index'. *International Journal of Business Competition and Growth* 3 (3): 174–88. https://doi.org/10.1504/IJBCG.2014.060304.

Tan, Khee Giap, Wing Thye Woo, and Kong Yam Tan. 2012. *Ranking The Liveability of the World's Major Cities: The Global Liveable Cities Index (Glci)*. World Scientific.

The Mori Memorial Foundation. 2017. 'Global Power City Index'. http://mori-m-foundation.or.jp/pdf/GPCI2017_en.pdf.

Xi, Jinping. 2017. 'Secure a Decisive Victory in Building a Moderately Prosperous Society in All Respects and Strive for the Great Success of Socialism with Chinese Characteristics for a New Era; Delivered at the 19th National Congress of the Communist Party of China'. http://www.xinhuanet.com/english/download/Xi_Jinping's_report_at_19th_CPC_National_Congress.pdf.

Xie, Shouhong. 2003. '湖南省中心城市竞争力分析 Study on Urban Competitive Capacities of Hunan Cities (in Chinese)'. *World Regional Studies* 12 (2): 92–98.

Zeleny, Milan. 1982. *Multiple Criteria Decision Making*. McGraw-Hill.

Zhao, Jingzhu. 2011. 'Towards Sustainable Cities in China: Analysis and Assessment of Some Chinese Cities in 2008'. *Springer*.

Zhu, Daocai, and Limin Yao. 2009. '安徽和谐城市竞争力实证研究 The Empirical Research of Harmonious Urban Competitiveness in Anhui Province (in Chinese)'. *East China Economic Management* 23 (2): 15–19.

Chapter 3
Empirical Findings of the Urban Composite Development Index for 17 Shandong Cities

As shown in Chapter 2, the Urban Composite Development Index (UCDI) is a comprehensive framework built on robust theoretical foundations and rigorous empirical methods. This chapter employs the methodology described to present the main empirical findings related to each environment, followed by the *What-if* simulation results. In particular, the chapter begins with an overview of the assignment of weights across the six environments by the Shapley and Equal weight methods before proceeding to present the ranking and *What-if* simulation results for the 17 cities in Shandong province.

3.1 Environment Weights

As mentioned in Section 2.6 of Chapter 2, the Equal and Shapley weight methods differ quite greatly. Figure 3.1 shows the computed Shapely weights for each of the six environments in the urban development framework.

Figure 3.1: Shapley Weight for Each Environment

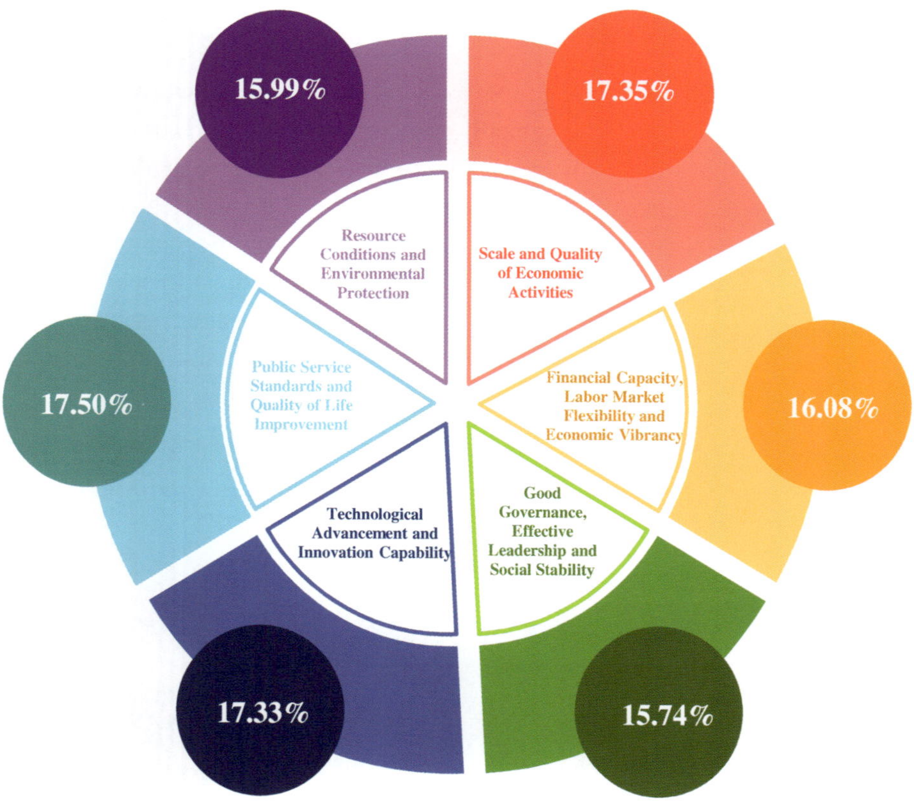

Source: Asia Competitiveness Institute.

Distinct from the Equal weight method, where each environment is considered to be equally important and therefore assigned a weight of 16.67% (or 1/6 equivalently), the Shapley weight method reveals some distribution of the environments' weight. The Shapely weights range from 15.74% for the environment of Good Governance, Effective Leadership and Social Stability to 17.50% for the environment of Public Service Standards and Quality of Life Improvement.

The Shapley weights assigned to each environment measures its unequal urban development performance among all the 17 Shandong cities. Consequently, the greater the divergence in performance of cities within a given environment, the higher its associated Shapley weight for that specific environment. Thus, the weight of an environment represents the relative importance of that environment in contributing to the overall urban development performance. A city will thus receive a higher score if it performs well in an environment in which there is higher inequality across all evaluated cities. Unequal development across different cities is therefore accounted for and captured by this Shapley weight approach. This correspondingly represents a significant change from the Equal weight method, where all environments are weighted at 16.67% (or 1/6) and unequal development is thus unaccounted for.

The comparatively high weight of 17.50% in the environment of Public Service Standards and Quality of Life Improvement reflects the unequal development of the 17 Shandong cities with regard to this specific environment. Correspondingly, the environment of Scale and Quality of Economic Activities has the second highest degree of unequal development, as indicated by its weight of 17.35%. The environment with the least divergent performance is thus the environment of Good Governance, Effective Leadership and Social Stability, as denoted by its relatively low weight of 15.74%.

Although the weights are different, the Shapley weights of each environment does not significantly deviate from 16.67%. Mathematically, there are two reasons that may account for this phenomenon. The first is that every surveyed city is equally developed in all aspects, and across all indicators, sub-environments, and hence environments. This is clearly not the case for Shandong, where regional inequality still exists. Thus, we come to the second explanation, which is that the aggregate dispersion (i.e. the Shapley value) of each indicator, sub-environment, and hence environment for all the cities has become equalised. The stronger performing cities excel in most aspects of the urban development, while the weaker performing cities expectedly lag behind for majority of the indicators.

3.2 Overall Urban Development Performance

Table 3.1: Overall Urban Development Performance

City	Rank		Score	
	Equal Weight Method	Shapley Weight Method	Equal Weight Method	Shapley Weight Method
Qingdao	1	1	1.753	1.628
Weihai	2	2	1.393	1.477
Yantai	3	3	1.312	1.404
Jinan	4	4	1.106	1.010
Weifang	5	5	0.855	0.872
Dongying	6	6	0.603	0.624
Zibo	7	7	0.403	0.464
Linyi	8	8	–0.002	0.005
Tai'an	9	9	–0.280	–0.278
Dezhou	10	10	–0.302	–0.326
Rizhao	11	11	–0.472	–0.482
Heze	12	12	–0.615	–0.639
Jining	13	13	–0.706	–0.782
Binzhou	14	14	–1.076	–1.032
Zaozhuang	15	15	–1.164	–1.154
Laiwu	16	16	–1.233	–1.186
Liaocheng	17	17	–1.576	–1.604

Source: Asia Competitiveness Institute.

Table 3.1 shows the overall urban development performance of 17 Shandong cities under both the equal and Shapley weight methods. There is no ranking difference between these two methods, which therefore highlights the robustness of equal weight approach. Even though the equal weight is a subjective assumption, the ranking remains consistent with the objective Shapley weight approach.

Since both methods offer consistent rankings, this section will employ the equal weight method in the ensuing discussion.

From the spread, it can be observed that the maximum score for the 17 Shandong cities is 1.753 and the minimum score is –1.576. Qingdao ranks 1st among the 17 Shandong cities with the highest score while Liaocheng ranks at 17th place. Qingdao performs best in urban development, with a gap followed by Weihai and Yantai. In terms of standardised score, there is a significant gap of 0.360 between Qingdao (rank 1st) and Weihai (rank 2nd). Weihai and Yantai score relatively close to each other. Jinan (rank 4th) leads Weifang (rank 5th) marginally by 0.251.

The average performing city (i.e. with a standardised score of 0) is somewhere between Zibo (0.403) at 7th place and Linyi (–0.002) at 8th place. The median belongs to Tai'an at 9th place with standardised score of –0.280. Clearly, the average score (0) is higher than the median score (–0.280). The average value is positioned in the upper half of the ranking, above the centre of the list, which indicates that more than half of the 17 cities obtained an overall performance that is weaker than the performance of the average performing city.

As for the distribution of the overall urban development scores, there are several gaps in scores between cities. For example, there is a relatively large gap between Zibo (0.403) (rank 7th) and Linyi (–0.002) (rank 8th), as well as between Jining (–0.706) (rank 13th) and Binzhou (–1.076) (rank 14th), and their scores differ by 0.405 and 0.370 respectively. These large gaps in scores are notable because the difference between their scores are sizeable despite being only one rank apart.

It can be observed that among the top five performing cities, Qingdao, Weihai, Yantai and Weifang are all coastal cities, while Jinan is the capital city of the province and holds Sub-Provincial administrative status since 1994. All the five cities have their own distinctive advantages that outperform the others. Qingdao excels in the sub-environment of Openness to Trade and Services. Weihai tops environmental management. Jinan performs well in the sub-environment of Financial Deepening and Business Efficiency, while Yantai has rich natural resources. Finally, yet importantly, Weifang has the highest economic vibrancy.

On the other hand, cities located in the central area of Shandong rank in the middle, while cities in Western Shandong tend to rank at the bottom (Figure 3.2). Zaozhuang, Laiwu and Liaocheng are relatively less developed cities. They are located farther in-land in Shandong province.

Figure 3.2: Overall Urban Development Performance Map of Shandong Province

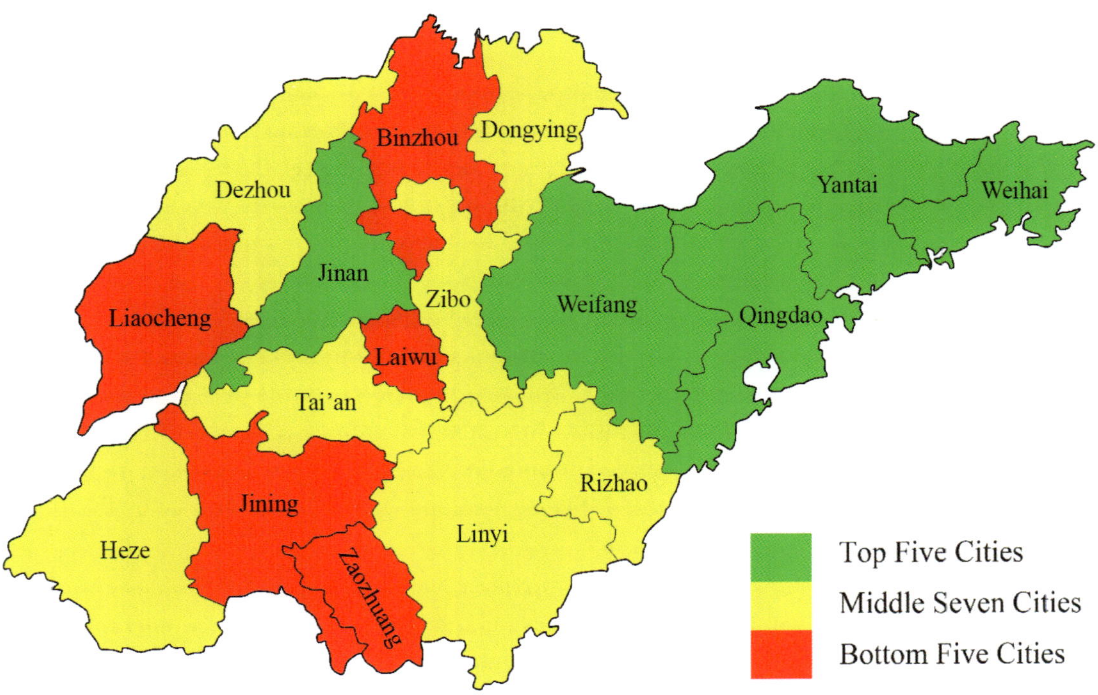

Source: Asia Competitiveness Institute.

The score difference between Liaocheng and Qingdao is more than 3.2, which indicates a large disparity between the two cities. As mentioned earlier in the introduction, Shandong is making notable effort to reduce inequality through regional integration via high-speed railway networks and the formation of various economic zones. The overlapping regional development strategies will offer new opportunities for cities beyond Shandong to narrow the development gap, while leaving room for them to specialise and differentiate.

3.3 Rankings by Environments

Table 3.2: Scale and Quality of Economic Activities Ranking

City	Rank		Score	
	Equal Weight Method	Shapley Weight Method	Equal Weight Method	Shapley Weight Method
Qingdao	1	2	1.987	1.608
Yantai	2	1	1.687	1.820
Heze	3	3	1.289	1.338
Weifang	4	4	1.021	1.079
Weihai	5	5	0.849	0.956
Linyi	6	6	0.447	0.451
Dezhou	7	7	0.096	0.175
Tai'an	8	8	–0.321	–0.251
Jinan	9	10	–0.364	–0.398
Zaozhuang	10	9	–0.412	–0.344
Binzhou	11	11	–0.573	–0.612
Liaocheng	12	13	–0.665	–0.689
Zibo	13	12	–0.674	–0.621
Dongying	14	14	–0.782	–0.722
Rizhao	15	15	–1.017	–0.998
Jining	16	17	–1.273	–1.469
Laiwu	17	16	–1.295	–1.322

Source: Asia Competitiveness Institute.

Table 3.2 shows the ranking for the environment of Scale and Quality of Economic Activities. The ranking for all the other cities are generally consistent, underscoring the robustness of the Equal weight approach. This discussion will focus on the results from the Equal weight method for the remainder of our discussion for this environment.

There are two possible explanations to account for the ranking differences between these two methods. Take, for instance, the case of Qingdao, where it ranks 2nd under the Shapley weight method, but ranks 1st under Equal weight method. The first reason suggests that Qingdao performs well in indicators associated with less weight. This means that all the other cities perform equally well in such indicators. The second reason is that the indicators Qingdao performs less well at are associated with higher weight, indicating that all the other cities perform varyingly in those indicators, and Qingdao is among the lower performing cities.

The city performing at the provincial average (i.e. with a standardised score of 0) for Scale and Quality of Economic Activities is between Dezhou (0.096) at 7th place and Tai'an (–0.321) at 8th place. The median is Jinan (–0.364), which ranks at 9th place. The average score (0) for the environment of Scale and Quality of Economic Activities is higher than the median score (–0.364).

It is worth noting that there is a marked drop in scores from Dezhou (0.096) (rank 7th) to Tai'an (–0.321) (rank 8th). The gap in scores between these two cities is 0.417. There are also considerable gaps between Weihai (0.849) (rank 5th) and Linyi (0.447) (rank 6th), as well as Yantai (1.687) (rank 2nd) and Heze (1.289) (rank 3rd). On the one hand, this shows that the performance of each city varies from each other even among the top-ranking cities. On the other hand, this suggests that the top seven cities considerably outperform the other 10 cities in the environment of Scale and Quality of Economic Activities.

Figure 3.3: Scale and Quality of Economic Activities Ranking Map

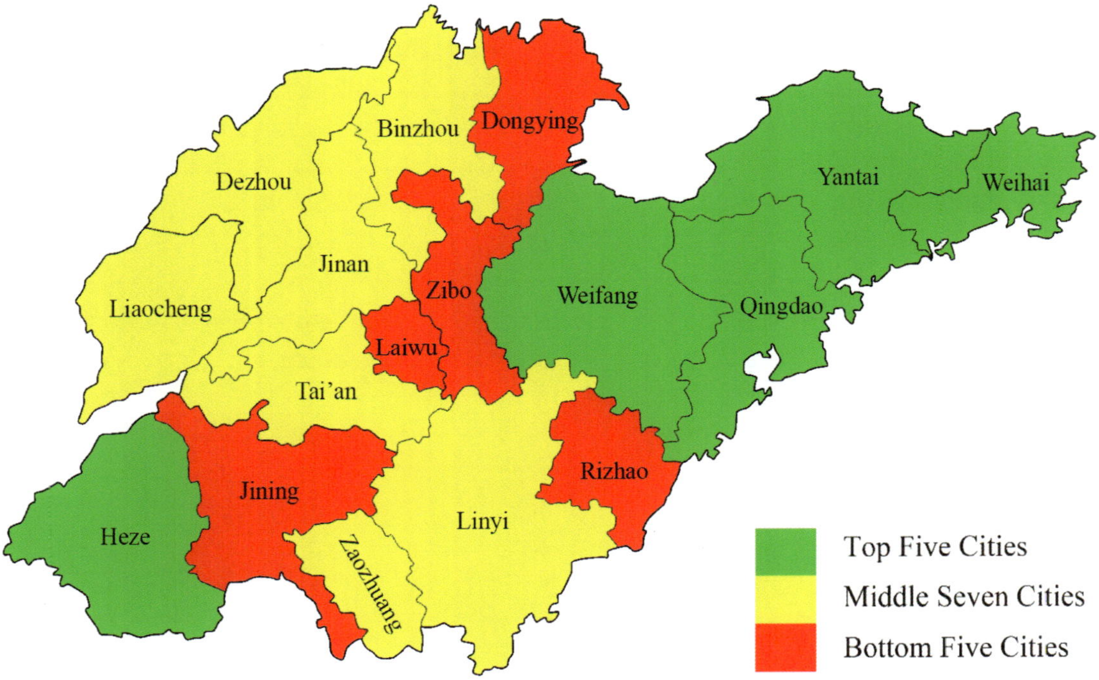

Source: Asia Competitiveness Institute.

Figure 3.3 provides a snapshot for the Scale and Quality of Economic Activities ranking. Similar to Figure 3.2, green represents the top five cities, yellow, the middle seven cities, and red, the five lowest ranking cities. We observe that the coastal area in Shandong as well as Heze are largely green. In general, the colour of the cities changes from green to red then to yellow as we move westwards towards inland areas in Shandong. However, Jining and Heze differ noticeably from this general pattern.

Table 3.3: **Financial Capacity, Labour Market Flexibility and Economic Vibrancy Ranking**

City	Rank		Score	
	Equal Weight Method	Shapley Weight Method	Equal Weight Method	Shapley Weight Method
Jinan	1	1	2.264	2.184
Qingdao	2	2	1.932	1.923
Yantai	3	3	1.271	1.334
Weifang	4	4	0.441	0.508
Linyi	5	5	0.387	0.436
Dongying	6	6	0.293	0.262
Zibo	7	7	0.089	0.133
Weihai	8	8	0.083	0.104
Jining	9	9	–0.171	–0.142
Binzhou	10	10	–0.329	–0.526
Rizhao	11	12	–0.619	–0.680
Heze	12	11	–0.638	–0.601
Tai'an	13	13	–0.763	–0.745
Zaozhuang	14	15	–0.894	–0.909
Liaocheng	15	14	–1.021	–0.900
Dezhou	16	16	–1.026	–1.009
Laiwu	17	17	–1.297	–1.371

Source: Asia Competitiveness Institute.

Table 3.3 shows the ranking for the environment of Financial Capacity, Labour Market Flexibility and Economic Vibrancy. Jinan ranks 1st under both the Equal weight method and Shapley weight method. The ranking for all the other cities are generally consistent, underscoring the robustness of the Equal weight approach. This discussion will focus on the results from the Equal weight method for the remainder of our discussion for this environment.

The city performing at the provincial average (i.e. with a standardised score of 0) for Financial Capacity, Labour Market Flexibility and Economic Vibrancy is between Weihai (0.083) at 8th place and Jining (–0.171) at 9th place. The median is Jining (–0.171), which ranks at 9th place. The average score (0) for the environment of Financial Capacity, Labour Market Flexibility and Economic Vibrancy is above the median score (–0.171).

It is worth noting that there is a marked drop in scores from Yantai (1.271) (rank 3rd) to Weifang (0.440) (rank 4th). The gap in scores between these two cities is as large as 0.831. There are also considerable gaps between Qingdao (1.932) (rank 2nd) and Yantai (1.271) (rank 3rd). On the one hand, this shows that the performance of each city varies from each other even among the top-ranking cities. On the other hand, this suggests that the top three cities, Jinan, Qingdao and Yantai, considerably outperform the other 17 cities in the environment of Financial Capacity, Labour Market Flexibility and Economic Vibrancy.

Figure 3.4: Financial Capacity, Labour Market Flexibility and Economic Vibrancy Ranking Map

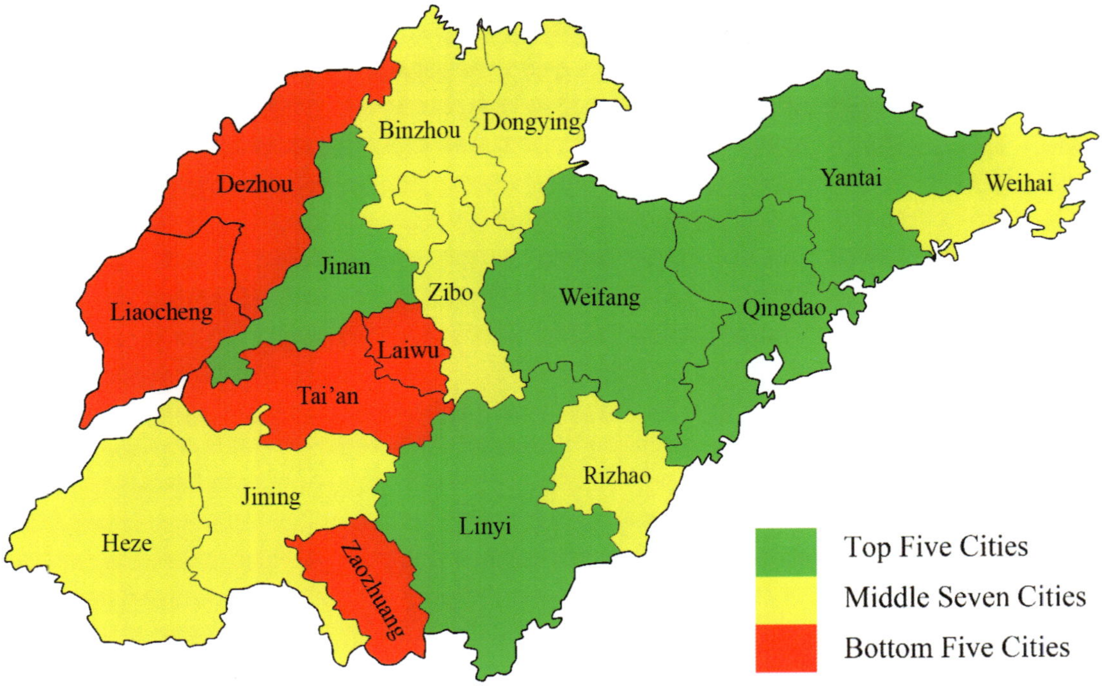

Source: Asia Competitiveness Institute.

Figure 3.4 provides a snapshot of the ranking for the environment of Financial Capacity, Labour Market Flexibility and Economic Vibrancy. Similar to Figure 3.2, green represents the top five cities, yellow, the middle seven cities, and red, the five lowest ranking cities. We observe that the coastal area in Shandong as well as Jinan and Linyi are largely green. In general, north-western cities are red, while the rest of the cities are yellow.

Table 3.4: Good Governance, Effective Leadership and Social Stability Ranking

City	Rank		Score	
	Equal Weight Method	Shapley Weight Method	Equal Weight Method	Shapley Weight Method
Dezhou	1	1	1.465	1.389
Weihai	2	2	1.134	1.180
Weifang	3	3	0.797	0.775
Qingdao	4	4	0.733	0.618
Jinan	5	5	0.532	0.533
Tai'an	6	6	0.498	0.526
Heze	7	9	0.435	0.324
Zibo	8	7	0.418	0.502
Linyi	9	8	0.321	0.326
Yantai	10	11	0.192	0.206

(*Continued*)

Table 3.4: (*Continued*)

City	Rank		Score	
	Equal Weight Method	Shapley Weight Method	Equal Weight Method	Shapley Weight Method
Dongying	11	10	0.173	0.271
Rizhao	12	12	0.042	0.085
Jining	13	13	–0.527	–0.564
Binzhou	14	14	–0.849	–0.774
Zaozhuang	15	15	–1.302	–1.297
Laiwu	16	16	–1.588	–1.530
Liaocheng	17	17	–2.473	–2.571

Source: Asia Competitiveness Institute.

Table 3.4 shows the ranking for the environment of Good Governance, Effective Leadership and Social Stability. Dezhou ranks 1st under both Equal weight method and Shapley weight method. The ranking for all the other cities are generally consistent, underscoring the robustness of the Equal weight approach. This discussion will focus on the results from the Equal weight method for the remainder of our discussion for this environment.

The city performing at the provincial average (i.e. with a standardised score of 0) for Good Governance, Effective Leadership and Social Stability is between Rizhao (0.042) at 12th place and Jining (–0.527) at 13th place. The median is Linyi (0.321), which ranks at 9th place. The average score (0) for the environment of Good Governance, Effective Leadership and Social Stability is lower than the median score (0.321).

It is worth noting that there is a marked drop in scores from Laiwu (–1.588) (rank 16th) to Liaocheng (–2.473) (rank 17th). The gap in scores between these two cities is as large as 0.885. There are also considerable gaps between Rizhao (0.042) (rank 12th) and Jining (–0.527) (rank 13th). This indicates that the cities which obtained scores below average have much weaker performance in the environment of Good Governance, Effective Leadership and Social Stability relative to all the other cities in Shandong.

Figure 3.5: Good Governance, Effective Leadership and Social Stability Ranking Map

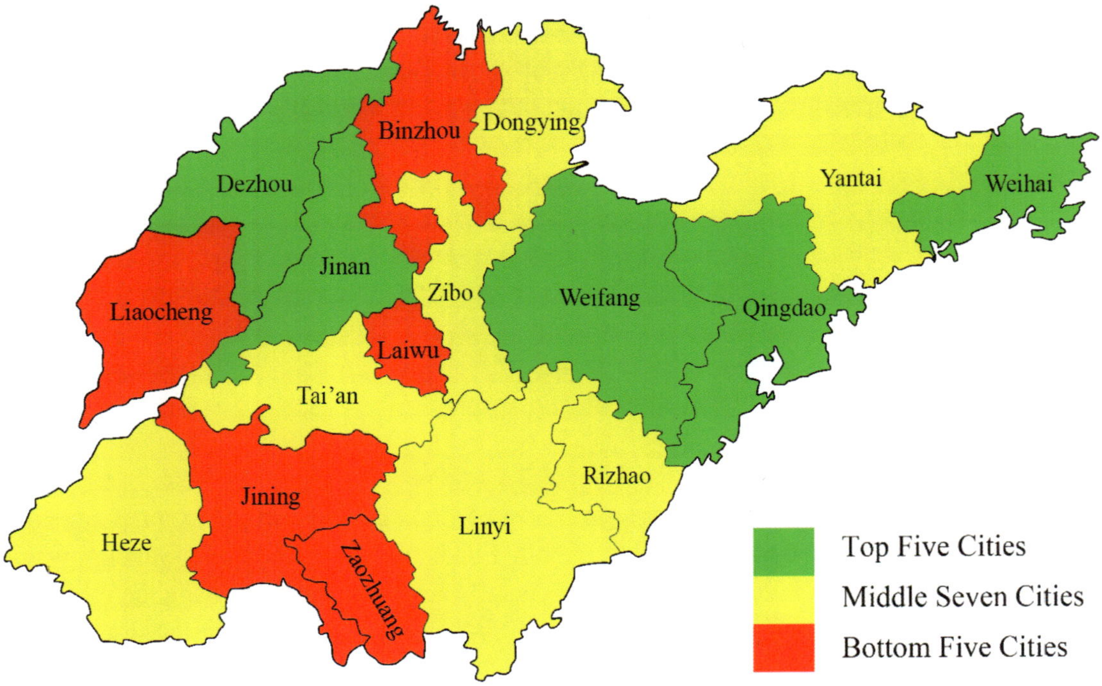

Source: Asia Competitiveness Institute.

Figure 3.5 provides a snapshot of the ranking for the environment of Good Governance, Effective Leadership and Social Stability. Similar to Figure 3.2, green represents the top five cities, yellow, the middle seven cities, and red, the five lowest ranking cities. We observe that the distribution of the cities follow no clear pattern. However, the southern and western Shandong cities are clearly lagging behind, as there is no green observed in those regions.

Table 3.5: Technological Advancement and Innovation Capability Ranking

City	Rank		Score	
	Equal Weight Method	Shapley Weight Method	Equal Weight Method	Shapley Weight Method
Qingdao	1	1	2.176	2.117
Weifang	2	2	1.417	1.429
Jinan	3	3	1.257	1.214
Yantai	4	4	1.009	1.049
Weihai	5	5	0.848	0.888
Zibo	6	6	0.492	0.521
Dongying	7	7	0.178	0.200
Jining	8	8	−0.222	−0.217
Linyi	9	9	−0.344	−0.342

(Continued)

Table 3.5: (*Continued*)

City	Rank		Score	
	Equal Weight Method	Shapley Weight Method	Equal Weight Method	Shapley Weight Method
Tai'an	10	10	–0.457	–0.453
Dezhou	11	11	–0.517	–0.507
Binzhou	12	12	–0.559	–0.551
Laiwu	13	13	–0.812	–0.816
Heze	14	14	–0.897	–0.906
Rizhao	15	15	–1.155	–1.175
Zaozhuang	16	16	–1.192	–1.206
Liaocheng	17	17	–1.221	–1.246

Source: Asia Competitiveness Institute.

Table 3.5 shows the ranking for the environment of Technological Advancement and Innovation Capability. Qingdao ranks 1st under both Equal weight method and Shapley weight method. The ranking for all the other cities are generally consistent, underscoring the robustness of the Equal weight approach. This discussion will focus on the results from the Equal weight method for the remainder of our discussion for this environment.

The city performing at the provincial average (i.e. with a standardised score of 0) for Technological Advancement and Innovation Capability is between Dongying (0.178) at 7th place and Jining (–0.222) at 8th place. The median is Linyi (–0.344), which ranks at 9th place. The average score (0) for the environment of Technological Advancement and Innovation Capability is higher than the median score (–0.344).

It is worth noting that there is a marked drop in scores from Qingdao (2.176) (rank 1st) to Weifang (1.417) (rank 2nd). The gap in scores between these two cities is as large as 0.759. There are also considerable gaps between Weihai (0.848) (rank 5th) and Zibo (0.492) (rank 6th). This indicates that Qingdao excels in the environment of Technological Advancement and Innovation Capability in Shandong.

Figure 3.6: Technological Advancement and Innovation Capability Ranking Map

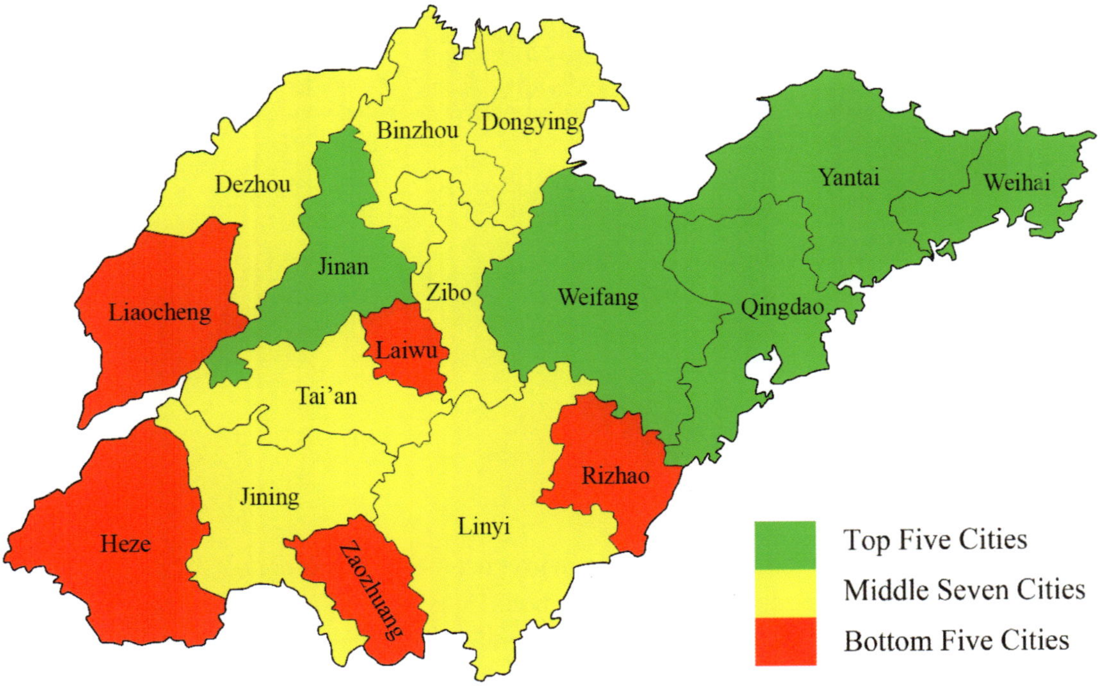

Source: Asia Competitiveness Institute.

Figure 3.6 provides a snapshot of the ranking for the environment of Technological Advancement and Innovation Capability. Similar to Figure 3.2, green represents the top five cities, yellow, the middle seven cities, and red, the five lowest ranking cities. We observe that the coastal area in Shandong as well as Jinan are largely green. In general, the colour of the cities changes from green to yellow, then to red as we move westwards towards inland areas in Shandong. Some cities that differ noticeably from this general pattern observed are Laiwu, Zaozhuang and Rizhao.

Table 3.6: Public Service Standards and Quality of Life Improvement Ranking

City	Rank		Score	
	Equal Weight Method	Shapley Weight Method	Equal Weight Method	Shapley Weight Method
Dongying	1	2	1.689	1.652
Weihai	2	1	1.616	1.689
Weifang	3	3	0.920	0.863
Jinan	4	4	0.919	0.831
Zibo	5	5	0.794	0.825
Laiwu	6	6	0.675	0.697
Qingdao	7	7	0.593	0.626

(Continued)

Table 3.6: (*Continued*)

City	Rank		Score	
	Equal Weight Method	Shapley Weight Method	Equal Weight Method	Shapley Weight Method
Yantai	8	8	0.251	0.305
Rizhao	9	9	–0.154	–0.153
Linyi	10	10	–0.307	–0.332
Tai'an	11	11	–0.567	–0.575
Heze	12	12	–0.766	–0.764
Jining	13	13	–0.819	–0.818
Binzhou	14	14	–0.862	–0.848
Zaozhuang	15	15	–0.954	–0.976
Dezhou	16	16	–1.066	–1.078
Liaocheng	17	17	–1.964	–1.945

Source: Asia Competitiveness Institute.

Table 3.6 shows the ranking for the environment of Public Service Standards and Quality of Life Improvement. The ranking for all the cities are generally consistent, underscoring the robustness of the Equal weight approach. This discussion will focus on the results from the Equal weight method for the remainder of our discussion for this environment.

The city performing at the provincial average (i.e. with a standardised score of 0) for Public Service Standards and Quality of Life Improvement is between Yantai (0.251) at 8th place and Rizhao (–0.154) at 9th place. The median is Rizhao (–0.154), which ranks at 9th place. The average score (0) for the environment of Public Service Standards and Quality of Life Improvement is higher than the median score (–0.154).

It is worth noting that there is an obvious drop in scores from Dezhou (–1.066) (rank 16th) to Liaocheng (–1.964) (rank 17th). The gap in scores between these two cities is as large as 0.898. There are also considerable gaps between Weihai (1.616) (rank 2nd) and Weifang (0.920) (rank 3rd). On the one hand, this shows that the performance of Liaocheng is lagged behind. On the other hand, this suggests that the top three cities, Dongying, Weihai and Weifang, considerably outperform the other 17 cities in the environment of Public Service Standards and Quality of Life Improvement.

Figure 3.7: Public Service Standards and Quality of Life Improvement Ranking Map

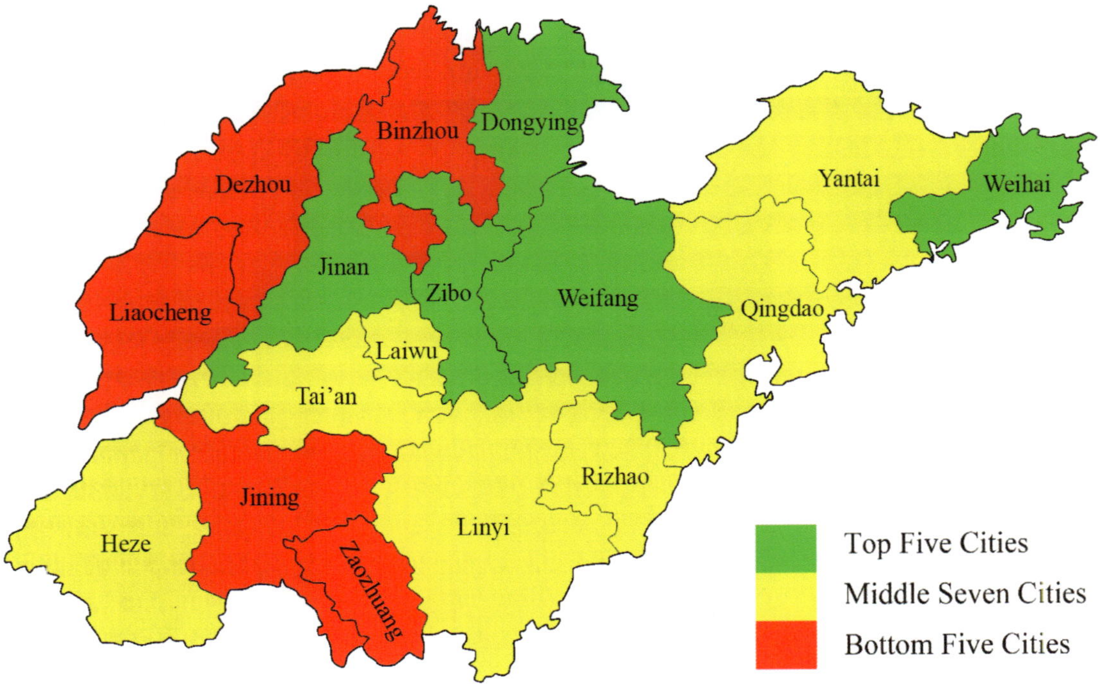

Source: Asia Competitiveness Institute.

Figure 3.7 provides a snapshot of the ranking for the environment of Public Service Standards and Quality of Life Improvement. Similar to Figure 3.2, green represents the top five cities, yellow, the middle seven cities, and red, the five lowest ranking cities. We observe that the distribution of the cities follow no clear pattern. However, southern and western cities are clearly lagging behind, as there is no green observed in those regions.

Table 3.7: Resource Conditions and Environmental Protection Ranking

City	Rank		Score	
	Equal Weight Method	Shapley Weight Method	Equal Weight Method	Shapley Weight Method
Weihai	1	1	1.632	1.677
Yantai	2	2	1.394	1.468
Dongying	3	3	1.118	1.098
Rizhao	4	4	0.817	0.906
Zibo	5	5	0.665	0.715
Liaocheng	6	7	0.376	0.284
Tai'an	7	6	0.370	0.344
Qingdao	8	8	0.330	0.221
Jinan	9	9	0.281	0.132
Jining	10	10	–0.112	–0.175

(*Continued*)

Table 3.7: *(Continued)*

City	Rank		Score	
	Equal Weight Method	Shapley Weight Method	Equal Weight Method	Shapley Weight Method
Dezhou	11	11	–0.287	–0.315
Zaozhuang	12	12	–0.393	–0.368
Linyi	13	13	–0.512	–0.492
Weifang	14	14	–0.814	–0.928
Laiwu	15	15	–1.136	–1.011
Binzhou	16	16	–1.586	–1.268
Heze	17	17	–2.142	–2.287

Source: Asia Competitiveness Institute.

Table 3.7 shows the ranking for the environment of Resource Conditions and Environmental Protection. Weihai ranks 1st under both the Equal weight method and Shapley weight method. The ranking for all the other cities are generally consistent, underscoring the robustness of the Equal weight approach. This discussion will focus on the results from the Equal weight method for the remainder of our discussion for this environment.

The city performing at the provincial average (i.e. with a standardised score of 0) for Resource Conditions and Environmental Protection is between Jinan (0.281) (rank 9th) and Jining (–0.112) (rank 10th). The median is Jinan (0.281), which ranks at 9th place. The average score (0) of Resource Conditions and Environmental Protection is lower than the median score (0.281).

It is worth noting that there is a marked drop in scores from Binzhou (–1.586) (rank 16th) to Heze (–2.142) (rank 17th). The gap in scores between these two cities is as large as 0.556. There are also considerable gaps between Jinan (0.281) (rank 9th) and Jining (–0.112) (rank 10th). This indicates that cities performing both above and below the provincial average have large disparities. In addition, the ranking highlights Heze's weakness in the environment of Resource Conditions and Environmental Protection.

Figure 3.8: Resource Conditions and Environmental Protection Ranking Map

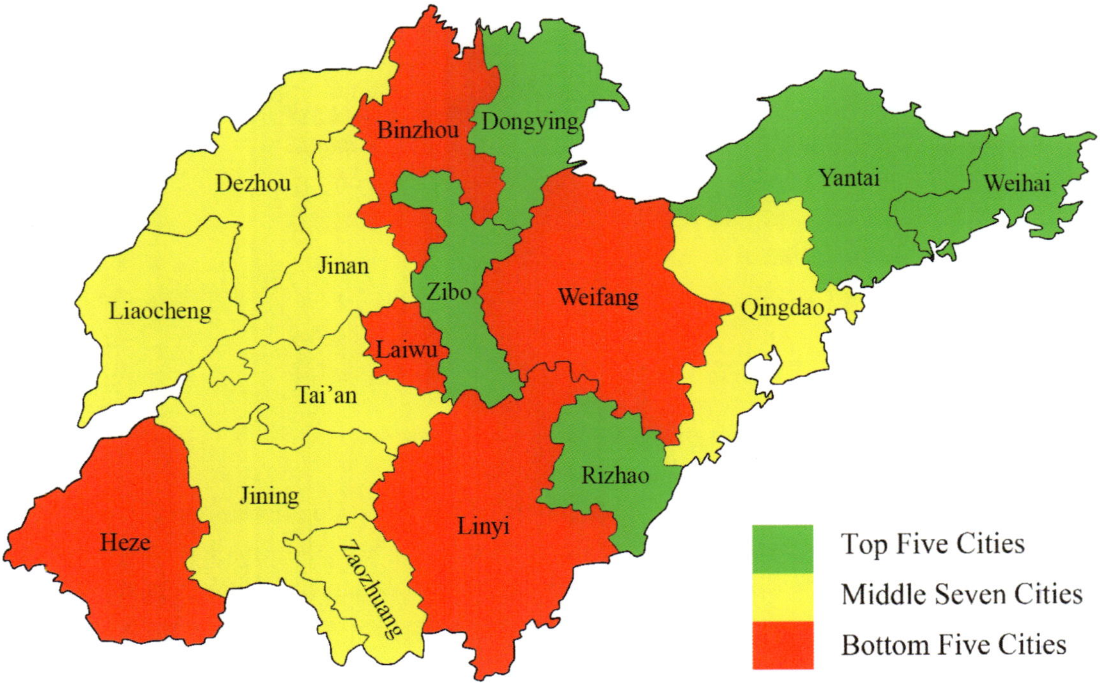

Source: Asia Competitiveness Institute.

Figure 3.8 provides a snapshot of the ranking for the environment of Resource Conditions and Environmental Protection. Similar to Figure 3.2, green represents the top five cities, yellow, the middle seven cities, and red, the five lowest ranking cities. We observe that the distribution of the cities follow no clear pattern. However, the southern and western cities are clearly lagging behind, as there is no green observed in those regions.

Overall, we observe that there exists large disparities across Shandong cities in terms of their urban development performance ranking, even within each environment. While cities like Qingdao and Weihai are generally high performers as they take the top positions in the overall performance in our ranking, they have been shown to perform weaker in some environments. Take Weihai as an example. It ranks 1st in Resource Conditions and Environmental Protection, with a score of 1.632, while only ranking 8th under Financial Capacity, Labour Market Flexibility and Economic Vibrancy, with a score of 0.083. For Qingdao, it drops to 8th place in the environment of Resource Conditions and Environmental Protection. At the same time, cities with weaker overall urban development performance are strong in some specific environments as well. Laiwu, for example, rises to 6th place in the environment of Public Service Standards and Quality of Life Improvement despite its rank of 16th in the overall urban development performance. These results therefore show that cities in Shandong should all strive towards greater urban development improvement, even among the best performers. Similarly, while the least performing cities have much more to improve on, they should take pride in their own specific strengths.

3.4 *What-if* Simulations and Analysis

As mentioned in Section 2.7 of Chapter 2, the *What-if* simulation allows ACI to analyse the data more closely to show the positive impact on each city if they manage to address their most pressing concerns. To do so, the 20% weakest indicators for each city was raised to the average level and recalculated to generate its new standardised score and rank, with every other city held constant.

The results for the *What-if* simulation were generated using the Equal weight method and presented in the remainder of this section.

Table 3.8: ***What-if* Urban Development Simulation on Overall Urban Development Performance**

City	*What-if* Simulation		Score Change	*What-if* Simulation		Rank Change
	Score Before	Score After		Rank Before	Rank After	
Qingdao	1.753	2.583	0.830	1	1	0
Weihai	1.393	1.849	0.455	2	1	1
Yantai	1.312	1.799	0.487	3	1	2
Jinan	1.106	2.078	0.973	4	1	3
Weifang	0.855	1.396	0.541	5	2	3
Dongying	0.603	1.597	0.994	6	2	4
Zibo	0.403	1.053	0.649	7	4	3
Linyi	–0.002	0.668	0.670	8	6	2
Tai'an	–0.280	0.378	0.659	9	7	2
Dezhou	–0.302	0.345	0.646	10	8	2
Rizhao	–0.472	0.301	0.773	11	8	3
Heze	–0.615	0.298	0.913	12	8	4
Jining	–0.706	0.169	0.875	13	8	5
Binzhou	–1.076	–0.035	1.041	14	8	6
Zaozhuang	–1.164	–0.369	0.795	15	11	4
Laiwu	–1.233	–0.116	1.117	16	9	7
Liaocheng	–1.576	–0.609	0.966	17	12	5

Source: Asia Competitiveness Institute.

An interesting result from this exercise is that the top four cities will rank first after the *What-if* Urban Development Simulation, as illustrated in Table 3.8. It shows that there exists intense competition among the top performing cities. Should the policymakers of Weihai, Yantai and Jinan improve their most significant weaknesses, all three cities will have the potential to become the best performer in terms of urban development, despite the initial score gaps between themselves and Qingdao. Consider Jinan as an example. The indicators of Satisfaction of Traffic Conditions, Satisfaction of Income Disparity and Satisfaction of Innovation Environment are among the worst performing indicators. Policies aimed at improving public transport, reducing income inequality and promoting R&D have the potential to improve Jinan's urban development performance tremendously.

If Qingdao improves its weakest indicators, its rank cannot improve further as it already holds the top position. However, its score will rise significantly from 1.753 to 2.583. The weakest performing indicators for Qingdao include the Satisfaction of Public Health Care Services, Satisfaction of Traffic Conditions, as well as the Green Coverage Ratio of Built-Up Area.

The *What-if* simulation also illustrates the great development potential that a city possesses. The most significant improvement is observed for Laiwu, where its rank improves from 16th place to 9th place while its corresponding score improves more than 1.1 points. In addition, policymakers at the city level should pay greater attention to and concern for environmental protection, since most of its weakest performing indicators are environment-related, including the indicators of Sulphur Dioxide Emission per RMB 10,000 GRDP, Nitrogen Oxides Emissions per RMB 10,000 GRDP and Urban Area Waste Water Treatment Rate. Although mining and steel production are industries that Laiwu continues to rely on for growth, there needs to be a greater emphasis on green and innovative development. To do so, Laiwu should seek greater structural reform to adopt and advance towards more environmentally friendly technologies.

Table 3.9: *What-if* Urban Development Simulation on Scale and Quality of Economic Activities

City	*What-if* Simulation		Score Change	*What-if* Simulation		Rank Change
	Score Before	Score After		Rank Before	Rank After	
Qingdao	1.987	2.700	0.713	1	1	0
Yantai	1.687	2.027	0.341	2	1	1
Heze	1.289	1.615	0.326	3	2	1
Weifang	1.021	1.254	0.233	4	3	1
Weihai	0.849	1.380	0.532	5	3	2
Linyi	0.447	0.802	0.354	6	6	0
Dezhou	0.096	0.284	0.188	7	7	0
Tai'an	–0.321	0.170	0.491	8	7	1
Jinan	–0.364	0.905	1.269	9	5	4
Zaozhuang	–0.412	0.116	0.528	10	7	3
Binzhou	–0.573	–0.042	0.531	11	8	3
Liaocheng	–0.665	–0.522	0.142	12	11	1
Zibo	–0.674	0.395	1.069	13	7	6
Dongying	–0.782	0.928	1.710	14	4	10
Rizhao	–1.017	–0.072	0.945	15	8	7
Jining	–1.273	–0.095	1.178	16	8	8
Laiwu	–1.295	–0.223	1.072	17	8	9

Source: Asia Competitiveness Institute.

Table 3.9 shows the *What-if* simulation results for the environment of Scale and Quality of Economic Activities for all 17 Shandong cities. Dongying and Laiwu have the potential for massive improvements, as they rise by 10 and nine ranks respectively. Although the rankings of Qingdao, Linyi and Dezhou remain unchanged after the simulation, their scores improve to a certain extent. The reason for these three cities' inability to improve their respective rankings after the simulation lies in the large gaps in scores between these cities and the cities that rank immediately ahead of them.

Table 3.10: *What-if* Urban Development Simulation on Financial Capacity, Labour Market Flexibility and Economic Vibrancy

City	*What-if* Simulation		Score Change	*What-if* Simulation		Rank Change
	Score Before	Score After		Rank Before	Rank After	
Jinan	2.264	2.264	0.000	1	1	0
Qingdao	1.932	1.972	0.040	2	2	0
Yantai	1.271	1.381	0.110	3	3	0
Weifang	0.441	0.634	0.194	4	4	0
Linyi	0.387	0.878	0.491	5	4	1
Dongying	0.293	0.892	0.600	6	4	2
Zibo	0.089	0.444	0.355	7	4	3
Weihai	0.083	0.464	0.382	8	4	4
Jining	–0.171	0.002	0.173	9	9	0
Binzhou	–0.329	0.269	0.598	10	6	4
Rizhao	–0.619	–0.108	0.511	11	9	2
Heze	–0.638	–0.061	0.577	12	9	3
Tai'an	–0.763	–0.359	0.404	13	10	3
Zaozhuang	–0.894	–0.330	0.564	14	10	4
Liaocheng	–1.021	–0.464	0.557	15	11	4
Dezhou	–1.026	–0.355	0.671	16	10	6
Laiwu	–1.297	–0.516	0.781	17	11	6

Source: Asia Competitiveness Institute.

Table 3.10 shows the *What-if* simulation results for the environment of Financial Capacity and Labour Market Flexibility and Economic Vibrancy for all 17 Shandong cities. Dezhou and Laiwu improve by six ranks after the simulation. Although the rankings of top four cities as well as Jining remain unchanged after the simulation, their scores improve to a certain extent. The reason for these five cities' inability to improve their respective rankings after the simulation lies in the large gaps in scores between these cities and the cities that rank immediately ahead of them.

Table 3.11: ***What-if*** **Urban Development Simulation on Good Governance, Effective Leadership and Social Stability**

City	*What-if* Simulation		Score Change	*What-if* Simulation		Rank Change
	Score Before	Score After		Rank Before	Rank After	
Dezhou	1.465	1.952	0.488	1	1	0
Weihai	1.134	1.591	0.457	2	1	1
Weifang	0.797	1.534	0.737	3	1	2
Qingdao	0.733	2.059	1.326	4	1	3
Jinan	0.532	1.749	1.217	5	1	4
Tai'an	0.498	1.442	0.944	6	1	5
Heze	0.435	0.578	0.144	7	5	2
Zibo	0.418	0.969	0.551	8	3	5
Linyi	0.321	0.897	0.576	9	3	6
Yantai	0.192	0.897	0.705	10	3	7
Dongying	0.173	1.113	0.940	11	2	9
Rizhao	0.042	0.730	0.688	12	3	9
Jining	–0.527	0.287	0.814	13	9	4
Binzhou	–0.849	–0.370	0.479	14	13	1
Zaozhuang	–1.302	–0.196	1.106	15	13	2
Laiwu	–1.588	–0.755	0.833	16	14	2
Liaocheng	–2.473	–0.255	2.217	17	13	4

Source: Asia Competitiveness Institute.

Table 3.11 shows the *What-if* simulation results for the environment of Good Governance, Effective Leadership and Social Stability for all 17 Shandong cities. Dongying and Rizhao have the potential for massive improvements, as it rises by nine ranks. Yantai improves by seven ranks after the simulation. We observe that all the Shandong cities have their 20% weakest indicators under this environment, as every city experiences an improvement in their score. This indicates the need for policymakers to improve the cities' governance, leadership and social stability.

Table 3.12: ***What-if*** **Urban Development Simulation on Technological Advancement and Innovation Capability**

City	*What-if* Simulation		Score Change	*What-if* Simulation		Rank Change
	Score Before	Score After		Rank Before	Rank After	
Qingdao	2.176	2.368	0.192	1	1	0
Weifang	1.417	1.417	0.000	2	2	0
Jinan	1.257	1.711	0.454	3	2	1
Yantai	1.009	1.079	0.069	4	4	0
Weihai	0.848	0.891	0.043	5	5	0
Zibo	0.492	0.492	0.000	6	6	0
Dongying	0.178	0.407	0.229	7	7	0

(*Continued*)

Table 3.12: (*Continued*)

City	*What-if* Simulation		Score Change	*What-if* Simulation		Rank Change
	Score Before	Score After		Rank Before	Rank After	
Jining	–0.222	0.087	0.310	8	8	0
Linyi	–0.344	0.150	0.494	9	8	1
Tai'an	–0.457	–0.067	0.390	10	8	2
Dezhou	–0.517	–0.308	0.209	11	9	2
Binzhou	–0.559	–0.322	0.237	12	9	3
Laiwu	–0.812	–0.155	0.656	13	8	5
Heze	–0.897	–0.492	0.404	14	11	3
Rizhao	–1.155	–0.284	0.871	15	9	6
Zaozhuang	–1.192	–0.825	0.367	16	13	3
Liaocheng	–1.221	–1.016	0.205	17	15	2

Source: Asia Competitiveness Institute.

Table 3.12 shows the *What-if* simulation results for the environment of Technological Advancement and Innovation Capability for all 17 Shandong cities. Rizhao has the potential for massive improvement, as it rises by six ranks after the simulation. Laiwu improves by five ranks after the simulation. Although the rankings for Qingdao, Yantai, Dongying and Jining remain unchanged after the simulation, their scores improve to a certain extent. The reason for these four cities' inability to improve their respective rankings after the simulation lies in the large gaps in scores between these cities and the cities that rank immediately ahead of them.

For Weifang and Zibo, both their scores and rankings are unaffected by the simulation. This is because none of their 20% weakest indicators belongs in this environment.

Table 3.13: *What-if* Urban Development Simulation on Public Service Standards and Quality of Life Improvement

City	*What-if* Simulation		Score Change	*What-if* Simulation		Rank Change
	Score Before	Score After		Rank Before	Rank After	
Dongying	1.689	2.067	0.378	1	1	0
Weihai	1.616	2.119	0.503	2	1	1
Weifang	0.920	1.240	0.320	3	3	0
Jinan	0.919	1.961	1.041	4	1	3
Zibo	0.794	1.335	0.540	5	3	2
Laiwu	0.675	0.847	0.172	6	5	1
Qingdao	0.593	1.619	1.026	7	1	6
Yantai	0.251	1.031	0.780	8	3	5
Rizhao	–0.154	0.138	0.291	9	9	0
Linyi	–0.307	0.251	0.559	10	8	2
Tai'an	–0.567	0.119	0.686	11	9	2

(*Continued*)

Table 3.13: (*Continued*)

City	*What-if* Simulation		Score Change	*What-if* Simulation		Rank Change
	Score Before	Score After		Rank Before	Rank After	
Heze	−0.766	0.240	1.007	12	8	4
Jining	−0.819	−0.168	0.651	13	9	4
Binzhou	−0.862	−0.302	0.560	14	10	4
Zaozhuang	−0.954	−0.628	0.326	15	12	3
Dezhou	−1.066	−0.035	1.031	16	9	7
Liaocheng	−1.964	−1.185	0.779	17	16	1

Source: Asia Competitiveness Institute.

Table 3.13 shows the *What-if* simulation results for the environment of Public Service Standards and Quality of Life Improvement for all 17 Shandong cities. Dezhou has the potential for massive improvements, as it rises by seven ranks. Although the ranking of Dongying, Weifang, and Rizhao remain unchanged after the simulation, their scores improve to a certain extent. The reason for the three cities' inability to improve their respective rankings after the simulation lies in the large gaps in scores between these cities and the cities that rank immediately ahead of them.

Table 3.14: *What-if* Urban Development Simulation on Resource Conditions and Environmental Protection

City	*What-if* Simulation		Score Change	*What-if* Simulation		Rank Change
	Score Before	Score After		Rank Before	Rank After	
Weihai	1.632	1.932	0.300	1	1	0
Yantai	1.394	1.798	0.404	2	1	1
Dongying	1.118	1.904	0.786	3	1	2
Rizhao	0.817	0.942	0.125	4	4	0
Zibo	0.665	1.086	0.422	5	4	1
Liaocheng	0.376	0.805	0.429	6	4	2
Tai'an	0.370	0.370	0.000	7	7	0
Qingdao	0.330	1.553	1.222	8	1	7
Jinan	0.281	1.078	0.797	9	3	6
Jining	−0.112	0.628	0.740	10	5	5
Dezhou	−0.287	−0.003	0.284	11	10	1
Zaozhuang	−0.393	0.253	0.647	12	9	3
Linyi	−0.512	−0.004	0.508	13	10	3
Weifang	−0.814	0.261	1.076	14	8	6
Laiwu	−1.136	0.293	1.429	15	8	7
Binzhou	−1.586	0.614	2.200	16	4	12
Heze	−2.142	−0.532	1.610	17	11	6

Source: Asia Competitiveness Institute.

Table 3.14 shows the *What-if* simulation results for the environment of Resource Conditions and Environmental Protection for all 17 Shandong cities. Binzhou has the potential for massive improvements, as it rises by 12 ranks. Although the rankings of Weihai and Rizhao remain unchanged after the simulation, their scores improve to a certain extent. The reason for these two cities' inability to improve their respective rankings after the simulation lies in the large gaps in scores between these cities and the cities that rank immediately ahead of them.

For Tai'an, both its scores and rankings are unaffected by the simulation. This is because none of its 20% weakest indicators belongs in this environment.

Overall, the *What-if* simulation exercise has shown that many cities, especially the least performing cities, have substantial room for improvement. For instance, Laiwu has the potential to move up seven ranks in its overall performance if it manages to address its 20% weakest indicators. Even for the overall best performing city, namely Qingdao, it has the potential for significant improvement in its urban development score despite no improvement in its rank.

Additionally, the *What-if* simulation by environment can motivate cities to focus their efforts in areas where they can find the largest improvement. As such, these results collectively show that urban development in Shandong province has yet to be fully realised. Extending from these results, we delve into the specific circumstances of each Shandong city in Part II of this book to illustrate their idiosyncrasies, as well as to offer evidence-based recommendations and analysis.

Discussant Note 1

Professor Yang Jinwei

Vice President, Shandong Academy of Social Sciences, People's Republic of China

This research project focuses on the remarkable Shandong Province. As Shandong is the third largest province by Gross Regional Domestic Product (GRDP) and the second largest province by population, it is noted as one of the most competitive provinces in China. In the 40 years of China's "Reform and Opening-Up" under the leadership of the Communist Party of China, the people of Shandong have embarked on a path of socialism with Chinese characteristics. While we have encountered difficulties and challenges along the way, we persevered and kept abreast with the times. In addition, through the dedicated, courageous and ingenious work in the province, Shandong has made great progress in its path towards greater development. In 2017, the GRDP of Shandong reached 7,268 billion yuan, accounting for nearly 9% of the country's GDP, 13% of its industrial output, 8% of its agricultural output and nurtured 7.2% of the country's population on less than 2% of the country's land. In recent years, the Asia Competitiveness Institute (ACI) at the Lee Kuan Yew School of Public Policy, National University of Singapore has paid close attention to the development of Shandong, especially after the robust collaboration with the Shandong Academy of Social Sciences. The research results of regional urban development evaluation in Shandong have provided an important reference for businesses, the government and the public to elucidate the opportunities and threats of Shandong's development.

1. Shandong's in-depth understanding of the Five Development Concepts: Promoting the construction of a pilot zone for industrial transformation

The Communist Party of China has identified a series of crucial ideas to guide development in its 13th Five-Year Plan. The first idea is the implementation of the Five Development Concepts, which are namely that of Innovative, Coordinated, Green, Open and Sharing development. These concepts are designed to facilitate the construction of a moderately prosperous society in all respects by 2020. Shandong Province actively implements these new development concepts while adapting its own development characteristics to promote the transformation of its economy by raising its economic potential. Specifically, the path of economic development will promote the reliance on innovation, rather than on low-tech industries. In doing so, these strategies hope to facilitate Shandong Province's modernisation process and building a moderately prosperous society.

The industries of Shandong are built on solid foundations and distinct categories, including traditional sectors such as food, metallurgy, textile, household appliances, chemicals and construction materials, as well as emerging sectors such as automobiles, locomotives, ship-building, information technology, bio-pharmaceutical and new materials. As such, it is clear that Shandong has a well-established population of both large as well as small and medium-sized enterprises. However, despite Shandong's remarkable achievements in economic development, serious concerns such as the regional development disparities remain. While the traditional industry has established a strong foundation, the overall industrial structure is biased towards the traditional sector as it continues to dominate. Despite systematic efforts to limit excess capacity and encourage bankruptcy reorganisation, relocation and upgrading, the task to reorganize unproductive resources remains a significant challenge.

In early 2018, the State Council officially approved the overall plan as part of its national strategy to construct a pilot zone in Shandong for industrial transformation. Moving forward, economic growth alone is not the answer. Instead, Shandong should advance structural reforms and explore new growth drivers and development paths, while balancing the needs of both its current and long-term objectives. To do so, there are several plans that Shandong should consider. First, Shandong should seize the opportunity presented by the new industrial revolution to promote growth and update its growth model via innovation. Second, Shandong should pursue an innovation-driven development strategy that incorporates smart manufacturing, the "Internet Plus" model, the digital economy and sharing economy. This technology-led approach will help Shandong stay ahead of the curve and facilitate the replacement of old growth drivers with new ones. Third, Shandong should eliminate impediments to economic progress through reform that both removes systemic and institutional barriers as well as rejuvenate the market, to achieve better quality, more resilient and sustainable growth.

2. The main characteristics and achievements of this research project

(1) The comprehensive development index of cities carried out by the project team is very meaningful.

Shandong is at a critical point of economic upgrading and restructuring. On the 40th anniversary of China's "Reform and Opening-Up", this project is a timely summary and reminder of the experiences of Shandong's urban development from a variety of perspectives. Specifically, this research highlights Shandong's idiosyncrasies, analyses its problems, explores solutions and looks forward to a better future. With ACI's research expertise amassed over the years, the team developed their very own theoretical framework and index system with a large amount of objective data. The resulting comprehensive development index was designed to make a detailed evaluation of the 17 cities in Shandong Province, including the measurement of the development patterns and competitiveness of the province as a whole. Despite the ongoing regional integration, Shandong's development is still geographically unbalanced, with large disparities between its rural and urban areas. With different local conditions, each of the 17 cities in Shandong have to explore dissimilar development discourses through cooperation and competition. In an increasingly competitive economic environment, local policymakers face the challenge of improving local economic conditions in a healthy and sustainable manner. This analysis is therefore important for governments, as it provides valuable research and insight that will help to inform their policy decisions.

(2) The design of the index system fully embodies the Five Development Concepts of Innovative, Coordinated, Green, Open and Sharing.

The Five Development Concepts were designed to address the current challenges facing China. I deeply admire the way the five concepts, namely that of Innovative, Coordinated, Green, Open and Sharing development, provide a clear blueprint for the country in the subsequent decades. This is a prime example of long-term strategic planning.

One of the biggest challenges that plagues all of China today is the need to achieve greater economic growth without negatively affecting the environment. I am confident that a sound process of development must be the underlying solution to solve Shandong's problems. In particular, there are several key points to note in order to do so. First, we must decisively pursue the vision of Innovative, Coordinated, Green, Open and Sharing development that benefits everyone. Second, we must continue to uphold and improve China's basic socialist economic system and socialist distribution system. Third, we must be committed to consolidate and develop the public sector while remaining resolute about working to encourage, support and guide the development of the non-public sector. Fourth, we must ensure that the market plays its role in resource allocation while the government plays its role to facilitate the process of industrialisation, IT application, urbanisation, and agricultural modernisation.

(3) Maintain a well-managed database that lays a good foundation for future research.
Data accumulation and management is a complex and tedious task. However, good data is necessary to conduct high-quality and objective research work. In ACI's research project for Shandong, a broad coverage of 265 ideal indicators were systematically identified across six categories, while 131 practical indicators were obtained. The data used were not only from publicly available sources, including China Statistical Yearbook, Shandong Statistical Yearbook, China Urban Statistical Yearbook, Shandong Urban Construction Statistical Yearbook and Regional Development Statistical Compilation, but also from survey data collected via random telephone interviews where 300 responses were successfully collected from each of the 17 Shandong cities included in the study. The combination of open statistical data and survey data will help to ensure that the data is reliable and objective, as it minimises errors and biases created from public opinion collected in the survey.

3. Several suggestions
(1) Include new and relevant indicators.
Although the coverage of the indicators in ACI's research project is sufficiently comprehensive, it stands to benefit from the inclusion of new and relevant indicators that reflect China's move towards finding new sources of growth via economic restructuring and upgrading under the Five Development Concepts. In doing so, the project will be able to more accurately track the development of Shandong Province while meaningfully incorporating the Five Development Concepts. In particular, indicators designed by the provincial government to assess local governments should be included, such as information technology expenditure per capita, PM10 concentration, amongst other indicators.

(2) Better reflect Shandong's urban agglomeration
Shandong is comprised of a network of cities and towns of all sizes, including city clusters that are closely linked to one another. These cities interact with each other through competition and have the potential to promote coordinated development. As such, given the powerful dynamics that exist between them that can influence development, achieve rural-urban integration and allow every city to perform at its economic potential, ACI should consider analysing clusters of cities in Shandong in addition to individual cities.

For instance, a nexus of cities around Jinan and Qingdao is being established, as they are the two most important cities in Shandong. Jinan, as the provincial capital of Shandong, is working to become a centre of regional economic, financial, logistics and technological innovation. In addition, Jinan hopes to remain the city that is able to highlight Shandong's economic and cultural strengths. Similarly, Qingdao is an important economic centre on the eastern coast of China as it is the economic centre of the Shandong Peninsula Economic Area, which includes Qingdao and seven other Shandong cities. Given its close ties and relationships with its neighbouring cities, Qingdao is a prime example of the urban agglomeration in the province.

(3) Broaden the sample of Shandong cities

There are more than the 17 cities identified in ACI's study in Shandong province. This is because various levels of cities exist within Shandong, which are the sub-provincial, prefecture and county levels. In Shandong, there are two sub-provincial cities, which are namely Jinan and Qingdao, and 15 prefecture level cities in Shandong. These two categories of cities form the 17 cities analysed in ACI's study.

However, it is worth noting that there are 26 county-level cities in Shandong as well. They are namely, Jiaozhou, Pingdu (under Qingdao jurisdiction), Laixi (under Qingdao jurisdiction), Tengzhou (under Zaozhuang jurisdiction), Penglai, Longkou, Zhaoyuan, Laizhou, Qixia, Haiyang (under Yantai jurisdiction), Laiyang (under Yantai jurisdiction), Qingzhou, Shouguang, Changyi, Anqiu, Zhucheng (under Weifang jurisdiction), Gaomi (under Weifang jurisdiction), Qufu (under Jining jurisdiction), Zoucheng (under Jining jurisdiction), Xintai (under Tai'an jurisdiction), Feicheng (under Tai'an jurisdiction), Rongcheng (under Weihai jurisdiction), Rushan (under Weihai jurisdiction), Laoling (under Dezhou jurisdiction), Yucheng (under Dezhou jurisdiction) and Linqing (under Liaocheng jurisdiction). In some these county-level cities, their economic strength and potential have even surpassed that of the prefecture level cities. As such, it is important and meaningful to analyse the development capacities of these smaller cities in ACI's research of the province.

Discussant Note 2

Dr Li Wei

Deputy Director, Institute of Applied Economics, Shanghai Academy of Social Sciences, People's Republic of China

In the presentation entitled "*Urban Composite Development Index for 17 Shandong Cities: Ranking and Simulation Analysis Based on China's Five Development Concepts*", we can see that Asia Competitiveness Institute (ACI) has adapted the Five Development Concepts of Innovation, Coordination, Green Development, Opening Up and Sharing proposed by President Xi Jinping into a well-developed competitiveness framework. Through a comprehensive analysis of the composite competitiveness of 17 Shandong cities, the presentation demonstrated high quality research that pushes back the frontiers of competitiveness analysis. Furthermore, with a solid foundation built over many years, ACI has made progress in innovating on urban development concepts, competitiveness frameworks and research methodologies, all of which will lead to their work having a much greater impact on research areas related to regional development and competitiveness.

In assessing regional composite competitiveness with the Five Development Concepts in mind, ACI has done pioneering work and produced important research that sheds more light on both the urban development concepts as well as the competitiveness framework. The Five Development Concepts of Innovation, Coordination, Green Development, Opening Up and Sharing, are derived from the seminal theory of development proposed by President Xi Jinping. Since the latter period of the 20th century, China has experienced rapid growth, which provides new impetus and information which will help to fuel further innovation in development theories. After the Global Financial Crisis, as we enter a new era of international development, there has surfaced a need in China for new development theories to assist in its active exploration of transformational development paths that retain uniquely Chinese characteristics.

The Five Development Concepts seek to assess and define China's transformational development through an understanding of new trends of economic and technological development. The frameworks of Green Development, Sharing and Coordination additionally provide impetus for specific, new development objectives and directions. In this presentation, ACI has integrated the groundbreaking properties of the Five Development Concepts into a competitiveness framework, quantifying and analyzing these concepts as competitiveness indicators. This model is therefore an important breakthrough for research in regional development and competitiveness.

Exploring city-level composite competitiveness in the context of a province is a new and important research area under regional competitiveness. Intra-provincial coordination and the balancing of regional development has always been the focus of both the theory and practice of development. This is especially important in the context of China's inter-regional development. Shandong province has high economic and cultural status in China, and plays an important role in China's development.

Balanced development among the province's 17 cities is thus not only important to Shandong, but can also function to provide a positive, instructional example for other provinces in China. In being based on the objectives and direction set by the Five Development Concepts, this research on the Urban Composite Development for 17 Shandong Cities is able to provide vital methodological support and outline policy implications to other cities, with regard to the effective implementation of the Five Development Concepts.

ACI has also proposed a new methodological approach to competitiveness studies — the Shapley Weightage Method. Originating in cooperative game theory, Shapley value has for the first time been applied to competitiveness studies, which in turn makes weightage methods more fundamentally objective. This is an important methodological innovation. In addition to the competitiveness analysis, ACI also undertakes *What-if* simulations, which are quantitative innovations designed to provide policy recommendations. These two innovations will no doubt make significant impressions on research in competitiveness studies.

Discussant Note 3

Mr Wang Kejian

Chairman, Urban Construction Press, People's Republic of China

The Asia Competitiveness Institute (ACI) delivered an insightful presentation on the project entitled "*Urban Composite Development Index for 17 Shandong Cities: Ranking and Simulation Analysis Based on China's Five Development Concepts*". The team provided a detailed description of President Xi Jinping's Five Development Concepts of Innovation, Coordination, Green Development, Opening Up and Sharing. By adapting these important elements into their framework, ACI has developed a novel and empirically rigorous composite index to critically analyse and evaluate key liveability indicators for the cities in Shandong province. As such, the high-quality research provides a useful platform for Shandong province to identify weaknesses and spearhead improvements necessary to engender growth and progress in the region and beyond.

The focus on the Five Development Concepts outlined by President Xi Jinping is the key feature that makes ACI's work such a breakthrough. While the rapid growth and development of China in recent decades is indicative of a prosperous and dynamic economy, it has also generated some notable challenges, including rising income inequality, environmental degradation and a strain on government finances. The Five Development Concepts provide the precise and innovative solution to these rising challenges. With these concepts as guiding principles, ACI constructed the six environments of (a) Scale and Quality of Economic Activities, (b) Financial Capacity, Labour Market Flexibility and Economic Vibrancy, (c) Good Governance, Effective Leadership and Social Stability, (d) Technological Advancement and Innovation Capability, (e) Public Service Standards and Quality of Life Improvement, and (f) Resource Conditions and Environmental Protection. Each identified environment is associated with at least one development concept. As such, the close alignment of ACI's Urban Composite Development Index with the strategic direction of the Chinese administration makes this study especially relevant and useful.

Another notable strength of the Urban Composite Development Index by ACI is its comprehensiveness. The index has an impressive coverage of 131 indicators across six environments and 23 sub-environments for all 17 Shandong cities. The meticulous construction of the index through careful consideration of the mix of indicators across the variety of environments makes the study particularly comprehensive and robust. In doing so, the Urban Composite Development Index provides a representative overview of the development conditions and standards in Shandong province. As such, with the critical assessment of each city under this framework, ACI is able to draw important policy implications and recommendations for the provincial and city-level administrations. As a result, policymakers across Shandong are empowered with the knowledge on how to leverage on its strengths while also addressing its weaknesses.

In addition, ACI has made an important contribution to the research methodology in the literature of index construction — the Shapley Weightage approach. The concept follows the work of Nobel Laurent Lloyd Shapley, and is widely applied in the field of applied game theory. The work by ACI is the first time the Shapley Weightage approach is being applied to the study of index construction. Departing from the subjective assumption that every category is weighted equally, this method is entirely objective, where all weights are computed from the raw data. This Shapley Weightage approach has thus strengthened the empirical rigour of Urban Composite Development Index.

Despite the many positive features of the Urban Composite Development Index, there are some recommendations that ACI can consider to improve further. First, the urban composite development framework and ranking can be extended to include cities beyond Shandong. For instance, the ACI team can apply the urban composite development framework to rank other provinces in China and even across the whole of China. Further, ranking within broader regional categories in China such as the Northern, Southern, Eastern and Western regions may be conducted to observe each city's performance relative to their regional neighbours. In doing so, ACI can offer useful insights to policymakers from other provinces and cities in China. Nevertheless, extending the study to the rest of China will be costly. Therefore, to accomplish such an ambitious feat, ACI will require strong collaboration with the research and governmental institutions in China for their support and guidance.

In addition, ACI should consider enhancing the data collection process by employing the use of websites and mobile application technology to conduct future surveys. Relative to telephone interviews, which can be costly and labour-intensive, the use of websites and mobile applications is less expensive and provides greater convenience to respondents. Such an extension will allow ACI to both reach out to more respondents and improve the response rate, hence providing a more comprehensive dataset for analysis. Nevertheless, promoting greater participation in the survey is challenging, as it requires finding the right incentives.

In summary, the ACI ranking and simulation analysis via the Urban Composite Development Index for 17 Shandong cities is an impressive framework that is empirically robust, comprehensive and relevant to the current growth trajectory of China. By highlighting the performance of cities in terms of its development and urbanisation, policymakers are better equipped with the knowledge and policies to facilitate necessary action. Nevertheless, some room for improvement still exists in terms of enhanced survey data collection methods and the application to the broader regions in China.

Looking ahead, the urban composite development framework developed from President Xi Jinping's Five Development Concepts will continue to be relevant to China's evolution as urbanisation increases across the country. Moreover, extending the analysis to include cities beyond Shandong is necessary to raise the overall development standards in China and encourage sustainable urbanisation practices that will eventually benefit everyone.

Part II

In-Depth Analysis on Patterns of Urban Development for 17 Cities in Shandong Province

Chapter 4: BINZHOU
Shandong Province

Location of City

Source: Asia Competitiveness Institute.

4.1 Profile of Binzhou City[1]

Well-known throughout China as the birthplace of the legendary strategist Sun Tzu, Binzhou today possesses administrative jurisdiction over five counties and two districts spanning a total land area of 9,172 square kilometres and a total population of 3,891,000. Administering a territory which extends from the banks of the Yellow River to the shores of the Bay of Bohai, Binzhou is also home to the famed Binzhou Shell Dyke Island, along with fertile and attractive agricultural holdings, all of which make the city a treat for the senses and contribute to the growth of tourism in the region.

In 2016, Binzhou's Gross Regional Domestic Product (GRDP) stood at around RMB 247 billion, and the city boasted a healthy growth rate of 7.2%, as can be seen in Table 4.1. Rich in natural resources including oil and natural gas, Binzhou derived 9.4% of its total GRDP from its primary sector. Binzhou's secondary sector, which comprised 46.3% of GRDP, focuses on several core industries including textiles, chemical engineering, machinery manufacturing and food processing, all of which continue to benefit greatly from the city's efforts to attract foreign

[1]The relevant city information are from the Department of Commerce of Shandong Province (n.d.) and Binzhou Municipal Government (n.d.).

investment. Finally, Binzhou's tertiary sector comprised 44.3% of GRDP, with a growing focus on information technology development spurring growth.

While it does not contain an airport, Binzhou benefits from its proximity to the Jinan Yaoqiang International Airport, and is also well connected to neighbouring areas by the high-speed rail network via the Jiaoji Railway Line. Binzhou's links abroad are also very numerous for a city of its size, with its investments outside of China amounting to approximately US $405 million. This in turn indicates the activity of the China Council for the Promotion of International Trade's Binzhou Subsidiary and the various initiatives it has embarked upon to encourage and facilitate transnational trade.

Table 4.1: Key Economic Indicators for Binzhou, 2016

Land Area (km²)	**9,172**
Population	
Total Population	3,891,000
Urbanisation Rate (%)	56.8
Average Life Expectancy (years)	74.1
Number of Employees (10,000)	289
Workforce Participation Rate (%)	81.4
Gross Regional Domestic Product (GRDP) — 2015 Prices	
GRDP (100 millions of RMB)	2,470
GRDP Per Capita (RMB)	63,745
GRDP Growth Rate (%)	7.2
Economic Composition	
Primary Sector (% of GRDP)	9.4
Secondary Sector (% of GRDP)	46.3
Tertiary Sector (% of GRDP)	44.3
Trade — 2016 Prices	
Exports (millions of RMB)	24,125
Imports (millions of RMB)	29,935
Dependency on Foreign Trade (%)	23.4
Infrastructure	
Per Capita Road Area (m²)	22.2
Growth in the Number of Passengers Transported (10,000)	7.0
Growth in the Volume of Cargo Transported (10,000 tons)	1,118
Environment	
Green Coverage Ratio of Built-up Area (%)	44.8
Environmental Expenditure (% of Total Fiscal Expenditure)	2.3

Source: Asia Competitiveness Institute from the 2017 Shandong Statistical Yearbook.

4.2 In-Depth Urban Development of Binzhou, 2016*

4.2.1 Overall Urban Development Performance

Overall Performance

2017 Rank

14th

Out of 17 Cities

Score: –1.076

Rank	City	Score
1	Qingdao	1.753
	...	
10	Dezhou	–0.302
11	Rizhao	–0.472
12	Heze	–0.615
13	Jining	–0.706
14	Binzhou	–1.076
15	Zaozhuang	–1.164
16	Laiwu	–1.233
17	Liaocheng	–1.576

Binzhou ranked 14th in its Overall Performance, with a standardised score of –1.076. This places the city in the Bottom Five Group of 17 cities. Binzhou is positioned between Jining (–0.706) at 13th place and Zaozhuang (–1.164) at 15th place.

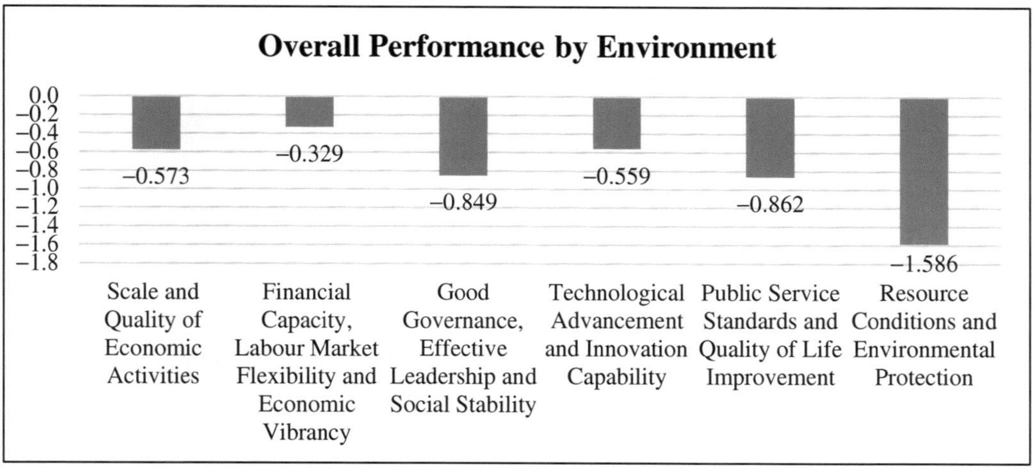

Among the six environments, Binzhou fares below the provincial average in all of them and especially weaker in the Resource Conditions and Environmental Protection environment. Other environments with lower scores include that of Good Governance, Effective Leadership and Social Stability and Public Service Standards and Quality of Life Improvement. Nevertheless, Binzhou scores relatively stronger in the environment of Financial Capacity, Labour Market Flexibility and Economic Vibrancy.

**For a complete list of rankings, see Tables 3.2 to 3.7 in Section 3.3 of Chapter 3.*

4.2.2 Urban Development within the Six Environments

Rank	City	Score
1	Qingdao	1.987
	...	
9	Jinan	–0.364
10	Zaozhuang	–0.412
11	Binzhou	–0.573
12	Liaocheng	–0.665
13	Zibo	–0.674
	...	
16	Jining	–1.273
17	Laiwu	–1.295

A: ***Scale and Quality of Economic Activities***

2017 Rank

11th

Out of 17 Cities

Score: –0.573

Binzhou ranks 11th for Scale and Quality of Economic Activities, with a standardised score of –0.573. This places the city in the Middle Seven Group of 17 cities. Binzhou is positioned behind Zaozhuang (–0.412) at 10th place and ahead of Liaocheng (–0.665) at 12th place.

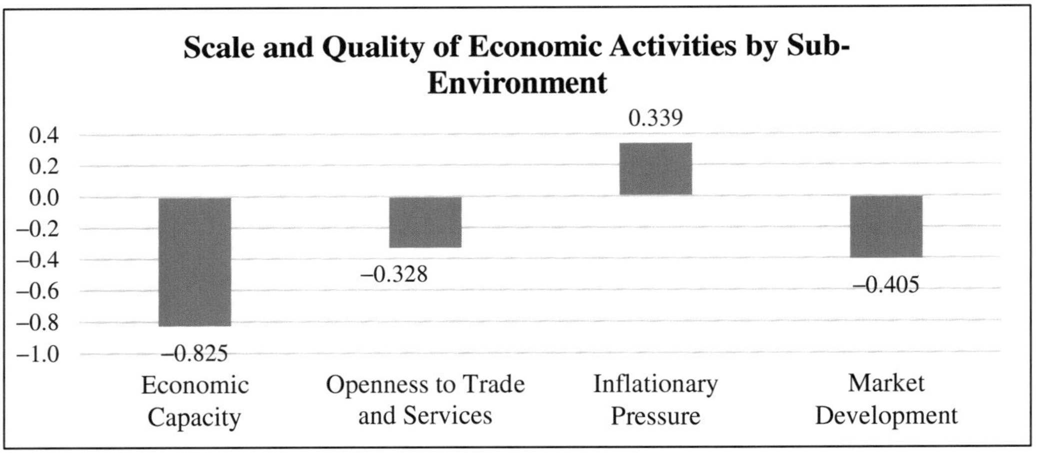

Looking at the four sub-environments of Scale and Quality of Economic Activities, Binzhou performs above the provincial average and relatively better for Inflationary Pressure, where it scores well in the indicators for Consumer Price Index and Producer Price Index. However, Binzhou performs below the provincial average in all the remaining sub-environments. Among them, Binzhou is the worst performing in terms of its Economic Capacity sub-environment, where the indicators GRDP Growth Rate and the Per Capita Volume of Retail Sales are particularly poor. In addition, the indicator Satisfaction with Business Environment in the Market Development sub-environment scores poorly as well.

B: *Financial Capacity, Labour Market Flexibility and Economic Vibrancy*

2017 Rank

10th

Out of 17 Cities

Score: –0.329

Rank	City	Score
1	Jinan	2.264
	...	
8	Weihai	0.083
9	Jining	–0.171
10	Binzhou	–0.329
11	Rizhao	–0.619
12	Heze	–0.638
	...	
16	Dezhou	–1.026
17	Laiwu	–1.297

Binzhou ranks 10th for Financial Capacity, Labour Market Flexibility and Economic Vibrancy, with a standardised score of –0.329. This places the city in the Middle Seven Group of 17 cities. Binzhou is positioned between Jining (–0.171) at 9th place and Rizhao (–0.619) at 11th place.

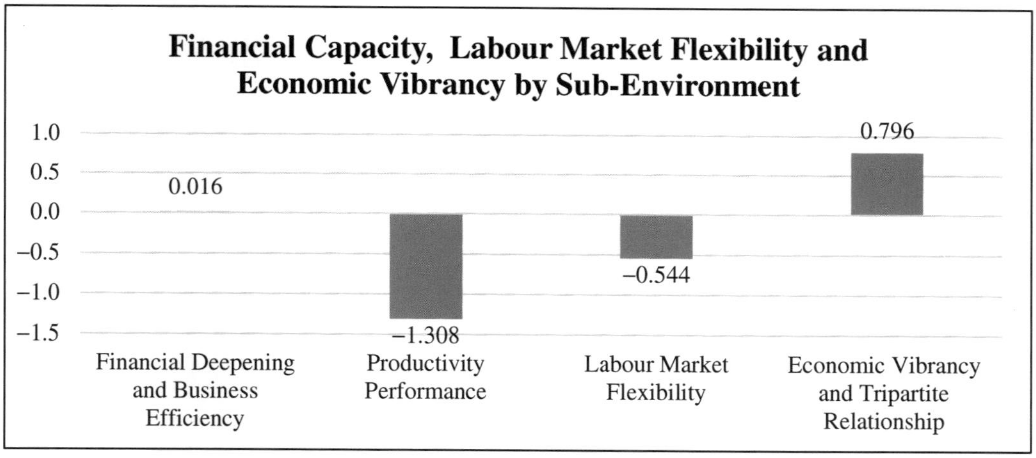

Among the four sub-environments of Financial Capacity, Labour Market Flexibility and Economic Vibrancy, Binzhou scores above the provincial average in two sub-environments and particularly well in Economic Vibrancy and Tripartite Relationship. This is due to an exceptionally high score in the indicator for the Growth in the Consumption of Electricity in that sub-environment. However, Binzhou performs below the provincial average in all the remaining sub-environments, especially in terms of its Productivity Performance where the indicator of Profit Margin of Enterprises above a Designated Size fares poorly. Other indicators that score poorly in this environment include the Proportion of Workforce Employed in the Service Sector from the Economic Vibrancy and Tripartite Relationship sub-environment.

BINZHOU

Shandong Province

Rank	City	Score
1	Dezhou	1.465
	...	
10	Yantai	0.192
11	Dongying	0.173
12	Rizhao	0.042
13	Jining	–0.527
14	Binzhou	–0.849
15	Zaozhuang	–1.302
16	Laiwu	–1.588
17	Liaocheng	–2.473

C: *Good Governance, Effective Leadership and Social Stability*

2017 Rank

14th

Out of 17 Cities

Score: –0.849

Binzhou ranks 14th for Good Governance, Effective Leadership and Social Stability with a standardised score of –0.849. This places the city in the Bottom Five Group of 17 cities. Binzhou is positioned behind Jining (–0.527) at 13th place and well ahead of Zaozhuang (–1.302) at 15th place.

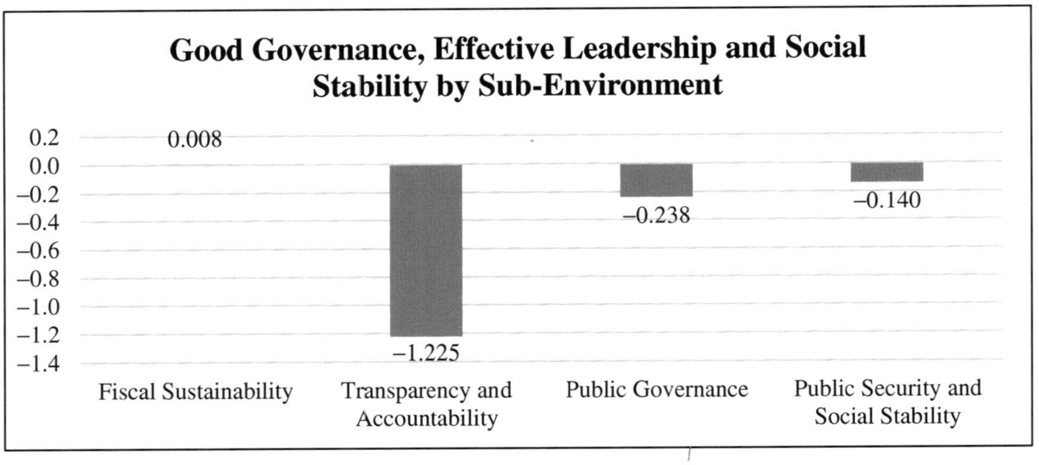

Looking at the four sub-environments of Good Governance, Effective Leadership and Social Stability, Binzhou scores marginally above the provincial average in Fiscal Sustainability, where the indicator of the Fiscal Revenue Growth Rate performs well. However, Binzhou scores below the provincial average in all the remaining sub-environments and substantially lower for Transparency and Accountability, where the indicators including the Number of Responses to Government Issues of Public Interest and the Number of Releases of Government Information for Public Viewing score especially poorly. Other indicators obtaining a low score also include the Growth Rate of the Number of Police Cases Solved from the Public Security and Social Stability sub-environment. Nevertheless, Binzhou scores relatively better in the indicator of the Number of Public Servants Per 10,000 Population from the Public Governance sub-environment.

D: ***Technological Advancement and Innovation Capability***

2017 Rank

12th

Out of 17 Cities

Score: –0.559

Rank	City	Score
1	Qingdao	2.176
	…	
10	Tai'an	–0.457
11	Dezhou	–0.517
12	Binzhou	–0.559
13	Laiwu	–0.812
14	Heze	–0.897
	…	
16	Zaozhuang	–1.192
17	Liaocheng	–1.221

Binzhou ranks 12th for Technological Advancement and Innovation Capability, with a standardised score of –0.559. This places the city in the Middle Seven Group of 17 cities. Binzhou is positioned narrowly between Dezhou (–0.517) at 11th place and Laiwu (–0.812) at 13th place.

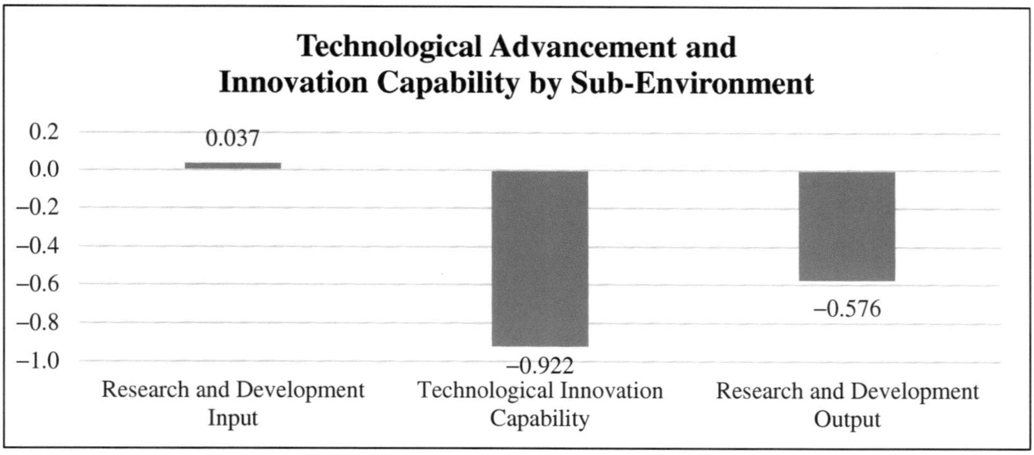

Among the three sub-environments of Technological Advancement and Innovation Capability, Binzhou performs slightly above the provincial average in Research and Development Input, where the indicator of Total Research and Development Expenditure of Enterprises Above Designated Size as a Percentage of Cash Flow performs well. However, Binzhou scores below the provincial average in the remaining sub-environments and particularly poorly for Technological Innovation Capability, where it obtains low scores in the indicators of the Number of Provincial-Level Science Parks and the Satisfaction with Innovation Environment. In addition, the indicator of the Number of Patents Granted from the Research and Development Output sub-environment performs poorly. Nevertheless, Binzhou scores better in the indicator of the Number of Research and Development Personnel Per 10,000 Population from the Technological Innovation Capability sub-environment.

BINZHOU

Shandong Province

Rank	City	Score
1	Dongying	1.689
	...	
10	Linyi	–0.307
11	Tai'an	–0.567
12	Heze	–0.766
13	Jining	–0.819
14	Binzhou	–0.862
15	Zaozhuang	–0.954
16	Dezhou	–1.066
17	Liaocheng	–1.964

E: *Public Service Standards and Quality of Life Improvement*

2017 Rank

14th

Out of 17 Cities

Score: –0.862

Binzhou ranks 14th for Public Service Standards and Quality of Life Improvement with a standardised score of –0.862. This places the city in the Bottom Five Group of 17 cities. Binzhou is positioned between Jining (–0.819) at 13th place and Zaozhuang (–0.954) at 15th place.

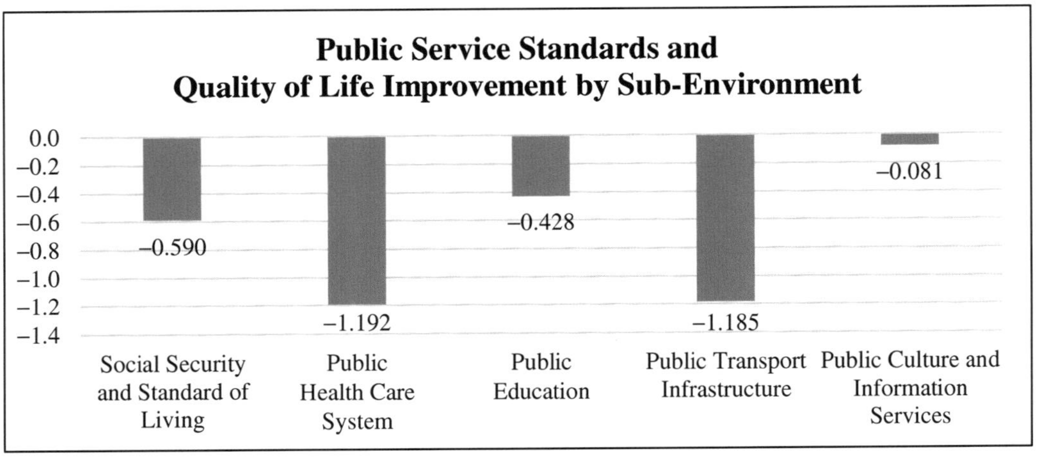

Among the five sub-environments of Public Service Standards and Quality of Life Improvement, Binzhou performs below the provincial average in all of them. This poor performance is largely due to the particularly low scores from the sub-environments of Public Health Care System and Public Transport Infrastructure. The indicators that contribute to the low scores in these sub-environments are the Average Life Expectancy, Satisfaction of Public Health Care Services, both from the Public Health Care System sub-environment, as well as the Per Capita Road Area and the Number of Passengers Transported, both from the Public Transport and Infrastructure sub-environment. On the other hand, the indicators of Public Health and Medical Service Expenses Per Capita from the Public Health Care System sub-environment and the Ratio of Teacher to Student in Primary and Secondary Schools from the Public Education sub-environment perform relatively better.

F: ***Resource Conditions and Environmental Protection***

2017 Rank

16th

Out of 17 Cities

Score: –1.586

Rank	City	Score
1	Weihai	1.632
	...	
10	Jining	–0.112
11	Dezhou	–0.287
12	Zaozhuang	–0.393
13	Linyi	–0.512
14	Weifang	–0.814
15	Laiwu	–1.136
16	Binzhou	–1.586
17	Heze	–2.142

Binzhou ranks 16th for Resource Conditions and Environmental Protection with a standardised score of –1.586. This places the city in the Bottom Five Group of 17 cities. Binzhou is positioned between Laiwu (–1.136) at 15th place and Heze (–2.142) at 17th place.

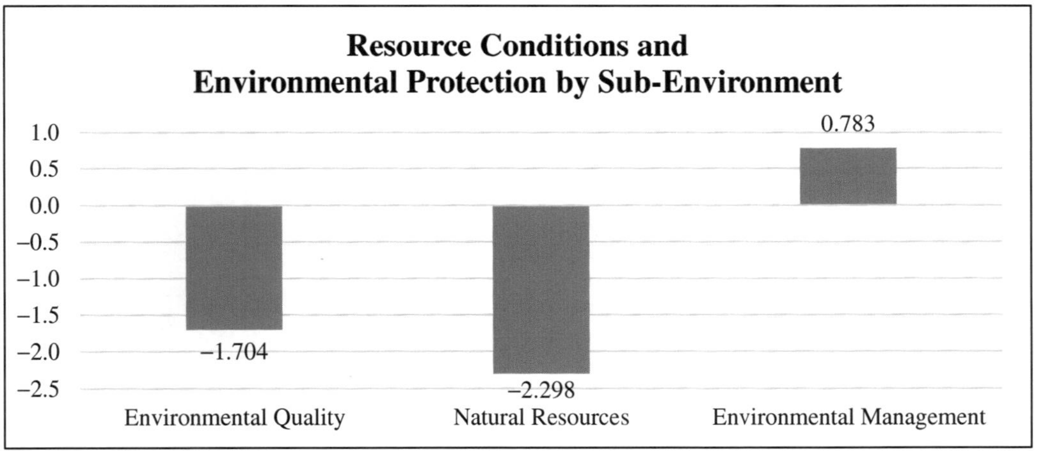

Among the three sub-environments of Resource Conditions and Environmental Protection, Binzhou scores above the provincial average in Environmental Management but below the provincial average in the remaining sub-environments and especially in Natural Resources, where the indicator of Forest Cover performs especially weak. Further, Binzhou scores unfavourably in the indicators of Sulphur Dioxide Per RMB 10,000 GRDP and Nitrogen Oxide Emissions Per RMB 10,000 GRDP, both from the Environmental Quality sub-environment. On the other hand, it performs better for the indicators of Per Capita Arable Land from the Natural Resources sub-environment, and Forest Land Growth from the Environmental Management sub-environment.

BINZHOU

Shandong Province

Figure 4.1: Median & Maximum Web for Binzhou

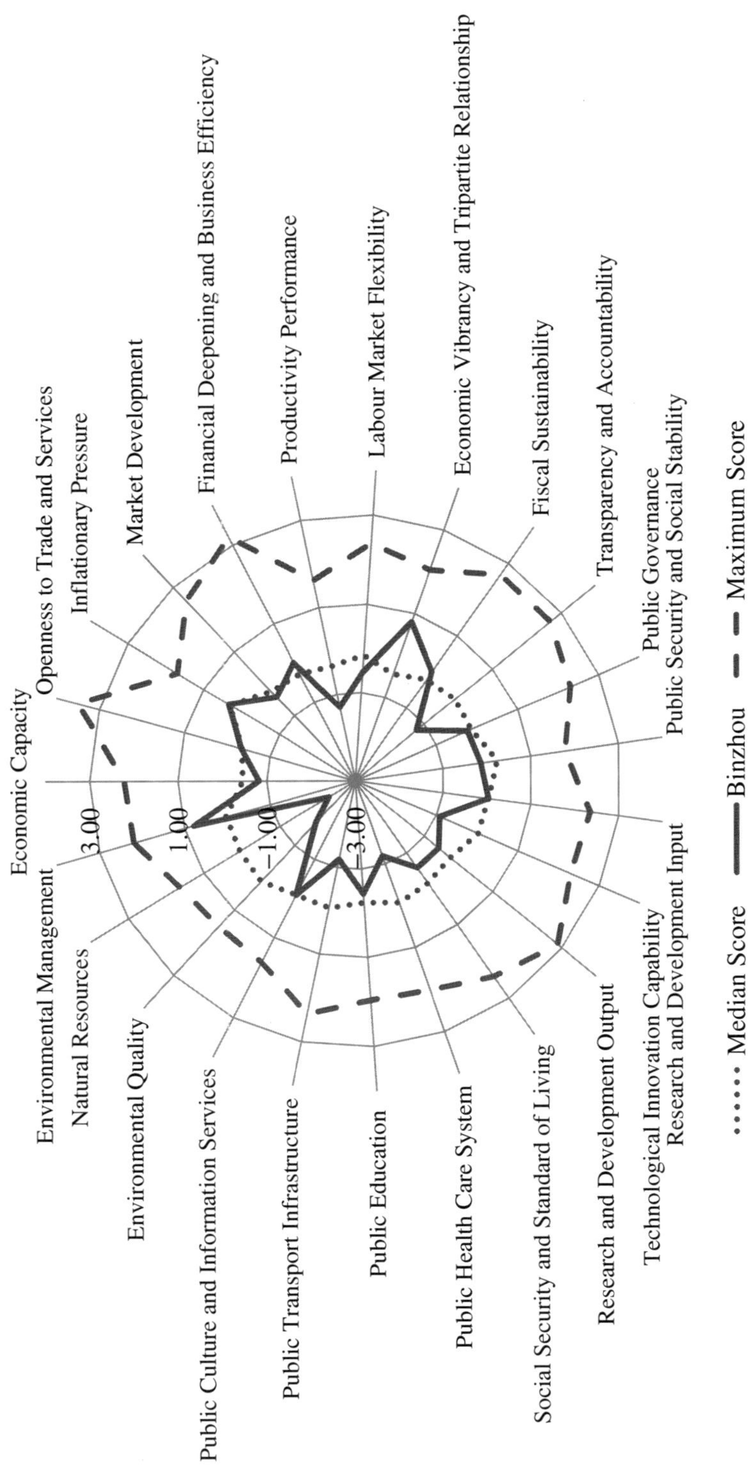

Source: Asia Competitiveness Institute.

4.2.3 Median and Maximum Web Analysis

To better understand Binzhou's relative strengths and weaknesses, it is useful to compare and contrast its scores for the 23 sub-environments against the median and maximum scores of Shandong's 17 cities.

In Figure 4.1, the median and maximum scores for 17 Shandong cities are shown as dotted and dashed lines respectively, while scores for Binzhou are shown as a solid line.

Comparison to Median Scores

Binzhou scores above the median for seven of the 23 sub-environments, most notably in Economic Vibrancy and Tripartite Relationship and Environmental Management.

On the other hand, Binzhou scores below the median for 15 of the 23 sub-environments, especially for Natural Resources and Environmental Quality, which are farthest below the median. The remaining sub-environment of Public Culture and Information Services is at the median.

Comparison to Maximum Scores

Binzhou scores below the provincial maximum of the 17 Shandong cities in all of the 23 sub-environments.

Binzhou's score in the Natural Resources (–2.298) sub-environment is farthest from the maximum, which is held by Rizhao (1.632). Further, Binzhou's score in Economic Vibrancy and Tripartite Relationship (0.796) is closest to the maximum, which is held by Linyi (2.054).

4.3 Summary of Empirical Findings of Binzhou and *What-if* Urban Development Simulation

4.3.1 Summary of Empirical Findings, 20% Strongest and Weakest Indicators

Overall Performance **14th** Score: –1.076		
Scale and Quality of Economic Activities **11th** Score: –0.573	Financial Capacity, Labour Market Flexibility and Economic Vibrancy **10th** Score: –0.329	Good Governance, Effective Leadership and Social Stability **14th** Score: –0.849
Technological Advancement and Innovation Capability **12th** Score: –0.559	Public Service Standards and Quality of Life Improvement **14th** Score: –0.862	Resource Conditions and Environmental Protection **16th** Score: –1.586

(Rank out of 17 cities)

Summary

Binzhou ranks 14th out of 17 Shandong cities in its Overall Performance. Binzhou performs below the provincial average in all of the six environments, where its worst performing environment is that of Resource Conditions and Environmental Protection (–1.586), at 16th place. However, Binzhou performs relatively better in the environment of Financial Capacity, Labour Market Flexibility and Economic Vibrancy (–0.329), at 10th place.

Strengths

As illustrated in Table 4.2, Binzhou performs well in the environment of Resource Conditions and Environmental Protection, with six out of 26 of its 20% Strongest Indicators included in this environment. Among Binzhou's best performing indicators are the Growth in the Consumption of Electricity, Per Capita Arable Land and Forest Land Growth.

Weaknesses

As observed in Table 4.3, Binzhou is also relatively weaker in the environments of Resource Conditions and Environmental Protection, with six out of 26 of its 20% Weakest Indicators under this environment. Among Binzhou's worst performing indicators are the Forest Cover, Sulphur Dioxide Emissions Per RMB 10,000 GRDP and Average Life Expectancy.

Table 4.2: 20% Strongest Indicators for Binzhou

Rank	20% Strongest Indicator	Score	SQEA	FCLMFEV	GGELSS	TAIC	PSSQLI	RCEP
1	Growth in Consumption of Electricity	3.304		✓				
2	Per Capita Arable Land	1.264						✓
3	Forest Land Growth	1.241						✓
4	Annual Loan Growth Rate	1.148		✓				
5	Area of Natural Reserves to Administrative Area (%)	1.098						✓
6	Urban Registered Unemployment Rate	1.084		✓				
7	Per Capita Freshwater Resource	1.057						✓
8	Total R&D Expenditure of Enterprises Above Designated Size as a Percentage of Cash Flow	0.994				✓		
9	Fiscal Revenue Growth Rate	0.988			✓			
10	Proportion of Urban Workers Employed in Private Enterprises	0.865		✓				
11	Traffic Accident Fatality Per 10,000 Population	0.829			✓			
12	Consumer Price Index (CPI)	0.828	✓					
13	Green Coverage Ratio of Built-up Area	0.803						✓
14	Producer Price Index (PPI)	0.678	✓					
15	Fire Fatality Per 10,000 Population	0.658			✓			
16	Government Expenditures as a Percentage of GRDP	0.606	✓					
17	Wetland Cover	0.582						✓
18	Residents' Satisfaction with Price Levels	0.544	✓					
19	Ratio of Teacher to Student in Primary and Secondary Schools	0.499					✓	
20	Proportion of Urban Workers Employed in State Enterprises	0.450		✓				
21	Number of Public Servants Per 10,000 Population	0.439			✓			
22	Public Health and Medical Service Expenses Per Capita	0.411					✓	
23	Internet Penetration Rate	0.339					✓	
24	Satisfaction of Traffic Conditions	0.335					✓	
25	Index for Quality of E-Government System	0.333			✓			
26	Research & Development Expenditure as a Share of Government Expenditure	0.227				✓		

Table 4.3: 20% Weakest Indicators for Binzhou

Rank	20% Weakest Indicator	Score	SQEA	FCLMFEV	GGELSS	TAIC	PSSQLI	RCEP
106	Growth Rate of the Number of Police Cases Solved	−0.725			✓			
107	Per Capita Volume of Retail Sales	−0.733	✓					
108	Number of Releases of Government Information for Public Viewing	−0.811			✓			
109	Number of Urban Taxis Per 10,000 Population	−0.820					✓	
110	Average Years of Education Received	−0.823					✓	
111	Growth Rate of Overall Labour Productivity	−0.863		✓				
112	COD (Chemical Oxygen Demand) Per RMB 10,000 GRDP	−0.892						✓
113	Number of Passengers Transported	−0.959					✓	
114	Per Capita Road Area	−0.996					✓	
115	Number of Responses to Government Issues of Public Interest	−1.031			✓			
116	GRDP Growth Rate	−1.040	✓					
117	Water Consumption Per RMB 10,000 GRDP	−1.047						✓
118	Number of Provincial-Level Science Parks	−1.056				✓		
119	Self-Employed as a Share of Total Employment	−1.063		✓				
120	Satisfaction of Public Health Care Services	−1.087					✓	
121	Workforce Participation Rate	−1.109		✓				
122	Built-up Area Population Density	−1.118						✓
123	Satisfaction with Business Environment	−1.155	✓					
124	Electricity Consumption Per RMB 10,000 GRDP	−1.202						✓
125	Proportion of Workforce Employed in Service Sector	−1.342		✓				
126	Growth in the Number of Passengers Transported	−1.454		✓				
127	Profit Margin of Enterprises Above Designated Size	−1.539		✓				
128	NO-X Emissions Per RMB 10,000 GRDP	−2.056						✓
129	Average Life Expectancy	−2.083					✓	
130	SO2 Emission Per RMB 10,000 GRDP	−2.837						✓
131	Forest Cover	−3.820						✓

Source: Asia Competitiveness Institute.

Notes: SQEA: Scale and Quality of Economic Activities; FCLMFEV: Financial Capacity, Labour Market Flexibility and Economic Vibrancy; GGELSS: Good Governance, Effective Leadership and Social Stability; TAIC: Technological Advancement and Innovation Capability; PSSQLI: Public Service Standards and Quality of Life Improvement; RCEP: Resource Conditions and Environmental Protection.

4.3.2 *What-if* Urban Development Simulation

ACI has devised a simulation methodology to improve the ranking of a particular city by improving on its 20% Weakest Indicators as shown in Table 4.3.[2] The figures below show Binzhou's ranking and standardised scores before and after the policy-induced simulation. Refer to Tables 3.8 to 3.14 in Section 3.4 of Chapter 3 for a complete list of simulation results for all cities.

Overall Performance

	Before		After
Rank	14th	▶	8th
Score	–1.076		–0.035

Scale and Quality of Economic Activities

	Before	After
Rank	11th	8th
Score	–0.573	–0.042

Financial Capacity, Labour Market Flexibility and Economic Vibrancy

	Before	After
Rank	10th	6th
Score	–0.329	0.269

Good Governance, Effective Leadership and Social Stability

	Before	After
Rank	14th	13th
Score	–0.849	–0.370

Technological Advancement and Innovation Capability

	Before	After
Rank	12th	9th
Score	–0.559	–0.322

Public Service Standards and Quality of Life Improvement

	Before	After
Rank	14th	10th
Score	–0.862	–0.302

Resource Conditions and Environmental Protection

	Before	After
Rank	16th	4th
Score	–1.586	0.614

After the *What-if* simulation, Binzhou improves its ranking from 14th to 8th in terms of its Overall Performance. Likewise, Binzhou's standardised score improves from –1.076 to –0.035. This leap is plausible if the city manages to successfully address its 20% Weakest Indicators.

The simulation further highlights substantial improvement for Binzhou in some of its environments, most notably for Resource Conditions and Environmental Protection, where its rank will rise from 16th to 4th. Such encouraging results should incentivise Binzhou to strive to improve the indicators under the 20% Weakest Indicators list. These indicators include the Forest Cover, Sulphur Dioxide Emissions Per RMB 10,000 GRDP and Nitrogen Oxide Emissions Per RMB 10,000 GRDP.

[2]The methodology for *What-if* simulation is thoroughly explained in Section 2.7 of Chapter 2.

4.4 Concluding Notes: Public Policy Implications[3]

Areas for Commendation

Binzhou performs well in the environments of Resource Conditions and Environmental Protection, Financial Capacity, Labour Market Flexibility and Economic Vibrancy and Good Governance, Effective Leadership and Social Stability with 16 out of 26 of the 20% Strongest Indicators falling in these environments, as indicated in Table 4.2.

While Binzhou does not hold the maximum score for any sub-environment, it scores above the provincial average in six out of 23 sub-environments.

Since 2016, Binzhou has made great strides in innovation, especially through the development of investment channels and optimisation of investment structures. The Binzhou government has also promoted the growth of consumption both quantitatively and qualitatively. The industries that reside in the city have improved the quality of consumer goods produced and have experienced rising growth rates, thereby generating a new impetus for the smooth and rapid development of consumer markets.

Areas for Improvement

As Binzhou scores below the provincial average in all of the six environments, there are plenty of areas for improvement for the city. Most crucially, Binzhou should address the environments of Resource Conditions and Environmental Protection, Public Service Standards and Quality of Life Improvement and Financial Capacity, Labour Market Flexibility and Economic Vibrancy, where they have a total of 19 out of 26 of the 20% Weakest Indicators under these environments, as shown in Table 4.3. Additionally, as gleaned from the *What-if* Urban Development Simulation, the environment for Resource Conditions and Environmental Protection should be prioritised because that is the environment in which Binzhou will achieve the greatest improvement in its ranking — 12 positions — relative to other environments.

Further, Binzhou obtains the weakest score in the sub-environments of Transparency and Accountability (–1.225), Public Transport Infrastructure (–1.185) and Natural Resources (–2.298), and scores below the provincial average in 17 out of 23 sub-environments.

In 2017, Binzhou worked vigorously to maintain and enforce regulations pertaining to the control and prevention of air pollution. The Binzhou government has even strengthened regulations relating to unauthorised emissions in high pollution industries such as steel, construction and thermal power, among others. As a result, firms with unauthorised excess supply capacity and incapable of reducing pollution were forced to close down. For example, Binzhou has cut illegal production of electrolytic aluminium by 2.69 million tons, crude steel by 1.82 million tons and power generation by 3 billion kiloWatt hour. As such, it is clear that Binzhou recognises the need to improve its environmental conservation efforts and has demonstrated its dedication towards doing so.

[3]The relevant statistical data and government policies are from Binzhou Statistical Information Net (2017) and Ministry of Environmental Protection of the People's Republic of China (2017).

Future Potential Development

In summary, Binzhou should focus on improving the environment of Resource Conditions and Environmental Protection by promoting the development of green spaces through reforestation efforts and limiting the emission of harmful gases by industries. In addition, Binzhou should look towards enhancing health care services and transport infrastructure to make meaningful progress in the environment of Public Service Standards and Quality of Life Improvement. Finally, Binzhou can afford to focus more on building up its human capital through comprehensive training programs, in order to strengthen the environment of Financial Capacity, Labour Market Flexibility and Economic Vibrancy.

Looking ahead, Binzhou should foster a better business environment for large enterprises through better market regulation and support. This will help bolster greater investment and consumption in the city. Further, the Binzhou government can help such firms through many strategies such as via the transformation and upgrading of traditional industries, the growth of emerging industries, cross-border integration of different industries through technological innovation, and the extension of supply chains and enhancing of value chains. In the meantime, Binzhou should continue to persist in its effort of environmental protection to ensure the sustainability of its environment to support future growth and success. Such a policy is aligned with China's direction of developing an ecological civilisation and building environmentally resilient and beautiful country.

References

Binzhou Municipal Government. n.d. 'History and Significant Figures'. Binzhou — Open for Business and Fun. Accessed 27 October 2017. http://www.binzhou.gov.cn/en/tourism/html/?271.html.

Binzhou Statistical Information Net. 2017. '五大理念引领滨州经济发展 — 2016年滨州市经济运行情况分析及形势展望 Five Development Concepts Led the Economic Growth of Binzhou — Analysis of Binzhou Economy in 2016 and Forecasts (in Chinese)'. Binzhou Statistical Information Net. 6 January 2017. http://www.bztj.gov.cn/bzstjjww/27/28/17010606135429681 1.html.

Department of Commerce of Shandong Province. n.d. 'Binzhou City Profile'. Department of Commerce of Shandong Province. Accessed 27 October 2017. http://en.shandongbusiness.gov.cn/city/80.

Ministry of Environmental Protection of the People's Republic of China. 2017. '滨州市综合施策整治突出环境问题 减产"减"来收入增一成 Binzhou Tackled Environmental Issues Comprehensively (in Chinese)'. Ministry of Environmental Protection of the People's Republic of China. 16 October 2017. http://www.mep.gov.cn/gkml/hbb/qt/201710/t20171016_423455_wap.shtml.

Chapter 5: DEZHOU
Shandong Province

Location of City

Source: Asia Competitiveness Institute.

5.1 Profile of Dezhou City[1]

Covering an area cut through by both the Yellow River and the Grand Canal, Dezhou is known as China's "Solar City" for the numerous initiatives which are being pursued to turn it into a centre for solar energy development. The city directly administers two districts, two county-level cities, seven counties and two development zones, all of which span a total area of 10,358 square kilometres and cover a total population of 5,792,300. The city of Dezhou is notably distinguished by a unique historical landmark — the tomb of Sultan Paduka Pahala of Sulu, constructed for him by the Yongle emperor after the Sultan passed away while returning home from China.

Dezhou's Gross Regional Domestic Product (GRDP) is RMB 293 billion in 2016, with the city boasting a GRDP growth rate of 7.2%, as can be seen in Table 5.1. Bolstered by a long, continuing history of agricultural abundance, Dezhou's primary sector contributes to 10.1% of its GRDP. Its secondary sector contrastingly constitutes 47.8% of GRDP, and is focused on food processing, equipment manufacturing, textile and garments, and chemical manufacturing. Finally, Dezhou's tertiary sector, which constitutes 42.1% of GRDP, is bolstered by emerging

[1]The relevant city information are from the Department of Commerce of Shandong Province (n.d.), Dezhou Municipal People's Government (2016) and Gao (2009).

industries including renewable energy, environmental protection, biotechnology, and information technology.

Dezhou is a regional rail transportation hub, and is located at the junctions of the Beijing-Shanghai Railway, Taiyuan-Qingdao Railway and Dezhou-Shijiazhuang Railway, among others. Dezhou has received significant praise for its part in facilitating a positive and welcoming environment for businesses, and correspondingly scores well relative to its peers in indicators relating to satisfaction with regard to business environment.

Table 5.1: Key Economic Indicators for Dezhou, 2016

Land Area (km²)	**10,358**
Population	
Total Population	5,792,300
Urbanisation Rate (%)	53.8
Average Life Expectancy (years)	75.0
Number of Employees (10,000)	358
Workforce Participation Rate (%)	83.9
Gross Regional Domestic Product (GRDP) — 2015 Prices	
GRDP (100 millions of RMB)	2,933
GRDP Per Capita (RMB)	50,856
GRDP Growth Rate (%)	7.2
Economic Composition	
Primary Sector (% of GRDP)	10.1
Secondary Sector (% of GRDP)	47.8
Tertiary Sector (% of GRDP)	42.1
Trade — 2016 Prices	
Exports (millions of RMB)	14,658
Imports (millions of RMB)	6,428
Dependency on Foreign Trade (%)	7.2
Infrastructure	
Per Capita Road Area (m²)	33.0
Growth in the Number of Passengers Transported (10,000)	28.0
Growth in the Volume of Cargo Transported (10,000 tons)	1,187
Environment	
Green Coverage Ratio of Built-up Area (%)	43.6
Environmental Expenditure (% of Total Fiscal Expenditure)	3.1

Source: Asia Competitiveness Institute from the 2017 Shandong Statistical Yearbook.

5.2 In-Depth Urban Development of Dezhou, 2016*

5.2.1 Overall Urban Development Performance

Overall Performance

2017 Rank

10th

Out of 17 Cities

Score: –0.302

Rank	City	Score
1	Qingdao	1.753
	...	
8	Linyi	–0.002
9	Tai'an	–0.280
10	Dezhou	–0.302
11	Rizhao	–0.472
12	Heze	–0.615
	...	
16	Laiwu	–1.233
17	Liaocheng	–1.576

Dezhou ranks 10th in its Overall Performance, with a standardised score of –0.302. This places the city in the Middle Seven Group of 17 cities. Dezhou is positioned closely between Tai'an (–0.280) at 9th place and Rizhao (–0.472) at 11th place.

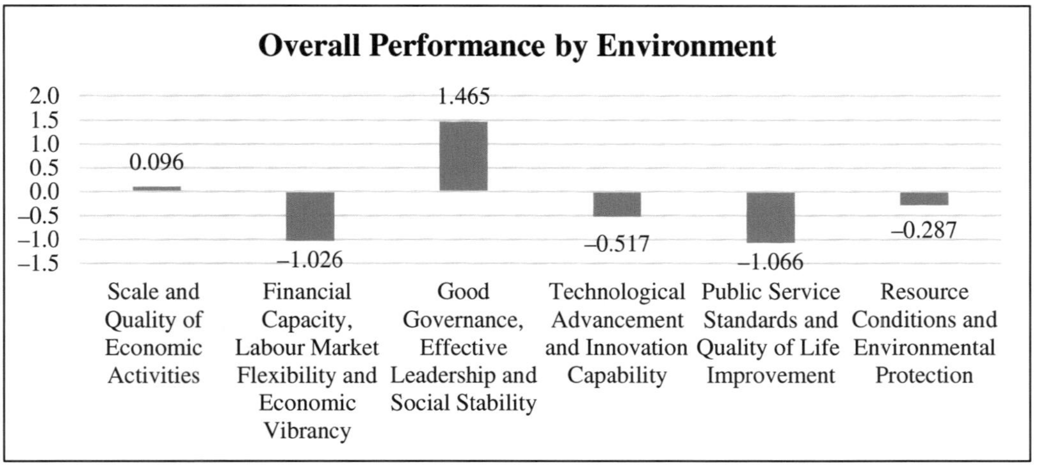

Among the six environments, Dezhou fares above the provincial average in two of them and the exceptionally well for Good Governance, Effective Leadership and Social Stability, which is the highest score among all 17 Shandong cities for that environment. However, Dezhou scores below the provincial average in the remaining four environments, especially in the environments of Financial Capacity, Labour Market Flexibility and Economic Vibrancy, as well as Public Service Standards and Quality of Life Improvement.

For a complete list of rankings, see Tables 3.2 to 3.7 in Section 3.3 of Chapter 3.

DEZHOU

Shandong Province

5.2.2 Urban Development within the Six Environments

Rank	City	Score
1	Qingdao	1.987
	...	
5	Weihai	0.849
6	Linyi	0.447
7	Dezhou	0.096
8	Tai'an	–0.321
9	Jinan	–0.364
	...	
16	Jining	–1.273
17	Laiwu	–1.295

A: ***Scale and Quality of Economic Activities***

2017 Rank

7th

Out of 17 Cities

Score: 0.096

Dezhou ranks 7th for Scale and Quality of Economic Activities, with a standardised score of 0.096. This places the city in the Middle Seven Group of 17 cities. Dezhou is positioned behind Linyi (0.447) at 6th place and ahead of Tai'an (–0.321) at 8th place.

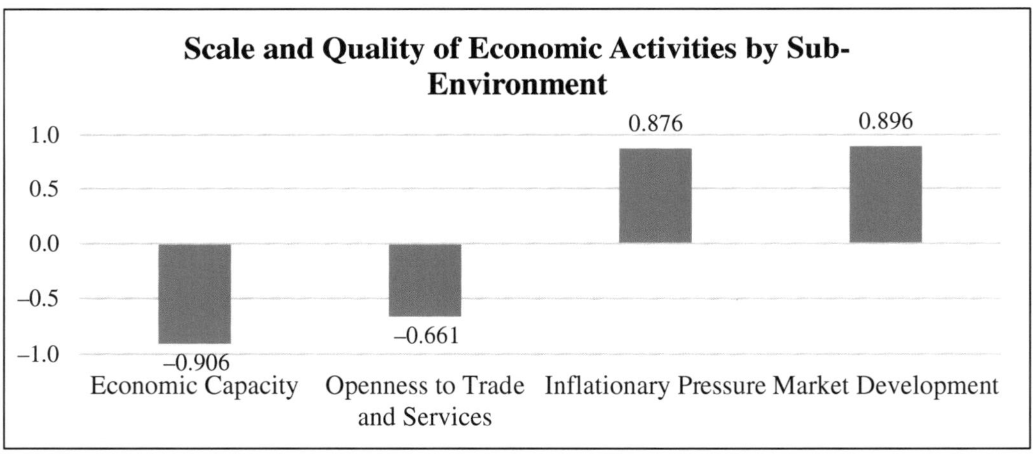

Looking at the four sub-environments of Scale and Quality of Economic Activities, Dezhou performs above the provincial average in Market Development and Inflationary Pressure, where it scores particularly better in the indicator of the Satisfaction with Business Environment from the Market Development sub-environment and Residents' Satisfaction with Price Levels from the Inflationary Pressure sub-environment. However, Dezhou performs below the provincial average in the remaining two sub-environments and especially weak in that of Economic Capacity, where the indicators of GRDP Growth Rate and Urbanisation Rate are poor. The indicator of the Dependency on Foreign Trade from the Openness to Trade and Services sub-environment has a particularly weak score as well.

DEZHOU

Shandong Province

B: ***Financial Capacity, Labour Market Flexibility and Economic Vibrancy***

2017 Rank

16th

Out of 17 Cities

Score: –1.026

Rank	City	Score
1	Jinan	2.264
	...	
10	Binzhou	–0.329
11	Rizhao	–0.619
12	Heze	–0.638
13	Tai'an	–0.763
14	Zaozhuang	–0.894
15	Liaocheng	–1.021
16	Dezhou	–1.026
17	Laiwu	–1.297

Dezhou ranks 16th for Financial Capacity, Labour Market Flexibility and Economic Vibrancy, with a standardised score of –1.026. This places the city in the Bottom Five Group of 17 cities. Dezhou is positioned closely behind Liaocheng (–1.021) at 15th place and ahead of Laiwu (–1.297) at 17th place.

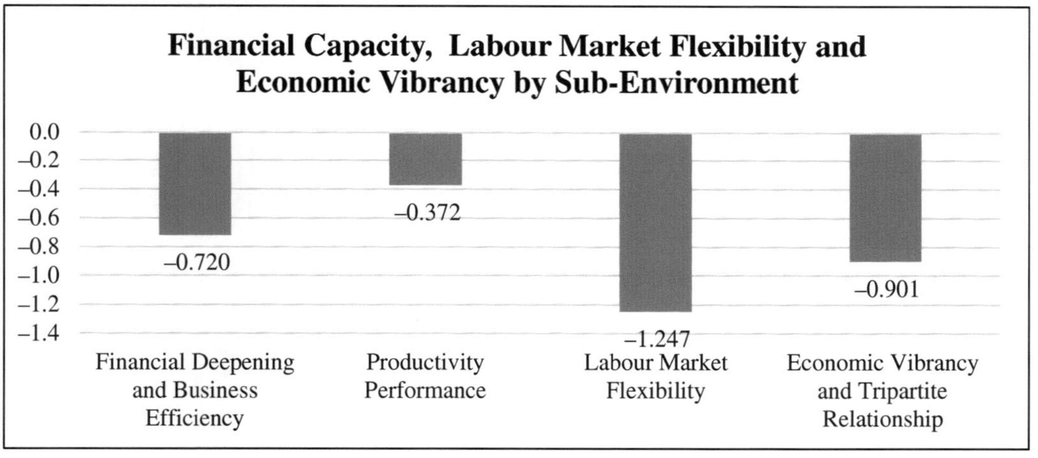

Among the four sub-environments of Financial Capacity, Economic Vibrancy and Harmony, Dezhou scores below the provincial average in all of them and particularly weak for Labour Market Flexibility, where the indicators of the Proportion of Workforce Employed in Agriculture Sector and Workforce Participation Rate perform especially poorly. The indicator of the Growth in the Number of Passengers Transported from the Economic Vibrancy and Tripartite Relationship sub-environment registered a low score as well. Nevertheless, Dezhou scores relatively better for the sub-environment Productivity Performance, where the indicator Secondary Industry Total Labour Productivity performs well. In addition, the indicator of Newly Increased Number of Employees from the Labour Market Flexibility sub-environment performs especially well.

DEZHOU

Shandong Province

Rank	City	Score
1	Dezhou	1.465
2	Weihai	1.134
3	Weifang	0.797
4	Qingdao	0.733
5	Jinan	0.532
6	Tai'an	0.498
7	Heze	0.435
	...	
16	Laiwu	−1.588
17	Liaocheng	−2.473

C: ***Good Governance, Effective Leadership and Social Stability***

2017 Rank

1st

Out of 17 Cities

Score: 1.465

Dezhou ranks 1st for Good Governance, Effective Leadership and Social Stability with a standardised score of 1.465. This places the city in the Top Five Group of 17 cities. Dezhou is ahead of Weihai (1.134) at 2nd place.

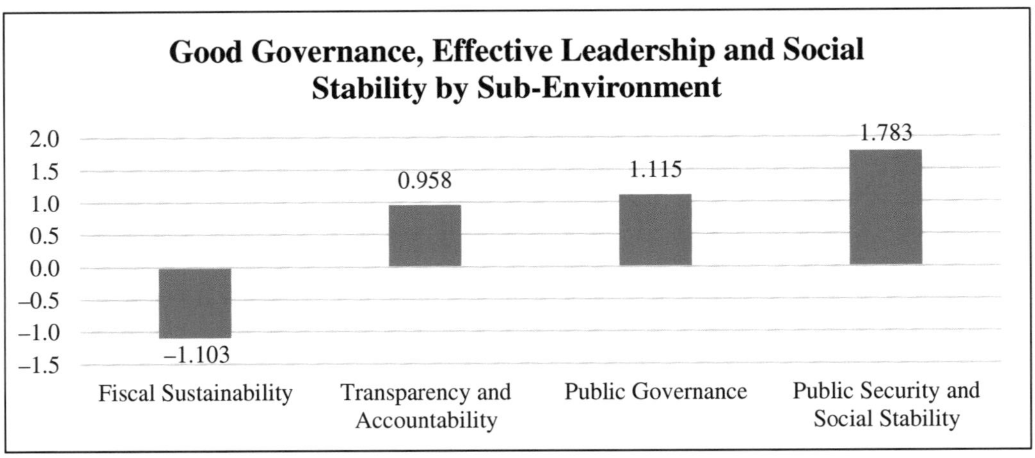

Among the four sub-environments of Good Governance, Effective Leadership and Social Stability, Dezhou scores above the provincial average and substantially better for Public Security and Social Stability, where the indicators of Growth Rate of the Number of Police Cases and Growth Rate of the Number of Police Cases Solved from the Public Security and Social Stability sub-environment perform exceptionally well. Other indicators that perform well include the Public Perception of Government Conduct and Number of Releases of Government Information for Public Viewing, both from the Transparency and Accountability sub-environment. However, the Fiscal Sustainability sub-environment scores relatively poorly and below the provincial average due to the low scores from the indicators of Fiscal Revenue Growth Rate and Government Fiscal Revenue Per Capita.

D: ***Technological Advancement and Innovation Capability***

2017 Rank

11th

Out of 17 Cities

Score: –0.517

Rank	City	Score
1	Qingdao	2.176
	...	
9	Linyi	–0.344
10	Tai'an	–0.457
11	Dezhou	–0.517
12	Binzhou	–0.559
13	Laiwu	–0.812
	...	
16	Zaozhuang	–1.192
17	Liaocheng	–1.221

Dezhou ranks 11th for Technological Advancement and Innovation Capability, with a standardised score of –0.517. This places the city in the Middle Seven Group of 17 cities. Dezhou is positioned after Tai'an (–0.457) at 10th place and followed closely by Binzhou (–0.559) at 12th place.

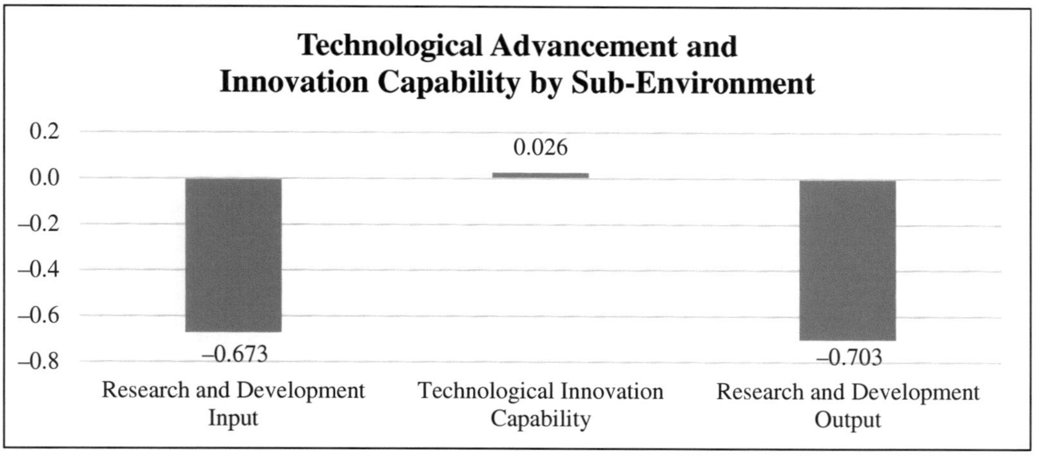

Among the three sub-environments of Technological Advancement and Innovation Capability, Dezhou performs slightly above the provincial average in Technological Innovation Capability, where the indicators of the Number of Provincial-Level Science Parks and Satisfaction of Innovation Environment perform relatively well. However, the remaining sub-environments score below the provincial average and especially for the Research and Development Output sub-environment, where the indicator of the Number of Existing Patents Per 10,000 Population scores poorly. In addition, the indicator of Per Capita Research and Development Expenditure from the Research and Development Input sub-environment registers a low score as well.

DEZHOU

Shandong Province

Rank	City	Score
1	Dongying	1.689
	...	
10	Linyi	–0.307
11	Tai'an	–0.567
12	Heze	–0.766
13	Jining	–0.819
14	Binzhou	–0.862
15	Zaozhuang	–0.954
16	Dezhou	–1.066
17	Liaocheng	–1.964

E: *Public Service Standards and Quality of Life Improvement*

2017 Rank

16th

Out of 17 Cities

Score: –1.066

Dezhou ranks 16th for Public Service Standards and Quality of Life Improvement with a standardised score of –1.066. This places the city in the Bottom Five Group of 17 cities. Dezhou is positioned between Zaozhuang (–0.954) at 15th place and Liaocheng (–1.964) at 17th place.

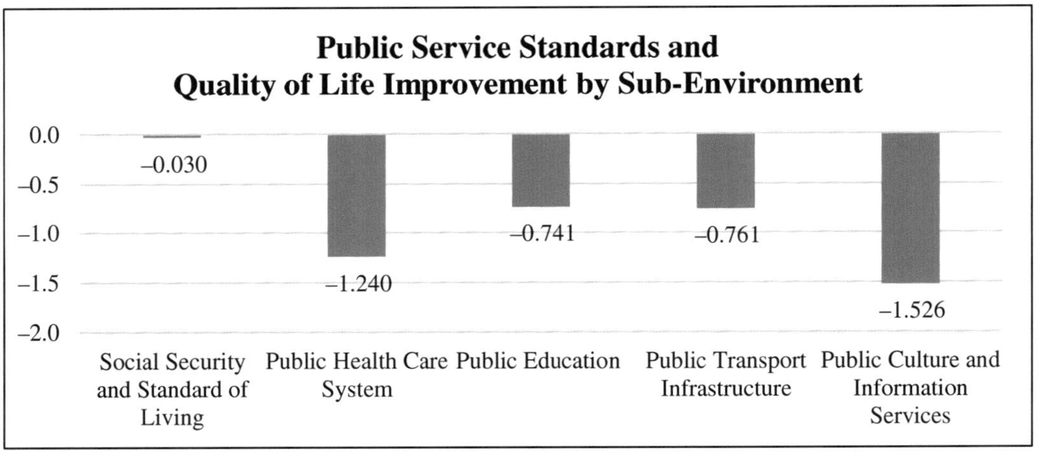

Among the five sub-environments of Public Service Standards and Quality of Life Improvement, Dezhou performs below the provincial average in all of them, especially in the sub-environments of Public Culture and Information Services and Public Health Care System. There are particularly low scores in the indicators of Number of Beds of Health Care Per 1,000 Population and Public Health and Average Life Expectancy, both from the Public Health Care System sub-environment. In addition, the weak performance in the Public Culture and Information Services sub-environment is largely due to the indicators of Percentage of Public Expenditure on Cultural Initiatives and Frequency of Using the Internet for Daily Convenience. Nevertheless, Dezhou performs relatively better in the Social Security and Standard of Living sub-environment, where the indicator of Resident's Perception of Happiness scores well.

F: ***Resource Conditions and Environmental Protection***

2017 Rank

11th

Out of 17 Cities

Score: –0.287

Rank	City	Score
1	Weihai	1.632
	...	
9	Jinan	0.281
10	Jining	–0.112
11	Dezhou	–0.287
12	Zaozhuang	–0.393
13	Linyi	–0.512
	...	
16	Binzhou	–1.586
17	Heze	–2.142

Dezhou ranks 11th for Resource Conditions and Environmental Protection with a standardised score of –0.287. This places the city in the Middle Seven Group of 17 cities. Dezhou is positioned between Jining (–0.112) at 10th place and Zaozhuang (–0.393) at 12th place.

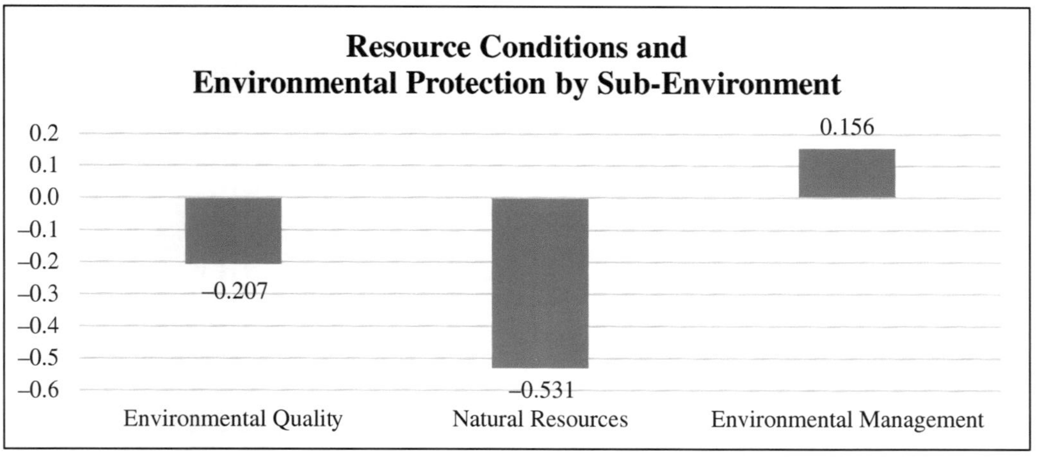

Among the three sub-environments of Resource Conditions and Environmental Protection, Dezhou scores above the provincial average in Environmental Management, where the indicators of Forest Land Growth and Urban Area Waste Water Treatment Rate perform well. On the other hand, Dezhou scores well below the provincial average in the two remaining sub-environments and particularly unfavourably in Natural Resources, where the indicators of Water Consumption Per RMB 10,000 GRDP scores particularly low. In addition, the indicator of Chemical Oxygen Demand Per RMB 10,000 from the Environmental Quality sub-environment registers a low score as well.

DEZHOU

Shandong Province

Figure 5.1: Median & Maximum Web for Dezhou

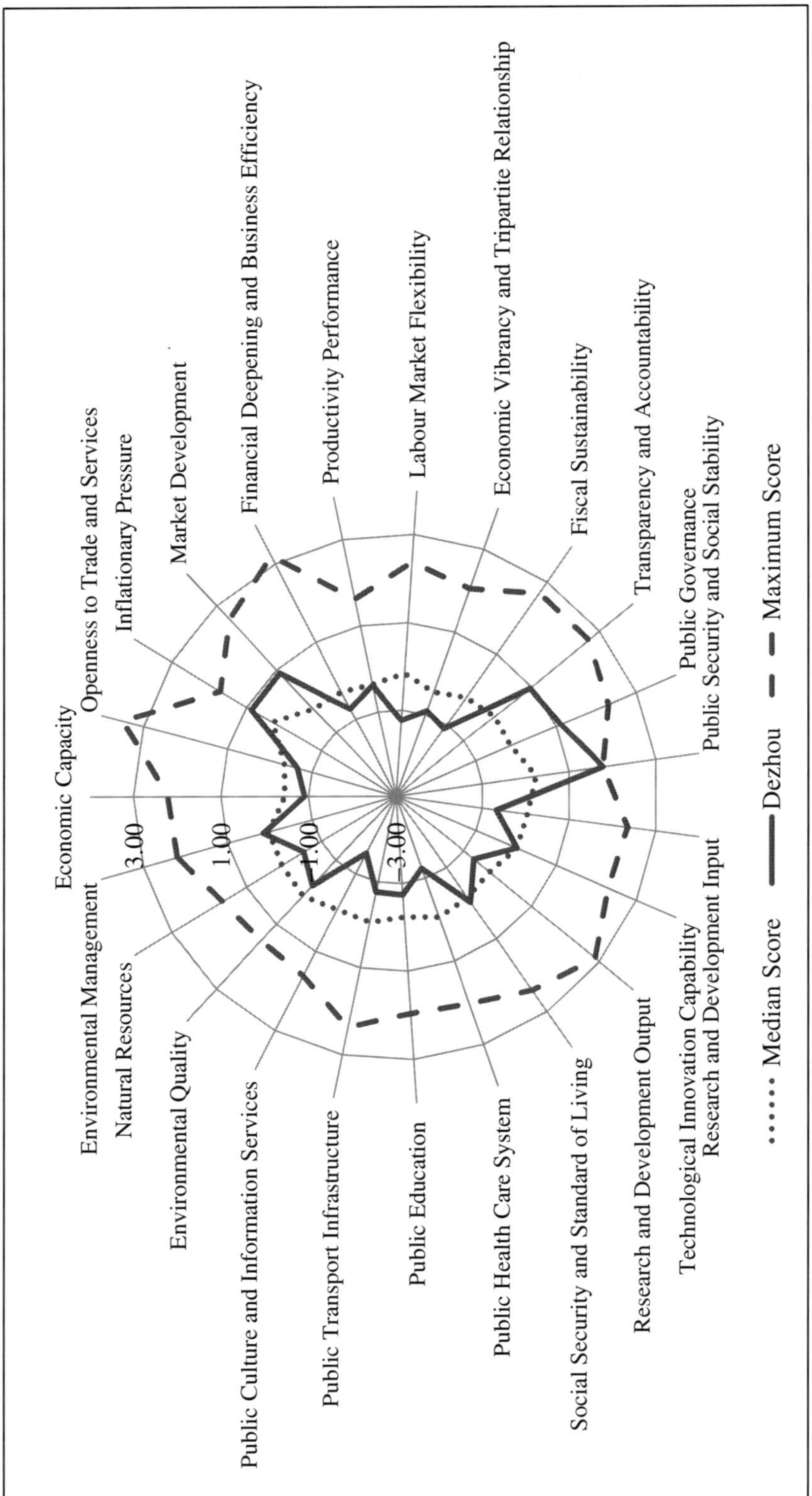

Source: Asia Competitiveness Institute.

5.2.3 Median and Maximum Web Analysis

To better understand Dezhou's relative strengths and weaknesses, it is useful to compare and contrast its scores for the 23 sub-environments against the median and maximum scores of Shandong's 17 cities.

In Figure 5.1, the median and maximum scores for 17 Shandong cities are shown as dotted and dashed lines respectively, while scores for Dezhou are shown as a solid line.

Comparison to Median Scores

Dezhou scores above the median for seven of the 23 sub-environments, most notably in Public Security and Social Stability, Public Governance and Market Development.

On the other hand, it scores below the median for 15 sub-environments, especially for Public Culture and Information Services, Labour Market Flexibility and Public Health Care System. The remaining sub-environment of Technological Innovation Capability is at the median.

Comparison to Maximum Scores

Dezhou scores below the provincial maximum of the 17 Shandong cities in all 23 sub-environments except for Public Security and Social Stability, where it obtains the standardised score of 1.783.

Dezhou's score in Openness to Trade and Services (–0.661) is farthest from the maximum, which is held by Qingdao (3.505). Dezhou's score in Inflationary Pressure (0.876) is closest to the maximum, which is held by Heze (1.696).

5.3 Summary of Empirical Findings of Dezhou and *What-if* Urban Development Simulation

5.3.1 Summary of Empirical Findings, 20% Strongest and Weakest Indicators

Overall Performance **10th** Score: –0.302		
Scale and Quality of Economic Activities **7th** Score: 0.096	Financial Capacity, Labour Market Flexibility and Economic Vibrancy **16th** Score: –1.026	Good Governance, Effective Leadership and Social Stability **1st** Score: 1.465
Technological Advancement and Innovation Capability **11th** Score: –0.517	Public Service Standards and Quality of Life Improvement **16th** Score: –1.066	Resource Conditions and Environmental Protection **11th** Score: –0.287

(Rank out of 17 cities)

Summary

Dezhou ranks 10th out of 17 Shandong cities in its Overall Performance. Dezhou scores below the provincial average in four out of the six environments, where the environments of Good Governance, Effective Leadership and Social Stability and Scale and Quality of Economic Activities are above the provincial average. Meanwhile, Dezhou is especially poor in the environments of Public Service Standards and Quality of Life Improvement as well as Financial Capacity, Labour Market Flexibility and Economic Vibrancy, both at 16th place.

Strengths

As illustrated in Table 5.2, Dezhou performs well in the environment of Good Governance, Effective Leadership and Social Stability, with 10 out of 26 of its 20% Strongest Indicators included in this environment. Among Dezhou's best performing indicators are the Growth Rate of the Number of Police Cases, Growth Rate of the Number of Police Cases Solved and Per Capita Road Area.

Weaknesses

As observed in Table 5.3, Dezhou is weak in the environments of Public Service Standards and Quality of Life Improvement, where 11 out of 26 of its 20% Weakest Indicators under this environment. Among Dezhou's worst performing indicators are the Proportion of Workforce Employed in Agriculture Sector, Number of Beds of Health Care Per 1,000 Population and Workforce Participation Rate.

DEZHOU

Shandong Province

Table 5.2: 20% Strongest Indicators for Dezhou

Rank	20% Strongest Indicator	Score	SQEA	FCLMFEV	GGELSS	TAIC	PSSQLI	RCEP
1	Growth Rate of the Number of Police Cases	3.272			✓			
2	Growth Rate of the Number of Police Cases Solved	3.011			✓			
3	Per Capita Road Area	1.544					✓	
4	Newly Increased Number of Employees	1.522		✓				
5	Satisfaction with Business Environment	1.450	✓					
6	Public Perception of Government Conduct	1.405			✓			
7	Number of Primary and Secondary Schools Per 10,000 Population	1.399					✓	
8	Forest Land Growth	1.365						✓
9	Number of Releases of Government Information for Public Viewing	1.295			✓			
10	Number of Public Servants Per 10,000 Population	1.244			✓			
11	Residents' Perception of Happiness	1.200					✓	
12	Number of Administration Action and Reconsideration Cases	1.159			✓			
13	Satisfaction with the Just of Judiciary	1.150			✓			
14	Satisfaction of Public Health Care Services	1.001					✓	
15	Urban Area Waste Water Treatment Rate	0.966						✓
16	Residents' Satisfaction with Price Levels	0.962	✓					
17	Urban Residents' Disposable Income Growth Rate	0.878	✓					
18	Public Perception of Security	0.808			✓			
19	Average Public Servant Salary	0.792			✓			
20	Retail Price Index	0.723	✓					
21	Index for Quality of E-Government System	0.722			✓			
22	Public Health and Medical Service Expenses as a Share of GRDP	0.716					✓	
23	Proportion of the Population Above 60 Years Old	0.617					✓	
24	Number of Provincial-Level Science Parks	0.576				✓		
25	Per Capita Arable Land	0.573						✓
26	Satisfaction of Income Disparity	0.503					✓	

Table 5.3: 20% Weakest Indicators for Dezhou

Rank	20% Weakest Indicator	Score	SQEA	FCLMFEV	GGELSS	TAIC	PSSQLI	RCEP
106	Proportion of Workforce Employed in Service Sector	–0.941		✓				
107	Number of R&D Personnel Per 10,000 Population	–0.955				✓		
108	Public Health and Medical Service Expenses Per Capita	–0.965					✓	
109	Dependency on Foreign Trade (Foreign Trade as a Share of GRDP)	–0.968	✓					
110	Percentage of the Employed Population with Tertiary Education	–0.983		✓				
111	Proportion of Urban Workers Employed in Private Enterprises	–1.003		✓				
112	Average Life Expectancy	–1.006					✓	
113	Average Years of Education Received	–1.012					✓	
114	GRDP Growth Rate	–1.040	✓					
115	Public Education Appropriation Per Capita	–1.064					✓	
116	Number of Investigations for Power Abuses Per 10,000 Population	–1.093			✓			
117	Mobile Phone Penetration Per Capita	–1.108					✓	
118	Number of Listed Items Under Executive Authority of the Government	–1.131			✓			
119	Rate of Migration Flow	–1.139		✓				
120	Growth in the Number of Passengers Transported	–1.157		✓				
121	Percentage of Public Expenditure on Cultural Initiatives	–1.183					✓	
122	Number of Urban Public Transport Vehicles Per 10,000 Population (Standard Number)	–1.212					✓	
123	Satisfaction of Public Transport Services	–1.247					✓	
124	Per Capita Annual Disposable Income	–1.275					✓	
125	Water Consumption Per RMB 10,000 GRDP	–1.301						✓
126	Frequency of Using the Internet for Daily Convenience	–1.338					✓	
127	Proportion of Urban Workers Employed in State Enterprises	–1.424		✓				
128	Fiscal Revenue Growth Rate	–1.466			✓			
129	Workforce Participation Rate	–1.666		✓				
130	Number of Beds of Health Care Per 1,000 Population	–1.984					✓	
131	Proportion of Workforce Employed in Agriculture Sector	–2.165		✓				

Source: Asia Competitiveness Institute.

Notes: SQEA: Scale and Quality of Economic Activities; FCLMFEV: Financial Capacity, Labour Market Flexibility and Economic Vibrancy; GGELSS: Good Governance, Effective Leadership and Social Stability; TAIC: Technological Advancement and Innovation Capability; PSSQLI: Public Service Standards and Quality of Life Improvement; RCEP: Resource Conditions and Environmental Protection.

5.3.2 *What-if* Urban Development Simulation

ACI has devised a simulation methodology to improve the ranking of a particular city by improving on its 20% Weakest Indicators as shown in Table 5.3.[2] The figures below show Dezhou's ranking and standardised scores before and after the policy-induced simulation. Refer to Tables 3.8 to 3.14 in Section 3.4 of Chapter 3 for a complete list of simulation results for all cities.

Overall Performance

	Before		After
Rank	10th	▶	8th
Score	–0.302		0.345

Scale and Quality of Economic Activities

	Before	After
Rank	7th	7th
Score	0.096	–0.285

Financial Capacity, Labour Market Flexibility and Economic Vibrancy

	Before	After
Rank	16th	10th
Score	–1.026	–0.356

Good Governance, Effective Leadership and Social Stability

	Before	After
Rank	1st	1st
Score	1.465	1.952

Technological Advancement and Innovation Capability

	Before	After
Rank	11th	9th
Score	–0.517	–0.308

Public Service Standards and Quality of Life Improvement

	Before	After
Rank	16th	9th
Score	–1.066	–0.035

Resource Conditions and Environmental Protection

	Before	After
Rank	11th	10th
Score	–0.287	–0.003

After the *What-if* simulation, Dezhou improves its ranking from 10th to 8th in terms of its Overall Performance. Likewise, Dezhou's standardised score increases from –0.302 to 0.345. This leap is plausible if the city manages to successfully address its 20% Weakest Indicators.

The simulation further highlights Dezhou potential for substantial improvement in some of its environments, most notably in Public Service Standards and Quality of Life Improvement, where its rank will rise from 16th to 9th. Such encouraging results should incentivise Dezhou to strive to improve the indicators under the 20% Weakest Indicators list. These indicators include Number of Beds of Health Care Per 1,000 Population and the Number of Urban Transport Vehicles Per 10,000 Population.

[2] The methodology for *What-if* simulation is thoroughly explained in Section 2.7 of Chapter 2.

5.4 Concluding Notes: Public Policy Implications[3]

Areas for Commendation

Dezhou performs well in the environment of Good Governance, Effective Leadership and Social Stability, with 10 out of 26 of its 20% Strongest Indicators contained in this environment alone, as indicated in Table 5.2.

Further, Dezhou holds the maximum score for the sub-environment of Public Security and Social Stability (1.868) and scores above the provincial average in seven of the 23 sub-environments.

In the past five years from 2012 to 2016, Dezhou has gradually completed the system of security prevention and control in both urban and rural areas. As a result, the social security in Dezhou has been improved. Moreover, Dezhou increased its fiscal expenditure in social welfare which of over 80% of its total fiscal expenditure during the same period. All these measures may explain Dezhou's good performance in the environment of Good Governance, Effective Leadership and Social Stability.

Areas for Improvement

As Dezhou scores below the provincial average in four out of the six environments, there are plenty of areas for improvement for the city. Most crucially, Dezhou should address the environment of Public Service Standards and Quality of Life Improvement, where it has a total of 11 out of 26 of the 20% Weakest Indicators under this environment, as shown in Table 5.3. Additionally, as gleaned from the *What-if* Urban Development Simulation, the environment for Public Service Standards and Quality of Life Improvement should be prioritised because that is the environment in which Dezhou will achieve the greatest improvement in its ranking — seven positions — relative to other environments.

Further, Dezhou obtains the weakest score in the sub-environment of Labour Market Flexibility (−1.247). In addition, Dezhou performs poorly in the sub-environments of Public Culture and Information Services (−1.526) and Public Health Care System (−1.240), and scores below the provincial average in 16 out of 23 sub-environments.

In November 2017, Dezhou initiated its plans for infrastructure investment in public education in rural areas. The project has invested over RMB 5 billion in dormitory buildings. Moreover, since 2016, Dezhou has invested almost RMB 7 billion in school infrastructure development to solve the issue of "Large Class Size". The projects mentioned provides evidence that the Dezhou administration is working on improving their weak public education system.

Regarding Dezhou's cultural development, the city government had announced its intention and plan to improve it in May 2017. However, the plan remains only on paper. More effort is

[3]The relevant statistical data and government policies are from Dezhou Municipal People's Government (2017a, 2017b, 2017c) and Yang, Dong, and Wu (2017).

required to implement the proposal to improve its public culture. In addition, the plan regarding enhancing public transport and infrastructure has yet to be executed.

Future Potential Development

In summary, Dezhou should focus on improving the environment of Public Service Standards and Quality of Life Improvement by enhancing access to education, quality of health Care services as well as transportation infrastructure.

Dezhou should also work on the environment of Financial Capacity, Labour Market Flexibility and Economic Vibrancy through policies that foster a better business environment. However, no significant measures on improving trade conditions have been observed. In the future, Dezhou should focus on improving its openness of trade by working on building both domestic and foreign trade partners. Successful improvement in its economic and trade conditions will have positive effects on the condition of its labour market as well. While improving its economic performance, Dezhou should also not neglect its environment as Dezhou's performance in the sub-environment of Environmental Quality is currently below the provincial average. For example, the government should enforce restrictions and regulations on the emission of chemicals from existing and future industrial plants. This is consistent with the goal of sustainable growth proposed during the 19th National Party Congress in October 2017.

References

Department of Commerce of Shandong Province. n.d. 'Dezhou City Profile'. Accessed 13 October 2017. http://en.shandongbusiness.gov.cn/city/77.

Dezhou Municipal People's Government. 2016. 'Dezhou Profile'. Dezhou Municipal People's Government. 6 June 2016. http://www.dezhou.gov.cn/en/n21661785/n21661772/c21854128/content.html.

———. 2017a. '2017年德州市政府工作报告（全文）- 德州宣传网 2017 Dezhou Annual Government Work Report (in Chinese)'. 3 March 2017. http://www.sddzxc.gov.cn/n24923121/c28486756/content.html.

———. 2017b. '《德州市关于加快构建现代公共文化服务体系的实施意见》 Suggestions on Accelerating the Construction of Modern Public Culture Service System in Dezhou (in Chinese)'. Dazhongwang Shandong. 11 May 2017. http://www.dzwww.com/shandong/sdnews/201705/t20170511_15907509.htm.

———. 2017c. '我市召开"全面改薄"规划调整部署会 Dezhou Held Planning Conference on "Comprehensive Improvement on Educational Infrastructure" (in Chinese)'. 9 November 2017. http://www.dzedu.gov.cn/n909426/c33720463/content.html.

Gao, Li. 2009. 'Dezhou'. Shandong China, the Hometown of Confucius. 24 July 2009. http://shandong.chinadaily.com.cn/e/2009-07/24/content_8469137.htm.

Yang, Fan, Xiaoshuang Dong, and Yajun Wu. 2017. '德州市教育局开展"全面改薄"工程 控制择校 Dezhou's Ministry of Education Carries out "Comprehensive Improvement on Educational Infrastructure" Project, Controlling School Selection (in Chinese)'. Qiluwang (齐鲁网). 10 November 2017. http://dezhou.iqilu.com/dzshizheng/2017/1110/3741805.shtml.

Chapter 6: DONGYING
Shandong Province

Location of City

Source: Asia Competitiveness Institute.

6.1 Profile of Dongying City[1]

Established in 1983 near a small village of the same name, Dongying was founded to capitalise on the vast amount of fossil fuel resources in the nearby Shengli Oil Field. The city now directly administers three districts and two counties spanning a total land area of 8,243 square kilometres, with a total population of 2,132,100. Dongying also sits astride the Yellow River's estuary region, and its wetlands are accordingly rich and fertile, with the Shandong Yellow River Delta National Nature Reserve boasting a remarkable ecological diversity.

In 2016, Dongying's Gross Regional Domestic Product (GRDP) stood at around RMB 348 billion, with the city boasting a GRDP growth rate of 7.0%, as can be seen in Table 6.1. While the areas surrounding Dongying are rich in oil and natural gas, the city's primary sector only comprised 3.5% of GRDP. Contrastingly, Dongying possesses a highly developed secondary sector, which comprised 62.2% of GRDP and capitalises on its wealth of fossil fuel resources by focusing on petrochemicals, rubber tire manufacturing and petroleum equipment manufacturing, with other significant secondary industries being non-ferrous metals smelting, salt chemicals

[1]The relevant city information are from the Department of Commerce of Shandong Province (n.d.), Dongying Municipal Government (2013) and Bai (2009).

and automobiles and auto parts. Dongying's tertiary sector plays a smaller role relative to its secondary sector, but still constituted 34.3% of GRDP in 2016 thanks to ongoing investments aimed at facilitating a greater focus on service industries.

Dongying is connected to the rest of China by the Dongying Shengli Airport, which caters to domestic flights, and is otherwise well-connected to neighbouring regions by the high-speed rail network and several expressways. Dongying is also notable for having managed to retain and maintain much of its ecological heritage despite the nature of its dominant industries, having been named in 2009 the "National Demonstration City for the Construction of Modern Forestry". Accordingly, its ratio of green coverage to built-up areas stands at a respectable 43.5%, while the city's efforts to upkeep its high percentage of wetland cover — 57.7% — has contributed to Dongying having one of the highest per capita park and green space acreages in the province, at 9.1 square metres.

Table 6.1: Key Economic Indicators for Dongying, 2016

Land Area (km²)	**8,243**
Population	
Total Population	2,132,100
Urbanisation Rate (%)	66.7
Average Life Expectancy (years)	77.8
Number of Employees (10,000)	151
Workforce Participation Rate (%)	74.3
Gross Regional Domestic Product (GRDP) — 2015 Prices	
GRDP (100 millions of RMB)	3,480
GRDP Per Capita (RMB)	164,024
GRDP Growth Rate (%)	7.0
Economic Composition	
Primary Sector (% of GRDP)	3.5
Secondary Sector (% of GRDP)	62.2
Tertiary Sector (% of GRDP)	34.3
Trade — 2016 Prices	
Exports (millions of RMB)	32,998
Imports (millions of RMB)	52,769
Dependency on Foreign Trade (%)	28.8
Infrastructure	
Per Capita Road Area (m²)	32.1
Growth in the Number of Passengers Transported (10,000)	57.0
Growth in the Volume of Cargo Transported (10,000 tons)	497
Environment	
Green Coverage Ratio of Built-up Area (%)	43.5
Environmental Expenditure (% of Total Fiscal Expenditure)	2.4

Source: Asia Competitiveness Institute from the 2017 Shandong Statistical Yearbook.

6.2 In-Depth Urban Development of Dongying, 2016*

6.2.1 Overall Urban Development Performance

Overall Performance

2017 Rank

6th

Out of 17 Cities

Score: 0.603

Rank	City	Score
1	Qingdao	1.753
	...	
4	Jinan	1.106
5	Weifang	0.855
6	Dongying	0.603
7	Zibo	0.403
8	Linyi	−0.002
	...	
16	Laiwu	−1.233
17	Liaocheng	−1.576

Dongying ranks 6th in its Overall Performance, with a standardised score of 0.603. This places the city in the Middle Seven Group of 17 cities. Dongying is positioned between Weifang (0.855) at 5th place and Zibo (0.403) at 7th place.

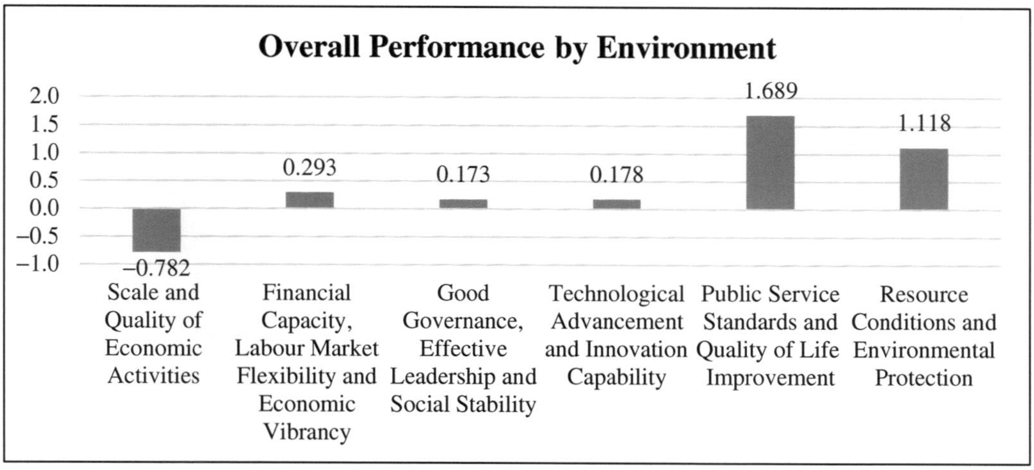

Across the six environments, Dongying fares above the provincial average in five of them and particularly well in the Public Service Standards and Quality of Life Improvement environment. Another particularly well performing environment includes that of Resource Conditions and Environmental Protection. In contrast, the environment of Scale and Quality of Economic Activities performs below the provincial average and especially weaker.

** For a complete list of rankings, see Tables 3.2 to 3.7 in Section 3.3 of Chapter 3.*

6.2.2 Urban Development within the Six Environments

Rank	City	Score
1	Qingdao	1.987
	...	
10	Zaozhuang	–0.412
11	Binzhou	–0.573
12	Liaocheng	–0.665
13	Zibo	–0.674
14	Dongying	–0.782
15	Rizhao	–1.017
16	Jining	–1.273
17	Laiwu	–1.295

A: ***Scale and Quality of Economic Activities***

2017 Rank

14th

Out of 17 Cities

Score: –0.782

Dongying ranks 14th for Scale and Quality of Economic Activities, with a standardised score of –0.782. This places the city in the Bottom Five Group of 17 cities. Dongying is positioned behind Zibo (–0.674) at 13th place and Rizhao (–1.017) at 15th place.

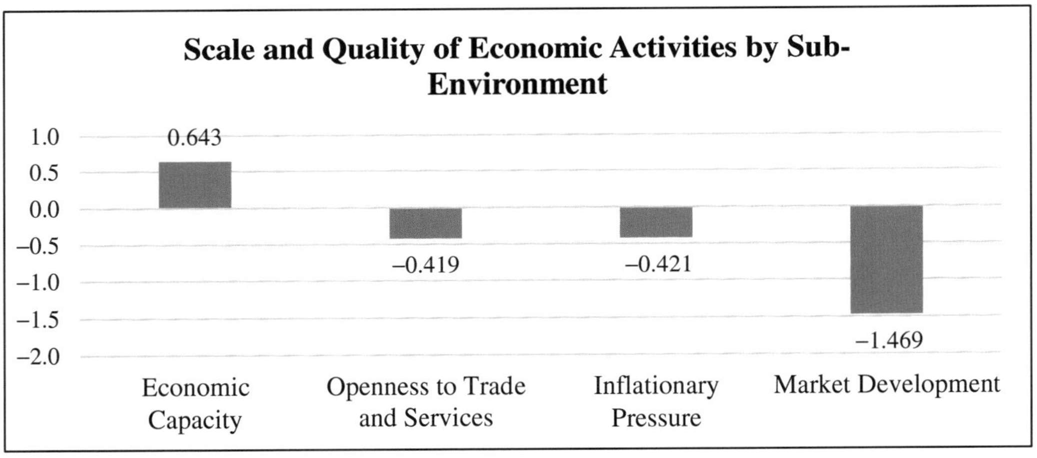

Looking at the four sub-environments of Scale and Quality of Economic Activities, Dongying performs above the provincial average and especially better for Economic Capacity, where the indicators of GRDP Per Capita and Manufacturing Sector as a Percentage of GRDP perform particularly well. Further, the indicator of Producer Price Index from the Inflationary Pressure sub-environment scores high as well. However, Dongying scores below the provincial average in all the remaining sub-environments and particularly weak in Market Development, where the indicator Government Expenditures as a Percentage of GRDP performed exceptionally weak. In addition, the indicator of Trade Surplus from the Openness to Trade and Services sub-environment scores poorly as well.

B: ***Financial Capacity, Labour Market Flexibility and Economic Vibrancy***

2017 Rank

6th

Out of 17 Cities

Score: 0.293

Rank	City	Score
1	Jinan	2.264
	…	
4	Weifang	0.441
5	Linyi	0.387
6	Dongying	0.293
7	Zibo	0.089
8	Weihai	0.083
	…	
16	Dezhou	−1.026
17	Laiwu	−1.297

Dongying ranks 6th for Financial Capacity, Labour Market Flexibility and Economic Vibrancy, with a standardised score of 0.293. This places the city in the Middle Seven Group of 17 cities. Dongying is positioned between Linyi (0.387) at 5th place and Zibo (0.089) at 7th place.

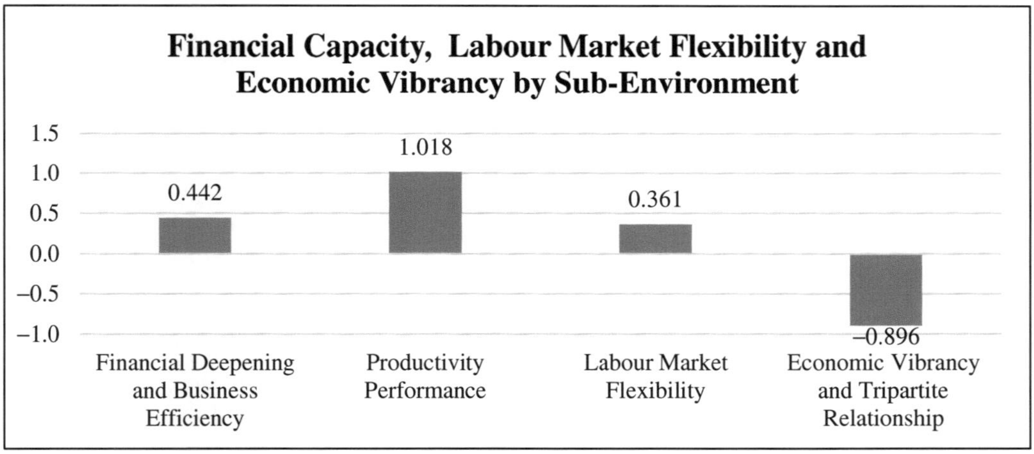

Among the four sub-environments of Financial Capacity, Labour Market Flexibility and Economic Vibrancy, Dongying fares above the provincial average in three of them and remarkably better in Productivity Performance, particularly due to the good performance in the indicators of Secondary Industry Total Labour Productivity and Percentage of the Employed Population with Tertiary Education. Further, the indicator or Loan Balance Per Capita and Deposit Balance Per Capita obtain high scores as well. Nevertheless, Dongying performs below the provincial average in the Economic Vibrancy and Tripartite Relationship sub-environment, where the indicator of Growth in the Volume of Cargo Transported scores poorly. In addition, the indicator of the Growth Rate of Overall Labour Productivity from the Productivity Performance sub-environment scores especially low.

DONGYING

Shandong Province

Rank	City	Score
1	Dezhou	1.465
	...	
9	Linyi	0.321
10	Yantai	0.192
11	Dongying	0.173
12	Rizhao	0.042
13	Jining	–0.527
	...	
16	Laiwu	–1.588
17	Liaocheng	–2.473

C: *Good Governance, Effective Leadership and Social Stability*

2017 Rank

11th

Out of 17 Cities

Score: 0.173

Dongying ranks 11th for Good Governance, Effective Leadership and Social Stability with a standardised score of 0.173. This places the city in the Middle Seven Group of 17 cities. Dongying is positioned closely behind Yantai (0.192) at 10th place and ahead of Rizhao (0.042) at 12th place.

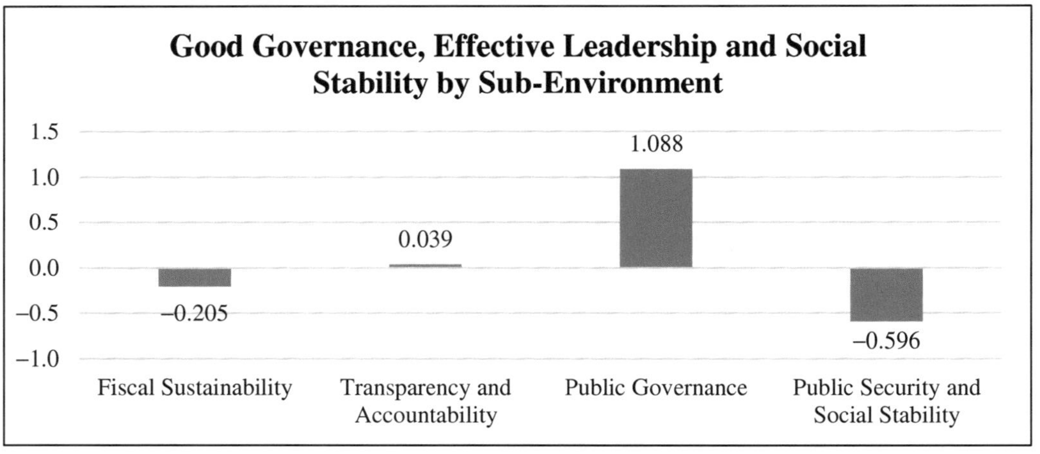

Across the four sub-environments of Good Governance, Effective Leadership and Social Stability, Dongying scores above the provincial average in two of them and particularly well for Public Governance, where the indicators of Number of Public Servants Per 10,000 Population and the Average Public Servant Salary performs well. In addition, the Government Fiscal Expenditure Per Capita from the Fiscal Sustainability sub-environment also scores well. However, Dongying performs below the provincial average in the remaining sub-environments and particularly weaker for Public Security and Social Stability, where the indicator of Traffic Accident Fatality Per 10,000 Population obtains a low score. Other indicators with poor performance include that of Fiscal Revenue Growth Rate from the Fiscal Sustainability sub-environment and Number of Investigations for Power Abuses Per 10,000 Population from the Transparency and Accountability sub-environment.

D: ***Technological Advancement and Innovation Capability***

2017 Rank

7th

Out of 17 Cities

Score: 0.178

Rank	City	Score
1	Qingdao	2.176
	...	
5	Weihai	0.848
6	Zibo	0.492
7	Dongying	0.178
8	Jining	–0.222
9	Linyi	–0.344
	...	
16	Zaozhuang	–1.192
17	Liaocheng	–1.221

Dongying ranks 7th for Technological Advancement and Innovation Capability, with a standardised score of 0.178. This places the city in the Middle Seven Group of 17 cities. Dongying is positioned between Zibo (0.492) at 6th place and Jining (–0.222) at 8th place.

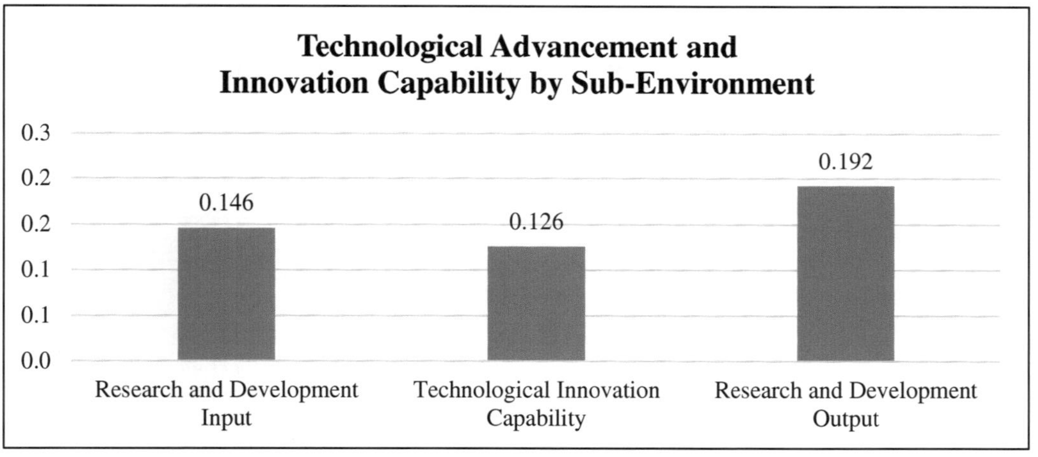

Among the three sub-environments of Technological Advancement and Innovation Capability, Dongying performs above the provincial average in all of them and relatively better for Research and Development Output, where the indicator of the Number of Existing Patents Per 10,000 Population scores relatively well. At the same time, the indicator of Per Capita Research and Development Expenditure from the Research and Development Output sub-environment scores exceptionally well among all indicators in this environment. However, Dongying performs comparatively weaker in the Technological Innovation Capability sub-environment, where there is weak performance in the indicator of the Number of Provincial-Level Science Parks.

DONGYING

Shandong Province

Rank	City	Score
1	Dongying	1.689
2	Weihai	1.616
3	Weifang	0.920
4	Jinan	0.919
5	Zibo	0.794
6	Laiwu	0.675
7	Qingdao	0.593
	...	
16	Dezhou	−1.066
17	Liaocheng	−1.964

E: ***Public Service Standards and Quality of Life Improvement***

2017 Rank

1st

Out of 17 Cities

Score: 1.689

Dongying ranks 1st for Public Service Standards and Quality of Life Improvement with a standardised score of 1.689. This places the city in the Top Five Group of 17 cities. Dongying is positioned ahead of Weihai (1.616) at 2nd place.

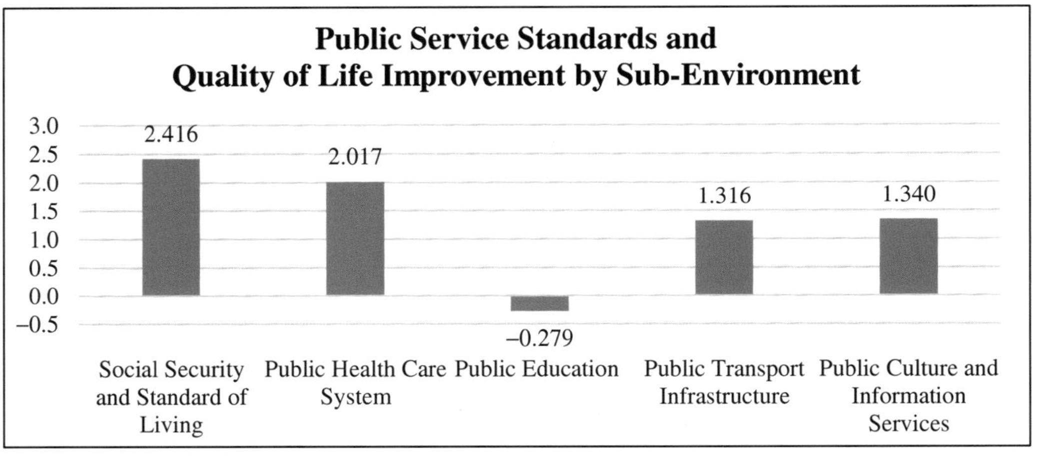

Among the five sub-environments of Public Service Standards and Quality of Life Improvement, Dongying performs well above the provincial average in four of them and exceptionally better for Social Security and Standard of Living and Public Health Care System. Dongying exhibits strong performance in the indicators of the Engel's Index and the Number of Private Cars Per 100 Households, both from the Social Security and Standard of Living sub-environment, as well as the indicators of Public Health and Medical Service Expenses Per Capita and Average Life Expectancy from the Public Health Care system sub-environment. However, Dongying scores marginally below the provincial average and relatively weaker in the Public Education sub-environment, where the indicator of the Ratio of Public Education Appropriation to GRDP scores especially poorly.

F: ***Resource Conditions and Environmental Protection***

2017 Rank

3rd

Out of 17 Cities

Score: 1.118

Rank	City	Score
1	Weihai	1.632
2	Yantai	1.394
3	Dongying	1.118
4	Rizhao	0.817
5	Zibo	0.665
6	Liaocheng	0.376
7	Tai'an	0.370
	...	
16	Binzhou	−1.586
17	Heze	−2.142

Dongying ranks 3rd for Resource Conditions and Environmental Protection with a standardised score of 1.118. This places the city in the Top Five Group of 17 cities. Dongying is positioned behind Yantai (1.394) at 2nd place and well ahead of Rizhao (0.817) at 4th place.

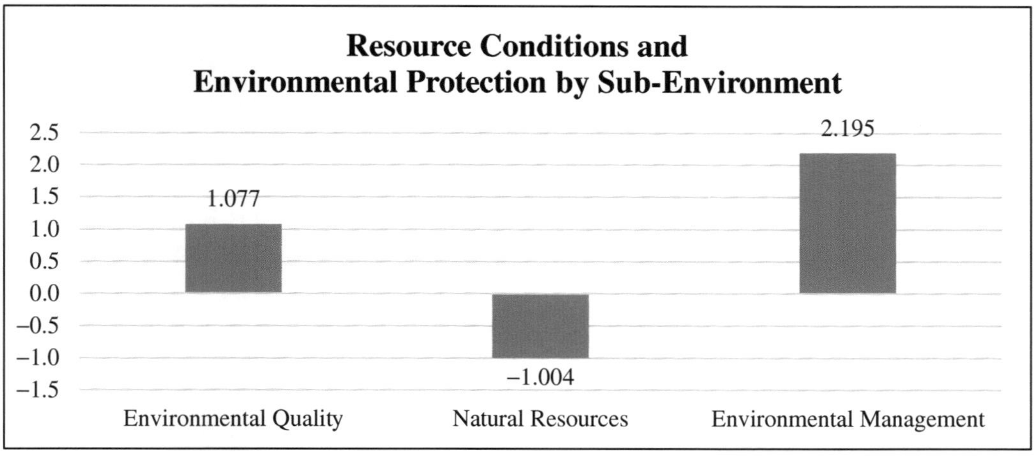

Among the three sub-environments of Resource Conditions and Environmental Protection, Dongying performs above the provincial average in two of them and remarkably well for Environmental Management, where the indicators of Wetland Cover and Area of Natural Reserves to Administrative Area score especially well. In addition, Dongying obtains a high score for the indicator of Ammoniacal Nitrogen Discharge Per RMB 10,000 GRDP from the Environmental Quality sub-environment as well. Nevertheless, Dongying performs below the provincial average in the Natural Resources sub-environment, where there are particularly weak scores from the indicators of the Electricity Consumption Per RMB 10,000 GRDP and Built-up Area Population Density. However, the indicator of Per Capita Arable Land from the Natural Resources sub-environment obtains a notably high score.

DONGYING

Shandong Province

Figure 6.1: Median & Maximum Web for Dongying

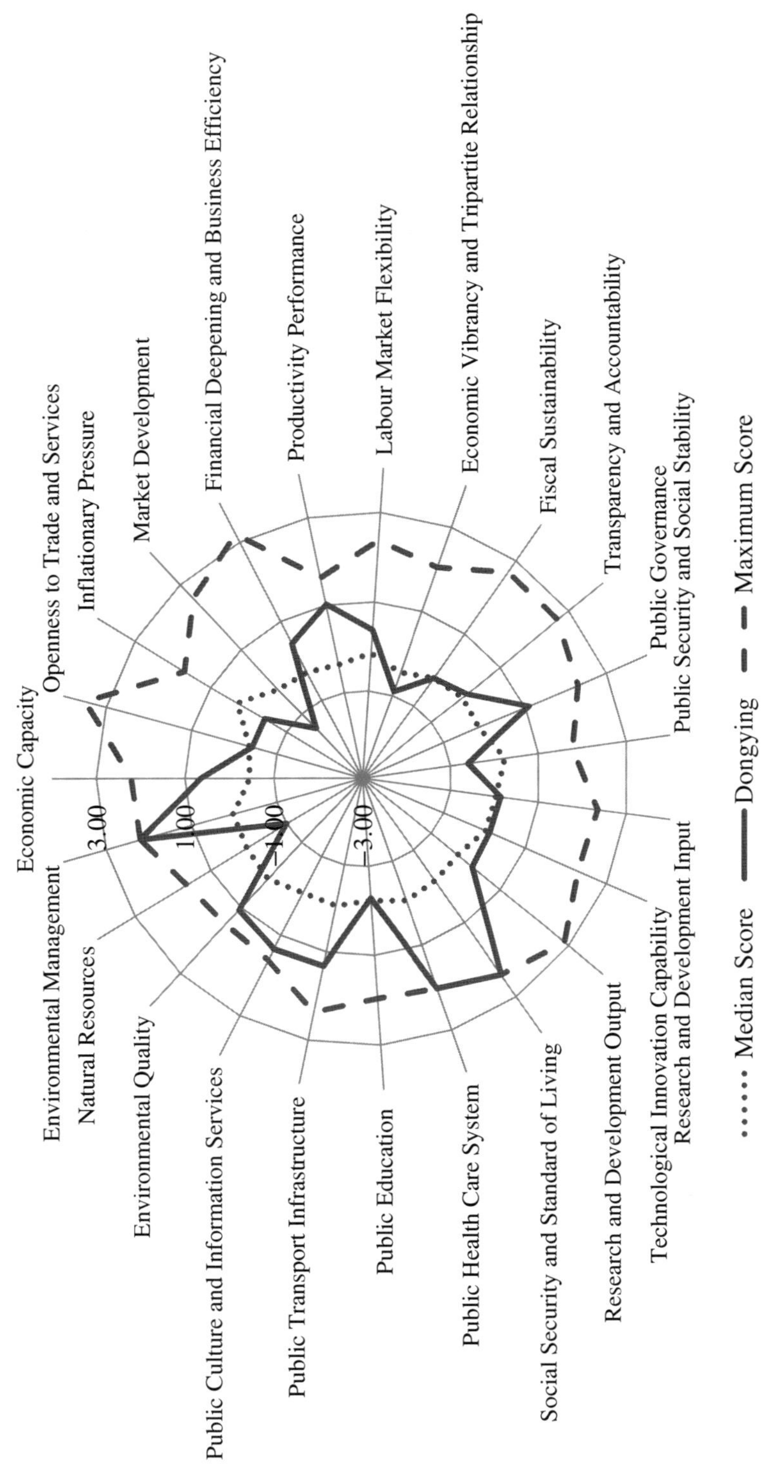

Source: Asia Competitiveness Institute.

6.2.3 Median and Maximum Web Analysis

To better understand Dongying's relative strengths and weaknesses, it is useful to compare and contrast its scores for the 23 sub-environments against the median and maximum scores of Shandong's 17 cities.

In Figure 6.1, the median and maximum scores for 17 Shandong cities are shown as dotted and dashed lines respectively, while scores for Dongying are shown as a solid line.

Comparison to Median Scores

Dongying scores above the median for 15 of the 23 sub-environments, most notably in Social Security and Standard of Living, Public Health Care System and Environmental Management.

On the other hand, Dongying scores below the median for seven of the 23 sub-environments, especially for Market Development and Natural Resources. The remaining sub-environment of Fiscal Sustainability is at the median.

Comparison to Maximum Scores

Dongying scores below the provincial maximum of the 17 Shandong cities in 20 out of 23 sub-environments. Dongying achieves the provincial maximum in three sub-environments, namely Social Security and Standard of Living (2.416), Public Health Care System (2.017) and Environmental Management (2.195).

Dongying's score in Market Development (−1.469) is farthest from the maximum, which is held by Heze (2.577). Further, Dongying's score in Public Culture and Information Services (1.340) is closest to the maximum, which is held by Weihai (1.617).

6.3 Summary of Empirical Findings of Dongying and *What-if* Urban Development Simulation

6.3.1 Summary of Empirical Findings, 20% Strongest and Weakest Indicators

Overall Performance **6th** Score: 0.603		
Scale and Quality of Economic Activities **14th** Score: –0.782	Financial Capacity, Labour Market Flexibility and Economic Vibrancy **6th** Score: 0.293	Good Governance, Effective Leadership and Social Stability **11th** Score: 0.173
Technological Advancement and Innovation Capability **7th** Score: 0.178	Public Service Standards and Quality of Life Improvement **1st** Score: 1.689	Resource Conditions and Environmental Protection **3rd** Score: 1.118

(Rank out of 17 cities)

Summary

Dongying ranks 6th out of 17 cities in its Overall Performance. Dongying performs above the provincial average in five out of the six environments, where the best performing environment is that of Public Service Standards and Quality of Life Improvement at 1st place. Meanwhile, Dongying is performs below the provincial average and weaker in the environment of Scale and Quality of Economic Activities at 7th place.

Strengths

As illustrated in Table 6.2, Dongying performs well in the environment of Public Service Standards and Quality of Life Improvement, with eight out of 26 of its 20% Strongest Indicators contained in this environment. Among Dongying's best performing indicators are the Wetland Cover, Secondary Industry Total Labour Productivity and GRDP Per Capita.

Weaknesses

As observed in Table 6.3, Dongying is weak in the environment of Scale and Quality of Economic Activities, with seven out of 26 of its 20% Weakest Indicators contained in this environment. Among Dongying's worst performing indicators are the Growth Rate of Overall Labour Productivity, Electricity Consumption Per RMB 10,000 GRDP and Public Perception of Security.

Table 6.2: 20% Strongest Indicators for Dongying

Rank	20% Strongest Indicator	Score	SQEA	FCLMFEV	GGELSS	TAIC	PSSQLI	RCEP
1	Wetland Cover	3.557						✓
2	Secondary Industry Total Labour Productivity	3.540		✓				
3	GRDP Per Capita	2.742	✓					
4	Manufacturing Sector as a Percentage of GRDP	2.707	✓					
5	Producer Price Index (PPI)	2.619	✓					
6	Per Capita R&D Expenditure	2.618				✓		
7	Per Capita Arable Land	2.382						✓
8	Average Life Expectancy	2.168					✓	
9	Loan Balance Per Capita	2.064		✓				
10	Public Health and Medical Service Expenses Per Capita	2.058					✓	
11	Engel's Index	1.969					✓	
12	Deposit Balance Per Capita	1.942		✓				
13	Number of Private Cars Per 100 Households	1.924					✓	
14	Number of Urban Taxis Per 10,000 Population	1.811					✓	
15	Percentage of the Employed Population with Tertiary Education	1.783		✓				
16	Area of Natural Reserves to Administrative Area (%)	1.734						✓
17	Tertiary Industry Total Labour Productivity	1.623		✓				
18	Average Salary of Urban Employees	1.600		✓				
19	Government Fiscal Revenue Per Capita	1.597			✓			
20	Public Education Appropriation Per Capita	1.526					✓	
21	Annual Loan Growth Rate	1.456		✓				
22	Number of Public Servants Per 10,000 Population	1.455			✓			
23	Per Capita Park and Green Space Acreage	1.450						✓
24	Internet Penetration Rate	1.413					✓	
25	Government Fiscal Expenditure Per Capita	1.344			✓			
26	Per Capita Road Area	1.332					✓	

Table 6.3: 20% Weakest Indicators for Dongying

Rank	20% Weakest Indicator	Score	SQEA	FCLMFEV	GGELSS	TAIC	PSSQLI	RCEP
106	Government Fiscal Expenditure	–0.758			✓			
107	Residents' Satisfaction with Price Levels	–0.912	✓					
108	Public Perception of Security	–0.981			✓			
109	Number of Vocational Education Institutions Per 10,000 Population	–1.008					✓	
110	Number of Passengers Transported	–1.012					✓	
111	Newly Increased Number of Employees	–1.031		✓				
112	Number of Primary and Secondary Schools Per 10,000 Population	–1.040					✓	
113	Number of Provincial-Level Science Parks	–1.056				✓		
114	Public Health and Medical Service Expenses as a Share of GRDP	–1.077					✓	
115	Growth in the Volume of Cargo Transported	–1.193		✓				
116	Tax Revenue as a Share of Fiscal Revenue	–1.303			✓			
117	Fiscal Revenue Growth Rate	–1.319			✓			
118	Number of Investigations for Power Abuses Per 10,000 Population	–1.332			✓			
119	Urban Residents' Disposable Income Growth Rate	–1.410	✓					
120	Number of Employees	–1.447		✓				
121	GRDP Growth Rate	–1.505	✓					
122	Retail Price Index	–1.537	✓					
123	Deepness of Insurance (Insurance Income as a Share of GRDP)	–1.561		✓				
124	Trade Surplus	–1.583	✓					
125	Traffic Accident Fatality Per 10,000 Population	–1.713			✓			
126	Service Sector as a Percentage of GRDP	–1.802	✓					
127	Ratio of Public Education Appropriation to GRDP	–1.849					✓	
128	Government Expenditures as a Percentage of GRDP	–2.011	✓					
129	Built-up Area Population Density	–2.025						✓
130	Electricity Consumption Per RMB 10,000 GRDP	–2.856						✓
131	Growth Rate of Overall Labour Productivity	–3.393		✓				

Source: Asia Competitiveness Institute.

Notes: SQEA: Scale and Quality of Economic Activities; FCLMFEV: Financial Capacity, Labour Market Flexibility and Economic Vibrancy; GGELSS: Good Governance, Effective Leadership and Social Stability; TAIC: Technological Advancement and Innovation Capability; PSSQLI: Public Service Standards and Quality of Life Improvement; RCEP: Resource Conditions and Environmental Protection.

6.3.2 *What-if* Urban Development Simulation

ACI has devised a simulation methodology to improve the ranking of a particular city by improving on its 20% Weakest Indicators as shown in Table 6.3.[2] The figures below show Dongying's ranking and standardised scores before and after the policy-induced simulation. Refer to Tables 3.8 to 3.14 in Section 3.4 of Chapter 3 for a complete list of simulation results for all cities.

Overall Performance

	Before		After
Rank	6th	▶	2nd
Score	0.603		1.597

Scale and Quality of Economic Activities

	Before	After
Rank	14th	4th
Score	–0.782	0.928

Financial Capacity, Labour Market Flexibility and Economic Vibrancy

	Before	After
Rank	6th	4th
Score	0.293	0.892

Good Governance, Effective Leadership and Social Stability

	Before	After
Rank	11th	2nd
Score	0.173	1.113

Technological Advancement and Innovation Capability

	Before	After
Rank	7th	7th
Score	0.178	0.407

Public Service Standards and Quality of Life Improvement

	Before	After
Rank	1st	1st
Score	1.689	2.067

Resource Conditions and Environmental Protection

	Before	After
Rank	3rd	1st
Score	1.118	1.904

After the *What-if* simulation, Dongying improves its ranking from 6th to 2nd in its Overall Performance. Likewise, Dongying's standardised score improves from 0.603 to 1.597. This leap is plausible if the city manages to successfully address its 20% Weakest Indicators.

The simulation further highlights substantial improvement for Dongying in some of its environments, most notably in Scale and Quality of Economic Activities where its rank will rise from 14th to 4th place. Such encouraging results should incentivise Dongying to strive to improve the indicators under the 20% Weakest Indicators list. These indicators include Government Expenditures as a Percentage of GRDP and Electricity Consumption Per RMB 10,000 GRDP.

[2] The methodology for *What-if* simulation is thoroughly explained in Section 2.7 of Chapter 2.

6.4 Concluding Notes: Public Policy Implications[3]

Areas for Commendation

Dongying performs well in the environment of Public Service Standards and Quality of Life Improvement with eight out of 26 of its 20% Strongest Indicators in this environment, as indicated in Table 6.2.

Further, Dongying holds the maximum score for three of the sub-environments, namely Social Security and Standard of Living, Public Health Care System and Environmental Management. In addition, it scores above the provincial average in 15 out of 23 sub-environments.

In the past five years, Dongying has been intensively focusing on improving the ecological environment with the ideology of "Big Space, Large Green Space, Large Water Surface and Large Wetland". The remarkable results from the ecological constructions, such as the Forest Wetlands Park and many other major ecological projects, have earned Dongying the China Habitat Environment Prize. Moreover, Dongying has also promoted the "Happiness Index of the People" by integrating basic medical insurance and providing temporary assistance. This explains why Dongying holds the maximum score for the sub-environments such as Environmental Management and Social Security and Standard of Living.

Areas for Improvement

Although Dongying scores above the provincial average in most of the environments, there remains room for improvement. Specifically, Dongying should target the environment of Scale and Quality of Economic Activities, where it has seven out of 26 of its 20% Weakest Indicators, as illustrated in Table 6.3. Additionally, as gleaned from the *What-if* Urban Development Simulation, the environment for Scale and Quality of Economic Activities should also be prioritised because that is the environment in which Dongying will achieve the greatest improvement in its ranking — 10 positions — relative to other environments.

Further, Dongying obtains the weakest score in the sub-environment of Market Development (−1.469) and scores below the provincial average in eight out of 23 sub-environments.

In 2017, the Dongying government has acknowledged its issues related to economic and social development. The slow progress in supply side structural reform, lack of innovative capacity, and the sluggish rate of industrial transformation have led to lower economic development efficiency, and hence increased pressure on public finances. These weaknesses are in line with our finding that the indicators of Tax Revenue as Share of Fiscal Revenue, Fiscal Revenue Growth Rate and Government Fiscal Expenditure are among the 20% Weakest Indicators for the city. Moreover, the Dongying government must also increase its Growth Rate of Overall Labour Productivity, as it has the lowest score in this indicator among the cities in Shandong.

[3]The relevant statistical data and government policies are from Dongying Municipal Government (2017) and Zhang (2017).

Future Potential Development

In conclusion, Dongying should focus on improving the environment of Scale and Quality of Economic Activities through deeper structural reform and industrial transformation. Dongying should also work on the environment of Scale and Quality of Economic Activities by maintaining greater control of public finances and by building the economy's various industries to boost economic growth.

In order to improve the public security and social stability, the government aims to establish the "One Village One Police Assistant" System and the "One Village One Legal Advisor" System. Dongying may also implement measures to strengthen workplace safety, scrutinise the implementation and accountability of safety, and improve risk identification and classification. The government should also improve Dongying's trade surplus and develop the service sector to boost the city's economyThese methods are aligned with China's goal of building a "moderately prosperous society".

References

Bai, Gao Li. 2009. "Dongying City Introduction." July 24, 2009. http://shandong.chinadaily.com.cn/e/2009-07/24/content_8468274.htm.

Department of Commerce of Shandong Province. n.d. "Dongying City." Accessed October 27, 2017. http://en.shandongbusiness.gov.cn/city/68.

Dongying Municipal Government. 2013. "About Dongying." April 11, 2013. http://www.dongying.gov.cn/html/AboutDongying/index.html.

Dongying Municipal Government. 2017. "2017年东营市政府工作报告 2017 Dongying Annual Government Work Report (in Chinese)." March 30, 2017. http://zfxxgk.dongying.gov.cn/gov/jcms_files/jcms1/web2/site/art/2017/3/30/art_9084_123699.html.

Zhang, Jun. 2017. "China's Vision for the Next 30 Years." Project Syndicate. November 14, 2017. https://www.project-syndicate.org/commentary/china-19th-congress-development-blueprint-by-zhang-jun-2017-11.

Chapter 7: HEZE
Shandong Province

Location of City

Source: Asia Competitiveness Institute.

7.1 Profile of Heze City[1]

Known as China's "Peony Capital", Heze is esteemed for the quality of the peonies it produces, as well as its long-standing significance to China's cultural history. Today, the city directly administers two districts and seven counties, covering a total area of 12,155 square kilometres and a total population of 8,622,600. Heze continues to contribute significantly to China's cultural heritage by functioning as a last refuge for well-beloved art forms such as Dingtao Shadow Puppetry and Shandong Bangzi (wooden clapper) Opera. These traditions are in turn kept alive by dedicated performers from the city, who often visit other regions in China to spread awareness and ensure that these aspects of China's intangible cultural heritage continue to exist for the benefit of future generations.

In 2016, Heze's Gross Regional Domestic Product (GRDP) stood at RMB 256 billion, and the city boasted a high GRDP growth rate of 8.5%, as can be seen in Table 7.1. The area surrounding Heze is rich in oil, coal, natural gas and iron ore, with the nearby Juye coal field being one of the largest in China. Correspondingly, the city's primary sector constituted 10.9% of its GRDP. Heze's secondary sector, which is based primarily on the petrochemicals, pharmaceuticals and

[1]The relevant city information are from the Department of Commerce of Shandong Province (n.d.), People's Government of Heze City (n.d.) and Wang (2009).

food manufacturing industries, constituted 51.3% of its total GRDP. Finally, Heze's tertiary sector constituted 37.8% of total GRDP, with service industries such as tourism and other service industries reporting steady growth and benefiting from initiatives to facilitate expansion.

Heze is relatively well connected to neighbouring cities and notably stands at the intersection of the Beijing–Jiulong railway and the New Eurasian Continental Bridge. The city is otherwise well-serviced by expressways and is located only a relatively short distance from both Jinan Yaoqiang International Airport and Zhengzhou Xinzheng International Airport. Heze also boasted the highest profit margin of enterprises over a designated size in the province for 2016, at 7.5%, which is a testament to the conditions the local government has created to maximise profitability for its enterprises.

Table 7.1: Key Economic Indicators for Heze, 2016

Land Area (km^2)	**12,155**
Population	
Total Population	8,622,600
Urbanisation Rate (%)	47.4
Average Life Expectancy (years)	76.2
Number of Employees (10,000)	517
Workforce Participation Rate (%)	81.7
Gross Regional Domestic Product (GRDP) — 2015 Prices	
GRDP (100 millions of RMB)	2,560
GRDP Per Capita (RMB)	29,904
GRDP Growth Rate (%)	8.5
Economic Composition	
Primary Sector (% of GRDP)	10.9
Secondary Sector (% of GRDP)	51.3
Tertiary Sector (% of GRDP)	37.8
Trade — 2016 Prices	
Exports (millions of RMB)	14,593
Imports (millions of RMB)	14,136
Dependency on Foreign Trade (%)	13.7
Infrastructure	
Per Capita Road Area (m^2)	25.4
Growth in the Number of Passengers Transported (10,000)	169
Growth in the Volume of Cargo Transported (10,000 tons)	1,176
Environment	
Green Coverage Ratio of Built-up Area (%)	40.1
Environmental Expenditure (% of Total Fiscal Expenditure)	1.8

Source: Asia Competitiveness Institute from the 2017 Shandong Statistical Yearbook.

7.2 In-Depth Urban Development of Heze, 2016*

7.2.1 Overall Urban Development Performance

Overall Performance

2017 Rank

12th

Out of 17 Cities

Score: –0.615

Rank	City	Score
1	Qingdao	1.753
	...	
10	Dezhou	–0.302
11	Rizhao	–0.472
12	Heze	–0.615
13	Jining	–0.706
14	Binzhou	–1.076
	...	
16	Laiwu	–1.233
17	Liaocheng	–1.576

Heze ranks 12th in its Overall Performance, with a standardised score of –0.615. This places the city in the Middle Seven Group of 17 cities. Heze is positioned between Rizhao (–0.472) at 11th place and Jining (–0.706) at 13th place.

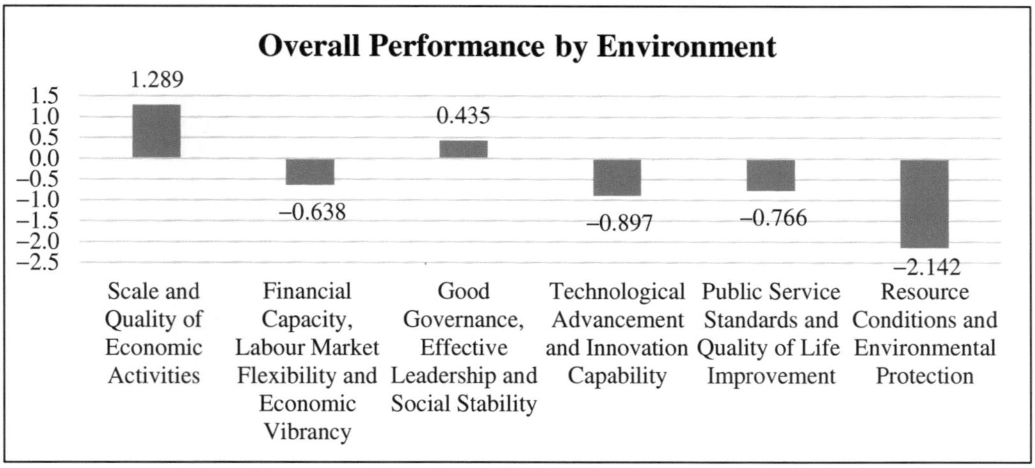

Among the six environments, Heze performs above the provincial average in the environments of Scale and Quality of Economic Activities and Good Governance, Effective Leadership and Social Stability, where the former scores particularly well. However, Heze performs below the provincial average in all the remaining environments and substantially weaker for Resource Conditions and Environmental Protection.

* *For a complete list of rankings, see Tables 3.2 to 3.7 in Section 3.3 of Chapter 3.*

7.2.2 Urban Development within the Six Environments

Rank	City	Score
1	Qingdao	1.987
2	Yantai	1.687
3	Heze	1.289
4	Weifang	1.021
5	Weihai	0.849
6	Linyi	0.447
7	Dezhou	0.096
	...	
16	Jining	−1.273
17	Laiwu	−1.295

A: ***Scale and Quality of Economic Activities***

2017 Rank

3rd

Out of 17 Cities

Score: 1.289

Heze ranks 3rd for Scale and Quality of Economic Activities, with a standardised score of 1.289. This places the city in the Top Five Group of 17 cities. Heze is positioned close behind Yantai (1.687) at 2nd place and ahead of Weifang (1.021) at 4th place.

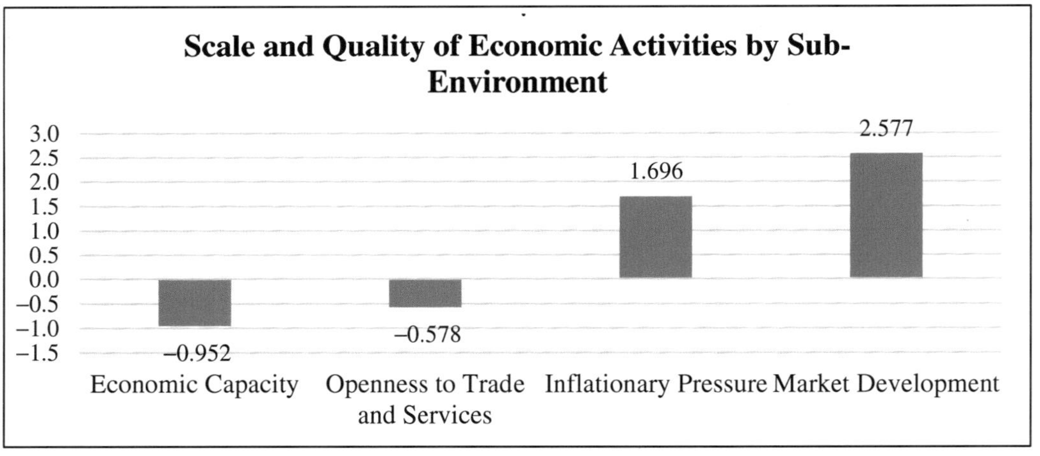

Looking at the four sub-environments of Scale and Quality of Economic Activities, Heze performs above the provincial average in two of them and exceptionally well for Market Development, where the indicator of Government Expenditures as a Percentage of GRDP performs the best among all Shandong cities. Other indicators that obtain particularly high scores include the Urban Residents' Disposable Income Growth Rate from the Inflationary Pressure sub-environment, as well as GRDP Groiwth Rate from the Economic Capacity sub-environment. However, Heze performs below the provincial average in all the remaining two sub-environments and particularly poorly for the Economic Capacity sub-environment, where the indicators of Urbanisation Rate, GRDP Per Capita and Per Capita Volume of Retail Sales obtain low scores.

B: *Financial Capacity, Labour Market Flexibility and Economic Vibrancy*

2017 Rank

12th

Out of 17 Cities

Score: –0.638

Rank	City	Score
1	Jinan	2.264
	...	
10	Binzhou	–0.329
11	Rizhao	–0.619
12	Heze	–0.638
13	Tai'an	–0.763
14	Zaozhuang	–0.894
	...	
16	Dezhou	–1.026
17	Laiwu	–1.297

Heze ranks 12th for Financial Capacity, Labour Market Flexibility and Economic Vibrancy, with a standardised score of –0.638. This places the city in the Middle Seven Group of 17 cities. Heze is positioned closely behind Rizhao (–0.619) at 11th place and ahead of Tai'an (–0.763) at 13th place.

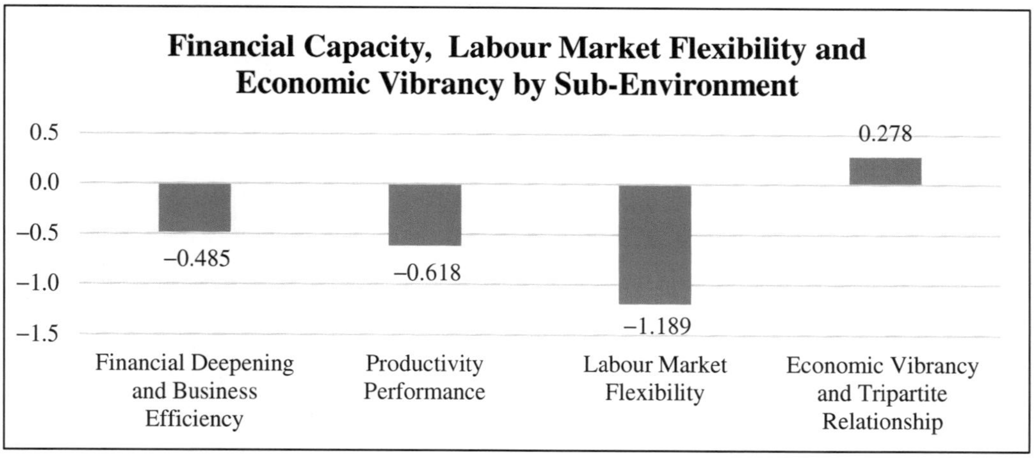

Looking at the four sub-environments of Financial Capacity, Labour Market Flexibility and Economic Vibrancy, Heze scores below the provincial average in three of them and substantially lower in the Labour Market Flexibility sub-environment, where the indicators including the Proportion of Urban Workers Employed in State Enterprises and Rate of Migration Flow score poorly. Another indicator that registers a particularly weak score is the Tertiary Industry Total Labour Productivity from the Productivity Performance sub-environment. Nevertheless, Heze scores above the provincial average in the sub-environment of Economic Vibrancy and Tripartite Relationship, where the indicator of Insurance Income as a Share of GRDP scores relatively better.

HEZE

Shandong Province

Rank	City	Score
1	Dezhou	1.465
	...	
5	Jinan	0.532
6	Tai'an	0.498
7	Heze	0.435
8	Zibo	0.418
9	Linyi	0.321
	...	
16	Laiwu	−1.588
17	Liaocheng	−2.473

C: ***Good Governance, Effective Leadership and Social Stability***

2017 Rank

7th

Out of 17 Cities

Score: 0.435

Heze ranks 7th for Good Governance, Effective Leadership and Social Stability with a standardised score of 0.435. This places the city in the Middle Seven Group of 17 cities. Heze is positioned between Tai'an (0.498) at 6th place and Zibo (0.418) at 8th place.

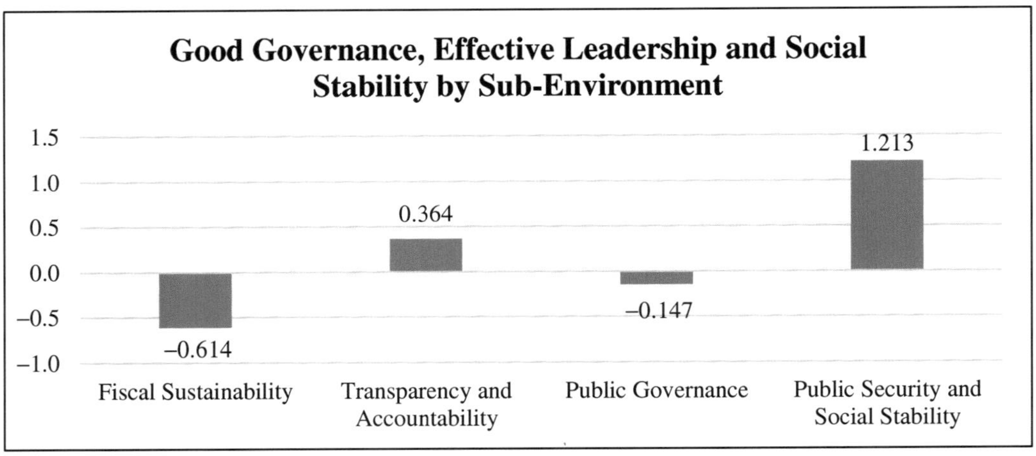

Among the four sub-environments of Good Governance, Effective Leadership and Social Stability, Heze scores above the provincial average in two of them and particularly so for Public Security and Social Stability, where the indicators of Traffic Accident Fatality Per 10,000 Population and Satisfaction of the Police Services perform relatively better. However, Heze scores below the provincial average in the remaining sub-environments of Fiscal Sustainability and Public Governance. Notably, Heze scores unfavorably in the indicators of Government Fiscal Revenue Per Capita and Government Fiscal Expenditure Per Capita from the Fiscal Sustainability sub-environment as well as the Average Public Servant Salary from the Public Governance sub-environment.

D: ***Technological Advancement and Innovation Capability***

2017 Rank

14th

Out of 17 Cities

Score: –0.897

Rank	City	Score
1	Qingdao	2.176
	...	
10	Tai'an	–0.457
11	Dezhou	–0.517
12	Binzhou	–0.559
13	Laiwu	–0.812
14	Heze	–0.897
15	Rizhao	–1.155
16	Zaozhuang	–1.192
17	Liaocheng	–1.221

Heze ranks 14th for Technological Advancement and Innovation Capability, with a standardised score of –0.897. This places the city in the Bottom Five Group of 17 cities. Heze is positioned between Laiwu (–0.812) at 13th place and Rizhao (–1.155) at 15th place.

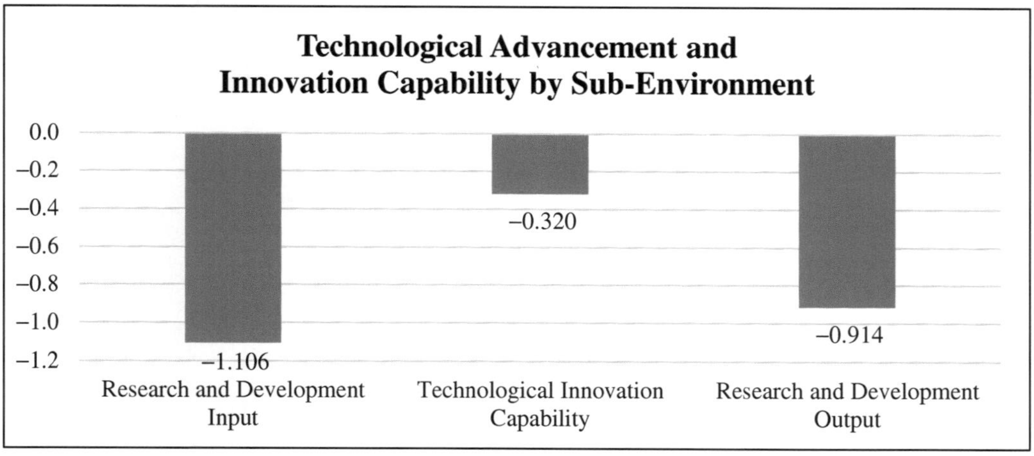

Among the three sub-environments of Technological Advancement and Innovation Capability, Heze performs below the provincial average in all of them and particularly poorly in the sub-environments of Research and Development Input and Research and Development Output. Specifically, Heze obtains low scores in the indicators of Per Capita Research and Development Expenditure from the Research and Development Input sub-environment as well as the Number of Existing Patents Per 10,000 Population from the Research and Development Output sub-environment. Additionally, the indicator the Number of Research and Development Personnel Per 10,000 Population from the Technological Innovation Capability sub-environment registers a low score as well. However, Heze performs relatively better in the indicator of Satisfaction with Innovation Environment from the Technological Innovation Capability sub-environment.

HEZE

Shandong Province

Rank	City	Score
1	Dongying	1.689
	…	
10	Linyi	–0.307
11	Tai'an	–0.567
12	Heze	–0.766
13	Jining	–0.819
14	Binzhou	–0.862
	…	
16	Dezhou	–1.066
17	Liaocheng	–1.964

E: *Public Service Standards and Quality of Life Improvement*

2017 Rank

12th

Out of 17 Cities

Score: –0.766

Heze ranks 12th for Public Service Standards and Quality of Life Improvement with a standardised score of –0.766. This places the city in the Middle Seven Group of 17 cities. Heze is positioned behind of Tai'an (–0.567) at 11th place and slightly ahead of Jining (–0.819) at 13th place.

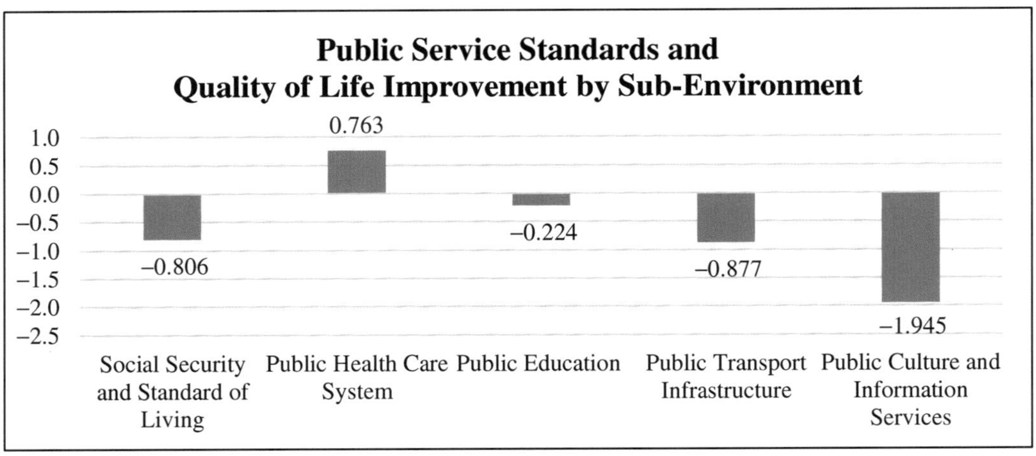

Among the five sub-environments of Public Service Standards and Quality of Life Improvement, Heze scores above the provincial average in Public Health Care System and registers remarkably higher scores in the indicators of Public Health and Medical Service Expenses as a Share of GRDP and Satisfaction of Public Health Care Services. However, Heze obtains scores below the provincial average in the remaining sub-environments and notably poor in Public Culture and Information Services, where many indicators including the Number of Books in Public Library Per Capita and Internet Penetration Rate score relatively weaker. Another indicator with particularly weaker performance include the Ratio of Teacher to Student in Primary and Secondary Schools from the Public Education sub-environment. Nevertheless, the indicator of Number of Primary and Secondary Schools Per 10,000 Population from the Public Education sub-environment scores exceptionally well.

F: ***Resource Conditions and Environmental Protection***

2017 Rank

17th

Out of 17 Cities

Score: –2.142

Rank	City	Score
1	Weihai	1.632
	...	
10	Jining	–0.112
11	Dezhou	–0.287
12	Zaozhuang	–0.393
13	Linyi	–0.512
14	Weifang	–0.814
15	Laiwu	–1.136
16	Binzhou	–1.586
17	Heze	–2.142

Heze ranks 17th for Resource Conditions and Environmental Protection with a standardised score of –2.142. This places the city in the Bottom Five Group of 17 cities. Heze is positioned well behind Binzhou (–1.586) at 16th place.

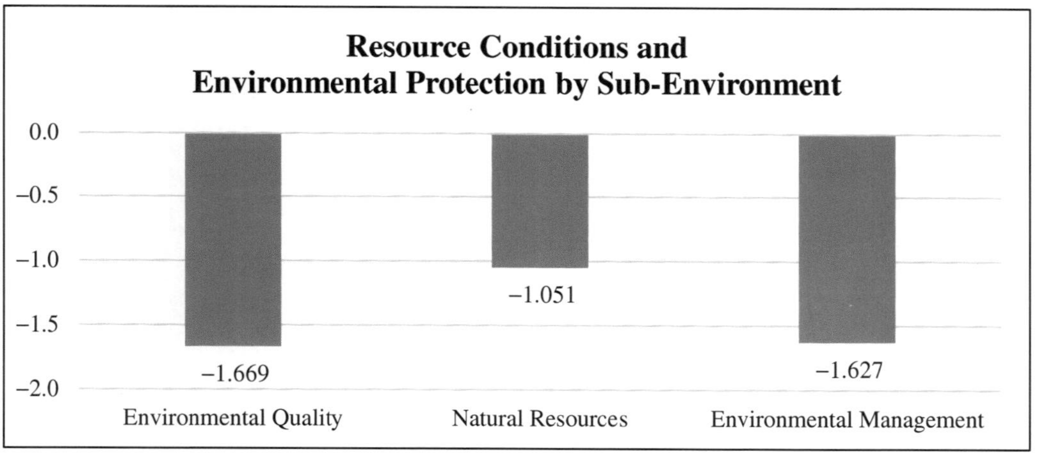

Among the three sub-environments of Resource Conditions and Environmental Protection, Heze performs below the provincial average in all of them and notably weaker for Environmental Quality and Environmental Management. Specifically, Heze obtains low scores in the indicators of Ammoniacal Nitrogen Discharge Per RMB 10,000 GRDP from the Environmental Quality sub-environment and Per Capita Park and Green Space Acreage from the Environmental Management sub-environment. Additionally, the indicator of Water Consumption Per RMB 10,000 GRDP from the Natural Resources sub-environment also scores particularly weak. Nevertheless, Heze performs more favorably in the indicator of Per Capita Freshwater Resource from the Natural Resources sub-environment and Urban Area Waste Water Treatment Rate from the Environmental Management sub-environment.

HEZE

Shandong Province

Figure 7.1: Median & Maximum Web for Heze

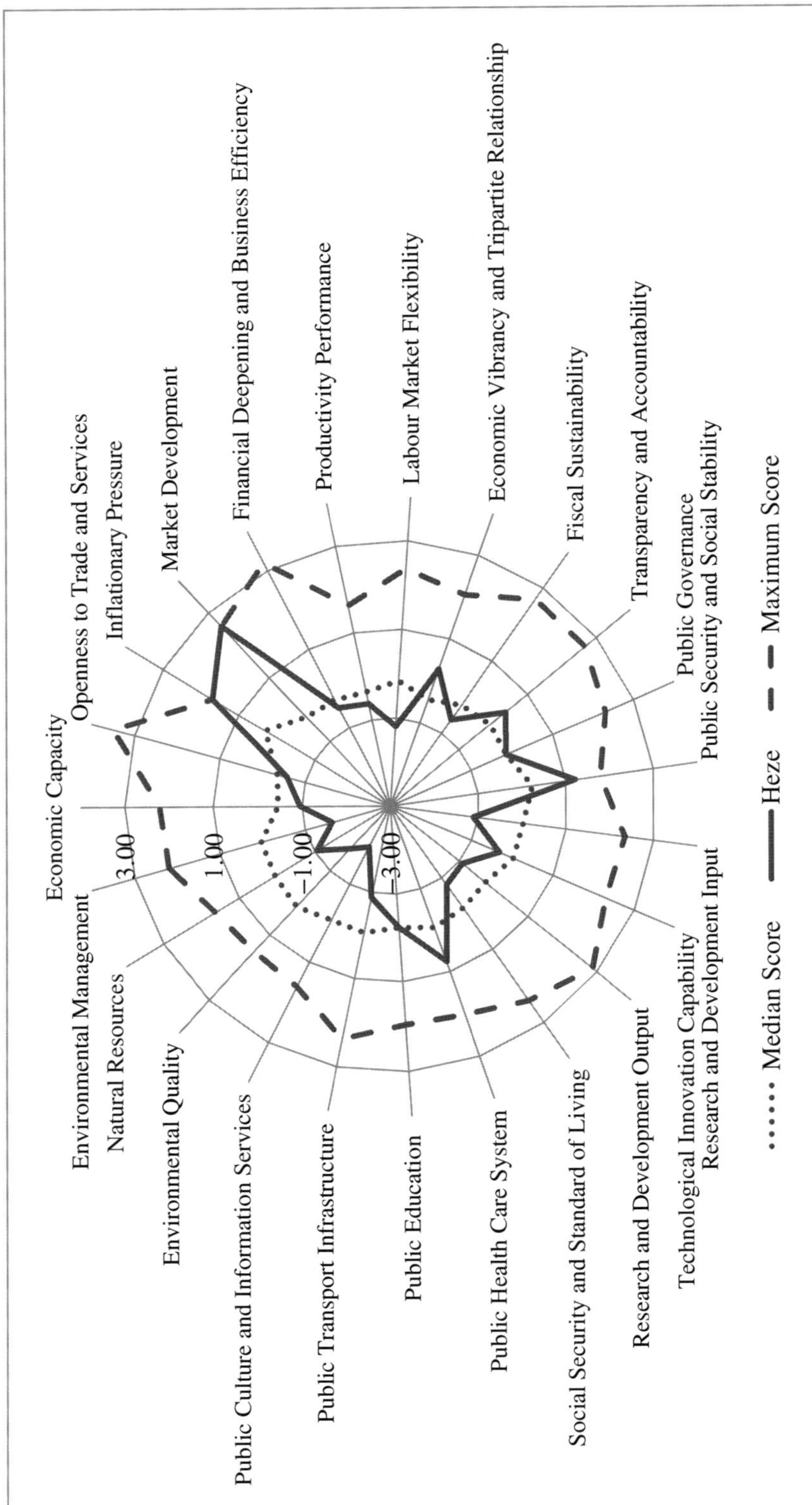

Source: Asia Competitiveness Institute.

7.2.3 Median and Maximum Web Analysis

To better understand Heze's relative strengths and weaknesses, it is useful to compare and contrast its scores for the 23 sub-environments against the median and maximum scores of Shandong's 17 cities.

In Figure 7.1, the median and maximum scores for 17 Shandong cities are shown as dotted and dashed lines respectively, while scores for Heze are shown as a solid line.

Comparison to Median Scores

Heze scores above the median for six of the 23 sub-environments, most notably for Market Development and Inflationary Pressure.

On the other hand, Heze scores below the median for 15 sub-environments, particularly for Public Culture and Information Services, Environmental Quality and Environmental Management. The remaining sub-environments of Public Governance and Public Education are at the median.

Comparison to Maximum Scores

Heze scores below the provincial maximum of the 17 Shandong cities in 21 out of 23 sub-environments. Heze scores the provincial maximum in the sub-environments of Market Development (2.577) and Inflationary Pressure (1.696).

Heze's score in Openness to Trade and Services (–0.578) is farthest from the maximum, which is held by Qingdao (3.505). Further, Heze's score in Public Security and Social Stability (1.213) is closest to the maximum, which is held by Dezhou (1.783).

7.3 Summary of Empirical Findings of Heze and *What-if* Urban Development Simulation

7.3.1 Summary of Empirical Findings, 20% Strongest and Weakest Indicators

Overall Performance		
12th Score: –0.615		
Scale and Quality of Economic Activities **3rd** Score: 1.289	Financial Capacity, Labour Market Flexibility and Economic Vibrancy **12th** Score: –0.638	Good Governance, Effective Leadership and Social Stability **7th** Score: 0.435
Technological Advancement and Innovation Capability **14th** Score: –0.897	Public Service Standards and Quality of Life Improvement **12th** Score: –0.766	Resource Conditions and Environmental Protection **17th** Score: –2.142

(Rank out of 17 cities)

Summary

Heze ranks 12th out of 17 cities in its Overall Performance. Heze performs below the provincial average in four out of the six environments. Heze's best performing environment is that of Scale and Quality of Economic Activities, ranked at 3rd place. Meanwhile, its least performing environment is that of Resource Conditions and Environmental Protection, at 17th place.

Strengths

As illustrated in Table 7.2, Heze performs well in the environment of Scale and Quality of Economic Activities, Good Governance, Effective Leadership and Social Stability as well as Public Service Standards and Quality of Life Improvement, where they collectively contain 19 out of 26 of Heze's 20% Strongest Indicators in these environments. Among Heze's best performing indicators are Government Expenditures as a Percentage of GRDP, Public Health and Medical Service Expenses as a Share of GRDP, and the Ratio of Public Education Appropriation to GRDP.

Weaknesses

As observed in Table 7.3, Heze is weak in the environment of Public Service Standards and Quality of Life Improvement, where it contains nine out of 26 of its 20% Weakest Indicators. Among the city's worst performing indicators are the Ammoniacal Nitrogen Discharge Per RMB 10,000, Water Consumption Per RMB 10,000 GRDP and Chemical Oxygen Demand Per RMB 10,000 GRDP.

Table 7.2: 20% Strongest Indicators for Heze

Rank	20% Strongest Indicator	Score	SQEA	FCLMFEV	GGELSS	TAIC	PSSQLI	RCEP
1	Government Expenditures as a Percentage of GRDP	2.491	✓					
2	Public Health and Medical Service Expenses as a Share of GRDP	2.455					✓	
3	Ratio of Public Education Appropriation to GRDP	2.176					✓	
4	Number of Primary and Secondary Schools Per 10,000 Population	2.088					✓	
5	Urban Residents' Disposable Income Growth Rate	2.031	✓					
6	GRDP Growth Rate	1.984	✓					
7	Number of Listed Items Under Executive Authority of the Government	1.647			✓			
8	Traffic Accident Fatality Per 10,000 Population	1.587			✓			
9	Satisfaction of Public Health Care Services	1.570					✓	
10	Self-Employed as a Share of Total Employment	1.435		✓				
11	Profit Margin of Enterprises Above Designated Size	1.427		✓				
12	Satisfaction of Income Disparity	1.399					✓	
13	Number of Investigations for Power Abuses Per 10,000 Population	1.041			✓			
14	Satisfaction with Business Environment	1.004	✓					
15	Satisfaction of the Police Services	0.999			✓			
16	Urban Residents' Per Capita Expenditure Growth Rate	0.861	✓					
17	Satisfaction with Innovation Environment	0.842				✓		
18	Growth in the Number of Passengers Transported	0.838		✓				
19	Residents' Perception of Happiness	0.812					✓	
20	Growth Rate of the Number of Police Cases Solved	0.799			✓			
21	Urban Area Waste Water Treatment Rate	0.772						✓
22	Number of Employees	0.759		✓				
23	Deepness of Insurance (Insurance Income as a Share of GRDP)	0.712		✓				
24	Manufacturing Sector as a Percentage of GRDP	0.669	✓					
25	Satisfaction with the Just of Judiciary	0.669			✓			
26	Public Perception of Government Conduct	0.664			✓			

Table 7.3: 20% Weakest Indicators for Heze

Rank	20% Weakest Indicator	Score	SQEA	FCLMFEV	GGELSS	TAIC	PSSQLI	RCEP
106	Engel's Index	−1.191					✓	
107	Per Capita Volume of Retail Sales	−1.214	✓					
108	Percentage of the Employed Population with Tertiary Education	−1.226		✓				
109	Mobile Phone Penetration Per Capita	−1.238					✓	
110	Per Capita R&D Expenditure	−1.261				✓		
111	Average Salary of Urban Employees	−1.265		✓				
112	Government Fiscal Revenue Per Capita	−1.277			✓			
113	Percentage of Public Expenditure on Cultural Initiatives	−1.299					✓	
114	GRDP Per Capita	−1.299	✓					
115	Number of R&D Personnel Per 10,000 Population	−1.385				✓		
116	Number of Books in Public Library Per Capita	−1.386					✓	
117	Green Coverage Ratio of Built-up area	−1.388						✓
118	Proportion of Workforce Employed in Agriculture Sector	−1.425		✓				
119	Tertiary Industry Total Labour Productivity	−1.440		✓				
120	Rate of Migration Flow	−1.448		✓				
121	Average Years of Education Received	−1.522					✓	
122	Per Capita Park and Green Space Acreage	−1.550						✓
123	Per Capita Annual Disposable Income	−1.574					✓	
124	Number of Private Cars Per 100 Households	−1.698					✓	
125	Urbanisation Rate	−1.783	✓					
126	Internet Penetration Rate	−1.806					✓	
127	Ratio of Teacher to Student in Primary and Secondary Schools	−1.939					✓	
128	Proportion of Urban Workers Employed in State Enterprises	−2.154		✓				
129	Water Consumption Per RMB 10,000 GRDP	−2.387						✓
130	COD (Chemical Oxygen Demand) Per RMB 10,000 GRDP	−2.467						✓
131	Ammoniacal Nitrogen Discharge Per RMB 10,000 GRDP	−2.669						✓

Source: Asia Competitiveness Institute.

Notes: SQEA: Scale and Quality of Economic Activities; FCLMFEV: Financial Capacity, Labour Market Flexibility and Economic Vibrancy; GGELSS: Good Governance, Effective Leadership and Social Stability; TAIC: Technological Advancement and Innovation Capability; PSSQLI: Public Service Standards and Quality of Life Improvement; RCEP: Resource Conditions and Environmental Protection.

7.3.2 *What-if* Urban Development Simulation

ACI has devised a simulation methodology to improve the ranking of a particular city by improving on its 20% Weakest Indicators as shown in Table 7.3.[2] The figures below show Heze's ranking and standardised scores before and after the policy-induced simulation. Refer to Tables 3.8 to 3.14 in Section 3.4 of Chapter 3 for a complete list of simulation results for all cities.

Overall Performance

	Before		After
Rank	12th	▶	8th
Score	–0.615		0.298

Scale and Quality of Economic Activities

	Before	After
Rank	3rd	2nd
Score	1.289	1.615

Financial Capacity, Labour Market Flexibility and Economic Vibrancy

	Before	After
Rank	12th	9th
Score	–0.638	–0.061

Good Governance, Effective Leadership and Social Stability

	Before	After
Rank	7th	5th
Score	0.435	0.578

Technological Advancement and Innovation Capability

	Before	After
Rank	14th	11th
Score	–0.897	–0.492

Public Service Standards and Quality of Life Improvement

	Before	After
Rank	12th	8th
Score	–0.766	0.240

Resource Conditions and Environmental Protection

	Before	After
Rank	17th	11th
Score	–2.142	–0.532

After the *What-if* simulation, Heze improved its ranking from 12th to 8th in terms of its Overall Performance. Likewise, Heze's standardised score increases from –0.615 to 0.298. This leap is plausible if the city manages to successfully address its 20% Weakest Indicators.

The simulation further indicates that Heze may achieve substantial improvement in some of its environments, most notably in Resource Conditions and Environmental Protection, where its ranks will rise from 17th to 11th. Such encouraging results should incentivise Heze to strive to improve the indicators under the 20% Weakest Indicators list. These indicators include the Ammoniacal Nitrogen Discharge Per RMB 10,000, Water Consumption Per RMB 10,000 GRDP and Per Capita Park and Green Space Acreage.

[2]The methodology for *What-if* simulation is thoroughly explained in Section 2.7 of Chapter 2.

7.4 Concluding Notes: Public Policy Implications[3]

Areas for Commendation

Heze performs well in the environments of Scale and Quality of Economic Activities, Good Governance, Effective Leadership and Social Stability as well as Public Service Standards and Quality of Life Improvement, where they collectively contain 19 out of 26 of Heze's 20% Strongest Indicators in these environments, as indicated in Table 7.2.

Further, Heze achieves the provincial maximum in the sub-environments of Market Development (2.577) and Inflationary Pressure (1.696), and scores above the provincial average in six out of 23 sub-environments.

Heze has comprehensively applied the Five Development Concepts through enhanced investment channels and innovation development. In 2016, the government increased its expenditure to create a better business environment, which promoted the development of emerging industries and e-commence.

Areas for Improvement

As Heze scores below the provincial average in four out of six environments, there is plenty of room for improvement for the city. Most crucially, Heze should address the environments of Public Service Standards and Quality of Life Improvement and Financial Capacity, Labour Market Flexibility and Economic Vibrancy, where they have a total of 15 out of 26 of the 20% Weakest Indicators under these environments, as shown in Table 7.3. Additionally, as gleaned from the *What-if* Urban Development Simulation, the environment for Resource Conditions and Environmental Protection should be prioritised because as Heze will achieve the greatest improvement in its ranking — six positions — relative to other environments.

Moreover, Heze obtained the weakest score in the sub-environments of Environmental Management (–1.078), Research and Development Output (–0.914) and Public Culture and Information Services (–1.627), and scores below the provincial average in 17 out of 23 sub-environments.

Currently, Heze has been actively focusing on the introduction of biological medicine, new energy and technology development to create new engine for growth for the city. As such, it is clear that Heze recognises the fundamental need to attract investment and large projects. For example, the construction of Danyang science and technology business incubator in the Heze City Development Zone has created more than 30 projects and generated at least 80 patents. Moreover, as Heze obtains the lowest scores for the indicators of Number of R&D Personnel Per 10,000 Population among all economies in Shandong province in our study, these efforts are a step in the right direction. In light of Heze's poor performance in the environment of Resource Conditions and Environmental Protection, the government has also recognised the need to improve Heze's environmental quality. In 2016, Heze successfully reduced its coal consumption

[3] The relevant statistical data and government policies are from People's Government of Heze City (2017a, 2017b, 2017c), Xinhua News (2017) and Phoenix New Media (2017).

by 15 ton and ensured that the water quality in its three major rivers complied with the national standards.

Future Potential Development

In summary, Heze should focus on improving the environment of Public Service Standards and Quality of Life Improvement by raising the residents' standard of living and disposable income. The government should also work on the environment of Financial Capacity, Labour Market Flexibility and Economic Vibrancy through greater investment towards education and training to develop its tertiary industry and raise wages and productivity.

While there is a steady progress in alleviating poverty through financial assistance for poor, this is not a long-term solution. In fact, Heze should focus on investing more in education and promoting entrepreneurship. This will help improve employment opportunities as a workforce with better qualifications and skills can raise job availability as businesses are incentivised to invest in the city. Furthermore, the Heze government can help support the development of various industries through many strategies via Research and Development, technological innovation and financial support.

At the same time, Heze should also strike a balance between economic growth and environmental protection as the poor environmental quality of Heze may impinge on its sustainable development in the long run. The government should implement measures to reduce water consumption in the city and enforce strict regulations on the discharge of chemicals from industrial plants.

References

Department of Commerce of Shandong Province. n.d. 'Heze City'. Accessed 27 October 2017. http://en.shandongbusiness.gov.cn/city/82.

People's Government of Heze City. 2017a. '菏泽市2017年政府工作报告 2017 Heze Annual Government Work Report (in Chinese)'. 27 February 2017. http://www.heze.gov.cn/art/2017/2/27/art_584_53088.html.

———. 2017b. '市政府全体（扩大）会议召开 The Municipal Government Held Expanded Conference (in Chinese)'. 17 July 2017. http://www.heze.gov.cn/art/2017/7/17/art_77_57125.html.

———. 2017c. '政务信息2017第35期 Government Information 2017 Issue 35 (in Chinese)'. 4 December 2017. http://zfxxgk.heze.gov.cn/xxgk/jcms_files/jcms1/web68/site/art/2017/12/4/art_10762_23319.html.

———. n.d. '菏泽市人民政府 牡丹之都 Heze People's Government The City of Peony (in Chinese)'. Accessed 27 October 2017. http://www.heze.gov.cn/col/col41/index.html.

Phoenix New Media. 2017. '菏泽市开发区丹阳街道办事处科学发展纪实 The Development Documentary of Danyang Street Office in Heze Development Zone (in Chinese)'. 27 November 2017. http://news.ifeng.com/a/20171127/53635039_0.shtml.

Wang, Xiaotao. 2009. 'Heze City Introduction'. 24 July 2009. http://shandong.chinadaily.com.cn/e/2009-07/24/content_8468084.htm.

Xinhua News. 2017. '恒丰银行济南分行因地制宜支持特色农业发展 Jinan Branch of Hengfeng Bank Supports the Development of Characteristic Agriculture According to Local Conditions (in Chinese)'. 10 April 2017. http://www.sd.xinhuanet.com/cj/2017-04/10/c_1120779953.htm.

Chapter 8: JINAN
Shandong Province

Location of City

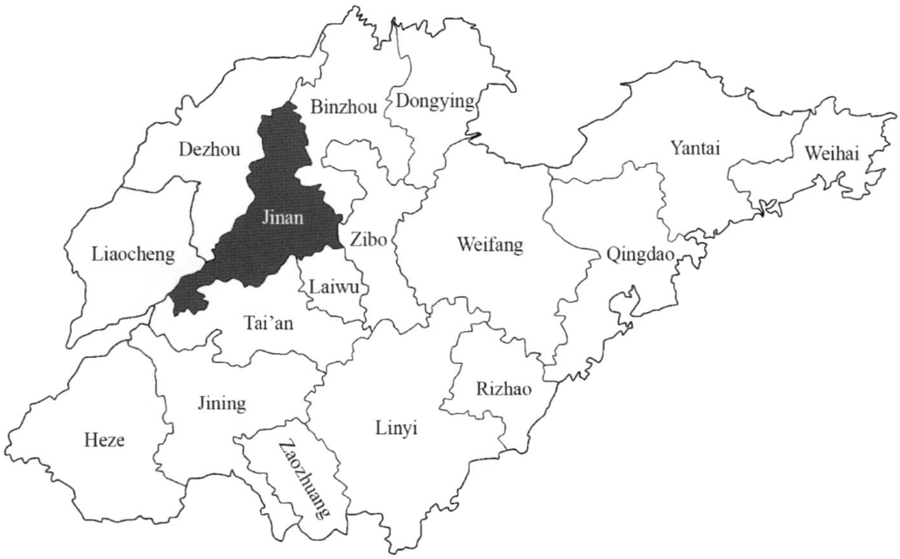

Source: Asia Competitiveness Institute.

8.1 Profile of Jinan City[1]

Jinan is the capital of Shandong province and has held sub-provincial administrative status since 1994, possessing direct jurisdiction over seven districts and three counties spanning a total land area of 7,998 square kilometres and a total population of 7,223,100. The city itself is located to the north of the Taishan massif, and to the south of the Yellow River. Jinan is renowned for its natural artesian springs, iconic scenery and historical significance as a cultural and religious centre, all of which have made the city extremely attractive to tourists. Jinan is noted for its 72 famous springs including Baotu Spring, which was highly regarded by renowned writers like Li Daoyuan and Yuan Haowen.

In 2016, Jinan's Gross Regional Domestic Product (GRDP) stood at around RMB 654 billion, and the city boasted a GRDP growth rate of 7.8%, as indicated in Table 8.1. The city and the area surrounding it is rich in energy resources and construction materials, and the city correspondingly derived 4.9% of its GRDP from its primary sector. Contrastingly, the city's secondary sector contributed to 36.2% of GRDP, significant proportions of which are drawn from

[1]The relevant city information are from the Department of Commerce of Shandong Province (n.d.), Jinan Municipal People's Government (2015) and Cheng (2009).

industries such as transportation equipment manufacturing, machinery manufacturing and solar energy. Ultimately, however, the greatest share of the city's GRDP is derived from its tertiary sector, which contributed 58.9% to GRDP. This is likely due to Jinan's growing focus on services, which has seen significant growth in such industries as software development, financial services, information services, cultural and creative activities, and tourism.

Jinan is a crucial transport hub and logistics centre and is served by the Jinan Yaoqiang International Airport. It is situated at the nexus of numerous national-level high-speed rail lines, expressway networks, and is even one of the six stations on the Beijing–Shanghai high-speed railway. With its strategic location and function, it is able to support the economic development along the Beijing–Shanghai axis. In addition, Jinan's downtown built area spans over 470 square kilometres and the urban population of the city stands at 69.3% — all of which serves to further underscore the high degree of urban development in the city.

Table 8.1: Key Economic Indicators for Jinan, 2016

Land Area (km^2)	**7,998**
Population	
Total Population	7,233,100
Urbanisation Rate (%)	69.5
Average Life Expectancy (years)	76.2
Number of Employees (10,000)	470
Workforce Participation Rate (%)	67.0
Gross Regional Domestic Product (GRDP) — 2015 Prices	
GRDP (100 millions of RMB)	6,536
GRDP Per Capita (RMB)	90,999
GRDP Growth Rate (%)	7.8
Economic Composition	
Primary Sector (% of GRDP)	4.9
Secondary Sector (% of GRDP)	36.2
Tertiary Sector (% of GRDP)	58.9
Trade — 2016 Prices	
Exports (millions of RMB)	39,828
Imports (millions of RMB)	26,009
Dependency on Foreign Trade (%)	11.0
Infrastructure	
Per Capita Road Area (m^2)	27.0
Growth in the Number of Passengers Transported (10,000)	113
Growth in the Volume of Cargo Transported (10,000 tons)	1,819
Environment	
Green Coverage Ratio of Built-up Area (%)	40.3
Environmental Expenditure (% of Total Fiscal Expenditure)	3.6

Source: Asia Competitiveness Institute from the 2017 Shandong Statistical Yearbook.

8.2 In-Depth Urban Development of Jinan, 2016*

8.2.1 Overall Urban Development Performance

Overall Performance

2017 Rank

4th

Out of 17 Cities

Score: 1.106

Rank	City	Score
1	Qingdao	1.753
2	Weihai	1.393
3	Yantai	1.312
4	Jinan	1.106
5	Weifang	0.855
6	Dongying	0.603
7	Zibo	0.403
	…	
16	Laiwu	−1.233
17	Liaocheng	−1.576

Jinan ranks 4th in its Overall Performance, with a standardised score of 1.106. This places the city in the Top Five Group of 17 cities. Jinan is positioned between Yantai (1.312) at 3rd place and Weifang (0.855) at 5th place.

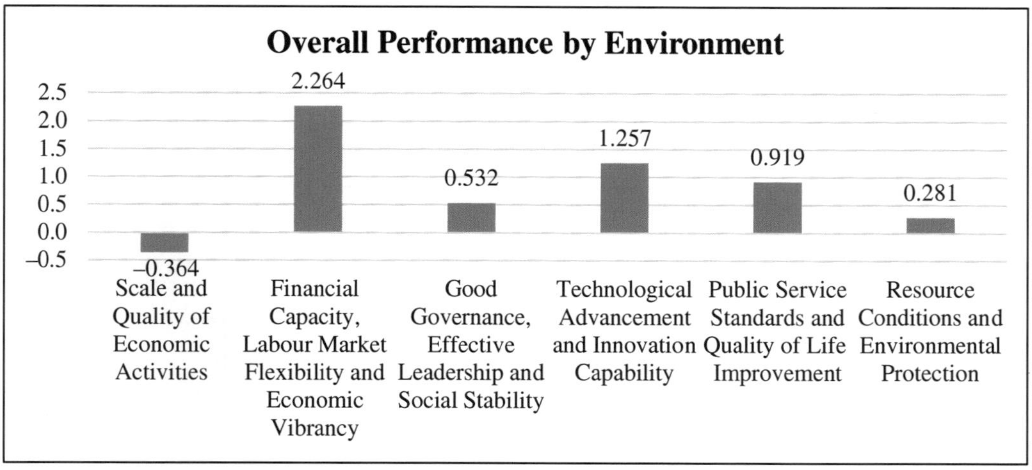

Among the six environments, Jinan scores above the provincial average in five of them and fares exceptionally better in Financial Capacity, Economic Vibrancy and Harmony. However, Jinan performs below the provincial average and relatively weaker in the environment of Scale and Quality of Economic Activities. On the other hand, the environments of Good Governance, Effective Leadership and Social Stability, and Resource Conditions and Environmental Protection also perform relatively weaker, but remain above the provincial average.

**For a complete list of rankings, see Tables 3.2 to 3.7 in Section 3.3 of Chapter 3.*

8.2.2 Urban Development within the Six Environments

Rank	City	Score
1	Qingdao	1.987
	...	
7	Dezhou	0.096
8	Tai'an	–0.321
9	Jinan	–0.364
10	Zaozhuang	–0.412
11	Binzhou	–0.573
	...	
16	Jining	–1.273
17	Laiwu	–1.295

A: ***Scale and Quality of Economic Activities***

2017 Rank

9th

Out of 17 Cities

Score: –0.364

Jinan ranks 9th for Scale and Quality of Economic Activities, with a standardised score of –0.364. This places the city in the Middle Seven Group of 17 cities. Jinan is positioned narrowly between Tai'an (–0.321) at 8th place and Zaozhuang (–0.412) at 10th place.

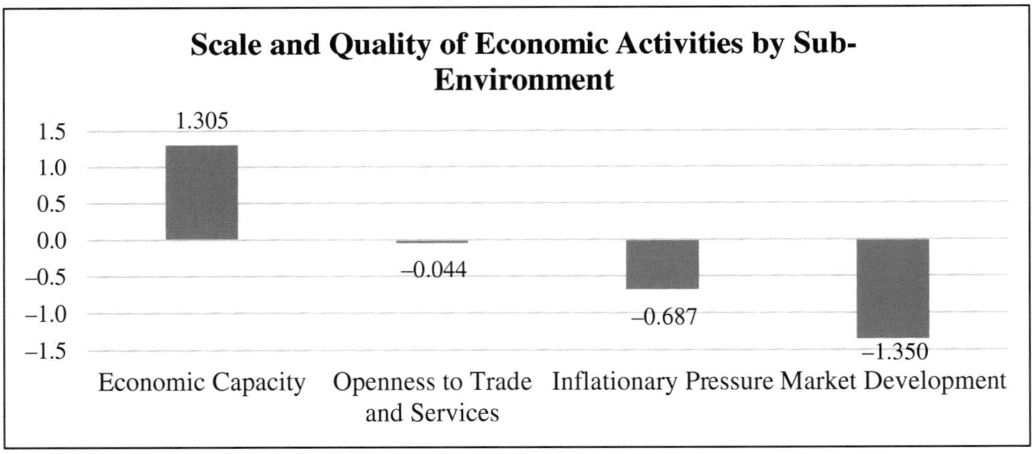

Looking at the four sub-environments of Scale and Quality of Economic Activities, Jinan performs above the provincial average and particularly better for Economic Capacity, where it scores especially well in the indicators of Service Sector as a Percentage of GRDP and Per Capita Volume of Retail Sales. However, Jinan performs below the provincial average in the remaining sub-environments and notably weaker in Market Development, where the indicator of Satisfaction with Business Environment scores especially poorly. In addition, the indicator of Manufacturing Sector as a Percentage of GRDP from the Economic Capacity sub-environment, and the Consumer Price Index from the Inflationary Pressure sub-environment score particularly low as well.

B: ***Financial Capacity, Labour Market Flexibility and Economic Vibrancy***

2017 Rank

1st

Out of 17 Cities

Score: 2.264

Rank	City	Score
1	Jinan	2.264
2	Qingdao	1.932
3	Yantai	1.271
4	Weifang	0.441
5	Linyi	0.387
6	Dongying	0.293
7	Zibo	0.089
	...	
16	Dezhou	−1.026
17	Laiwu	−1.297

Jinan ranks 1st for Financial Capacity, Labour Market Flexibility and Economic Vibrancy, with a standardised score of 2.264. This places the city in the Top Five Group of 17 cities. Jinan is positioned ahead of Qingdao (1.932) at 2nd place.

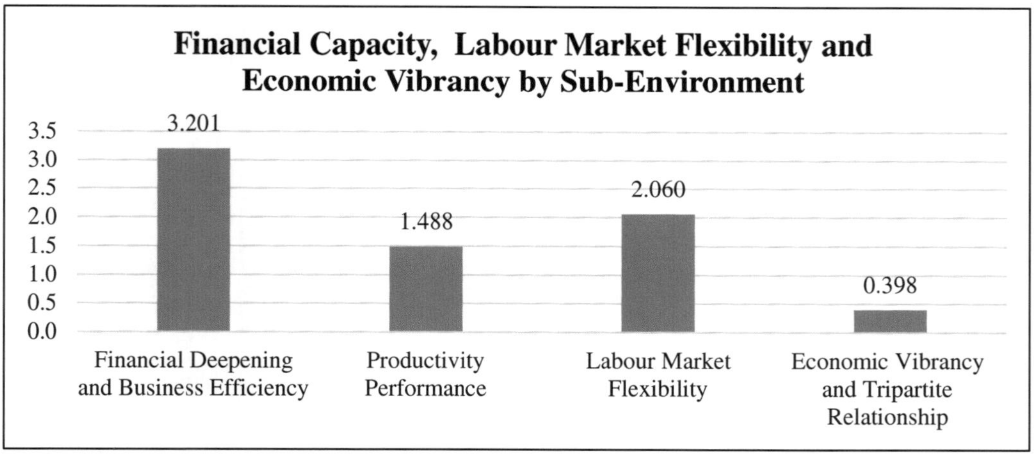

Among the four sub-environments of Financial Capacity, Labour Market Flexibility and Economic Vibrancy, Jinan performs above the provincial average in all of them and scores remarkably well in Financial Deepening and Business Efficiency, where many indicators including the Financed Amount in Stock Market, Insurance Net Income and Financial Sector Value-Added all score well above the provincial average. Other indicators with good performance include the Workforce Participation Rate and Proportion of Workforce in Service Sector from the Labour Market Flexibility sub-environment. However, Jinan scores relatively weaker in the Economic Vibrancy and Tripartite Relationship sub-environment, due to the indicator of Growth in Consumption of Electricity.

JINAN

Shandong Province

Rank	City	Score
1	Dezhou	1.465
2	Weihai	1.134
3	Weifang	0.797
4	Qingdao	0.733
5	Jinan	0.532
6	Tai'an	0.498
7	Heze	0.435
	...	
16	Laiwu	−1.588
17	Liaocheng	−2.473

C: *Good Governance, Effective Leadership and Social Stability*

2017 Rank

5th

Out of 17 Cities

Score: 0.532

Jinan ranks 5th for Good Governance, Effective Leadership and Social Stability with a standardised score of 0.532. This places the city in the Top Five Group of 17 cities. Jinan is positioned between Qingdao (0.733) at 4th place and Tai'an (0.498) at 6th place.

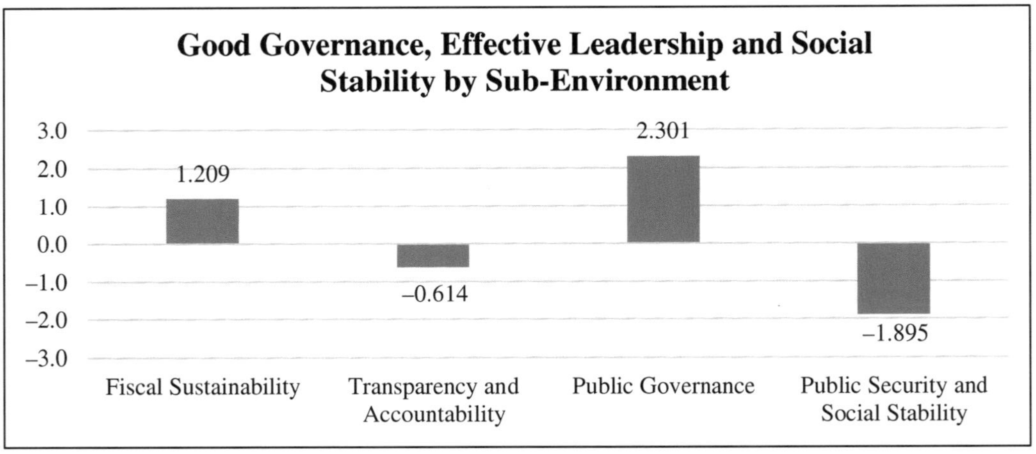

Among the four sub-environments of Good Governance, Effective Leadership and Social Stability, Jinan scores above the provincial average in two of them and especially for Public Governance, where the indicators of the Number of Administration Action and Reconsideration Cases and Number of Public Servants Per 10,000 Population score particularly well. However, Jinan performs below the provincial average in the remaining two sub-environments and especially unfavorably in the Public Security and Social Stability sub-environment, where the indicators of Fire Fatality Per 10,000 Population and the Satisfaction with Urban Management Personnel perform substantially weaker. Further, the indicators of Public Perception of Government Conduct and Satisfaction with the Just of Judiciary also register low scores.

D: ***Technological Advancement and Innovation Capability***

2017 Rank

3rd

Out of 17 Cities

Score: 1.257

Rank	City	Score
1	Qingdao	2.176
2	Weifang	1.417
3	Jinan	1.257
4	Yantai	1.009
5	Weihai	0.848
6	Zibo	0.492
7	Dongying	0.178
	...	
16	Zaozhuang	–1.192
17	Liaocheng	–1.221

Jinan ranks 3rd for Technological Advancement and Innovation Capability, with a standardised score of 1.257. This places the city in the Top Five Group of 17 cities. Jinan is positioned between Weifang (1.417) at 2nd place and Yantai (1.009) at 4th place.

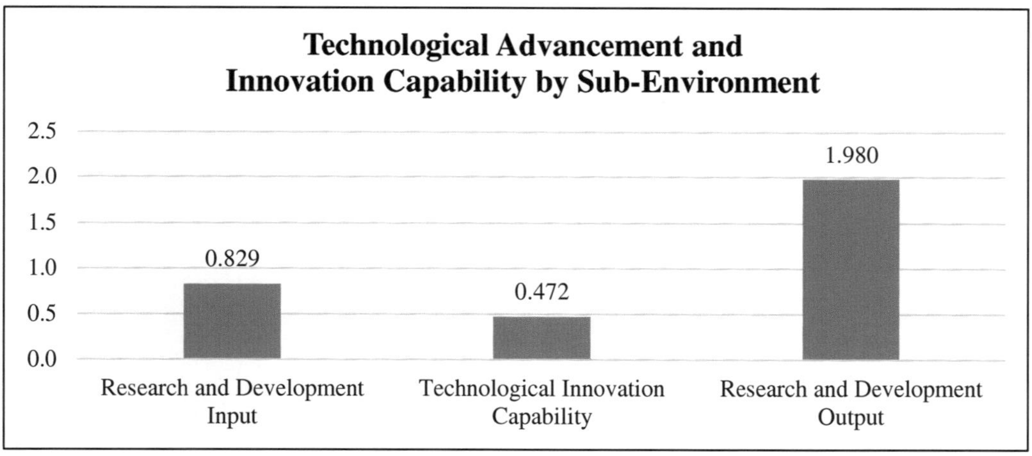

Among the three sub-environments of Technological Advancement and Innovation Capability, Jinan performs above the provincial average in all of them and particularly well in Research and Development Output, where it obtains high scores in the indicators of Number of Patents Granted and Number of Existing Patents Per 10,000 Population. In addition, the indicators of Total Research and Development Man-Hour and Number of Science and Technology Personnel from the Research and Development Input sub-environment score exceptionally well. However, Jinan performs relatively weaker in the Technological Innovation and Capability sub-environment due in large part to the poor performance in the indicator of Satisfaction with the Innovation Environment.

JINAN

Shandong Province

Rank	City	Score
1	Dongying	1.689
2	Weihai	1.616
3	Weifang	0.920
4	Jinan	0.919
5	Zibo	0.794
6	Laiwu	0.675
7	Qingdao	0.593
	...	
16	Dezhou	−1.066
17	Liaocheng	−1.964

E: *Public Service Standards and Quality of Life Improvement*

2017 Rank

4th

Out of 17 Cities

Score: 0.919

Jinan ranks 4th for Public Service Standards and Quality of Life Improvement with a standardised score of 0.919. This places the city in the Top Five Group of 17 cities. Jinan is positioned closely behind Weifang (0.920) at 3rd place and Zibo (0.794) at 5th place.

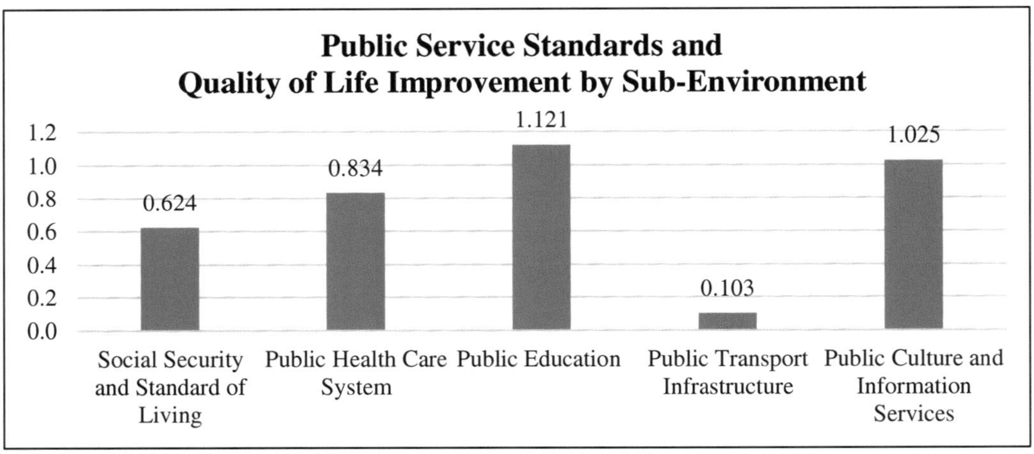

Among the five sub-environments of Public Service Standards and Quality of Life Improvement, Jinan scores above the provincial average in all of them and relatively better in Public Education and Public Culture and Information Services. Specifically, the indicators of Average Years of Education Received from the Public Education sub-environment, as well as the Internet Penetration Rate from the Public Culture and Information Services sub-environment score exceptionally better. Other indicators that perform remarkably well are the Number of Tertiary Education Attendees Per 10,000 Population and Number of Beds of Health Care Per 1,000 Population from the Public Health Care System sub-environment. However, Jinan scores relatively lower in the Public Transport Infrastructure sub-environment, where the indicators of Satisfaction of Traffic Conditions and Satisfaction of Public Transport Services score especially weak.

F: ***Resource Conditions and Environmental Protection***

2017 Rank

9th

Out of 17 Cities

Score: 0.281

Rank	City	Score
1	Weihai	1.632
	...	
7	Tai'an	0.370
8	Qingdao	0.330
9	Jinan	0.281
10	Jining	–0.112
11	Dezhou	–0.287
	...	
16	Binzhou	–1.586
17	Heze	–2.142

Jinan ranks 9th for Resource Conditions and Environmental Protection with a standardised score of 0.281. This places the city in the Middle Seven Group of 17 cities. Jinan is positioned between Qingdao (0.330) at 8th place and Jining (–0.112) at 10th place.

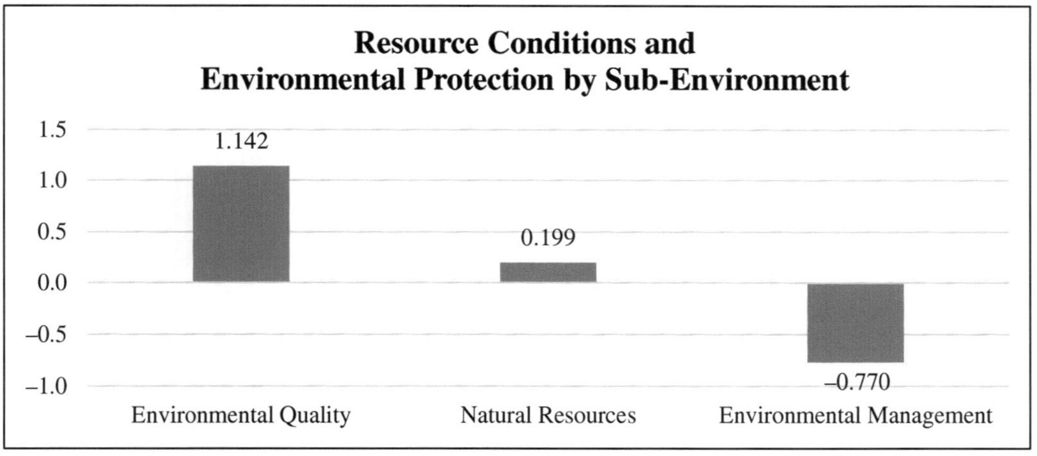

Among the three sub-environments of Resource Conditions and Environmental Protection, Jinan scores above the provincial average in two of them and particularly better in Environmental Quality, where the indicators of Ammoniacal Nitrogen Discharge Per RMB 10,000 GRDP and Chemical Oxygen Demand Per RMB 10,000 GRDP perform better. However, Jinan scores below the provincial average and significantly weaker in the Environmental Management sub-environment, where it scores unfavourably in the indicators of Green Coverage Ratio of Built-up Area and Forest Land Growth. Further, the indicator of Per Capita Arable Land from the Natural Resources sub-environment scores poorly as well. Nevertheless, the indicator of Urban Area Waste Water Treatment Rate from the Environmental Management sub-environment obtains a high score.

Figure 8.1: Median & Maximum Web for Jinan

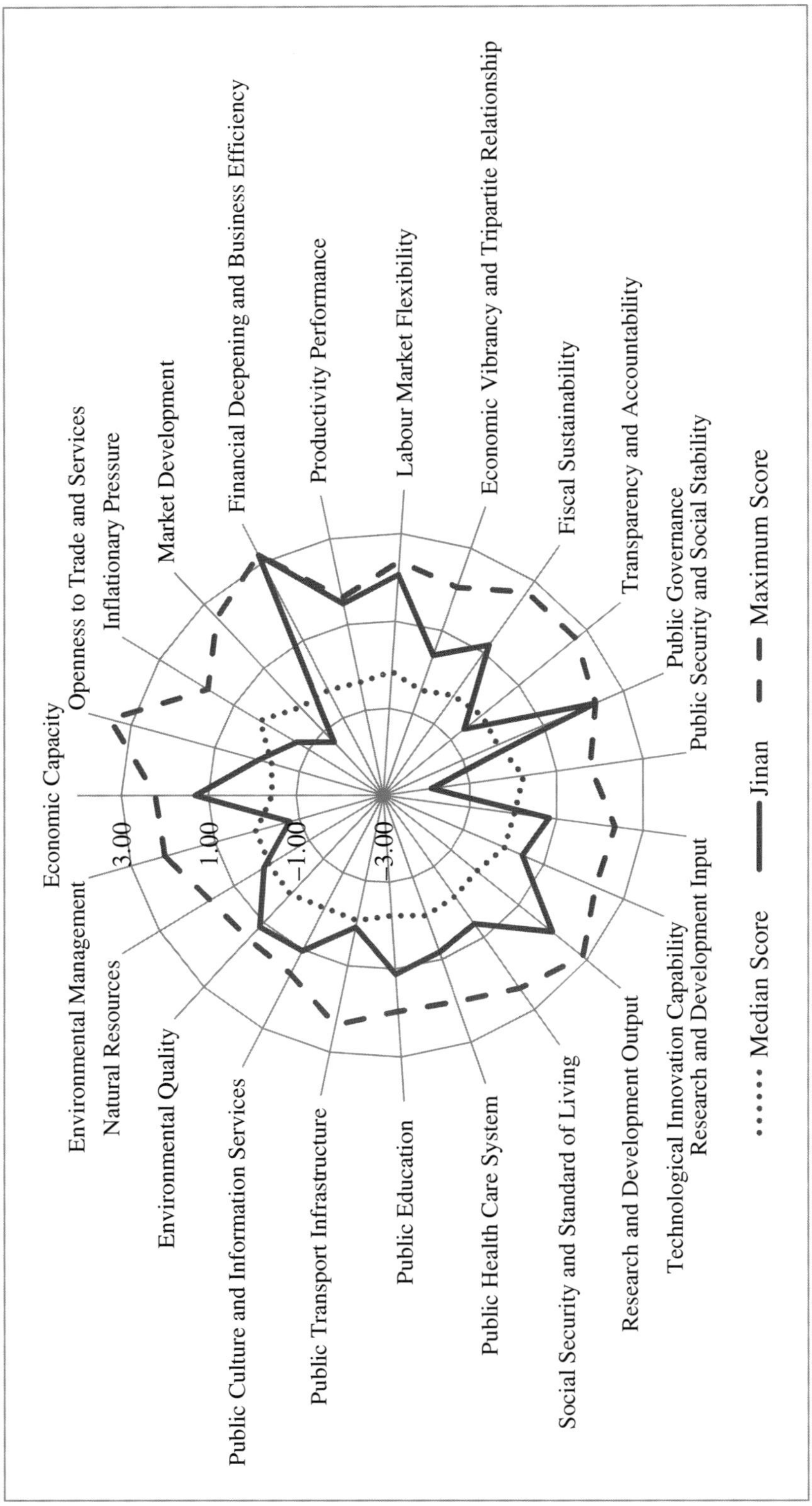

Source: Asia Competitiveness Institute.

8.2.3 Median and Maximum Web Analysis

To better understand Jinan's relative strengths and weaknesses, it is useful to compare and contrast its scores for the 23 sub-environments against the median and maximum scores of Shandong's 17 cities.

In Figure 8.1, the median and maximum scores for 17 Shandong cities are shown as dotted and dashed lines respectively, while scores for Jinan are shown as a solid line.

Comparison to Median Scores

Jinan scores above the median for 18 of the 23 sub-environments, most notably in Financial Deepening and Business Efficiency, Labour Market Flexibility and Economic Capacity.

On the other hand, it scores below the median for the remaining five sub-environments, most notably for Public Security and Social Stability, Market Development and Environmental Management.

Comparison to Maximum Scores

Jinan scores below the provincial maximum of the 17 Shandong cities in 21 out of 23 sub-environments. Jinan achieves the provincial maximum in the sub-environments of Financial Deepening and Business Efficiency (3.201) and Public Governance (2.301).

Jinan's score in Market Development (–1.350) is farthest from the maximum, which is held by Heze (2.577). Further, Jinan's score in Productivity Performance (1.488) is closest to the maximum, which is held by Qingdao (1.628).

8.3 Summary of Empirical Findings of Jinan and *What-if* Urban Development Simulation

8.3.1 Summary of Empirical Findings, 20% Strongest and Weakest Indicators

Overall Performance **4th** Score: 1.106		
Scale and Quality of Economic Activities **9th** Score: –0.364	Financial Capacity, Labour Market Flexibility and Economic Vibrancy **1st** Score: 2.264	Good Governance, Effective Leadership and Social Stability **5th** Score: 0.532
Technological Advancement and Innovation Capability **3rd** Score: 1.257	Public Service Standards and Quality of Life Improvement **4th** Score: 0.919	Resource Conditions and Environmental Protection **9th** Score: 0.281

(Rank out of 17 cities)

Summary

Jinan ranks 4th out of 17 cities in terms of its Overall Performance and scores above the provincial average in five out of the six environments. Further, it ranks 1st in Financial Capacity, Labour Market Flexibility and Economic Vibrancy. Meanwhile, Jinan's weakest environments are that of Scale and Quality of Economic Activities and Resource Conditions and Environmental Protection, where they both rank at 9th place.

Strengths

As illustrated in Table 8.2, Jinan performs especially well in the environment of Financial Capacity, Labour Market Flexibility and Economic Vibrancy, with 10 out of 26 of its 20% Strongest Indicators in that environment. Among Jinan's best performing indicators are Number of Tertiary Education Attendees Per 10,000 Population, Financed Amount in Stock Market and Number of Administration Action and Reconsideration Cases.

Weaknesses

As observed in Table 8.3, Jinan is weaker in the environment of Public Service Security and Quality of Life Improvement, with 10 out of 26 of its 20% Weakest Indicators under this environment. Among Jinan's lowest scoring indicators are the Fire Fatality Per 10,000 Population, Satisfaction of Traffic Conditions and Consumer Price Index.

JINAN

Shandong Province

Table 8.2: 20% Strongest Indicators for Jinan

Rank	20% Strongest indicator	Score	SQEA	FCLMFEV	GGELSS	TAIC	PSSQLI	RCEP
1	Number of Tertiary Education Attendees Per 10,000 Population	3.784					✓	
2	Financed Amount in Stock Market	3.243		✓				
3	Number of Administration Action and Reconsideration Cases	3.027			✓			
4	Deepness of Insurance (Insurance Income as a Share of GRDP)	2.760		✓				
5	Insurance Net Income	2.725		✓				
6	Financial Sector Value-Added	2.691		✓				
7	Number of Doctors Per 1,000 Persons	2.686					✓	
8	Proportion of Workforce Employed in Service Sector	2.594		✓				
9	Service Sector as a Percentage of GRDP	2.544	✓					
10	Deposit Balance Per Capita	2.486		✓				
11	Number of Science and Technology Personnel	2.429				✓		
12	Number of Beds of Health Care Per 1,000 Population	2.424					✓	
13	Loan Balance Per Capita	2.415		✓				
14	Number of R&D Personnel Per 10,000 Population	2.281				✓		
15	Percentage of the Employed Population with Tertiary Education	2.279		✓				
16	Number of Releases of Government Information for Public Viewing	2.274			✓			
17	Internet Penetration Rate	2.222					✓	
18	Total R&D Man-Hour	2.200				✓		
19	Average Salary of Urban Employees	2.053		✓				
20	Workforce Participation Rate	2.040		✓				
21	Number of Public Servants Per 10,000 Population	1.899			✓			
22	Average Years of Education Received	1.872					✓	
23	Number of Existing Patents Per 10,000 Population	1.862				✓		
24	Per Capita Volume of Retail Sales	1.849	✓					
25	Number of Patents Granted	1.844				✓		
26	Mobile Phone Penetration Per Capita	1.739					✓	

Table 8.3: 20% Weakest Indicators for Jinan

Rank	20% Weakest Indicator	Score	SQEA	FCLMFEV	GGELSS	TAIC	PSSQLI	RCEP
106	Public Health and Medical Service Expenses as a Share of GRDP	−0.726					✓	
107	Area of Natural Reserves to Administrative Area (%)	−0.826						✓
108	Satisfaction of the Police Services	−0.889			✓			
109	Ratio of Public Education Appropriation to GRDP	−0.906					✓	
110	Forest Land Growth	−1.219						✓
111	Frequency of Using the Internet for Daily Convenience	−1.222					✓	
112	Residents' Satisfaction with Price Levels	−1.230	✓					
113	Green Coverage Ratio of Built-up Area	−1.290						✓
114	Per Capita Arable Land	−1.438						✓
115	Traffic Accident Fatality Per 10,000 Population	−1.444			✓			
116	Satisfaction with the Just of Judiciary	−1.494			✓			
117	Public Perception of Government Conduct	−1.523			✓			
118	Satisfaction with Urban Management Personnels	−1.543			✓			
119	Satisfaction with Business Environment	−1.625	✓					
120	Cleanliness of Public Toilets	−1.655					✓	
121	Total R&D Expenditure of Enterprises Above Designated Size as a Percentage of Cash Flow	−1.670				✓		
122	Satisfaction of Public Transport Services	−1.677					✓	
123	Satisfaction of Public Education System	−1.682					✓	
124	Satisfaction of Public Health Care Services	−1.724					✓	
125	Residents' Perception of Happiness	−1.796					✓	
126	Satisfaction with Innovation Environment	−1.831				✓		
127	Satisfaction of Income Disparity	−2.072					✓	
128	Manufacturing Sector as a Percentage of GRDP	−2.155	✓					
129	Consumer Price Index (CPI)	−2.233	✓					
130	Satisfaction of Traffic Conditions	−2.647					✓	
131	Fire Fatality Per 10,000 Population	−3.405			✓			

Source: Asia Competitiveness Institute.

Notes: SQEA: Scale and Quality of Economic Activities; FCLMFEV: Financial Capacity, Labour Market Flexibility and Economic Vibrancy; GGELSS: Good Governance, Effective Leadership and Social Stability; TAIC: Technological Advancement and Innovation Capability; PSSQLI: Public Service Standards and Quality of Life Improvement; RCEP: Resource Conditions and Environmental Protection.

8.3.2 *What-if* Urban Development Simulation

ACI has devised a simulation methodology to improve the ranking of a particular city by improving on its 20% Weakest Indicators as shown in Table 8.3.[2] The figures below show Jinan's ranking and standardised scores before and after the policy-induced simulation. Refer to Tables 3.8 to 3.14 in Section 3.4 of Chapter 3 for a complete list of simulation results for all cities.

Overall Performance

	Before		After
Rank	4th	▶	1st
Score	1.106		2.078

Scale and Quality of Economic Activities

	Before	After
Rank	9th	5th
Score	–0.364	0.905

Financial Capacity, Labour Market Flexibility and Economic Vibrancy

	Before	After
Rank	1st	1st
Score	2.264	2.264

Good Governance, Effective Leadership and Social Stability

	Before	After
Rank	5th	1st
Score	0.532	1.749

Technological Advancement and Innovation Capability

	Before	After
Rank	3rd	2nd
Score	1.257	1.711

Public Service Standards and Quality of Life Improvement

	Before	After
Rank	4th	1st
Score	0.919	1.961

Resource Conditions and Environmental Protection

	Before	After
Rank	9th	3rd
Score	0.281	1.078

After the *What-if* simulation, Jinan improved its ranking from 4th place to 1st place in terms of its Overall Performance. Likewise, Jinan's standardised score increases from 1.106 to 2.078. This leap is plausible if the city manages to successfully address its 20% Weakest Indicators.

The simulation further indicates that Jinan may achieve substantial improvement in some of its environments, most notably in Resource Conditions and Environmental Protection, where its rank will rise from 9th to 3rd. Such encouraging results should incentivise Jinan to strive to improve the indicators under the 20% Weakest Indicators list. These indicators include Green Coverage Ratio of Built-up Area and the Area of Natural Reserves to Administrative Area.

[2]The methodology for *What-if* simulation is thoroughly explained in Section 2.7 of Chapter 2.

8.4 Concluding Notes: Public Policy Implications[3]

Areas for Commendation

Jinan performs especially well in the environment of Financial Capacity, Labour Market Flexibility and Economic Vibrancy, with 10 out of 26 of its 20% Strongest Indicators contained in this environment, as indicated in Table 8.2.

Further, Jinan holds the maximum score for the sub-environment of Financial Deepening and Business Efficiency (3.201) and Public Governance (2.301) and scores above the provincial average in 17 out of 23 sub-environments.

In 2016, Jinan further improved its innovative development through the extensive promotion of green agricultural science, construction of marine science and technology and technological innovation platform. In addition, the government also has the advantage of Cloud Computing and Big Data Technologies to support the construction of a "smart city" that leverages on technology in daily activities. To further raise employment opportunities in the city, Jinan built a new material industrial park, which generated more than 180,000 jobs.

Areas for Improvement

While Jinan performs above the provincial average in majority of the environments, there is still room for improvement, especially in the environment of Public Service Standards and Quality of Life Improvement, where it contributes 10 out of 26 of its 20% Weakest Indicators, as shown in Table 8.3. Additionally, as gleaned from the *What-if* Urban Development Simulation, the environment of Resource Conditions and Environmental Protection should be prioritised because that is the environment in which Jinan will achieve the greatest improvement in its rankings — six positions — relative to other environments.

Moreover, Jinan obtains substantially lower scores in the sub-environments of Public Security and Social Stability (−1.895) and Market Development (−1.350), and scores below the provincial average in six out of 23 sub-environments.

Jinan has acknowledged its weakness in public transport before. In 2016, the government launched 17 new public bus routes, while several other urban rail transits, high-speed railways and high ways were also under construction. Further, Jinan had vigorously promoted the integration of its government information systems and government service platforms to constantly improve its "Internet + Government Services" standard.

[3]The relevant statistical data and government policies are from Jinan Municipal People's Government (2017), Jinan Urban Planning (2017), Ministry of Commerce of the People's Republic of China (2017), The State Council of the People's Republic of China (2017), Phoenix New Media (2017), Tencent (2017), Fan (2017) and Qilu Network and Liu (2016).

JINAN

Shandong Province

Future Potential Development

In summary, Jinan should strive to maintain its high and exemplary position in Shandong, as shown from our index and ranking. Specifically, Jinan should focus on improving its public service standards and quality by investing more towards transport, education and health care services, which are among Jinan's 20% Weakest Indicators.

In addition, to improve its scores in the sub-environment of Public Security and Social Stability, Jinan policymakers should focus on reducing traffic accidents and improve the efficiency of police forces. Some strategies Jinan may consider include the increase in the penalty for traffic violations and the number of surveillance cameras on the roads. Furthermore, with the "Belt and Road Initiative", Jinan is positioned to become a strategically important international intermediary, whether for goods or logistics. As such, this will help bolster greater investment and tourism. Taking advantage of the "Belt and Road Initiative", Jinan should aim to develop itself as a hub for business, tourism, as well as advanced manufacturing and marine industries. At the same time, the Jinan government should focus its efforts on the construction of a "smart city" so as to further improve its international reputation.

References

Cheng, Weihong. 2009. 'Jinan City Introduction'. 24 July 2009. http://shandong.chinadaily.com.cn/e/2009-07/24/content_8467836.htm.

Department of Commerce of Shandong Province. n.d. 'Jinan City'. Accessed 27 October 2017. http://en.shandongbusiness.gov.cn/city/67.

Fan, Lixin. 2017. '政策利好力挺济南 Government Policies Promote Jinan Development (in Chinese)'. 23 November 2017. http://news.163.com/17/1123/11/D3U397I400018AOP.html.

Jinan Municipal People's Government. 2015. 'Introduction of Jinan'. 22 August 2015. http://english.jinan.gov.cn/col/col2231/index.html.

———. 2017. '济南市政府信息公开-市规划局2017年规划工作要点Jinan Municipal Government Information Released 2017 Working Focuses of Urban Planning Bureau (in Chinese)'. 25 April 2017. http://xxgk.jinan.gov.cn/xxgk/jcms_files/jcms1/web15/site/art/2017/4/25/art_17716_193097.html.

Jinan Urban Planning. 2017. '大数据时代的城市设计模式 Urban Design Patterns in Big Data Era (in Chinese)'. 10 November 2017. http://jnup.jinan.gov.cn/art/2017/11/10/art_38738_939019.html.

Ministry of Commerce of the People's Republic of China. 2017. '济南出台政策力争打造'一带一路'核心城市 Jinan Introduced Policies to Strive to Create a Core City under 'Belt and Road Initiative' (in Chinese)'. 6 March 2017. http://www.mofcom.gov.cn/article/difang/201703/20170302527573.shtml.

Phoenix New Media. 2017. '2017年济南市政府工作报告（全文）2017 Jinan Annual Government Work Report (in Chinese)'. 9 April 2017. http://sd.ifeng.com/a/20170409/5537641_1.shtml.

Qilu Network, and Yan Liu. 2016. '济南2030年要成特大城市 未来15年中心城区再扩容 Jinan Will Become A Megacity in 2030, Its Downtown Area Will Be Further Expanded in the Next 15 Years (in Chinese)'. 22 February 2016. http://news.iqilu.com/shandong/yuanchuang/2016/0222/2695027.shtml.

Tencent. 2017. '未来山东版图啥样看这里 2030年济南将成为特大城市 How Shandong Will Grow In The Future? Jinan Will Become A Megacity in 2030 (in Chinese)'. 7 April 2017. http://jn.house.qq.com/a/20170407/007598.htm.

The State Council, The People's Republic of China. 2017. '"济南：'互联网+政务服务''打造功能最强政务服务平台 Jinan: 'Internet + Government Services' to Create the Most Powerful Government Service Platform (in Chinese)"'. 13 December 2017. http://www.gov.cn/zhengce/2017-12/13/content_5246577.htm.

Chapter 9: JINING
Shandong Province

Location of City

Source: Asia Competitiveness Institute.

9.1 Profile of Jining City[1]

Jining has been an economic, cultural and political centre throughout much of Chinese history and today directly administers two districts, two county-level cities and seven counties spanning a total land area of 11,187 square kilometres, and a total population of 8,354,400. The wider region which the city of Jining administers also encompasses Qufu and Zoucheng, which are renowned for having respectively been the birthplaces of Confucius and Mencius, China's most venerated sages and the most significant figures in Confucian philosophy.

In 2016, Jining's Gross Regional Domestic Product (GRDP) stood at RMB 430 billion, with the city also boasting a healthy GRDP growth rate of 8.0%, as is reflected in Table 9.1. Jining and its surrounding regions are rich in mineral resources and land for agricultural cultivation. The city is notably one of China's eight coal bases and holds 25 billion tons of reserves. Jining's primary sector correspondingly contributed to 11.2% of GRDP. Jining also benefits from an advanced manufacturing base, specialising in machinery manufacturing, textiles and garments, new energy and materials, pharmaceuticals, food production, and coal-chemical processing.

[1]The relevant city information are from the Department of Commerce of Shandong Province (n.d.), Jining People's Government (2016) and Xiaotao (2009).

Jining's secondary sector accordingly accounted for 45.3% of total GRDP. Jining's tertiary sector constituted 43.5% of GRDP and continues to be bolstered by developments in its National High-tech Industrial Zone and ongoing investments into its tourism and vacation zone.

Jining is served by the Jining Qufu Airport, which caters to domestic flights. The city is also well served by five expressways and three railway lines, which in combination with its existing links to the south of China via the Grand Canal, makes the city exceptionally well connected on the whole. Jining is also the city which spent the greatest amount on cultural initiatives relative to total expenditure in 2016, with such initiatives taking up 2.0% of total public expenditure. This is in turn a testament to the city's dedication to doing its historical and cultural legacy justice and ensuring that it remains alive for future generations.

Table 9.1: Key Economic Indicators for Jining, 2016

Land Area (km^2)	**11,187**
Population	
Total Population	8,354,400
Urbanisation Rate (%)	55.2
Average Life Expectancy (years)	76.0
Number of Employees (10,000)	554
Workforce Participation Rate (%)	77.1
Gross Regional Domestic Product (GRDP) — 2015 Prices	
GRDP (100 millions of RMB)	4,302
GRDP Per Capita (RMB)	51,662
GRDP Growth Rate (%)	8.0
Economic Composition	
Primary Sector (% of GRDP)	11.2
Secondary Sector (% of GRDP)	45.3
Tertiary Sector (% of GRDP)	43.5
Trade — 2016 Prices	
Exports (millions of RMB)	22,814
Imports (millions of RMB)	13,298
Dependency on Foreign Trade (%)	8.4
Infrastructure	
Per Capita Road Area (m^2)	29.5
Growth in the Number of Passengers Transported (10,000)	168
Growth in the Volume of Cargo Transported (10,000 tons)	1,360
Environment	
Green Coverage Ratio of Built-up Area (%)	42.4
Environmental Expenditure (% of Total Fiscal Expenditure)	2.7

Source: Asia Competitiveness Institute from the 2017 Shandong Statistical Yearbook.

9.2 In-Depth Urban Development of Jining, 2016*

9.2.1 Overall Urban Development Performance

Overall Performance

2017 Rank

13th

Out of 17 Cities

Score: –0.706

Rank	City	Score
1	Qingdao	1.753
	...	
10	Dezhou	–0.302
11	Rizhao	–0.472
12	Heze	–0.615
13	Jining	–0.706
14	Binzhou	–1.076
15	Zaozhuang	–1.164
16	Laiwu	–1.233
17	Liaocheng	–1.576

Jining ranks 13th in its Overall Performance, with a standardised score of –0.706. This places the city in the Bottom Five Group of 17 cities. Jining is positioned between Heze (–0.615) at 12th place and Binzhou (–1.076) at 14th place.

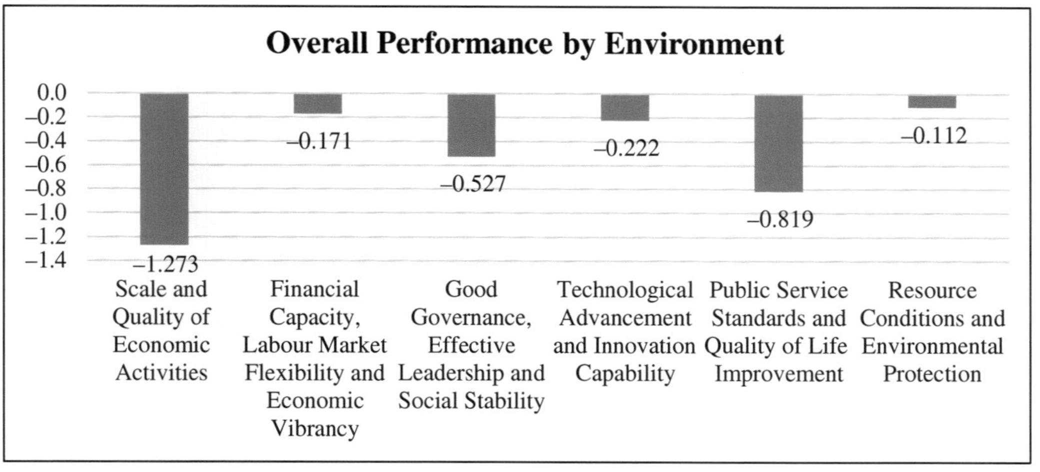

Among the six environments, Jining performs below the provincial average in all of them. In particular, Jining performs substantially further below the provincial average in the environments of Scale and Quality of Economic Activities and Public Service Standards and Quality of Life Improvement. On the other hand, Jining performs relatively better in the environments of Financial Capacity, Labour Market Flexibility and Economic Vibrancy as well as Resource Conditions and Environmental Protection.

** For a complete list of rankings, see Tables 3.2 to 3.7 in Section 3.3 of Chapter 3.*

9.2.2 Urban Development within the Six Environments

Rank	City	Score
1	Qingdao	1.987
	...	
10	Zaozhuang	–0.412
11	Binzhou	–0.573
12	Liaocheng	–0.665
13	Zibo	–0.674
14	Dongying	–0.782
15	Rizhao	–1.017
16	Jining	–1.273
17	Laiwu	–1.295

A: ***Scale and Quality of Economic Activities***

2017 Rank

16th

Out of 17 Cities

Score: –1.273

Jining ranks 16th for Scale and Quality of Economic Activities, with a standardised score of –1.273. This places the city in the Bottom Five Group of 17 cities. Jining is positioned between Rizhao (–1.017) at 15th place and Laiwu (–1.295) at 17th place.

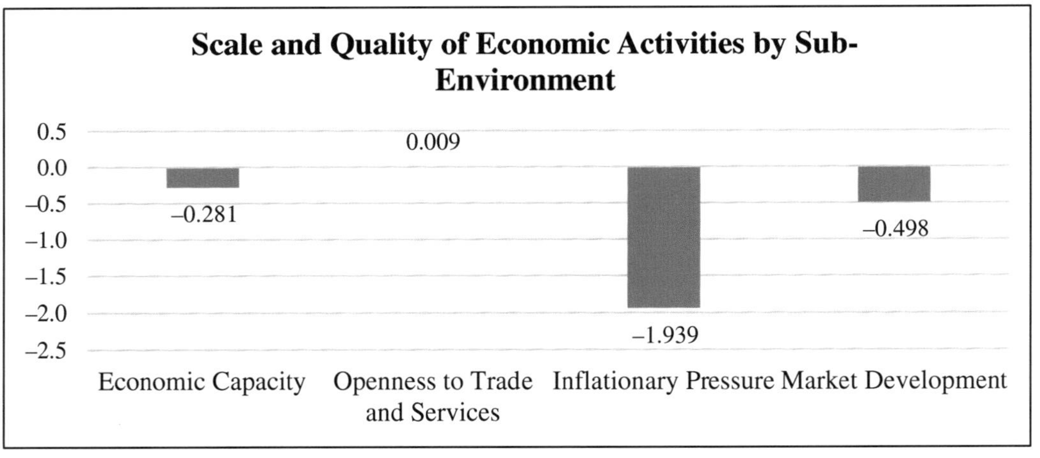

Among the four sub-environments of Scale and Quality of Economic Activities, Jining performs marginally above the provincial average in Openness to Trade and Services, where it has a significantly high score in the indicator for Investment Abroad. However, the Jining scores below the provincial average in all the remaining three sub-environments and especially poorly for Inflationary Pressure, where the indicators of Retail Price Index and Urban Residents' Per Capita Expenditure Growth Rate register particularly low scores. In addition, the indicator of Satisfaction with Business Environment from the Market Development sub-environment is weak as well.

B: *Financial Capacity, Labour Market Flexibility and Economic Vibrancy*

2017 Rank

9th

Out of 17 Cities

Score: –0.171

Rank	City	Score
1	Jinan	2.264
	...	
7	Zibo	0.089
8	Weihai	0.083
9	Jining	–0.171
10	Binzhou	–0.329
11	Rizhao	–0.619
	...	
16	Dezhou	–1.026
17	Laiwu	–1.297

Jining ranks 9th for Financial Capacity, Labour Market Flexibility and Economic Vibrancy, with a standardised score of –0.171. This places the city in the Middle Seven Group of 17 cities. Jining is positioned between Weihai (0.083) at 8th place and Binzhou (–0.329) at 10th place.

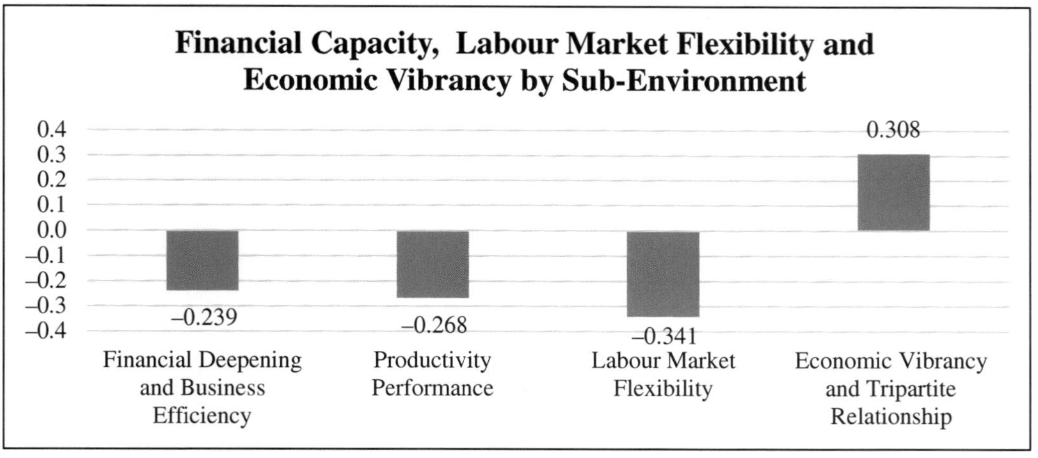

Among the four sub-environments of Financial Capacity, Labour Market Flexibility and Economic Vibrancy, Jining scores above the provincial average in Economic Vibrancy and Tripartite Relationship, where the indicator of Growth in the Number of Passengers Transported performs well. However, Jining performs below the provincial average in the remaining three sub-environments and most notably in Labour Market Flexibility, where it obtains low scores in the indicator for Urban Registered Unemployment Rate and Rate of Migration Flow. Nevertheless, the indicator of Number of Employees also from the sub-environment of Labour Market Flexibility registers a strong score.

JINING

Shandong Province

Rank	City	Score
1	Dezhou	1.465
	...	
10	Yantai	0.192
11	Dongying	0.173
12	Rizhao	0.042
13	Jining	–0.527
14	Binzhou	–0.849
15	Zaozhuang	–1.302
16	Laiwu	–1.588
17	Liaocheng	–2.473

C: ***Good Governance, Effective Leadership and Social Stability***

2017 Rank

13th

Out of 17 Cities

Score: –0.527

Jining ranks 13th for Good Governance, Effective Leadership and Social Stability with a standardised score of –0.527. This places the city in the Bottom Five Group of 17 cities. Jining is positioned between Rizhao (0.042) at 12th place and Binzhou (–0.849) at 14th place.

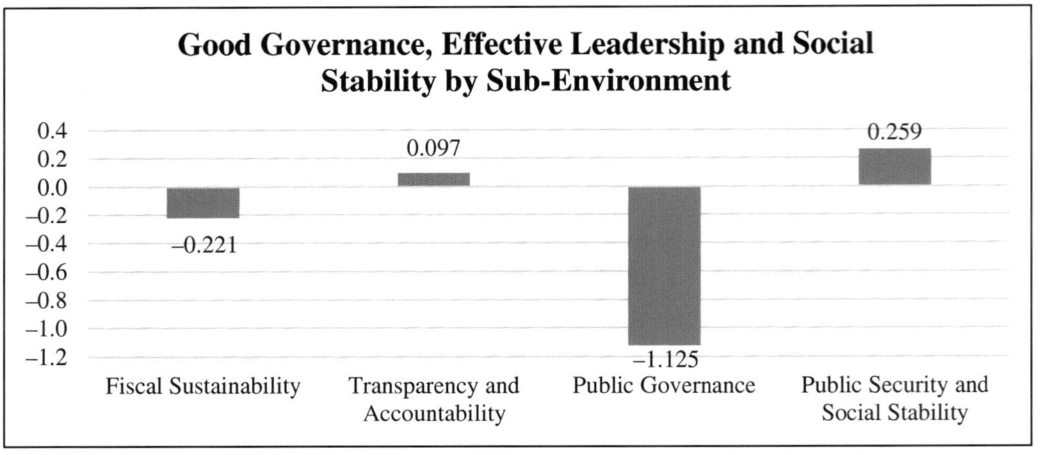

Among the four sub-environments of Good Governance, Effective Leadership and Social Stability, Jining scores above the provincial average in Transparency and Accountability, and Public Security and Social Stability. Specifically, the indicators of the Number of Responses to Government Issues of Public Interest from the Transparency and Accountability sub-environment and Growth Rate of Police Cases Solved from the Public Security and Social Stability sub-environment perform exceptionally well. However, Jining scores below the provincial average in the remaining two sub-environments and especially weaker in Public Governance, where it performs particularly unfavorably in the indicator of Average Public Servant Salary. Further, the indicator of Tax Revenue as a Share of Fiscal Revenue from the Fiscal Sustainability sub-environment registers a low score as well.

D: ***Technological Advancement and Innovation Capability***

2017 Rank

8th

Out of 17 Cities

Score: –0.222

Rank	City	Score
1	Qingdao	2.176
	…	
6	Zibo	0.492
7	Dongying	0.178
8	Jining	–0.222
9	Linyi	–0.344
10	Tai'an	–0.457
	…	
16	Zaozhuang	–1.192
17	Liaocheng	–1.221

Jining ranks 8th for Technological Advancement and Innovation Capability, with a standardised score of –0.222. This places the city in the Middle Seven Group of 17 cities. Jining is positioned between Dongying (0.178) at 7th place and Linyi (–0.344) at 9th place.

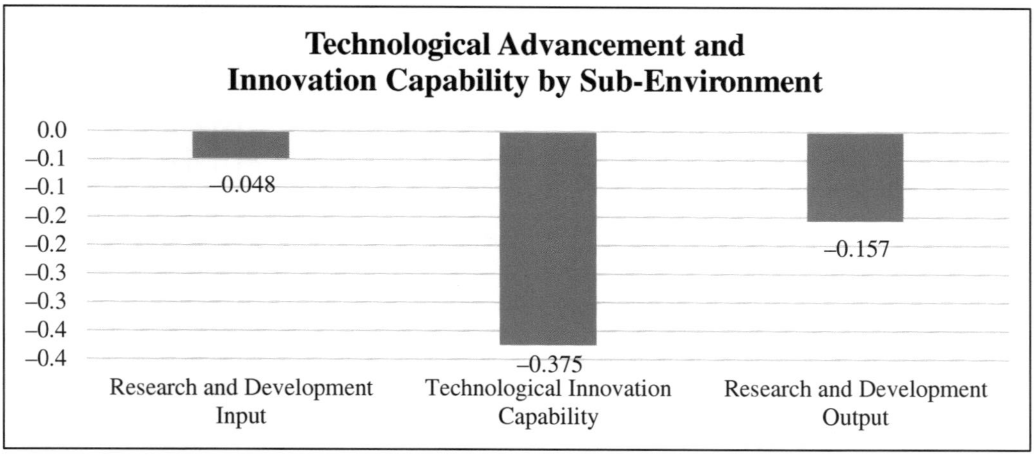

Looking at the three sub-environments of Technological Advancement and Innovation Capability, Jining performs below the provincial average in all of them and most notably in Technological Innovation Capability, where it obtains a low score in the indicator of the Satisfaction with Innovation Environment. Nevertheless, Jining scores more favourably in the indicator of Number of Provincial-Level Science Parks also from the Technological Innovation Capability sub-environment. In addition, the indicators of Total Research and Development Expenditure of Enterprises above Designated Size as a Percentage of Cash Flow from the Research and Development Input sub-environment also scores relatively well.

JINING

Shandong Province

Rank	City	Score
1	Dongying	1.689
	...	
10	Linyi	–0.307
11	Tai'an	–0.567
12	Heze	–0.766
13	Jining	–0.819
14	Binzhou	–0.862
15	Zaozhuang	–0.954
16	Dezhou	–1.066
17	Liaocheng	–1.964

E: *Public Service Standards and Quality of Life Improvement*

2017 Rank

13th

Out of 17 Cities

Score: –0.819

Jining ranks 13th for Public Service Standards and Quality of Life Improvement with a standardised score of –0.819. This places the city in the Middle Seven Group of 17 cities. Jining is positioned between Heze (–0.766) at 12th place and Binzhou (–0.862) at 14th place.

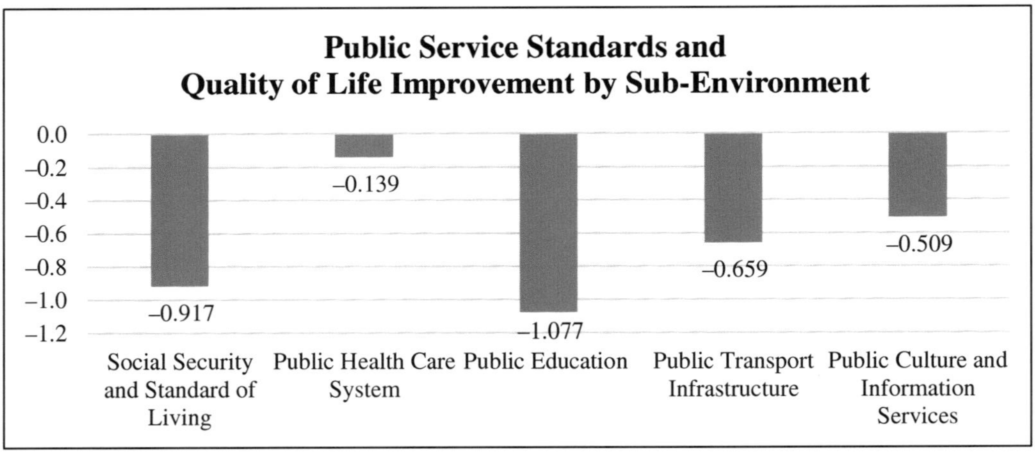

Across the five sub-environments of Public Service Standards and Quality of Life Improvement, Jining performs below the provincial average in all of them and particularly poorly in Public Education, where the indicators of Satisfaction of Public Education System and Number of Vocational Education Institutions Per 10,000 Population obtain exceptionally low scores. In addition, the indicators of Number of Private Cars Per 100 Households and Engel's Index from the Social Security and Standard of Living sub-environment score relatively low. Nevertheless, the indicator of the Percentage of Public Expenditure on Cultural Initiatives from the Public Culture and Information Services sub-environment performs remarkably well.

F: ***Resource Conditions and Environmental Protection***

2017 Rank

10th

Out of 17 Cities

Score: –0.112

Rank	City	Score
1	Weihai	1.632
	...	
8	Qingdao	0.330
9	Jinan	0.281
10	Jining	–0.112
11	Dezhou	–0.287
12	Zaozhuang	–0.393
	...	
16	Binzhou	–1.586
17	Heze	–2.142

Jining ranks 10th for Resource Conditions and Environmental Protection with a standardised score of –0.112. This places the city in the Middle Seven Group of 17 cities. Jining is positioned behind Jinan (0.281) at 9th place and well ahead of Dezhou (–0.287) at 11th place.

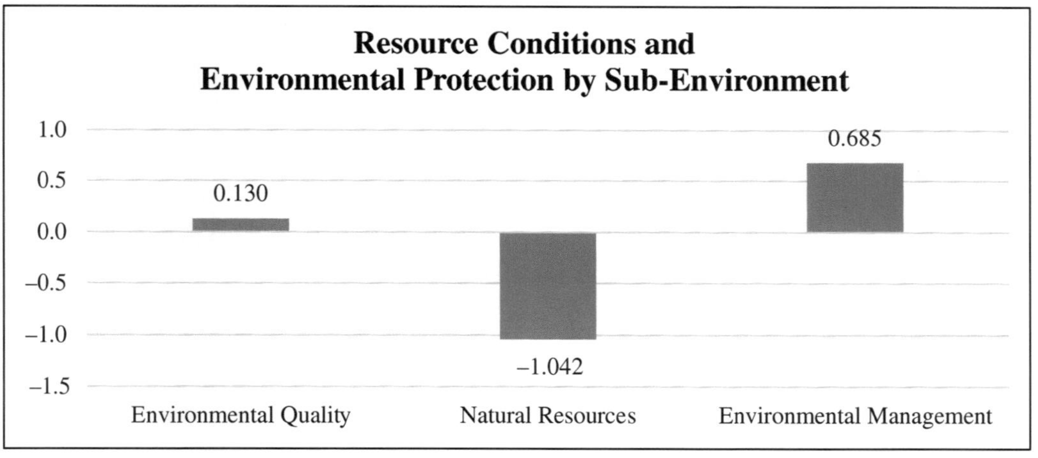

Among the three sub-environments of Resource Conditions and Environmental Protection, Jining performs above the provincial average in two of them and relatively better for Environmental Management, where the indicators of Forest Land Growth and Area of Natural Reserves to Administrative Areas score particularly well. On the other hand, the Natural Resources sub-environment performs below the provincial average and is brought down by low scores in the indicators of Electricity Consumption Per RMB 10,000 GRDP and Per Capita Arable Land.

JINING

Shandong Province

Figure 9.1: Median & Maximum Web for Jining

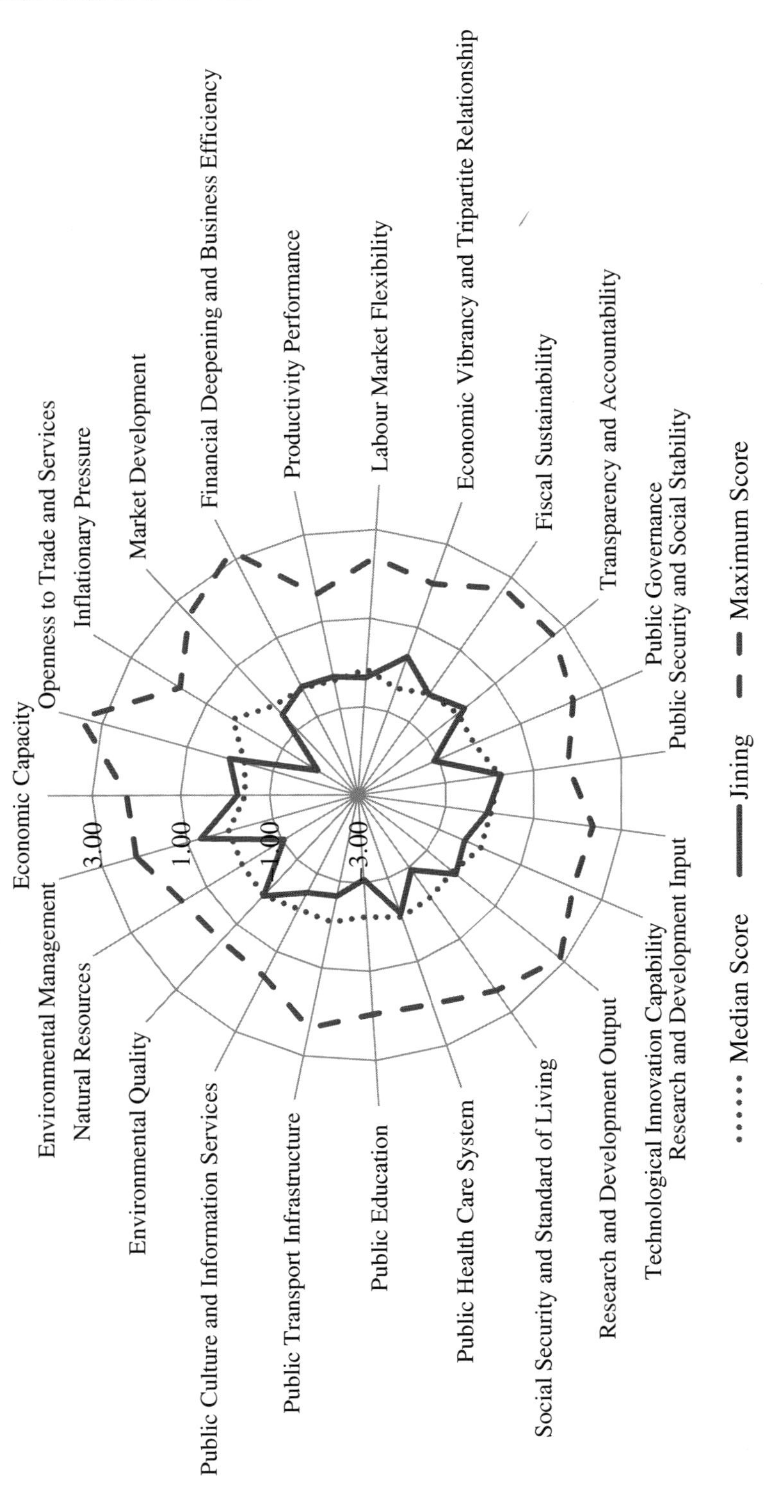

Source: Asia Competitiveness Institute.

9.2.3 Median and Maximum Web Analysis

To better understand Jining's relative strengths and weaknesses, it is useful to compare and contrast its scores for the 23 sub-environments against the median and maximum scores of Shandong's 17 cities.

In Figure 9.1, the median and maximum scores for 17 Shandong cities are shown as dotted and dashed lines respectively, while scores for Jining are shown as a solid line.

Comparison to Median Scores

Jining scores above the median for 10 of the 23 sub-environments, most notably in Economic Vibrancy and Tripartite Relationship and Environmental Management.

On the other hand, it scores below the median in the remaining 13 sub-environments, especially for Inflationary Pressure, Public Governance and Natural Resources.

Comparison to Maximum Scores

Jining scores below the provincial maximum of the 17 Shandong cities in all 23 sub-environments.

Jining's score in the Inflationary Pressure (–1.939) sub-environment is farthest from the maximum, which is held by Heze (1.696). Likewise, Jining's score in the Openness to Trade and Services (0.009) sub-environment is substantially below the provincial maximum, which is held by Qingdao (3.505).

Jining's score in the Environmental Quality (0.130) sub-environment is closest to the maximum, which is held by Qingdao (1.521).

9.3 Summary of Empirical Findings of Jining and *What-if* Urban Development Simulation

9.3.1 Summary of Empirical Findings, 20% Strongest and Weakest Indicators

Overall Performance 13th Score: –0.706		
Scale and Quality of Economic Activities 16th Score: –1.273	Financial Capacity, Labour Market Flexibility and Economic Vibrancy 9th Score: –0.171	Good Governance, Effective Leadership and Social Stability 13th Score: –0.527
Technological Advancement and Innovation Capability 8th Score: –0.222	Public Service Standards and Quality of Life Improvement 13th Score: –0.819	Resource Conditions and Environmental Protection 10th Score: –0.112

(Rank out of 17 cities)

Summary

Jining ranks 13th out of 17 cities in its Overall Performance and performs below the provincial average in all of the six environments. Nevertheless, Jining achieves relatively favourable positions in the environments of Technological Advancement and Innovation Capability, and Financial Capacity, Labour Market Flexibility and Economic Vibrancy, at 8th place and 9th place respectively. In contrast, Jining performs weaker in all the remaining environments, most notably for the environment of Scale and Quality of Economic Activities.

Strengths

As illustrated in Table 9.2, Jining's strengths are spread across the environments of Financial Capacity, Labour Market Flexibility and Economic Vibrancy, Good Governance, Effective Leadership and Social Stability, and Public Service Standards and Quality of Life Improvement, where each of them has six out of 26 of its 20% Strongest Indicators in these environments. Among Jining's best performing indicators are the Percentage of Public Expenditure on Cultural Initiatives, Investment Abroad and Forest Land Growth.

Weaknesses

As observed in Table 9.3, majority of Jining's weakest indicators are in the environment of Public Service Standards and Quality of Life Improvement, with eight out of 26 of its 20% Weakest Indicators falling in this environment. Among Jining's weakest indicators are the Urban Residents' Per Capita Expenditure Growth Rate, Number of Vocational Education Institutions Per 10,000 Population and Satisfaction with Innovation Environment.

JINING

Shandong Province

Table 9.2: 20% Strongest Indicators for Jining

Rank	20% Strongest Indicator	Score	SQEA	FCLMFEV	GGELSS	TAIC	PSSQLI	RCEP
1	Percentage of Public Expenditure on Cultural Initiatives	2.055					✓	
2	Investment Abroad	1.935	✓					
3	Forest Land Growth	1.876						✓
4	Number of Responses to Government Issues of Public Interest	1.564			✓			
5	Number of Provincial-Level Science Parks	1.392				✓		
6	Growth Rate of the Number of Police Cases Solved	1.317			✓			
7	Area of Natural Reserves to Administrative Area (%)	1.030						✓
8	Total R&D Expenditure of Enterprises Above Designated Size as a Percentage of Cash Flow	1.009				✓		
9	Proportion of the Population Above 60 Years Old	0.986					✓	
10	Number of Employees	0.981		✓				
11	Traffic Accident Fatality Per 10,000 Population	0.892			✓			
12	Number of Primary and Secondary Schools Per 10,000 Population	0.838					✓	
13	Ratio of Public Education Appropriation to GRDP	0.826					✓	
14	Growth in the Number of Passengers Transported	0.824		✓				
15	GRDP Growth Rate	0.821	✓					
16	Per Capita Road Area	0.721					✓	
17	Profit Margin of Enterprises Above Designated Size	0.609		✓				
18	Government Expenditures as a Percentage of GRDP	0.576	✓					
19	Growth Rate of Overall Labour Productivity	0.555		✓				
20	Newly Increased Number of Employees	0.501		✓				
21	Fiscal Revenue Growth Rate	0.499			✓			
22	Deepness of Insurance (Insurance Income as a Share of GRDP)	0.387		✓				
23	Fire Fatality Per 10,000 Population	0.387			✓			
24	Public Health and Medical Service Expenses as a Share of GRDP	0.375					✓	
25	Urban Area Waste Water Treatment Rate	0.374						✓
26	Growth Rate of the Number of Police Cases	0.371			✓			

Table 9.3: 20% Weakest Indicators for Jining

Rank	20% Weakest Indicator	Score	SQEA	FCLMFEV	GGELSS	TAIC	PSSQLI	RCEP
106	Number of Urban Taxis Per 10,000 Population	−0.746					✓	
107	Rate of Migration Flow	−0.757		✓				
108	Index For Quality of E-Government System	−0.763			✓			
109	Water Consumption Per RMB 10,000 GRDP	−0.772						✓
110	Public Perception of Government Conduct	−0.791			✓			
111	Tertiary Industry Total Labour Productivity	−0.797		✓				
112	Engel's Index	−0.811					✓	
113	Public Perception of Security	−0.828			✓			
114	Ratio of Teacher to Student in Primary and Secondary Schools	−0.863					✓	
115	Dependency on Foreign Trade (Foreign Trade as a Share of GRDP)	−0.881	✓					
116	Number of Private Cars Per 100 Households	−0.897					✓	
117	Per Capita Arable Land	−0.897						✓
118	Urban Residents' Disposable Income Growth Rate	−0.902	✓					
119	Per Capita Park and Green Space Acreage	−0.936						✓
120	Number of Books in Public Library Per Capita	−0.945					✓	
121	Satisfaction of Public Education System	−1.094					✓	
122	Urban Registered Unemployment Rate	−1.110		✓				
123	Tax Revenue as a Share of Fiscal Revenue	−1.113			✓			
124	Electricity Consumption Per RMB 10,000 GRDP	−1.133						✓
125	Frequency of Using the Internet for Daily Convenience	−1.151					✓	
126	Satisfaction with Business Environment	−1.252	✓					
127	Retail Price Index	−1.342	✓					
128	Average Public Servant Salary	−1.372			✓			
129	Satisfaction with Innovation Environment	−1.389				✓		
130	Number of Vocational Education Institutions Per 10,000 Population	−1.739					✓	
131	Urban Residents' Per Capita Expenditure Growth Rate	−1.847	✓					

Source: Asia Competitiveness Institute.

Notes: SQEA: Scale and Quality of Economic Activities; FCLMFEV: Financial Capacity, Labour Market Flexibility and Economic Vibrancy; GGELSS: Good Governance, Effective Leadership and Social Stability; TAIC: Technological Advancement and Innovation Capability; PSSQLI: Public Service Standards and Quality of Life Improvement; RCEP: Resource Conditions and Environmental Protection.

9.3.2 *What-if* Urban Development Simulation

ACI has devised a simulation methodology to improve the ranking of a particular city by improving on its 20% Weakest Indicators as shown in Table 9.3.[2] The figures below show Jining's ranking and standardised scores before and after the policy-induced simulation. Refer to Tables 3.8 to 3.14 in Section 3.4 of Chapter 3 for a complete list of simulation results for all cities.

Overall Performance

	Before		After
Rank	13th	▶	8th
Score	–0.706		0.169

Scale and Quality of Economic Activities

	Before	After
Rank	16th	8th
Score	–1.273	–0.095

Financial Capacity, Labour Market Flexibility and Economic Vibrancy

	Before	After
Rank	9th	9th
Score	–0.171	0.002

Good Governance, Effective Leadership and Social Stability

	Before	After
Rank	13th	9th
Score	–0.527	0.287

Technological Advancement and Innovation Capability

	Before	After
Rank	8th	8th
Score	–0.222	0.087

Public Service Standards and Quality of Life Improvement

	Before	After
Rank	13th	9th
Score	–0.819	–0.168

Resource Conditions and Environmental Protection

	Before	After
Rank	10th	5th
Score	–0.112	0.628

After the *What-if* simulation, Jining improves its ranking from 13th place to 8th place in terms of its Overall Performance. Likewise, Jining's standardised score increases from –0.706 to 0.169. This leap is plausible if the city manages to successfully address its 20% Weakest Indicators.

The simulation further indicates that Jining may achieve substantial improvement in some of its environments, most notably in Scale and Quality of Economic Activities, and Resource Conditions and Environmental Protection, whose ranks will rise from 16th to 8th and 10th to 5th respectively. Such encouraging results should incentivise Jining to strive to improve the indicators under the 20% Weakest Indicators list. These indicators include the Dependency on Foreign Trade and Electricity Consumption Per RMB 10,000 GRDP.

[2]The methodology for *What-if* simulation is thoroughly explained in Section 2.7 of Chapter 2.

9.4 Concluding Notes: Public Policy Implications[3]

Areas for Commendation

Jining is strongest in the environments of Financial Capacity, Labour Market Flexibility and Economic Vibrancy, Good Governance, Effective Leadership and Social Stability, and Public Service Standards and Quality of Life Improvement, where they collectively contain 18 out of 26 of its 20% Strongest Indicators in these environments, as indicated in Table 9.2.

While Jining does not achieve the maximum score for any sub-environment, it scores above the provincial average in six out of the 23 sub-environments.

As gleaned from the analysis, Jining performs particularly well in the Percentage of Public Expenditure on Cultural Initiatives. This is due in part to the Jining government's investment in cultural activities, such as the Confucius and Mencius cultural tour. In addition, the number of provincial cultural enterprises in Jining is the second best of the 17 Shandong cities, at 407 in 2015. As Jining recognised the need to improve its public education system, it has built, reformed and extended more than 1,300 schools between 2012 and 2016. During the same period, the government had also improved its environmental conditions, including the complete reform of 119 polluted projects and increase in forestland coverage to 30.8%.

Areas for Improvement

As Jining scores below the provincial average in all of the six environments, there is plenty of room for improvement. Most crucially, Jining should address the environment for Public Service Standards and Quality of Life Improvement, as it contains eight out of 26 of its 20% Weakest Indicators, as shown in Table 9.3. Additionally, as gleaned from the *What-if* Urban Development Simulation, the environment for Scale and Quality of Economic Activities should be prioritised because that is the environment in which Jining will achieve the greatest improvement in its ranking — eight positions — relative to other environments.

Moreover, Jining's weakest scores are from the sub-environments of Inflationary Pressure (−1.939) and Public Governance (−1.125).

Despite the fact that the Jining government invested a total of RMB 4.6 billion in primary and secondary schools between 2012 and 2016, it still performs poorly in public education. This suggests that the Jining government should explore other established and effective strategies to improve its public education. For instance, Jining may work on improving the number of vocational education institutions as well as the ratio of teacher to student in primary and secondary schools to achieve this goal.

[3] The relevant statistical data and government policies are from Jining People's Government (2017), China Inspection and Quarantine Times (2017), Phoenix New Media (2017), Cao (2017), Yang (2017), Zheng (2017) and Zhu (2017).

Future Potential Development

In summary, Jining should focus on improving the environment of Public Service Standards and Quality of Life Improvement through greater investment in education and infrastructure. In addition, Jining should look towards developing a more vibrant business sector to improve the environment of Scale and Quality of Economic Activities.

In an effort to strengthen its development in public services, Jining decided to construct 100 Public Service Centres for the Rural Express E-commerce with the purpose of alleviating poverty and strengthening the electronic commerce in 2017. Jining is also working on related industries, such as agricultural products, to deeply integrate with e-commerce. Such an amalgamation can promote agricultural supply-side reform and continuously optimise the economic structure.

Going forward, Jining should implement more measures to push for more business enterprise development by promoting quality management and active consultation. This encourages higher fixed investment and economic activity as a whole. Moreover, the Jining government can also help firms to raise productivity and cost efficiency by providing more training grants for employees as well as to help firms to establish a comprehensive management system. At the same time, as Jining's performance in the sub-environment of Environmental Quality is only slightly above the provincial average, Jining should remember not to sacrifice its environment as it aims to achieve higher economic growth.

References

Cao, Li. 2017. "济宁高新区打造'一刻钟便民生活圈' 居民在社区生活便捷又舒心 Jining High-Tech Industrial Development Zone Has Built a Convenient Living Zone (in Chinese)." November 29, 2017. http://jining.sdchina.com/show/4233592.html.

China Inspection and Quarantine Times. 2017. "山东济宁检验检疫局多措并举服务企业发展 Shandong Jining Inspection and Quarantine Bureau's Efforts on Supporting Enterprise Development (in Chinese)." November 15, 2017. http://www.cqn.com.cn/zggmsb/content/2017-11/15/content_5111328.htm.

Department of Commerce of Shandong Province. n.d. "Jining City." Accessed October 27, 2017. http://en.shandongbusiness.gov.cn/city/73.

Jining People's Government. 2017. "济宁市人民政府2017年政府工作报告 2017 Jining Annual Government Work Report (in Chinese)." February 23, 217AD. http://www.jining.gov.cn/art/2017/3/3/art_2639_246855.html.

———. 2016. "Overview of Jining." March 25, 2016. http://www.jining.gov.cn/col/col6751/index.html.

Phoenix New Media. 2017. "济宁，一座资源型城市的环保转型之路 Transformation of Environmental Protection of a Resource-Based City, Jining (in Chinese)." December 18, 2017. http://finance.ifeng.com/a/20171218/15874999_0.shtml.

Xiaotao, Wang. 2009. "Jining City Introduction." July 23, 2009. http://shandong.chinadaily.com.cn/e/2009-07/23/content_8465382.htm.

Yang, Shulin. 2017. "济宁将建设100处农村快递电商公共服务中心 Jining Will Build 100 Rural Public Service Centers for E-Commerce Express Delivery (in Chinese)." December 12, 2017. http://jining.dzwww.com/2017/xjdnzh/kjn/xwbd/201712/t20171212_16287199.htm.

Zheng, Yan Yan. 2017. "文化济宁:全力推进旅游厕所革命 Cultural Development in Jining: To Improve the Hygiene of Public Toilet (in Chinese)." December 14, 2017. http://tour.dzwww.com/lvnews/201712/t20171214_16779143.htm.

Zhu, Xianping. 2017. "过去五年，济宁都取得了哪些成绩？What Has Jining Acheived in the Past Five Years? (In Chinese)." February 25, 2017. http://jining.dzwww.com/news/jnxw/201702/t20170225_15593678.htm.

Chapter 10: LAIWU
Shandong Province

Location of City

Source: Asia Competitiveness Institute.

10.1 Profile of Laiwu City[1]

Located to the east of the Taishan massif, the geography of the area around the city of Laiwu, which accommodates a total population of 1,375,800 people, is alternatingly mountainous and hilly. While having administrative jurisdiction over only two districts spanning a total area of 2,246 square kilometres — the smallest territory of any city in the province — Laiwu boasts a heritage that extends all the way to the Shang and Zhou Dynasties of early Chinese history. It is particularly well known for its long history as a centre for the smelting and processing of iron, and the production of steel.

In 2016, Laiwu's Gross Regional Domestic Product (GRDP) stood at RMB 70 billion, with the city also boasting a healthy GRDP growth rate of 7.2%, as is reflected in Table 10.1. As noted, Laiwu is rich in iron as well as coal, while also being rich in other mineral resources such as copper, gold, aluminium and zinc. Accordingly, Laiwu's primary sector constituted 7.8% of total GRDP. Laiwu's secondary sector, which constituted 50.2% of GRDP, is strongly dependent on the industries which have served as the backbone of its economy for millennia — iron

[1]The relevant city information are from the Department of Commerce of Shandong Province (n.d.), People's Government of Laiwu City (n.d.) and Yue (2009).

processing and steel production. Finally, the city's tertiary sector is undergoing significant development in the tourism and logistics industries, and constituted 42.0% of total GRDP.

Laiwu is located relatively near to Jinan and thus benefits from easy access to the Jinan Yaoqiang International Airport. Several expressways also run through Laiwu, and while the two railways that service the city cater mainly to freight transport, plans for a rail line which connects Laiwu directly with Jinan are moving forward. Laiwu has also demonstrated a particular dedication towards social welfare, and in 2016 dedicated significant portions of GRDP to both public health care and public education — at a share of 11.6% and a ratio of 2.9% respectively — relative to other cities in the province.

Table 10.1: Key Economic Indicators for Laiwu, 2016

Land Area (km^2)	**2,246**
Population	
Total Population	1,375,800
Urbanisation Rate (%)	61.1
Average Life Expectancy (years)	76.0
Number of Employees (10,000)	112
Workforce Participation Rate (%)	77.7
Gross Regional Domestic Product (GRDP) — 2015 Prices	
GRDP (100 millions of RMB)	703
GRDP Per Capita (RMB)	51,533
GRDP Growth Rate (%)	7.2
Economic Composition	
Primary Sector (% of GRDP)	7.8
Secondary Sector (% of GRDP)	50.2
Tertiary Sector (% of GRDP)	42.0
Trade — 2016 Prices	
Exports (millions of RMB)	6,537
Imports (millions of RMB)	6,064
Dependency on Foreign Trade (%)	16.1
Infrastructure	
Per Capita Road Area (m^2)	29.1
Growth in the Number of Passengers Transported (10,000)	12.0
Growth in the Volume of Cargo Transported (10,000 tons)	582
Environment	
Green Coverage Ratio of Built-up Area (%)	45.2
Environmental Expenditure (% of Total Fiscal Expenditure)	2.1

Source: Asia Competitiveness Institute from the 2017 Shandong Statistical Yearbook.

10.2 In-Depth Urban Development of Laiwu, 2016*

10.2.1 Overall Urban Development Performance

Overall Performance

2017 Rank

16th

Out of 17 Cities

Score: –1.233

Rank	City	Score
1	Qingdao	1.753
	...	
10	Dezhou	–0.302
11	Rizhao	–0.472
12	Heze	–0.615
13	Jining	–0.706
14	Binzhou	–1.076
15	Zaozhuang	–1.164
16	Laiwu	–1.233
17	Liaocheng	–1.576

Laiwu ranks 16th in its Overall Performance, with a standardised score of –1.233. This places the city in the Bottom Five Group of 17 cities. Laiwu is positioned between Zaozhuang (–1.164) at 15th place and Liaocheng (–1.576) at 17th place.

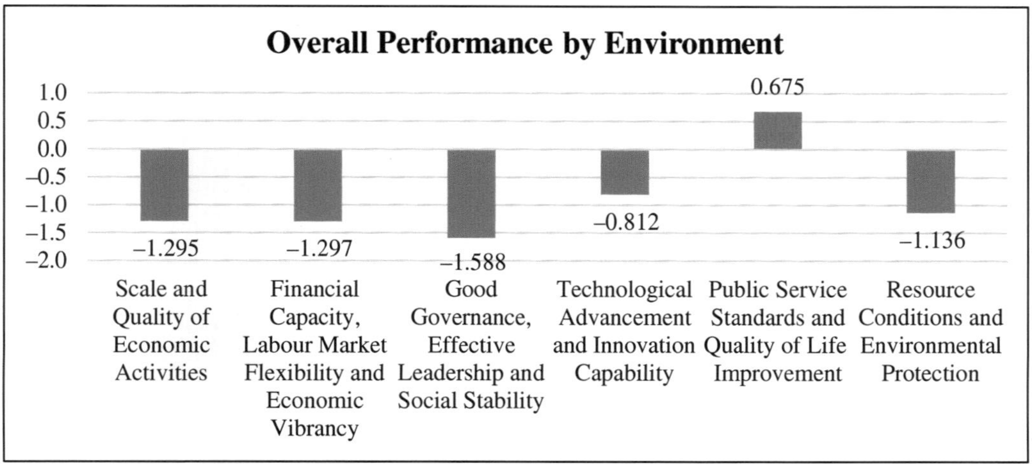

Among the six environments, Laiwu performs above the provincial average in Public Service Standards and Quality of Life Improvement. However, all the remaining environments score well below the provincial average, especially for the environments of Good Governance, Effective Leadership and Social Stability, Financial Capacity, Labour Market Flexibility and Economic Vibrancy and Scale and Quality of Economic Activities.

** For a complete list of rankings, see Tables 3.2 to 3.7 in Section 3.3 of Chapter 3.*

10.2.2 Urban Development within the Six Environments

Rank	City	Score
1	Qingdao	1.987
	...	
10	Zaozhuang	–0.412
11	Binzhou	–0.573
12	Liaocheng	–0.665
13	Zibo	–0.674
14	Dongying	–0.782
15	Rizhao	–1.017
16	Jining	–1.273
17	Laiwu	–1.295

A: ***Scale and Quality of Economic Activities***

2017 Rank

17th

Out of 17 Cities

Score: –1.295

Laiwu ranks 17th for Scale and Quality of Economic Activities, with a standardised score of –1.295. This places the city in the Bottom Five Group of 17 cities. Laiwu is positioned closely behind Jining (–1.273) at 16th place.

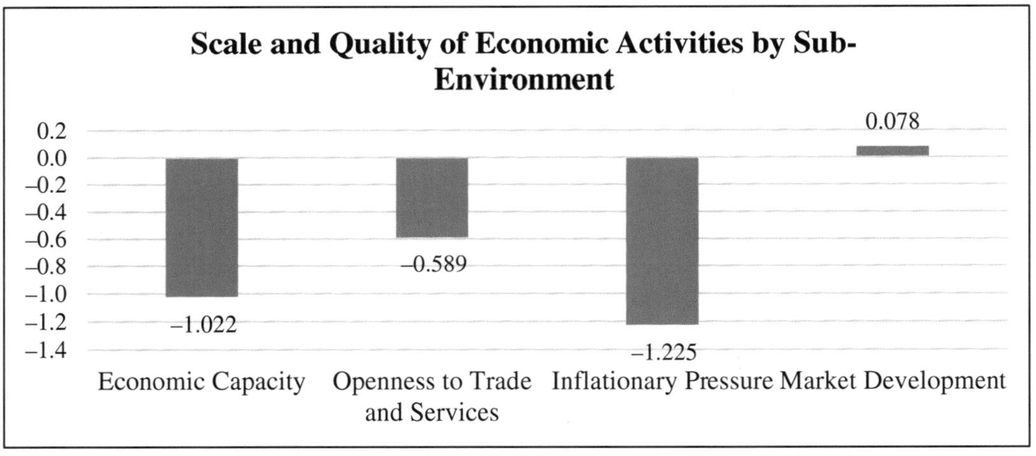

Looking at the four sub-environments of Scale and Quality of Economic Activities, Laiwu performs marginally above the provincial average in Market Development, where there is a relatively good score in the indicator of Government Expenditure as a Percentage of GRDP. However, Laiwu scores below the provincial average in the remaining three sub-environments and especially weaker for Inflationary Pressure and Economic Capacity. Specifically, the indicators of Urban Residents' Disposable Income Growth Rate and Producer Price Index from the Inflationary Pressure sub-environment, as well as the indicators of Gross Regional Domestic Product and Per Capita Fixed Investment from the Economic Capacity sub-environment are significantly low. Nevertheless, the indicator of Consumer Price Index from the Inflationary Pressure sub-environment performs particularly well.

B: *Financial Capacity, Labour Market Flexibility and Economic Vibrancy*

2017 Rank

17th

Out of 17 Cities

Score: –1.297

Rank	City	Score
1	Jinan	2.264
	...	
10	Binzhou	–0.329
11	Rizhao	–0.619
12	Heze	–0.638
13	Tai'an	–0.763
14	Zaozhuang	–0.894
15	Liaocheng	–1.021
16	Dezhou	–1.026
17	Laiwu	–1.297

Laiwu ranks 17th for Financial Capacity, Labour Market Flexibility and Economic Vibrancy, with a standardised score of –1.297. This places the city at the last place and in the Bottom Five Group of 17 cities. Laiwu is positioned behind Dezhou (–1.026) at 16th place.

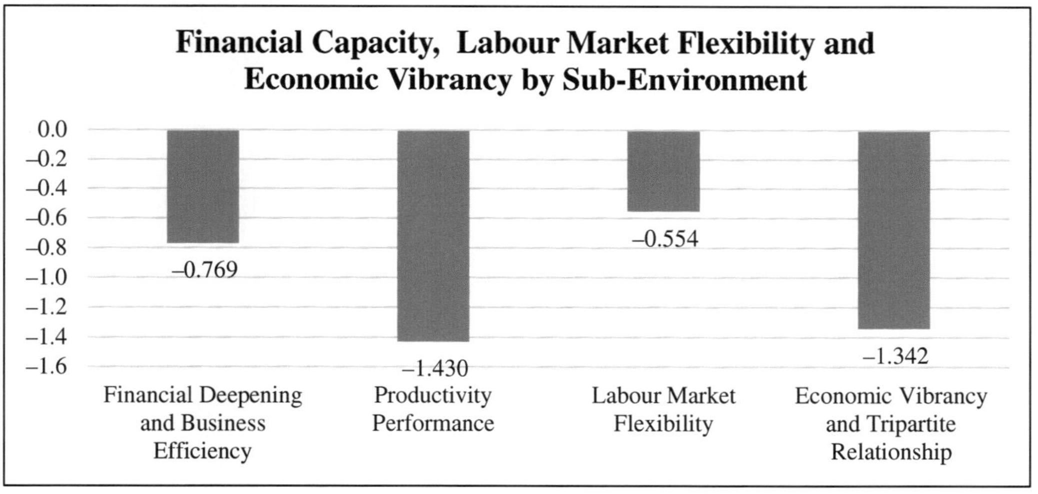

Looking at the four sub-environments of Financial Capacity, Labour Market Flexibility and Economic Vibrancy, Laiwu scores well below the provincial average in all of them and notably poorer for Productivity Performance and Economic Vibrancy and Tripartite Relationship. In particular, the indicators of Profit Margin of Enterprises Above Designated Size from the Productivity Performance sub-environment and Growth in Number of Passengers Transported register significantly low scores. In addition, the indicators of Number of Employees and Newly Increased Number of Employees from the Labour Market Flexibility sub-environment obtain low scores as well. However, the indicator of Proportion of Urban Workers Employed in State Enterprises from the Labour Market Flexibility sub-environment performs exceptionally well.

LAIWU

Shandong Province

Rank	City	Score
1	Dezhou	1.465
	...	
10	Yantai	0.192
11	Dongying	0.173
12	Rizhao	0.042
13	Jining	–0.527
14	Binzhou	–0.849
15	Zaozhuang	–1.302
16	Laiwu	–1.588
17	Liaocheng	–2.473

C: ***Good Governance, Effective Leadership and Social Stability***

2017 Rank

16th

Out of 17 Cities

Score: –1.588

Laiwu ranks 16th for Good Governance, Effective Leadership and Social Stability with a standardised score of –1.588. This places the city in the Bottom Five Group of 17 cities. Laiwu is positioned between Zaozhuang (–1.302) at 15th place and well ahead of Liaocheng (–2.473) at 17th place.

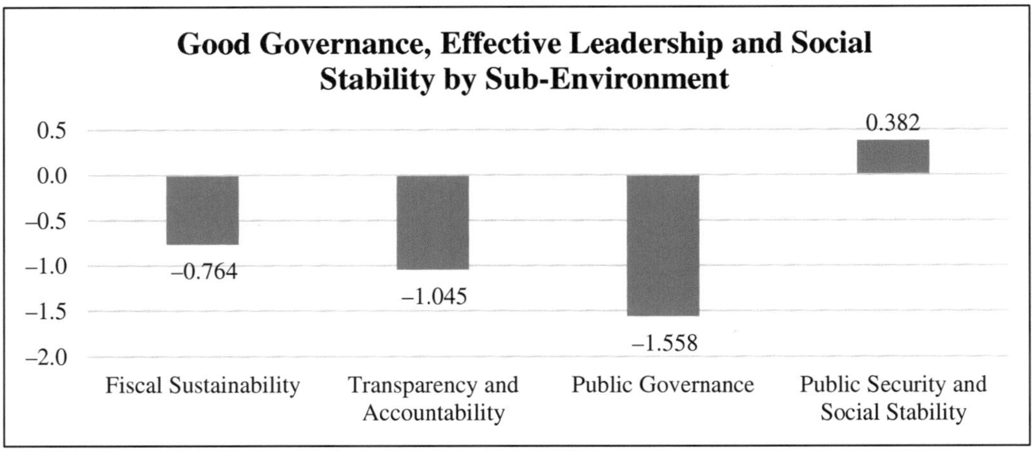

Among the four sub-environments of Good Governance, Effective Leadership and Social Stability, Laiwu scores above the provincial average and relatively better in Public Security and Social Stability, where the indicators for Growth Rate of the Number of Police Cases Solved and Fire Fatality Per 10,000 Population perform relatively well. However, Laiwu scores below the provincial average in the remaining three sub-environments and most notably for Public Governance, where the indicator of the Number of Public Servants Per 10,000 Population scores especially weaker. In addition, the indicator of the Number of Releases of Government Information for Public Viewing from the Transparency and Accountability sub-environment performs particularly poorly.

D: *Technological Advancement and Innovation Capability*

2017 Rank

13th

Out of 17 Cities

Score: –0.812

Rank	City	Score
1	Qingdao	2.176
	...	
10	Tai'an	–0.457
11	Dezhou	–0.517
12	Binzhou	–0.559
13	Laiwu	–0.812
14	Heze	–0.897
15	Rizhao	–1.155
16	Zaozhuang	–1.192
17	Liaocheng	–1.221

Laiwu ranks 13th for Technological Advancement and Innovation Capability, with a standardised score of –0.812. This places the city in the Bottom Five Group of 17 cities. Laiwu is positioned between Binzhou (–0.559) at 12th place and Heze (–0.897) at 14th place.

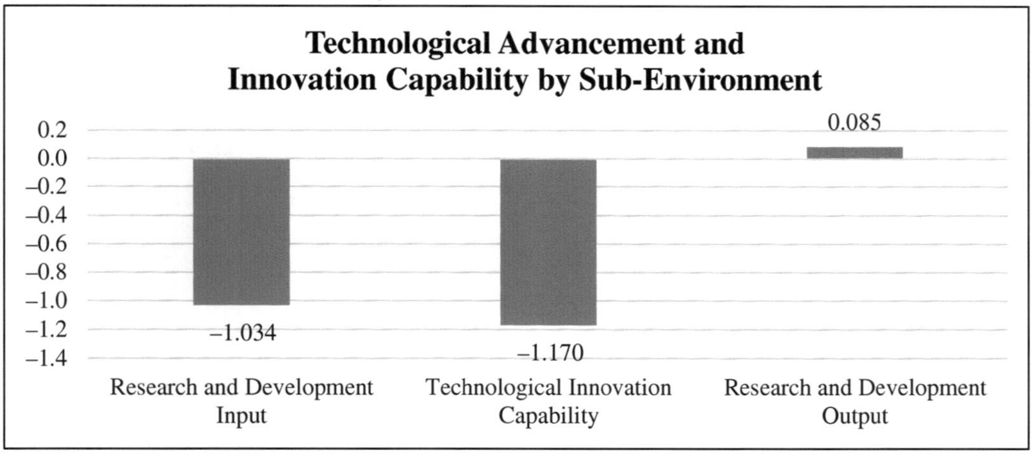

Among the three sub-environments of Technological Advancement and Innovation Capability, Laiwu performs above the provincial average in Research and Development Output, where the indicator of the Number of Existing Patents Per 10,000 Population scores well. However, Laiwu performs well below the provincial average in the remaining two sub-environments, where the indicators of Total Research and Development Expenditure of Enterprises above Designated Size as a Percentage of Cash Flow from the Research and Development Input sub-environment and Number of Provincial-Level Science Parks from the Technological Innovation Capability sub-environment score poorly.

LAIWU

Shandong Province

Rank	City	Score
1	Dongying	1.689
	...	
4	Jinan	0.919
5	Zibo	0.794
6	Laiwu	0.675
7	Qingdao	0.593
8	Yantai	0.251
	...	
16	Dezhou	−1.066
17	Liaocheng	−1.964

E: *Public Service Standards and Quality of Life Improvement*

2017 Rank

6th

Out of 17 Cities

Score: 0.675

Laiwu ranks 6th for Public Service Standards and Quality of Life Improvement with a standardised score of 0.675. This places the city in the Middle Seven Group of 17 cities. Laiwu is positioned between Zibo (0.794) at 5th place and Qingdao (0.593) at 7th place.

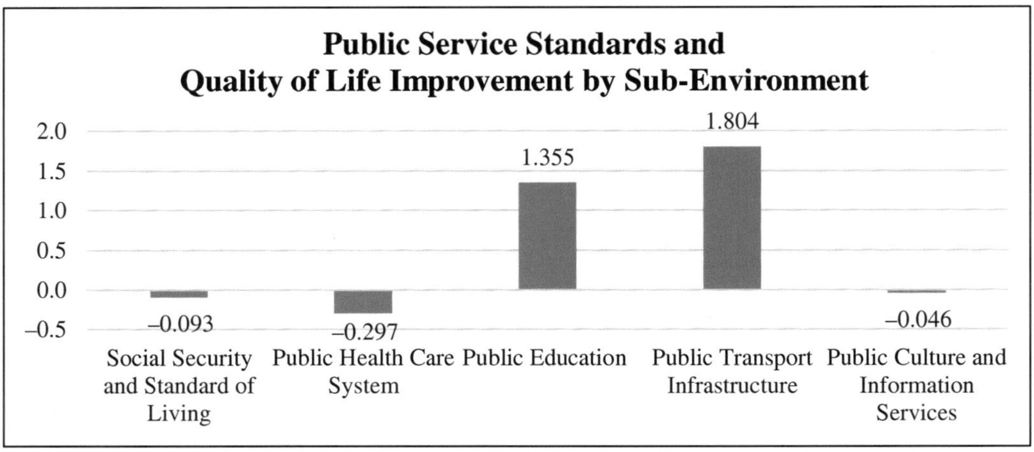

Among the five sub-environments of Public Service Standards and Quality of Life Improvement, Laiwu performs above the provincial average in two of them and exceptionally well in Public Transport Infrastructure, where the indicators of Number of Urban Public Transport Vehicles Per 10,000 Population and Satisfaction of Public Transport Services register high scores. Further, Laiwu scores exceptionally well in the indicator of Number of Vocational Education Institutions Per 10,000 Population from the Public Education sub-environment. However, Laiwu scores relatively lower and below the provincial average in the remaining three sub-environments. In particular, the indicator of Percentage of Public Expenditure on Cultural Intiatives in the Public Culture and Information Services sub-environment is notably low.

F: ***Resource Conditions and Environmental Protection***

2017 Rank

15th

Out of 17 Cities

Score: –1.136

Rank	City	Score
1	Weihai	1.632
	...	
10	Jining	–0.112
11	Dezhou	–0.287
12	Zaozhuang	–0.393
13	Linyi	–0.512
14	Weifang	–0.814
15	Laiwu	–1.136
16	Binzhou	–1.586
17	Heze	–2.142

Laiwu ranks 15th for Resource Conditions and Environmental Protection with a standardised score of –1.136. This places the city at the in the Bottom Five Group of 17 cities. Laiwu is positioned between Weifang (–0.814) at 14th place and Binzhou (–1.586) at 16th place.

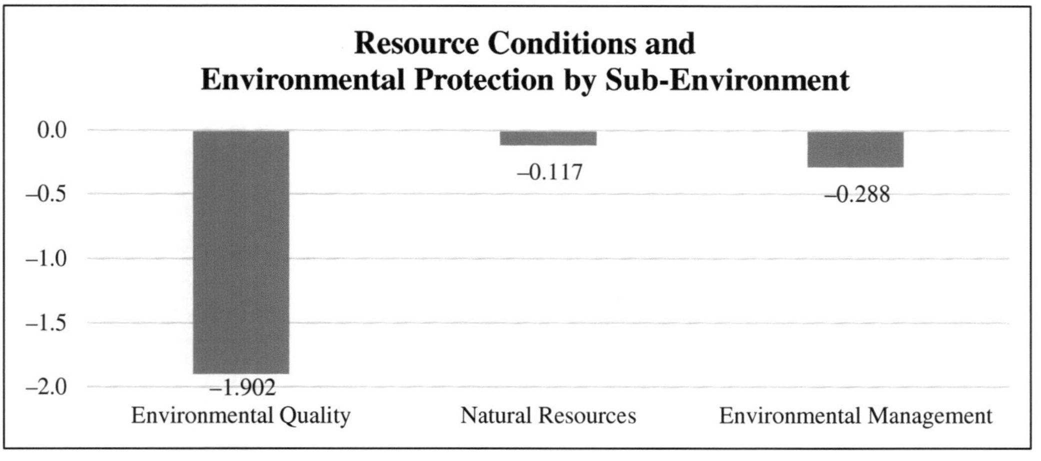

Looking at the three sub-environments of Resource Conditions and Environmental Protection, Laiwu performs below the provincial average in all of them and exceptionally weaker in the sub-environment of Environmental Quality, where the indicators of Sulphur Dioxide Emissions Per RMB 10,000 GRDP and Nitrogen Oxide Emissions Per RMB 10,000 GRDP score particularly low. In addition, the indicators of Urban Area Waste Water Treatment Rate and Forest Land Growth from the Environmental Management sub-environment perform poorly as well. Nevertheless, Laiwu performs relatively better in the Natural Resources sub-environment, where the indicator of Per Capita Freshwater Resource obtains a particularly high score. Further, the indicator of Per Capita Park and Green Space Acreage from the Environmental Management sub-environment registers a high score as well.

LAIWU

Shandong Province

Figure 10.1: Median & Maximum Web for Laiwu

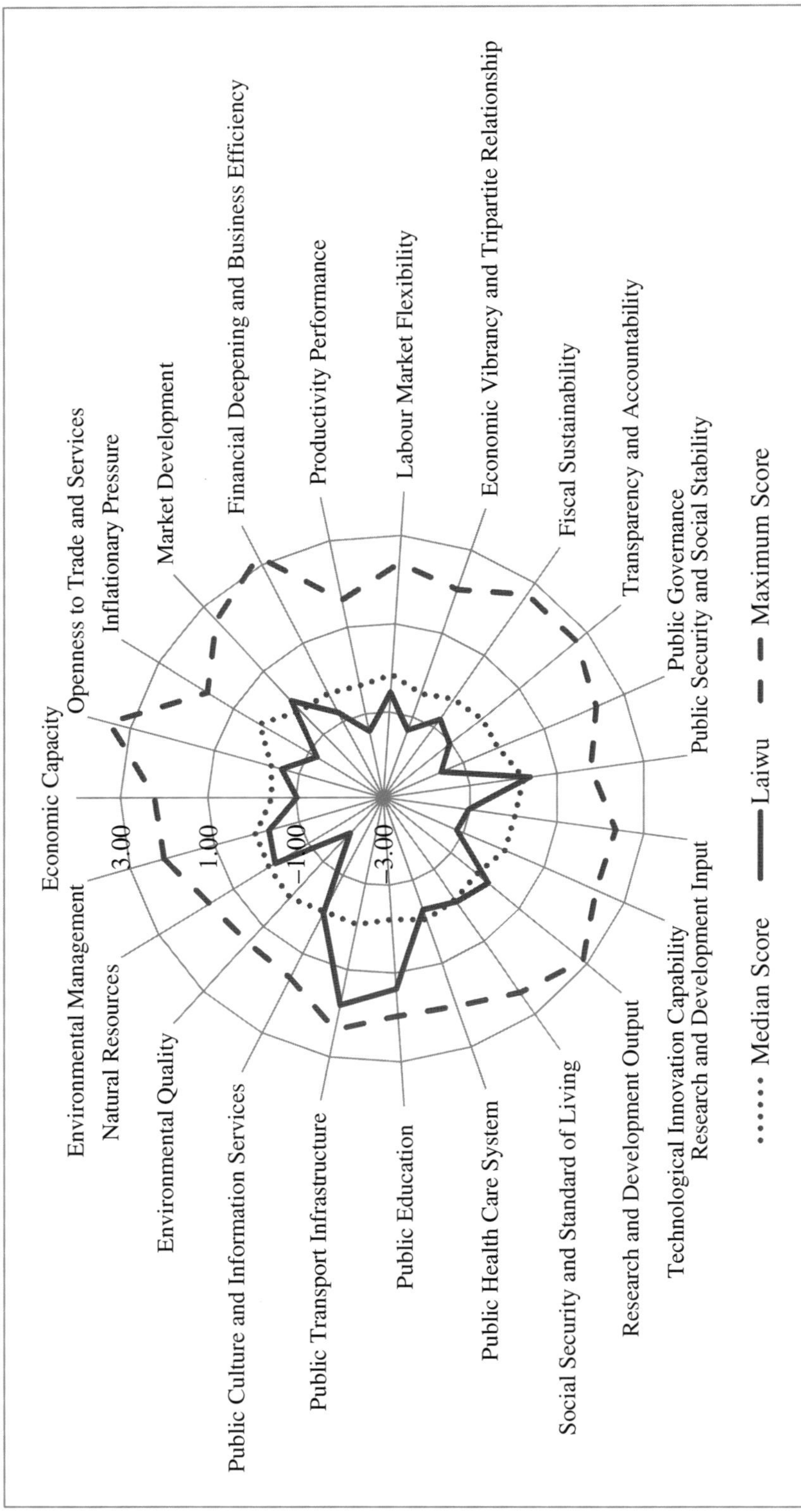

Source: Asia Competitiveness Institute.

10.2.3 Median and Maximum Web Analysis

To better understand Laiwu's relative strengths and weaknesses, it is useful to compare and contrast its scores for the 23 sub-environments against the median and maximum scores of Shandong's 17 cities.

In Figure 10.1, the median and maximum scores for 17 Shandong cities are shown as dotted and dashed lines respectively, while scores for Laiwu are shown as a solid line.

Comparison to Median Scores

Laiwu scores above the median for seven of the 23 sub-environments, most notably in Public Transport Infrastructure and Public Education.

On the other hand, it scores below the median for 16 of the 23 sub-environments, especially for Public Governance, Environmental Quality and Inflationary Pressure.

Comparison to Maximum Scores

Laiwu scores below the provincial maximum of the 17 Shandong cities in all 23 sub-environments.

Laiwu's score in Openness to Trade and Services (–0.589) is farthest from the maximum, which is held by Qingdao (3.505). Further, Laiwu's score in Public Transport Infrastructure (1.804) is closest to the maximum, which is held by Weihai (2.368).

10.3 Summary of Empirical Findings of Laiwu and *What-if* Urban Development Simulation

10.3.1 Summary of Empirical Findings, 20% Strongest and Weakest Indicators

Overall Performance **16th** Score: –1.233		
Scale and Quality of Economic Activities **17th** Score: –1.295	Financial Capacity, Labour Market Flexibility and Economic Vibrancy **17th** Score: –1.297	Good Governance, Effective Leadership and Social Stability **16th** Score: –1.588
Technological Advancement and Innovation Capability **13th** Score: –0.812	Public Service Standards and Quality of Life Improvement **6th** Score: 0.675	Resource Conditions and Environmental Protection **15th** Score: –1.136

(Rank out of 17 cities)

Summary

Laiwu ranks 16th out of 17 cities in its Overall Performance. Further, Laiwu performs below the provincial average in five out of six environments, of which its weakest environments are the Scale and Quality of Economic Activities, Financial Capacity, Labour Market Flexibility and Economic Vibrancy, both at 17th place. On the other hand, the environment of Public Service Standards and Quality of Life Improvement performs above the provincial average at 6th place.

Strengths

As illustrated in Table 10.2, Laiwu's strength lies in the environment of Public Service Standards and Quality of Life Improvement, with 13 out of 26 of its 20% Strongest Indicators under this environment. Among its best performing indicators are the Number of Museums Per 10,000 Population, Per Capita Freshwater Resource and Number of Vocational Education Institutions Per 10,000 Population.

Weaknesses

As observed in Table 10.3, Laiwu is weak in the environments of Financial Capacity, Labour Market Flexibility and Economic Vibrancy and Resource Conditions and Environmental Protection, with each having six out of 26 of the city's 20% Weakest Indicators. Among Laiwu's worst performing indicators are the Nitrogen Oxide Emissions Per RMB 10,000 GRDP, Profit Margin of Enterprises Above Designated Size and Urban Residents' Disposable Income Growth Rate.

Table 10.2: 20% Strongest Indicators for Laiwu

Rank	20% Strongest Indicator	Score	SQEA	FCLMFEV	GGELSS	TAIC	PSSQLI	RCEP
1	Number of Museums Per 10,000 Population	2.340					✓	
2	Per Capita Freshwater Resource	2.309						✓
3	Number of Vocational Education Institutions Per 10,000 Population	2.269					✓	
4	Number of Urban Public Transport Vehicles Per 10,000 Population (Standard Number)	2.072					✓	
5	Proportion of Urban Workers Employed in State Enterprises	1.995		✓				
6	Per Capita Park and Green Space Acreage	1.922						✓
7	Satisfaction of Public Transport Services	1.672					✓	
8	Consumer Price Index (CPI)	1.444	✓					
9	Number of Urban Taxis Per 10,000 Population	1.330					✓	
10	Green Coverage Ratio of Built-up Area	0.986						✓
11	Number of Existing Patents Per 10,000 Population	0.857				✓		
12	Growth Rate of the Number of Police Cases Solved	0.855			✓			
13	Satisfaction of Public Education System	0.847					✓	
14	Ratio of Public Education Appropriation to GRDP	0.845					✓	
15	Engel's Index	0.760					✓	
16	Research & Development Expenditure as a Share of Government Expenditure	0.709				✓		
17	Public Health and Medical Service Expenses as a Share of GRDP	0.684					✓	
18	Fire Fatality Per 10,000 Population	0.658			✓			
19	Per Capita Road Area	0.627					✓	
20	Satisfaction of Traffic Conditions	0.621					✓	
21	Ratio of Teacher to Student in Primary and Secondary Schools	0.593					✓	
22	Manufacturing Sector as a Percentage of GRDP	0.463	✓					
23	Satisfaction with Urban Management Personnels	0.438			✓			
24	Average Years of Education Received	0.438					✓	
25	Satisfaction of the Police Services	0.364			✓			
26	Fiscal Revenue Growth Rate	0.314			✓			

Table 10.3: 20% Weakest Indicators for Laiwu

Rank	20% Weakest Indicator	Score	SQEA	FCLMFEV	GGELSS	TAIC	PSSQLI	RCEP
106	Growth in the Volume of Cargo Transported	−1.067		✓				
107	Forest Land Growth	−1.077						✓
108	Insurance Net Income	−1.115		✓				
109	Government Fiscal Revenue	−1.128			✓			
110	Ammoniacal Nitrogen Discharge Per RMB 10,000 GRDP	−1.133						✓
111	Total R&D Expenditure of Enterprises Above Designated Size	−1.187				✓		
112	Urban Residents' Per Capita Expenditure Growth Rate	−1.258	✓					
113	Built-up Area Population Density	−1.286						✓
114	Government Fiscal Expenditure	−1.331			✓			
115	Producer Price Index (PPI)	−1.346	✓					
116	Newly Increased Number of Employees	−1.372		✓				
117	Percentage of Public Expenditure on Cultural Initiatives	−1.379					✓	
118	Growth in the Number of Passengers Transported	−1.383		✓				
119	Number of Public Servants Per 10,000 Population	−1.403			✓			
120	Number of Passengers Transported	−1.430					✓	
121	Number of Releases of Government Information for Public Viewing	−1.458			✓			
122	Urban Area Waste Water Treatment Rate	−1.476						✓
123	Gross Regional Domestic Product	−1.489	✓					
124	Per Capita Fixed Investment	−1.507	✓					
125	Number of Employees	−1.684		✓				
126	Total R&D Expenditure of Enterprises Above Designated Size as a Percentage of Cash Flow	−1.714				✓		
127	SO2 Emission Per RMB 10,000 GRDP	−1.807						✓
128	Number of Provincial-Level Science Parks	−1.872				✓		
129	Urban Residents' Disposable Income Growth Rate	−2.086	✓					
130	Profit Margin of Enterprises Above Designated Size	−2.160		✓				
131	NO-X Emissions Per RMB 10,000 GRDP	−2.687						✓

Source: Asia Competitiveness Institute.

Notes: SQEA: Scale and Quality of Economic Activities; FCLMFEV: Financial Capacity, Labour Market Flexibility and Economic Vibrancy; GGELSS: Good Governance, Effective Leadership and Social Stability; TAIC: Technological Advancement and Innovation Capability; PSSQLI: Public Service Standards and Quality of Life Improvement; RCEP: Resource Conditions and Environmental Protection.

10.3.2 *What-if* Urban Development Simulation

ACI has devised a simulation methodology to improve the ranking of a particular city by improving on its 20% Weakest Indicators as shown in Table 10.3.[2] The figures below show Laiwu's ranking and standardised scores before and after the policy-induced simulation. Refer to Tables 3.8 to 3.14 in Section 3.4 of Chapter 3 for a complete list of simulation results for all cities.

Overall Performance

	Before		After
Rank	16th	▶	9th
Score	–1.233		–0.116

Scale and Quality of Economic Activities

	Before	After
Rank	17th	8th
Score	–1.295	–0.223

Financial Capacity, Labour Market Flexibility and Economic Vibrancy

	Before	After
Rank	17th	11th
Score	–1.297	–0.516

Good Governance, Effective Leadership and Social Stability

	Before	After
Rank	16th	14th
Score	–1.588	–0.755

Technological Advancement and Innovation Capability

	Before	After
Rank	13th	8th
Score	–0.812	–0.155

Public Service Standards and Quality of Life Improvement

	Before	After
Rank	6th	5th
Score	0.675	0.847

Resource Conditions and Environmental Protection

	Before	After
Rank	15th	8th
Score	–1.136	0.293

After the *What-if* simulation, Laiwu improves its ranking from 16th to 9th in terms of its Overall Performance. Likewise, its standardised score increases from –1.233 to –0.116. This leap is plausible if the city manages to successfully address its 20% Weakest Indicators.

The simulation further underscores Laiwu's potential for substantial improvement in some of its environments, most notably in Scale and Quality of Economic Activities and Resource Conditions and Environmental Protection, where its rank rises from 17th to 8th and 15th to 8th respectively. Such encouraging results should incentivise Laiwu to strive to improve the indicators under its 20% Weakest Indicators list. These indicators include Per Capita Fixed Investment, Nitrogen Oxide Emissions Per 10,000 GRDP and Forest Land Growth.

[2]The methodology for *What-if* simulation is thoroughly explained in Section 2.7 of Chapter 2.

10.4 Concluding Notes: Public Policy Implications[3]

Areas for Commendation

Laiwu performs well in the environment of Public Service Standards and Quality of Life Improvement, with 13 out of 26 of its 20% Strongest Indicators in this environment, as indicated in Table 10.2.

While Laiwu does not achieve the maximum score for any sub-environment, it scores above the provincial average in five out of 23 sub-environments.

In the period from 2012 to 2016, Laiwu has made measurable progress in the quality of life of its residents. Laiwu's disposable income per capita growth rate of its urban and rural residents was 9.06% and 10.65% respectively on average across the five years. Moreover, in the same period, the Laiwu government's poverty reduction campaign successfully raised the standard of living of 43,000 residents. Laiwu's strength in Public Service Standards and Quality of Life lies primarily in its provision of public transportation and education. The road density in Laiwu has increased by 13% from 2012 to 2016. In terms of education, the Laiwu government has invested RMB 1.12 billion since 2015 to address the issue of "Large Class Size" in primary and middle schools. By the end of 2017, the number of teachers have increased by 1000 and 22 new schools have been constructed.

Areas for Improvement

As Laiwu scores below the provincial average in five out of the six environments, there are plenty of areas for improvement for the city. Most crucially, Laiwu should address the environments of Financial Capacity, Labour Market Flexibility and Economic Vibrancy, and Resource Conditions and Environmental Protection, as they collectively contain 12 out of 26 of its 20% Weakest Indicators, as shown in Table 10.3. Additionally, as gleaned from the *What-if* Urban Development Simulation, the environments of Scale and Quality of Economic Activities and Resource Conditions and Environmental Protection should be prioritised as those are the environments Laiwu may achieve the greatest improvement in rankings — nine and seven positions respectively — relative to other environments.

Further, Laiwu scores below the provincial average in 18 out of 23 sub-environments and obtains the weakest score among all Shandong cities in six out of the 23 sub-environments, namely Environmental Quality (−1.902), Public Governance (−1.558), Productivity Performance (−1.430) and Economic Vibrancy and Tripartite Relationship (−1.342).

As our analysis shows that Laiwu performs poorly in the indicator of Per Capita Fixed Investment, it suggests a lack of investment activities in the city that constraints its economic capacity. In view of this, the Laiwu administration has promised to innovate its financial industry and expand financing channels for both the local government and enterprises to stimulate

[3]The relevant statistical data and government policies are from Laiwu Municipal Bureau of Statistics (2017) and People's Government of Laiwu City (2017).

investment in the economy. The Laiwu government also understands the necessity for environmental protection. As such, it plans to afforest more than 26 square kilometres, so that the forest coverage ratio will reach 36%.

Future Potential Development

In summary, Laiwu's results and ranking exhibit a general weakness across all environments. Nevertheless, as noted in our analysis, Laiwu has a few areas to focus on. First, Laiwu may focus on improving the environment of Financial Capacity, Labour Market Flexibility and Economic Vibrancy by investing more in human capital and promoting a more business-friendly environment. Second, Laiwu should look to improve the environment of Resource Conditions and Environmental Protection by enforcing regulations that prohibit the emission of harmful gases while at the same time promoting more green spaces. Finally, Laiwu should work on the environment of Good Governance, Effective Leadership and Social Stability by raising the standards of its civil service while ensuring that its public finances are kept in check.

The Laiwu government should strive for a solid foundation for future growth and development by promoting technological innovation and incentives for enterprises to upgrade themselves. For example, allocating more funds and support for start-ups in Laiwu will encourage innovation in the city, which can bring positive impact to its economy. The Laiwu government should also aim to strengthen the environment of Resource Conditions and Environmental Protection. For instance, it should strengthen its pollution regulations, promote the efficient and environment-friendly utilisation of coal, and refrain from stubble burning. To improve the standard of government service, the Laiwu administration should increase its transparency by releasing more information for public reviewing. Moreover, Laiwu should continue its efforts to reduce poverty in rural areas through skills upgrading workshops for its rural residents.

References

Department of Commerce of Shandong Province. n.d. 'Laiwu City'. Accessed 3 November 2017. http://en.shandongbusiness.gov.cn/city/75.

Laiwu Municipal Bureau of Statistics. 2017. '2016年莱芜市国民经济和社会发展统计公报 2016 Laiwu Economic and Social Development Statistical Report (in Chinese)'. 10 March 2017. http://www.lwtjj.gov.cn/art/2017/3/10/art_1851_156831.html.

People's Government of Laiwu City. 2017. '2017年莱芜市政府工作报告 2017 Laiwu Annual Government Work Report (in Chinese)'. 28 February 2017. http://www.laiwu.gov.cn/art/2017/2/28/art_783_155651.html.

People's Government of Laiwu City. 2017. '我市大班额消控任务基本完成 The Groundwork for Eliminating and Controlling Large Class Size in Our City has been Completed (in Chinese)'. 22 December 2017. http://www.laiwu.gov.cn/art/2017/12/22/art_21_196952.html.

———. n.d. 'Laiwu Info'. Accessed 3 November 2017. http://en.laiwu.gov.cn/.

Yue, Yuan. 2009. 'Laiwu'. Shandong China, the Hometown of Confucius. 23 July 2009. http://www.chinadaily.com.cn/m/shandong/e/2009-07/23/content_8465204.htm.

Chapter 11: LIAOCHENG
Shandong Province

Location of City

Source: Asia Competitiveness Institute.

11.1 Profile of Liaocheng City[1]

Situated on the Grand Canal, which threads through the centre of the city alongside several other rivers, Liaocheng is known as "the water city" and boasts a heritage that echoes far back into Chinese history. The city directly administers one district, one county-level city and six counties, spanning a total land area of 8,628 square kilometres and a total population of 6,036,800. The city is also notably located on Shandong's border with both Henan and Hebei provinces, making it a vital artery by which goods and people flow into and out of the province.

In 2016, Liaocheng's Gross Regional Domestic Product (GRDP) stood at RMB 286 billion, and the city boasted a healthy GRDP growth rate of 7.3%, as is reflected in Table 11.1. Liaocheng is rich in mineral and energy resources, and its primary sector constituted 11.8% of total GRDP. The city's secondary sector, which constituted 49.5% of total GRDP, is dependent on industries, such as aluminium and copper processing, energy, automobile manufacturing, textiles and food processing. Finally, Liaocheng's tertiary sector, which is dependent on its extant advantages as a commercial and logistics hub as well as its popularity with tourists, constituted 38.7% of GRDP.

Liaocheng is located relatively near to Jinan and thus benefits from relative ease of access to Jinan Yaoqiang International Airport. Because of Liaocheng's advantageous location and

[1] The relevant city information are from the Department of Commerce of Shandong Province (n.d.) and Shi (2017).

status as a regional transport hub, it benefits from connectivity to nearby cities in the region and is well situated on regional high-speed rail and highway networks. Liaocheng is also the city which devoted the greatest proportion of its total fiscal expenditure in 2016 to initiatives and programs relating to environmental concerns, with environmental expenditure comprising 8.9% of total expenditures. This in turn demonstrates the city's dedication to maintaining and improving its natural environment, so as to ensure that it remains sustainable for future generations.

Table 11.1: Key Economic Indicators for Liaocheng, 2016

Land Area (km^2)	**8,628**
Population	
Total Population	6,036,800
Urbanisation Rate (%)	48.5
Average Life Expectancy (years)	75.1
Number of Employees (10,000)	411
Workforce Participation Rate (%)	81.0
Gross Regional Domestic Product (GRDP) — 2015 Prices	
GRDP (100 millions of RMB)	2,859
GRDP Per Capita (RMB)	47,624
GRDP Growth Rate (%)	7.3
Economic Composition	
Primary Sector (% of GRDP)	11.8
Secondary Sector (% of GRDP)	49.5
Tertiary Sector (% of GRDP)	38.7
Trade — 2016 Prices	
Exports (millions of RMB)	16,850
Imports (millions of RMB)	16,847
Dependency on Foreign Trade (%)	13.0
Infrastructure	
Per Capita Road Area (m^2)	27.7
Growth in the Number of Passengers Transported (10,000)	86.0
Growth in the Volume of Cargo Transported (10,000 tons)	1,473
Environment	
Green Coverage Ratio of Built-up Area (%)	44.8
Environmental Expenditure (% of Total Fiscal Expenditure)	8.9

Source: Asia Competitiveness Institute from the 2017 Shandong Statistical Yearbook.

11.2 In-Depth Urban Development of Liaocheng, 2016*

11.2.1 Overall Urban Development Performance

Overall Performance

2017 Rank

17th

Out of 17 Cities

Score: –1.576

Rank	City	Score
1	Qingdao	1.753
	...	
10	Dezhou	–0.302
11	Rizhao	–0.472
12	Heze	–0.615
13	Jining	–0.706
14	Binzhou	–1.076
15	Zaozhuang	–1.164
16	Laiwu	–1.233
17	Liaocheng	–1.576

Liaocheng ranks 17th in its Overall Performance, with a standardised score of –1.576. This places the city at the last place and in the Bottom Five Group of 17 cities. Liaocheng is positioned below Laiwu (–1.233) at 16th place.

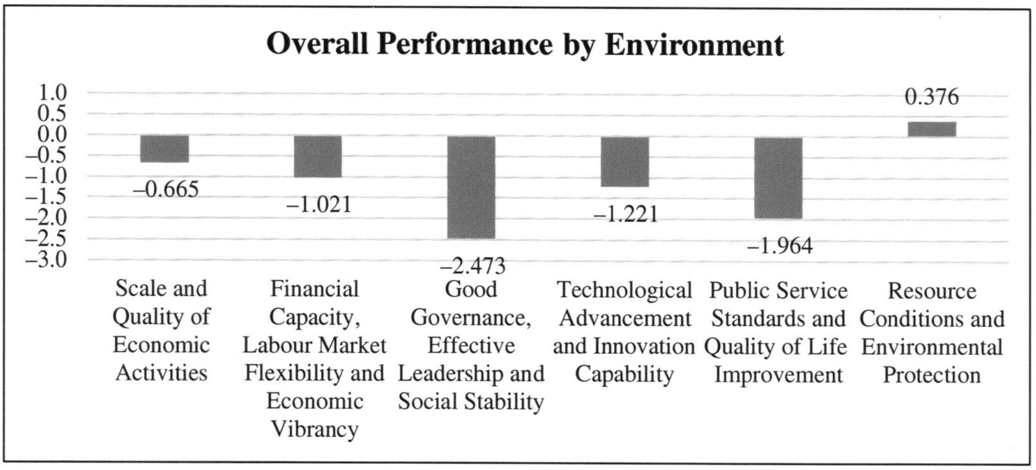

Among the six environments, Liaocheng performs below the provincial average in five of them and most notably in three environments, which all rank last among the 17 Shandong cities. They are namely the environments of Good Governance, Effective Leadership and Social Stability, Technological Advancement and Innovation Capability, and Public Service Standards and Quality of Life Improvement. Liaocheng performs above the provincial average only in the environment of Resource Condition and Environmental Protection.

For a complete list of rankings, see Tables 3.2 to 3.7 in Section 3.3 of Chapter 3.

11.2.2 Urban Development within the Six Environments

Rank	City	Score
1	Qingdao	1.987
	...	
10	Zaozhuang	–0.412
11	Binzhou	–0.573
12	Liaocheng	–0.665
13	Zibo	–0.674
14	Dongying	–0.782
	...	
16	Jining	–1.273
17	Laiwu	–1.295

A: ***Scale and Quality of Economic Activities***

2017 Rank

12th

Out of 17 Cities

Score: –0.665

Liaocheng ranks 12th for Scale and Quality of Economic Activities, with a standardised score of –0.665. This places the city in the Middle Seven Group of 17 cities. Liaocheng is positioned between Binzhou (–0.573) at 11th place and Zibo (–0.674) at 13th place.

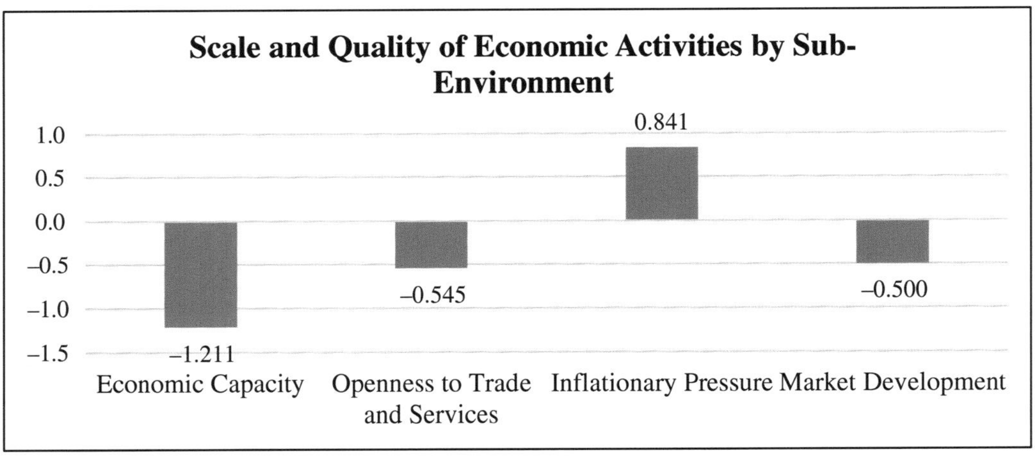

Looking at the four sub-environments of Scale and Quality of Economic Activities, Liaocheng performs above the provincial average in Inflationary Pressure, where the indicators of Urban Residents' Per Capita Expenditure Growth Rate and Consumer Price Index perform relatively well. However, Liaocheng performs below the provincial average in the remaining three sub-environments and particularly poorly in Economic Capacity, where the indicators of Urbanisation Rate and Per Capita Volume of Retail Sales score poorly. Additionally, the indicator of Satisfaction with Business Environment from the Economic Capacity sub-environment has a notably low score.

B: ***Financial Capacity, Labour Market Flexibility and Economic Vibrancy***

2017 Rank

15th

Out of 17 Cities

Score: –1.021

Rank	City	Score
1	Jinan	2.264
	…	
10	Binzhou	–0.329
11	Rizhao	–0.619
12	Heze	–0.638
13	Tai'an	–0.763
14	Zaozhuang	–0.894
15	Liaocheng	–1.021
16	Dezhou	–1.026
17	Laiwu	–1.297

Liaocheng ranks 15th for Financial Capacity, Labour Market Flexibility and Economic Vibrancy, with a standardised score of –1.021. This places the city in the Bottom Five Group of 17 cities. Liaocheng is positioned behind Zaozhuang (–0.894) at 14th place and narrowly ahead of Dezhou (–1.026) at 16th place.

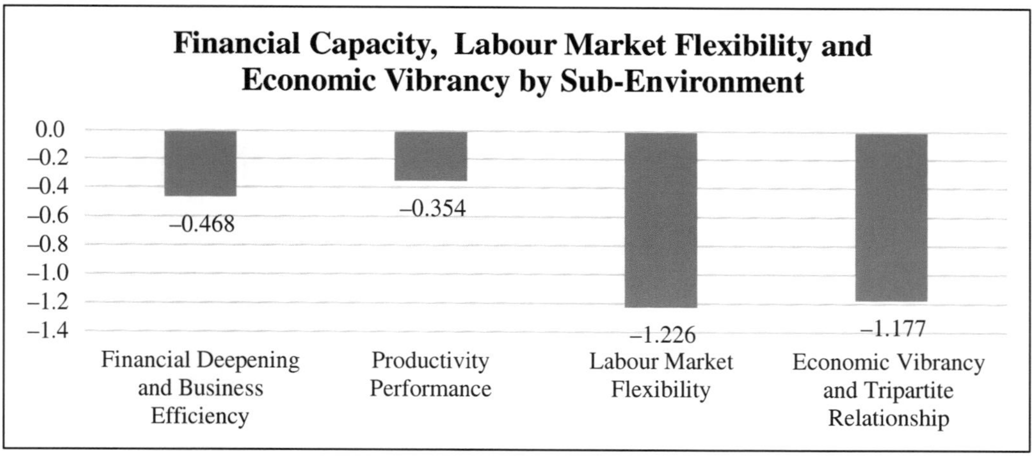

Looking at the four sub-environments of Financial Capacity, Labour Market Flexibility and Economic Vibrancy, Liaocheng scores below the provincial average in all of them and especially weaker for Labour Market Flexibility and Economic Vibrancy and Tripartite Relationship. Notably, the indicators of Proportion of Urban Workers Employed in Private Enterprises and Urban Registered Unemployment Rate from the Labour Market Flexibility sub-environment, as well as the indicator of Growth in Consumption of Electricity in the Economic Vibrancy and Tripartite Relationship sub-environment have exceptionally poor scores. On the other hand, the indicator of Annual Loan Growth Rate in the Financial Deepening and Business Efficiency sub-environment obtains a relatively high score.

LIAOCHENG

Shandong Province

Rank	City	Score
1	Dezhou	1.465
	...	
10	Yantai	0.192
11	Dongying	0.173
12	Rizhao	0.042
13	Jining	–0.527
14	Binzhou	–0.849
15	Zaozhuang	–1.302
16	Laiwu	–1.588
17	Liaocheng	–2.473

C: ***Good Governance, Effective Leadership and Social Stability***

2017 Rank

17th

Out of 17 Cities

Score: –2.473

Liaocheng ranks 17th for Good Governance, Effective Leadership and Social Stability with a standardised score of –2.473. This places the city at the last place and in the Bottom Five Group of 17 cities. Liaocheng is positioned behind Laiwu (–1.588) at 16th place.

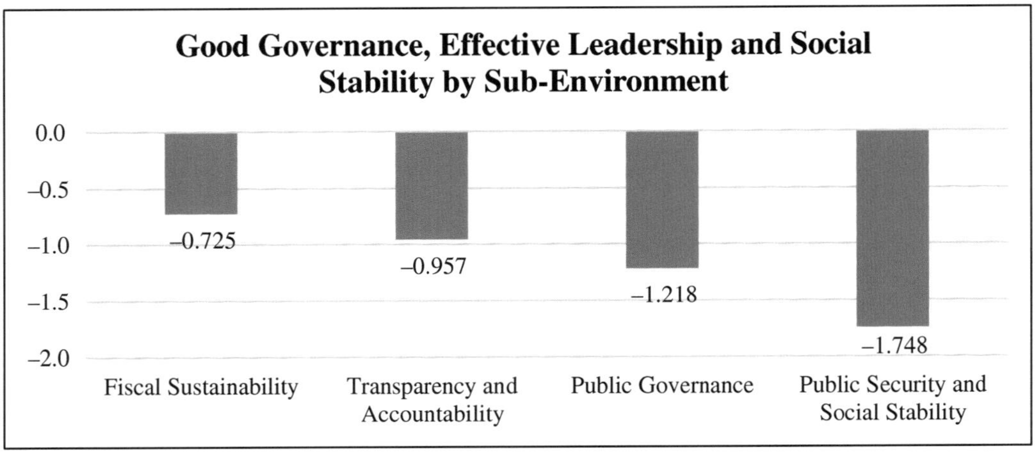

Looking at the four sub-environments of Good Governance, Effective Leadership and Social Stability, Liaocheng scores below the provincial average in all of them and most notably for Public Security and Social Stability, where the indicators of Public Perception of Security, Satisfaction of the Police Services and Satisfaction with Urban Management Personnel score especially poorly. In addition, the indicators of Index For Quality of E-Government System and Average Public Servant Salary from the Public Governance sub-environment as well as the Satisfaction with the Just of Judiciary from the Transparency and Accountability sub-environment register especially low scores. Nevertheless, the indicator of Number of Investigations for Power Abuses Per 10,000 Population from the Transparency and Accountability sub-environment performs remarkably well.

D: ***Technological Advancement and Innovation Capability***

2017 Rank

17th

Out of 17 Cities

Score: –1.221

Rank	City	Score
1	Qingdao	2.176
	...	
10	Tai'an	–0.457
11	Dezhou	–0.517
12	Binzhou	–0.559
13	Laiwu	–0.812
14	Heze	–0.897
15	Rizhao	–1.155
16	Zaozhuang	–1.192
17	Liaocheng	–1.221

Liaocheng ranks 17th for Technological Advancement and Innovation Capability, with a standardised score of –1.221. This places the city at the last place and in the Bottom Five Group of 17 cities. Liaocheng is positioned behind Zaozhuang (–1.192) at 16th place.

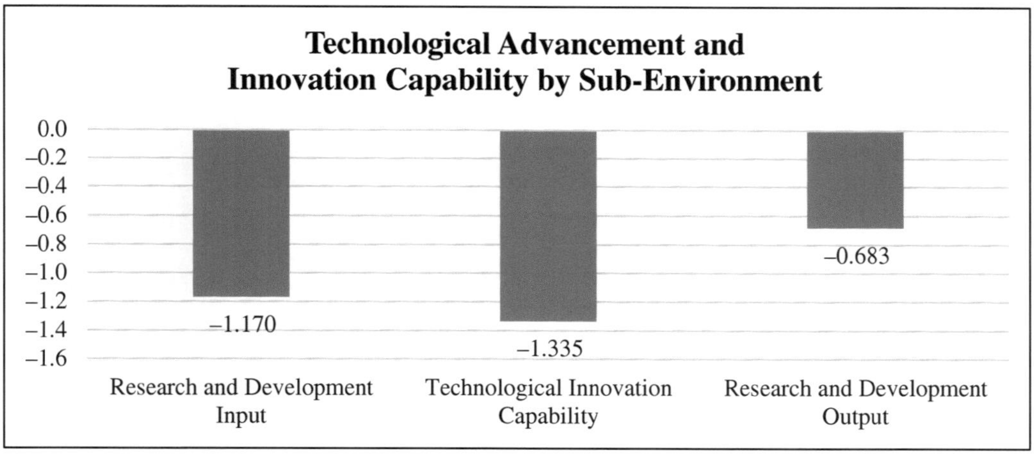

Looking at the three sub-environments of Technological Advancement and Innovation Capability, Liaocheng scores below the provincial average in all of them and particularly weaker for Technological Innovation Capability, where the indicators including the Number of Research and Development Personnel Per 10,000 Population and Satisfaction with Innovation Environment score poorly. Further, the indicators of Research & Development Expenditure as a Share of Government Expenditure and Total Research and Development Expenditure of Enterprises Above Designated Size as a Percentage of Cash Flow, both from the Research and Development Input sub-environment, as well as Number of Existing Patents Per 10,000 population from Research and Development Output sub-environment obtain low scores.

LIAOCHENG

Shandong Province

Rank	City	Score
1	Dongying	1.689
	...	
10	Linyi	–0.307
11	Tai'an	–0.567
12	Heze	–0.766
13	Jining	–0.819
14	Binzhou	–0.862
15	Zaozhuang	–0.954
16	Dezhou	–1.066
17	Liaocheng	–1.964

E: *Public Service Standards and Quality of Life Improvement*

2017 Rank

17th

Out of 17 Cities

Score: –1.964

Liaocheng ranks 17th for Public Service Standards and Quality of Life Improvement with a standardised score of –1.964. This places the city at the last place and in the Bottom Five Group of 17 cities. Liaocheng is positioned well behind Dezhou (–1.066) at 16th place.

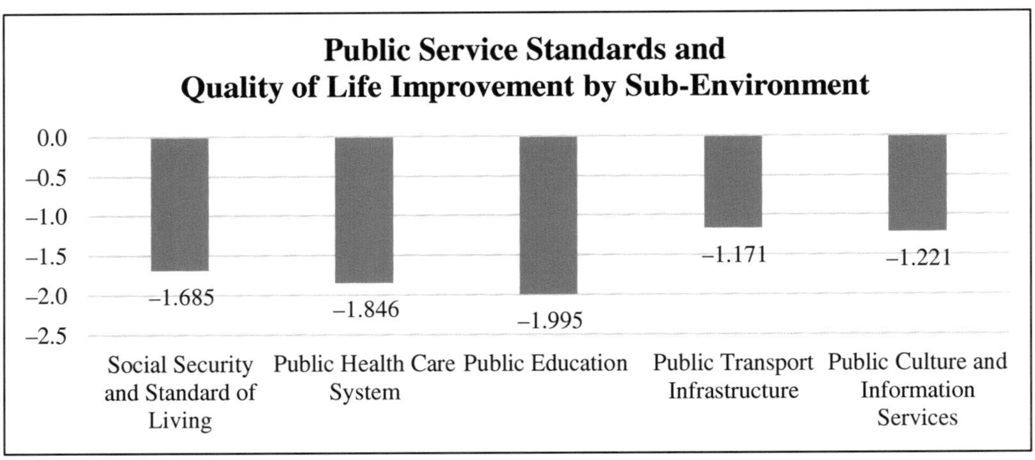

Among the five sub-environments of Public Service Standards and Quality of Life Improvement, Liaocheng performs below the provincial average in all of them, especially in the sub-environments of Public Education, Public Health Care System and Social Security and Standard of Living. The indicators with especially low scores in these sub-environments include the Cleanliness of Public Toilets and Number of Doctors Per 1,000 Persons from the Public Health Care System sub-environment, Satisfaction of Public Education System and Ratio of Teacher to Student in Primary and Secondary Schools from the Public Education sub-environment, as well as the Per Capita Annual Disposable Income from the Social Security and Standard of Living sub-environment. On the other hand, the indicator of Proportion of the Population Above 60 Years Old from the Social Security and Standard of Living sub-environment performs relatively better and above the provincial average.

F: ***Resource Conditions and Environmental Protection***

2017 Rank

6th

Out of 17 Cities

Score: 0.376

Rank	City	Score
1	Weihai	1.632
	...	
4	Rizhao	0.817
5	Zibo	0.665
6	Liaocheng	0.376
7	Tai'an	0.370
8	Qingdao	0.330
	...	
16	Binzhou	–1.586
17	Heze	–2.142

Liaocheng ranks 6th for Resource Conditions and Environmental Protection with a standardised score of 0.376. This places the city in the Middle Seven Group of 17 cities. Liaocheng is positioned behind Zibo (0.665) at 5th place and slightly ahead of Tai'an (0.370) at 7th place.

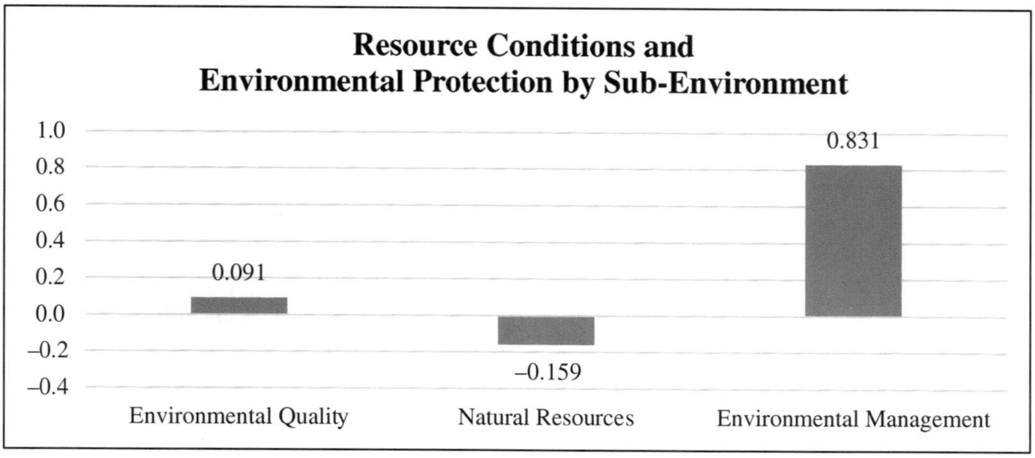

Among the three sub-environments of Resource Conditions and Environmental Protection, Liaocheng scores above the provincial average in two of them and particularly well for Environmental Management, where it obtains exceptional scores in the indicators of Environmental Expenditure as a Percentage of Total Fiscal Expenditure and Forest Land Growth. However, Liaocheng performs below the provincial average in the sub-environment of Natural Resources, where it obtains a low score for the indicator of Water Consumption Per RMB 10,000 GRDP. Further, the indicator of Per Capita Park and Green Space Acreage from the Environmental Management sub-environment registers a weak score as well.

LIAOCHENG

Shandong Province

Figure 11.1: Median & Maximum Web for Liaocheng

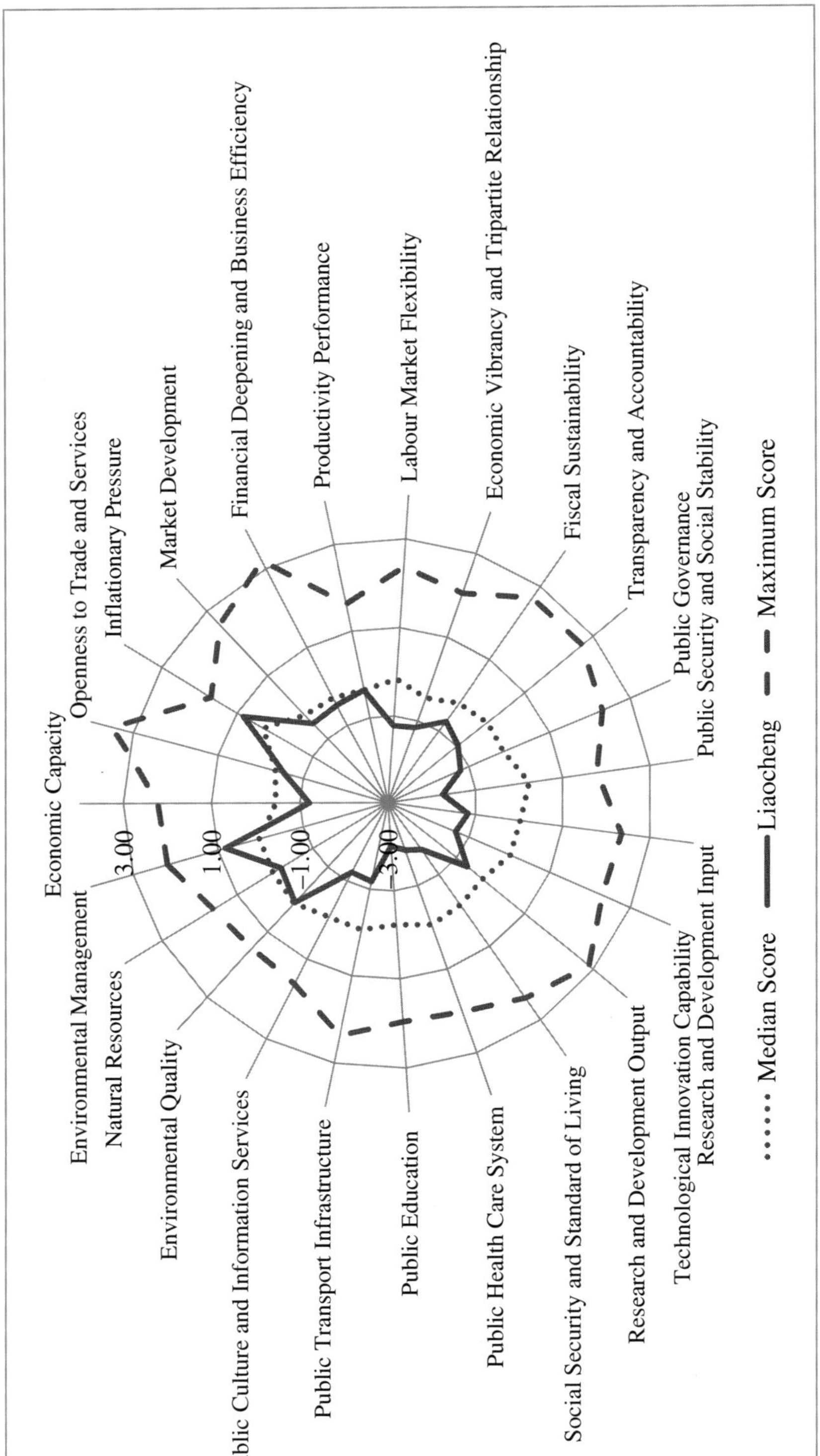

Source: Asia Competitiveness Institute.

11.2.3 Median and Maximum Web Analysis

To better understand Liaocheng's relative strengths and weaknesses, it is useful to compare and contrast its scores for the 23 sub-environments against the median and maximum scores of Shandong's 17 cities.

In Figure 11.1, the median and maximum scores for 17 Shandong cities are shown as dotted and dashed lines respectively, while scores for Liaocheng are shown as a solid line.

Comparison to Median Scores

Liaocheng scores above the median in two of the 23 sub-environments, namely Inflationary Pressure and Environmental Management.

On the other hand, it scores below the median in 20 sub-environments, especially for Public Security and Social Stability, Public Health Care System and Public Education, which are furthest below the median. The remaining sub-environment of Productivity Performance is at the median.

Comparison to Maximum Scores

Liaocheng scores below the provincial maximum of the 17 Shandong cities in all 23 sub-environments.

In addition, Liaocheng's score in Social Security and Standard of Living (−1.685) is farthest from the maximum, which is held by Dongying (2.416). Further, Liaocheng's score in Inflationary Pressure (0.841) is closest to the maximum, which is held by Heze (1.696).

11.3 Summary of Empirical Findings of Liaocheng and *What-if* Urban Development Simulation

11.3.1 Summary of Empirical Findings, 20% Strongest and Weakest Indicators

Overall Performance 17th Score: –1.576		
Scale and Quality of Economic Activities 12th Score: –0.665	Financial Capacity, Labour Market Flexibility and Economic Vibrancy 15th Score: –1.021	Good Governance, Effective Leadership and Social Stability 17th Score: –2.473
Technological Advancement and Innovation Capability 17th Score: –1.221	Public Service Standards and Quality of Life Improvement 17th Score: –1.964	Resource Conditions and Environmental Protection 6th Score: 0.376

(Rank out of 17 cities)

Summary

Liaocheng ranks 17th out of 17 cities in its Overall Performance. Liaocheng performs below the provincial average in five out of six environments and especially poorly in Good Governance, Effective Leadership and Social Stability, Technological Advancement and Innovation Capability, and Public Service Standards and Quality of Life Improvement, all of which rank last among the 17 cities in Shandong at 17th place. In contrast, the environment of Resource Conditions and Environmental Protection performs above the provincial average.

Strengths

As illustrated in Table 11.2, Liaocheng performs well in the environments of Scale and Quality of Economic Activities, and Resource Conditions and Environmental Protection, where of them each contains seven out of 26 of its 20% Strongest Indicators falling in these environments. Among Liaocheng's best performing indicators are the Environmental Expenditure as a Percentage of Total Fiscal Expenditure, Forest Land Growth, and Annual Loan Growth Rate.

Weaknesses

As observed in Table 11.3, Liaocheng is weak in the environments of Good Governance, Effective Leadership and Social Stability and Public Service Standards and Quality of Life Improvement, where each of them has have eight out of 26 of its 20% Weakest Indicators in these environments. Among Liaocheng's worst performing indicators are the Satisfaction of the Police Services, Public Perception of Security and Growth in Consumption of Electricity.

Table 11.2: 20% Strongest Indicators for Liaocheng

Rank	20% Strongest Indicator	Score	SQEA	FCLMFEV	GGELSS	TAIC	PSSQLI	RCEP
1	Environmental Expenditure as a Percentage of Total Fiscal Expenditure	3.521						✓
2	Number of Investigations for Power Abuses Per 10,000 Population	2.324			✓			
3	Forest Land Growth	1.087						✓
4	Proportion of the Population Above 60 Years Old	1.058					✓	
5	Annual Loan Growth Rate	1.047		✓				
6	Urban Residents' Per Capita Expenditure Growth Rate	0.986	✓					
7	Profit Margin of Enterprises Above Designated Size	0.862		✓				
8	Electricity Consumption Per RMB 10,000 GRDP	0.859						✓
9	Number of Primary and Secondary Schools Per 10,000 Population	0.840					✓	
10	Green Coverage Ratio of Built-up Area	0.789						✓
11	Number of Listed Items Under Executive Authority of the Government	0.780			✓			
12	Consumer Price Index (CPI)	0.739	✓					
13	Growth Rate of Overall Labour Productivity	0.673		✓				
14	Built-up Area Population Density	0.671						✓
15	Fiscal Revenue Growth Rate	0.614			✓			
16	Public Health and Medical Service Expenses as a Share of GRDP	0.553					✓	
17	Government Expenditures as a Percentage of GRDP	0.377	✓					
18	Retail Price Index	0.365	✓					
19	Manufacturing Sector as a Percentage of GRDP	0.332	✓					
20	COD (Chemical Oxygen Demand) Per RMB 10,000 GRDP	0.327						✓
21	Per Capita Road Area	0.297					✓	
22	Fire Fatality Per 10,000 Population	0.283			✓			
23	Producer Price Index (PPI)	0.265	✓					
24	Growth in the Volume of Cargo Transported	0.251		✓				
25	Urban Residents' Disposable Income Growth Rate	0.149	✓					
26	Ammoniacal Nitrogen Discharge Per RMB 10,000 GRDP	0.128						✓

Table 11.3: 20% Weakest Indicators for Liaocheng

Rank	20% Weakest Indicator	Score	SQEA	FCLMFEV	GGELSS	TAIC	PSSQLI	RCEP
106	Tax Revenue as a Share of Fiscal Revenue	−1.063			✓			
107	Rate of Migration Flow	−1.070		✓				
108	Average Years of Education Received	−1.102					✓	
109	Total R&D Expenditure of Enterprises Above Designated Size as a Percentage of Cash Flow	−1.110				✓		
110	Urban Registered Unemployment Rate	−1.110		✓				
111	Number of Books in Public Library Per Capita	−1.139					✓	
112	Satisfaction of Income Disparity	−1.174					✓	
113	Water Consumption Per RMB 10,000 GRDP	−1.203						✓
114	Number of Doctors Per 1,000 Persons	−1.212					✓	
115	Per Capita Park and Green Space Acreage	−1.265						✓
116	Proportion of Urban Workers Employed in State Enterprises	−1.311		✓				
117	Proportion of Urban Workers Employed in Private Enterprises	−1.360		✓				
118	Public Perception of Government Conduct	−1.396			✓			
119	Per Capita Annual Disposable Income	−1.400					✓	
120	Ratio of Teacher to Student in Primary and Secondary Schools	−1.445					✓	
121	Cleanliness of Public Toilets	−1.453					✓	
122	Satisfaction of Public Education System	−1.455					✓	
123	Average Public Servant Salary	−1.471			✓			
124	Research & Development Expenditure as a Share of Government Expenditure	−1.489				✓		
125	Urbanisation Rate	−1.616	✓					
126	Satisfaction with Urban Management Personnels	−1.931			✓			
127	Index for Quality of E-Government System	−1.943			✓			
128	Satisfaction with the Just of Judiciary	−1.991			✓			
129	Growth in Consumption of Electricity	−2.245		✓				
130	Public Perception of Security	−2.246			✓			
131	Satisfaction of the Police Services	−2.335			✓			

Source: Asia Competitiveness Institute.

Notes: SQEA: Scale and Quality of Economic Activities; FCLMFEV: Financial Capacity, Labour Market Flexibility and Economic Vibrancy; GGELSS: Good Governance, Effective Leadership and Social Stability; TAIC: Technological Advancement and Innovation Capability; PSSQLI: Public Service Standards and Quality of Life Improvement; RCEP: Resource Conditions and Environmental Protection.

11.3.2 *What-if* Urban Development Simulation

ACI has devised a simulation methodology to improve the ranking of a particular city by improving on its 20% Weakest Indicators as shown in Table 11.3.[2] The figures below show Liaocheng's ranking and standardised scores before and after the policy-induced simulation. Refer to Tables 3.8 to 3.14 in Section 3.4 of Chapter 3 for a complete list of simulation results for all cities.

Overall Performance

	Before		After
Rank	17th	▶	12th
Score	–1.576		–0.609

Scale and Quality of Economic Activities

	Before	After
Rank	12th	11th
Score	–0.665	–0.522

Financial Capacity, Labour Market Flexibility and Economic Vibrancy

	Before	After
Rank	15th	11th
Score	–1.021	–0.464

Good Governance, Effective Leadership and Social Stability

	Before	After
Rank	17th	13th
Score	–2.473	–0.255

Technological Advancement and Innovation Capability

	Before	After
Rank	17th	15th
Score	–1.221	–1.016

Public Service Standards and Quality of Life Improvement

	Before	After
Rank	17th	16th
Score	–1.964	–1.185

Resource Conditions and Environmental Protection

	Before	After
Rank	6th	4th
Score	0.376	0.805

After the *What-if* simulation, Liaocheng improves its ranking from 17th to 12th in terms of its Overall Performance. Likewise, its standardised score increases from –1.576 to –0.609. This leap is plausible if the city manages to successfully address its 20% Weakest Indicators.

The simulation further indicates Liaocheng's potential for substantial improvement in some of its environments, most notably in Financial Capacity, Labour Market Flexibility and Economic Vibrancy and Good Governance, Effective Leadership and Social Stability, where its ranks will rise from 15th to 11th and 17th to 13th respectively. Such encouraging results should incentivise Liaocheng to strive to improve the indicators under its 20% Weakest Indicators list. These indicators include Rate of Migration Flow, Index for Quality of E-government System and Tax Revenue as a Share of Fiscal Revenue.

[2]The methodology for *What-if* simulation is thoroughly explained in Section 2.7 of Chapter 2.

11.4 Concluding Notes: Public Policy Implications[3]

Areas for Commendation

Liaocheng performs well in the environments Scale and Quality of Economic Activities and Resource Conditions and Environmental Protection, as each of them has seven out of 26 of its 20% Strongest Indicators in these environments, as indicated in Table 11.2.

While Liaocheng does not achieve the maximum score for any sub-environment, it scores above the provincial average in three of the 23 sub-environments.

In 2016, Liaocheng has made further progress at improving its environmental conditions. It began initiatives to improve eight national forests and completed the afforestation of a total area of 1.4 billion square metres. As of 2016, the green space coverage ratio reached 40% in Liaocheng. Moreover, Liaocheng has continued its development in energy conservation and environment protection. The government spent over RMB 2.3 billion in 2016, a 32.26% increase compared to that in 2015.

Areas for Improvement

As Liaocheng scores below the provincial average in five of the six environments, there is plenty of room for improvement for the city. Most crucially, Liaocheng should address the environments of Good Governance, Effective Leadership and Social Stability and Public Service Standards and Quality of Life Improvement, where each of them has a total of 16 out of 26 of its 20% Weakest Indicators under these environments, as shown in Table 11.3. Additionally, as gleaned from the *What-if* Urban Development Simulation, the environments of Financial Capacity, Labour Market Flexibility and Economic Vibrancy and Good Governance, Effective Leadership and Social Stability should be prioritised because those are the environments where Liaocheng may achieve the greatest improvement in its ranking — four positions — relative to other environments.

Furthermore, Liaocheng obtains the weakest scores in the sub-environments of Public Education (–1.995), Public Health Care System (–1.846), Public Security and Social Stability (–1.748) and Social Security and Standard of Living (–1.685). In addition, Liaocheng scores below the provincial average in 20 out of 23 sub-environments.

As indicated by the study, Liaocheng performs badly in the indicator of Satisfaction of Public Education System. In 2016, Liaocheng increased its public education spending by 2.51% relative to that in 2015. The government has also recognised the lack of public education in rural areas and have allocated more funds towards it. In addition, Liaocheng has actively tried to invest in education resources such as schools and educators to reduce the class size of primary and secondary schools in urban areas. In the future, Liaocheng may also look into other areas, such as vocational education in primary and secondary schools.

[3]The relevant statistical data and government policies are from Liaocheng Bureau of Finance (2017) and Liaocheng Municipal People's Government (2017).

Future Potential Development

In summary, Liaocheng should improve the environment of Good Governance, Effective Leadership and Social Stability by investing more towards social security, police services and its judiciary system. In addition, Liaocheng should expand its public education and health care provision to make progress in the environment of Public Service Standards and Quality of Life Improvement.

Moving forward, the Liaocheng administration should focus on its tax collection processes while enforcing strict auditing standards of every company's financial statements to effectively address the loopholes in the management of its public finances. Only with an increase in its fiscal revenue can Liaocheng be able to allocate more funds towards the upgrading of its education, health care and transportation services. Besides, the government should take the initiative to release more information for public reviewing and engage the people more actively through conversations and various media platforms. These actions will help improve Liaocheng's public perception of government services.

References

Department of Commerce of Shandong Province. n.d. 'Liaocheng City'. Accessed 10 November 2017. http://en.shandongbusiness.gov.cn/city/79.

Liaocheng Bureau of Finance. 2017. '关于聊城市 2016 年预算执行情况 和 2017 年预算草案的报告 Report on Liaocheng's Implementation of 2016 Budget and Proposal of 2017 Budget (in Chinese)'. 14 June 2017. http://www.lcczj.gov.cn/uploads/1/file/public/201705/20170512143927_9rq7wsy1fp.pdf.

Liaocheng Municipal People's Government. 2017. '2017年聊城市政府工作报告（全文）聊城新闻网 2017 Liaocheng Annual Government Work Report (in Chinese)'. 23 February 2017. http://www.lcxw.cn/news/liaocheng/yaowen/20170301/737066.html.

Shi, Zhiban. 2017. '中国聊城 China Liaocheng (in Chinese)'. 29 March 2017. http://www.liaocheng.gov.cn/col/col795/index.html.

Chapter 12: LINYI
Shandong Province

Location of City

Source: Asia Competitiveness Institute.

12.1 Profile of Linyi City[1]

Situated at the confluence of the Yihe and Benghe rivers, Linyi is the largest prefecture-level city in southern Shandong. The city directly administers three districts and nine counties spanning a total land area of 17,191 square kilometres and a total population of 10,443,000. Boasting a long and rich history, Linyi is especially renowned as a centre for the development of calligraphy, as well as for having been the birthplace of historical figures such as Zhuge Liang — the famed sage of China's Three Kingdoms period. The area surrounding Linyi is also well known for its scenic natural landscapes which in combination with Linyi's numerous sites of historical interest have made the city very attractive to tourists.

Linyi's Gross Regional Domestic Product (GRDP) stands at RMB 403 billion, with the city also boasting a GRDP growth rate of 7.6%, as can be seen in Table 12.1. Linyi benefits significantly from its agricultural sector, and the abundant mineral wealth of the areas surrounding the city, and its primary sector accordingly accounts for 8.9% of overall GRDP. Linyi's secondary sector is also dependent on its abundant mineral wealth, as well as its network of wholesale

[1]The relevant city information are from the Department of Commerce of Shandong Province (n.d.), the People's Government of Linyi (n.d.) and Li (2009).

markets, and constitutes 43.1% of total GRDP. Finally, Linyi's tertiary sector constitutes 48.0% of total GRDP, due to new initiatives by the Linyi government to focus on high-tech services and urban development.

Linyi is served by Linyi Shubuling International Airport, which caters to both domestic and international flights. The city is also well served by high-speed rail networks, including the Yanzhou–Shijiu Railway and the Jiaozhou–Xinyi Railways, as well as numerous highways. The scale of investment that Linyi has put into public education relative to the size of its economy can be discerned from the fact that its ratio of public education appropriation to overall GRDP is 3.3 — the second highest of the 17 cities in this study. Linyi additionally ranks second in terms of expenditure on public health care relative to overall GRDP at 12.0%, reflecting its dedication to safeguarding the welfare of its people, even as it continues to develop its economy.

Table 12.1: Key Economic Indicators for Linyi, 2016

Land Area (km^2)	**17,191**
Population	
Total Population	10,443,000
Urbanisation Ratio (%)	55.8
Average Life Expectancy (years)	75.5
Number of Employees (10,000)	723
Workforce Participation Rate (%)	81.9
Gross Regional Domestic Product (GRDP) — 2015 Prices	
GRDP (100 millions of RMB)	4,027
GRDP Per Capita (RMB)	38,803
GRDP Growth Rate (%)	7.6
Economic Composition	
Primary Sector (% of GRDP)	8.9
Secondary Sector (% of GRDP)	43.1
Tertiary Sector (% of GRDP)	48.0
Trade — 2016 Prices	
Exports (millions of RMB)	40,229
Imports (millions of RMB)	17,841
Dependency on Foreign Trade (%)	14.2
Infrastructure	
Per Capita Road Area (m^2)	21.3
Growth in the Number of Passengers Transported (10,000)	227
Growth in the Volume of Cargo Transported (10,000 tons)	2,576
Environment	
Green Coverage Ratio of Built-up Area (%)	40.7
Environmental Expenditure (% of Total Fiscal Expenditure)	2.5

Source: Asia Competitiveness Institute from the 2017 Shandong Statistical Yearbook.

12.2 In-Depth Urban Development of Linyi, 2016*

12.2.1 Overall Urban Development Performance

Overall Performance

2017 Rank

8th

Out of 17 Cities

Score: –0.002

Rank	City	Score
1	Qingdao	1.753
	...	
6	Dongying	0.603
7	Zibo	0.403
8	Linyi	–0.002
9	Tai'an	–0.280
10	Dezhou	–0.302
	...	
16	Laiwu	–1.233
17	Liaocheng	–1.576

Linyi ranks 8th in its Overall Performance, with a standardised score of –0.002. This places the city among the Middle Seven Group of 17 cities. Linyi is positioned between Zibo (0.403) at 7th place and Tai'an (–0.280) at 9th place.

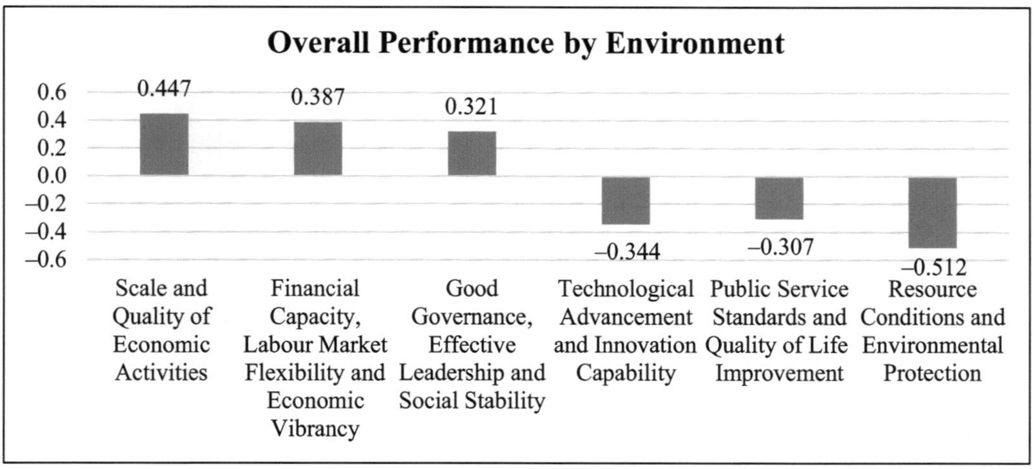

Among the six environments, Linyi fares above the provincial average in three of them, with its highest score in Scale and Quality of Economic Activities. However, Linyi scores below the provincial average in the remaining three environments and weakest in the environment of Resource Conditions and Environmental Protection.

For a complete list of rankings, see Tables 3.2 to 3.7 in Section 3.3 of Chapter 3.

12.2.2 Urban Development within the Six Environments

Rank	City	Score
1	Qingdao	1.987
	…	
4	Weifang	1.021
5	Weihai	0.849
6	Linyi	0.447
7	Dezhou	0.096
8	Tai'an	−0.321
	…	
16	Jining	−1.273
17	Laiwu	−1.295

A: ***Scale and Quality of Economic Activities***

2017 Rank

6th

Out of 17 Cities

Score: 0.447

Linyi ranks 6th for Scale and Quality of Economic Activities, with a standardised score of 0.447. This places the city in the Middle Seven Group of 17 cities. Linyi is positioned behind Weihai (0.849) at 5th place and ahead of Dezhou (0.096) at 7th place.

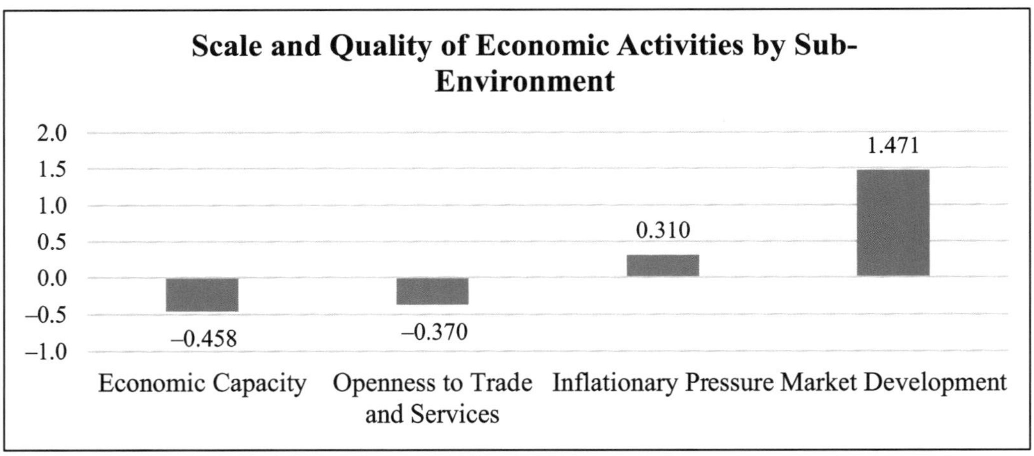

Looking at the four sub-environments of Scale and Quality of Economic Activities, Linyi performs above the provincial average in two of them and particularly well for Market Development, where the indicator of Government Expenditures as a Percentage of GRDP scores well. However, Linyi performs below the provincial average in the remaining two sub-environments and weaker for Economic Capacity, where the indicator of GRDP Per Capita is particularly poor. Further, the indicator of Retail Price Index from the Inflationary Pressure sub-environment performs poorly as well.

B: ***Financial Capacity, Labour Market Flexibility and Economic Vibrancy***

2017 Rank

5th

Out of 17 Cities

Score: 0.387

Rank	City	Score
1	Jinan	2.264
2	Qingdao	1.932
3	Yantai	1.271
4	Weifang	0.441
5	Linyi	0.387
6	Dongying	0.293
7	Zibo	0.089
	...	
16	Dezhou	−1.026
17	Laiwu	−1.297

Linyi ranks 5th for Financial Capacity, Labour Market Flexibility and Economic Vibrancy, with a standardised score of 0.387. This places the city in the Top Five Group of 17 cities. Linyi is positioned between Weifang (0.441) at 4th place and Dongying (0.293) at 6th place.

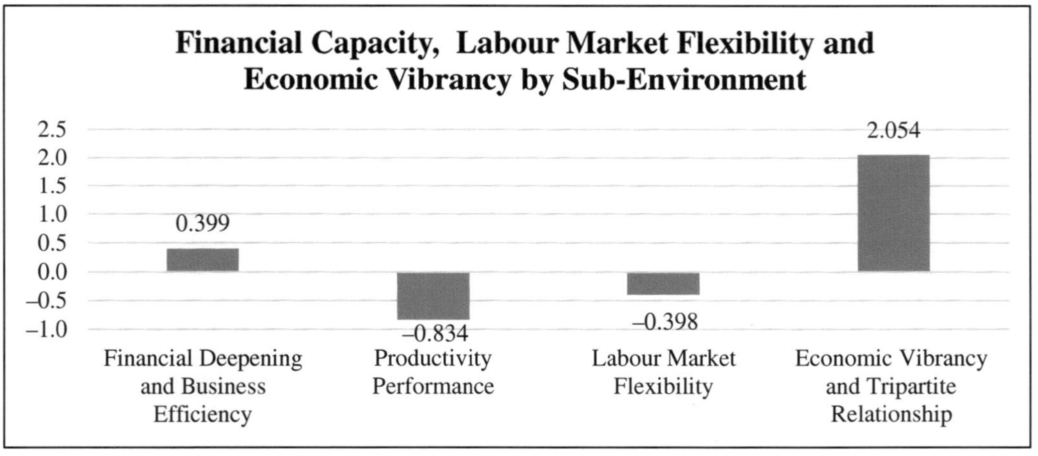

Among the four sub-environments of Financial Capacity, Labour Market Flexibility and Economic Vibrancy, Linyi scores above the provincial average in two of them and remarkably well for Economic Vibrancy and Tripartite Relationship, where the indicators of Growth in Volume of Cargo Transported and Growth in the Number of Passengers Transported report especially high scores. In addition, the indicator of Annual Loan Growth Rate from the Financial Deepening and Business Efficiency sub-environment performs well too. However, Linyi's scores below the provincial average in the remaining two sub-environments and weaker in Productivity Performance, where the indicators of Tertiary Industry Total Labour Productivity register low scores. Further, the indicators of Self-Employed as a Share of Total Employment and the Workforce Participation Rate from the Labour Market Flexibility sub-environment perform poorly as well.

LINYI

Shandong Province

Rank	City	Score
1	Dezhou	1.465
	...	
7	Heze	0.435
8	Zibo	0.418
9	Linyi	0.321
10	Yantai	0.192
11	Dongying	0.173
	...	
16	Laiwu	−1.588
17	Liaocheng	−2.473

C: *Good Governance, Effective Leadership and Social Stability*

2017 Rank

9th

Out of 17 Cities

Score: 0.321

Linyi ranks 9th for Good Governance, Effective Leadership and Social Stability with a standardised score of 0.321. This places the city in the Middle Seven Group of 17 cities. Linyi is positioned behind Zibo (0.418) at 8th place and well ahead of Yantai (0.192) at 10th place.

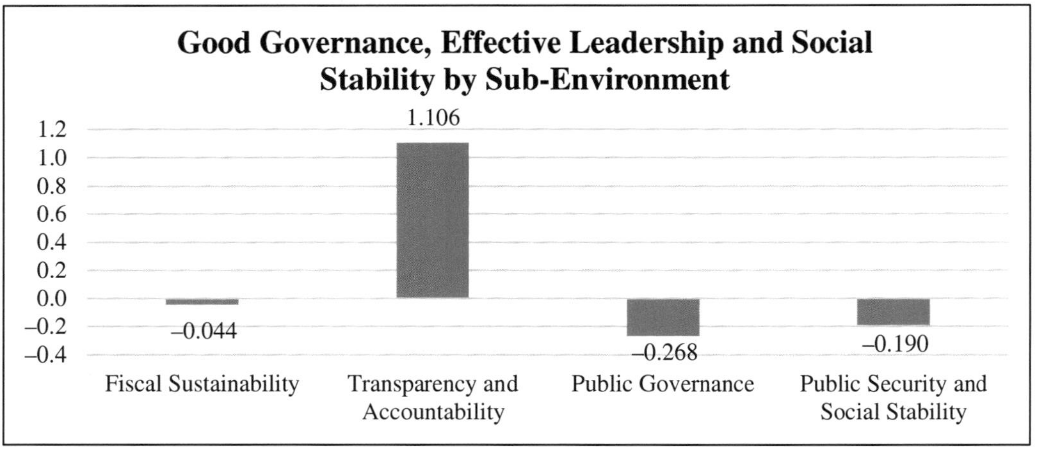

Among the four sub-environments of Good Governance, Effective Leadership and Social Stability, Linyi scores above the provincial average in the sub-environment of Transparency and Accountability, where the indicator of Number of Responses to Government Issues of Public Interest performs particularly well. Further, the indicator for Tax Revenue as a Share of Fiscal Revenue from the Fiscal Sustainability sub-environment obtains an especially high score. However, Linyi fares below the provincial average in the remaining three sub-environments and most notably in Public Governance, where the indicator of Number of Public Servants Per 10,000 Population scores poorly. In addition, the indicator of Government Fiscal Revenue Per Capita from the Fiscal Sustainability sub-environment performs poorly as well.

D: ***Technological Advancement and Innovation Capability***

2017 Rank

9th

Out of 17 Cities

Score: –0.344

Rank	City	Score
1	Qingdao	2.176
	...	
7	Dongying	0.178
8	Jining	–0.222
9	Linyi	–0.344
10	Tai'an	–0.457
11	Dezhou	–0.517
	...	
16	Zaozhuang	–1.192
17	Liaocheng	–1.221

Linyi ranks 9th for Technological Advancement and Innovation Capability, with a standardised score of –0.344. This places the city in the Middle Seven Group of 17 cities. Linyi is positioned between Jining (–0.222) at 8th place and Tai'an (–0.457) at 10th place.

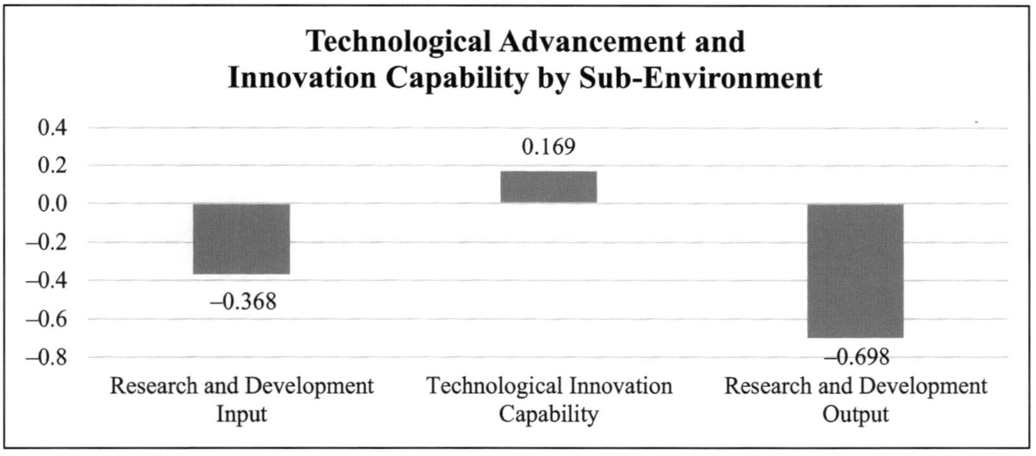

Among the three sub-environments of Technological Advancement and Innovation Capability, Linyi scores above the provincial average in Technological Innovation Capability, where it has a relatively high score in the indicator of Number of Provincial-level Science Parks. However, the Linyi's scores below the provincial average in the remaining two sub-environments and notably weaker for Research and Development Output, where the indicator of the Number of Existing Patents Per 10,000 Population scores poorly. Other indicators with weak scores include Research and Development Expenditure as a Share of Government Expenditure and Per Capita Research and Development Expenditure, both from the Research and Development Input sub-environment.

LINYI

Shandong Province

Rank	City	Score
1	Dongying	1.689
	...	
8	Yantai	0.251
9	Rizhao	–0.154
10	Linyi	–0.307
11	Tai'an	–0.567
12	Heze	–0.766
	...	
16	Dezhou	–1.066
17	Liaocheng	–1.964

E: *Public Service Standards and Quality of Life Improvement*

2017 Rank

10th

Out of 17 Cities

Score: –0.307

Linyi ranks 10th for Public Service Standards and Quality of Life Improvement with a standardised score of –0.307. This places the city in the Middle Seven Group of 17 cities. Linyi is positioned between Rizhao (–0.154) at 9th place and Tai'an (–0.567) at 11th place.

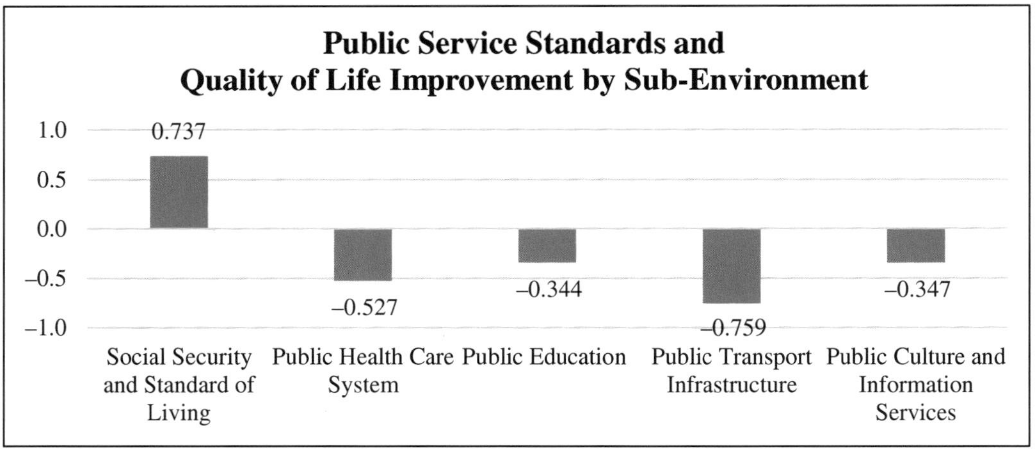

Among the five sub-environments of Public Service Standards and Quality of Life Improvement, Linyi performs above the provincial average in the sub-environment of Social Security and Standard of Living, where the indicator of Satisfaction of Income Disparity scores particularly better. Further, the indicator of Ratio of Public Education Appropriation to GRDP from the Public Education sub-environment also performs well. However, Linyi performs below the provincial average in the remaining four sub-environments and notably weaker in Public Transport Infrastructure and Public Health Care System, where the indicators of Per Capita Road Area from the Public Transport Infrastructure sub-environment and Number of Doctors Per 1,000 Persons from the Public Health Care System sub-environment contribute to their low scores.

F: ***Resource Conditions and Environmental Protection***

2017 Rank

13th

Out of 17 Cities

Score: –0.512

Rank	City	Score
1	Weihai	1.632
	...	
10	Jining	–0.112
11	Dezhou	–0.287
12	Zaozhuang	–0.393
13	Linyi	–0.512
14	Weifang	–0.814
15	Laiwu	–1.136
16	Binzhou	–1.586
17	Heze	–2.142

Linyi ranks 13th for Resource Conditions and Environmental Protection with a standardised score of –0.512. This places the city in the Bottom Five Group of 17 cities. Linyi is positioned between Zaozhuang (–0.393) at 12th place and Weifang (–0.814) at 14th place.

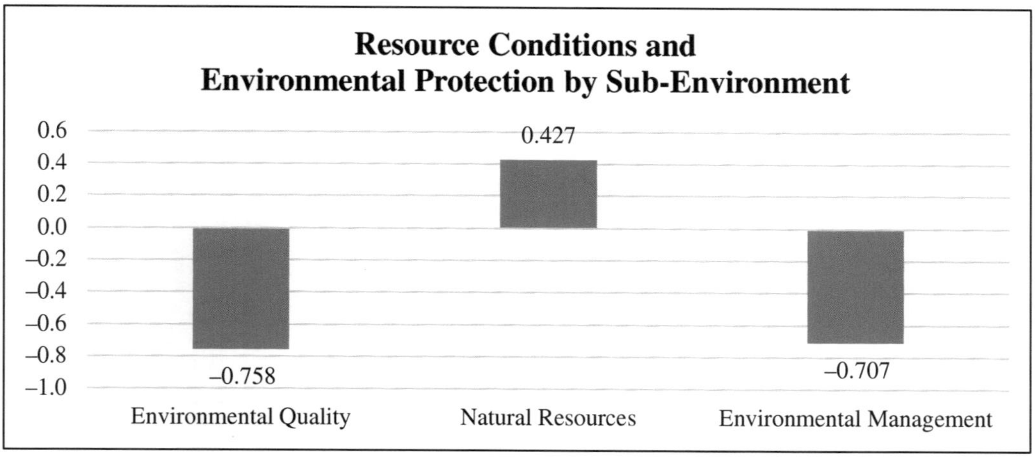

Among the three sub-environments of Resource Conditions and Environmental Protection, Linyi scores above the provincial average in Natural Resources, where the indicator of Per Capita Freshwater Resource scores exceptionally well. However, Linyi performs below the provincial average in the remaining two sub-environments and weaker in the Environmental Quality sub-environment, where the indicator of Ammoniacal Nitrogen Discharge Per RMB 10,000 GRDP performs poorly. In addition, the indicator of Green Coverage Ratio of Built-up Area from the Environmental Management sub-environment also registers a low score.

LINYI

Shandong Province

Figure 12.1: Median & Maximum Web for Linyi

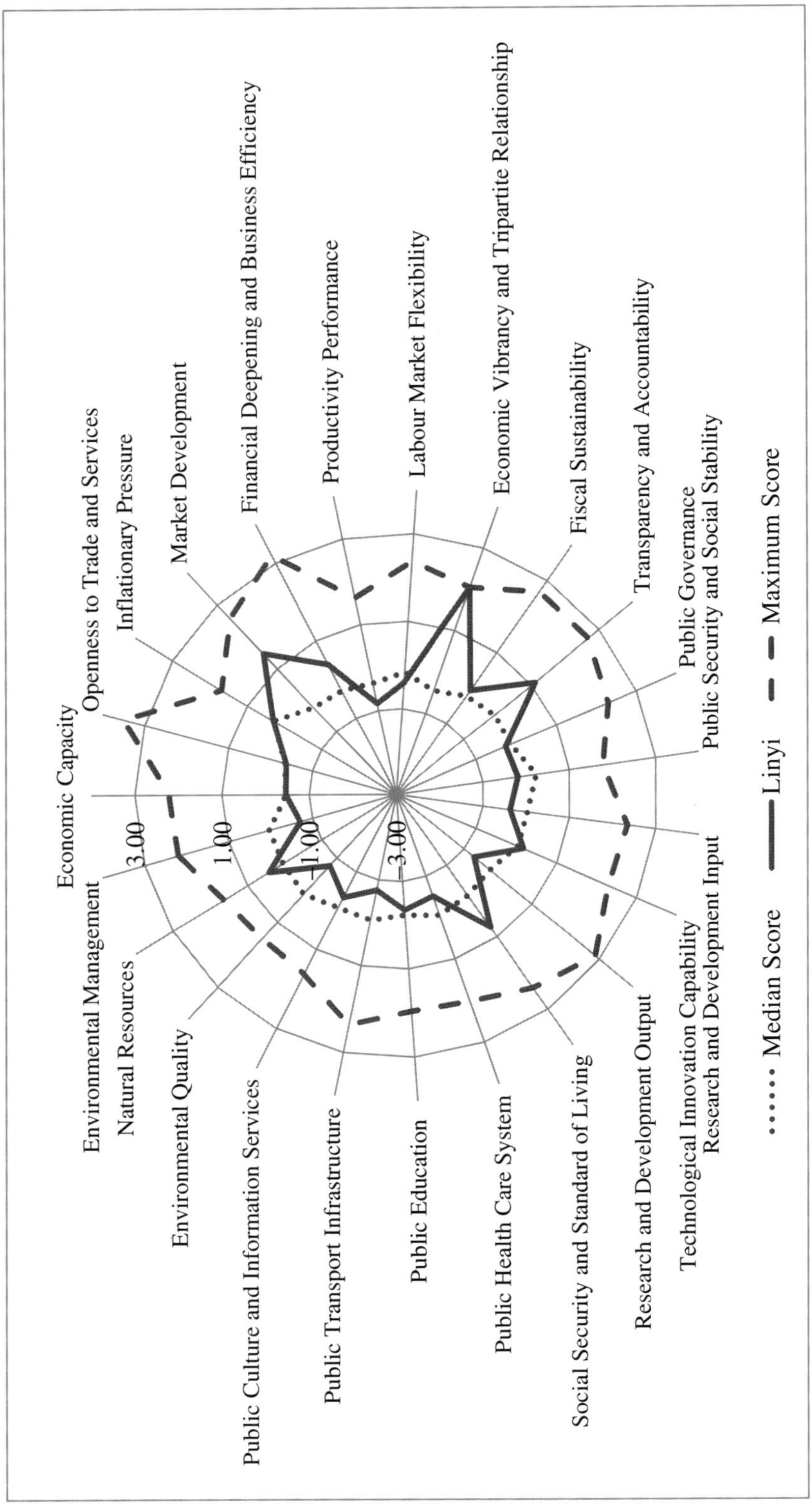

Source: Asia Competitiveness Institute.

12.2.3 Median and Maximum Web Analysis

To better understand Linyi's relative strengths and weaknesses, it is useful to compare and contrast its scores for the 23 sub-environments against the median and maximum scores of Shandong's 17 cities.

In Figure 12.1, the median and maximum scores for 17 Shandong cities are shown as dotted and dashed lines respectively, while scores for Linyi are shown as a solid line.

Comparison to Median Scores

Linyi scores above the median for eight of the 23 sub-environments, most notably in Economic Vibrancy and Tripartite Relationship, Market Development and Transparency and Accountability.

On the other hand, Linyi scores below the median for 13 sub-environments, especially for the Environmental Quality sub-environment, which is farthest below the median. The remaining two sub-environments of Economic Capacity and Inflationary Pressure are at the median.

Comparison to Maximum Scores

Linyi achieves the provincial maximum score of the 17 Shandong cities in Economic Vibrancy and Tripartite Relationship.

Further, Linyi's score in Openness to Trade and Services (–0.370) is farthest from the maximum, which is held by Qingdao (3.505). Further, Linyi's score in Market Development (1.471) is closest to the maximum, which is held by Heze (2.577).

12.3 Summary of Empirical Findings of Linyi and *What-if* Urban Development Simulation

12.3.1 Summary of Empirical Findings, 20% Strongest and Weakest Indicators

Overall Performance		
8th Score: –0.002		
Scale and Quality of Economic Activities **6th** Score: 0.447	Financial Capacity, Labour Market Flexibility and Economic Vibrancy **5th** Score: 0.387	Good Governance, Effective Leadership and Social Stability **9th** Score: 0.321
Technological Advancement and Innovation Capability **9th** Score: –0.344	Public Service Standards and Quality of Life Improvement **10th** Score: –0.307	Resource Conditions and Environmental Protection **13th** Score: –0.512

(Rank out of 17 cities)

Summary

Linyi ranks 8th out of 17 Shandong cities in its Overall Performance. Linyi performs above the provincial average in three out of the six environments and performs best in the environment of Financial Capacity, Labour Market Flexibility and Economic Vibrancy at 5th place. Meanwhile, Linyi's worst performing environment is that of Resource Conditions and Environmental Protection, ranked at 13th place.

Strengths

As illustrated in Table 12.2, Linyi performs well in the environments of Public Service Standards and Quality of Life Improvement, with nine out of 26 of its 20% Strongest Indicators falling in this environment. Among Linyi's best performing indicators are the Number of Employees, Tax Revenue as a Share of Fiscal Revenue and Growth in the Volume of Cargo Transported.

Weaknesses

As observed in Table 12.3, Linyi is weak in the environment of Financial Capacity, Labour Market Flexibility and Economic Vibrancy, where it has and seven out of 26 of its 20% Weakest Indicators in this environment. Among Linyi's worst performing indicators are the Number of Doctors Per 1,000 Persons, Self-Employed as a Share of Total Employment and Ammoniacal Nitrogen Discharge Per RMB 10,000 GRDP.

Table 12.2: 20% Strongest Indicators for Linyi

Rank	20% Strongest Indicator	Score	SQEA	FCLMFEV	GGELSS	TAIC	PSSQLI	RCEP
1	Number of Employees	1.998		✓				
2	Tax Revenue as a Share of Fiscal Revenue	1.935			✓			
3	Growth in the Volume of Cargo Transported	1.884		✓				
4	Deepness of Insurance (Insurance Income as a Share of GRDP)	1.875		✓				
5	Number of Responses to Government Issues of Public Interest	1.756			✓			
6	Growth in the Number of Passengers Transported	1.658		✓				
7	Ratio of Public Education Appropriation to GRDP	1.641					✓	
8	Annual Loan Growth Rate	1.623		✓				
9	Per Capita Freshwater Resource	1.371						✓
10	Government Expenditures as a Percentage of GRDP	1.245	✓					
11	Residents' Satisfaction with Price Levels	1.205	✓					
12	Newly Increased Number of Employees	1.181		✓				
13	Forest Land Growth	1.048						✓
14	Satisfaction of Income Disparity	0.945					✓	
15	Percentage of Public Expenditure on Cultural Initiatives	0.938					✓	
16	Traffic Accident Fatality Per 10,000 Population	0.917			✓			
17	Satisfaction of Public Education System	0.916					✓	
18	Consumer Price Index (CPI)	0.893	✓					
19	Number of Passengers Transported	0.889					✓	
20	Satisfaction of Public Health Care Services	0.887					✓	
21	Public Health and Medical Service Expenses as a Share of GRDP	0.884					✓	
22	Number of Provincial-Level Science Parks	0.848				✓		
23	Satisfaction with Business Environment	0.749	✓					
24	Frequency of Using the Internet for Daily Convenience	0.740					✓	
25	Number of Releases of Government Information for Public Viewing	0.740			✓			
26	Number of Primary and Secondary Schools Per 10,000 Population	0.720					✓	

Table 12.3: 20% Weakest Indicators for Linyi

Rank	20% Weakest Indicator	Score	SQEA	FCLMFEV	GGELSS	TAIC	PSSQLI	RCEP
106	Per Capita R&D Expenditure	−0.864				✓		
107	Manufacturing Sector as a Percentage of GRDP	−0.864	✓					
108	Secondary Industry Total Labour Productivity	−0.883		✓				
109	Internet Penetration Rate	−0.886					✓	
110	Proportion of Workforce Employed in Agriculture Sector	−0.900		✓				
111	Percentage of the Employed Population with Tertiary Education	−0.931		✓				
112	Government Fiscal Expenditure Per Capita	−0.943			✓			
113	Growth Rate of the Number of Police Cases Solved	−0.962			✓			
114	Proportion of Urban Workers Employed in State Enterprises	−0.971		✓				
115	COD (Chemical Oxygen Demand) Per RMB 10,000 GRDP	−1.008						✓
116	Number of Existing Patents Per 10,000 Population	−1.011				✓		
117	Public Health and Medical Service Expenses Per Capita	−1.017					✓	
118	Tertiary Industry Total Labour Productivity	−1.025		✓				
119	GRDP Per Capita	−1.031	✓					
120	Government Fiscal Revenue Per Capita	−1.044			✓			
121	Number of R&D Personnel Per 10,000 Population	−1.048				✓		
122	Ratio of Teacher to Student in Primary and Secondary Schools	−1.126					✓	
123	Green Coverage Ratio of Built-up Area	−1.128						✓
124	Retail Price Index	−1.146	✓					
125	Per Capita Road Area	−1.208					✓	
126	Workforce Participation Rate	−1.225		✓				
127	Average Years of Education Received	−1.278					✓	
128	Number of Public Servants Per 10,000 Population	−1.311			✓			
129	Ammoniacal Nitrogen Discharge Per RMB 10,000 GRDP	−1.431						✓
130	Self–Employed as a Share of Total Employment	−1.457		✓				
131	Number of Doctors Per 1,000 Persons	−1.603					✓	

Source: Asia Competitiveness Institute.

Notes: SQEA: Scale and Quality of Economic Activities; FCLMFEV: Financial Capacity, Labour Market Flexibility and Economic Vibrancy; GGELSS: Good Governance, Effective Leadership and Social Stability; TAIC: Technological Advancement and Innovation Capability; PSSQLI: Public Service Standards and Quality of Life Improvement; RCEP: Resource Conditions and Environmental Protection.

12.3.2 *What-if* Urban Development Simulation

ACI has devised a simulation methodology to improve the ranking of a particular city by improving on its 20% Weakest Indicators as shown in Table 12.3.[2] The figures below show Linyi's ranking and standardised scores before and after the policy-induced simulation. Refer to Tables 3.8 to 3.14 in Section 3.4 of Chapter 3 for a complete list of simulation results for all cities.

Overall Performance

8th	▶	**6th**
–0.002		**0.668**

Scale and Quality of Economic Activities

	Before	After
Rank	6th	6th
Score	0.447	0.802

Financial Capacity, Labour Market Flexibility and Economic Vibrancy

	Before	After
Rank	5th	4th
Score	0.387	0.878

Good Governance, Effective Leadership and Social Stability

	Before	After
Rank	9th	3rd
Score	0.321	0.897

Technological Advancement and Innovation Capability

	Before	After
Rank	9th	8th
Score	–0.344	0.150

Public Service Standards and Quality of Life Improvement

	Before	After
Rank	10th	8th
Score	–0.307	0.251

Resource Conditions and Environmental Protection

	Before	After
Rank	13th	10th
Score	–0.512	–0.004

After the *What-if* simulation, Linyi improves its ranking from 8th to 6th in its Overall Performance. Likewise, Linyi's standardised score increases from –0.002 to 0.668. This leap is plausible if the city manages to successfully address its top 20% Weakest Indicators.

The simulation further highlights substantial improvement for Linyi in some of its environments, most notably in Good Governance, Effective Leadership and Social Stability, where its ranks will rise from 9th to 3rd. Such encouraging results should incentivise Linyi to strive to improve the indicators under the 20% Weakest Indicators list. These indicators include the Government Fiscal Expenditure Per Capita, Government Fiscal Revenue Per Capita and Number of Public Servants Per 10,000 Population.

[2]The methodology for *What-if* simulation is thoroughly explained in Section 2.7 of Chapter 2.

12.4 Concluding Notes: Public Policy Implications[3]

Areas for Commendation

Linyi performs relatively well in areas of the environment of Public Service Standards and Quality of Life Improvement, with nine out of 26 of its 20% Strongest Indicators falling in this environment, as shown in Table 12.2.

Further, Linyi achieves the provincial maximum score in the sub-environment of Economic Vibrancy and Tripartite Relationship (2.054) and scores above the provincial average in eight out of the 23 sub-environments.

In the past five years from 2012 to 2016, Linyi has been working on improving its scale and quality of economic activities as well as its financial capacity. For example, Linyi's aggregate trade has improved its value of trade to US $100 million by August 2017, a 483.3% increase by a year on year basis. The huge increase is largely due to the reduction in tariff and improvement in the ease of conducting trade.

As for its labour market conditions, Linyi has announced a few measures to encourage employment, such as migrating rural labour to urban area and better training for its tertiary students. The government also aims to improve employment by encouraging entrepreneurship through policies creating more start-up platforms for undergraduates. These measures may account for Linyi's good performance in both Scale and Quality of Economic Activities and Financial Capacity, Labour Market Flexibility and Economic Vibrancy.

Areas for Improvement

As Linyi scores below the provincial average in three of the six environments, there are plenty of areas for improvement for the city. Most crucially, Linyi should address its weaknesses in the environments of Public Service Standards and Quality of Life Improvement and Financial Capacity, Labour Market Flexibility and Economic Vibrancy, where they collectively have 13 out of 26 of its 20% Weakest Indicators, as shown in Table 12.3. Additionally, as gleaned from the *What-if* Urban Development Simulation, the environment of Good Governance, Effective Leadership and Social Stability should be prioritised because that is the environment in which Linyi will achieve the greatest improvement in its ranking — six positions — relative to other environments.

Further, Linyi obtains its weakest score in the sub-environment of Productivity Performance (–0.834) and scores below the provincial average in 15 out of 23 sub-environments.

From 2012 to 2016, Linyi made progress in terms of its residents' quality of life. The government spent RMB 189 billion during this period to improve public education and public health. The spending has been rising sharply to an estimated 11.2% of the government's total fiscal expenditure. Meanwhile, Linyi government collaborates closely with media to release

[3] The relevant statistical data and government policies are from the People's Government of Linyi (2017a, 2017b) and Yimengwanbao (沂蒙晚报) (2017).

environment-protection information on a regular basis in order to address its poor environmental quality and environmental management. This demonstrates the government's aim to improve its Public Service Standards and Quality of Life Improvement, and Resource Condition and Environmental Protection.

Future Potential Development

In summary, Linyi should focus on improving the environment of Resource Conditions and Environmental Protection by enforcing environmental standards and raising the amount of green coverage. In addition, Linyi should look towards investing more in its human capital by stimulating employment and raising its workforce participation rate to progress in the environment of Financial Capacity, Labour Market Flexibility and Economic Vibrancy.

Although plans have been laid out to stimulate entrepreneurship and employment, the effectiveness of these plans are under observation. To support the growth of its labour market and economic activity, Linyi should also work towards improving its technological advancement and innovation capabilities, which is fundamental for high-quality growth. Meanwhile, given the relative poor performance in Linyi's environmental conditions, Linyi should implement policies to maintain the balance between economic growth and environmental sustainability.

References

Department of Commerce of Shandong Province. n.d. 'Linyi City Profile'. Department of Commerce of Shandong Province. Accessed 20 October 2017. http://en.shandongbusiness.gov.cn/city/81.

Li, Ruoxi. 2009. 'Shandong China, the Hometown of Confucius — Linyi'. 30 July 2009. http://shandong.chinadaily.com.cn/e/2009-07/30/content_8493114.htm.

The People's Government of Linyi. 2017a. '张术平同志在临沂市第十九届人民代表大会第一次会议上的政府工作报告 2017 Linyi Annual Government Work Report (in Chinese)'. The People's Government of Linyi. 24 February 2017. http://www.linyi.gov.cn/info/egovinfo/1105/gk/zwgk_page/004448101-02_gzbg/2017-0228001.htm.

———. 2017b. '临沂综保区：强化便利化服务单月进出口总额首次突破1亿美元 Linyi Free Trade Zone: Total Trade Value of August Exceeded 100 Million USD for the First Time (in Chinese)'. The People's Government of Linyi. 27 October 2017. http://www.linyi.gov.cn/info/egovinfo/1332/gk/zwgk_page/004448101-02_gzdt_/2017-1027002.htm.

———. n.d. '市情 Overview of Linyi City (in Chinese)'. The People's Government of Linyi (临沂市人民政府). Accessed 20 October 2017. http://linyi.gov.cn/sq.htm.

Yimengwanbao (沂蒙晚报). 2017. '2017年临沂市将新增农村劳动力转移就业10万人 Linyi Plans to Transfer 100 Thousands Rural Labor to Urban Area (in Chinese)'. IFeng News. 21 March 2017. http://news.ifeng.com/a/20170321/50808538_0.shtml.

Chapter 13: QINGDAO
Shandong Province

Location of City

Source: Asia Competitiveness Institute.

13.1 Profile of Qingdao City[1]

Located on the eastern coast of Shandong facing the Yellow Sea, Qingdao is the largest city in the province. Qingdao is renowned for its remarkable economic vibrancy and overall excellence as a lifestyle and tourism hub. Designated a Special Economic Zone (SEZ) by the Chinese government in 1984, Qingdao was in 2006 named one of the World Bank's six 'Golden Cities', in which were found the ideal conditions for strong and sustainable economic development. Qingdao currently retains sub-provincial administrative status and directly governs seven districts and three county-level cities, covering a total land area of 11,282 square kilometres and a population of 9,204,000.

In 2016, Qingdao's Gross Regional Domestic Product (GRDP) stood at RMB 1001 billion, with the city continuing to enjoy a healthy GRDP growth rate of 7.9%, as is reflected in Table 13.1. Qingdao's primary sector only constituted 3.7% of total GRDP. Contrastingly, its secondary sector constituted 41.6% of total GRDP, with specialisations in secondary industries such as maritime engineering, electronics, textiles, biotechnology, and food and beverage production and processing. Qingdao's tertiary sector constituted 54.7% of the city's GRDP, significant portions

[1]The relevant city information are from the Department of Commerce of Shandong Province (n.d.) and Wang (2009).

of which were derived from tourism-related service industries, with the city also continuing to nurture growing industries such as software development, information technology, and finance.

Qingdao is served by the Qingdao Liuting International Airport, a major regional aviation hub which caters to flights from several major cities around the world. Qingdao is also home to one of the world's largest container ports and is located at a nexus of road and rail networks. Qingdao also led its peers in terms of per capita public education appropriation, at RMB 2,749 per student in 2016. Additionally, at 7.2 billion passenger-kilometres, Qingdao's public transport network also led those of Shandong's other cities by a considerable margin in terms of passenger numbers and distance travelled.

Table 13.1: Key Economic Indicators for Qingdao, 2016

Land Area (km^2)	**11,282**
Population	
Total Population	9,204,000
Urban Population Ratio (%)	71.5
Average Life Expectancy (years)	77.2
Number of Employees (10,000)	591
Workforce Participation Rate (%)	70.8
Gross Regional Domestic Product (GRDP) — 2015 Prices	
GRDP (100 millions of RMB)	10,011
GRDP Per Capita (RMB)	109,407
GRDP Growth Rate (%)	7.9
Economic Composition	
Primary Sector (% of GRDP)	3.7
Secondary Sector (% of GRDP)	41.6
Tertiary Sector (% of GRDP)	54.7
Trade — 2016 Prices	
Exports (millions of RMB)	301,075
Imports (millions of RMB)	165,209
Dependency on Foreign Trade (%)	43.5
Infrastructure	
Per Capita Road Area (m^2)	18.2
Growth in the Number of Passengers Transported (10,000)	97.0
Growth in the Volume of Cargo Transported (10,000 tons)	2,080
Environment	
Green Coverage Ratio of Built-up Area (%)	38.6
Environmental Expenditure (% of Total Fiscal Expenditure)	1.6

Source: Asia Competitiveness Institute from the 2017 Shandong Statistical Yearbook.

13.2 In-Depth Urban Development of Qingdao, 2016*

13.2.1 Overall Urban Development Performance

Overall Performance

2017 Rank

1st

Out of 17 Cities

Score: 1.753

Rank	City	Score
1	Qingdao	1.753
2	Weihai	1.393
3	Yantai	1.312
4	Jinan	1.106
5	Weifang	0.855
6	Dongying	0.603
7	Zibo	0.403
	...	
16	Laiwu	–1.233
17	Liaocheng	–1.576

Qingdao ranks 1st in its Overall Performance, with a standardised score of 1.753. This places the city at the top in Shandong province and in the Top Five Group of 17 cities. Qingdao is followed by Weihai (1.393) at 2nd place.

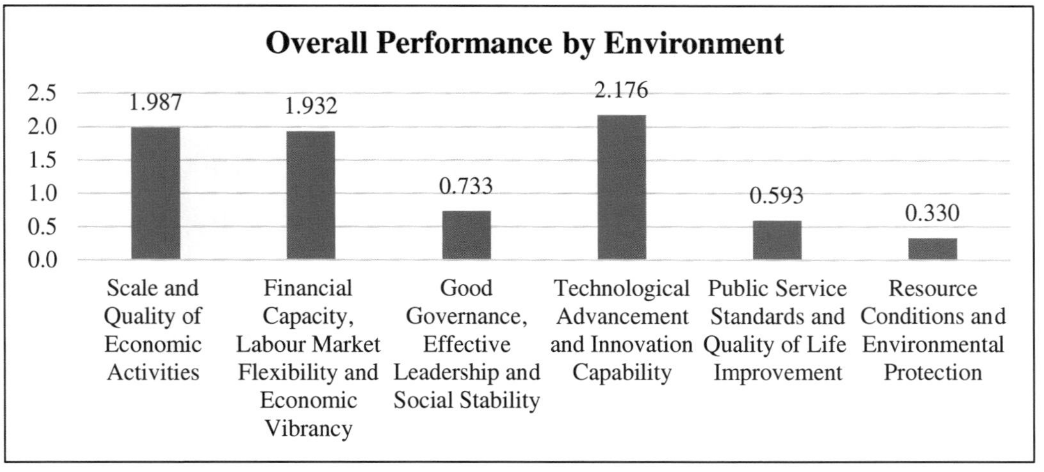

Among the six environments, Qingdao fares above the provincial average in all of them and particularly well in Technological Advancement and Innovation Capability, Scale and Quality of Economic Activities, and Financial Capacity, Labour Market Flexibility and Economic Vibrancy. Qingdao's lowest score is in the environment of Resource Conditions and Environmental Protection.

** For a complete list of rankings, see Tables 3.2 to 3.7 in Section 3.3 of Chapter 3.*

13.2.2 Urban Development within the Six Environments

Rank	City	Score
1	Qingdao	1.987
2	Yantai	1.687
3	Heze	1.289
4	Weifang	1.021
5	Weihai	0.849
6	Linyi	0.447
7	Dezhou	0.096
	...	
16	Jining	−1.273
17	Laiwu	−1.295

A: ***Scale and Quality of Economic Activities***

2017 Rank

1st

Out of 17 Cities

Score: 1.987

Qingdao ranks 1st for Scale and Quality of Economic Activities, with a standardised score of 1.987. This places the city in the Top Five Group of 17 cities. Qingdao is positioned ahead of Yantai (1.687) at 2nd place.

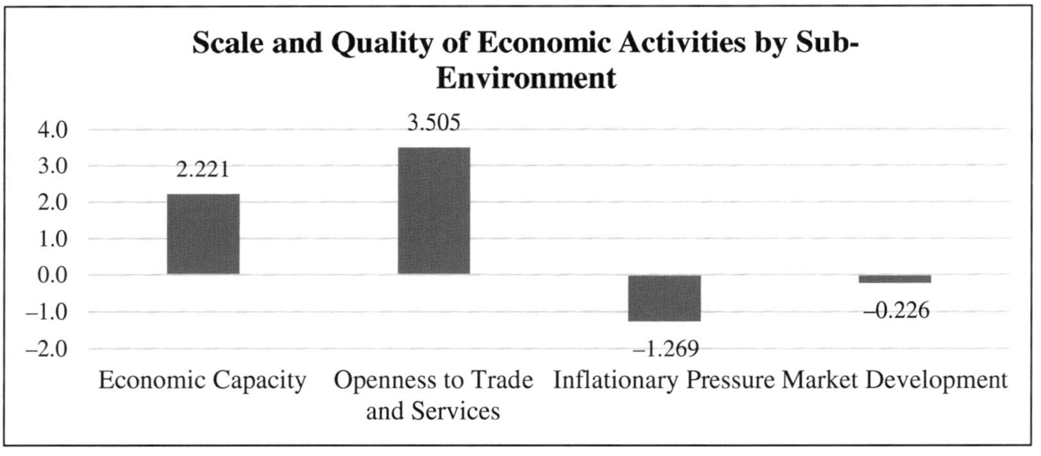

Looking at the four sub-environments of Scale and Quality of Economic Activities, Qingdao performs above the provincial average in two of them and remarkably well for Openness to Trade and Services, where it scores extremely well in the indicators of Trade Surplus, Total Trade Volumes, Investment Abroad and Foreign Investment in Actual Use. However, Qingdao performs below the provincial average in the remaining two sub-environments of Inflationary Pressure and Market Development. Among them, Qingdao is notably weaker for in the Inflationary Pressure sub-environment, where the indicators of Consumer Price Index, Retail Price Index and Residents' Satisfaction with Price Levels are particularly weak. In addition, the indicator of Satisfaction with Business Environment from the Market Development sub-environment performs poorly.

B: ***Financial Capacity, Labour Market Flexibility and Economic Vibrancy***

2017 Rank

2nd

Out of 17 Cities

Score: 1.932

Rank	City	Score
1	Jinan	2.264
2	Qingdao	1.932
3	Yantai	1.271
4	Weifang	0.441
5	Linyi	0.387
6	Dongying	0.293
7	Zibo	0.089
	...	
16	Dezhou	−1.026
17	Laiwu	−1.297

Qingdao ranks 2nd for Financial Capacity, Labour Market Flexibility and Economic Vibrancy, with a standardised score of 1.932. This places the city in the Top Five Group of 17 cities. Qingdao is positioned behind Jinan (2.264) at 1st place and well ahead of Yantai (1.271) at 3rd place.

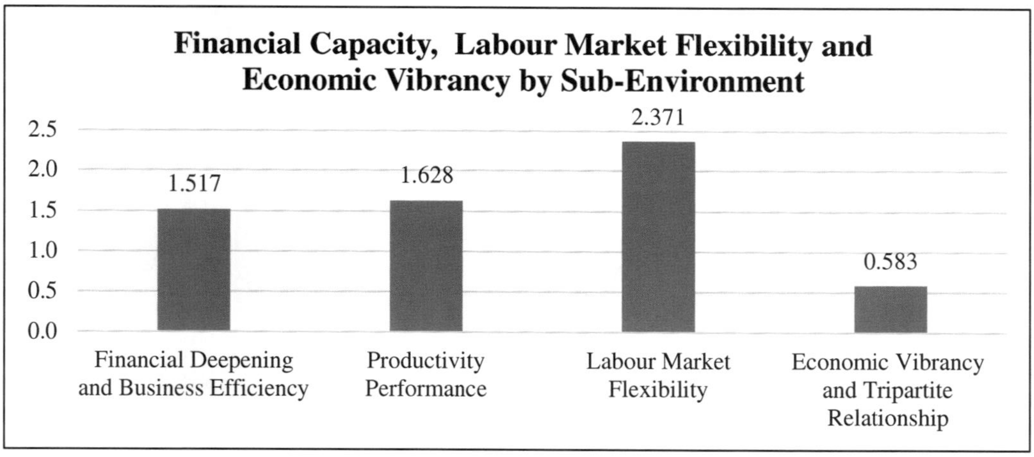

Among the four sub-environments of Financial Capacity, Labour Market Flexibility and Economic Vibrancy, Qingdao scores above the provincial average in all of them and especially better in Labour Market Flexibility, which has significantly high scores in the indicators of Proportion of Urban Workers Employed in Private Enterprises, Average Salary of Urban Employees and Rate of Migration Flow. Additionally, the indicators of the Financial Sector Value-added from the Financial Deepening and Business Efficiency sub-environment and Tertiary Industry Total Labour Productivity in the Productivity Performance sub-environment perform particularly well. However, Qingdao has a noticeably poor score in the indicator for Urban Registered Unemployment Rate in the Labour Market Flexibility sub-environment.

QINGDAO

Shandong Province

Rank	City	Score
1	Dezhou	1.465
2	Weihai	1.134
3	Weifang	0.797
4	Qingdao	0.733
5	Jinan	0.532
6	Tai'an	0.498
7	Heze	0.435
	...	
16	Laiwu	−1.588
17	Liaocheng	−2.473

C: *Good Governance, Effective Leadership and Social Stability*

2017 Rank

4th

Out of 17 Cities

Score: 0.733

Qingdao ranks 4th for Good Governance, Effective Leadership and Social Stability with a standardised score of 0.733. This places the city in the Top Five Group of 17 cities. Qingdao is positioned between Weifang (0.797) at 3rd place and Jinan (0.532) at 5th place.

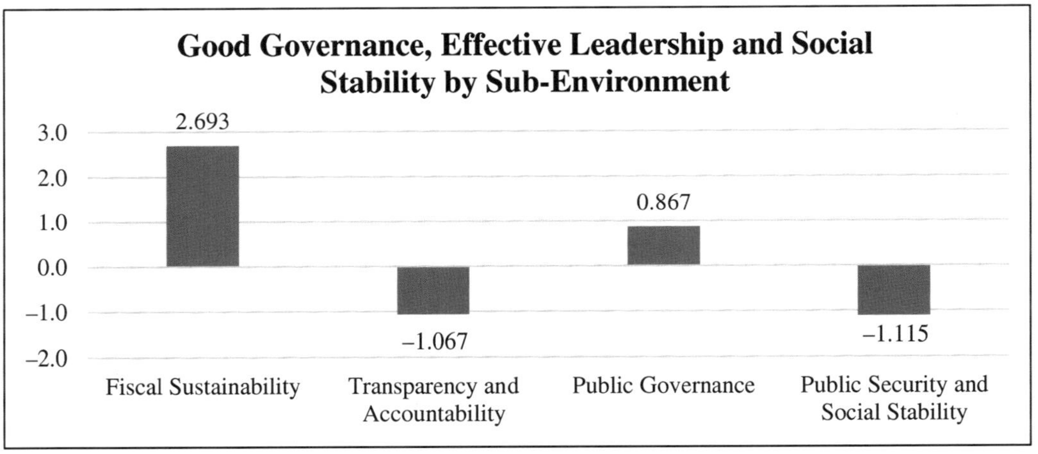

Looking at the four sub-environments of Good Governance, Effective Leadership and Social Stability, Qingdao scores above the provincial average in two of them and substantially better in the Fiscal Sustainability sub-environment, where the indicators of Government Fiscal Revenue and Government Fiscal Expenditure score remarkably well. Further, the indicator of Average Public Servant Salary from the Public Governance sub-environment also performs well. However, Qingdao scores below the provincial average in the sub-environments of Transparency and Accountability as well as Public Security and Social Stability. Specifically, the indicators of Public Perception of Government Conduct and Satisfaction with the Just of Judiciary, both from the Transparency and Accountability sub-environment score especially poorly. The indicator of Satisfaction of the Police Services in the Public Security and Social Stability sub-environment also obtains a weak score.

D: ***Technological Advancement and Innovation Capability***

2017 Rank

1st

Out of 17 Cities

Score: 2.176

Rank	City	Score
1	Qingdao	2.176
2	Weifang	1.417
3	Jinan	1.257
4	Yantai	1.009
5	Weihai	0.848
6	Zibo	0.492
7	Dongying	0.178
	...	
16	Zaozhuang	−1.192
17	Liaocheng	−1.221

Qingdao ranks 1st for Technological Advancement and Innovation Capability, with a standardised score of 2.176. This places the city in the Top Five Group of 17 cities. Qingdao is positioned well ahead of Weifang (1.417) at 2nd place.

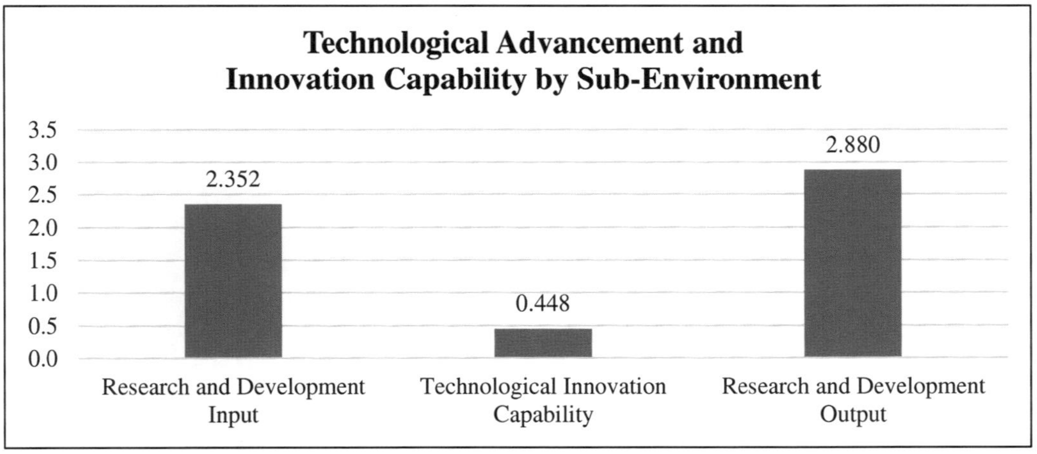

Among the three sub-environments of Technological Advancement and Innovation Capability, Qingdao performs above the provincial average in all of them and particularly well for Research Development Input and Research and Development Output. Specifically, the indicator of the Number of Patents Granted from the Research and Development Output registers an exceptionally high score. Other indicators that perform well include the Total Research and Development Expenditure of Enterprises Above Designated Size, Total Research and Development Man-Hour, and Number of Science and Technology Personnel, all from the Research and Development Input sub-environment. Nevertheless, Qingdao performs relatively weaker in the Technological Innovation Capability sub-environment, where the indicator of the Satisfaction with Innovation Environment registers a low score.

QINGDAO

Shandong Province

Rank	City	Score
1	Dongying	1.689
	...	
5	Zibo	0.794
6	Laiwu	0.675
7	Qingdao	0.593
8	Yantai	0.251
9	Rizhao	–0.154
	...	
16	Dezhou	–1.066
17	Liaocheng	–1.964

E: *Public Service Standards and Quality of Life Improvement*

2017 Rank

7th

Out of 17 Cities

Score: 0.593

Qingdao ranks 7th for Public Service Standards and Quality of Life Improvement with a standardised score of 0.593. This places the city in the Middle Seven Group of 17 cities. Qingdao is positioned between Laiwu (0.675) at 6th place and Yantai (0.251) at 8th place.

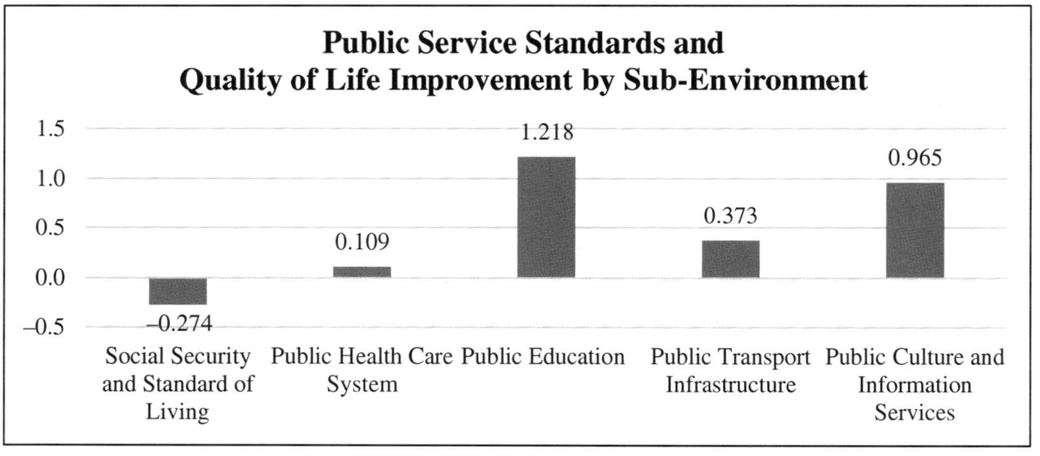

Among the five sub-environments of Public Service Standards and Quality of Life Improvement, Qingdao performs above the provincial average in four of them and particularly well for Public Education, where the indicator of the Public Education Appropriation Per Capita performs especially well. Other indicators with good scores include the Mobile Phone Penetration Per Capita from the Public Culture and Information Services sub-environment, as well as the Number of Urban Public Transport Vehicles Per 10,000 Population and Number of Passengers Transported, both from the Public Transport Infrastructure sub-environment. However, Qingdao scores below the provincial average in the Social Security and Standard of Living sub-environment, where the indicators of Residents' Perception of Happiness and Satisfaction of Income Disparity score especially poorly.

F: ***Resource Conditions and Environmental Protection***

2017 Rank

8th

Out of 17 Cities

Score: 0.330

Rank	City	Score
1	Weihai	1.632
	...	
6	Liaocheng	0.376
7	Tai'an	0.370
8	Qingdao	0.330
9	Jinan	0.281
10	Jining	–0.112
	...	
16	Binzhou	–1.586
17	Heze	–2.142

Qingdao ranks 8th for Resource Conditions and Environmental Protection with a standardised score of 0.330. This places the city in the Middle Seven Group of 17 cities. Qingdao is positioned between Tai'an (0.370) at 7th place and ahead of Jinan (0.281) at 9th place.

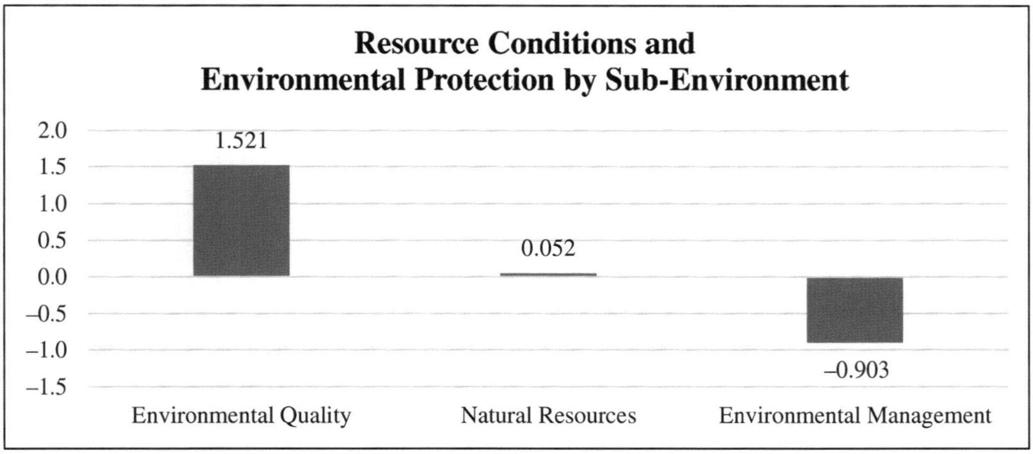

Among the three sub-environments of Resource Conditions and Environmental Protection, Qingdao scores above the provincial average in two of them and especially better for Environmental Quality, where the indicators of Ammoniacal Nitrogen Discharge Per RMB 10,000 GRDP and Chemical Oxygen Demand Per RMB 10,000 GRDP score well. Further, the indicator of Water Consumption Per RMB 10,000 GRDP from the Natural Resources sub-environment also registers a good score. However, Qingdao performs below the provincial average in the sub-environment of Environmental Management, where it scores particularly unfavourably in the indicators of Forest Land Growth and Green Coverage Ratio of Built-up Area. In addition, the indicator of Per Capita Freshwater Resource from the Natural Resources sub-environment performs poorly as well.

QINGDAO

Shandong Province

Figure 13.1: Median & Maximum Web for Qingdao

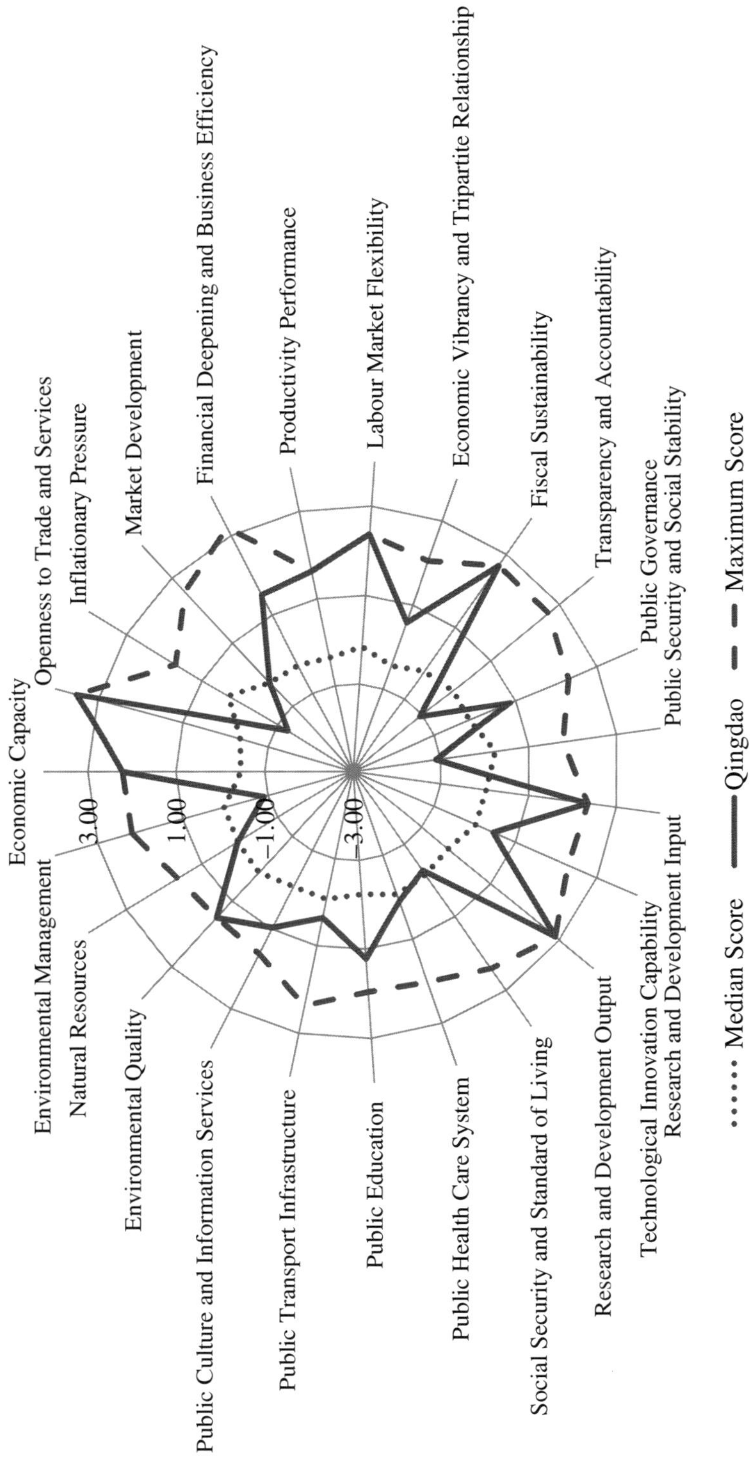

Source: Asia Competitiveness Institute.

13.2.3 Median and Maximum Web Analysis

To better understand Qingdao's relative strengths and weaknesses, it is useful to compare and contrast its scores for the 23 sub-environments against the median and maximum scores of Shandong's 17 cities.

In Figure 13.1, the median and maximum scores for 17 Shandong cities are shown as dotted and dashed lines respectively, while scores for Qingdao are shown as a solid line.

Comparison to Median Scores

Qingdao scores above the median for 16 of the 23 sub-environments, most notably in Openness to Trade and Services, Fiscal Sustainability and Research and Development Output.

On the other hand, Qingdao scores below the median for five sub-environments, especially for Public Security and Social Stability, and Inflationary Pressure. The remaining two sub-environments of Natural Resources and Market Development are at the median.

Comparison to Maximum Scores

Qingdao scores below the provincial maximum of the 17 Shandong cities in 15 out of the 23 sub-environments. Qingdao achieves the provincial maximum score in eight sub-environments, namely Economic Capacity (2.221), Openness to Trade and Services (3.505), Productivity Performance (1.628), Labour Market Flexibility (2.371), Fiscal Sustainability (2.693), Research and Development Input (2.352), Research and Development Output (2.880), and Environmental Quality (1.521).

Qingdao's score in the Transparency and Accountability (−1.067) is farthest from the maximum, which is held by Tai'an (2.676). Further, Qingdao's score in Public Culture and Information Services (0.965) is closest to the maximum, which is held by Weihai (1.617).

13.3 Summary of Empirical Findings of Qingdao and *What-if* Urban Development Simulation

13.3.1 Summary of Empirical Findings, 20% Strongest and Weakest Indicators

Overall Performance 1st Score: 1.753		
Scale and Quality of Economic Activities 1st Score: 1.987	Financial Capacity, Labour Market Flexibility and Economic Vibrancy 2nd Score: 1.932	Good Governance, Effective Leadership and Social Stability 4th Score: 0.733
Technological Advancement and Innovation Capability 1st Score: 2.176	Public Service Standards and Quality of Life Improvement 7th Score: 0.593	Resource Conditions and Environmental Protection 8th Score: 0.330

(Rank out of 17 cities)

Summary

Qingdao ranks 1st out of 17 Shandong cities in its Overall Performance. Qingdao performs above the provincial average in all of the six environments, where the environments of Scale and Quality of Economic Activities and Technological Advancement and Innovation Capability perform exceptionally better. Meanwhile Qingdao's worst performing environment is that of the Resource Conditions and Environmental Protection, although it remains above the provincial average.

Strengths

As observed in Table 13.2, Qingdao performs especially well in the Scale and Quality of Economic Activities, with seven out of 26 of its 20% Strongest Indicators in that environment. Among Qingdao's best performing indicators are Foreign Investment in Actual Use, Investment Abroad and Trade Surplus.

Weaknesses

As observed in Table 13.3, Qingdao is weaker in the environment of Public Service Standards and Quality of Life Improvement, where it has eight out of 26 of its 20% Weakest Indicators under this environment. Among Qingdao's worst performing indicators are Public Perception of Government Conduct, Satisfaction of Public Health Care Services and Green Coverage Ratio of Built-up Area.

Table 13.2: 20% Strongest Indicators for Qingdao

Rank	20% Strongest Indicator	Score	SQEA	FCLMFEV	GGELSS	TAIC	PSSQLI	RCEP
1	Foreign Investment in Actual Use	3.746	✓					
2	Investment Abroad	3.236	✓					
3	Trade Surplus	3.233	✓					
4	Total Trade Volumes	3.187	✓					
5	Government Fiscal Expenditure	3.157			✓			
6	Number of Patents Granted	3.099				✓		
7	Government Fiscal Revenue	3.086			✓			
8	Total R&D Expenditure of Enterprises Above Designated Size	2.886				✓		
9	Gross Regional Domestic Product	2.774	✓					
10	Per Capita Fixed Investment	2.697	✓					
11	Proportion of Urban Workers Employed in Private Enterprises	2.678		✓				
12	Total R&D Man-Hour	2.540				✓		
13	Government Fiscal Expenditure Per Capita	2.485			✓			
14	Financial Sector Value-Added	2.419		✓				
15	Number of Science and Technology Personnel	2.368				✓		
16	Number of Passengers Transported	2.341					✓	
17	Average Public Servant Salary	2.307			✓			
18	Number of Existing Patents Per 10,000 Population	2.291				✓		
19	Average Salary of Urban Employees	2.185		✓				
20	Government Fiscal Revenue Per Capita	2.135			✓			
21	Public Education Appropriation Per Capita	2.075					✓	
22	Insurance Net Income	2.018		✓				
23	Rate of Migration Flow	2.007		✓				
24	Number of Urban Public Transport Vehicles Per 10,000 Population (Standard Number)	1.869					✓	
25	Service Sector as a Percentage of GRDP	1.802	✓					
26	Per Capita Annual Disposable Income	1.801					✓	

Table 13.3: 20% Weakest Indicators for Qingdao

Rank	20% Weakest Indicator	Score	SQEA	FCLMFEV	GGELSS	TAIC	PSSQLI	RCEP
106	Environmental Expenditure as a Percentage of Total Fiscal Expenditure	–0.934						✓
107	Per Capita Arable Land	–1.056						✓
108	Frequency of Using the Internet for Daily Convenience	–1.098					✓	
109	Manufacturing Sector as a Percentage of GRDP	–1.145	✓					
110	Retail Price Index	–1.146	✓					
111	Satisfaction with Business Environment	–1.180	✓					
112	Satisfaction with Innovation Environment	–1.195				✓		
113	Fire Fatality Per 10,000 Population	–1.307			✓			
114	Urban Registered Unemployment Rate	–1.330		✓				
115	Satisfaction with Urban Management Personnels	–1.361			✓			
116	Forest Land Growth	–1.385						✓
117	Consumer Price Index (CPI)	–1.620	✓					
118	Satisfaction of Income Disparity	–1.653					✓	
119	Satisfaction of Public Education System	–1.702					✓	
120	Residents' Satisfaction with Price Levels	–1.746	✓					
121	Public Health and Medical Service Expenses as a Share of GRDP	–1.771					✓	
122	Residents' Perception of Happiness	–1.824					✓	
123	Satisfaction of Traffic Conditions	–1.840					✓	
124	Satisfaction of the Police Services	–1.861			✓			
125	Index for Quality of E-Government System	–1.902			✓			
126	Per Capita Freshwater Resource	–1.909						✓
127	Per Capita Road Area	–1.937					✓	
128	Satisfaction with the Just of Judiciary	–1.984			✓			
129	Green Coverage Ratio of Built-up Area	–2.102						✓
130	Satisfaction of Public Health Care Services	–2.110					✓	
131	Public Perception of Government Conduct	–2.203			✓			

Source: Asia Competitiveness Institute.

Notes: SQEA: Scale and Quality of Economic Activities; FCLMFEV: Financial Capacity, Labour Market Flexibility and Economic Vibrancy; GGELSS: Good Governance, Effective Leadership and Social Stability; TAIC: Technological Advancement and Innovation Capability; PSSQLI: Public Service Standards and Quality of Life Improvement; RCEP: Resource Conditions and Environmental Protection.

13.3.2 *What-if* Urban Development Simulation

ACI has devised a simulation methodology to improve the ranking of a particular city by improving on its 20% Weakest Indicators as shown in Table 13.3.[2] The figures below show Qingdao's ranking and standardised scores before and after the policy-induced simulation. Refer to Tables 3.8 to 3.14 in Section 3.4 of Chapter 3 for a complete list of simulation results for all cities.

Overall Performance

	Before		After
Rank	1st	▶	1st
Score	1.753		2.583

Scale and Quality of Economic Activities

	Before	After
Rank	1st	1st
Score	1.987	2.700

Financial Capacity, Labour Market Flexibility and Economic Vibrancy

	Before	After
Rank	2nd	2nd
Score	1.932	1.972

Good Governance, Effective Leadership and Social Stability

	Before	After
Rank	4th	1st
Score	0.733	2.059

Technological Advancement and Innovation Capability

	Before	After
Rank	1st	1st
Score	2.176	2.368

Public Service Standards and Quality of Life Improvement

	Before	After
Rank	7th	1st
Score	0.593	1.619

Resource Conditions and Environmental Protection

	Before	After
Rank	8th	1st
Score	0.330	1.553

After the *What-if* simulation, Qingdao remains at 1st place in terms of its Overall Performance. However, Qingdao's standardised score improves from 1.753 to 2.583. This leap is plausible if the city manages to successfully address its 20% Weakest Indicators.

The simulation further highlights substantial improvement for Qingdao in some of its environments, most notably in Resource Conditions and Environmental Protection, where its rank will rise from 8th to 1st. Such encouraging results should incentivise Qingdao to strive to improve the indicators under the 20% Weakest Indicators list. These indicators include Green Coverage Ratio of Built-up Area, Per Capita Freshwater Resource and Forest Land Growth.

[2]The methodology for *What-if* simulation is thoroughly explained in Section 2.7 of Chapter 2.

13.4 Concluding Notes: Public Policy Implications[3]

Areas for Commendation

Qingdao performs especially well in the environment of Scale and Quality of Economic Activities, which has eight out of 26 of its 20% Strongest Indicators in this environment, as indicated in Table 13.2.

Qingdao holds the maximum score for eight sub-environments, namely Economic Capacity (2.221), Openness to Trade and Services (3.505), Productivity Performance (1.628), Labour Market Flexibility (2.371), Fiscal Sustainability (2.693), Research and Development Input (2.352), Research and Development Output (2.880) and Environmental Quality (1.521). In addition, Qingdao scores above the provincial average in 17 out of 23 sub-environments.

In the past five years from 2012 to 2016, Qingdao performed well in building its financial capacity, economic vibrancy and harmony. Its financial sector value-added contributed approximately 6.7% of its GRDP. Moreover, it obtained direct financing of more than RMB 45 billion during this period. These achievements were largely influenced by the designation of the wealth management financial reform pilot area.

Areas for Improvement

While Qingdao does not score below the provincial average in any of the six environments, it has an incentive to address its weaknesses to maintain its strong position in Shandong, such as the environment of Resource Conditions and Environmental Protection. Most crucially, Qingdao should address the environment of Public Service Standards and Quality of Life Improvement, where it contributes eight out of 26 of Qingdao's 20% Weakest Indicators, as shown in Table 13.3. Additionally, as gleaned from the *What-if* Urban Development Simulation, the environment of Resource Conditions and Environmental Protection should be prioritised because that is the environment in which Qingdao will achieve the greatest improvement in its ranking — seven positions — relative to other environments.

Moreover, Qingdao obtains a low score in the sub-environment of Inflationary Pressure (−1.269), and scores below the provincial average in six out of 23 sub-environments.

The Qingdao government had plans to address the relatively weak position of the manufacturing sector in the economy. Specifically, it aimed to promote Qingdao as an advanced manufacturing hub by promoting intelligent, premium, environment-friendly and service manufacturing. In addition, there were plans to build four provincial-level manufacturing innovation centres and cultivate 60 municipal-level enterprise technology centres and industrial design centres in 2017. In this way, the manufacturing sector as a share of GRDP is expected to increase steadily if these measures are executed effectively.

[3]The relevant statistical data and government policies are from Qingdao Environmental Protection Bureau (2017), Qingdao Municipal People's Government (2017) and Xu (2017).

QINGDAO

Shandong Province

In 2017, Qingdao has made progress at improving its environmental conditions where its air and water quality both increased on a year on year basis. Further, it has resolved over 1,000 environmental issues brought up by the Central Environmental Inspectorate and rectified more than 2,400 polluting firms reported by the public. Moreover, the government strengthened its accountability system on the civil servants. This is a good sign suggesting that the city is now working towards a better environmental condition.

Future Potential Development

In summary, Qingdao should focus on improving the environment of Public Service Standards and Quality of Life Improvement by raising public health standards and medical service expenditure. In addition, Qingdao should look towards improving the quality of its environment by increasing its green coverage in urban spaces and consider raising environmental expenditure to improve the Resource Conditions and Environmental Protection environment.

In September 2017, the government of Qingdao convened for its first meeting to discuss public health. The meeting was very impressive in terms of its scale. During the meeting, the objective and plan for public health in Qingdao were announced and deployed. The government also promised to consider public health in all aspects of public policies. In the future, more development and government spending in this sector are expected.

References

Department of Commerce of Shandong Province. n.d. 'Qingdao City Profile'. Department of Commerce of Shandong Province. Accessed 27 October 2017. http://en.shandongbusiness.gov.cn/city/65.

Qingdao Environmental Protection Bureau. 2017. '青岛以硬措施打好污染防治攻坚战 Qingdao Tackled Environmental Pollution with Tough Measures (in Chinese)'. Qingdao Environmental Protection Bureau. 7 December 2017. http://www.qepb.gov.cn/m2/view.aspx?n=11af4b91-1a82-4c70-b2ce-e60f0620a174#auto.

Qingdao Municipal People's Government. 2017. '2017年政府工作报告 2017 Qingdao Annual Government Work Report (in Chinese)'. 24 April 2017. http://www.qingdao.gov.cn/n172/n25685095/n25685320/n25685925/n25687788/170424094634803311.html.

Wang, Qian. 2009. 'Qingdao'. Shandong China, the Hometown of Confucius. 23 July 2009. http://shandong.chinadaily.com.cn/e/2009-07/23/content_8464637.htm.

Xu, Jun. 2017. '您心中2017年卫生计生便民惠民十件大事有哪些? What Are the Top Ten Policies of Healthcare in 2017 (in Chinese)'. Dazhongwang Qingdao (大众网青岛). 14 December 2017. http://qingdao.dzwww.com/xinwen/qingdaonews/201712/t20171214_16291039.htm.

Chapter 14: RIZHAO
Shandong Province

Location of City

Source: Asia Competitiveness Institute.

14.1 Profile of Rizhao City[1]

The area surrounding Rizhao is renowned in archaeological circles as a cradle of ancient human habitation and is home to some of the largest discovered settlements of the Neolithic Dawenkou and Longshan cultures. Today, Rizhao directly administers two districts and two counties, spanning a total land area of 5,359 square kilometres and a total population of 2,901,100. The city also plays host to one of the world's largest seaports and sets an example to its neighbours in terms of its dedication to improving urban liveability — an endeavour for which the city's municipal government was awarded a UN-Habitat Scroll of Honour in 2009.

In 2016, Rizhao's Gross Regional Domestic Product (GRDP) stood at RMB 180 billion, with the city boasting a healthy GRDP growth rate of 8.1%, as is reflected in Table 14.1. Rizhao is rich in marine resources, and its primary sector constituted 8.1% of GRDP. It is also a manufacturing hub, with its secondary sector constituting 47.3% of GRDP for 2016, due to the highly developed secondary industries, including steel production, automobile manufacturing, petrochemical processing and food processing. Finally, Rizhao's tertiary sector constituted 44.6% of

[1] The relevant city information are from the Department of Commerce of Shandong Province (n.d.), Rizhao Municipal People's Government (n.d.) and China Daily (2009).

GRDP and has benefited from developments in industries such as e-commerce, service outsourcing and information technology.

Rizhao is served by the Rizhao Shanzihe Airport, which caters to domestic flights. The city also benefits from linkages enabled by its large seaport, which offers passenger services to the port of Pyeongtaek in South Korea. Rizhao is also well connected to regional high-speed rail and highway networks due to its importance as a seaport and looks to benefit from several forthcoming railway projects involving Shandong's coastline. Rizhao has also invested heavily into public security and in 2016 scored highly with regard to public perceptions of security, as well as overall satisfaction with police services.

Table 14.1: Key Economic Indicators for Rizhao, 2016

Land Area (km²)	**5,359**
Population	
Total Population	2,901,100
Urbanisation Ratio (%)	56.9
Average Life Expectancy (years)	76.0
Number of Employees (10,000)	210
Workforce Participation Rate (%)	75.6
Gross Regional Domestic Product (GRDP) — 2015 Prices	
GRDP (100 millions of RMB)	1,802
GRDP Per Capita (RMB)	62,357
GRDP Growth Rate (%)	8.1
Economic Composition	
Primary Sector (% of GRDP)	8.1
Secondary Sector (% of GRDP)	47.3
Tertiary Sector (% of GRDP)	44.6
Trade — 2016 Prices	
Exports (millions of RMB)	27,458
Imports (millions of RMB)	73,403
Dependency on Foreign Trade (%)	45.8
Infrastructure	
Per Capita Road Area (m²)	22.4
Growth in the Number of Passengers Transported (10,000)	96.0
Growth in the Volume of Cargo Transported (10,000 tons)	662
Environment	
Green Coverage Ratio of Built-up Area (%)	45.4
Environmental Expenditure (% of Total Fiscal Expenditure)	3.1

Source: Asia Competitiveness Institute from the 2017 Shandong Statistical Yearbook.

14.2 In-Depth Urban Development of Rizhao, 2016*

14.2.1 Overall Urban Development Performance

Overall Performance

2017 Rank

11th

Out of 17 Cities

Score: –0.472

Rank	City	Score
1	Qingdao	1.753
	...	
9	Tai'an	–0.280
10	Dezhou	–0.302
11	Rizhao	–0.472
12	Heze	–0.615
13	Jining	–0.706
	...	
16	Laiwu	–1.233
17	Liaocheng	–1.576

Rizhao ranks 11th in its Overall Performance, with a standardised score of –0.472. This places the city in the Middle Seven Group of 17 cities. Rizhao is positioned between Dezhou (–0.302) at 10th place and Heze (–0.615) at 12th place.

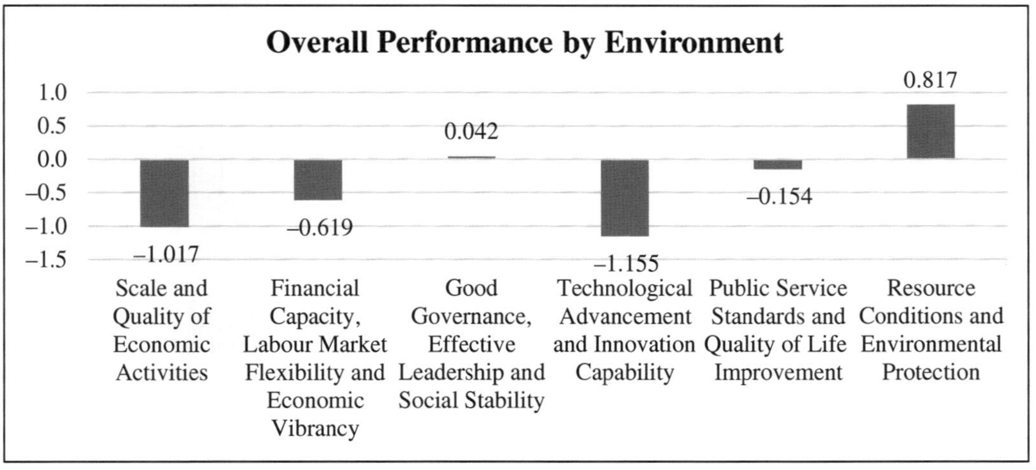

Among the six environments, Rizhao scores below the provincial average in four of them and fares particularly weaker for Technological Advancement and Innovation Capability and Scale and Quality of Economic Activities. On the other hand, Rizhao scores above the provincial average in two environments and notably better in Resource Conditions and Environmental Protection. The Good Governance, Effective Leadership and Social Stability environment performs marginally above the provincial average.

** For a complete list of rankings, see Tables 3.2 to 3.7 in Section 3.3 of Chapter 3.*

14.2.2 Urban Development within the Six Environments

Rank	City	Score
1	Qingdao	1.987
	...	
10	Zaozhuang	–0.412
11	Binzhou	–0.573
12	Liaocheng	–0.665
13	Zibo	–0.674
14	Dongying	–0.782
15	Rizhao	–1.017
16	Jining	–1.273
17	Laiwu	–1.295

A: ***Scale and Quality of Economic Activities***

2017 Rank

15th

Out of 17 Cities

Score: –1.017

Rizhao ranks 15th for Scale and Quality of Economic Activities, with a standardised score of –1.017. This places the city in the Bottom Five Group of 17 cities. Rizhao is positioned between Dongying (–0.782) at 14th place and Jining (–1.273) at 16th place.

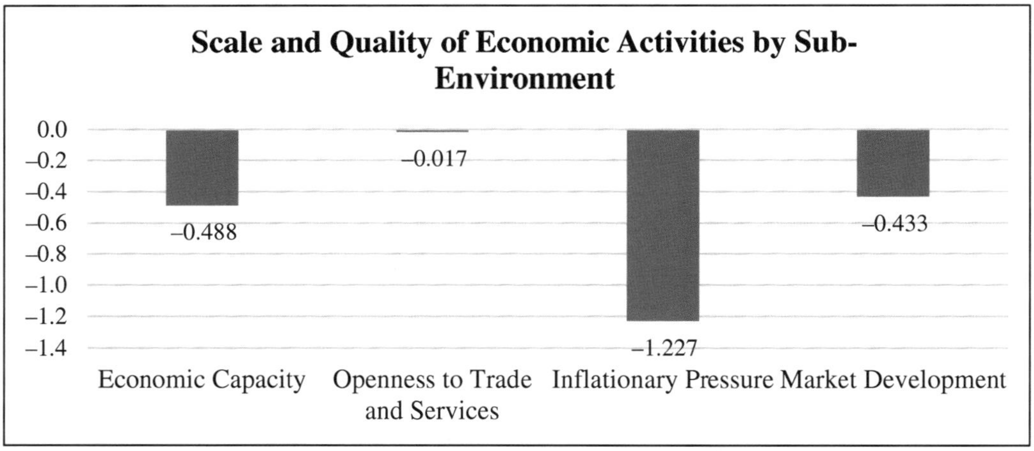

Looking at the four sub-environments of Scale and Quality of Economic Activities, Rizhao performs below the provincial average in all of them and particularly poorly for Inflationary Pressure, where it has low scores in the indicators of Producer Price Index and Urban Residents' Per Capita Expenditure Growth Rate. In addition, the indicator of Trade Surplus from the Openness to Trade and Services sub-environment obtains a low score as well. However, Rizhao has a noticeably high score for the indicator of Dependency on Foreign Trade (Foreign Trade as a Share of GDRP) from the Openness to Trade and Services sub-environment.

B: ***Financial Capacity, Labour Market Flexibility and Economic Vibrancy***

2017 Rank

11th

Out of 17 Cities

Score: –0.619

Rank	City	Score
1	Jinan	2.264
	...	
9	Jining	–0.171
10	Binzhou	–0.329
11	Rizhao	–0.619
12	Heze	–0.638
13	Tai'an	–0.763
	...	
16	Dezhou	–1.026
17	Laiwu	–1.297

Rizhao ranks 11th for Financial Capacity, Labour Market Flexibility and Economic Vibrancy, with a standardised score of –0.619. This places the city in the Middle Seven Group of 17 cities. Rizhao is positioned behind Binzhou (–0.329) at 10th place and slightly ahead of Heze (–0.638) at 12th place.

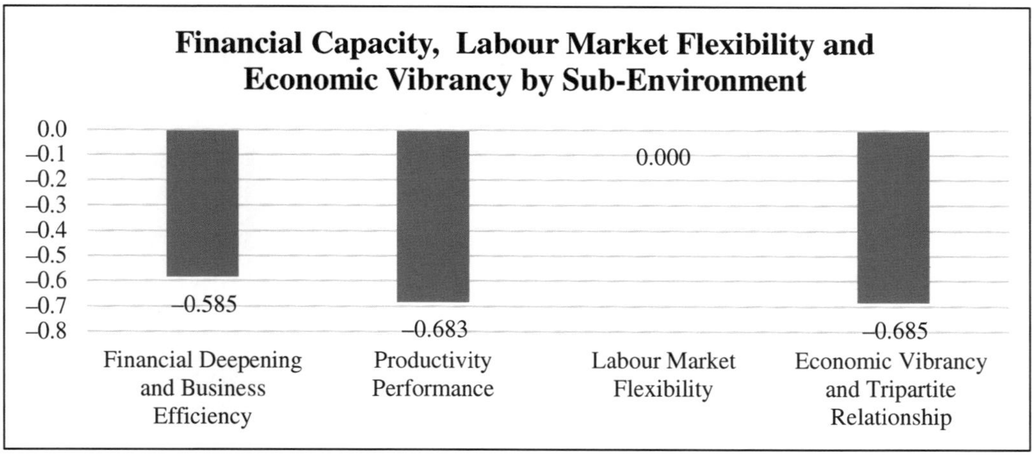

Among the four sub-environments of Financial Capacity, Labour Market Flexibility and Economic Vibrancy, Rizhao scores below the provincial average in all of them and weakest for Economic Vibrancy and Tripartite Relationship, where the indicator of Growth in the Volume of Cargo Transported scores relatively low. In addition, the indicators of Profit Margin of Enterprises Above Designated Size from the Productivity Performance sub-environment as well as the Insurance Net Income from the Financial Deepening and Business Efficiency sub-environment score poorly as well. However, the sub-environment for Labour Market Flexibility performs relatively better and only marginally below the provincial average, with a strong score in the indicator of Proportion of Workforce Employed in Service Sector.

RIZHAO

Shandong Province

Rank	City	Score
1	Dezhou	1.465
	...	
10	Yantai	0.192
11	Dongying	0.173
12	Rizhao	0.042
13	Jining	–0.527
14	Binzhou	–0.849
	...	
16	Laiwu	–1.588
17	Liaocheng	–2.473

C: *Good Governance, Effective Leadership and Social Stability*

2017 Rank

12th

Out of 17 Cities

Score: 0.042

Rizhao ranks 12th for Good Governance, Effective Leadership and Social Stability with a standardised score of 0.042. This places the city in the Middle Seven Group of 17 cities. Rizhao is positioned between Dongying (0.173) at 11th place and Jining (–0.527) at 13th place.

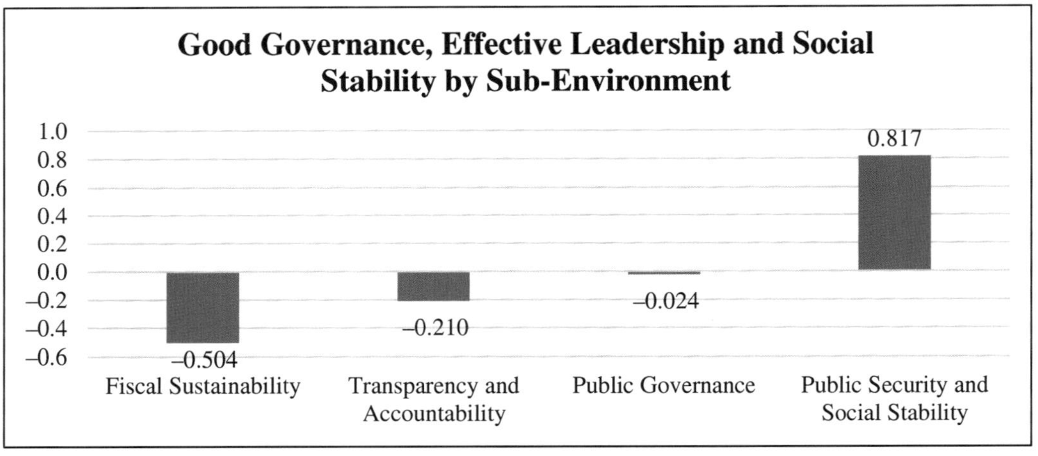

Looking at the four sub-environments of Good Governance, Effective Leadership and Social Stability, Rizhao scores above the provincial average only in Public Security and Social Stability, where the indicators of Public Perception of Security and Satisfaction of the Police Services score relatively well. However, Rizhao scores below the provincial average in the remaining three sub-environments and relatively weaker for Fiscal Sustainability, where the indicators of Government Fiscal Expenditure and Government Fiscal Revenue score poorly. Other indicators with low scores include the Number of Releases of Government Information for Public Viewing and Number of Responses to Government Issues of Public Interest, both from the Transparency and Accountability sub-environment.

D: *Technological Advancement and Innovation Capability*

2017 Rank

15th

Out of 17 Cities

Score: –1.155

Rank	City	Score
1	Qingdao	2.176
	...	
10	Tai'an	–0.457
11	Dezhou	–0.517
12	Binzhou	–0.559
13	Laiwu	–0.812
14	Heze	–0.897
15	Rizhao	–1.155
16	Zaozhuang	–1.192
17	Liaocheng	–1.221

Rizhao ranks 15th for Technological Advancement and Innovation Capability, with a standardised score of –1.155. This places the city in the Bottom Five Group of 17 cities. Rizhao is positioned between Heze (–0.897) at 14th place and Zaozhuang (–1.192) at 16th place.

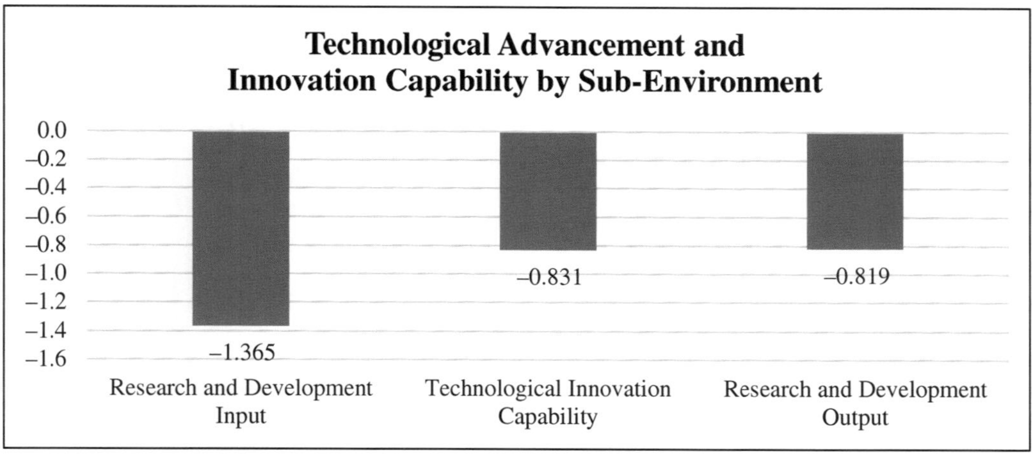

Among the three sub-environments of Technological Advancement and Innovation Capability, Rizhao performs below the provincial average in all of them and particularly poor in the Research and Development Input sub-environment, where it registers low scores in many indicators including Total Research and Development Expenditure of Enterprises Above Designated Size as a Percentage of Cash Flow and Number of Science and Technology Personnel. Other indicators with weak performance include the Number of Provincial-level Science Parks from the Technological Innovation Capability sub-environment and Number of Patents Granted from Research and Development Output sub-environment. Nevertheless, the indicator of Satisfaction with Innovation Environment in the Technological Innovation Capability sub-environment performs relatively better.

RIZHAO

Shandong Province

Rank	City	Score
1	Dongying	1.689
	...	
7	Qingdao	0.593
8	Yantai	0.251
9	Rizhao	–0.154
10	Linyi	–0.307
11	Tai'an	–0.567
	...	
16	Dezhou	–1.066
17	Liaocheng	–1.964

E: *Public Service Standards and Quality of Life Improvement*

2017 Rank

9th

Out of 17 Cities

Score: –0.154

Rizhao ranks 9th for Public Service Standards and Quality of Life Improvement with a standardised score of –0.154. This places the city in the Middle Seven Group of 17 cities. Rizhao is positioned between Yantai (0.251) at 8th place and Linyi (–0.307) at 10th place.

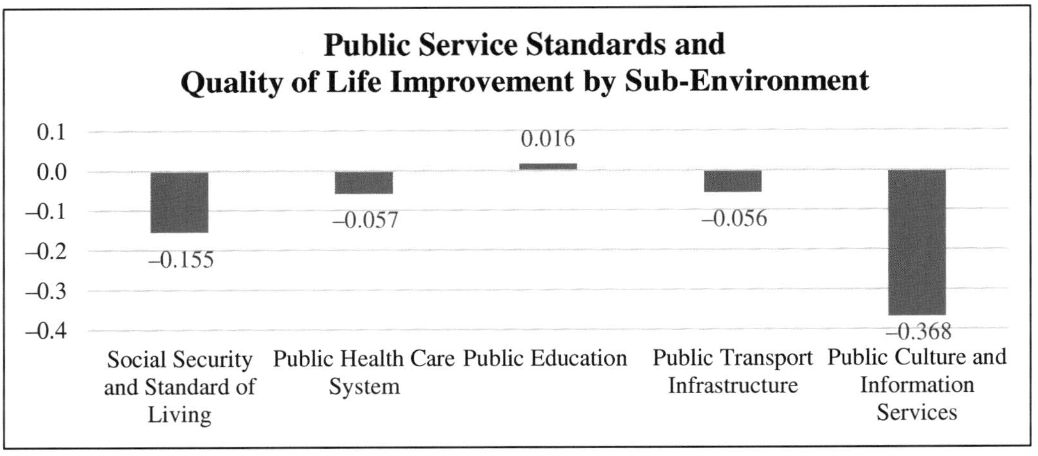

Among the five sub-environments of Public Service Standards and Quality of Life Improvement, Rizhao performs slightly above the provincial average in Public Education, where the indicator of Satisfaction of Public Education System scores relatively well. However, Rizhao performs below the provincial average in the remaining four sub-environments and relatively worse in Public Culture and Information Services, where the indicator of Percentage of Public Expenditure on Cultural Initiatives scores relatively low. Nevertheless, the indicators of Cleanliness of Public Toilets from the Public Health Care System sub-environment, Satisfaction of Public Transport Services from the Public Transport Infrastructure sub-environment, and Frequency of Using the Internet for Daily Convenience from the Public Culture and Information Services sub-environment score especially well.

F: ***Resource Conditions and Environmental Protection***

2017 Rank

4th

Out of 17 Cities

Score: 0.817

Rank	City	Score
1	Weihai	1.632
2	Yantai	1.394
3	Dongying	1.118
4	Rizhao	0.817
5	Zibo	0.665
6	Liaocheng	0.376
7	Tai'an	0.370
	...	
16	Binzhou	−1.586
17	Heze	−2.142

Rizhao ranks 4th for Resource Conditions and Environmental Protection with a standardised score of 0.817. This places the city in the Top Five Group of 17 cities. Rizhao is positioned between Dongying (1.118) at 3rd place and Zibo (0.665) at 5th place.

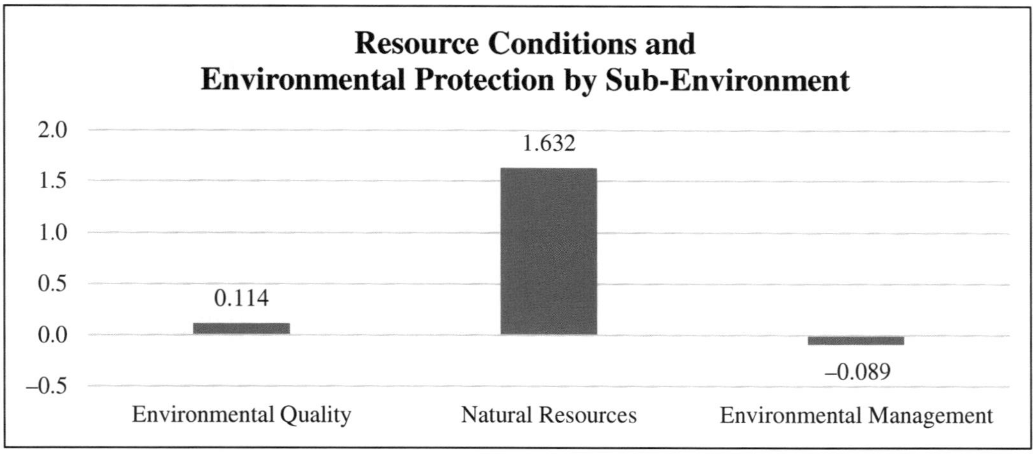

Among the three sub-environments of Resource Conditions and Environmental Protection, Rizhao scores above the provincial average in two of them and significantly better for Natural Resources, where the indicators of Electricity Consumption Per RMB 10,000 GDRP and Per Capita Arable Land perform especially well. However, Rizhao performs slightly below the provincial average in Environmental Management, where it scores unfavourably in the indicator of Forest Land Growth. Nevertheless, Rizhao performs relatively well in the indicator of Green Coverage Ratio of Built-up Area from the Environmental Management sub-environment.

RIZHAO

Shandong Province

Figure 14.1: Median & Maximum Web for Rizhao

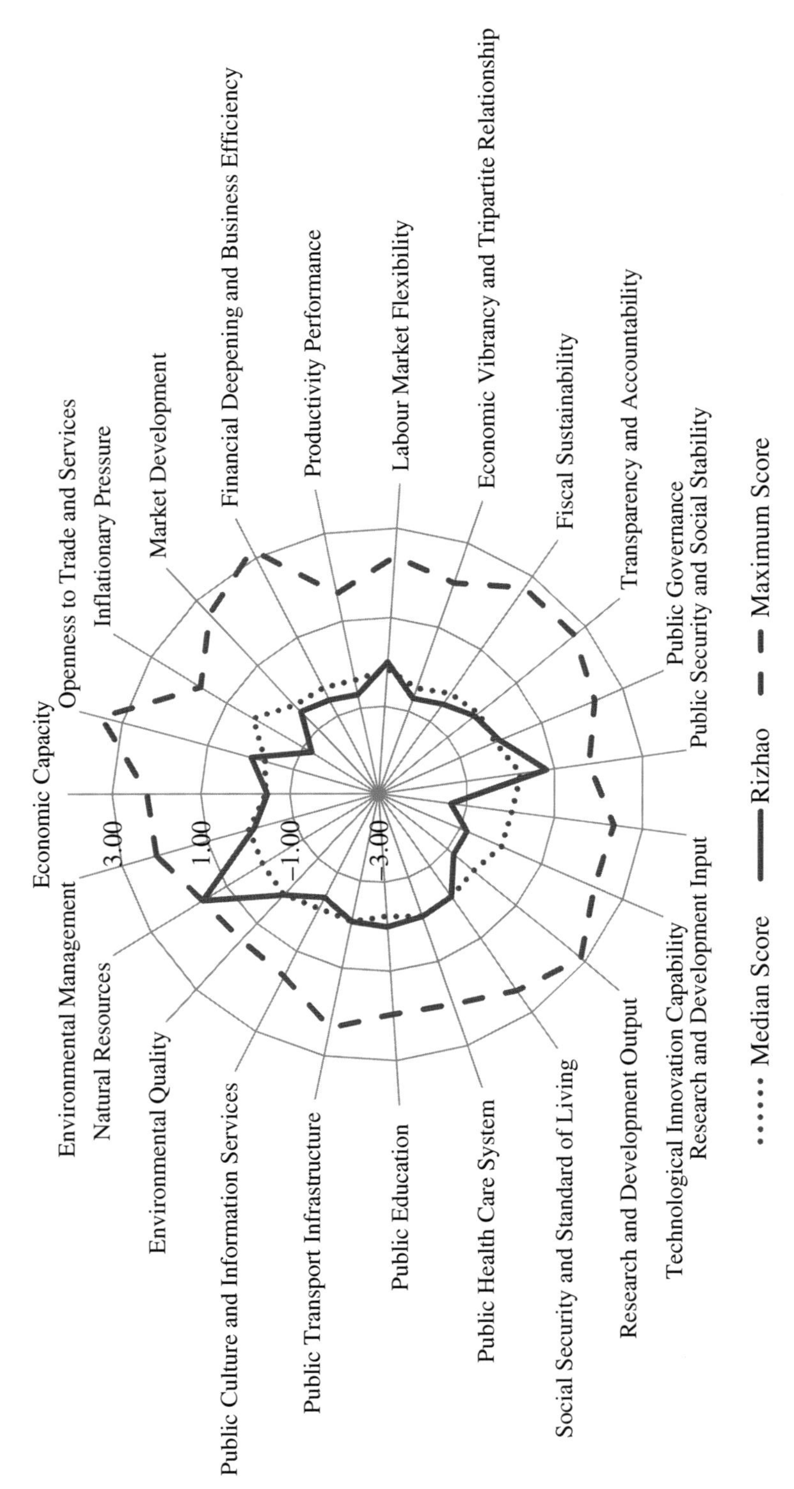

Source: Asia Competitiveness Institute.

14.2.3 Median and Maximum Web Analysis

To better understand Rizhao's relative strengths and weaknesses, it is useful to compare and contrast its scores for the 23 sub-environments against the median and maximum scores of Shandong's 17 cities.

In Figure 14.1, the median and maximum scores for 17 Shandong cities are shown as dotted and dashed lines respectively, while scores for Rizhao are shown as a solid line.

Comparison to Median Scores

Rizhao scores above the median for six of the 23 sub-environments, most notably in Natural Resources and Public Security and Social Stability.

On the other hand, Rizhao scores below the median for 13 of the 23 sub-environments, especially for Inflationary Pressure, which scores farthest below the median. Rizhao scores at median for the remaining four sub-environments, namely Social Security and Standard of Living, Public Health Care System, Public Transport Infrastructure, and Environmental Quality.

Comparison to Maximum Scores

Rizhao scores below the provincial maximum of the 17 Shandong cities in 22 of the 23 sub-environments. Rizhao achieves the maximum score in the Natural Resources (1.632) sub-environment.

Rizhao's score in the sub-environment of Financial Deepening and Business Efficiency (–0.585) is farthest from the maximum, which is held by Jinan (3.201). Further, Rizhao's score in Public Security and Social Stability (0.817) is closest to the maximum, which is held by Dezhou (1.783).

14.3 Summary of Empirical Findings of Rizhao and *What-if* Urban Development Simulation

14.3.1 Summary of Empirical Findings, 20% Strongest and Weakest Indicators

Overall Performance **11th** Score: –0.472		
Scale and Quality of Economic Activities **15th** Score: –1.017	Financial Capacity, Labour Market Flexibility and Economic Vibrancy **11th** Score: –0.619	Good Governance, Effective Leadership and Social Stability **12th** Score: 0.042
Technological Advancement and Innovation Capability **15th** Score: –1.155	Public Service Standards and Quality of Life Improvement **9th** Score: –0.154	Resource Conditions and Environmental Protection **4th** Score: 0.817

(Rank out of 17 cities)

Summary

Rizhao ranks 11th out of 17 Shandong cities in its Overall Performance. Rizhao performs above the provincial average in two of the six environments, namely Resource Conditions and Environmental Protections and Good Governance, Effective Leadership and Social Stability. Meanwhile, Rizhao performs below the provincial average in four environments and fares weakest in the environments of Technological Advancement and Innovation Capability and Scale and Quality of Economic Activities environments, which are both at 15th place.

Strengths

As observed in Table 14.2, Rizhao performs especially well in the environments of Public Service Standards and Quality of Life Improvement and Good Governance, Effective Leadership and Social Stability, with each containing seven out of 26 of its 20% Strongest Indicators. Among Rizhao's best performing indicators are the Dependency on Foreign Trade (Foreign Trade as a Share of GDRP), Satisfaction of Public Transport Services and the Proportion of Workforce Employed in the Service Sector.

Weaknesses

As observed in Table 14.3, Rizhao is weaker in the environments of Technological Advancement and Innovation Capability and Financial Capacity, Labour Market Flexibility and Economic Vibrancy, as each of them contains six out of 26 of its 20% Weakest Indicators. Among Rizhao's worst performing indicators are the Producer Price Index, Profit Margin of Enterprises Above Designated Size and Urban Residents' Per Capita Expenditure Growth Rate.

Table 14.2: 20% Strongest Indicators for Rizhao

Rank	20% Strongest Indicator	Score	SQEA	FCLMFEV	GGELSS	TAIC	PSSQLI	RCEP
1	Dependency on Foreign Trade (Foreign Trade as a Share of GRDP)	1.859	✓					
2	Satisfaction of Public Transport Services	1.476					✓	
3	Proportion of Workforce Employed in Service Sector	1.454		✓				
4	Cleanliness of Public Toilets	1.315					✓	
5	Public Perception of Security	1.284			✓			
6	Frequency of Using the Internet for Daily Convenience	1.281					✓	
7	Electricity Consumption Per RMB 10,000 GRDP	1.242						✓
8	Green Coverage Ratio of Built-up Area	1.106						✓
9	GRDP Growth Rate	1.054	✓					
10	Residents' Perception of Happiness	0.989					✓	
11	Growth Rate of Overall Labour Productivity	0.978		✓				
12	Satisfaction of the Police Services	0.977			✓			
13	Satisfaction with Innovation Environment	0.919				✓		
14	Urban Registered Unemployment Rate	0.865		✓				
15	Satisfaction with the Just of Judiciary	0.855			✓			
16	Satisfaction of Traffic Conditions	0.849					✓	
17	Satisfaction of Income Disparity	0.833					✓	
18	Satisfaction with Urban Management Personnels	0.771			✓			
19	Index for Quality of E-Government System	0.765			✓			
20	Public Perception of Government Conduct	0.731			✓			
21	Per Capita Arable Land	0.728						✓
22	Fire Fatality Per 10,000 Population	0.658			✓			
23	Urban Residents' Disposable Income Growth Rate	0.653	✓					
24	Per Capita Freshwater Resource	0.637						✓
25	Satisfaction of Public Education System	0.484					✓	
26	Built-up Area Population Density	0.475						✓

Table 14.3: 20% Weakest Indicators for Rizhao

Rank	20% Weakest Indicator	Score	SQEA	FCLMFEV	GGELSS	TAIC	PSSQLI	RCEP
106	Forest Land Growth	−0.823						✓
107	Government Fiscal Revenue	−0.823			✓			
108	Newly Increased Number of Employees	−0.861		✓				
109	Insurance Net Income	−0.863		✓				
110	Government Fiscal Expenditure	−0.911			✓			
111	Per Capita Fixed Investment	−0.914	✓					
112	Number of R&D Personnel Per 10,000 Population	−0.919				✓		
113	Number of Beds of Health Care Per 1,000 Population	−0.923					✓	
114	Growth in the Volume of Cargo Transported	−0.949		✓				
115	Per Capita Road Area	−0.949					✓	
116	Total R&D Man-Hour	−0.962				✓		
117	Percentage of Public Expenditure on Cultural Initiatives	−0.962					✓	
118	Number of Science and Technology Personnel	−0.973				✓		
119	Number of Doctors Per 1,000 Persons	−0.980					✓	
120	Gross Regional Domestic Product	−0.985	✓					
121	Number of Responses to Government Issues of Public Interest	−1.017			✓			
122	Total R&D Expenditure of Enterprises Above Designated Size	−1.068				✓		
123	Number of Employees	−1.093		✓				
124	Trade Surplus	−1.205	✓					
125	Number of Releases of Government Information for Public Viewing	−1.290			✓			
126	Number of Provincial-Level Science Parks	−1.328				✓		
127	Self-Employed as a Share of Total Employment	−1.443		✓				
128	Urban Residents' Per Capita Expenditure Growth Rate	−1.455	✓					
129	Profit Margin of Enterprises Above Designated Size	−1.549		✓				
130	Total R&D Expenditure of Enterprises Above Designated Size as a Percentage of Cash Flow	−1.579				✓		
131	Producer Price Index (PPI)	−2.337	✓					

Source: Asia Competitiveness Institute.

Notes: SQEA: Scale and Quality of Economic Activities; FCLMFEV: Financial Capacity, Labour Market Flexibility and Economic Vibrancy; GGELSS: Good Governance, Effective Leadership and Social Stability; TAIC: Technological Advancement and Innovation Capability; PSSQLI: Public Service Standards and Quality of Life Improvement; RCEP: Resource Conditions and Environmental Protection.

14.3.2 *What-if* Urban Development Simulation

ACI has devised a simulation methodology to improve the ranking of a particular city by improving on its 20% Weakest Indicators as shown in Table 14.3.[2] The figures below show Rizhao's ranking and standardised scores before and after the policy-induced simulation. Refer to Tables 3.8 to 3.14 in Section 3.4 of Chapter 3 for a complete list of simulation results for all cities.

Overall Performance

Before		After
11th	▶	**8th**
–0.472		**0.301**

Economic Size and Quality

	Before	After
Rank	15th	8th
Score	–1.017	–0.072

Financial Capacity, Labour Market Flexibility and Economic Vibrancy

	Before	After
Rank	11th	9th
Score	–0.619	–0.108

Good Governance, Effective Leadership and Social Stability

	Before	After
Rank	12th	3rd
Score	0.042	0.730

Technological Advancement and Innovation Capability

	Before	After
Rank	15th	9th
Score	–1.155	–0.284

Public Service Standards and Quality of Life Improvement

	Before	After
Rank	9th	9th
Score	–0.154	0.138

Resource Conditions and Environmental Protection

	Before	After
Rank	4th	4th
Score	0.817	0.942

After the *What-if* simulation, Rizhao improves its ranking from 11th to 8th in terms of its Overall Performance. Likewise, Rizhao's standardised score improves from –0.472 to 0.301. This leap is plausible if the city manages to successfully address its 20% Weakest Indicators.

The simulation further highlights substantial improvement for Rizhao in some of its environments, most notably in Good Governance, Effective Leadership and Social Stability, where its rank will rise from 12th to 3rd. Such encouraging results should incentivise Rizhao to strive to improve the indicators under the 20% Weakest Indicators list. These indicators include the Number of Releases of Government Information for Public Viewing and Government Fiscal Expenditure.

[2]The methodology for *What-if* simulation is thoroughly explained in Section 2.7 of Chapter 2.

14.4 Concluding Notes: Public Policy Implications[3]

Areas for Commendation

Rizhao performs especially well in the environments of Good Governance, Effective Leadership and Social Stability as well as Public Service Standards and Quality of Life Improvement, where they collectively account for 14 out of 26 of its 20% Strongest Indicators, as indicated in Table 14.2.

Rizhao achieves the maximum score for the Natural Resources sub-environment (1.632) and scores above the provincial average in four out of the 23 sub-environments.

From 2012 to 2016, the government fiscal revenue of Rizhao has experienced a 12.3% increase on average. Moreover, the total expenditure spent on social welfare increased from 63% in 2012 to 80.3% in 2016. The annual disposable income per capita for urban and rural residents grew by 9.9% and 11.4% on average respectively. Furthermore, Rizhao's Air Quality Index reached Moderate level and above by 74.5% during the first nine months of 2017, which made the greatest improvement in Shandong province. The above achievements indicate that Rizhao has performed well in the environment of Resource Conditions and Environmental Protection and made efforts in the environment of Good Governance, Effective Leadership and Social Stability.

Areas for Improvement

As Rizhao scores below the provincial average in five out of the six environments, there is much room for improvement. Most crucially, Rizhao should address the environments of Financial Capacity, Labour Market Flexibility and Economic Vibrancy as well as Technological Advancement and Innovation Capability as they collectively contribute 12 out of 26 of Rizhao's 20% Weakest Indicators, as shown in Table 14.3. Additionally, as gleaned from the *What-if* Urban Development Simulation, the environment of Good Governance, Effective Leadership and Social Stability should be prioritised because that is the environment in which Rizhao will achieve the greatest improvement in its ranking — nine positions — relative to other environments.

Moreover, Rizhao obtains its lowest score in the sub-environment of Research and Development Input (−1.365) and scores below the provincial average in 19 out of 23 sub-environments.

In 2017, to address the environments of Financial Capacity, Labour Market Flexibility and Economic Vibrancy as well as Technological Advancement and Innovation Capability, the Rizhao government promised to boost the real economy by emphasising on industrial development through structural reform of enterprises, expansion of manufacturing industry, and optimisation of service environment and innovation of financial services. The initiative to support the industrial development included supporting large-scale technological advancement of

[3]The relevant statistical data and government policies are from Rizhao Economic and Information Technology Commission (2017), Rizhao Human Resources and Social Security Bureau (2017) and Rizhao Municipal People's Government (2017).

enterprises by giving subsidies and rewards, encouraging mergers and acquisitions, as well as public listings of enterprises.

Future Potential Development

In summary, Rizhao should focus on improving the environment of Technological Advancement and Innovation Capability by investing more towards Research and Development on emerging enterprises and building provincial-level science parks. In addition, Rizhao should look towards encouraging economic vibrancy through greater support for businesses to improve the environment of Financial Capacity, Labour Market Flexibility and Economic Vibrancy.

In 2017, the Rizhao government-subsidised enterprises innovation projects with a minimum project budget of RMB 10 million. This has the potential to encourage R&D expenditure in enterprises. As businesses may deliberately inflate the budget on purpose to receive rewards and subsidies, the effectiveness of this policy is uncertain.

In June 2017, the Rizhao government announced its policy to increase employment by supporting entrepreneurship with subsidies. The government promised more than RMB 40 million for subsidies relating to entrepreneurial activities.

References

Department of Commerce of Shandong Province. n.d. 'Rizhao City Profile'. Department of Commerce of Shandong Province. Accessed 3 November 2017. http://en.shandongbusiness.gov.cn/city/78.

Li, Ruoxi. 2009. 'Rizhao'. Shandong China, the Hometown of Confucius. 30 July 2009. http://www.chinadaily.com.cn/m/shandong/e/2009-07/30/content_8490823_3.htm.

Rizhao Economic and Information Technology Commission. 2017. '《关于加快工业强市建设的意见》政策解读 Interpretation of "Suggestions on Accelerating the Construction of Industrial City" (in Chinese)'. Rizhao Economic and Information Technology Commission. 25 July 2017. http://www.rzeic.gov.cn/ctnshow.php/aid/7535.

Rizhao Human Resources and Social Security Bureau. 2017. '关于印发《日照市创业带动就业扶持资金管理实施办法》的通知 Regarding to "Rizhao's Policies on Encouraging Employment by Incentivizing Entrepreneurship with Subsidies" (in Chinese)'. Rizhao Human Resources and Social Security Bureau. 7 September 2017. http://www.rzhrss.gov.cn/rz12333/fwyd/ywzn/ldjybgs/zcwj/12386.html.

Rizhao Municipal People's Government. 2017. '政府工作报告（2017年2月24日在日照市第十八届人民代表大会第一次会议上）2017 Rizhao Annual Government Work Report (in Chinese)'. Rizhao Municipal People's Government. 24 February 2017. http://www.rizhao.gov.cn/ContShowZwgk.php?category_id=1147&aiticle_id=8860.

———. n.d. 'About Rizhao'. Rizhao Municipal People's Government. Accessed 3 November 2017. http://english.rizhao.gov.cn/aboutnew.php.

Rizhao Environmental Protection Bureau. 2017. '日照市蓝天保卫战集中攻坚行动成效显著 Rizhao has Significant Achievements in the Act of Blue Sky Battle (in Chinese)'. Accessed 22 June 2018. http://www.rzhb.gov.cn/ctnshow.php/aid/9420.

Chapter 15: TAI'AN
Shandong Province

Location of City

Source: Asia Competitiveness Institute.

15.1 Profile of Tai'an City[1]

Situated at the foot of the venerated United Nations Educational, Scientific and Cultural Organisation (UNESCO) World Heritage Site Mount Taishan, Tai'an is additionally esteemed as a cradle of early Chinese civilisation, having been a focal point for settlement by the ancient Dawenkou culture up to six millennia ago. Today, Tai'an directly administers two districts, two county-level cities and two counties over a total land area of 7,761 square kilometres, with a total population of 5,637,400. Tai'an is also known for being an important transportation hub, as well as a significant manufacturing base.

In 2016, Tai'an's Gross Regional Domestic Product (GRDP) stood at RMB 332 billion and the city enjoyed a healthy GRDP growth rate of 7.2%, as is reflected in Table 15.1. Tai'an is known as a major exporter of construction materials, such as plaster and granite. Accordingly, the city's primary sector accounted for 8.5% of total GRDP. The city's secondary sector, which is dependent on industries, such as mechanical manufacturing, textiles, building materials and energy, comprised 44.8% of total GRDP. Finally, Tai'an's tertiary sector, which is strongly based on tourism, constituted 46.7% of GRDP.

---

[1]The relevant city information are from the Department of Commerce of Shandong Province (n.d.), Travel China Guide (2017) and Yuan (2009).

TAI'AN

Shandong Province

The closest airport to Tai'an is Jinan Yaoqiang International Airport. The city is also located on several important railroads, such as the Beijing–Shanghai high-speed rail line. Tai'an also benefits from having several expressways run through it, enhancing its connectivity to nearby regions considerably. Tai'an's e-government systems, which broadly refer to administrative functions hosted online for residents of the city and surrounding territories, received significant praise in 2015 for their overall reliability and usability. This in turn reflects well on the municipal government's dedication to ensuring that residents are able to seamlessly access important government functions and its competence in organising and maintaining those vital systems online.

Table 15.1: Key Economic Indicators for Tai'an, 2016

Land Area (km²)	**7,761**
Population	
Total Population	5,637,400
Urban Population Ratio (%)	59.1
Average Life Expectancy (years)	74.8
Number of Employees (10,000)	411
Workforce Participation Rate (%)	76.5
Gross Regional Domestic Product (GRDP) — 2015 Prices	
GRDP (100 millions of RMB)	3,317
GRDP Per Capita (RMB)	59,027
GRDP Growth Rate (%)	7.2
Economic Composition	
Primary Sector (% of GRDP)	8.5
Secondary Sector (% of GRDP)	44.8
Tertiary Sector (% of GRDP)	46.7
Trade — 2016 Prices	
Exports (millions of RMB)	11,616
Imports (millions of RMB)	3,552
Dependency on Foreign Trade (%)	4.0
Infrastructure	
Per Capita Road Area (m²)	27.6
Growth in the Number of Passengers Transported (10,000)	108
Growth in the Volume of Cargo Transported (10,000 tons)	588
Environment	
Green Coverage Ratio of Built-up Area (%)	45.0
Environmental Expenditure (% of Total Fiscal Expenditure)	2.3

Source: Asia Competitiveness Institute from the 2017 Shandong Statistical Yearbook.

15.2 In-Depth Urban Development of Tai'an, 2016*

15.2.1 Overall Urban Development Performance

Overall Performance

2017 Rank

9th

Out of 17 Cities

Score: –0.280

Rank	City	Score
1	Qingdao	1.753
	...	
7	Zibo	0.403
8	Linyi	–0.002
9	Tai'an	–0.280
10	Dezhou	–0.302
11	Rizhao	–0.472
	...	
16	Laiwu	–1.233
17	Liaocheng	–1.576

Tai'an ranks 9th in its Overall Performance, with a standardised score of –0.280. This places the city in the Middle Seven Group of 17 cities. Tai'an is positioned between Linyi (–0.002) at 8th place and Dezhou (–0.302) at 10th place.

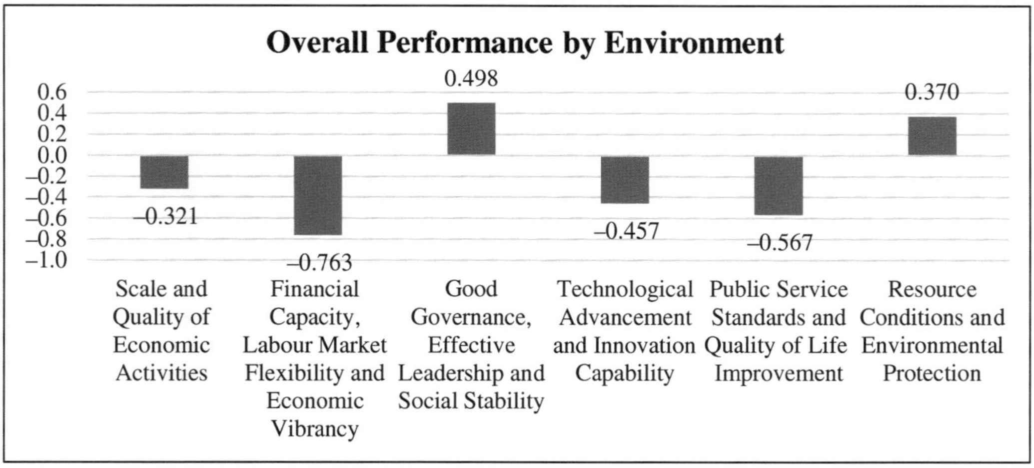

Among the six environments, Tai'an scores above the provincial average in two of them, which are specifically the environments of Good Governance, Effective Leadership and Social Stability as well as Resource Conditions and Environmental Protection. However, Tai'an scores below the provincial average in the remaining four environments and notably weaker for that of Financial Capacity, Labour Market Flexibility and Economic Vibrancy.

** For a complete list of rankings, see Tables 3.2 to 3.7 in Section 3.3 of Chapter 3.*

15.2.2 Urban Development within the Six Environments

Rank	City	Score
1	Qingdao	1.987
	…	
6	Linyi	0.447
7	Dezhou	0.096
8	Tai'an	–0.321
9	Jinan	–0.364
10	Zaozhuang	–0.412
	…	
16	Jining	–1.273
17	Laiwu	–1.295

A: ***Scale and Quality of Economic Activities***

2017 Rank

8th

Out of 17 Cities

Score: –0.321

Tai'an ranks 8th for Scale and Quality of Economic Activities, with a standardised score of –0.321. This places the city in the Middle Seven Group of 17 cities. Tai'an is positioned behind Dezhou (0.096) at 7th place and ahead of Jinan (–0.364) at 9th place.

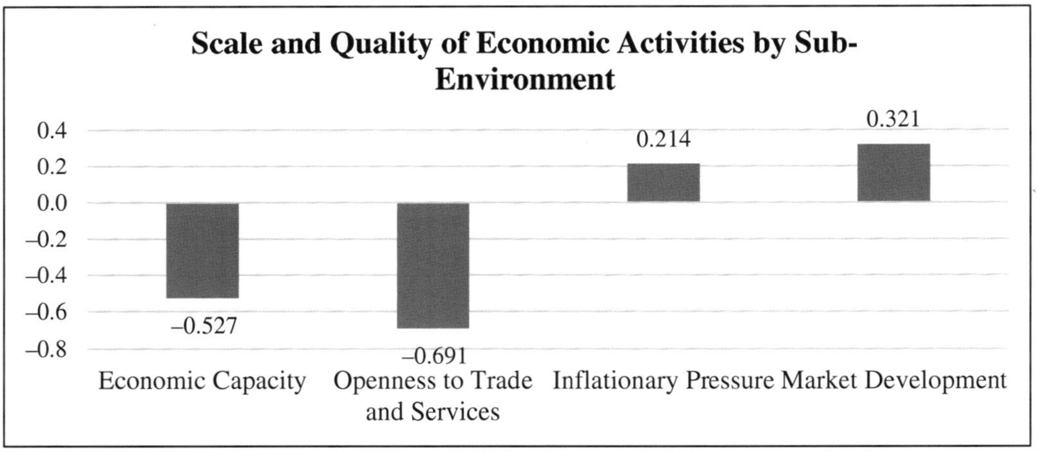

Among the four sub-environments of Scale and Quality of Economic Activities, Tai'an performs above the provincial average in two of them, namely the sub-environments of Inflationary Pressure and Market Development. In particular, Tai'an scores well in the indicator of Residents' Satisfaction with Price Levels from the Inflationary Pressure sub-environment and the indicator of Satisfaction with Business Environment from the Market Development sub-environment. On the other hand, Tai'an performs below the provincial average and especially weaker in the remaining two sub-environments, where it fares poorly in the indicators of GRDP Growth Rate from the Economic Capacity sub-environment and Dependency on Foreign Trade from the Openness to Trade and Services sub-environment.

B: ***Financial Capacity, Labour Market Flexibility and Economic Vibrancy***

2017 Rank

13th

Out of 17 Cities

Score: –0.763

Rank	City	Score
1	Jinan	2.264
	...	
10	Binzhou	–0.329
11	Rizhao	–0.619
12	Heze	–0.638
13	Tai'an	–0.763
14	Zaozhuang	–0.894
15	Liaocheng	–1.021
16	Dezhou	–1.026
17	Laiwu	–1.297

Tai'an ranks 13th for Financial Capacity, Labour Market Flexibility and Economic Vibrancy, with a standardised score of –0.763. This places the city in the Bottom Five Group of 17 cities. Tai'an is positioned between Heze (–0.638) at 12th place and Zaozhuang (–0.894) at 14th place.

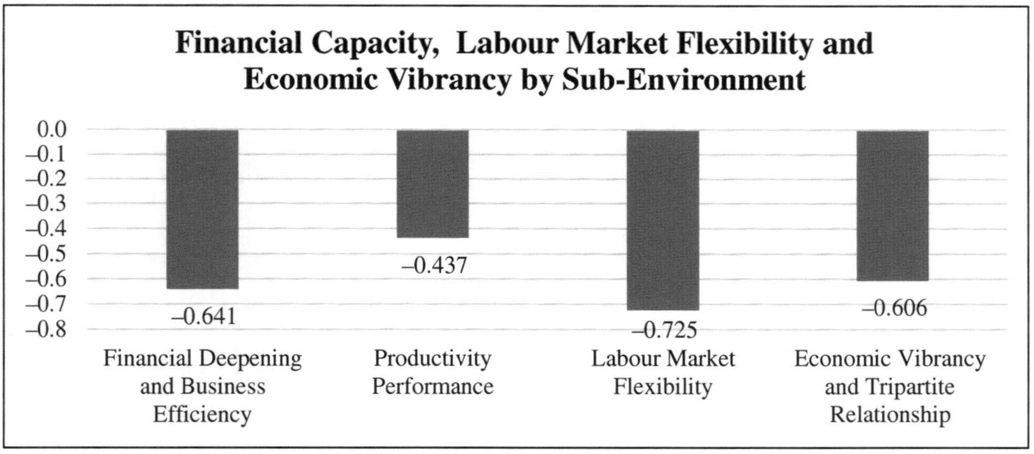

Across the four sub-environments of Financial Capacity, Labour Market Flexibility and Economic Vibrancy, Tai'an performs below the provincial average in all of them and weaker for Labour Market Flexibility, where the indicators of Self-Employed as a Share of Total Employment, Proportion of Workforce Employed in Agricultural Sector and Proportion of Workforce Employed in Service Sector register low scores. In addition, the indicators of Loan Balance Per Capita from the Financial Deepening and Business Efficiency sub-environment and Growth in the Volume of Cargo Transported from the Economic Vibrancy and Tripartite Relationship sub-environment fares poorly as well. However, Tai'an performs comparatively better in the sub-environment of Productivity Performance, where the indicator of Profit Margin of Enterprises Above Designated Size scores relatively well.

TAI'AN

Shandong Province

Rank	City	Score
1	Dezhou	1.465
	...	
4	Qingdao	0.733
5	Jinan	0.532
6	Tai'an	0.498
7	Heze	0.435
8	Zibo	0.418
	...	
16	Laiwu	−1.588
17	Liaocheng	−2.473

C: ***Good Governance, Effective Leadership and Social Stability***

2017 Rank

6th

Out of 17 Cities

Score: 0.498

Tai'an ranks 6th for Good Governance, Effective Leadership and Social Stability with a standardised score of 0.498. This places the city in the Middle Seven Group of 17 cities. Tai'an is positioned between Jinan (0.532) at 5th place and Heze (0.435) at 7th place.

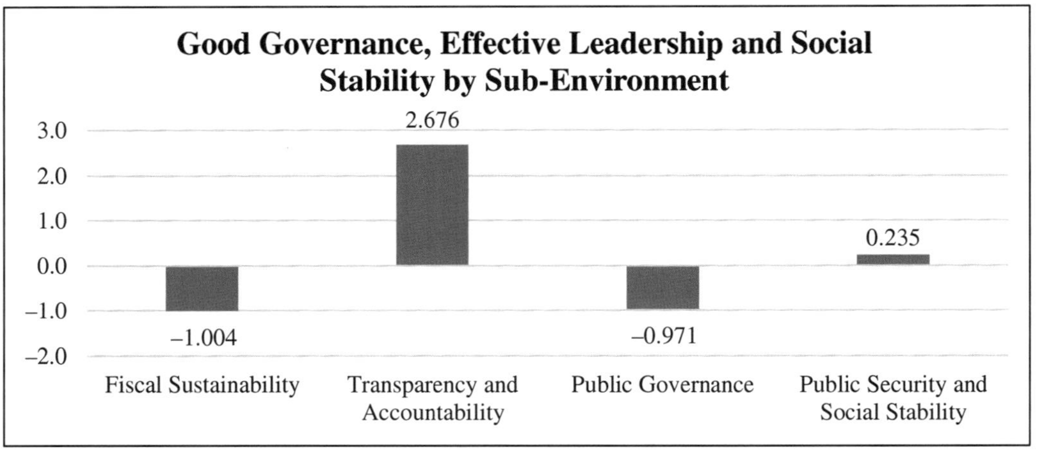

Across the four sub-environments of Good Governance, Effective Leadership and Social Stability, Tai'an scores above the provincial average in two of them and exceptionally well for Transparency and Accountability, where majority of the indicators such as the Satisfaction with the Just of Judiciary, Number of Responses to Government Issues of Public Interest and Number of Investigations for Power Abuses Per 10,000 Population score well. On the other hand, Tai'an performs below the provincial average and notably weaker in the remaining two sub-environments of Fiscal Sustainability and Public Governance. Under these two sub-environments, the indicators of Fiscal Revenue Growth Rate from the Fiscal Sustainability sub-environment and Number of Public Servants Per 10,000 Population under Public Governance sub-environment perform especially poorly.

D: ***Technological Advancement and Innovation Capability***

2017 Rank

10th

Out of 17 Cities

Score: –0.457

Rank	City	Score
1	Qingdao	2.176
	...	
8	Jining	–0.222
9	Linyi	–0.344
10	Tai'an	–0.457
11	Dezhou	–0.517
12	Binzhou	–0.559
	...	
16	Zaozhuang	–1.192
17	Liaocheng	–1.221

Tai'an ranks 10th for Technological Advancement and Innovation Capability, with a standardised score of –0.457. This places the city in the Middle Seven Group of 17 cities. Tai'an is positioned between Linyi (–0.344) at 9th place and Dezhou (–0.517) at 11th place.

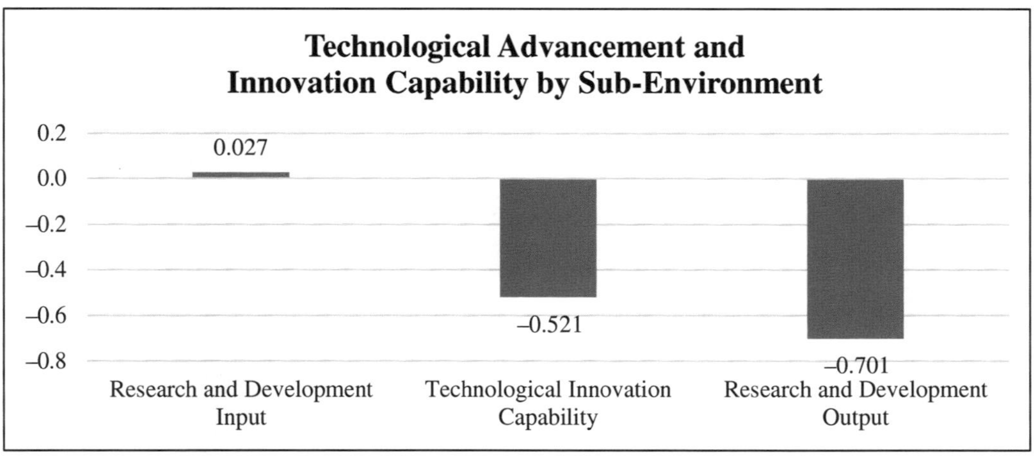

Among the three sub-environments of Technological Advancement and Innovation Capability, Tai'an performs slightly above the provincial average in that of Research and Development Input, where the indicator of Total Research and Development Expenditure of Enterprises Above Designated Size as a Percentage of Cash Flow performs especially well. On the other hand, Tai'an scores below the provincial average in the remaining two sub-environments, faring notably worse for Research and Development Output where the indicator of the Number of Existing Patents Per 10,000 Population scores poorly. In addition, the indicator of the Number of Provincial-Level Science Parks from the Technological Innovation Capability sub-environment registers a weak score as well.

TAI'AN

Shandong Province

Rank	City	Score
1	Dongying	1.689
	...	
9	Rizhao	–0.154
10	Linyi	–0.307
11	Tai'an	–0.567
12	Heze	–0.766
13	Jining	–0.819
	...	
16	Dezhou	–1.066
17	Liaocheng	–1.964

E: *Public Service Standards and Quality of Life Improvement*

2017 Rank

11th

Out of 17 Cities

Score: –0.567

Tai'an ranks 11th for Public Service Standards and Quality of Life Improvement with a standardised score of –0.567. This places the city in the Middle Seven Group of 17 cities. Tai'an is positioned between Linyi (–0.307) at 10th place and Heze (–0.766) at 12th place.

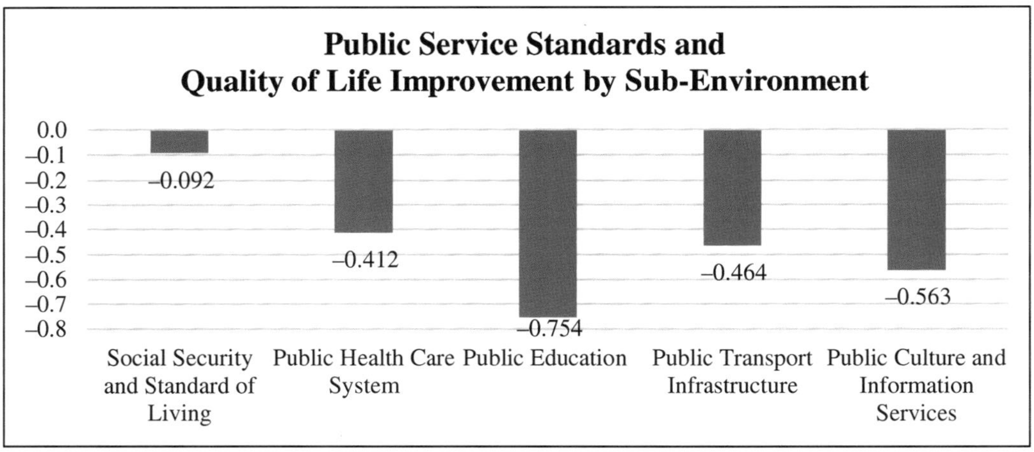

Looking at the five sub-environments of Public Service Standards and Quality of Life Improvement, Tai'an performs below the provincial average in all of them and fares especially weaker in the sub-environments of Public Education, where the indicators of Public Education Appropriation Per Capita score poorly. In addition, the indicators of the Number of Private Cars Per 100 Households under the Social Security and Standard of Living sub-environment and the Average Life Expectancy under the Public Health Care System sub-environment score particularly weaker as well. On the other hand, the sub-environment of Social Security and Standard of Living sub-environment scores relatively better, where the indicator of Residents' Perception of Happiness performs well. Further, the indicator of Satisfaction of Public Health Care Services from the Public Health Care System sub-environment scores well.

F: ***Resource Conditions and Environmental Protection***

2017 Rank

7th

Out of 17 Cities

Score: 0.370

Rank	City	Score
1	Weihai	1.632
	...	
5	Zibo	0.665
6	Liaocheng	0.376
7	Tai'an	0.370
8	Qingdao	0.330
9	Jinan	0.281
	...	
16	Binzhou	−1.586
17	Heze	−2.142

Tai'an ranks 7th for Resource Conditions and Environmental Protection with a standardised score of 0.370. This places the city in the Middle Seven Group of 17 cities. Tai'an is positioned between Liaocheng (0.376) at 6th place and ahead of Qingdao (0.330) at 8th place.

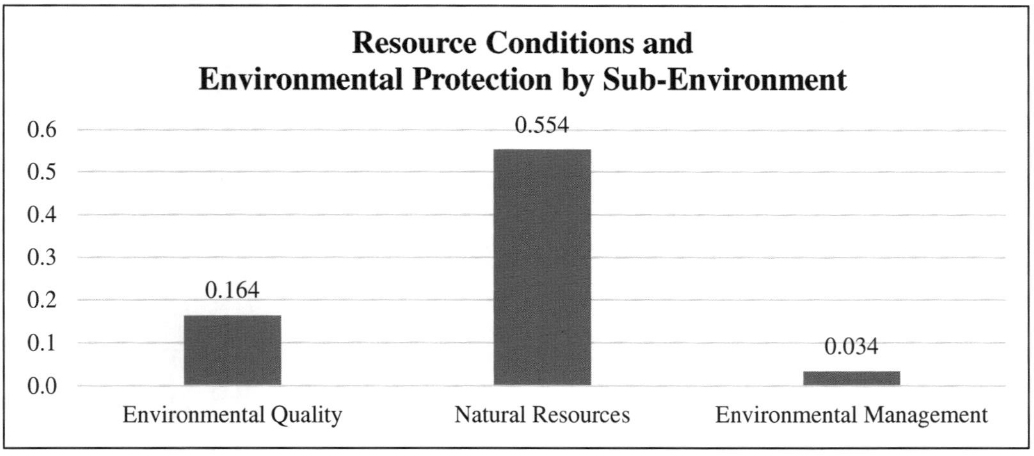

Looking at the three sub-environments of Resources Conditions and Environmental Protection, Tai'an scores above the provincial average in all of them and fares notably better for Natural Resources, where the indicators of Electricity Consumption Per RMB 10,000 GRDP scores well. Further, Tai'an attains high scores in the indicators of Green Coverage Ratio of Built-up Area and the Urban Area Waste Water Treatment Rate, both from the sub-environment of Environmental Management. On the other hand, the indicators of Chemical Oxygen Demand Per RMB 10,000 GRDP from the Environmental Quality sub-environment, Per Capita Arable Land from the Natural Resources sub-environment and Environmental Expenditure as a Percentage of Total Fiscal Expenditure from the Environmental Management sub-environment score comparatively weaker.

TAI'AN

Shandong Province

Figure 15.1: Median & Maximum Web for Tai'an

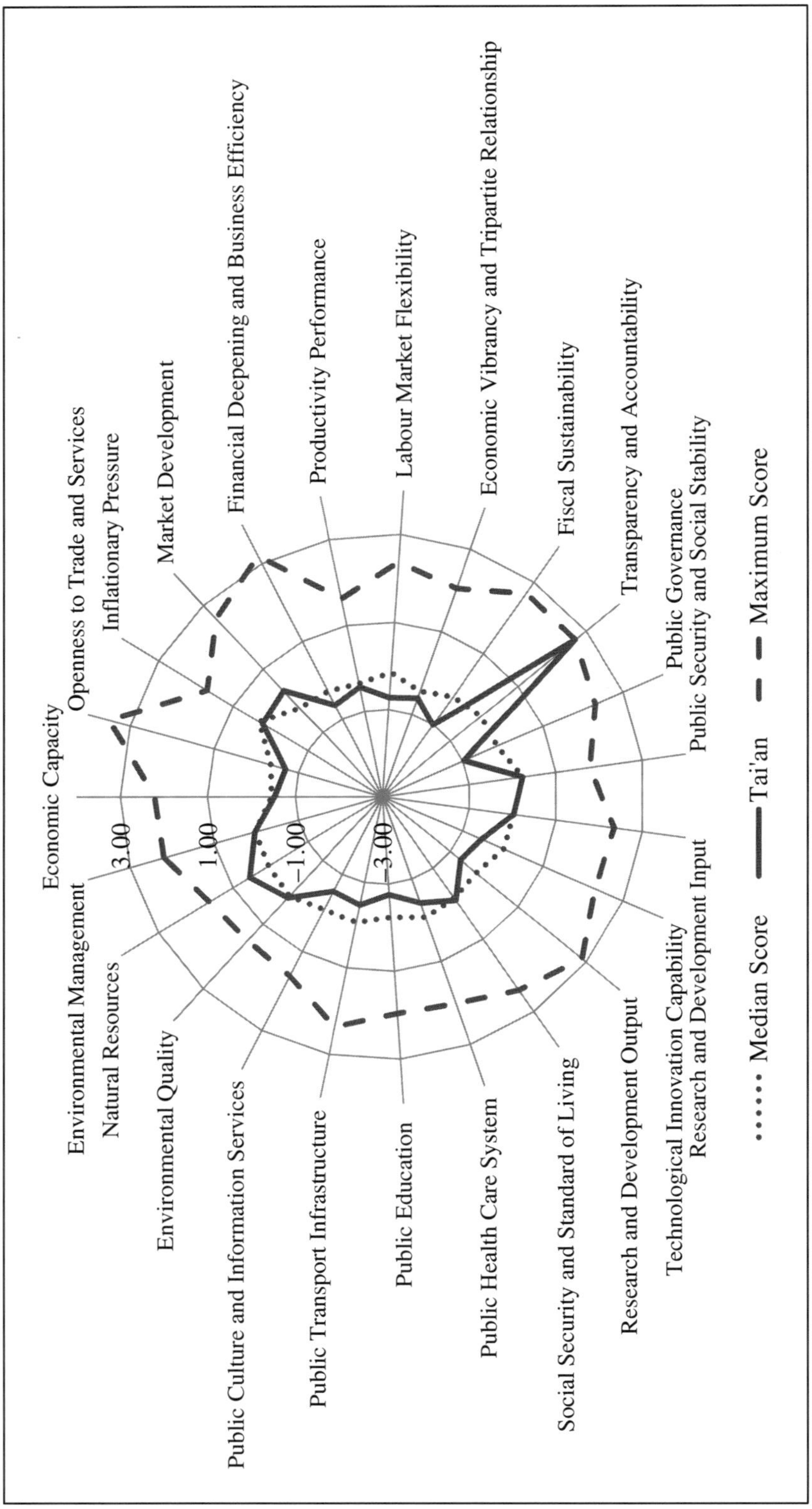

Source: Asia Competitiveness Institute.

15.2.3 Median and Maximum Web Analysis

To better understand Tai'an's relative strengths and weaknesses, it is useful to compare and contrast its scores for the 23 sub-environments against the median and maximum scores of Shandong's 17 cities.

In Figure 15.1, the median and maximum scores for 17 Shandong cities are shown as dotted and dashed lines respectively, while scores for Tai'an are shown as a solid line.

Comparison to Median Scores

Tai'an scores above the median for five of the 23 sub-environments, most notably in Transparency and Accountability.

On the other hand, it scores below the median for 15 of the 23 sub-environments, especially for Public Governance and Fiscal Sustainability. Tai'an achieves the median score for the remaining three sub-environments of Public Security and Social Stability, Research and Development Input and Environmental Management.

Comparison to Maximum Scores

Tai'an scores below the provincial maximum of the 17 Shandong cities in 22 out of the 23 sub-environments. Tai'an achieves the provincial maximum score in the sub-environment of Transparency and Accountability, with standardised score of 2.676.

Tai'an's score in the Openness to Trade and Services (–0.691) sub-environment is farthest from the maximum, which is held by Qingdao (3.505). Further, Tai'an's score in Natural Resources (0.554) is closest to the maximum, which is held by Rizhao (1.632).

15.3 Summary of Empirical Findings of Tai'an and *What-if* Urban Development Simulation

15.3.1 Summary of Empirical Findings, 20% Strongest and Weakest Indicators

Overall Performance 9th Score: –0.280		
Scale and Quality of Economic Activities 8th Score: –0.321	**Financial Capacity, Labour Market Flexibility and Economic Vibrancy** 13th Score: –0.763	**Good Governance, Effective Leadership and Social Stability** 6th Score: 0.498
Technological Advancement and Innovation Capability 10th Score: –0.457	**Public Service Standards and Quality of Life Improvement** 11th Score: –0.567	**Resource Conditions and Environmental Protection** 7th Score: 0.370

(Rank out of 17 cities)

Summary

Tai'an ranks 9th out of 17 Shandong cities in its Overall Performance. Tai'an performs above the provincial average in two out of the six environments, where the environment of Good Governance, Effective Leadership and Social Stability scores the highest. Meanwhile, Tai'an performs below the provincial average in the remaining four environments and fares especially weaker for Financial Capacity, Labour Market Flexibility and Economic Vibrancy and Public Service Standards and Quality of Life Improvement.

Strengths

As observed in Table 15.2, Tai'an performs especially well in Good Governance, Effective Leadership and Social Stability environment, with nine out of 26 of its 20% Strongest Indicators included in that environment. Among Tai'an's best performing indicators are Number of Investigations for Power Abuses Per 10,000 Population, Total Research and Development Expenditure of Enterprises Above Designated Size as a Percentage of Cash Flow and Satisfaction of Public Health Care Services.

Weaknesses

As observed in Table 15.3, Tai'an is weaker in the environment of Public Service Standards and Quality of Life Improvement with a total of nine out of 26 of its 20% Weakest Indicators under this environment. Among Tai'an's worst performing indicators are Growth Rate of the Number of Police Cases, Number of Public Servants Per 10,000 Population and Fiscal Revenue Growth Rate.

Table 15.2: 20% Strongest Indicators for Tai'an

Rank	20% Strongest Indicator	Score	SQEA	FCLMFEV	GGELSS	TAIC	PSSQLI	RCEP
1	Number of Investigations for Power Abuses Per 10,000 Population	2.206			✓			
2	Total R&D Expenditure of Enterprises Above Designated Size as a Percentage of Cash Flow	1.558				✓		
3	Satisfaction of Public Health Care Services	1.517					✓	
4	Number of Responses to Government Issues of Public Interest	1.473			✓			
5	Satisfaction with the Just of Judiciary	1.428			✓			
6	Satisfaction with Business Environment	1.324	✓					
7	Index for Quality of E-Government System	1.296			✓			
8	Satisfaction with Urban Management Personnels	1.240			✓			
9	Residents' Perception of Happiness	1.213					✓	
10	Public Perception of Government Conduct	1.122			✓			
11	Residents' Satisfaction with Price Levels	1.032	✓					
12	Satisfaction of the Police Services	1.032			✓			
13	Satisfaction of Public Education System	1.002					✓	
14	Urban Area Waste Water Treatment Rate	0.913						✓
15	Green Coverage Ratio of Built-up Area	0.906						✓
16	NO-X Emissions Per RMB 10,000 GRDP	0.763						✓
17	Electricity Consumption Per RMB 10,000 GRDP	0.763						✓
18	SO2 Emission Per RMB 10,000 GRDP	0.737						✓
19	Public Health and Medical Service Expenses as a Share of GRDP	0.644					✓	
20	Public Perception of Security	0.565			✓			
21	Profit Margin of Enterprises Above Designated Size	0.473		✓				
22	Traffic Accident Fatality Per 10,000 Population	0.469			✓			
23	Satisfaction of Traffic Conditions	0.455					✓	
24	Forest Cover	0.439						✓
25	Service Sector as a Percentage of GRDP	0.389	✓					
26	Engel's Index	0.387					✓	

Table 15.3: 20% Weakest Indicators for Tai'an

Rank	20% Weakest Indicator	Score	SQEA	FCLMFEV	GGELSS	TAIC	PSSQLI	RCEP
106	Number of Books in Public Library Per Capita	–0.754					✓	
107	Research & Development Expenditure as a Share of Government Expenditure	–0.756				✓		
108	Number of Provincial-Level Science Parks	–0.784				✓		
109	Number of Urban Taxis Per 10,000 Population	–0.785					✓	
110	Number of Existing Patents Per 10,000 Population	–0.789				✓		
111	Number of Vocational Education Institutions Per 10,000 Population	–0.790					✓	
112	Growth Rate of Overall Labour Productivity	–0.798		✓				
113	Government Fiscal Expenditure Per Capita	–0.807			✓			
114	Cleanliness of Public Toilets	–0.847					✓	
115	Public Health and Medical Service Expenses Per Capita	–0.884					✓	
116	Average Public Servant Salary	–0.888			✓			
117	Government Expenditures as a Percentage of GRDP	–0.888	✓					
118	Ratio of Public Education Appropriation to GRDP	–0.907					✓	
119	Number of Listed Items Under Executive Authority of the Government	–0.912			✓			
120	Public Education Appropriation Per Capita	–0.963					✓	
121	GRDP Growth Rate	–1.040	✓					
122	Growth in the Volume of Cargo Transported	–1.058		✓				
123	Self-Employed as a Share of Total Employment	–1.110		✓				
124	Proportion of Workforce Employed in Service Sector	–1.141		✓				
125	Proportion of Workforce Employed in Agriculture Sector	–1.160		✓				
126	Dependency on Foreign Trade (Foreign Trade as a Share of GRDP)	–1.199	✓					
127	Number of Private Cars Per 100 Households	–1.225					✓	
128	Average Life Expectancy	–1.269					✓	
129	Fiscal Revenue Growth Rate	–1.365			✓			
130	Number of Public Servants Per 10,000 Population	–1.422			✓			
131	Growth Rate of the Number of Police Cases	–1.427			✓			

Source: Asia Competitiveness Institute.

Notes: SQEA: Scale and Quality of Economic Activities; FCLMFEV: Financial Capacity, Labour Market Flexibility and Economic Vibrancy; GGELSS: Good Governance, Effective Leadership and Social Stability; TAIC: Technological Advancement and Innovation Capability; PSSQLI: Public Service Standards and Quality of Life Improvement; RCEP: Resource Conditions and Environmental Protection.

15.3.2 *What-if* Urban Development Simulation

ACI has devised a simulation methodology to improve the ranking of a particular city by improving on its 20% Weakest Indicators as shown in Table 15.3.[2] The figures below show Tai'an's ranking and standardised scores before and after the policy-induced simulation. Refer to Tables 3.8 to 3.14 in Section 3.4 of Chapter 3 for a complete list of simulation results for all cities.

Overall Performance

	Before		After
Rank	9th	▶	7th
Score	–0.280		0.378

Scale and Quality of Economic Activities

	Before	After
Rank	8th	7th
Score	–0.321	0.170

Financial Capacity, Labour Market Flexibility and Economic Vibrancy

	Before	After
Rank	13th	10th
Score	–0.763	–0.359

Good Governance, Effective Leadership and Social Stability

	Before	After
Rank	6th	1st
Score	0.498	1.443

Technological Advancement and Innovation Capability

	Before	After
Rank	10th	8th
Score	–0.457	–0.067

Public Service Standards and Quality of Life Improvement

	Before	After
Rank	11th	9th
Score	–0.567	0.119

Resource Conditions and Environmental Protection

	Before	After
Rank	7th	7th
Score	0.370	0.370

After the *What-if* simulation, Tai'an improves its ranking from 9th to 7th in its Overall Performance. Likewise, Tai'an's standardised score increases from –0.280 to 0.378. This leap is plausible if the city manages to successfully address its 20% Weakest Indicators.

The simulation further highlights substantial improvement for Tai'an in some of its environments, most notably in Good Governance, Effective Leadership and Social Stability where its rank will rise from 6th place to 1st place. Such encouraging results should incentivise Tai'an to strive to improve the indicators under the 20% Weakest Indicators list. These indicators include Number of Public Servants Per 10,000 Population, Fiscal Revenue Growth Rate and Number of Listed Items Under the Executive Authority of the Government.

[2]The methodology for *What-if* simulation is thoroughly explained in Section 2.7 of Chapter 2.

15.4 Concluding Notes: Public Policy Implications[3]

Areas for Commendation

Tai'an performs especially well in the environments of Good Governance, Effective Leadership and Social Stability, Public Service Standards and Quality of Life Improvement and Resource Conditions and Environmental Protection, where they collectively contain 21 out of 26 of its 20% Strongest Indicators in these environments, as indicated in Table 15.2.

Tai'an holds the maximum score for the sub-environment of Transparency and Accountability (2.676) and scores above the provincial average in eight out of 23 sub-environments.

Tai'an has performed well in managing its environment from 2012 to 2016. The air quality in Tai'an was noted as one of the best in Shandong, while its river water quality remains high. Moreover, the forest coverage in Tai'an reached 39.6% in 2016. There were three National Wetland Parks and one National Forest Park. The city was also awarded the China Habitat Environment Prize, National Forest City and National Water-Efficient City. These achievements explain the good performance of Tai'an in the environment of Resource Conditions and Environmental Protection.

Areas for Improvement

As Tai'an scores below the provincial average in four out of the six environments, there is much room for improvement. Most crucially, Tai'an should address the environments of Good Governance, Effective Leadership and Social Stability and Public Service Standards and Quality of Life Improvement, where they collectively contribute 15 out of 26 of Tai'an's 20% Weakest Indicators, as shown in Table 15.3. Additionally, as gleaned from the *What-if* Urban Development Simulation, the environment of Good Governance, Effective Leadership and Social Stability should be prioritised because that is the environment in which Tai'an will achieve the greatest improvement in its ranking — five positions — relative to other environments.

Moreover, Tai'an obtains a low score in the sub-environment Fiscal Sustainability (−1.004) and performs below the provincial average in 15 out of 23 sub-environments.

In December 2017, Tai'an government issued an official document detailing its plan to integrate and share public service information systems. This plan aims to achieve preliminary integration and sharing of major public service information systems by the end of 2017, while completing the set-up of the proposed public service cloud system by the end of April 2018. By successfully completing this plan, the Tai'an government expects to achieve a public service system that is able to serve its residents more conveniently and efficiently. This can help improve its Public Service Standards and Quality of Life Improvement.

[3] The relevant statistical data and government policies are from Tai'an Municipal People's Government (2017a, 2017b) and Gao (2017).

Future Potential Development

In summary, Tai'an should look towards encouraging healthier lifestyles and investment in education to improve the environment of Public Service Standards and Quality of Life Improvement. In addition, Tai'an should focus on improving the environment of Good Governance, Effective Leadership and Social Stability by better managing its public finances while at the same time investing more in its public sector.

Looking forward, Tai'an should put more emphasis on improving the quality of life of its residents. For instance, it may invest more in cultural infrastructure and organise more cultural events. As of November 2017, Tai'an has built 3,200 comprehensive cultural service centres in the urban areas. In December 2017, the Tai'an government announced plans to raise RMB 8 million to support the cultural needs in rural areas. With more funding and effort invested in cultural infrastructure, Tai'an's urban and rural residents can expect to realise an improvement in their quality of life.

References

Department of Commerce of Shandong Province. n.d. 'Heaven on Earth — Tai'an'. Department of Commerce of Shandong Province. Accessed 10 November 2017. http://en.shandongbusiness.gov.cn/city/76.

Gao, Ying. 2017. '泰安市文广新局：基层公共文化服务增强百姓"获得感" Tai'an Aimed to Improve Public Culture Infrastructure (in Chinese)'. Taishanwang. 21 December 2017. http://www.1545ts.com/taiannews/contents/697/326708.html.

Tai'an Municipal People's Government. 2017a. '2017年泰安市政府工作报告 2017 Tai'an Annual Government Work Report (in Chinese)'. Libaiwu. 28 March 2017. https://www.libaiwu.com/23785.htm.

———. 2017b. '我市政务信息系统整合共享实施方案下发 Tai'an's Plan on Public Service Information System Integration and Sharing (in Chinese)'. Tai'an Municipal People's Government. 12 December 2017. http://www.taian.gov.cn/zwgk/jrta/201712/t20171212_751722.html.

Travel China Guide. 2017. 'Beijing Shanghai High Speed Trains'. Travel China Guide. 17 October 2017. https://www.travelchinaguide.com/china-trains/beijing-shanghai-highspeed.htm.

Yuan, Hao. 2009. 'Tai'an'. Shandong China, the Hometown of Confucius. 23 July 2009. http://www.chinadaily.com.cn/m/shandong/e/2009-07/23/content_8464514_3.htm.

Chapter 16: WEIFANG
Shandong Province

Location of City

Source: Asia Competitiveness Institute.

16.1 Profile of Weifang City[1]

Weifang is renowned as the "Kite Capital of the World" and plays host to the annual Weifang International Kite Festival. Several waterways including the Bailang, Zhangmian and Yuhe rivers run through the city, which directly administers four districts, six county-level cities and two counties spanning a total land area of 16,143 square kilometres and a total population of 9,357,000. Weifang and the regions that surround it are additionally noted for their specific contributions to China's cultural and scientific heritage, with Gaomi being the home city of China's first Nobel Laureate for Literature Mo Yan and the primary setting for many of his novels and Zhucheng being renowned as a uniquely prolific source of paleontological discoveries.

In 2016, Weifang's Gross Regional Domestic Product (GRDP) stood at RMB 552 billion, with the city also boasting a GRDP growth rate of 8.0%, as is reflected in Table 16.1. The regions surrounding Weifang are rich in natural resources and notably contain large quantities of sapphires, as well as reserves of bittern water. Weifang's primary sector correspondingly constituted 8.6% of its GRDP. The city's secondary sector, which has traditionally depended on industries, such as mechanical equipment, automobile manufacturing, textiles, and food processing,

[1]The relevant city information are from the Department of Commerce of Shandong Province (n.d.), Weifang Municipal People's Government (n.d.) and Shen (2009).

constituted 46.4% of GRDP. Finally, Weifang's tertiary sector constituted 45.0% of total GRDP and looks to continue expanding, with investments fuelling the growth of service industries, such as financial services, tourism and service outsourcing.

Weifang is served by Weifang Airport, which offers domestic flights. It is also serviced by a class one seaport, and an abundance of well connected rail and road networks. Weifang's admirable dedication to public welfare is evident in the high levels of satisfaction among the population with regard to both the public education system and public health care, with the city scoring one of the highest in the province for both metrics in 2016. This undoubtedly contributes to the fact that Weifang scored the highest among its peers for residents' perceptions of overall happiness in 2016, underlining the city's achievements in ensuring that it is liveable for its residents.

Table 16.1: Key Economic Indicators for Weifang, 2016

Land Area (km^2)	**16,143**
Population	
Total Population	9,357,000
Urbanisation Rate (%)	58.2
Average Life Expectancy (years)	76.5
Number of Employees (10,000)	573
Workforce Participation Rate (%)	76.4
Gross Regional Domestic Product (GRDP) — 2015 Prices	
GRDP (100 millions of RMB)	5,523
GRDP Per Capita (RMB)	59,275
GRDP Growth Rate (%)	8.0
Economic Composition	
Primary Sector (% of GRDP)	8.6
Secondary Sector (% of GRDP)	46.4
Tertiary Sector (% of GRDP)	45.0
Trade — 2016 Prices	
Exports (millions of RMB)	86,242
Imports (millions of RMB)	39,438
Dependency on Foreign Trade (%)	22.6
Infrastructure	
Per Capita Road Area (m^2)	28.6
Growth in the Number of Passengers Transported (10,000)	217
Growth in the Volume of Cargo Transported (10,000 tons)	2,193
Environment	
Green Coverage Ratio of Built-up Area (%)	41.9
Environmental Expenditure (% of Total Fiscal Expenditure)	3.5

Source: Asia Competitiveness Institute from the 2017 Shandong Statistical Yearbook.

16.2 In-Depth Urban Development of Weifang, 2016*

16.2.1 Overall Urban Development Performance

Overall Performance

2017 Rank

5th

Out of 17 Cities

Score: 0.855

Rank	City	Score
1	Qingdao	1.753
2	Weihai	1.393
3	Yantai	1.312
4	Jinan	1.106
5	Weifang	0.855
6	Dongying	0.603
7	Zibo	0.403
	...	
16	Laiwu	–1.233
17	Liaocheng	–1.576

Weifang ranks 5th in its Overall Performance, with a standardised score of 0.855. This places the city in the Top Five Group of 17 cities. Weifang is positioned between Jinan (1.106) at 4th place and Dongying (0.603) at 6th place.

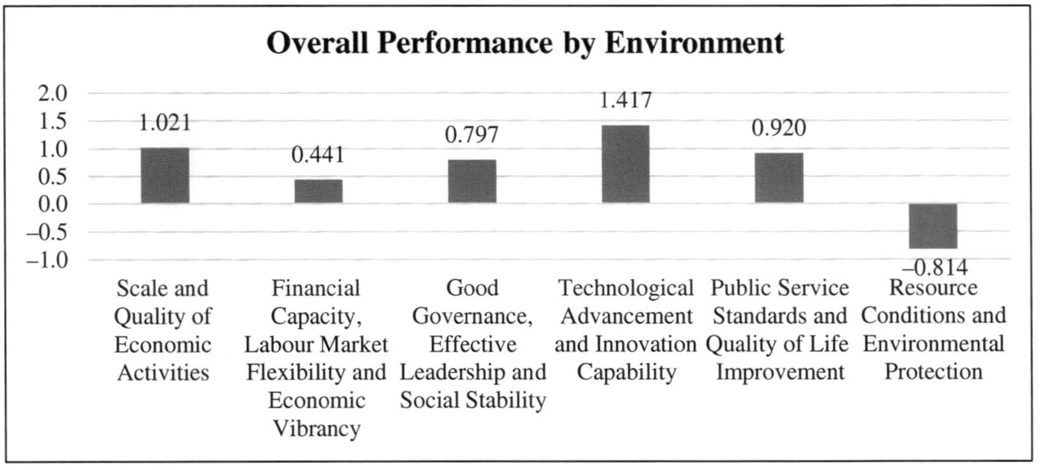

Among the six environments, Weifang scores above the provincial average in five of them, performing especially better in the environments of Scale and Quality of Economic Activities and Technological Advancement and Innovation Capability. However, Weifang scores below the provincial average and particularly weaker in the remaining environment of Resource Conditions and Environmental Protection.

**For a complete list of rankings, see Tables 3.2 to 3.7 in Section 3.3 of Chapter 3.*

16.2.2 Urban Development within the Six Environments

Rank	City	Score
1	Qingdao	1.987
2	Yantai	1.687
3	Heze	1.289
4	Weifang	1.021
5	Weihai	0.849
6	Linyi	0.447
7	Dezhou	0.096
	...	
16	Jining	−1.273
17	Laiwu	−1.295

A: ***Scale and Quality of Economic Activities***

2017 Rank

4th

Out of 17 Cities

Score: 1.021

Weifang ranks 4th for Scale and Quality of Economic Activities, with a standardised score of 1.021. This places the city in the Top Five Group of 17 cities. Weifang is positioned behind Heze (1.289) at 3rd place and ahead of Weihai (0.849) at 5th place.

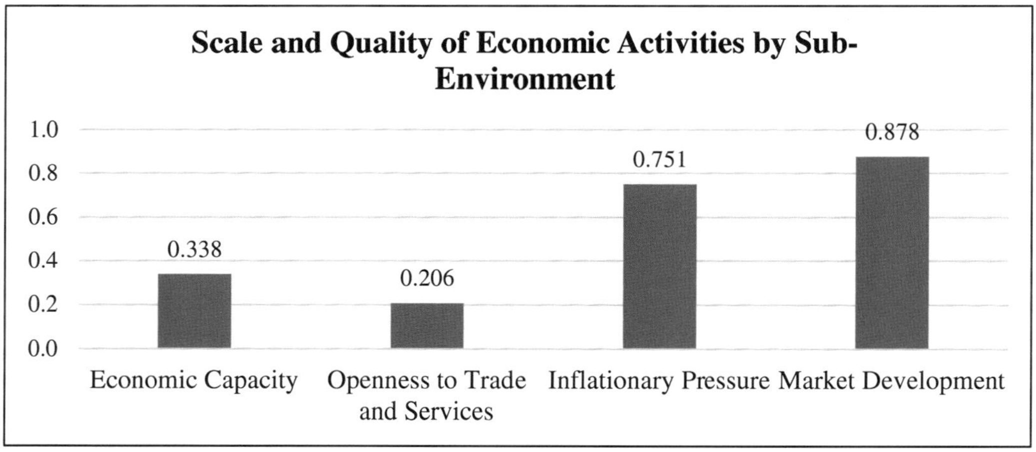

Looking at the four sub-environments of Scale and Quality of Economic Activities, Weifang performs above the provincial average in all of them and fares exceptionally well in the sub-environments of Inflationary Pressure and Market Development. In particular, it scores well in the indicator of Residents' Satisfaction with Price Levels under the Inflationary Pressure sub-environment and the indicator of Satisfaction with Business Environment under the Market Development sub-environment. The indicator of Per Capita Fixed Investment under the sub-environment of Economic Capacity also performs relatively well. However, the indicator of Consumer Price Index from the sub-environment of Inflationary Pressure scores relatively poorly.

B: *Financial Capacity, Labour Market Flexibility and Economic Vibrancy*

2017 Rank

4th

Out of 17 Cities

Score: 0.441

Rank	City	Score
1	Jinan	2.264
2	Qingdao	1.932
3	Yantai	1.271
4	Weifang	0.441
5	Linyi	0.387
6	Dongying	0.293
7	Zibo	0.089
	...	
16	Dezhou	−1.026
17	Laiwu	−1.297

Weifang ranks 4th for Financial Capacity, Labour Market Flexibility and Economic Vibrancy, with a standardised score of 0.441. This places the city in the Top Five Group of 17 cities. Weifang is positioned well behind Yantai (1.271) at 3rd place and ahead of Linyi (0.387) at 5th place.

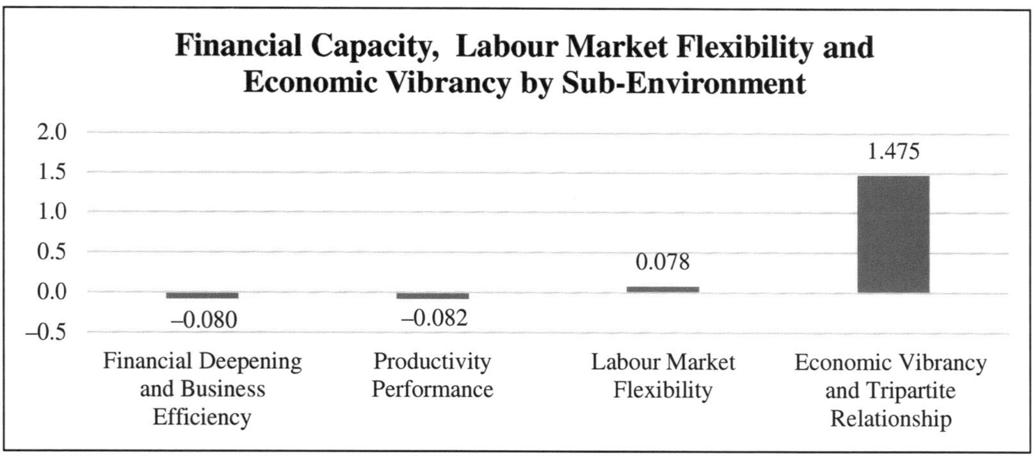

Among the four sub-environments of Financial Capacity, Labour Market Flexibility and Economic Vibrancy, Weifang performs above the provincial average in two of them and especially well for Economic Vibrancy and Tripartite Relationship, where it scores well in the indicators of Growth in the Number of Passengers Transported and Growth in the Volume of Cargo Transported. In addition, the Number of Employees and Newly Increased Number of Employees under the sub-environment of Labour Market Flexibility also score well. On the other hand, Weifang performs marginally below the provincial average in the remaining two sub-environments, where it scores especially poorly in the indicator of Annual Loan Growth Rate from the Financial Deepening and Business Efficiency sub-environment.

WEIFANG

Shandong Province

Rank	City	Score
1	Dezhou	1.465
2	Weihai	1.134
3	Weifang	0.797
4	Qingdao	0.733
5	Jinan	0.532
6	Tai'an	0.498
7	Heze	0.435
	...	
16	Laiwu	–1.588
17	Liaocheng	–2.473

C: *Good Governance, Effective Leadership and Social Stability*

2017 Rank

3rd

Out of 17 Cities

Score: 0.797

Weifang ranks 3rd for Good Governance, Effective Leadership and Social Stability with a standardised score of 0.797. This places the city in the Top Five Group of 17 cities. Weifang is positioned between Weihai (1.134) at 2nd place and Qingdao (0.733) at 4th place.

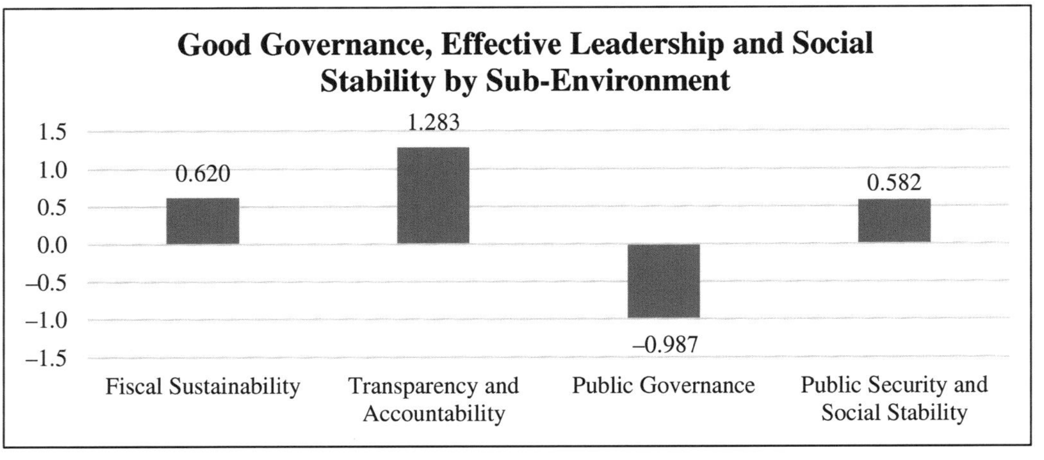

Looking at the four sub-environments of Good Governance, Effective Leadership and Social Stability, Weifang scores above the provincial average in three of them and particularly better for Transparency and Accountability, where the indicators of Public Perception of Government Conduct and Satisfaction with the Just of Judiciary score remarkably well. The indicator of Public Perception of Security under the Public Security and Social Stability sub-environment also scores well. On the other hand, Weifang performs below the provincial average in the remaining sub-environment of Public Governance, where the indicators of Number of Public Servants Per 10,000 Population and Average Public Servant Salary fare especially poorly.

D: ***Technological Advancement and Innovation Capability***

2017 Rank

2nd

Out of 17 Cities

Score: 1.417

Rank	City	Score
1	Qingdao	2.176
2	Weifang	1.417
3	Jinan	1.257
4	Yantai	1.009
5	Weihai	0.848
6	Zibo	0.492
7	Dongying	0.178
	...	
16	Zaozhuang	–1.192
17	Liaocheng	–1.221

Weifang ranks 2nd for Technological Advancement and Innovation Capability, with a standardised score of 1.417. This places the city in the Top Five Group of 17 cities. Weifang is positioned between Qingdao (2.176) at 1st place and Jinan (1.257) at 3rd place.

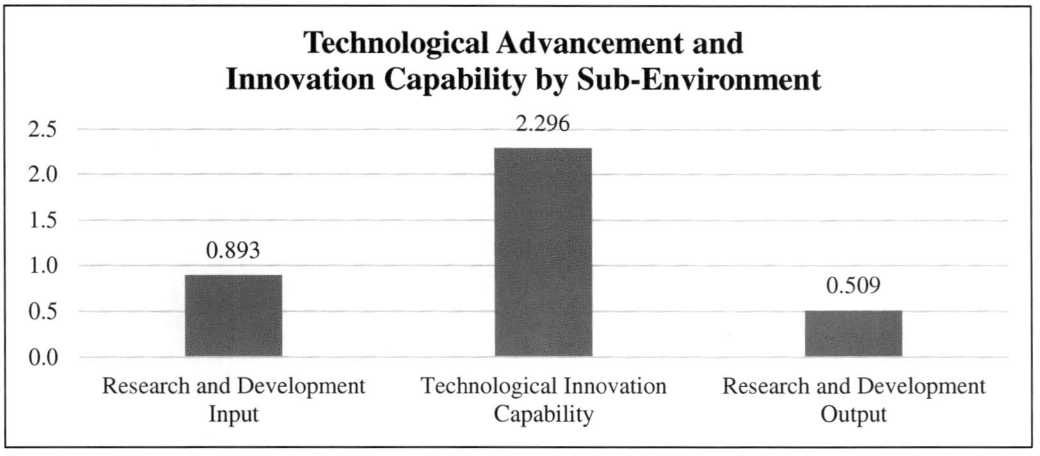

In the three sub-environments of Technological Advancement and Innovation Capability, Weifang performs above the provincial average in all of them and exceptionally well for Technological Innovation Capability, the indicators of the Satisfaction with Innovation Environment and Number of Provincial-Level Science Parks record particularly high scores. In addition, the indicators of Total Research and Development Expenditure of Enterprises above Designated Size as well as the Research and Development Expenditure as a Share of Government Expenditure, both from the Research and Development Input sub-environment, perform relatively well.

WEIFANG

Shandong Province

Rank	City	Score
1	Dongying	1.689
2	Weihai	1.616
3	Weifang	0.920
4	Jinan	0.919
5	Zibo	0.794
6	Laiwu	0.675
7	Qingdao	0.593
	...	
16	Dezhou	–1.066
17	Liaocheng	–1.964

E: *Public Service Standards and Quality of Life Improvement*

2017 Rank

3rd

Out of 17 Cities

Score: 0.920

Weifang ranks 3rd for Public Service Standards and Quality of Life Improvement with a standardised score of 0.920. This places the city in the Top Five Group of 17 cities. Weifang is positioned well behind Weihai (1.616) at 2nd place and marginally ahead of Jinan (0.919) at 4th place.

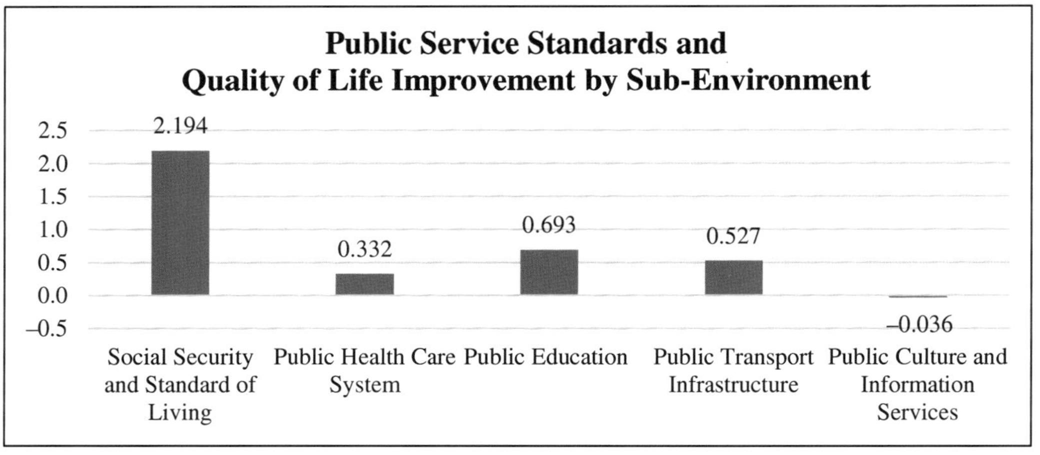

Among the five sub-environments of Public Service Standards and Quality of Life Improvement, Weifang performs above the provincial average in four of their and exceptionally well for Social Security and Standard of Living, where the indicators of Engel's Index, Residents' Perception of Happiness and Satisfaction of Income Disparity attain relatively high scores. Other well performing indicators include the Satisfaction of Public Health Care Services from the Public Health Care System sub-environment and Satisfaction of Public Education System from the Public Education sub-environment. However, the sub-environment of Public Culture and Information Services fares slightly below the provincial average, where the indicator of Number of Museums Per 10,000 Population scores relatively poorly. In addition, the indicator of Number of Urban Public Transport Vehicles Per 10,000 Population from the Public Transport Infrastructure sub-environment is weaker as well.

F: ***Resource Conditions and Environmental Protection***

2017 Rank

14th

Out of 17 Cities

Score: –0.814

Rank	City	Score
1	Weihai	1.632
	...	
10	Jining	–0.112
11	Dezhou	–0.287
12	Zaozhuang	–0.393
13	Linyi	–0.512
14	Weifang	–0.814
15	Laiwu	–1.136
16	Binzhou	–1.586
17	Heze	–2.142

Weifang ranks 14th for Resource Conditions and Environmental Protection with a standardised score of –0.814. This places the city in the Bottom Five Group of 17 cities. Weifang is positioned between Linyi (–0.512) at 13th place and Laiwu (–1.136) at 15th place.

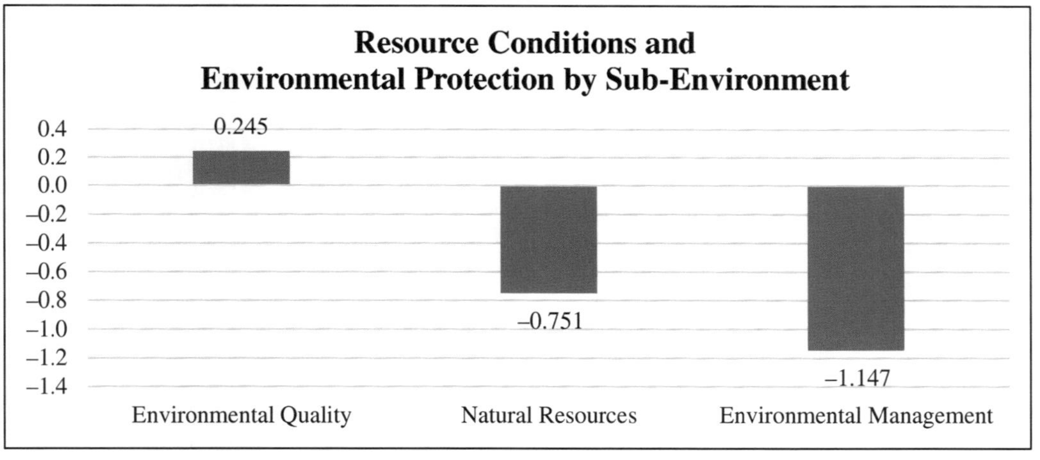

Among the three sub-environments in Resource Conditions and Environmental Protection, Weifang performs below the provincial average in two of them and especially weaker for Environmental Management, where the indicators of Per Capita Park and Green Space Acreage and Forest Land Growth perform weaker. In addition, the indicator of Built-up Area Population Density from the sub-environment of Natural Resources records a relatively low score. On the other hand, Weifang performs slightly above the provincial average in the remaining sub-environment of Environmental Quality, where the indicator of Sulphur Dioxide Emissions Per RMB 10,000 GRDP performs relatively better.

WEIFANG

Shandong Province

Figure 16.1: Median & Maximum Web for Weifang

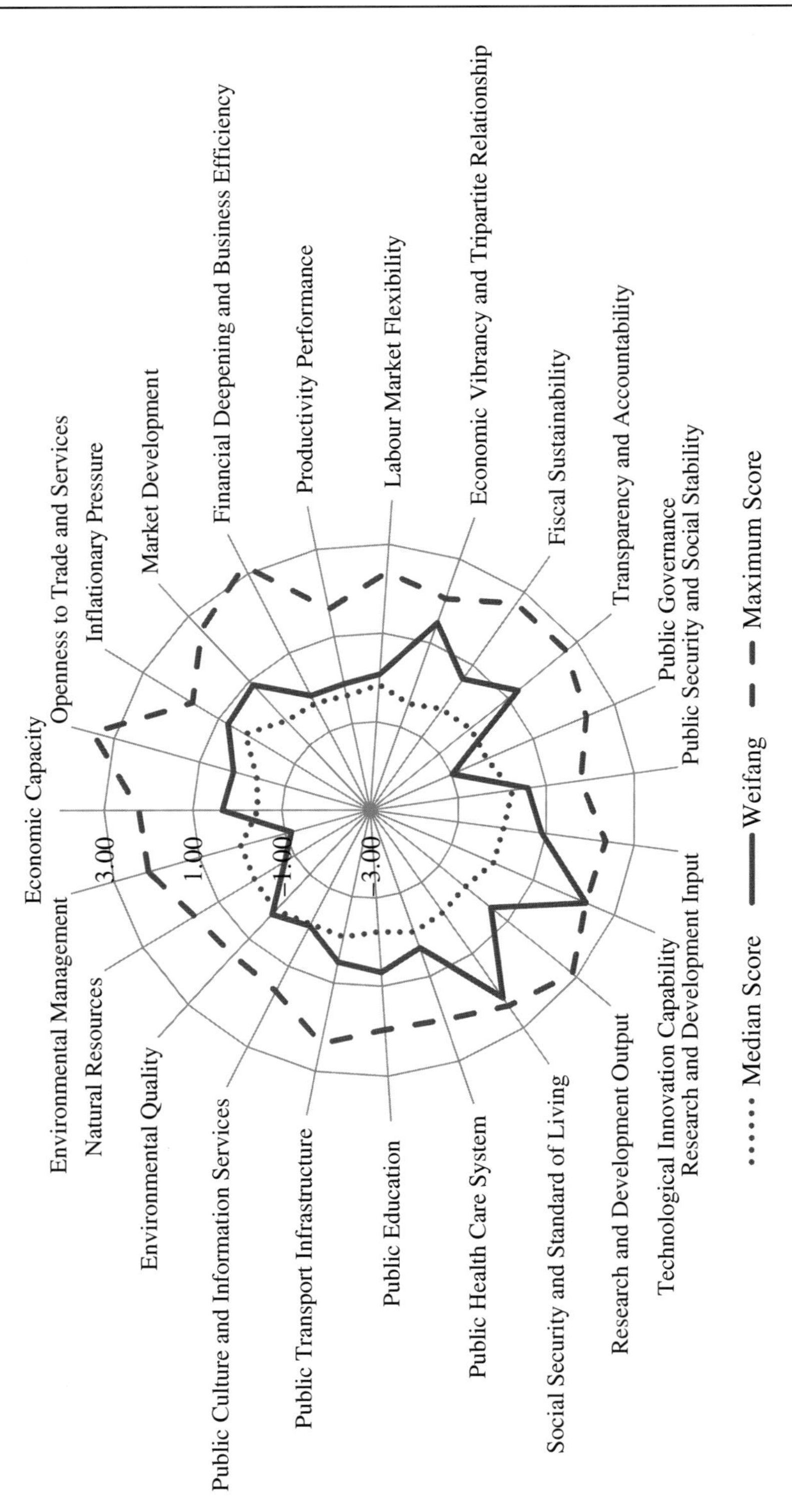

Source: Asia Competitiveness Institute.

16.2.3 Median and Maximum Web Analysis

To better understand Weifang's relative strengths and weaknesses, it is useful to compare and contrast its scores for the 23 sub-environments against the median and maximum scores of Shandong's 17 cities.

In Figure 16.1, the median and maximum scores for 17 Shandong cities are shown as dotted and dashed lines respectively, while scores for Weifang are shown as a solid line.

Comparison to Median Scores

Weifang scores above the median for 20 of the 23 sub-environments, most notably in Social Security and Standard of Living and Technological Innovation Capability.

On the other hand, it scores below the median for the remaining three sub-environments, especially for Environmental Management and Natural Resources.

Comparison to Maximum Scores

Weifang scores below the provincial maximum of the 17 Shandong cities in 22 out of the 23 sub-environments. Weifang achieves the provincial maximum score in the sub-environment of Technological Innovation Capability, with a standardised score of 2.296.

Weifang's score in the Environmental Management (–1.147) is the farthest from the maximum, which is held by Dongying (2.195). Further, Weifang's score in Social Security and Standard of Living (2.194) is closest to the maximum, which is held by Dongying (2.416).

16.3 Summary of Empirical Findings of Weifang and *What-if* Urban Development Simulation

16.3.1 Summary of Empirical Findings, 20% Strongest and Weakest Indicators

Overall Performance		
5th Score: 0.855		
Scale and Quality of Economic Activities **4th** Score: 1.021	Financial Capacity, Labour Market Flexibility and Economic Vibrancy **4th** Score: 0.441	Good Governance, Effective Leadership and Social Stability **3rd** Score: 0.797
Technological Advancement and Innovation Capability **2nd** Score: 1.417	Public Service Standards and Quality of Life Improvement **3rd** Score: 0.920	Resource Conditions and Environmental Protection **14th** Score: –0.814

(Rank out of 17 cities)

Summary

Weifang ranks 5th out of 17 Shandong cities in its Overall Performance. Weifang performs above the provincial average in five out of the six environments, where the environment of Technological Advancement and Innovation Capability performs exceptionally better. Meanwhile Weifang's worst performing environment is that of Resource Conditions and Environmental Protection, which is the only environment performing below the provincial average.

Strengths

As observed in Table 16.2, Weifang performs especially well in the environment of Public Service Standards and Quality of Life Improvement, with eight out of 26 of its 20% Strongest Indicators in that environment. Among Weifang's best performing indicators are the Satisfaction with Innovation Environment, the Number of Provincial-Level Science Parks and Residents' Perception of Happiness.

Weaknesses

As observed in Table 16.3, Weifang is weaker in the environment of Resource Conditions and Environmental Protection, with seven out of 26 of its 20% Weakest Indicators under this environment. Among Weifang's worst performing indicators are the Number of Public Servants Per 10,000 Population, Consumer Price Index and Annual Loan Growth Rate.

Table 16.2: 20% Strongest Indicators for Weifang

Rank	20% Strongest Indicator	Score	SQEA	FCLMFEV	GGELSS	TAIC	PSSQLI	RCEP
1	Satisfaction with Innovation Environment	2.201				✓		
2	Number of Provincial-Level Science Parks	1.664				✓		
3	Residents' Perception of Happiness	1.609					✓	
4	Engel's Index	1.552					✓	
5	Satisfaction of Income Disparity	1.525					✓	
6	Growth in the Number of Passengers Transported	1.517		✓				
7	Residents' Satisfaction with Price Levels	1.509	✓					
8	Public Perception of Government Conduct	1.425			✓			
9	Satisfaction of Public Education System	1.330					✓	
10	Growth in the Volume of Cargo Transported	1.317		✓				
11	Satisfaction with Business Environment	1.295	✓					
12	Satisfaction with the Just of Judiciary	1.285			✓			
13	Frequency of Using the Internet for Daily Convenience	1.263					✓	
14	Per Capita Fixed Investment	1.253	✓					
15	Index for Quality of E-Government System	1.113			✓			
16	Number of Employees	1.096		✓				
17	Public Perception of Security	1.080			✓			
18	Satisfaction of Public Health Care Services	1.077					✓	
19	Total R&D Expenditure of Enterprises Above Designated Size	1.050				✓		
20	Self-Employed as a Share of Total Employment	1.043		✓				
21	Newly Increased Number of Employees	1.011		✓				
22	Ratio of Public Education Appropriation to GRDP	0.992					✓	
23	Urban Residents' Disposable Income Growth Rate	0.951	✓					
24	Fiscal Revenue Growth Rate	0.949			✓			
25	Research & Development Expenditure as a Share of Government Expenditure	0.934				✓		
26	Number of Passengers Transported	0.909					✓	

Table 16.3: 20% Weakest Indicators for Weifang

Rank	20% Weakest Indicator	Score	SQEA	FCLMFEV	GGELSS	TAIC	PSSQLI	RCEP
106	Percentage of Public Expenditure on Cultural Initiatives	–0.404					✓	
107	Urban Area Waste Water Treatment Rate	–0.407						✓
108	GRDP Per Capita	–0.414	✓					
109	Government Fiscal Expenditure Per Capita	–0.453			✓			
110	Number of Administration Action and Reconsideration Cases	–0.483			✓			
111	Proportion of Workforce Employed in Agriculture Sector	–0.504		✓				
112	Proportion of Urban Workers Employed in Private Enterprises	–0.526		✓				
113	Green Coverage Ratio of Built-up Area	–0.539						✓
114	Growth Rate of the Number of Police Cases Solved	–0.641			✓			
115	Urban Registered Unemployment Rate	–0.671		✓				
116	Number of Listed Items Under Executive Authority of the Government	–0.714			✓			
117	Number of Vocational Education Institutions Per 10,000 Population	–0.720					✓	
118	Number of Urban Taxis Per 10,000 Population	–0.746					✓	
119	Number of Museums Per 10,000 Population	–0.755					✓	
120	Number of Urban Public Transport Vehicles Per 10,000 Population (Standard Number)	–0.773					✓	
121	Average Public Servant Salary	–0.866			✓			
122	Area of Natural Reserves to Administrative Area (%)	–0.894						✓
123	Forest Land Growth	–0.927						✓
124	Per Capita Freshwater Resource	–0.994						✓
125	Per Capita Park and Green Space Acreage	–1.017						✓
126	Proportion of Workforce Employed in Service Sector	–1.045		✓				
127	Built-up Area Population Density	–1.151						✓
128	Public Health and Medical Service Expenses Per Capita	–1.156					✓	
129	Annual Loan Growth Rate	–1.226		✓				
130	Consumer Price Index (CPI)	–1.314	✓					
131	Number of Public Servants Per 10,000 Population	–1.515			✓			

Source: Asia Competitiveness Institute.

Notes: SQEA: Scale and Quality of Economic Activities; FCLMFEV: Financial Capacity, Labour Market Flexibility and Economic Vibrancy; GGELSS: Good Governance, Effective Leadership and Social Stability; TAIC: Technological Advancement and Innovation Capability; PSSQLI: Public Service Standards and Quality of Life Improvement; RCEP: Resource Conditions and Environmental Protection.

16.3.2 *What-if* Urban Development Simulation

ACI has devised a simulation methodology to improve the ranking of a particular city by improving on its 20% Weakest Indicators as shown in Table 16.3.[2] The figures below show Weifang's ranking and standardised scores before and after the policy-induced simulation. Refer to Tables 3.8 to 3.14 in Section 3.4 of Chapter 3 for a complete list of simulation results for all cities.

Overall Performance

5th	▶	**2nd**
0.855		**1.396**

Scale and Quality of Economic Activities

	Before	After
Rank	4th	3rd
Score	1.021	1.254

Financial Capacity, Labour Market Flexibility and Economic Vibrancy

	Before	After
Rank	4th	4th
Score	0.441	0.634

Good Governance, Effective Leadership and Social Stability

	Before	After
Rank	3rd	1st
Score	0.797	1.534

Technological Advancement and Innovation Capability

	Before	After
Rank	2nd	2nd
Score	1.417	1.417

Public Service Standards and Quality of Life Improvement

	Before	After
Rank	3rd	3rd
Score	0.920	1.240

Resource Conditions and Environmental Protection

	Before	After
Rank	14th	8th
Score	–0.814	0.261

After the *What-if* Simulation, Weifang improved its ranking from 5th to 2nd in terms of its Overall Performance. Likewise, Weifang's standardised score improved from 0.855 to 1.396. This leap is plausible if the city manages to successfully address its 20% Weakest Indicators.

The simulation further highlights substantial improvement for Weifang in some of its environments, most notably in Resource Conditions and Environmental Protection where its rank will rise from 14th to 8th. Such encouraging results should incentivise Weifang to strive to improve the indicators under the 20% Weakest Indicators list. These indicators include the Built-up Area Population Density, Per Capita Park and Green Space Acreage and Per Capita Freshwater Resource.

[2]The methodology for *What-if* Simulation is thoroughly explained in Section 2.7 of Chapter 2.

16.4 Concluding Notes: Public Policy Implications[3]

Areas for Commendation

Weifang performs especially well in the environments of Financial Capacity, Labour Market Flexibility and Economic Vibrancy, Public Service Standards and Quality of Life Improvement and Good Governance, Effective Leadership and Social Stability, where 18 out of 26 of its 20% Strongest Indicators are contained in these environments, as indicated in Table 16.2.

Weifang holds the maximum score for the sub-environment of Technological Innovation Capability (2.296) and scores above the provincial average in 17 out of 23 sub-environments.

From 2012 to 2016, the Weifang government has been forging ahead to boost innovation in the city, where the proportion of Research and Development investment in GRDP is expected to reach 2.6% by 2016. For instance, Sheng Rui Transmission Corporation Limited, an automatic transmissions manufacturer based in Weifang, won the first price for National Improvement in Science and Technology with their Eight Gear Automatic Transmission (8AT) and Industrial Project. With regard to the good performance in the sub-environment of Inflationary Pressure, Weifang's Consumer Price Index increased by approximately 3% in 2015. However, the per capita disposable income of urban and rural residents increased by about 8% and 8.5% respectively in 2016, on a year on year basis. These developments reveal Weifang's strength in the sub-environments of Technological Innovation Capability and Inflationary Pressure respectively.

Areas for Improvement

Weifang scores below the provincial average in one out of the six environments. Most crucially, Weifang should address the environments of Good Governance, Effective Leadership and Social Stability, Public Service Standards and Quality of Life Improvement and Resource Conditions and Environmental Protection, which collectively contribute 19 out of 26 of Weifang's 20% Weakest Indicators, as shown in Table 16.3. Additionally, as gleaned from the *What-if* Urban Development Simulation, the environment of Resource Conditions and Environmental Protection should be prioritised because that is the environment in which Weifang will achieve the greatest improvement in its ranking — six positions — relative to other environments.

Moreover, Weifang obtains one of the lowest scores in the sub-environment of Environmental Management (–1.147) and scores below the provincial average in six out of 23 sub-environments.

The Weifang government should make efforts in the environment of Resource Conditions and Environmental Protection. For example, the government should increase the city's green space and increase freshwater resource for residents. In addition, there is a significant downward pressure in the economy, protruding structural contradiction and noticeable differentiation of

[3]The relevant statistical data and government policies are from Weifang Municipal People's Government (n.d.), Dazhong Newspaper (2017) and Han (2017).

industry enterprises. For example, the capacity to innovate is weak and the constraints of natural resources from the environment are tightening. As such, the Weifang government places great emphasis on these problems and have taken pertinent measures to solve them seriously.

Future Potential Development

In summary, Weifang should focus on implementing better urban waste treatment, as well as investing in more green spaces to improve the environment of Resource Conditions and Environmental Protection. In addition, Weifang should look towards improving the environment of Financial Capacity, Labour Market Flexibility and Economic Vibrancy by developing its service sector and financial institutions.

In 2016, the Weifang government reached a record high of RMB 15.88 billion in its investment in transport infrastructure. However, Weifang still obtains negative growth in the number of passengers transported in our analysis. Nevertheless, as Weifang strives to achieve the goal of being an integrated transportation hub, it has committed to the investment in public transport in 2017 by a total of RMB 23.85 billion. In addition, Weifang needs to focus on the development of service industries, such as tourism and e-commerce.

References

Dazhong Newspaper. 2017. '潍坊市政府工作报告 2017 Weifang Annual Government Work Report (in Chinese)'. 7 March 2017. http://weifang.dzwww.com/wfxwn/201703/t20170307_15636044.htm.

Department of Commerce of Shandong Province. n.d. 'Weifang City'. Accessed 27 October 2017. http://en.shandongbusiness.gov.cn/city/72.

Han, Beibei. 2017. '潍坊市召开2017年全市交通运输工作会议 Weifang Held 2017 Municipal Work Conference on Transportation (in Chinese)'. 12 April 2017. http://weifang.sdchina.com/show/4086279.html.

Shen, Hong. 2009. 'Weifang City Introduction'. 23 July 2009. http://shandong.chinadaily.com.cn/e/2009-07/23/content_8464120_2.htm.

Weifang Municipal People's Government. n.d. '中国潍坊 China Weifang (in Chinese)'. Accessed 27 October 2017. http://www.weifang.gov.cn/.

Chapter 17: WEIHAI
Shandong Province

Location of City

Source: Asia Competitiveness Institute.

17.1 Profile of Weihai City[1]

Weihai is located at the eastern tip of Shandong Province and faces the Korean peninsula across the Yellow Sea. Once famed for hosting the Qing Dynasty's massive Beiyang Fleet, the city and its surrounding territories are today famed for their picturesque qualities, with many tourists being drawn to the region by its scenic vistas, temperate weather and well-developed infrastructure. Weihai presently administers two districts and two county-level cities, covering a total land area of 5,797 square kilometres and a total population of 2,819,300. The city's municipal government has been commended for its comprehensive approach to urban liveability, and was awarded a Scroll of Honour by UN-Habitat in 2003 for its work in this regard.

In 2016, Weihai's Gross Regional Domestic Product (GRDP) stood at RMB 321 billion, with the city also enjoying a healthy GRDP growth rate of 8.0%, as reflected in Table 17.1. Weihai is a major fishing port which boasts an output of around 2.5 million tons — which accounts for 4% of China's total output of aquatic products. Correspondingly, Weihai's primary sector comprised 7.1% of total GRDP. Weihai's secondary sector constituted 45.6% of GRDP and is focused on several general industrial clusters, including food processing, machine manufacturing,

[1]The relevant city information are from the Department of Commerce of Shandong Province (n.d.), Weihai Foreign Investment Promotion Centre (n.d.) and Yuan (2009).

transportation equipment, textiles, pharmaceuticals and medical apparatuses. Finally, Weihai's tertiary sector, which constituted 47.3% of GRDP, is dependent on tourism, while also being bolstered by ongoing investments into Research and Development (R&D) and education.

Weihai is served by Weihai Dashuibo Airport. The city is also a major seaport, which offers passenger lines to South Korea. Moreover, Weihai is connected via the high-speed rail network, as well as multiple expressways, to Beijing, Jinan, and other cities in neighbouring regions. Weihai is additionally distinguished by the fact that it was the city with one of the highest rates of growth for urban residents' disposable income in 2016, at 8.3%. Weihai additionally spent the greatest proportion of public expenditure on R&D of any of Shandong's cities, at 3.8% in 2016, reflecting the city's drive to ensure that it remains on the cutting edge of scientific and technological development.

Table 17.1: Key Economic Indicators for Weihai, 2016

Land Area (km²)	**5,797**
Population	
Total Population	2,819,300
Urbanisation Rate (%)	65.0
Average Life Expectancy (years)	75.5
Number of Employees (10,000)	201
Workforce Participation Rate (%)	71.9
Gross Regional Domestic Product (GRDP) — 2015 Prices	
GRDP (100 millions of RMB)	3,212
GRDP Per Capita (RMB)	114,220
GRDP Growth Rate (%)	8.0
Economic Composition	
Primary Sector (% of GRDP)	7.1
Secondary Sector (% of GRDP)	45.6
Tertiary Sector (% of GRDP)	47.3
Trade — 2016 Prices	
Exports (millions of RMB)	83,832
Imports (millions of RMB)	28,674
Dependency on Foreign Trade (%)	36.7
Infrastructure	
Per Capita Road Area (m²)	33.6
Growth in the Number of Passengers Transported (10,000)	87.0
Growth in the Volume of Cargo Transported (10,000 tons)	735
Environment	
Green Coverage Ratio of Built-up Area (%)	46.0
Environmental Expenditure (% of Total Fiscal Expenditure)	3.3

Source: Asia Competitiveness Institute from the 2017 Shandong Statistical Yearbook.

17.2 In-Depth Urban Development of Weihai, 2016*

17.2.1 Overall Urban Development Performance

Overall Performance

2017 Rank

2nd

Out of 17 Cities

Score: 1.393

Rank	City	Score
1	Qingdao	1.753
2	Weihai	1.393
3	Yantai	1.312
4	Jinan	1.106
5	Weifang	0.855
6	Dongying	0.603
7	Zibo	0.403
	...	
16	Laiwu	–1.233
17	Liaocheng	–1.576

Weihai ranks 2nd in its Overall Performance, with a standardised score of 1.393. This places the city in the Top Five Group of 17 cities. Weihai is positioned between Qingdao (1.753) at 1st place and Yantai (1.312) at 3rd place.

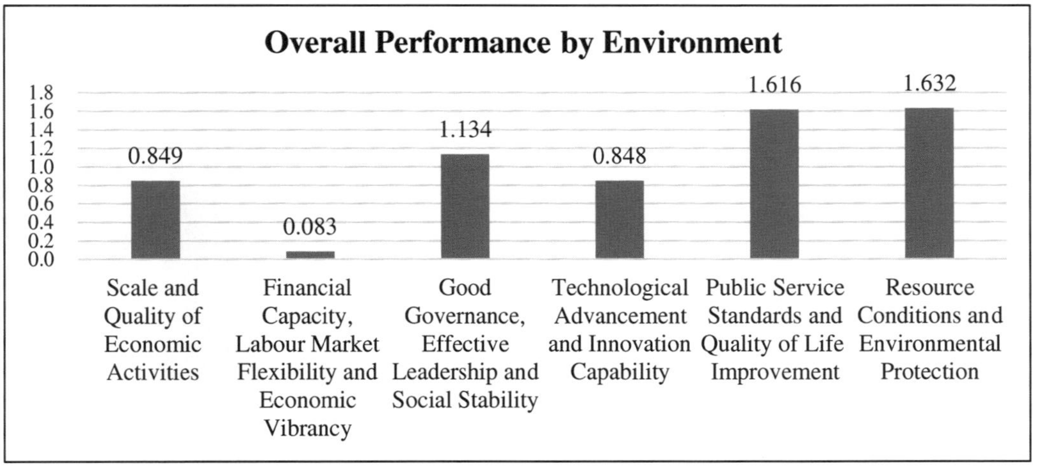

Across the six environments, Weihai scores above the provincial average in all of them and especially well in the environments of Good Governance, Effective Leadership and Social Stability, Public Service Standards and Quality of Life Improvement and Resource Conditions and Environmental Protection. In contrast, the environment of Financial Capacity, Labour Market Flexibility and Economic Vibrancy exhibits a relatively weaker performance.

**For a complete list of rankings, see Tables 3.2 to 3.7 in Section 3.3 of Chapter 3.*

17.2.2 Urban Development within the Six Environments

Rank	City	Score
1	Qingdao	1.987
2	Yantai	1.687
3	Heze	1.289
4	Weifang	1.021
5	Weihai	0.849
6	Linyi	0.447
7	Dezhou	0.096
	...	
16	Jining	–1.273
17	Laiwu	–1.295

A: ***Scale and Quality of Economic Activities***

2017 Rank

5th

Out of 17 Cities

Score: 0.849

Weihai ranks 5th for Scale and Quality of Economic Activities, with a standardised score of 0.849. This places the city in the Top Five Group of 17 cities. Weihai is positioned behind Weifang (1.021) at 4th place and ahead of Linyi (0.447) at 6th place.

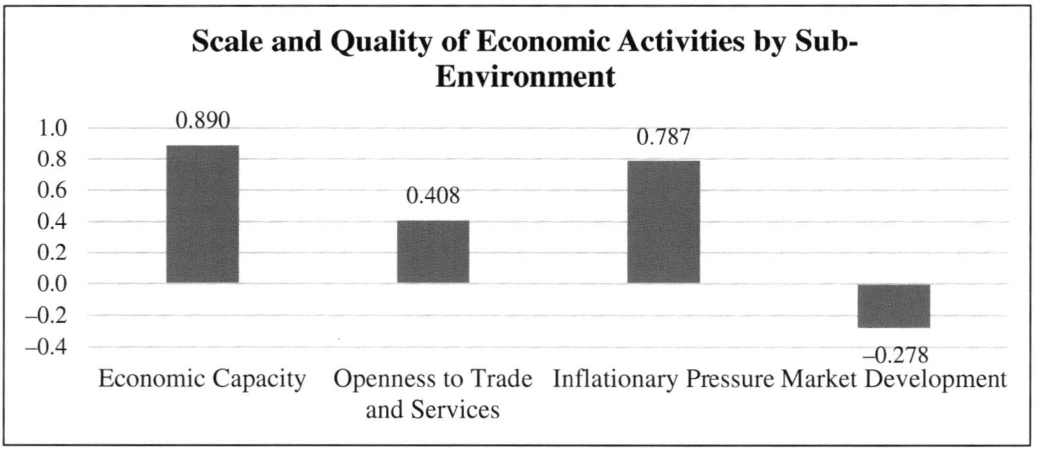

Looking at the four sub-environments of Scale and Quality of Economic Activities, Weihai performs above the provincial average in three of them and especially better in Economic Capacity and Inflationary Pressure. Specifically, the indicators of GRDP Per Capita and Per Capita Volume of Retail Sales from the Economic Capacity sub-environment, as well as the indicator of Urban Residents' Disposable Income Growth Rate from the Inflationary Pressure sub-environment record high scores. However, Weihai performs below the provincial average in the remaining sub-environment of Market Development, where it fares weakly in the indicator of Government Expenditures as a Percentage of GRDP. In addition, the indicator of Residents' Satisfaction with Price Levels from the sub-environment of Inflationary Pressure registers a particularly weak score as well.

B: *Financial Capacity, Labour Market Flexibility and Economic Vibrancy*

2017 Rank

8th

Out of 17 Cities

Score: 0.083

Rank	City	Score
1	Jinan	2.264
	...	
6	Dongying	0.293
7	Zibo	0.089
8	Weihai	0.083
9	Jining	–0.171
10	Binzhou	–0.329
	...	
16	Dezhou	–1.026
17	Laiwu	–1.297

Weihai ranks 8th for Financial Capacity, Labour Market Flexibility and Economic Vibrancy, with a standardised score of 0.083. This places the city in the Middle Seven Group of 17 cities. Weihai is positioned marginally behind Zibo (0.089) at 7th place and ahead of Jining (–0.171) at 9th place.

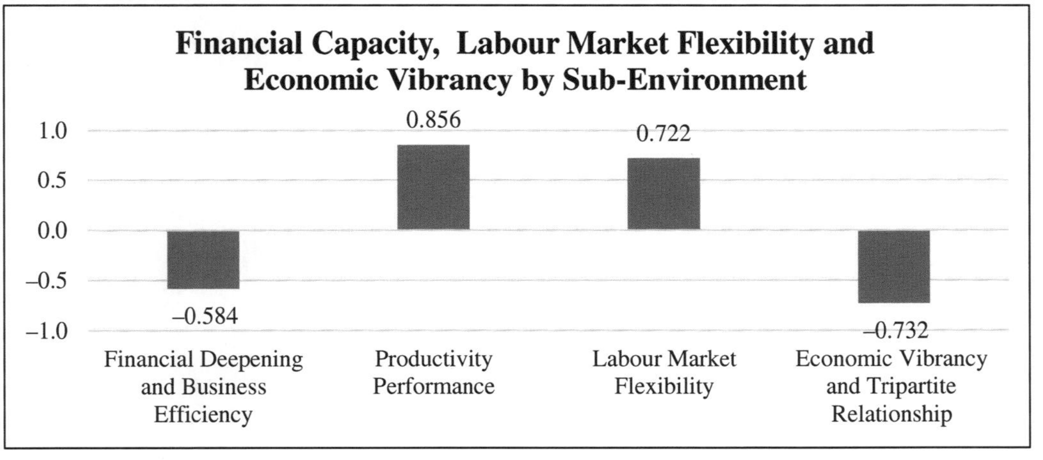

Among the four sub-environments of Financial Capacity, Labour Market Flexibility and Economic Vibrancy, Weihai performs above the provincial average in Productivity Performance and Labour Market Flexibility. Specifically, the indicators of Tertiary Industry Total Labour Productivity from the Productivity Performance sub-environment and the indicators of Rate of Migration Flow and Urban Registered Unemployment Rate from the Labour Market Flexibility sub-environment score especially well. On the other hand, Weihai fares below the provincial average in the remaining two sub-environments of Financial Deepening and Business Efficiency and Economic Vibrancy and Tripartite Relationship. In particular, indicators Annual Loan Growth Rate from the Financial Deepening and Business Efficiency sub-environment and Number of Employees from the Labour Market Flexibility sub-environment register low scores.

WEIHAI

Shandong Province

Rank	City	Score
1	Dezhou	1.465
2	Weihai	1.134
3	Weifang	0.797
4	Qingdao	0.733
5	Jinan	0.532
6	Tai'an	0.498
7	Heze	0.435
	...	
16	Laiwu	–1.588
17	Liaocheng	–2.473

C: *Good Governance, Effective Leadership and Social Stability*

2017 Rank

2nd

Out of 17 Cities

Score: 1.134

Weihai ranks 2nd for Good Governance, Effective Leadership and Social Stability with a standardised score of 1.134. This places the city in the Top Five Group of 17 cities. Weihai is positioned behind Dezhou (1.465) at 1st place and ahead of Weifang (0.797) at 3rd place.

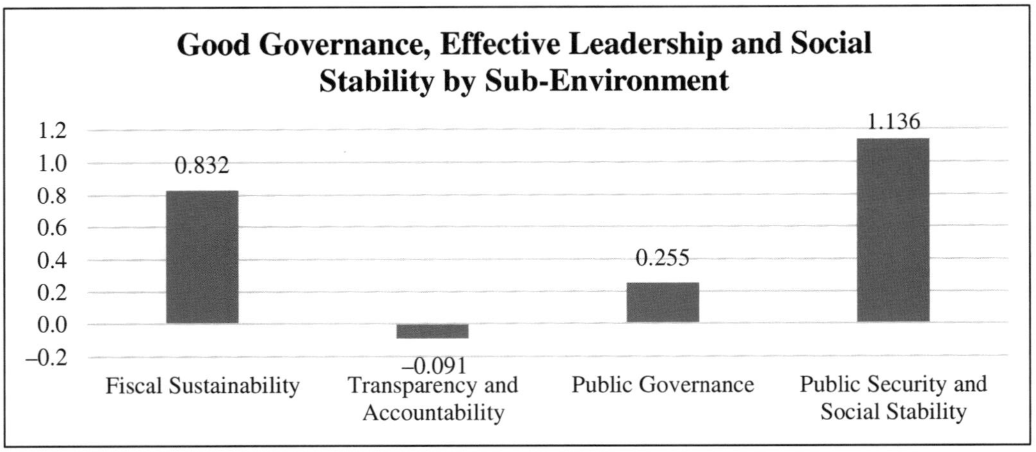

Looking at the four sub-environments of Good Governance, Effective Leadership and Social Stability, Weihai scores above the provincial average in three of them and especially well for Public Security and Social Stability, where the indicators of Public Perception of Security and Satisfaction with Urban Management Personnel score especially well. In addition, the indicators of Tax Revenue as a Share of Fiscal Revenue, Government Fiscal Expenditure Per Capita and Government Fiscal Revenue Per Capita, all under the sub-environment of Fiscal Sustainability, also fare well. However, Weihai performs slightly below the provincial average in the remaining sub-environment of Transparency and Accountability, where the indicator of the Number of Responses to Government Issues of Public Interest scores relatively poorly.

D: ***Technological Advancement and Innovation Capability***

2017 Rank

5th

Out of 17 Cities

Score: 0.848

Rank	City	Score
1	Qingdao	2.176
2	Weifang	1.417
3	Jinan	1.257
4	Yantai	1.009
5	Weihai	0.848
6	Zibo	0.492
7	Dongying	0.178
	...	
16	Zaozhuang	–1.192
17	Liaocheng	–1.221

Weihai ranks 5th for Technological Advancement and Innovation Capability, with a standardised score of 0.848. This places the city in the Top Five Group of 17 cities. Weihai is positioned behind Yantai (1.009) at 4th place and is followed by Zibo (0.492) at 6th place.

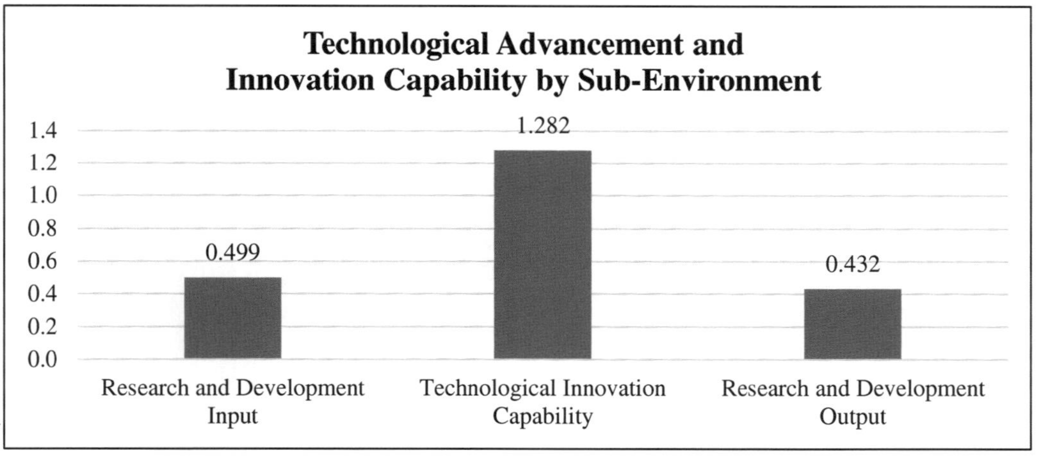

Among the three sub-environments of Technological Advancement and Innovation Capability, Weihai performs above the provincial average in all of them and exceedingly better for Technological Innovation Capability, where the indicators of the Number of Research and Development Personnel Per 10,000 Population and Satisfaction with Innovation Environment record high scores. Further, the indicators of Research and Development Expenditure as a Share of Government Expenditure and Per Capita Research and Development Expenditure from the Research and Development Input sub-environment, as well as the indicator of the Number of Existing Patents Per 10,000 Population from the Research and Development Output sub-environment perform relatively well.

WEIHAI

Shandong Province

Rank	City	Score
1	Dongying	1.689
2	Weihai	1.616
3	Weifang	0.920
4	Jinan	0.919
5	Zibo	0.794
6	Laiwu	0.675
7	Qingdao	0.593
	...	
16	Dezhou	−1.066
17	Liaocheng	−1.964

E: *Public Service Standards and Quality of Life Improvement*

2017 Rank

2nd

Out of 17 Cities

Score: 1.616

Weihai ranks 2nd for Public Service Standards and Quality of Life Improvement with a standardised score of 1.616. This places the city in the Top Five Group of 17 cities. Weihai is positioned between Dongying (1.689) at 1st place and Weifang (0.920) at 3rd place.

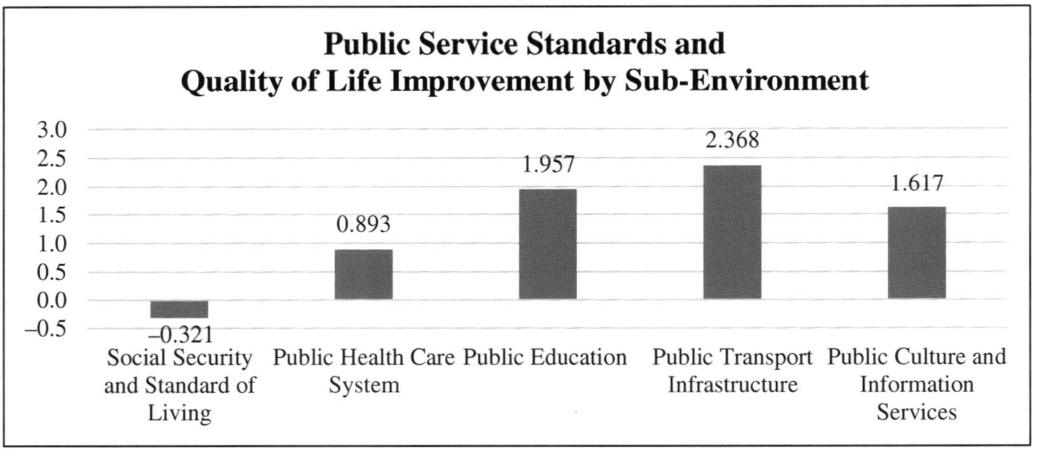

Among the five sub-environments of Public Service Standards and Quality of Life Improvement, Weihai performs above the provincial average in four of them and especially well for Public Transport Infrastructure, where the indicators of Satisfaction of Public Transport Services and Satisfaction of Traffic Conditions attain particularly high scores. Other well performing indicators include the Cleanliness of Public Toilets from the Public Health Care System sub-environment, and the indicators of Public Education Appropriation Per Capita and Number of Vocational Education Institutions Per 10,000 Population from the Public Education sub-environment. On the other hand, the Social Security and Standard of Living sub-environment fares below the provincial average, where the indicator of Proportion of the Population Above 60 Years Old performs especially poorly.

F: ***Resource Conditions and Environmental Protection***

2017 Rank

1st

Out of 17 Cities

Score: 1.632

Rank	City	Score
1	Weihai	1.632
2	Yantai	1.394
3	Dongying	1.118
4	Rizhao	0.817
5	Zibo	0.665
6	Liaocheng	0.376
7	Tai'an	0.370
	...	
16	Binzhou	–1.586
17	Heze	–2.142

Weihai ranks 1st for Resource Conditions and Environmental Protection with a standardised score of 1.632. This places the city in the Top Five Group and the best in the environment across the 17 Shandong cities. Weihai is positioned ahead of Yantai (1.394) at 2nd place.

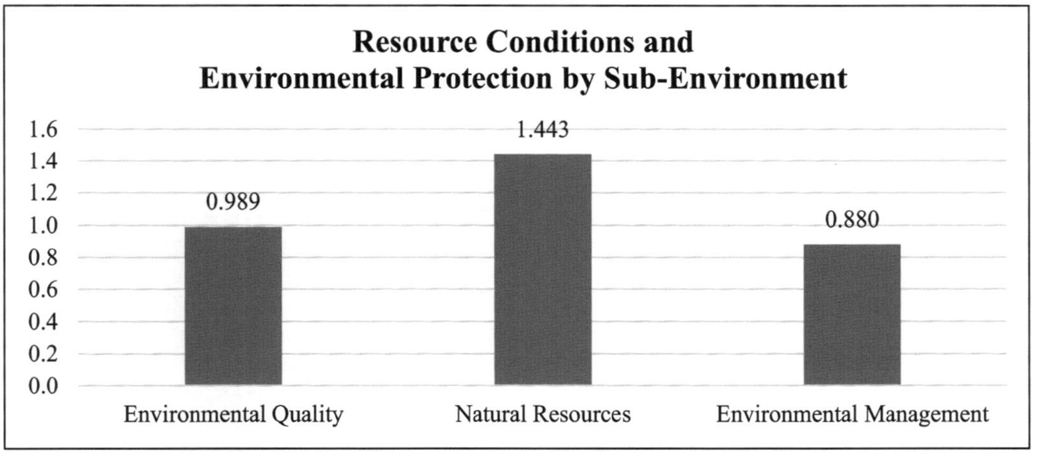

Among the three sub-environments of Resource Conditions and Environmental Protection, Weihai scores above the provincial average in all of them and especially well for Natural Resources, where the indicators of Electricity Consumption Per RMB 10,000 GRDP and Water Consumption Per RMB 10,000 GRDP perform especially well. Other well performing indicators include the Green Coverage Ratio of Built-up Area and Per Capita Park and Green Space Acreage from the Environmental Management sub-environment, and Chemical Oxygen Demand Per RMB 10,000 GRDP from the Environmental Quality sub-environment. On the other hand, the indicators of Per Capita Freshwater Resource from the Natural Resources sub-environment and Forest Land Growth under the Environmental Management sub-environment obtain comparatively weaker scores.

WEIHAI

Shandong Province

Figure 17.1: Median & Maximum Web for Weihai

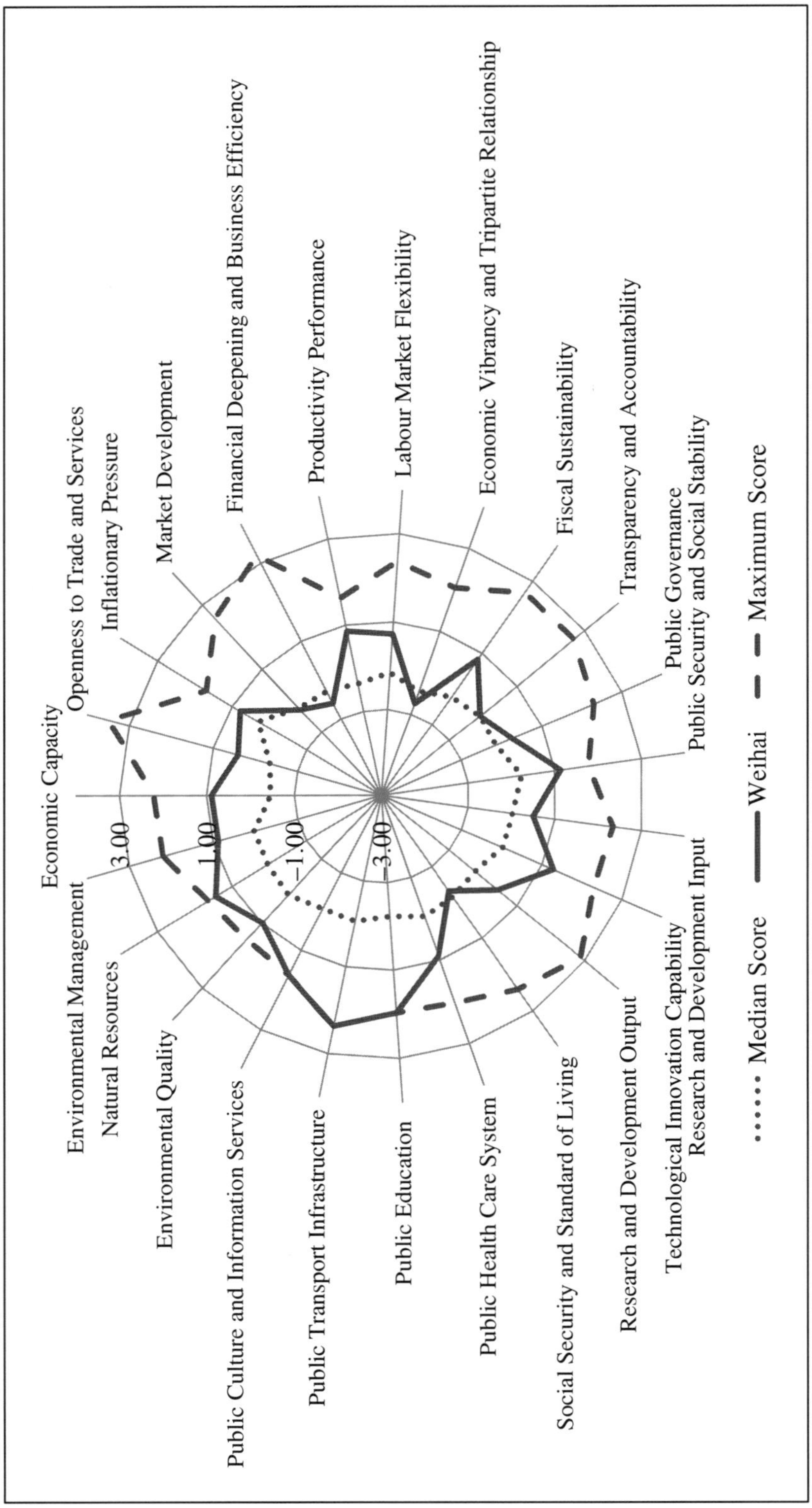

Source: Asia Competitiveness Institute.

17.2.3 Median and Maximum Web Analysis

To better understand Weihai's relative strengths and weaknesses, it is useful to compare and contrast its scores for the 23 sub-environments against the median and maximum scores of Shandong's 17 cities.

In Figure 17.1, the median and maximum scores for 17 Shandong cities are shown as dotted and dashed lines respectively, while scores for Weihai are shown as a solid line.

Comparison to Median Scores

Weihai scores above the median for 18 of the 23 sub-environments, most notably in Public Education and Public Transport Infrastructure.

On the other hand, it scores below the median for four of the 23 sub-environments, especially for Financial Deepening and Business Efficiency, and Economic Vibrancy and Tripartite Relationship. The remaining sub-environment of Transparency and Accountability is at the median.

Comparison to Maximum Scores

Weihai scores below the provincial maximum of the 17 Shandong cities in 20 out of the 23 sub-environments. Weihai achieves the provincial maximum score in three sub-environments, namely Public Education (1.957), Public Transport Infrastructure (2.368) and Public Culture and Information Services (1.617).

Weihai's score in the sub-environment of Financial Deepening and Business Efficiency (–0.584) is farthest from the maximum, which is held by Jinan (3.201). Further, Weihai's score in Natural Resources (1.443) is closest to the maximum, which is held by Rizhao (1.632).

17.3 Summary of Empirical Findings of Weihai and *What-if* Urban Development Simulation

17.3.1 Summary of Empirical Findings, 20% Strongest and Weakest Indicators

Overall Performance		
	2nd Score: 1.393	
Scale and Quality of Economic Activities 5th Score: 0.849	Financial Capacity, Labour Market Flexibility and Economic Vibrancy 8th Score: 0.083	Good Governance, Effective Leadership and Social Stability 2nd Score: 1.134
Technological Advancement and Innovation Capability 5th Score: 0.848	Public Service Standards and Quality of Life Improvement 2nd Score: 1.616	Resource Conditions and Environmental Protection 1st Score: 1.632

(Rank out of 17 cities)

Summary

Weihai ranks 2nd out of 17 cities in its Overall Performance. Weihai performs above the provincial average in all of the six environments, where the environments of Resource Conditions and Environmental Protection, Public Service Standards and Quality of Life Improvement and Good Governance, Effective Leadership and Social Stability perform exceptionally well. Meanwhile Weihai's worst performing environment is that of the Financial Capacity, Labour Market Flexibility and Economic Vibrancy.

Strengths

As observed in Table 17.2, Weihai performs especially well in the environment of Public Service Standards and Quality of Life Improvement, with 12 out of 26 of its 20% Strongest Indicators in that environment. Among Weihai's best performing indicators are the Urban Registered Unemployment Rate, Cleanliness of Public Toilets as well as Research and Development Expenditure as a Share of Government Expenditure.

Weaknesses

As observed in Table 17.3, Weihai is weaker in the environment of Financial Capacity, Labour Market Flexibility and Economic Vibrancy, with seven out of 26 of its 20% Weakest Indicators under this environment. Among Weihai's worst performing indicators are the Proportion of Population Above 60 Years Old, Residents' Satisfaction with Price Levels and the Number of Primary and Secondary Schools Per 10,000 Population.

Table 17.2: 20% Strongest Indicators for Weihai

Rank	20% Strongest Indicator	Score	SQEA	FCLMFEV	GGELSS	TAIC	PSSQLI	RCEP
1	Urban Registered Unemployment Rate	2.401		✓				
2	Cleanliness of Public Toilets	2.347					✓	
3	Research & Development Expenditure as a Share of Government Expenditure	2.206				✓		
4	Satisfaction of Public Transport Services	2.163					✓	
5	Public Education Appropriation Per Capita	1.912					✓	
6	Public Perception of Security	1.884			✓			
7	Number of Vocational Education Institutions Per 10,000 Population	1.834					✓	
8	Per Capita Volume of Retail Sales	1.815	✓					
9	Satisfaction with Urban Management Personnels	1.792			✓			
10	Tax Revenue as a Share of Fiscal Revenue	1.756			✓			
11	Per Capita Road Area	1.685					✓	
12	Ratio of Teacher to Student in Primary and Secondary Schools	1.673					✓	
13	Frequency of Using the Internet for Daily Convenience	1.635					✓	
14	Government Fiscal Expenditure Per Capita	1.496			✓			
15	Number of Books in Public Library Per Capita	1.479					✓	
16	Satisfaction of Traffic Conditions	1.423					✓	
17	Satisfaction of Public Education System	1.409					✓	
18	Percentage of Public Expenditure on Cultural Initiatives	1.394					✓	
19	Green Coverage Ratio of Built-up Area	1.363						✓
20	Mobile Phone Penetration Per Capita	1.346					✓	
21	Tertiary Industry Total Labour Productivity	1.335		✓				
22	Per Capita Park and Green Space Acreage	1.333						✓
23	Urban Residents' Disposable Income Growth Rate	1.291	✓					
24	Electricity Consumption Per RMB 10,000 GRDP	1.280						✓
25	COD (Chemical Oxygen Demand) Per RMB 10,000 GRDP	1.277						✓
26	Number of R&D Personnel Per 10,000 Population	1.258				✓		

Table 17.3: 20% Weakest Indicators for Weihai

Rank	20% Weakest Indicator	Score	SQEA	FCLMFEV	GGELSS	TAIC	PSSQLI	RCEP
106	Manufacturing Sector as a Percentage of GRDP	–0.397	✓					
107	Built-up Area Population Density	–0.415						✓
108	Government Fiscal Expenditure	–0.434			✓			
109	Investment Abroad	–0.438	✓					
110	Number of Administration Action and Reconsideration Cases	–0.475			✓			
111	Number of Investigations for Power Abuses Per 10,000 Population	–0.493			✓			
112	Number of Museums Per 10,000 Population	–0.500					✓	
113	Average Life Expectancy	–0.524					✓	
114	Engel's Index	–0.541					✓	
115	Total R&D Expenditure of Enterprises Above Designated Size as a Percentage of Cash Flow	–0.548				✓		
116	Insurance Net Income	–0.571		✓				
117	Government Expenditures as a Percentage of GRDP	–0.603	✓					
118	Financial Sector Value-Added	–0.689		✓				
119	Newly Increased Number of Employees	–0.691		✓				
120	Per Capita Freshwater Resource	–0.706						✓
121	Number of Responses to Government Issues of Public Interest	–0.775			✓			
122	Growth in the Volume of Cargo Transported	–0.841		✓				
123	Deepness of Insurance (Insurance Income as a Share of GRDP)	–0.843		✓				
124	Forest Land Growth	–0.952						✓
125	Traffic Accident Fatality Per 10,000 Population	–0.960			✓			
126	Number of Employees	–1.147		✓				
127	Annual Loan Growth Rate	–1.182		✓				
128	Public Health and Medical Service Expenses as a Share of GRDP	–1.448					✓	
129	Number of Primary and Secondary Schools Per 10,000 Population	–1.798					✓	
130	Residents' Satisfaction with Price Levels	–1.992	✓					
131	Proportion of the Population Above 60 Years Old	–2.599					✓	

Source: Asia Competitiveness Institute.

Notes: SQEA: Scale and Quality of Economic Activities; FCLMEV: Financial Capacity, Labour Market Flexibility and Economic Vibrancy; GGELSS: Good Governance, Effective Leadership and Social Stability; TAIC: Technological Advancement and Innovation Capability; PSSQLI: Public Service Standards and Quality of Life Improvement; RCEP: Resource Conditions and Environmental Protection.

17.3.2 *What-if* Urban Development Simulation

ACI has devised a simulation methodology to improve the ranking of a particular city by improving on its 20% Weakest Indicators as shown in Table 17.3.[2] The figures below show Weihai's ranking and standardised scores before and after the policy-induced simulation. Refer to Tables 3.8 to 3.14 in Section 3.4 of Chapter 3 for a complete list of simulation results for all cities.

Overall Performance

	Before		After
Rank	2nd	▶	1st
Score	1.393		1.849

Scale and Quality of Economic Activities

	Before	After
Rank	5th	3rd
Score	0.849	1.380

Financial Capacity, Labour Market Flexibility and Economic Vibrancy

	Before	After
Rank	8th	4th
Score	0.083	0.464

Good Governance, Effective Leadership and Social Stability

	Before	After
Rank	2nd	1st
Score	1.134	1.591

Technological Advancement and Innovation Capability

	Before	After
Rank	5th	5th
Score	0.848	0.891

Public Service Standards and Quality of Life Improvement

	Before	After
Rank	2nd	1st
Score	1.616	2.119

Resource Conditions and Environmental Protection

	Before	After
Rank	1st	1st
Score	1.632	1.932

After the *What-if* Simulation, Weihai improves its ranking from 2nd to 1st in terms of its Overall Performance. Likewise, Weihai's standardised score improves from 1.393 to 1.849. This leap is plausible if the city manages to successfully address its 20% Weakest Indicators.

The simulation further highlights substantial improvement for Weihai in some of its environments, most notably in Financial Capacity, Labour Market Flexibility and Economic Vibrancy where its rank will rise from 8th place to 4th place. Such encouraging results should incentivise Weihai to strive to improve the indicators under its 20% Weakest Indicators list. These indicators include the Annual Loan Growth Rate, Number of Employees and Deepness of Insurance.

[2] The methodology for *What-if* Simulation is thoroughly explained in Section 2.7 of Chapter 2.

17.4 Concluding Notes: Public Policy Implications[3]

Areas for Commendation

Weihai performs especially well in the environment of Public Service Standards and Quality of Life Improvement, where 12 out of 26 of its 20% Strongest Indicators fall under this environment, as indicated in Table 17.2.

Weihai holds the maximum score in the three sub-environments of Public Education (1.957), Public Transport Infrastructure (2.368) and Public Culture and Information Services (1.617). In addition, Weihai scores above the provincial average in 18 out of 23 sub-environments.

From 2012 to 2016, Weihai has been pushing to promote economic restructuring and upgrading, improving the quality of public services and focusing on its development needs. In 2016, the city received RMB 8.48 billion education funding and spent RMB 8.47 billion on education. The Weihai government is working to strengthen its overall vocational education development plan by improving the training of skilled personnel, while at the same time promote deeper integration between the school and firms. Such efforts reveal why Weihai does well in the sub-environment of Public Education.

Areas for Improvement

While Weihai does not score below the provincial average in any of the six environments, it has an incentive to address its weaknesses to maintain its strong position in Shandong. Specifically, Weihai should address the environments of Financial Capacity, Labour Market Flexibility and Economic Vibrancy and Public Service Standards and Quality of Life Improvement as they collectively contribute 13 out of 26 of Weihai's 20% Weakest Indicators, as shown in Table 17.3. Additionally, as gleaned from the *What-if* Urban Development Simulation, the environment of Financial Capacity, Labour Market Flexibility and Economic Vibrancy should be prioritised because that is the environment in which Weihai will achieve the greatest improvement in its ranking — four positions — relative to other environments.

Moreover, Weihai obtains particularly lower scores in the sub-environment of Economic Vibrancy and Tripartite Relationship (–0.732), and Financial Deepening and Business Efficiency (–0.584). Further, it scores below the provincial average in five out of 23 sub-environments.

Since 2017, regional economic development has continued to decline, causing the slowdown in the growth of loans in Weihai. By September 2017, total loans dropped by 1.38% from the beginning of the year. Moreover, local enterprises continue to face financial pressure due to the notable increase in non-performing loans as well. Therefore, the Weihai government should aim to improve the regional economic development through entrepreneurship and innovation. As economic development improves, demand for loans will increase as well, which will be able to support growth.

[3]The relevant statistical data and government policies are from China Economic Net (2017) and Weihai Municipal Government (2017a, 2017b).

Future Potential Development

In summary, while Weihai performs well in general, it should continue to focus on improving its weaker environments. In particular, Weihai should emphasise improvements to the environment of Financial Capacity, Labour Market Flexibility and Economic Vibrancy by developing its financial institutions and insurance sector. In addition, Weihai should improve the environment of Scale and Quality of Economic Activities by promoting a business-friendly environment that leads to increased market development.

The Weihai administration should focus on promoting innovations in financial reform by encouraging more firms to enter the capital market and cultivate bond issuance from enterprises. At the same time, Weihai should continue to strengthen its oversight of online financial regulations to reduce the risk when conducting internet-banking transactions.

References

China Economic Net. 2017. '威海农商行评级展望调整为负面：不良贷款率5.27%超出监管红线 Negative Outlook of Weihai Agricultural and Commercial Banks' Rating: Non-Performing Loan Rate (5.27%) beyond the Regulatory Red Line (in Chinese)'. 19 December 2017. http://finance.ce.cn/rolling/201712/19/t20171219_27327611.shtml.

Department of Commerce of Shandong Province. n.d. 'Weihai City'. Accessed 27 October 2017. http://en.shandongbusiness.gov.cn/city/70.

Weihai Foreign Investment Promotion Centre. n.d. 'Brief of Weihai'. Accessed 27 October 2017. http://60.212.191.137/english/showContext_374.html.

Weihai Municipal Government. 2017a. '威海政府工作报告 2017 Weihai Annual Government Work Report (in Chinese)'. 28 March 2017. http://www.weihai.gov.cn/art/2017/3/28/art_16965_914654.html.

———. 2017b. '威海市人民政府-教育 Weihai Municipal People's Government — Education (in Chinese)'. 27 September 2017. http://www.weihai.gov.cn/col/col17100/index.html.

Yuan, Hao. 2009. 'Weihai City Introduction'. 23 July 2009. http://shandong.chinadaily.com.cn/e/2009-07/23/content_8464218_3.htm.

Chapter 18: YANTAI
Shandong Province

Location of City

Source: Asia Competitiveness Institute.

18.1 Profile of Yantai City[1]

The city of Yantai is famed across China for its fruit orchards, majestic scenery, and for playing host to China's oldest and most venerated winery Changyu. It directly administers four districts, seven county-level cities, one county and one development zone across a total land area of 13,852 square kilometres, within which resides a total population of 7,064,000. Furthermore, boasting a proud heritage derived from its significance throughout the mid-to-late Imperial and Republican periods of Chinese history, the city is today one of China's largest fishing ports, a manufacturing powerhouse and an increasingly attractive location for both domestic and international tourists.

In 2016, Yantai's Gross Regional Domestic Product (GRDP) stood at RMB 693 billion, with the city enjoying a healthy GRDP growth rate of 8.1%, as is reflected in Table 18.1. Apart from its agricultural bounty, Yantai is also rich in mineral resources such as magnesium and molybdenum, while additionally being particularly rich in gold. Yantai's primary sector accordingly accounted for 6.7% of GRDP. Yantai's secondary sector, which constituted 50.0% of GRDP, capitalises on its wealth of natural resources and is based on industries, such as food processing,

[1]The relevant city information are from the Department of Commerce of Shandong Province (n.d.), China Daily (n.d.), Yantai Municipal People's Government (2015) and Shen (2009).

gold processing, automobile manufacturing and electronics. Finally, Yantai's tertiary sector, which constituted 43.3% of GRDP, depends strongly on expanding service industries, such as finance, logistics, commercial services, and culture and creativity.

Yantai is served by the Yantai Penglai International Airport, which caters to both international flights and domestic flights to other cities in China. Yantai is well connected to nearby cities by the highways and high-speed rail network, and is notably situated on the Qingdao–Yantai–Weihai–Rongcheng intercity railway. Yantai has demonstrated an exceptional openness to trade, and in 2016 boasted the second highest total trade volumes of any city in the province, at US $43.9 billion. The city's public transport network is also well developed and comprehensive, with 5.3 billion passenger-kilometres registered in the province over the same year.

Table 18.1: Key Economic Indicators for Yantai, 2016

Land Area (km²)	**13,852**
Population	
Total Population	7,064,000
Urbanisation Ratio (%)	62.1
Average Life Expectancy (years)	76.1
Number of Employees (10,000)	463
Workforce Participation Rate (%)	74.1
Gross Regional Domestic Product (GRDP) — 2015 Prices	
GRDP (100 millions of RMB)	6,929
GRDP Per Capita (RMB)	98,388
GRDP Growth Rate (%)	8.1
Economic Composition	
Primary Sector (% of GRDP)	6.7
Secondary Sector (% of GRDP)	50.0
Tertiary Sector (% of GRDP)	43.3
Trade — 2016 Prices	
Exports (millions of RMB)	186,282
Imports (millions of RMB)	141,760
Dependency on Foreign Trade (%)	42.1
Infrastructure	
Per Capita Road Area (m²)	21.9
Growth in the Number of Passengers Transported (10,000)	208
Growth in the Volume of Cargo Transported (10,000 tons)	2,306
Environment	
Green Coverage Ratio of Built-up Area (%)	42.5
Environmental Expenditure (% of Total Fiscal Expenditure)	2.1

Source: Asia Competitiveness Institute from the 2017 Shandong Statistical Yearbook.

18.2 In-Depth Urban Development of Yantai, 2016*

18.2.1 Overall Urban Development Performance

Overall Performance

2017 Rank

3rd

Out of 17 Cities

Score: 1.312

Rank	City	Score
1	Qingdao	1.753
2	Weihai	1.393
3	Yantai	1.312
4	Jinan	1.106
5	Weifang	0.855
6	Dongying	0.603
7	Zibo	0.403
	...	
16	Laiwu	–1.233
17	Liaocheng	–1.576

Yantai ranks 3rd in its Overall Performance, with a standardised score of 1.312. This places the city in the Top Five Group of 17 cities. Yantai is positioned behind Weihai (1.393) at 2nd place and ahead of Jinan (1.106) at 4th place.

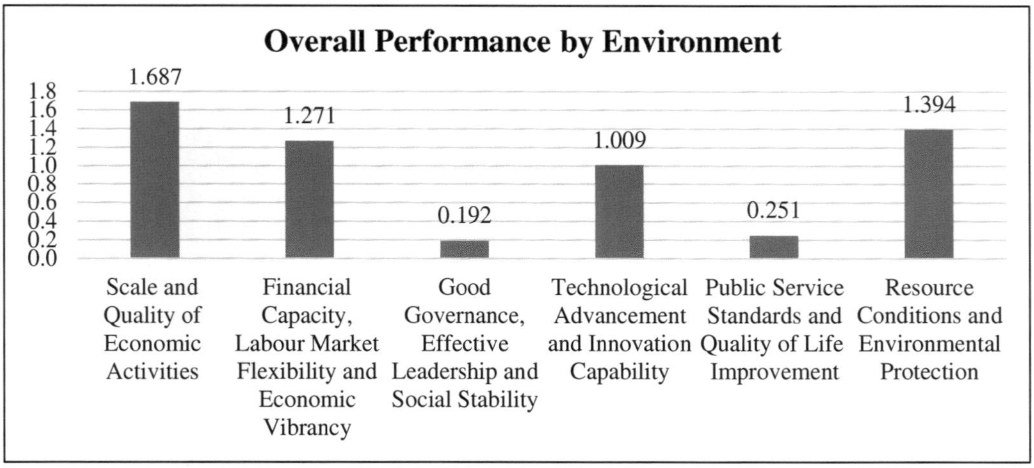

Among the six environments, Yantai scores above the provincial average in all of them, faring especially well in the environments of Scale and Quality of Economic Activities, and Resource Conditions and Environmental Protection. In contrast, the environments of Good Governance, Effective Leadership and Social Stability, and Public Service Standards and Quality of Life Improvement exhibit relatively weaker performance.

* *For a complete list of rankings, see Tables 3.2 to 3.7 in Section 3.3 of Chapter 3.*

18.2.2 Urban Development within the Six Environments

Rank	City	Score
1	Qingdao	1.987
2	Yantai	1.687
3	Heze	1.289
4	Weifang	1.021
5	Weihai	0.849
6	Linyi	0.447
7	Dezhou	0.096
	…	
16	Jining	−1.273
17	Laiwu	−1.295

A: ***Scale and Quality of Economic Activities***

2017 Rank

2nd

Out of 17 Cities

Score: 1.687

Yantai ranks 2nd for Scale and Quality of Economic Activities, with a standardised score of 1.687. This places the city in the Top Five Group of 17 cities. Yantai is positioned behind Qingdao (1.987) at 1st place and ahead of Heze (1.289) at 3rd place.

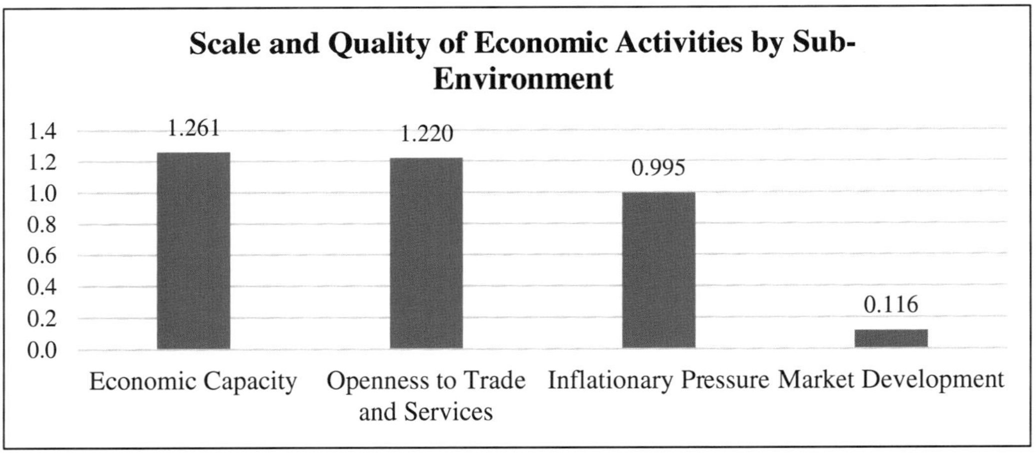

Looking at the four sub-environments of Scale and Quality of Economic Activities, Yantai performs above the provincial average in all of them, faring exceptionally well in the sub-environments of Economic Capacity and Openness to Trade and Services. In particular, it scores well in the indicators of Gross Regional Domestic Product and Per Capita Fixed Investment from the sub-environment of Economic Capacity, and Total Trade Volumes and Dependency on Foreign Trade from the sub-environment of Openness to Trade and Services. The indicator of Urban Residents' Per Capita Expenditure Growth Rate under the sub-environment of Inflationary Pressure also performs relatively well. On the other hand, the sub-environment of Market Development fares comparatively poorly, with the indicator of Government Expenditures as a Percentage of GRDP recording a relatively lower score.

B: *Financial Capacity, Labour Market Flexibility and Economic Vibrancy*

2017 Rank

3rd

Out of 17 Cities

Score: 1.271

Rank	City	Score
1	Jinan	2.264
2	Qingdao	1.932
3	Yantai	1.271
4	Weifang	0.441
5	Linyi	0.387
6	Dongying	0.293
7	Zibo	0.089
	...	
16	Dezhou	–1.026
17	Laiwu	–1.297

Yantai ranks 3rd for Financial Capacity, Labour Market Flexibility and Economic Vibrancy, with a standardised score of 1.271. This places the city in the Top Five Group of 17 cities. Yantai is positioned behind Qingdao (1.932) at 2nd place and well ahead of Weifang (0.441) at 4th place.

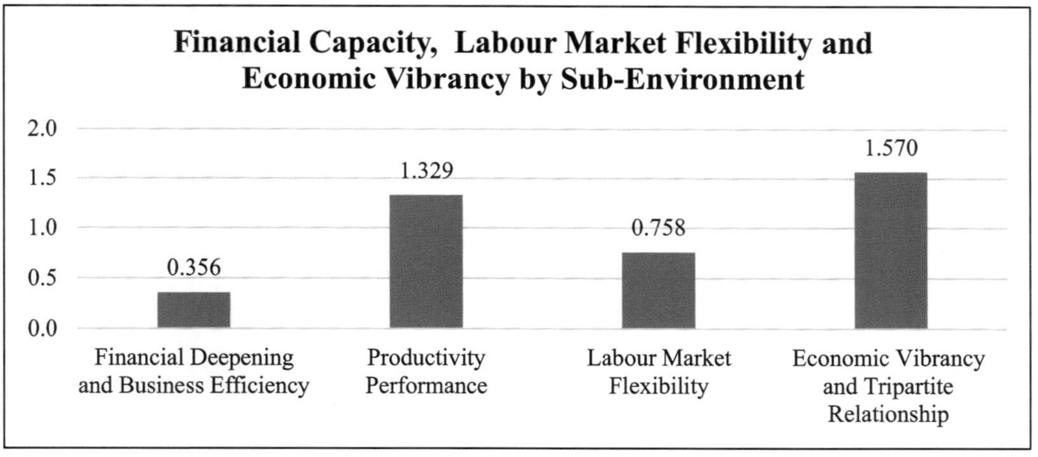

Among the four sub-environments of Financial Capacity, Labour Market Flexibility and Economic Vibrancy, Yantai performs above the provincial average in all of them and especially well in Productivity Performance and Economic Vibrancy and Tripartite Relationship. In particular, it scores well in the indicators of Growth in the Number of Passengers Transported and Growth in the Volume of Cargo Transported from the sub-environment of Economic Vibrancy and Tripartite Relationship. Further, the indicator of the Financed Amount in Stock Market from the Financial Deepening and Business Efficiency sub-environment also scores well. However, Yantai performs comparatively poorly in the sub-environment of Financial Deepening and Business Efficiency and the indicator of Urban Registered Unemployment Rate under the sub-environment of Labour Market Flexibility.

YANTAI

Shandong Province

Rank	City	Score
1	Dezhou	1.465
	...	
8	Zibo	0.418
9	Linyi	0.321
10	Yantai	0.192
11	Dongying	0.173
12	Rizhao	0.042
	...	
16	Laiwu	–1.588
17	Liaocheng	–2.473

C: ***Good Governance, Effective Leadership and Social Stability***

2017 Rank

10th

Out of 17 Cities

Score: 0.192

Yantai ranks 10th for Good Governance, Effective Leadership and Social Stability with a standardised score of 0.192. This places the city in the Middle Seven Group of 17 cities. Yantai is positioned between Linyi (0.321) at 9th place and Dongying (0.173) at 11th place.

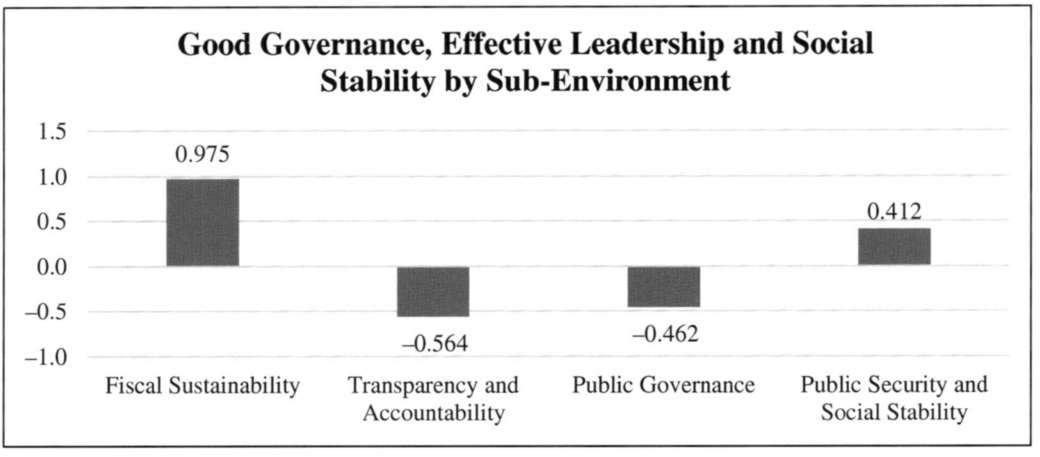

Looking at the four sub-environments of Good Governance, Effective Leadership and Social Stability, Yantai performs above the provincial average in Fiscal Sustainability, and Public Security and Social Stability. In particular, the indicators of Government Fiscal Revenue and Government Fiscal Revenue Per Capita under the sub-environment of Fiscal Sustainability and the indicator of Satisfaction with Urban Management Personnel under the sub-environment of Public Security and Social Stability record relatively high scores. On the other hand, Yantai fares below the provincial average in the remaining two sub-environments of Transparency and Accountability and Public Governance, where the indicators of the Number of Releases of Government Information for Public Viewing and the Number of Responses to Government Issues of Public Interest, both from the Transparency and Accountability sub-environment, record relatively low scores.

D: ***Technological Advancement and Innovation Capability***

2017 Rank

4th

Out of 17 Cities

Score: 1.009

Rank	City	Score
1	Qingdao	2.176
2	Weifang	1.417
3	Jinan	1.257
4	Yantai	1.009
5	Weihai	0.848
6	Zibo	0.492
7	Dongying	0.178
	...	
16	Zaozhuang	–1.192
17	Liaocheng	–1.221

Yantai ranks 4th for Technological Advancement and Innovation Capability, with a standardised score of 1.009. This places the city in the Top Five Group of 17 cities. Yantai is positioned behind Jinan (1.257) at 3rd place and ahead of Weihai (0.848) at 5th place.

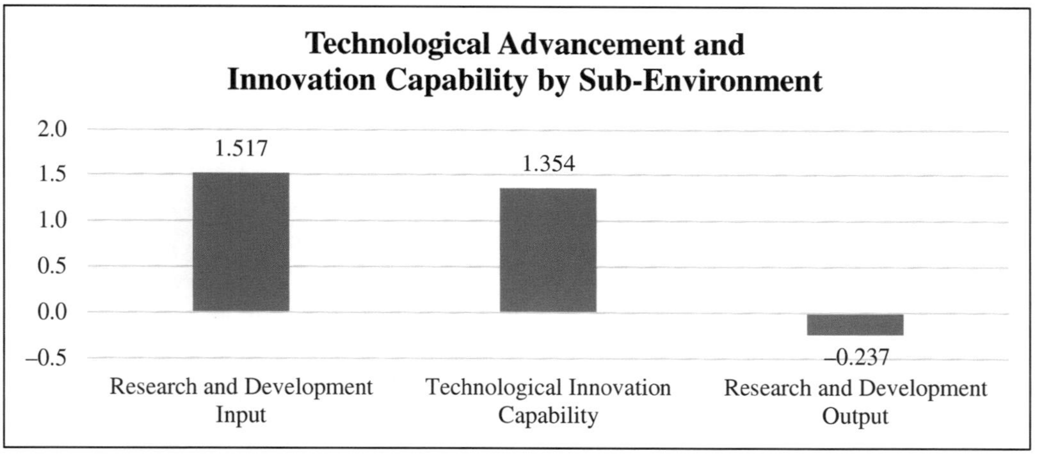

Among the three sub-environments of Technological Advancement and Innovation Capability, Yantai scores above the provincial average in Research and Development Input and Technological Innovation Capability. In particular, the indicators Research and Development Expenditure as a Share of Government Expenditure and Total Research and Development Expenditure of Enterprises Above Designated Size from the sub-environment of Research and Development Input, and the indicator of the Number of Provincial-Level Science Parks under the sub-environment of Technological Innovation Capability fare relatively well. On the other hand, the remaining sub-environment of Research and Development Output scores below the provincial average, with the indicator of the Number of Existing Patents Per 10,000 Population performing comparatively poorly.

YANTAI

Shandong Province

Rank	City	Score
1	Dongying	1.689
	...	
6	Laiwu	0.675
7	Qingdao	0.593
8	Yantai	0.251
9	Rizhao	–0.154
10	Linyi	–0.307
	...	
16	Dezhou	–1.066
17	Liaocheng	–1.964

E: *Public Service Standards and Quality of Life Improvement*

2017 Rank

8th

Out of 17 Cities

Score: 0.251

Yantai ranks 8th for Public Service Standards and Quality of Life Improvement with a standardised score of 0.251. This places the city in the Middle Seven Group of 17 cities. Yantai is positioned between Qingdao (0.593) at 7th place and Rizhao (–0.154) at 9th place.

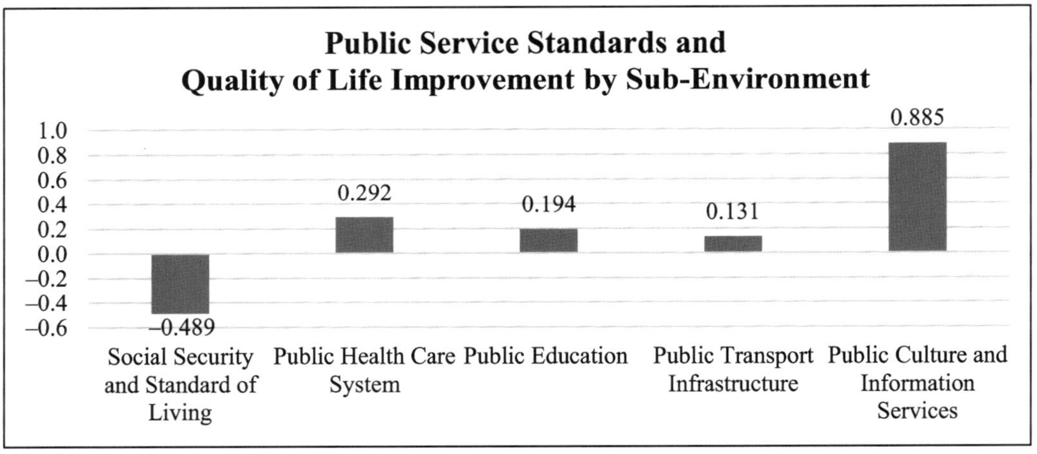

Among the five sub-environments of Public Service Standards and Quality of Life Improvement, Yantai performs above the provincial average in four of them and exceptionally well for Public Culture and Information Services, where the indicator of the Number of Books in Public Library Per Capita attains a high score. Other well performing indicators include the Ratio of Teacher to Student in Primary and Secondary Schools from the Public Education sub-environment and the Number of Passengers Transported from the Public Transport Infrastructure sub-environment. However, the Social Security and Standard of Living sub-environment fares below the provincial average, with the indicators of the Proportion of the Population Above 60 Years Old and the Engel's Index scoring especially poorly. Further, the Number of Primary and Secondary Schools Per 10,000 Population from the Public Education sub-environment also records a low score.

F: ***Resource Conditions and Environmental Protection***

2017 Rank

2nd

Out of 17 Cities

Score: 1.394

Rank	City	Score
1	Weihai	1.632
2	Yantai	1.394
3	Dongying	1.118
4	Rizhao	0.817
5	Zibo	0.665
6	Liaocheng	0.376
7	Tai'an	0.370
	...	
16	Binzhou	–1.586
17	Heze	–2.142

Yantai ranks 2nd for Resource Conditions and Environmental Protection with a standardised score of 1.394. This places the city in the Top Five Group of 17 cities. Yantai is positioned between Weihai (1.632) at 1st place and Dongying (1.118) at 3rd place.

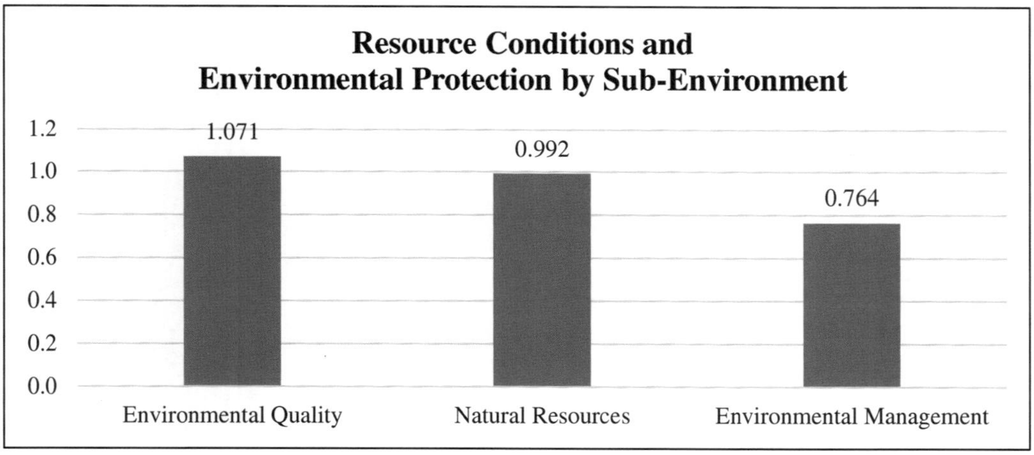

Among the three sub-environments of Resource Conditions and Environmental Protection, Yantai performs above the provincial average in all of them and exceedingly well in the sub-environments of Environmental Quality and Natural Resources. Under this environment, the indicators of Ammoniacal Nitrogen Discharge Per RMB 10,000 GRDP, Water Consumption Per RMB 10,000 GRDP and Area of Natural Reserves to Administrative Area under the respective sub-environments of Environmental Quality, Natural Resources and Environmental Management score notably well. On the other hand, the indicator of Per Capita Freshwater Resource under the Natural Resources sub-environment fares comparatively poorly.

YANTAI

Shandong Province

Figure 18.1: Median & Maximum Web for Yantai

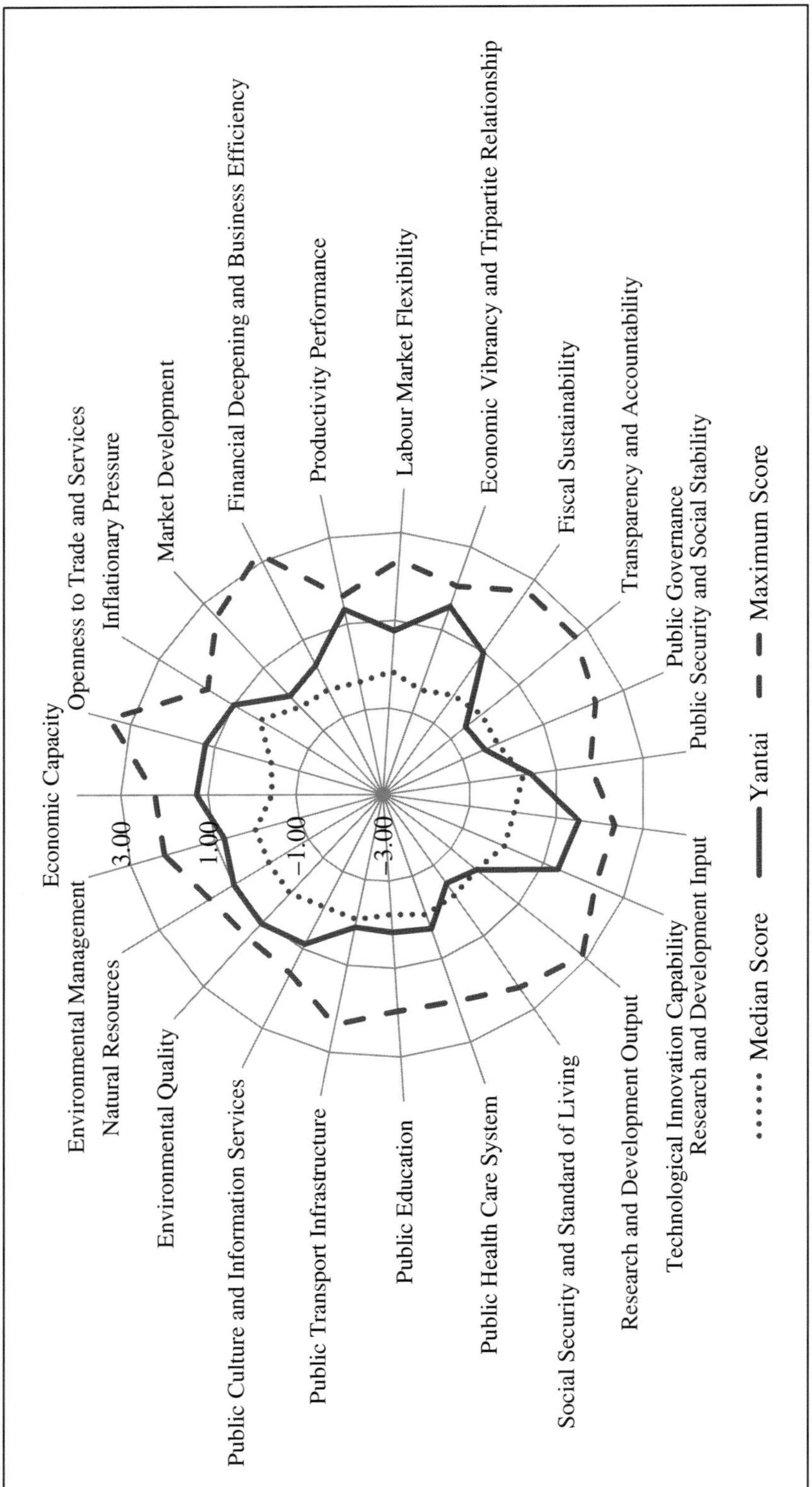

Source: Asia Competitiveness Institute.

18.2.3 Median and Maximum Web Analysis

To better understand Yantai's relative strengths and weaknesses, it is useful to compare and contrast its scores for the 23 sub-environments against the median and maximum scores of Shandong's 17 cities.

In Figure 18.1, the median and maximum scores for 17 Shandong cities are shown as dotted and dashed lines respectively, while scores for Yantai are shown as a solid line.

Comparison to Median Scores

Yantai scores above the median for 19 of the 23 sub-environments, most notably in the sub-environment of Economic Vibrancy and Tripartite Relationship, Productivity Performance and Research and Development Input.

On the other hand, it scores below the median in the three sub-environments of Transparency and Accountability, Public Governance, and Social Security and Standard of Living. Yantai performs at the median in the remaining sub-environment of Research and Development Output.

Comparison to Maximum Scores

Yantai scores below the provincial maximum of the 17 Shandong cities in all of the 23 sub-environments.

Yantai's score in the Transparency and Accountability (–0.564) is farthest from the maximum, which is held by Tai'an (2.676). Further, Yantai's score in Productivity Performance (1.329) is closest to the maximum, which is held by Qingdao (1.628).

YANTAI

Shandong Province

18.3 Summary of Empirical Findings of Yantai and *What-if* Urban Development Simulation

18.3.1 Summary of Empirical Findings, 20% Strongest and Weakest Indicators

Overall Performance 3rd Score: 1.312		
Scale and Quality of Economic Activities 2nd Score: 1.687	Financial Capacity, Labour Market Flexibility and Economic Vibrancy 3rd Score: 1.271	Good Governance, Effective Leadership and Social Stability 10th Score: 0.192
Technological Advancement and Innovation Capability 4th Score: 1.009	Public Service Standards and Quality of Life Improvement 8th Score: 0.251	Resource Conditions and Environmental Protection 2nd Score: 1.394

(Rank out of 17 cities)

Summary

Yantai ranks 3rd out of 17 Shandong cities in its Overall Performance. Yantai performs above the provincial average in all of the six environments, where the environments of Scale and Quality of Economic Activities, and Resource Conditions and Environmental Protection perform exceptionally better. Meanwhile, Yantai performs relatively weaker in some environments, namely Good Governance, Effective Leadership and Social Stability and Public Service Standards and Quality of Life Improvement.

Strengths

As observed in Table 18.2, Yantai performs well in the environment of Scale and Quality of Economic Activities which contains eight out of 26 of Yantai's 20% Strongest Indicators. Among Yantai's best performing indicators are the Area of Natural Reserves to Administrative Area, Urban Residents' Per Capita Expenditure Growth Rate and the Number of Books in Public Library Per Capita.

Weaknesses

As observed in Table 18.3, Yantai is weaker in the environment of Public Service Standards and Quality of Life Improvement, where it has 10 out of 26 of its 20% Weakest Indicators under this environment. Among Yantai's worst performing indicators are the Proportion of the Population Above 60 Years Old, Per Capita Freshwater Resource and the Number of Primary and Secondary Schools Per 10,000 Population.

Table 18.2: 20% Strongest Indicators for Yantai

Rank	20% Strongest Indicator	Score	SQEA	FCLMFEV	GGELSS	TAIC	PSSQLI	RCEP
1	Area of Natural Reserves to Administrative Area (%)	2.657						✓
2	Urban Residents' Per Capita Expenditure Growth Rate	2.116	✓					
3	Number of Books in Public Library Per Capita	1.953					✓	
4	Total Trade Volumes	1.854	✓					
5	Research & Development Expenditure as a Share of Government Expenditure	1.829				✓		
6	Financed Amount in Stock Market	1.648		✓				
7	Dependency on Foreign Trade (Foreign Trade as a Share of GRDP)	1.590	✓					
8	Proportion of Urban Workers Employed in Private Enterprises	1.581		✓				
9	Total R&D Expenditure of Enterprises Above Designated Size	1.555				✓		
10	Growth in the Volume of Cargo Transported	1.484		✓				
11	Growth in the Number of Passengers Transported	1.390		✓				
12	Per Capita Fixed Investment	1.367	✓					
13	Gross Regional Domestic Product	1.362	✓					
14	Self-Employed as a Share of Total Employment	1.361		✓				
15	Ratio of Teacher to Student in Primary and Secondary Schools	1.358					✓	
16	Number of Passengers Transported	1.321					✓	
17	Profit Margin of Enterprises Above Designated Size	1.305		✓				
18	Frequency of Using the Internet for Daily Convenience	1.248					✓	
19	Water Consumption Per RMB 10,000 GRDP	1.196						✓
20	Satisfaction with Business Environment	1.126	✓					
21	Number of Provincial-Level Science Parks	1.120				✓		
22	Ammoniacal Nitrogen Discharge Per RMB 10,000 GRDP	1.086						✓
23	Total R&D Expenditure of Enterprises Above Designated Size as a Percentage of Cash Flow	1.075				✓		
24	GRDP Growth Rate	1.054	✓					
25	Government Fiscal Revenue	0.981			✓			
26	Per Capita Volume of Retail Sales	0.971	✓					

Table 18.3: 20% Weakest Indicators for Yantai

Rank	20% Weakest Indicator	Score	SQEA	FCLMFEV	GGELSS	TAIC	PSSQLI	RCEP
106	Service Sector as a Percentage of GRDP	–0.212	✓					
107	Percentage of Public Expenditure on Cultural Initiatives	–0.231					✓	
108	Green Coverage Ratio of Built-up Area	–0.260						✓
109	Number of Urban Public Transport Vehicles Per 10,000 Population (Standard Number)	–0.275					✓	
110	Number of Museums Per 10,000 Population	–0.302					✓	
111	Number of Listed Items Under Executive Authority of the Government	–0.317			✓			
112	Number of Existing Patents Per 10,000 Population	–0.391				✓		
113	Deepness of Insurance (Insurance Income as a Share of GRDP)	–0.469		✓				
114	Growth Rate of the Number of Police Cases Solved	–0.487			✓			
115	Number of Administration Action and Reconsideration Cases	–0.531			✓			
116	Average Public Servant Salary	–0.557			✓			
117	Environmental Expenditure as a Percentage of Total Fiscal Expenditure	–0.592						✓
118	Number of Urban Taxis Per 10,000 Population	–0.609					✓	
119	Annual Loan Growth Rate	–0.612		✓				
120	Producer Price Index (PPI)	–0.685	✓					
121	Number of Responses to Government Issues of Public Interest	–0.783			✓			
122	Government Expenditures as a Percentage of GRDP	–0.969	✓					
123	Number of Releases of Government Information for Public Viewing	–1.011			✓			
124	Public Health and Medical Service Expenses as a Share of GRDP	–1.039					✓	
125	Per Capita Road Area	–1.067					✓	
126	Ratio of Public Education Appropriation to GRDP	–1.108					✓	
127	Engel's Index	–1.327					✓	
128	Urban Registered Unemployment Rate	–1.330		✓				
129	Number of Primary and Secondary Schools Per 10,000 Population	–1.501					✓	
130	Per Capita Freshwater Resource	–1.634						✓
131	Proportion of the Population Above 60 Years Old	–1.915					✓	

Source: Asia Competitiveness Institute.

Notes: SQEA: Scale and Quality of Economic Activities; FCLMFEV: Financial Capacity, Labour Market Flexibility and Economic Vibrancy; GGELSS: Good Governance, Effective Leadership and Social Stability; TAIC: Technological Advancement and Innovation Capability; PSSQLI: Public Service Standards and Quality of Life Improvement; RCEP: Resource Conditions and Environmental Protection.

18.3.2 *What-if* Urban Development Simulation

ACI has devised a simulation methodology to improve the ranking of a particular city by improving on its 20% Weakest Indicators as shown in Table 18.3.[2] The figures below show Yantai's ranking and standardised scores before and after the policy-induced simulation. Refer to Tables 3.8 to 3.14 in Section 3.4 of Chapter 3 for a complete list of simulation results for all cities.

Overall Performance

	Before		After
Rank	3rd	▶	1st
Score	1.312		1.799

Scale and Quality of Economic Activities

	Before	After
Rank	2nd	1st
Score	1.687	2.028

Financial Capacity, Labour Market Flexibility and Economic Vibrancy

	Before	After
Rank	3rd	3rd
Score	1.271	1.381

Good Governance, Effective Leadership and Social Stability

	Before	After
Rank	10th	3rd
Score	0.192	0.897

Technological Advancement and Innovation Capability

	Before	After
Rank	4th	4th
Score	1.009	1.079

Public Service Standards and Quality of Life Improvement

	Before	After
Rank	8th	3rd
Score	0.251	1.031

Resource Conditions and Environmental Protection

	Before	After
Rank	2nd	1st
Score	1.394	1.798

After the *What-if* simulation, Yantai improves its ranking from 3rd to 1st in terms of its Overall Performance. Likewise, Yantai's standardised score improves from 1.312 to 1.799. This leap is plausible if the city manages to successfully address its 20% Weakest Indicators.

The simulation further highlights substantial improvement for Yantai in some of its environments, most notably in Good Governance, Effective Leadership and Social Stability where its rank will rise from 10th to 3rd. Such encouraging results should incentivise Yantai to strive to improve the indicators under the 20% Weakest Indicators list. These indicators include the Number of Releases of Government Information for Public Viewing, the Number of Responses to Government Issues of Public Interest and the Average Public Servant Salary.

[2]The methodology for *What-if* Simulation is thoroughly explained in Section 2.7 of Chapter 2.

18.4 Concluding Notes: Public Policy Implications[3]

Areas for Commendation

Yantai performs especially well in the environments of Scale and Quality of Economic Activities and Financial Capacity, Labour Market Flexibility and Economic Vibrancy, where 14 out of 26 of its 20% Strongest Indicators fall in these environments, as indicated in Table 18.2.

While Yantai does not achieve the maximum score for any sub-environment, it scores above the provincial average in 19 out of the 23 sub-environments.

In the past five years from 2012 to 2016, Yantai achieved spectacular results in the areas captured in the environment of Scale and Quality of Economic Activities. For instance, the average growth rate of GRDP of Yantai was 9.2% during this period. Moreover, the average growth rate of fixed assets investment was 16.7% while the average growth rate of retail sales was 13% during the same period. In particular for 2016, the GRDP of Yantai ranks 19th among all the cities in China, at RMB 692 billion. These economic data indicate the strong momentum of Yantai's economic activities, which is consistent with our results.

Areas for Improvement

Yantai does not score below the provincial average in any of the six environments. However, to maintain and improve its position, Yantai should address the environment of Public Service Standards and Quality of Life Improvement which contributes 10 out of 26 of Yantai's 20% Weakest Indicators, as shown in Table 18.3. In addition, the *What-if* Urban Development Simulation supports the emphasis on the Good Governance, Effective Leadership and Social Stability environment as it shows that it is the environment in which Yantai will achieve the greatest improvement in its ranking — seven positions — relative to other environments.

Moreover, Yantai obtains its weakest score in the sub-environment of Transparency and Accountability (–0.564) and performs below the provincial average in four out of the 23 sub-environments.

Yantai performs relatively poor in the environments of Public Service Standards and Quality of Life Improvement and Good Governance, Effective Leadership and Social Stability. In 2017, the Yantai government promised to increase public spending in areas such as health care, education and cultural activities in order to improve the quality of life of Yantai's residents. Such efforts include the coverage of 18 types of targeted drugs in health care insurance, resolving the issue of "Large Class Size" in public schools and building public exercising facilities in both rural and urban regions.

Future Potential Development

In summary, Yantai should focus on improving the environment of Public Service Standards and Quality of Life Improvement by investing more in public goods, such as education, infrastructure

[3] The relevant statistical data and government policies are from Yantai Municipal People's Government (2017).

and health care. In addition, Yantai should progress in its environment of Good Governance, Effective Leadership and Social Stability by improving the transparency and accountability of the government.

Yantai should promote activities beyond simply funding workout facilities. For instance, Yantai may raise cultural sophistication and awareness by building more museums of different themes to improve the quality of life and to address its poor performance in the indicator of the Number of Museums Per 10,000 Population. Besides policies on health care, education and cultural activities, the government should direct more efforts towards developing its public transport infrastructure. To do so, Yantai should construct more roads in the rural areas to increase its road area per capita, which aims to provide more convenience to residents.

References

China Daily. n.d. 'Yantai, a Gold City in China'. China Daily. Accessed 3 November 2017. http://www.chinadaily.com.cn/m/shandong/yantai/2015-03/16/content_19791005.htm.

Department of Commerce of Shandong Province. n.d. 'Yantai City Profile'. Department of Commerce of Shandong Province. Accessed 3 November 2017. http://en.shandongbusiness.gov.cn/city/69.

Shen, Hong. 2009. 'Yantai'. Shandong China, the Hometown of Confucius. 28 July 2009. http://www.chinadaily.com.cn/m/shandong/e/2009-07/28/content_8481945_3.htm.

Yantai Municipal People's Government. 2015. 'About Yantai — Overview'. Wonderland Yantai. 31 March 2015. http://shandong.chinadaily.com.cn/yantai/overview.html.

———. 2017. '2017年烟台市政府工作报告 2017 Yantai Annual Government Work Report (in Chinese)'. 27 March 2017. http://www.yantai.gov.cn/art/2017/3/27/art_6063_747785.html.

Chapter 19: ZAOZHUANG
Shandong Province

Location of City

Source: Asia Competitiveness Institute.

19.1 Profile of Zaozhuang City[1]

Home to excavated settlements attributed to the Neolithic Beixin culture and the city in which the ancient philosopher Mozi was born, the region surrounding Zaozhuang features sites of great significance to the study of early Chinese history. Today, the city directly administers five districts and one county-level city, covering a total land area of 4,564 square kilometres and a total population of 3,915,600. Zaozhuang is a rising industrial hub surrounded by natural environments and historical sites that make it attractive to tourists.

In 2016, Zaozhuang's Gross Regional Domestic Product (GRDP) stood at RMB 214 billion and the city enjoyed a healthy GRDP growth rate of 7.2%, as is reflected in Table 19.1. Abundant in fertile land for agriculture while also being rich in natural resources such as coal and iron, Zaozhuang's primary sector constituted 7.6% of GRDP. The city's secondary sector, which constituted 51.2% of GRDP, is dependent on industries, including metallurgy, food processing and pharmaceuticals. Finally, Zaozhuang's tertiary sector, which constituted 41.2% of GRDP, benefits from investments into industries, such as financial services and insurance, e-commerce and service outsourcing.

[1]The relevant city information are from the Department of Commerce of Shandong Province (n.d.) and Xu (2009).

ZAOZHUANG

Shandong Province

Zaozhuang is situated on the Shanghai–Beijing high-speed rail line and possesses easy access to nearby airports such as Jinan Yaoqiang International Airport and Linyi Shubuling International Airport. It is also well connected to surrounding regions by highways. In addition, Zaozhuang dedicates a proportionately high amount of its total expenditures in public health care relative to its peers. For instance, Zaozhuang in 2016 spent a full 10.0% of total GRDP on expenses relating to public health. This reflects the city's willingness to channel significant resources to ensuring that its population retains easy access to comprehensive health care services.

Table 19.1: Key Economic Indicators for Zaozhuang, 2016

Land Area (km^2)	**4,564**
Population	
Total Population	3,915,600
Urbanisation Rate (%)	55.5
Average Life Expectancy (years)	75.8
Number of Employees (10,000)	296
Workforce Participation Rate (%)	76.3
Gross Regional Domestic Product (GRDP) — 2015 Prices	
GRDP (100 millions of RMB)	2,143
GRDP Per Capita (RMB)	54,984
GRDP Growth Rate (%)	7.2
Economic Composition	
Primary Sector (% of GRDP)	7.6
Secondary Sector (% of GRDP)	51.2
Tertiary Sector (% of GRDP)	41.2
Trade — 2016 Prices	
Exports (millions of RMB)	9,317
Imports (millions of RMB)	1,275
Dependency on Foreign Trade (%)	4.2
Infrastructure	
Per Capita Road Area (m^2)	25.8
Growth in the Number of Passengers Transported (10,000)	169
Growth in the Volume of Cargo Transported (10,000 tons)	334
Environment	
Green Coverage Ratio of Built-up Area (%)	42.3
Environmental Expenditure (% of Total Fiscal Expenditure)	2.8

Source: Asia Competitiveness Institute from the 2017 Shandong Statistical Yearbook.

19.2 In-Depth Urban Development of Zaozhuang, 2016*

19.2.1 Overall Urban Development Performance

Overall Performance

2017 Rank

15th

Out of 17 Cities

Score: –1.164

Rank	City	Score
1	Qingdao	1.753
	...	
10	Dezhou	–0.302
11	Rizhao	–0.472
12	Heze	–0.615
13	Jining	–0.706
14	Binzhou	–1.076
15	Zaozhuang	–1.164
16	Laiwu	–1.233
17	Liaocheng	–1.576

Zaozhuang ranks 15th in its Overall Performance, with a standardised score of –1.164. This places the city in the Bottom Five Group of 17 cities. Zaozhuang is positioned between Binzhou (–1.076) at 14th place and Laiwu (–1.233) at 16th place.

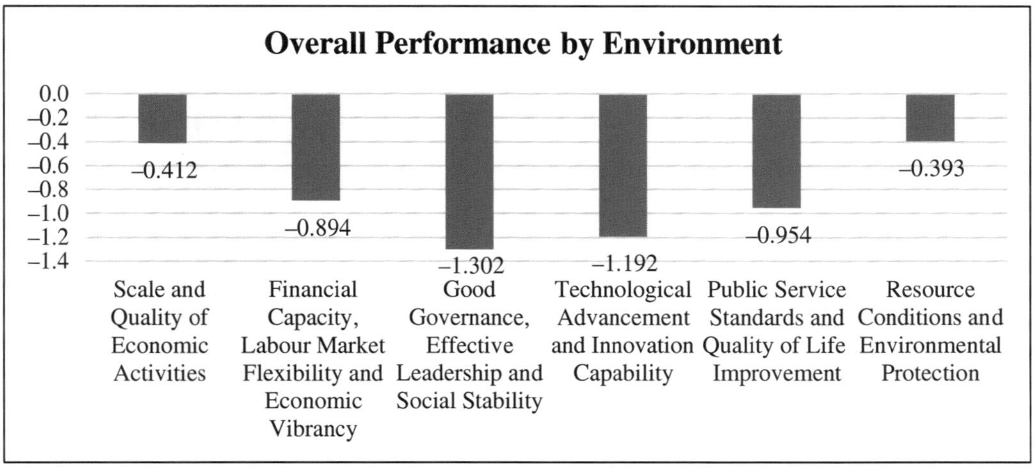

Among the six environments, Zaozhuang scores below the provincial average in all of them and especially poorly in the environments of Good Governance, Effective Leadership and Social Stability, and Technological Advancement and Innovation Capability. Nevertheless, the environments of Scale and Quality of Economic Activities, and Resource Conditions and Environmental Protection exhibit comparatively stronger performance.

---

* *For a complete list of rankings, see Tables 3.2 to 3.7 in Section 3.3 of Chapter 3.*

ZAOZHUANG

Shandong Province

19.2.2 Urban Development within the Six Environments

Rank	City	Score
1	Qingdao	1.987
	…	
8	Tai'an	–0.321
9	Jinan	–0.364
10	Zaozhuang	–0.412
11	Binzhou	–0.573
12	Liaocheng	–0.665
	…	
16	Jining	–1.273
17	Laiwu	–1.295

A: ***Scale and Quality of Economic Activities***

2017 Rank

10th

Out of 17 Cities

Score: –0.412

Zaozhuang ranks 10th for Scale and Quality of Economic Activities, with a standardised score of –0.412. This places the city in the Middle Seven Group of 17 cities. Zaozhuang is positioned behind Jinan (–0.364) at 9th place and ahead of Binzhou (–0.573) at 11th place.

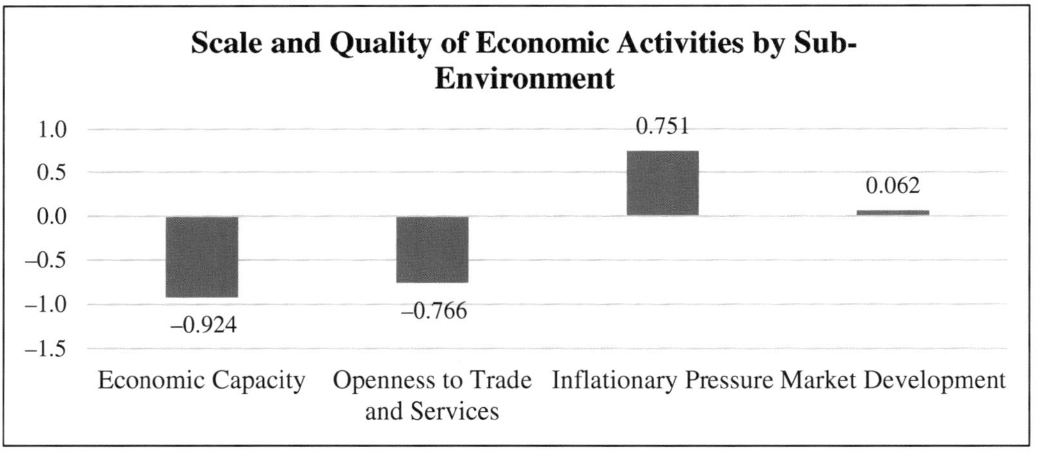

Looking at the four sub-environments of Scale and Quality of Economic Activities, Zaozhuang performs above the provincial average in the sub-environments of Inflationary Pressure and Market Development. In particular, the indicator of the Retail Price Index from the sub-environment of Inflationary Pressure records a notably high score. On the other hand, Zaozhuang fares below the provincial average in the remaining two sub-environments of Economic Capacity and Openness to Trade and Services, attaining a poor score in the respective indicators of GRDP Growth Rate and Dependency on Foreign Trade. The indicator of Urban Residents' Disposable Income Growth Rate under the sub-environment of Inflationary Pressure also records a low score.

B: ***Financial Capacity, Labour Market Flexibility and Economic Vibrancy***

2017 Rank

14th

Out of 17 Cities

Score: –0.894

Rank	City	Score
1	Jinan	2.264
	...	
10	Binzhou	–0.329
11	Rizhao	–0.619
12	Heze	–0.638
13	Tai'an	–0.763
14	Zaozhuang	–0.894
15	Liaocheng	–1.021
16	Dezhou	–1.026
17	Laiwu	–1.297

Zaozhuang ranks 14th for Financial Capacity, Labour Market Flexibility and Economic Vibrancy, with a standardised score of –0.894. This places the city in the Bottom Five Group of 17 cities. Zaozhuang is positioned between Tai'an (–0.763) at 13th place and Liaocheng (–1.021) at 15th place.

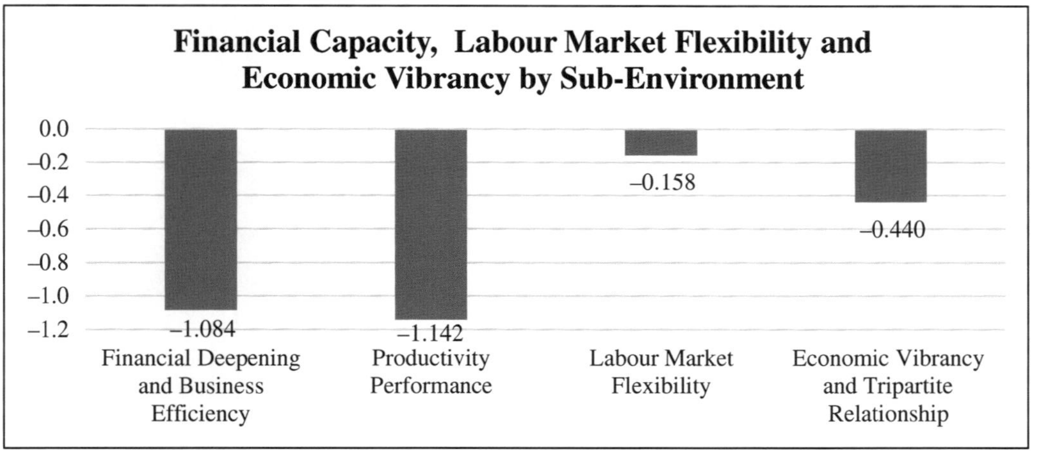

Among the four sub-environments of Financial Capacity, Labour Market Flexibility and Economic Vibrancy, Zaozhuang performs below the provincial average in all of them and fares especially poorly in Financial Deepening and Business Efficiency, and Productivity Performance. In particular, it scores poorly in the indicators of Annual Loan Growth Rate from the Financial Deepening and Business Efficiency sub-environment and Tertiary Industry Total Labour Productivity from the Productivity Performance sub-environment. Nevertheless, Zaozhuang performs comparatively better in the sub-environment of Labour Market Flexibility, where the indicator of Self-Employed as a Share of Total Employment records a relatively high score.

ZAOZHUANG

Shandong Province

Rank	City	Score
1	Dezhou	1.465
	...	
10	Yantai	0.192
11	Dongying	0.173
12	Rizhao	0.042
13	Jining	–0.527
14	Binzhou	–0.849
15	Zaozhuang	–1.302
16	Laiwu	–1.588
17	Liaocheng	–2.473

C: ***Good Governance, Effective Leadership and Social Stability***

2017 Rank

15th

Out of 17 Cities

Score: –1.302

Zaozhuang ranks 15th for Good Governance, Effective Leadership and Social Stability with a standardised score of –1.302. This places the city in the Bottom Five Group of 17 cities. Zaozhuang is positioned between Binzhou (–0.849) at 14th place and Laiwu (–1.588) at 16th place.

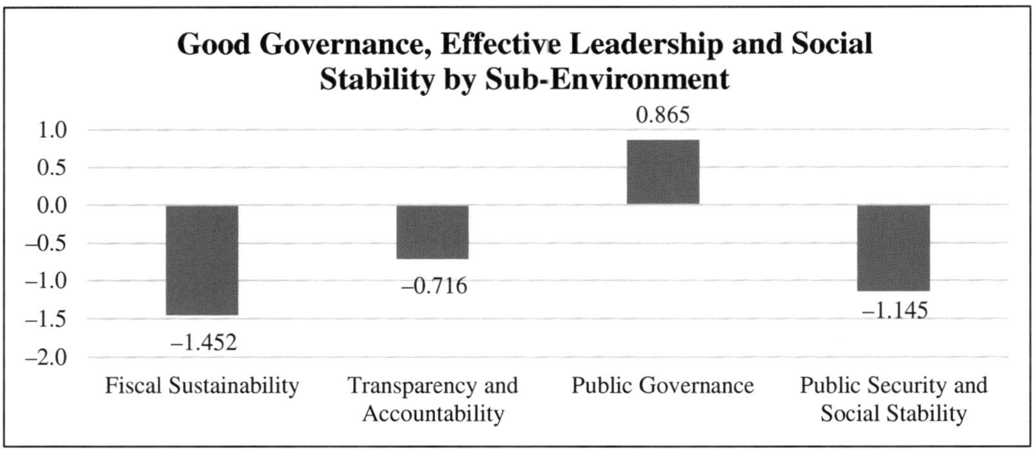

Looking at the four sub-environments of Good Governance, Effective Leadership and Social Stability, Zaozhuang scores below the provincial average in three of them and especially weaker for Fiscal Sustainability and Public Security and Social Stability. In particular, the indicators of Tax Revenue as a Share of Fiscal Revenue and Fiscal Revenue Growth Rate, both from the Fiscal Sustainability sub-environment, as well as the indicators of Public Perception of Security and Growth Rate of the Number of Police Cases from the Public Security and Social Stability sub-environment fare relatively poorly. On the other hand, the remaining sub-environment of Public Governance scores above the provincial average and relatively better, where the indicator of the Number of Listed Items Under Executive Authority of the Government performs comparatively well.

D: ***Technological Advancement and Innovation Capability***

2017 Rank

16th

Out of 17 Cities

Score: –1.192

Rank	City	Score
1	Qingdao	2.176
	...	
10	Tai'an	–0.457
11	Dezhou	–0.517
12	Binzhou	–0.559
13	Laiwu	–0.812
14	Heze	–0.897
15	Rizhao	–1.155
16	Zaozhuang	–1.192
17	Liaocheng	–1.221

Zaozhuang ranks 16th for Technological Advancement and Innovation Capability, with a standardised score of –1.192. This places the city in the Bottom Five Group of 17 cities. Zaozhuang is positioned behind Rizhao (–1.155) at 15th place and ahead of Liaocheng (–1.221) at 17th place.

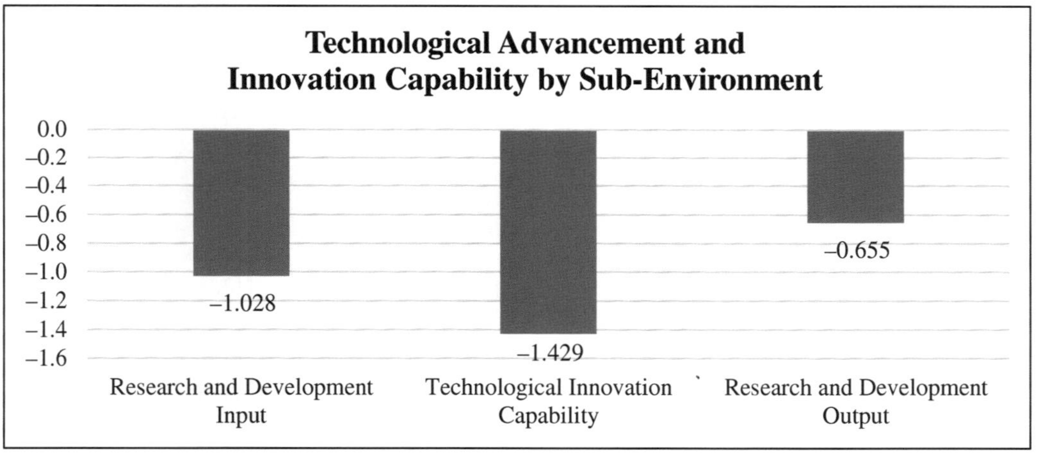

Among the three sub-environments of Technological Advancement and Innovation Capability, Zaozhuang scores below the provincial average in all of them and especially poorly in the sub-environment of Technological Innovation Capability, where the indicator of the Number of Research and Development Personnel Per 10,000 Population fares poorly. Other poor performing indicators include the Research and Development Expenditure as a Share of Government Expenditure, the Number of Science and Technology Personnel and the Total Research and Development Expenditure of Enterprises Above Designated Size, all from the sub-environment of Research and Development Input. In contrast, the sub-environment of Research and Development Output performs comparatively better.

ZAOZHUANG

Shandong Province

Rank	City	Score
1	Dongying	1.689
	...	
10	Linyi	–0.307
11	Tai'an	–0.567
12	Heze	–0.766
13	Jining	–0.819
14	Binzhou	–0.862
15	Zaozhuang	–0.954
16	Dezhou	–1.066
17	Liaocheng	–1.964

E: *Public Service Standards and Quality of Life Improvement*

2017 Rank

15th

Out of 17 Cities

Score: –0.954

Zaozhuang ranks 15th for Public Service Standards and Quality of Life Improvement with a standardised score of –0.954. This places the city in the Bottom Five Group of 17 cities. Zaozhuang is positioned between Binzhou (–0.862) at 14th place and Dezhou (–1.066) at 16th place.

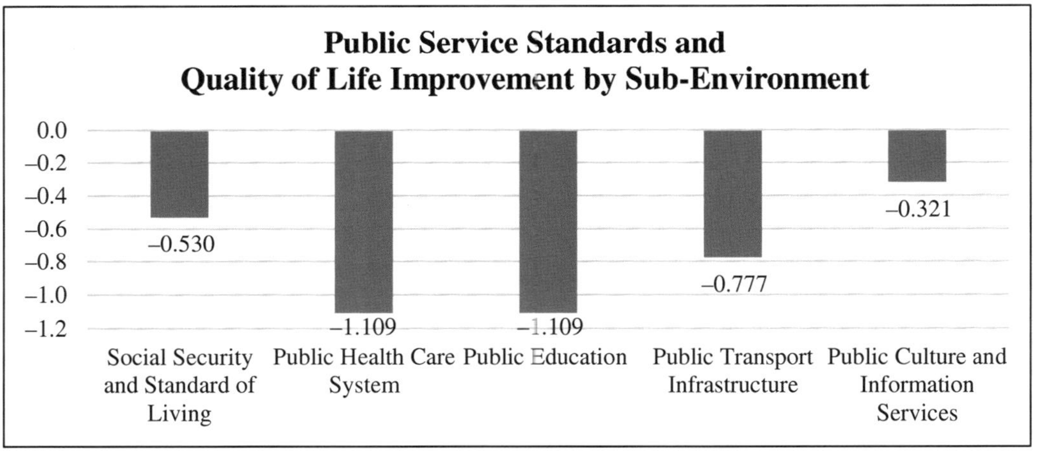

Among the five sub-environments of Public Service Standards and Quality of Life Improvement, Zaozhuang performs below the provincial average in all of them and especially poorly in the Public Health Care System and Public Education. In particular, it scores poorly in the indicators of Public Health and Medical Service Expenses Per Capita and Cleanliness of Public Toilets from the Public Health Care System sub-environment, as well as the Ratio of Teacher to Student in Primary and Secondary Schools from the Public Education sub-environment. On the other hand, the sub-environments of Social Security and Standard of Living, and Public Culture and Information Services perform comparatively better. Specifically, the indicator of the Proportion of the Population Above 60 Years Old under the Social Security and Standard of Living sub-environment attains a relatively high score.

F: *Resource Conditions and Environmental Protection*

2017 Rank

12th

Out of 17 Cities

Score: –0.393

Rank	City	Score
1	Weihai	1.632
	...	
10	Jining	–0.112
11	Dezhou	–0.287
12	Zaozhuang	–0.393
13	Linyi	–0.512
14	Weifang	–0.814
	...	
16	Binzhou	–1.586
17	Heze	–2.142

Zaozhuang ranks 12th for Resource Conditions and Environmental Protection with a standardised score of –0.393. This places the city in the Middle Seven Group of 17 cities. Zaozhuang is positioned between Dezhou (–0.287) at 11th place and Linyi (–0.512) at 13th place.

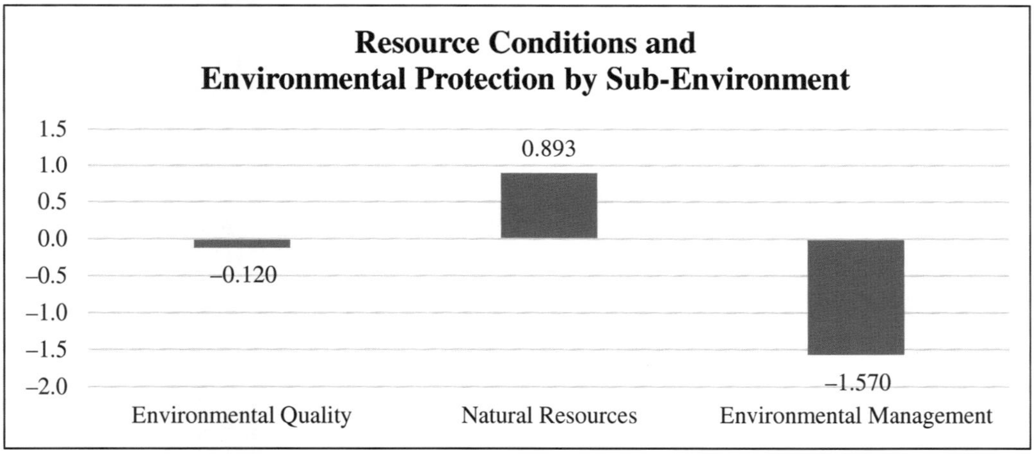

Among the three sub-environments of Resource Conditions and Environmental Protection, Zaozhuang scores below the provincial average in two of them and notably weaker for Environmental Management, where the indicator of Urban Area Waste Water Treatment Rate attains an especially low score. Another weaker performing indicator includes that of Nitrogen Oxide Emissions Per RMB 10,000 GRDP from the Environmental Quality sub-environment. On the other hand, Zaozhuang scores above the provincial average in the remaining sub-environment of Natural Resources, where the indicator of Built-up Area Population Density fares exceptionally well.

ZAOZHUANG

Shandong Province

Figure 19.1: Median & Maximum Web for Zaozhuang

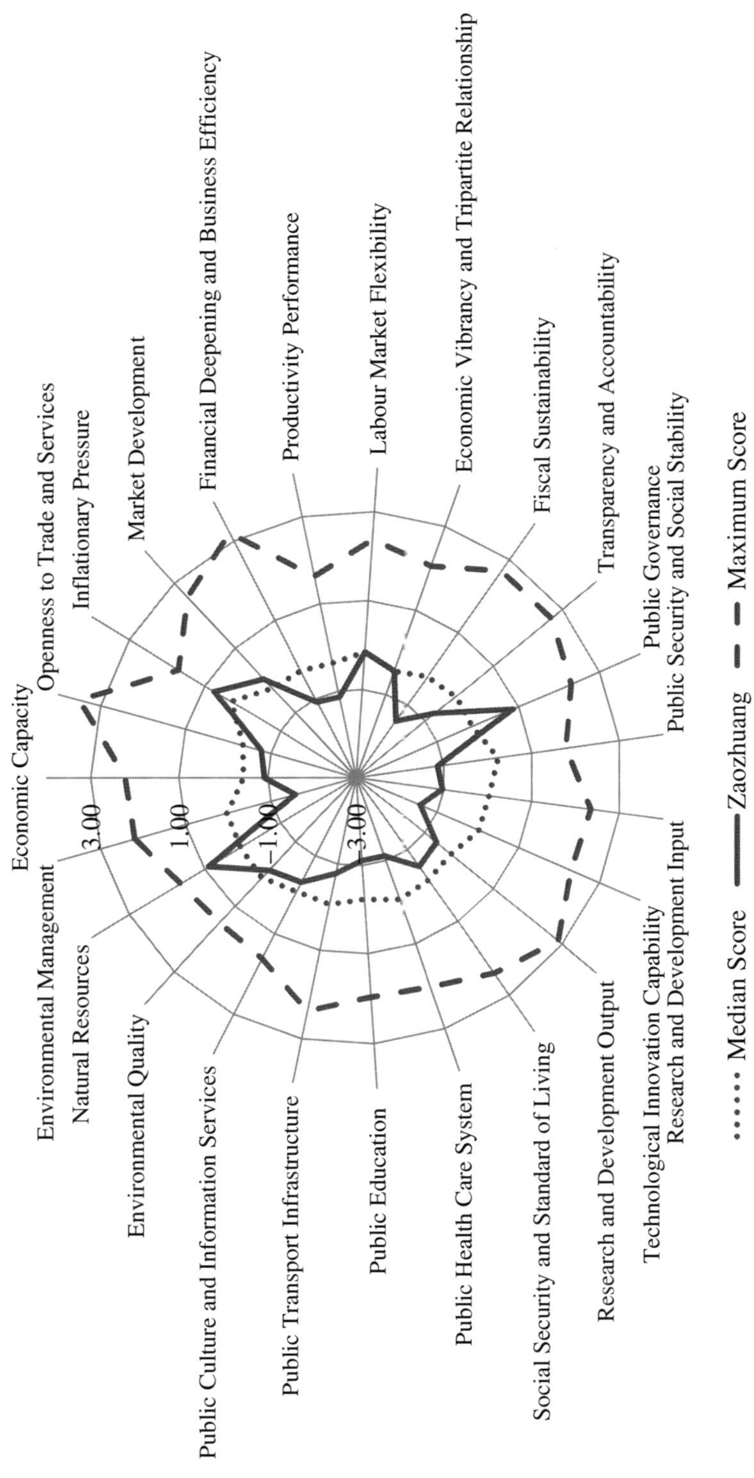

Source: Asia Competitiveness Institute.

19.2.3 Median and Maximum Web Analysis

To better understand Zaozhuang's relative strengths and weaknesses, it is useful to compare and contrast its scores for the 23 sub-environments against the median and maximum scores of Shandong's 17 cities.

In Figure 19.1, the median and maximum scores for 17 Shandong cities are shown as dotted and dashed lines respectively, while scores for Zaozhuang are shown as a solid line.

Comparison to Median Scores

Zaozhuang scores above the median in four of the 23 sub-environments, most notably in Public Governance.

On the other hand, Zaozhuang scores below the median in 17 of the 23 sub-environments, especially for Environmental Management, which scores the farthest below the median. Zaozhuang performs at the median in the remaining two sub-environments of Labour Market Flexibility, and Economic Vibrancy and Tripartite Relationship.

Comparison to Maximum Scores

Zaozhuang scores below the provincial maximum of the 17 Shandong cities in all 23 sub-environments.

Zaozhuang's score in the Financial Deepening and Business Efficiency (–1.084) is farthest from the maximum, which is held by Jinan (3.201). Further, Zaozhuang's score in Natural Resources (0.893) is closest to the maximum, which is held by Rizhao (1.632).

19.3 Summary of Empirical Findings of Zaozhuang and *What-if* Urban Development Simulation

19.3.1 Summary of Empirical Findings, 20% Strongest and Weakest Indicators

Overall Performance 15th Score: –1.164		
Scale and Quality of Economic Activities 10th Score: –0.412	Financial Capacity, Labour Market Flexibility and Economic Vibrancy 14th Score: –0.894	Good Governance, Effective Leadership and Social Stability 15th Score: –1.302
Technological Advancement and Innovation Capability 16th Score: –1.192	Public Service Standards and Quality of Life Improvement 15th Score: –0.954	Resource Conditions and Environmental Protection 12th Score: –0.393

(Rank out of 17 cities)

Summary

Zaozhuang ranks 15th out of 17 Shandong cities in its Overall Performance. Zaozhuang performs below the provincial average in all the six environments, where the environments of Good Governance, Effective Leadership and Social Stability, and Technological Advancement and Innovation Capability perform especially poorly. Meanwhile, Zaozhuang performs relatively better in the environments of Scale and Quality of Economic Activities and Resource Conditions and Environmental Protection.

Strengths

As observed in Table 19.2, Zaozhuang performs well in the environment of Public Service Standards and Quality of Life Improvement which contains seven out of 26 of Zaozhuang's 20% Strongest Indicators. Among Zaozhuang's best performing indicators are the Number of Listed Items Under Executive Authority of the Government, Retail Price Index and Built-up Area Population Density.

Weaknesses

As observed in Table 19.3, Zaozhuang is weaker in the environment of Good Governance, Effective Leadership and Social Stability which contains seven out of 26 of Zaozhuang's 20% Weakest Indicators. Among Zaozhuang's worst performing indicators are the Urban Area Waste Water Treatment Rate, Fiscal Revenue Growth Rate and Annual Loan Growth Rate.

ZAOZHUANG

Shandong Province

Table 19.2: 20% Strongest Indicators for Zaozhuang

Rank	20% Strongest Indicator	Score	SQEA	FCLMFEV	GGELSS	TAIC	PSSQLI	RCEP
1	Number of Listed Items Under Executive Authority of the Government	2.999			✓			
2	Retail Price Index	2.570	✓					
3	Built-up Area Population Density	2.055						✓
4	Self-Employed as a Share of Total Employment	1.469		✓				
5	Proportion of the Population Above 60 Years Old	1.383					✓	
6	Number of Primary and Secondary Schools Per 10,000 Population	0.939					✓	
7	Growth in the Number of Passengers Transported	0.838		✓				
8	Consumer Price Index (CPI)	0.831	✓					
9	Traffic Accident Fatality Per 10,000 Population	0.700			✓			
10	Number of Public Servants Per 10,000 Population	0.675			✓			
11	Forest Land Growth	0.670						✓
12	Manufacturing Sector as a Percentage of GRDP	0.650	✓					
13	Residents' Satisfaction with Price Levels	0.638	✓					
14	Water Consumption Per RMB 10,000 GRDP	0.488						✓
15	Proportion of Workforce Employed in Service Sector	0.483		✓				
16	Percentage of Public Expenditure on Cultural Initiatives	0.469					✓	
17	Urban Registered Unemployment Rate	0.426		✓				
18	Forest Cover	0.402						✓
19	Number of Urban Public Transport Vehicles Per 10,000 Population (Standard Number)	0.226					✓	
20	Satisfaction with Business Environment	0.197	✓					
21	Proportion of Urban Workers Employed in State Enterprises	0.187		✓				
22	Proportion of Workforce Employed in Agriculture Sector	0.168		✓				
23	Electricity Consumption Per RMB 10,000 GRDP	0.135						✓
24	Satisfaction of Income Disparity	0.135					✓	
25	Number of Vocational Education Institutions Per 10,000 Population	0.072					✓	
26	Number of Museums Per 10,000 Population	0.071					✓	

Table 19.3: 20% Weakest Indicators for Zaozhuang

Rank	20% Weakest Indicator	Score	SQEA	FCLMFEV	GGELSS	TAIC	PSSQLI	RCEP
106	Profit Margin of Enterprises Above Designated Size	–0.872		✓				
107	Mobile Phone Penetration Per Capita	–0.890					✓	
108	Producer Price Index (PPI)	–0.892	✓					
109	Total R&D Expenditure of Enterprises Above Designated Size	–0.895				✓		
110	Average Salary of Urban Employees	–0.896		✓				
111	Deposit Balance Per Capita	–0.900		✓				
112	Satisfaction with Urban Management Personnels	–0.914			✓			
113	Tertiary Industry Total Labour Productivity	–0.918		✓				
114	Number of R&D Personnel Per 10,000 Population	–0.944				✓		
115	Cleanliness of Public Toilets	–1.005					✓	
116	Number of Responses to Government Issues of Public Interest	–1.009			✓			
117	Growth Rate of the Number of Police Cases Solved	–1.035			✓			
118	GRDP Growth Rate	–1.040	✓					
119	Ratio of Teacher to Student in Primary and Secondary Schools	–1.139					✓	
120	Per Capita Arable Land	–1.141						✓
121	Research & Development Expenditure as a Share of Government Expenditure	–1.155				✓		
122	Urban Residents' Disposable Income Growth Rate	–1.180	✓					
123	Dependency on Foreign Trade (Foreign Trade as a Share of GRDP)	–1.188	✓					
124	Public Health and Medical Service Expenses Per Capita	–1.264					✓	
125	Growth Rate of the Number of Police Cases	–1.276			✓			
126	Tax Revenue as a Share of Fiscal Revenue	–1.331			✓			
127	Public Perception of Security	–1.358			✓			
128	Growth in the Volume of Cargo Transported	–1.434		✓				
129	Annual Loan Growth Rate	–1.498		✓				
130	Fiscal Revenue Growth Rate	–2.077			✓			
131	Urban Area Waste Water Treatment Rate	–2.910						✓

Source: Asia Competitiveness Institute.

Notes: SQEA: Scale and Quality of Economic Activities; FCLMFEV: Financial Capacity, Labour Market Flexibility and Economic Vibrancy; GGELSS: Good Governance, Effective Leadership and Social Stability; TAIC: Technological Advancement and Innovation Capability; PSSQLI: Public Service Standards and Quality of Life Improvement; RCEP: Resource Conditions and Environmental Protection.

19.3.2 *What-if* Urban Development Simulation

ACI has devised a simulation methodology to improve the ranking of a particular city by improving on its 20% Weakest Indicators as shown in Table 19.3.[2] The figures below show Zaozhuang's ranking and standardised scores before and after the policy-induced simulation. Refer to Tables 3.8 to 3.14 in Section 3.4 of Chapter 3 for a complete list of simulation results for all cities.

Overall Performance

	Before		After
Rank	15th	▶	11th
Score	–1.164		–0.369

Scale and Quality of Economic Activities

	Before	After
Rank	10th	7th
Score	–0.412	0.116

Financial Capacity, Labour Market Flexibility and Economic Vibrancy

	Before	After
Rank	14th	10th
Score	–0.894	–0.330

Good Governance, Effective Leadership and Social Stability

	Before	After
Rank	15th	13th
Score	–1.302	–0.196

Technological Advancement and Innovation Capability

	Before	After
Rank	16th	13th
Score	–1.192	–0.825

Public Service Standards and Quality of Life Improvement

	Before	After
Rank	15th	12th
Score	–0.954	–0.628

Resource Conditions and Environmental Protection

	Before	After
Rank	12th	9th
Score	–0.393	0.254

After the *What-if* Simulation, Zaozhuang improves its ranking from 15th to 11th in terms of its Overall Performance. Likewise, Zaozhuang's standardised score improves from –1.164 to –0.369. This leap is plausible if the city manages to successfully address its 20% Weakest Indicators.

The simulation further highlights substantial improvement for Zaozhuang in some of its environments, most notably in Financial Capacity, Labour Market Flexibility and Economic Vibrancy where its rank will rise from 14th to 10th. Such encouraging results should incentivise Zaozhuang to strive to improve the indicators under its 20% Weakest Indicators list. These indicators include the Annual Loan Growth Rate, Growth in the Volume of Cargo Transported and Tertiary Industry Total Labour Productivity.

[2]The methodology for *What-if* Simulation is thoroughly explained in Section 2.7 of Chapter 2.

19.4 Concluding Notes: Public Policy Implications[3]

Areas for Commendation

Zaozhuang performs relatively well in the environments of Public Service Standards and Quality of Life Improvement, and Financial Capacity, Labour Market Flexibility and Economic Vibrancy, with 13 out of 26 of its 20% Strongest Indicators falling in these environments, as indicated in Table 19.2.

While Zaozhuang does not achieve the maximum score for any sub-environment, it scores above the provincial average in four of the 23 sub-environments.

Over the past five years from 2012 to 2016, Zaozhuang has made progress in the environment of Resource Conditions and Environmental Protection. It represented Shandong province for the national assessment of water quality along the Huai River and achieved first place in that assessment. Moreover, Zaozhuang received the titles of both the National Forest City and National Landscape City, hence showing its exemplary environmental conditions.

Areas for Improvement

As Zaozhuang scores below the provincial average in all of the six environments, there are many potential areas for improvement for the city. Zaozhuang should address the environments of Good Governance, Effective Leadership and Social Stability, and Financial Capacity, Labour Market Flexibility and Economic Vibrancy as they collectively contribute 13 out of 26 of Zaozhuang's Weakest Indicators, as shown in Table 19.3. In addition, the *What-if* Urban Development Simulation supports the emphasis on the Financial Capacity, Labour Market Flexibility and Economic Vibrancy environment as it shows that it is the environment in which Zaozhuang will achieve the greatest improvement in its ranking — four positions — relative to other environments.

Moreover, Zaozhuang's weakest scores are in the sub-environments of Environmental Management (–1.570), Fiscal Sustainability (–1.452) and Technological Innovation Capability (–1.429). Further, Zaozhuang scores below the provincial average in 19 out of 23 sub-environments.

In 2017, the Zaozhuang administration has expressed its plans to boost the development of its industrial innovation. In the plan, the Zaozhuang government noted its support for a number of technological innovation projects initiated by local industrial enterprises. Moreover, the government aimed to achieve an increase of investment in technological innovation of 12% in 2017. All these measures will be effective in improving the environment of Technological Advancement and Innovation Capability.

[3]The relevant statistical data and government policies are from Zaozhuang Municipal People's Government (2017).

ZAOZHUANG

Shandong Province

Future Potential Development

In summary, Zaozhuang should focus on improving the environment of Technological Advancement and Innovation Capability by developing its Research and Development infrastructure as well as investing more towards the development of the sector. In addition, Zaozhuang should improve the environment of Good Governance, Effective Leadership and Social Stability by solving the problems of fiscal sustainability and public security. Nevertheless, Zaozhuang has a general weakness across all of its environments from our analysis. As such, it should diversify its strategies to tackle each one of them.

While the government of Zaozhuang had plans to encourage industrial innovation for economic growth, it did not make concrete plans in the development of science and high-tech industry. Therefore, given the poor performance of Zaozhuang in the environment of Technological Advancement and Innovation Capability, especially in the field of science and technology, Zaozhuang should stress the innovation of science and high-tech industry by raising investment in high-skilled professionals in the sector and the building of provincial-level science parks to foster a conducive innovation environment.

References

Department of Commerce of Shandong Province. n.d. 'Zaozhuang City Profile'. Department of Commerce of Shandong Province. Accessed 10 November 2017. http://en.shandongbusiness.gov.cn/city/74.

Xu, Fen. 2009. 'Zaozhuang'. Shandong China, the Hometown of Confucius. 23 July 2009. http://www.chinadaily.com.cn/m/shandong/e/2009-07/23/content_8463729_3.htm.

Zaozhuang Municipal People's Government. 2017. '权威发布：2017年枣庄市政府工作报告 2017 Zaozhuang Annual Government Work Report (in Chinese)'. China Shandong Website (中国山东网). 1 March 2017. http://zaozhuang.sdchina.com/show/4056677.html.

Chapter 20: ZIBO
Shandong Province

Location of City

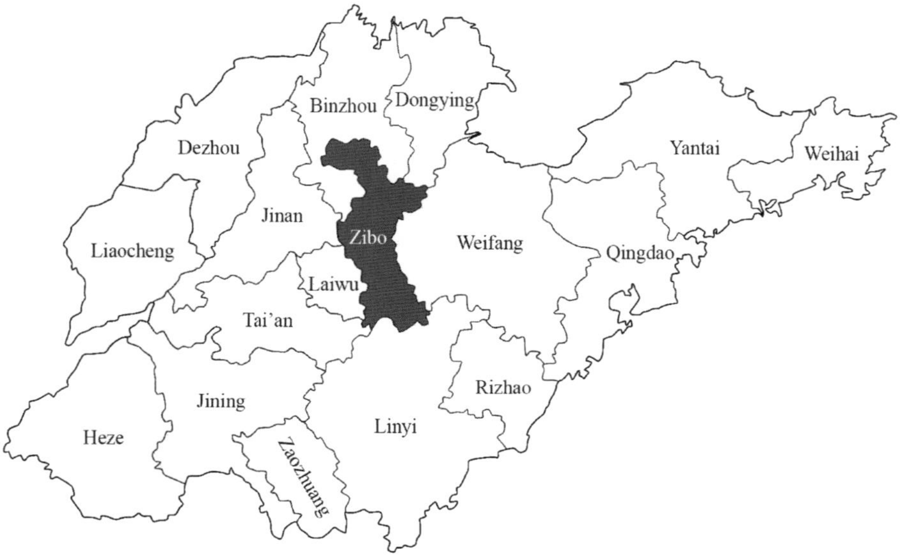

Source: Asia Competitiveness Institute.

20.1 Profile of Zibo City[1]

Best known among historians for being situated on the site of Linzi, capital of the ancient state of Qi, Zibo is home to numerous important historical sites, bearing testament to its long-standing and continuing importance to Chinese history. The city today possesses direct administrative authority over five districts and three counties, which cover a total land area of 5,965 square kilometres and a total population of 4,686,900. Zibo is a recognised hub for ceramic manufacturing and petrochemical processing, and has a historical legacy and beautiful landscape that attracts tourists from around the world.

In 2016, Zibo's Gross Regional Domestic Product (GRDP) stood at RMB 441 billion, with the city also boasting a respectable GRDP growth rate of 7.7%, as is reflected in Table 20.1.While rich in natural resources, Zibo's primary sector constituted just 3.4% of its GRDP. Contrastingly, Zibo's secondary sector constituted 52.5% of GRDP, being fuelled by its aforementioned strengths in the petrochemicals and ceramics industries, along with other industries like automobile manufacturing and equipment manufacturing. Zibo's tertiary sector constituted 44.1% of

[1]The relevant city information are from the Department of Commerce of Shandong Province (n.d.), Zibo Municipal People's Government (n.d.) and Li (2009).

GRDP, and is mainly derived from tertiary industries, such as tourism, information technology, Research and Development, and education, among others.

Zibo benefits from its proximity to both the Jinan Yaoqiang International Airport and the Qingdao Liuting International Airport. The city is also located at a crossroad of railways and highways going through Shandong province and functions as a provincial transport hub, being well connected to nearby regions and provinces. Zibo is known for its many museums, including the Qi Dynasty Memorial Museum and the Linzi Football Museum. This in turn reflects the city's place as one of the main cultural centres in the province.

Table 20.1: Key Economic Indicators for Zibo, 2016

Land Area (km²)	**5,965**
Population	
Total Population	4,686,900
Urbanisation Rate (%)	69.1
Average Life Expectancy (years)	76.9
Number of Employees (10,000)	321
Workforce Participation Rate (%)	70.0
Gross Regional Domestic Product (GRDP) — 2015 Prices	
GRDP (100 millions of RMB)	4,412
GRDP Per Capita	94,587
GRDP Growth Rate (%)	7.7
Economic Composition	
Primary Sector (% of GRDP)	3.4
Secondary Sector (% of GRDP)	52.5
Tertiary Sector (% of GRDP)	44.1
Trade — 2016 Prices	
Exports (millions of RMB)	38,441
Imports (millions of RMB)	12,236
Dependency on Foreign Trade (%)	11.9
Infrastructure	
Per Capita Road Area (m²)	24.0
Growth in the Number of Passengers Transported (10,000)	17.0
Growth in the Volume of Cargo Transported (10,000 tons)	1,466
Environment	
Green Coverage Ratio of Built-up Area (%)	45.1
Environmental Expenditure (% of Total Fiscal Expenditure)	5.0

Source: Asia Competitiveness Institute from the 2017 Shandong Statistical Yearbook.

20.2 In-Depth Urban Development of Zibo, 2016*

20.2.1 Overall Urban Development Performance

Overall Performance

2017 Rank

7th

Out of 17 Cities

Score: 0.403

Rank	City	Score
1	Qingdao	1.753
	...	
5	Weifang	0.855
6	Dongying	0.603
7	Zibo	0.403
8	Linyi	–0.002
9	Tai'an	–0.280
	...	
16	Laiwu	–1.233
17	Liaocheng	–1.576

Zibo ranks 7th in its Overall Performance, with a standardised score of 0.403. This places the city in the Middle Seven Group of 17 cities. Zibo is positioned between Dongying (0.603) at 6th place and Linyi (–0.002) at 8th place.

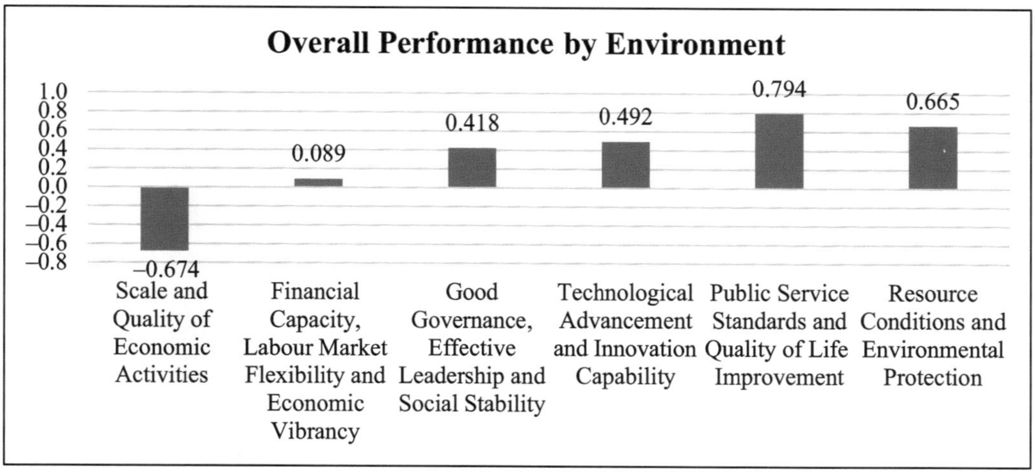

Among the six environments, Zibo scores above the provincial average in five of them and fares particularly better in the environments of Public Service Standards and Quality of Life Improvement, and Resource Conditions and Environmental Protection. Nevertheless, Zibo's score in Scale and Quality of Economic Activities is below the provincial average.

For a complete list of rankings, see Tables 3.2 to 3.7 in Section 3.3 of Chapter 3.

20.2.2 Urban Development within the Six Environments

Rank	City	Score
1	Qingdao	1.987
	...	
10	Zaozhuang	–0.412
11	Binzhou	–0.573
12	Liaocheng	–0.665
13	Zibo	–0.674
14	Dongying	–0.782
15	Rizhao	–1.017
16	Jining	–1.273
17	Laiwu	–1.295

A: ***Scale and Quality of Economic Activities***

2017 Rank

13th

Out of 17 Cities

Score: –0.674

Zibo ranks 13th for Scale and Quality of Economic Activities, with a standardised score of –0.674. This places the city in the Bottom Five Group of 17 cities. Zibo is positioned slightly behind Liaocheng (–0.665) at 12th place and ahead of Dongying (–0.782) at 14th place.

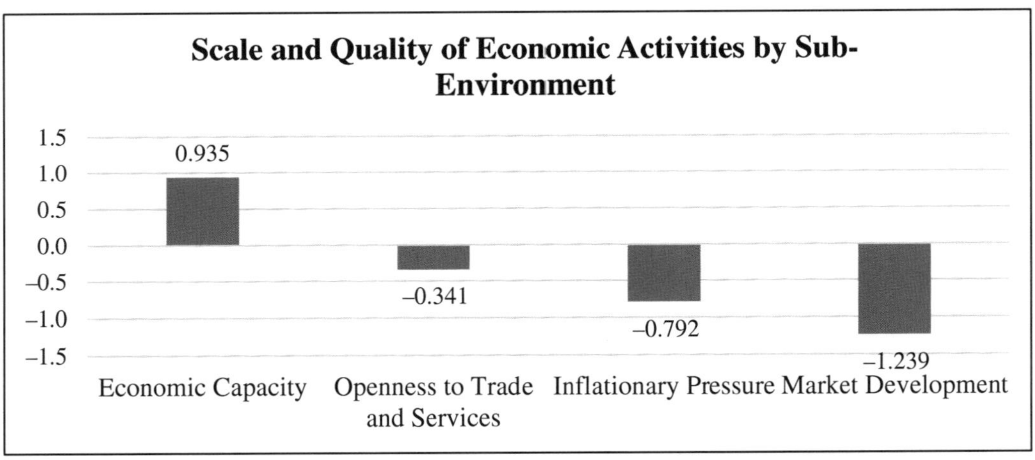

Looking at the four sub-environments of Scale and Quality of Economic Activities, Zibo scores above the provincial average in Economic Capacity, where the indicators of Per Capita Volume of Retail Sales and Urbanisation Rate perform exceptionally well. However, it performs below the provincial average in the remaining three sub-environments and particularly poorly in Market Development, where the indicator of Government Expenditures as a Percentage of GDRP performs relatively poorly. Additionally, the indicators of Consumer Price Index and Urban Residents' Per Capita Expenditure Growth Rate in the Inflationary Pressure sub-environment are particularly low as well.

B: ***Financial Capacity, Labour Market Flexibility and Economic Vibrancy***

2017 Rank

7th

Out of 17 Cities

Score: 0.089

Rank	City	Score
1	Jinan	2.264
	...	
5	Linyi	0.387
6	Dongying	0.293
7	Zibo	0.089
8	Weihai	0.083
9	Jining	–0.171
	...	
16	Dezhou	–1.026
17	Laiwu	–1.297

Zibo ranks 7th for Financial Capacity, Labour Market Flexibility and Economic Vibrancy, with a standardised score of 0.089. This places the city in the Middle Seven Group of 17 cities. Zibo is positioned behind Dongying (0.293) at 6th place and slightly ahead of Weihai (0.083) at 8th place.

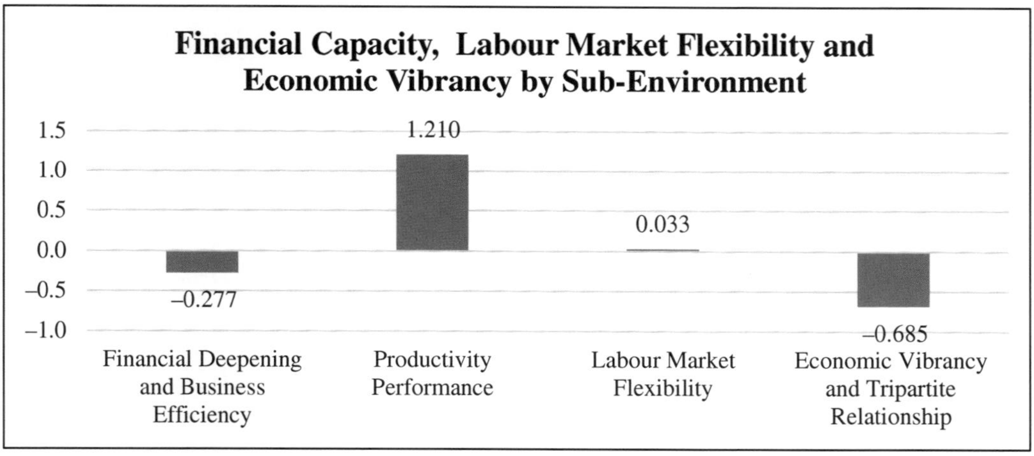

Among the four sub-environments of Financial Capacity, Labour Market Flexibility and Economic Vibrancy, Zibo scores above the provincial average in two of them and particularly well in Productivity Performance, where the indicator of Tertiary Industry Total Labour Productivity scores well. In addition, the indicator of Workforce Participation Rate from the Labour Market Flexibility sub-environment performs well too. However, Zibo scores below the provincial average in the remaining sub-environments, registering an especially low score in the indicator of Growth in Number of Passengers Transported in the Economic Vibrancy and Tripartite Relationship sub-environment.

ZIBO

Shandong Province

Rank	City	Score
1	Dezhou	1.465
	...	
6	Tai'an	0.498
7	Heze	0.435
8	Zibo	0.418
9	Linyi	0.321
10	Yantai	0.192
	...	
16	Laiwu	–1.588
17	Liaocheng	–2.473

C: *Good Governance, Effective Leadership and Social Stability*

2017 Rank

8th

Out of 17 Cities

Score: 0.418

Zibo ranks 8th for Good Governance, Effective Leadership and Social Stability with a standardised score of 0.418. This places the city in the Middle Seven Group of 17 cities. Zibo is positioned slightly behind Heze (0.435) at 7th place and ahead of Linyi (0.321) at 9th place.

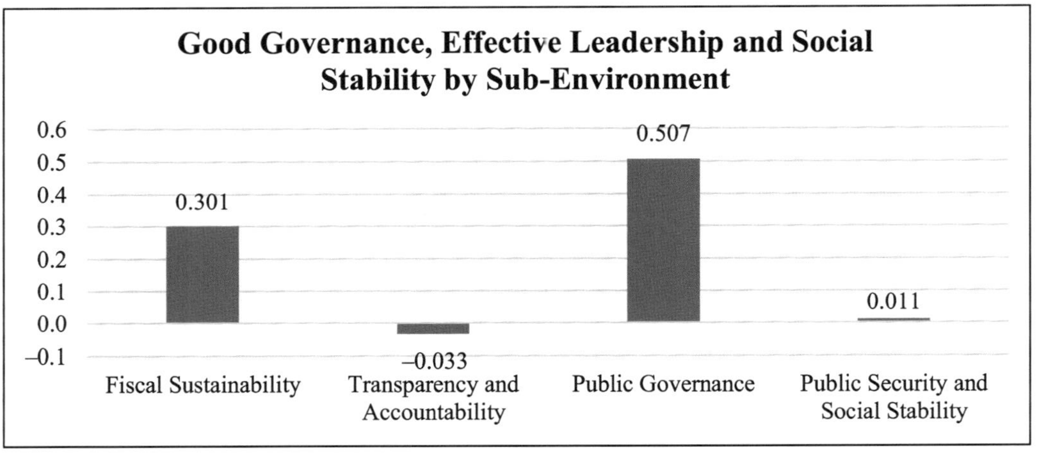

Looking at the four sub-environments of Good Governance, Effective Leadership and Social Stability, Zibo scores above the provincial average in three of them and better in the Public Governance sub-environment, where the indicator of the Index for Quality of E-Government System performs well. Additionally, the indicator of Fiscal Revenue Growth Rate from the Fiscal Sustainability sub-environment also scores particularly well. However, Zibo performs below the provincial average in the Transparency and Accountability sub-environment, where the indicator of Number of Investigations for Power Abuses Per 10,000 Population scores especially poorly. Further, the indicator of Traffic Accidents Fatalities Per 10,000 Population from the Public Security and Social Stability sub-environment performs particularly weak as well.

D: ***Technological Advancement and Innovation Capability***

2017 Rank

6th

Out of 17 Cities

Score: 0.492

Rank	City	Score
1	Qingdao	2.176
	...	
4	Yantai	1.009
5	Weihai	0.848
6	Zibo	0.492
7	Dongying	0.178
8	Jining	–0.222
	...	
16	Zaozhuang	–1.192
17	Liaocheng	–1.221

Zibo ranks 6th for Technological Advancement and Innovation Capability, with a standardised score of 0.492. This places the city in the Middle Seven Group of 17 cities. Zibo is positioned behind Weihai (0.848) at 5th place and ahead of Dongying (0.178) at 7th place.

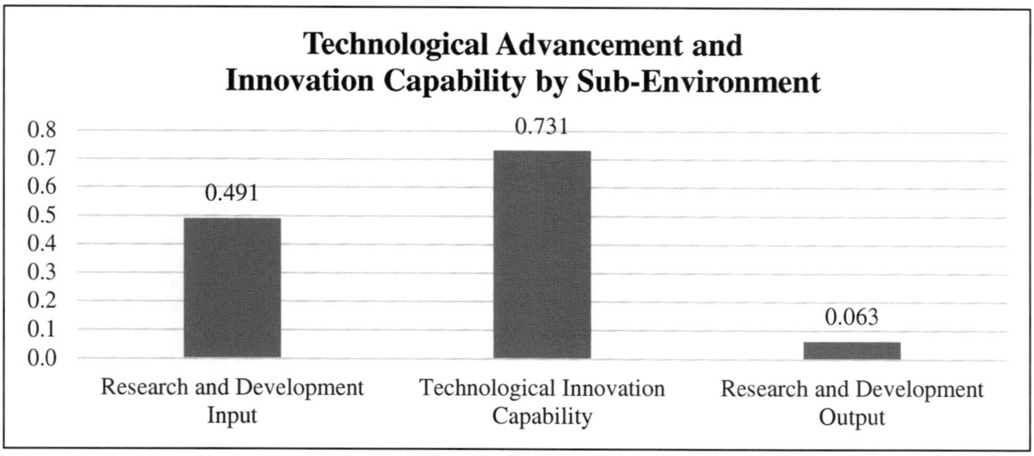

Among the three sub-environments of Technological Advancement and Innovation Capability, Zibo performs above the provincial average in all of them and especially well in the Technological Innovation Capability sub-environment, where the indicators of the Number of Provincial-Level Science Parks as well as the Number of Research and Development Personnel Per 10,000 Population perform particularly well. Zibo also has a relatively high score for the indicator of Research and Development Expenditure as a Share of Government Expenditure in the Research and Development Input sub-environment. However, the city has relatively lower scores in the indicators of Satisfaction with Innovation Environment in the Technological Innovation Capability sub-environment, as well as the Number of Patents Granted in the Research and Development Output sub-environment.

ZIBO

Shandong Province

Rank	City	Score
1	Dongying	1.689
2	Weihai	1.616
3	Weifang	0.920
4	Jinan	0.919
5	Zibo	0.794
6	Laiwu	0.675
7	Qingdao	0.593
	...	
16	Dezhou	–1.066
17	Liaocheng	–1.964

E: *Public Service Standards and Quality of Life Improvement*

2017 Rank

5th

Out of 17 Cities

Score: 0.794

Zibo ranks 5th for Public Service Standards and Quality of Life Improvement with a standardised score of 0.794. This places the city in the Top Five Group of 17 cities. Zibo is positioned between Jinan (0.919) at 4th place and Laiwu (0.675) at 6th place.

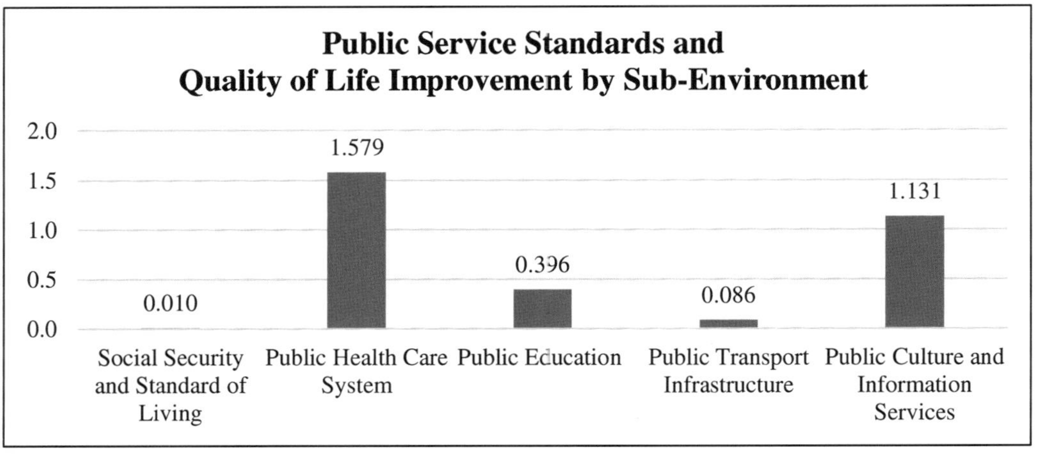

Among the five sub-environments of Public Service Standards and Quality of Life Improvement, Zibo performs above the provincial average in all of them and particularly well for the Public Health Care System and Public Culture and Information Services sub-environments. Noteworthy performance is seen in the indicators of the Number of Beds of Health Care Per 10,000 Population and Average Life Expectancy, both from the Public Health Care System sub-environment, as well as the Number of Museums Per 10,000 Population from the Public Culture and Information Services sub-environment. However, the Social Security and Standard of Living sub-environment is the city's weakest sub-environment in this area, where the indicator of Satisfaction of Income Disparity scores particularly poorly.

F: ***Resource Conditions and Environmental Protection***

2017 Rank

5th

Out of 17 Cities

Score: 0.665

Rank	City	Score
1	Weihai	1.632
2	Yantai	1.394
3	Dongying	1.118
4	Rizhao	0.817
5	Zibo	0.665
6	Liaocheng	0.376
7	Tai'an	0.370
	...	
16	Binzhou	–1.586
17	Heze	–2.142

Zibo ranks 5th for Resource Conditions and Environmental Protection with a standardised score of 0.665. This places the city in the Top Five Group of 17 cities. Zibo is positioned well behind Rizhao (0.817) at 4th place and ahead of Liaocheng (0.376) at 6th place.

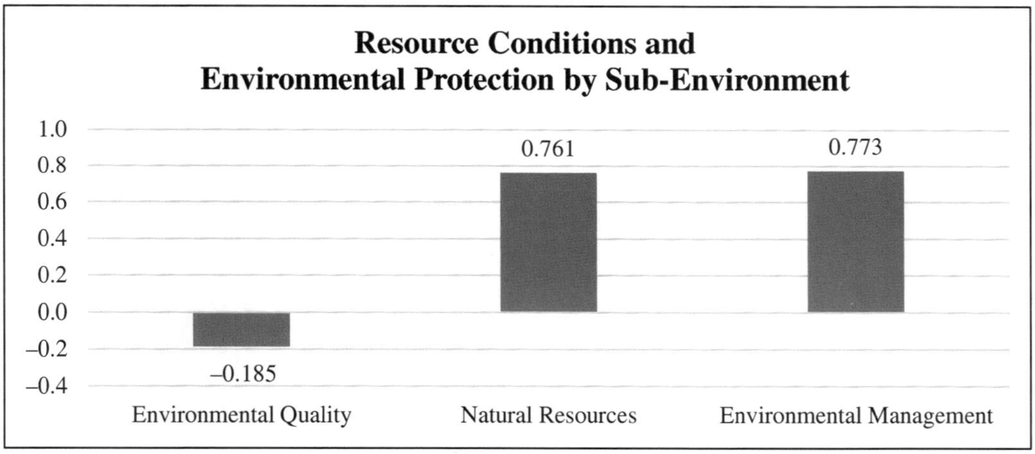

Among the three sub-environments of Resource Conditions and Environmental Protection, Zibo scores above the provincial average in two of them and slightly better in the Environmental Management sub-environment, where the indicator of Environmental Expenditure as a Percentage of Total Fiscal Expenditure performs well. In addition, the indicator of the Built-up Area Population Density from the Natural Resources sub-environment also performs particularly well. Nevertheless, the city performs below the provincial average in the Environmental Quality sub-environment, where the indicator of Sulphur Dioxide Emissions Per RMB 10,000 GRDP registers a particularly low score.

ZIBO

Shandong Province

Figure 20.1: Median & Maximum Web for Zibo

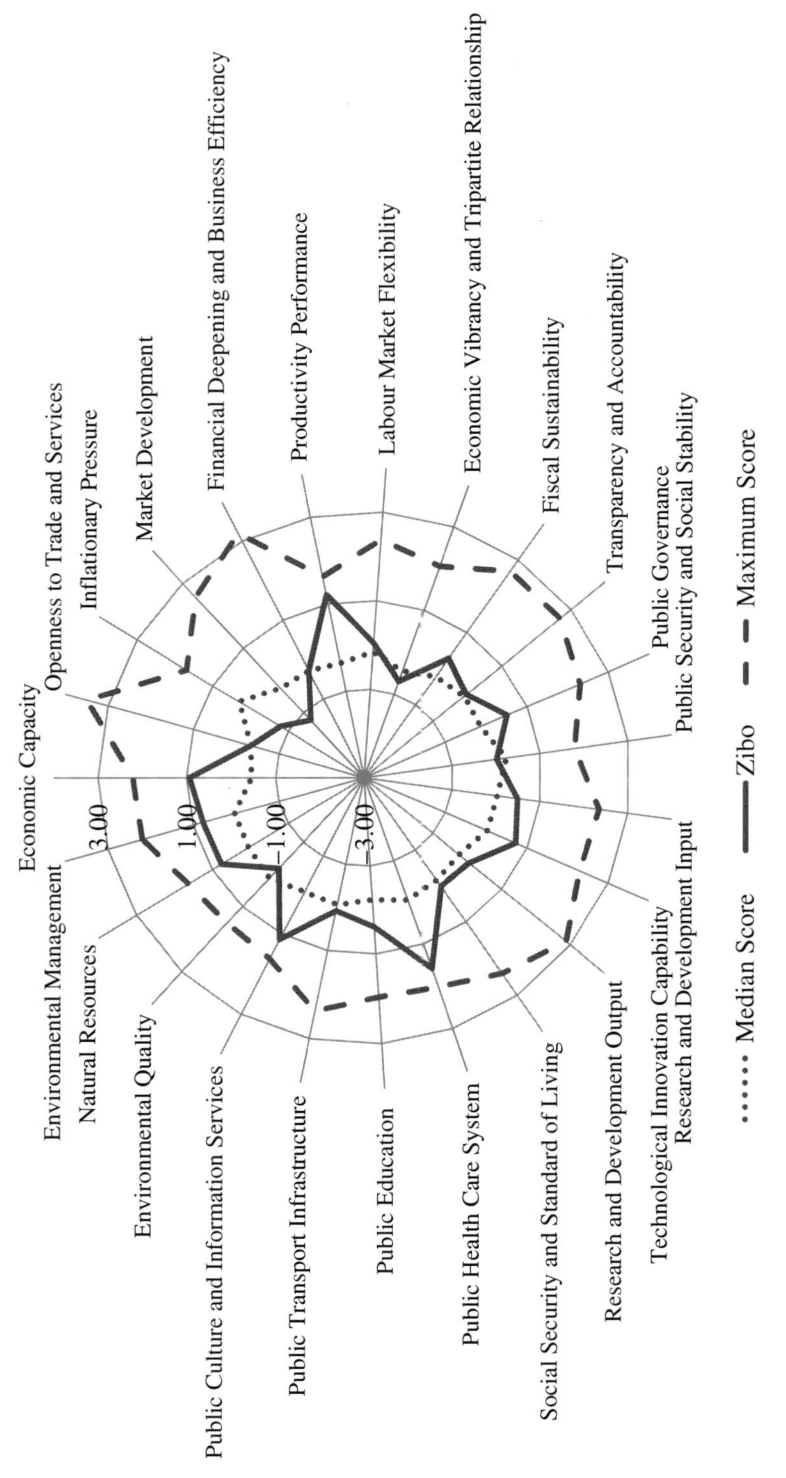

Source: Asia Competitivness Institute.

20.2.3 Median and Maximum Web Analysis

To better understand Zibo's relative strengths and weaknesses, it is useful to compare and contrast its scores for the 23 sub-environments against the median and maximum scores of Shandong's 17 cities.

In Figure 20.1, the median and maximum scores for 17 Shandong cities are shown as dotted and dashed lines respectively, while scores for Zibo are shown as a solid line.

Comparison to Median Scores

Zibo scores above the median for 16 of the 23 sub-environments, most notably in the sub-environments of Public Health Care System, Productivity Performance and Economic Capacity.

On the other hand, Zibo scores below the median in five sub-environments, most notably for Inflationary Pressure and Market Development. The remaining two sub-environments of Openness to Trade and Services, and Financial Deepening and Business Efficiency are at the median.

Comparison to Maximum Scores

Zibo scores below the provincial maximum of the 17 Shandong cities in all of the 23 sub-environments.

Zibo's score in the sub-environment of Openness to Trade and Services (–0.341) is farthest from the maximum, which is held by Qingdao (3.505). Further, Zibo's score in Productivity Performance (1.210) is closest to the maximum, which is held by Qingdao (1.628).

20.3 Summary of Empirical Findings of Zibo and *What-if* Urban Development Simulation

20.3.1 Summary of Empirical Findings, 20% Strongest and Weakest Indicators

Overall Performance **7th** Score: 0.403		
Scale and Quality of Economic Activities **13th** Score: –0.674	Financial Capacity, Labour Market Flexibility and Economic Vibrancy **7th** Score: 0.089	Good Governance, Effective Leadership and Social Stability **8th** Score: 0.418
Technological Advancement and Innovation Capability **6th** Score: 0.492	Public Service Standards and Quality of Life Improvement **5th** Score: 0.794	Resource Conditions and Environmental Protection **5th** Score: 0.665

(Rank out of 17 cities)

Summary

Zibo ranks 7th out of 17 Shandong cities in its Overall Performance. Zibo performs above the provincial average in five of the six environments, where the environments of Resource Conditions and Environmental Protection, and Public Service Standards and Quality of Life Improvement perform better. Meanwhile, Zibo performs below the provincial average in the environment of Scale and Quality of Economic Activities.

Strengths

As observed in Table 20.2, Zibo performs especially well in the environments of Public Service Standards and Quality of Life Improvement, where it contains 10 out of 26 of Zibo's 20% Strongest Indicators. Among Zibo's best performing indicators are the Number of Museums Per 10,000 Population, Number of Urban Taxis Per 10,000 Population and Number of Beds of Health Care Per 1,000 Population.

Weaknesses

As observed in Table 20.3, Zibo is at the same time weak in the environment of Public Service Standards and Quality of Life Improvement, where it has 10 out of 26 of its 20% Weakest Indicators under this environment. Among Zibo's worst performing indicators are the Traffic Accident Fatality Per 10,000 Population, Newly Increased Number of Employees and Growth in the Number of Passengers Transported.

Table 20.2: 20% Strongest Indicators for Zibo

Rank	20% Strongest Indicator	Score	SQEA	FCLMFEV	GGELSS	TAIC	PSSQLI	RCEP
1	Number of Museums Per 10,000 Population	2.453					✓	
2	Number of Urban Taxis Per 10,000 Population	1.636					✓	
3	Number of Beds of Health Care Per 1,000 Population	1.582					✓	
4	Percentage of Public Expenditure on Cultural Initiatives	1.570					✓	
5	Built-up Area Population Density	1.521						✓
6	Number of Responses to Government Issues of Public Interest	1.442			✓			
7	Urbanisation Rate	1.403	✓					
8	Workforce Participation Rate	1.385		✓				
9	Per Capita Volume of Retail Sales	1.312	✓					
10	Fiscal Revenue Growth Rate	1.255			✓			
11	Average Years of Education Received	1.229					✓	
12	Proportion of Workforce Employed in Agriculture Sector	1.215		✓				
13	Tertiary Industry Total Labour Productivity	1.175		✓				
14	Environmental Expenditure as a Percentage of Total Fiscal Expenditure	1.133						✓
15	Engel's Index	1.128					✓	
16	Average Life Expectancy	1.103					✓	
17	Public Health and Medical Service Expenses Per Capita	1.008					✓	
18	Number of Doctors Per 1,000 Persons	1.002					✓	
19	Index for Quality of E-Government System	0.998			✓			
20	Green Coverage Ratio of Built-up Area	0.950						✓
21	Profit Margin of Enterprises Above Designated Size	0.915		✓				
22	Manufacturing Sector as a Percentage of GRDP	0.893	✓					
23	Number of Provincial-Level Science Parks	0.848				✓		
24	Research & Development Expenditure as a Share of Government Expenditure	0.838				✓		
25	Ratio of Teacher to Student in Primary and Secondary Schools	0.820					✓	
26	Percentage of the Employed Population with Tertiary Education	0.786		✓				

Table 20.3: 20% Weakest Indicators for Zibo

Rank	20% Weakest Indicator	Score	SQEA	FCLMFEV	GGELSS	TAIC	PSSQLI	RCEP
106	Satisfaction of Public Health Care Services	–0.490					✓	
107	Number of Vocational Education Institutions Per 10,000 Population	–0.550					✓	
108	Satisfaction with Business Environment	–0.552	✓					
109	Retail Price Index	–0.559	✓					
110	Per Capita Road Area	–0.573					✓	
111	Dependency on Foreign Trade (Foreign Trade as a Share of GRDP)	–0.622	✓					
112	Number of Passengers Transported	–0.634					✓	
113	Deepness of Insurance (Insurance Income as a Share of GRDP)	–0.647		✓				
114	Satisfaction of Public Transport Services	–0.647					✓	
115	Ratio of Public Education Appropriation to GRDP	–0.666					✓	
116	Wetland Cover	–0.667						✓
117	Tax Revenue as a Share of Fiscal Revenue	–0.725			✓			
118	Frequency of Using the Internet for Daily Convenience	–0.779					✓	
119	Number of Primary and Secondary Schools Per 10,000 Population	–0.782					✓	
120	Residents' Perception of Happiness	–0.920					✓	
121	Proportion of Workforce Employed in Service Sector	–0.960		✓				
122	Per Capita Arable Land	–1.000						✓
123	SO2 Emission Per RMB 10,000 GRDP	–1.006						✓
124	Satisfaction of Income Disparity	–1.007					✓	
125	Consumer Price Index (CPI)	–1.007	✓					
126	Urban Residents' Per Capita Expenditure Growth Rate	–1.111	✓					
127	Number of Investigations for Power Abuses Per 10,000 Population	–1.120			✓			
128	Government Expenditures as a Percentage of GRDP	–1.128	✓					
129	Growth in the Number of Passengers Transported	–1.312		✓				
130	Newly Increased Number of Employees	–1.712		✓				
131	Traffic Accident Fatality Per 10,000 Population	–2.156			✓			

Source: Asia Competitiveness Institute.

Notes: SQEA: Scale and Quality of Economic Activities; FCLMFEV: Financial Capacity, Labour Market Flexibility and Economic Vibrancy; GGELSS: Good Governance, Effective Leadership and Social Stability; TAIC: Technological Advancement and Innovation Capability; PSSQLI: Public Service Standards and Quality of Life Improvement; RCEP: Resource Conditions and Environmental Protection.

20.3.2 *What-if* Urban Development Simulation

ACI has devised a simulation methodology to improve the ranking of a particular city by improving on its 20% Weakest Indicators as shown in Table 20.3.[2] The figures below show Zibo's ranking and standardised scores before and after the policy-induced simulation. Refer to Tables 3.8 to 3.14 in Section 3.4 of Chapter 3 for a complete list of simulation results for all cities.

Overall Performance

	Before		After
Rank	7th	▶	4th
Score	0.403		1.053

Scale and Quality of Economic Activities

	Before	After
Rank	13th	7th
Score	–0.674	0.395

Financial Capacity, Labour Market Flexibility and Economic Vibrancy

	Before	After
Rank	7th	4th
Score	0.089	0.444

Good Governance, Effective Leadership and Social Stability

	Before	After
Rank	8th	3rd
Score	0.418	0.969

Technological Advancement and Innovation Capability

	Before	After
Rank	6th	6th
Score	0.492	0.492

Public Service Standards and Quality of Life Improvement

	Before	After
Rank	5th	3rd
Score	0.794	1.335

Resource Conditions and Environmental Protection

	Before	After
Rank	5th	4th
Score	0.665	1.086

After the *What-if* Simulation, Zibo improves its ranking from 7th to 4th in terms of its Overall Performance. Likewise, Zibo's standardised score improves from 0.403 to 1.053. This leap is plausible if the city manages to successfully address its 20% Weakest Indicators.

The simulation further highlights substantial improvement for Zibo in some of its environments, most notably in Scale and Quality of Economic Activities, where its rank will rise from 13th to 7th. Such encouraging results should incentivise Zibo to strive to improve the indicators under the 20% Weakest Indicators list. These indicators include the Government Expenditures as a Percentage of GRDP and the Satisfaction with Business Environment.

[2] The methodology for *What-if* Simulation is thoroughly explained in Section 2.7 of Chapter 2.

20.4 Concluding Notes: Public Policy Implications[3]

Areas for Commendation

Zibo performs especially better in the environments of Public Service Standards and Quality of Life Improvement, where it has 10 out of 26 of its 20% Strongest Indicators in this environment, as indicated in Table 20.2.

While Zibo does not achieve the maximum score for any sub-environment, it scores above the provincial average in 16 out of the 23 sub-environments.

For the past five years from 2012 to 2016, the government of Zibo has continued to improve the environment of Resource Conditions and Environmental Protection. It has completed 7,035 environment management projects and reduced its yearly consumption of coal by 10 million tons. Moreover, the average concentration of sulphur dioxide in 2016 reduced by 50.4% compared to the level in 2014. The average concentration of chemical oxygen demand and ammoniacal nitrogen decreased by 24% and 43.3% respectively as compared to 2011. The forest cover and green coverage ratio of built-up area of Zibo reached 37% and 45.2% respectively as of 2016.

Areas for Improvement

Zibo scores below the provincial average in Scale and Quality of Economic Activities. Additionally, to improve its position, Zibo should also address the environment of Public Service Standards and Quality of Life Improvement, where it contributes 10 out of 26 of Zibo's 20% Weakest Indicators, as shown in Table 20.3. This is despite the fact that the environment of Public Service Standards and Quality of Life Improvement has the most number of strong indicators. In addition, as gleaned from the *What-if* Urban Development Simulation, Zibo should focus on the environment of Scale and Quality of Economic Activities as it is the environment in which Zibo will achieve the greatest improvement in its ranking — six positions — relative to other environments.

Moreover, Zibo obtains its weakest score in the sub-environment of Market Development (–1.239) and scores below the provincial average in seven out of 23 sub-environments.

According to the 2017 plan, the government of Zibo planned to boost its tertiary industry which may increase the proportion of workforce employed in service sector and thus improve the environment of Financial Capacity, Labour Market Flexibility and Economic Vibrancy. Moreover, as part of its development plan, the Zibo government aimed to raise the number of publicly listed companies in its main board and the "New Third Board" by 28 and 55 respectively. The realisation of these goals will provide a significant boost to Zibo's financial capacity.

The Zibo administration also announced its plan to build a more vibrant and robust business environment to remedy its poor performance in the areas captured in the sub-environment of

[3] The relevant statistical data and government policies are from Zibo Municipal People's Government (2017).

Market Development. Its plan includes simplifying the administrative process, strengthening the regulation of misconduct of businesses and improving the public credit information platform.

Future Potential Development

In summary, Zibo should focus on improving the environment of Scale and Quality of Economic Activities by promoting market development, reducing inflationary pressure and adopting open policies for trade and services. In addition, the government should improve Public Service Standards and Quality of Life Improvement by investing more in public goods such as education and transport infrastructure.

One of Zibo's weakest indicators is the Number of Vocational Education Institutions Per 10,000 Population. As such, the Zibo government should extend its development plan beyond the generic primary, secondary and university education system to include vocational education as well. Such a move will better equip its workforce with specific skills demanded in the job market, thereby raising employment and productivity.

References

Department of Commerce of Shandong Province. n.d. 'Zibo City Profile'. Department of Commerce of Shandong Province. Accessed 10 November 2017. http://en.shandongbusiness.gov.cn/city/71.

Li, Jiaxia. 2009. 'Zibo'. Shandong China, the Hometown of Confucius. 23 July 2009. http://shandong.chinadaily.com.cn/e/2009-07/23/content_8463020.htm.

Zibo Municipal People's Government. 2017. '2017年淄博市政府工作报告 2017 Zibo Annual Government Work Report (in Chinese)'. 28 February 2017. http://www.zibo.gov.cn/art/2017/2/28/art_1579_748610.html.

———. n.d. '走进淄博 Introduction to Zibo (in Chinese)'. 淄博市人民政府 Zibo Municipal People's Government (in Chinese). Accessed 10 November 2017. http://www.zibo.gov.cn/col/col4/index.html.

Part III
Tentative Conclusion on the Urban Development of 17 Shandong Cities

Chapter 21
Conclusion and the Way Forward

The prior section in this book illustrated the complex development trajectories, differences and appropriate recommendations for each of the 17 Shandong cities. In summary, there is a great diversity of development conditions across the cities within Shandong province. For instance, Qingdao and Weihai are consistently better performing cities compared to others, such as Laiwu and Liaocheng. In addition, there are notable gaps between the ranks in the city as well. For example, between Zibo and Linyi, there is a considerable disparity in the scores of their overall performance despite their ranks being in succession of each other.

Furthermore, looking at the six environments, there can be significant movement for cities. For instance, while Qingdao is top in the environments of Scale and Quality of Economic Activities-and Technological Advancement and Innovation Capability, it falls to 8th place in the environment of Resource Conditions and Environmental Protection. As such, there is a need for policymakers across the various localities to provide a targeted approach to address their unique circumstances.

In contrast to the analysis in Part II where we explained each city's strongest and weakest indicators, sub-environments and environments, this chapter will take a step further to summarise and consolidate critical development challenges across Shandong province as a whole by analysing each city's performance in terms of particular indicators and sub-environments. In addition, this chapter proposes relevant evidence-based recommendations for the provincial government to implement in order to support urban development in Shandong province. Finally, this book will close with possible extensions of the framework, which may be applied to other sub-national economies in China, as well as the future research agenda of the Urban Composite Development Index (UCDI).

21.1 Identifying Key Factors Affecting the Development of Shandong Cities

As illustrated in Chapter 3, each city's urban development performance was ranked by Shapley weights as a robustness check to the conventional equal weight ranking. Beyond this, the Shapley weight method may provide additional insight on the development inequalities of cities across the indicators, sub-environments and environments. This is because, as explained in Chapter 3, the greater the variance in the performance of cities for a given indicator, sub-environment or environment, the higher its associated Shapley weight for that specific indicator, sub-environment or environment. As such, higher Shapley weights imply greater development inequalities while lower Shapley imply greater development equality.

The weights of 131 indicators range from 0.52% to 0.88%, significantly different from 0.76%, if the weights were to assign equally. Figure 21.1 lists 10 indicators with lowest weights by the Shapley weight method. The disparities among the 17 cities are the lowest under the 10 indicators.

Figure 21.1: 10 Indicators with the Lowest Shapley Weights

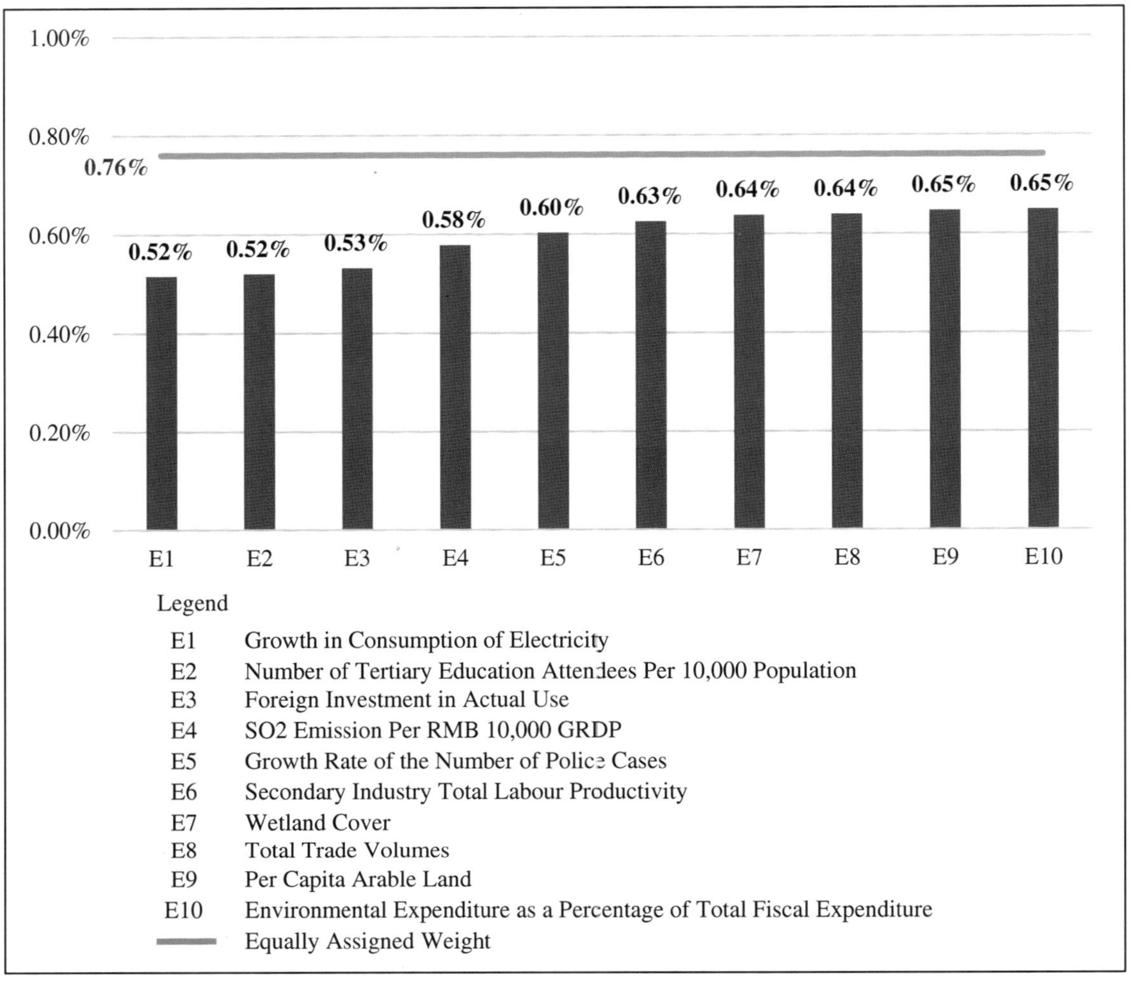

Source: Asia Competitiveness Institute.

As shown in Figure 21.1, electricity-related indicators, such as Growth in Consumption of Electricity (E1) and Electricity Consumption Per RMB 10,000 GRDP (E2), have the lowest Shapley weight of approximately 0.52%. This indicates that all the cities have developed with the least disparity for this indicator. Excluding Binzhou and Liaocheng, all cities have no significant differences in their growth of the electricity consumption. The exceptional growth in electricity consumption for Binzhou and Liaocheng are 73.3 and 10.1 billion kilowatt hour in 2015 respectively, relative to the other cities ranging from –1.23 to 1.44 billion kilowatt hour. This anomaly is because the presence of large industrial facilities in Binzhou and Liaocheng requires huge amounts of electricity. For example, Weiqiao Pioneering Group in Binzhou has expanded to become the world's largest producer of aluminium (Clean Air Alliance of China 2017). With an annual growth of international aluminum demand at an average of 5% between 2012 and 2015, Weiqiao expanded its capacity by 31% on average to capture market share. As a result, such developments significantly raise electricity consumption for these cities.

The indicator Number of Tertiary Education Attendees Per 10,000 Population (E3) has the Shapley weight of 0.53% (Figure 21.1). Excluding Jinan, the number of tertiary students ranges from 52 to 347 per 10,000 population. However, Jinan has 1134 tertiary students per 10,000 population. This is primarily because most of the top 10 universities in Shandong are located in Jinan (uniRank 2018). For example, Shandong University is a top university in China located in Jinan, with one of the largest student population of an estimated 59,500 in 2015 (Report on the Quality of Higher Education in China 2016). Further, Shandong University was recognised and involved in national education projects, such as Project 985 and Project 211 (Report on the Quality of Higher Education in China 2016), where there was an increased emphasis on raising education standards and research capabilities in China.

Apart from the indicators with lowest disparity, we can observe the 10 indicators with the highest disparity by the Shapley weight method, as shown in Figure 21.2.

The indicator Number of Urban Taxis Per 10,000 Population (U1) has the highest Shapley weight of 0.88%, as observed in Figure 21.1. This indicates that all cities have developed with the most disparity under this indicator. In particular, Dongying has the largest number of urban taxis per 10,000 population, with a standardised score of 1.589. In contrast, Heze performs the weakest, with a standardised score of –0.760. As one of the important components of "Sharing Economy", the emergence of carpooling has brought great challenges to the traditional taxis

Figure 21.2: 10 Indicators with the Highest Shapley Weights

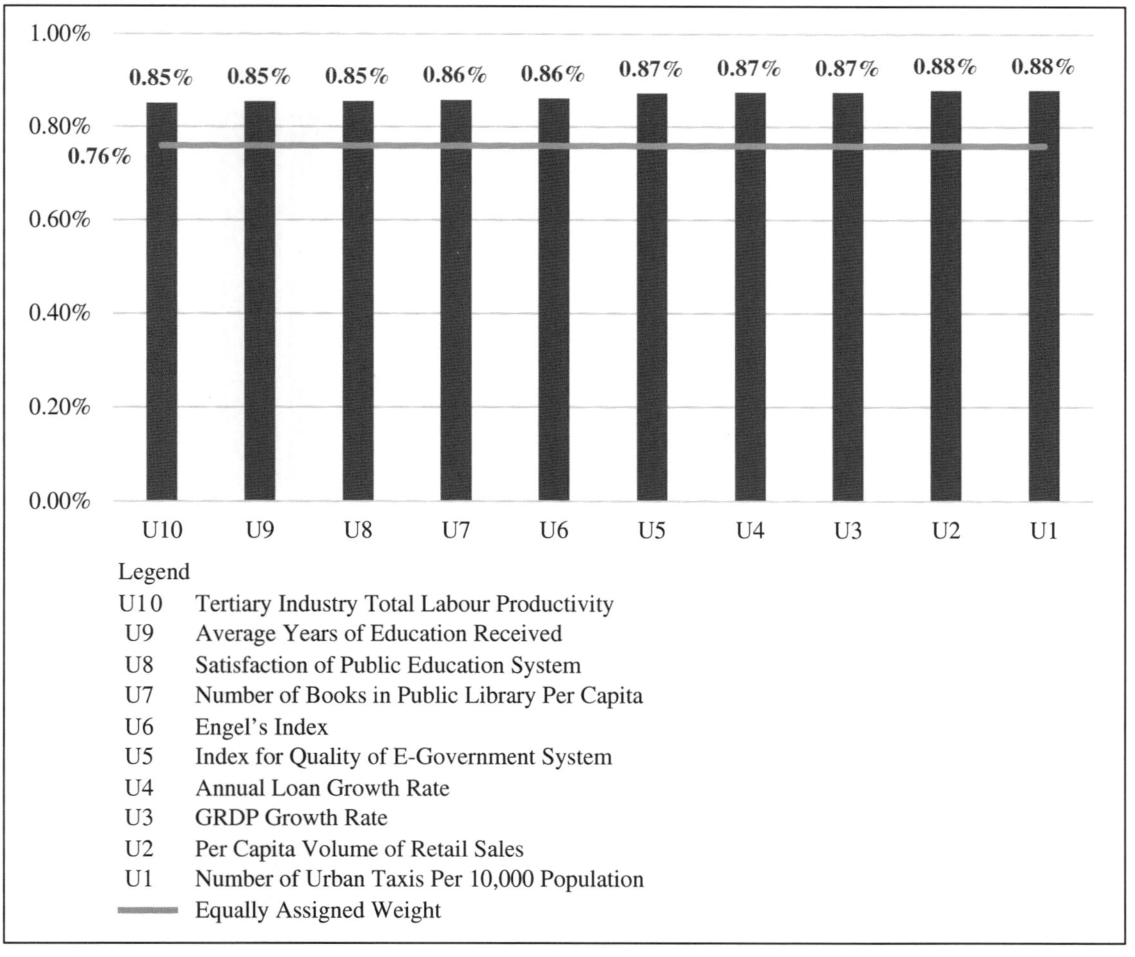

Source: Asia Competitiveness Institute.

markets. On the one hand, one of the underlying reasons for Dongying's greater supply of taxis is the lack of development in the carpooling market. It was only until July 2017 that the DiDi ChuXing (the dominant carpooling company in China) had entered Dongying. On the other hand, higher standard of living and economic activities in the cities, such as Qingdao and Jinan, drive the faster development in the carpooling market, competing with the traditional taxis for the market share and leading to relatively lower supply of taxis in those cities. (http://www.sohu.com/a/158912170_671031)

The indicator Per Capita Volume of Retail Sales (U2) has a Shapley weight of 0.88%. Jinan has the largest per capita volume of retail sales, with a standardised score of 1.873. In contrast, Heze ranks lowest, with a standardised score of –1.231. Both the development of traditional retail industries and e-commence have contributed to the disparity observed in the region. For instance, Jinan as the provincial capital has large shopping malls to attract international brands (Hong Kong Trade Development Council 2015), while Heze is known as a traditional agricultural base city with the fifth smallest economy in Shandong Province by GRDP in 2015. In addition, with the rapid growth of e-commence, residents in Jinan can enjoy quicker delivery services, where goods bought online will be delivered within one or two days. Moreover, the per capita annual disposable income of Jinan is RMB 33,274, while that of Heze is RMB 14,571 in 2015, which indicates the disparities in purchasing power between Jinan and Heze.

Beyond indicators, we can better understand the development inequalities at the sub-environment level. The weights of the 23 sub-environments range from 3.5% to 4.9%, which significantly differ from 4.3%, if the weights were to assign equally. Table 21.1 shows the

Table 21.1: Sub-Environment with the Lowest Shapley Weight — Openness to Trade and Services

City	Standardised Score by Shapley Weight Method	
Qingdao	3.444	
Yantai	1.283	
Weihai	0.475	
Weifang	0.211	
Rizhao	0.115	
Jining	–0.043	
Jinan	–0.101	
Binzhou	–0.296	
Dongying	–0.355	
Zibo	–0.369	
Linyi	–0.380	
Liaocheng	–0.555	
Laiwu	–0.583	
Heze	–0.586	
Dezhou	–0.697	
Tai'an	–0.748	
Zaozhuang	–0.814	

Source: Asia Competitiveness Institute.

performance of cities under the sub-environment with the lowest weight by the Shapley weight method.

As shown in Table 21.1, the performance of cities in Openness to Trade and Services is the least diverse, with the lowest Shapley weight of 3.5%. However, Qingdao stands out in its performance with a standardised score of 3.444. The exceptional performance of Qingdao is primarily due to its geographical advantages as a coastal region and belonging to the Special Economic Zone since 1984. Qingdao is also setting up the Free Trade Zone, and the targeted year of completion is 2020, which will further excel its trade performance. Despite the exceptional performance of Qingdao, all the other cities perform relatively equal, with their standardised scores ranging from –0.814 to 1.283.

Apart from the sub-environment with the least disparity, we can observe the performance of cities under the sub-environment with the most diversity by the Shapley weight method, as shown in Table 21.2.

As shown in Table 21.2, the performance of cities in the Inflationary Pressure sub-environment is the most diverse, with the highest Shapley weight of 4.9%. Majority of the cities (10 out of 17) perform above the provincial average in this sub-environment. Heze has the highest standardised score of 1.673, while Jining has the lowest standardised score of –1.950. It is worth noting that because inflation-related measures such as the consumer price index, producer price index and retail price index are included in this sub-environment, the inequality indicates that all the cities are at different stages of their economic development. In particular, the lower rankings of Qingdao and Jinan indicate that there is excess demand in the cities which drive up the price of goods and services. The fact that Heze ranks 1st under this sub-environment reflects that Heze government should incentivise the consumers and firms to stimulate the local demand and production.

Table 21.2: Sub-Environment with the Highest Shapley Weight — Inflationary Pressure

City	Standardised Score by Shapley Weight Method	
Heze	1.673	
Yantai	1.039	
Dezhou	0.907	
Liaocheng	0.827	
Zaozhuang	0.815	
Weifang	0.739	
Weihai	0.700	
Linyi	0.356	
Binzhou	0.332	
Tai'an	0.248	
Dongying	–0.553	
Jinan	–0.755	
Zibo	–0.807	
Laiwu	–1.106	
Rizhao	–1.122	
Qingdao	–1.343	
Jining	–1.950	

Source: Asia Competitiveness Institute.

21.2 Evidence-Based Policy Evaluation and Recommendations for Shandong

Given our prior analysis of the most unequal indicators by Shapley weights, the two main areas the city and provincial-level administration should be directing their efforts at include the push for environmental protection through green spaces and the promotion of online retail sales.

The municipal governments in Shandong province should reinforce their efforts on green development. To improve the green coverage ratio, local governments should encourage both state-owned and private enterprises to participate and do more. With the increased amount of green spaces, it can help alleviate serious air pollution caused by urban activities. Therefore, policymakers should demarcate more green spaces in its cities by building more parks and increasing the amount of greenery in hotels and high-rise buildings (Massachusetts Institute of Technology Senseable City Lab 2018). For example, as Qingdao has one of the most vibrant business environments in Shandong, the government can encourage more firms there to lead this initiative by increasing the amount of green spaces around their businesses. Such an initiative over the long run will help foster a sustainable city for people to live in.

As shown in our analysis, the per capita volume of retail sales is the second most unequal indicator by Shapley weight, suggesting the need for greater investment in this area across the province. According to the China E-Retail Market Report (2016), the "Internet Plus" initiative has greatly promoted the development of e-commerce industry in the country. However, in terms of geographical distribution, the financing of e-commerce industry is highly concentrated in first-tier cities such as Beijing, Shanghai, and Guangzhou and eastern coastal areas in 2015. E-retail is the major driver for the growth of China's retail market due to the rise of digitisation and use of the Internet (Deloitte 2018). Thus, in order for Shandong to leverage on the growing demand and popularity of online retail sales, the municipal governments in Shandong must boost investment in the e-commerce market. The provincial governments can provide this support by allocating more funds to promote infrastructure construction, enhanced supply-chain processes and guidance through management advice.

In addition to these specific areas of focus, we propose a number of policy objectives that the provincial government must aim to achieve on a broader level to support and maintain sustainable growth and management of the increasingly urbanising Shandong province.

First, urban planning needs to be prioritised. Fundamental to a liveable and prosperous city is how the urban space is developed and used. Planning that focuses on creating communities, accommodating growth and fostering abundant recreational and lifestyle activities are crucial to the development of a vibrant urban environment. The investment in meticulous design of the province will generate a boost to Shandong's attractiveness as a centre of not just economic growth, but also a lively and comfortable place to reside as well. To do so, the provincial- and city-level governments must come together to address the various infrastructural, educational, technological and architectural needs in the province to detail coherent and comprehensive long-term plans that will benefit its people and the entire province as a whole.

Second, the provincial government needs to tackle the issue of inequality with good management. As apparent from the empirical results, there exists notable inequalities between the cities in Shandong province. As such, the provincial government needs to boost and channel greater aid towards the less developed regions in Shandong, such as Laiwu and Liaocheng. Such development should include the improvement towards infrastructure and promotion of investment activities in these specific cities.

Third, the provincial government needs to boost urban governance. This includes the increased management of processes and enforcement of policies within the cities. In order to achieve the objectives of the Five Development Concepts, the progress of urban development in Shandong must be carefully managed with effective and broad-based governance within its cities. This is necessary in order to meet the set requirements and restrict non-compliance to standards, especially in terms of environmental sustainability standards and unlawful business practices. Moreover, the policies implemented and enforced need to be sensitive to the needs of the city and demands of its people to maintain sustainable growth. This can be facilitated through the conduct of comprehensive surveys to obtain feedback on the unique circumstances of each city.

Fourth, the provincial government needs to focus on a coordinated regional development strategy. This is one of the visions of development of a modernised economy mentioned by President Xi Jinping at the 19th National Congress (Xi 2017). While the cities in Shandong are unique, a coordinated strategy that complements cities throughout the region will inevitably aid its sustainable growth. As such, the provincial government of Shandong needs to both harmonise the development between cities in Shandong as well as between the regions neighbouring Shandong, including Hebei, Shanxi, Henan and Jiangsu. Nurturing and aligning the growth strategies both within and around the region will develop synergies that will support the long-term success of Shandong.

While these policy goals and recommendations are useful, they must come with the firm support and dedication from the government and private entities alike. It is only when the community and institutions share common goals can Shandong proceed with a plan to revitalise its urban spaces and push forward to achieve the goals for the province.

21.3 Urban Development Framework for Other Sub-National Economies in China

Given the robust urban development framework constructed based on China's Five Development Concepts, sub-national economies beyond Shandong stand to benefit as well. As the framework is tailor-made for China, it is intuitive to consider other provinces in China to extend the analysis. In addition, it will be useful to benchmark the urban development of cities across China with this framework over time, as other government bodies understand their urban development performance and standards relative to their counterparts. In this regard, it has the potential to spur other provinces to improve as they strive to remain competitive relative to each other.

This study may extend its coverage and analysis to other provinces with larger population sizes like Guangdong and Henan. Such a people-centred criteria will be useful for the national and provincial government as the urban development needs would be most pressing in those areas where the urban populations are larger. Subsequently, the study should aim to rank cities across provinces in China to provide a broader benchmark for governments of different provinces. For example, a ranking of cities in Eastern China may be developed after each individual province in the region has been separately evaluated. By adopting this approach, the UCDI will benefit each city as they are empowered with a better understanding of their performance and standards relative to the broader context in China. The ultimate goal of the UCDI is to provide an assessment across China as a whole.

To accomplish such ambitious goals, it must be accompanied with support both from public and private entities alike. The significant investment in data collection will require extensive partnerships with research and data-collection agencies across China. Further, policy insights from interactions with academics and experts across the various provinces in China will contribute to the analysis of specific local-level policies as well. In doing so, we will be closer to attaining a broader application of our framework to obtain more profound insights and evaluations of urban development performance in China.

21.4 Concluding Remarks

Overall, Shandong has made tremendous progress in managing its urban development in recent years. From greater economic vibrancy through trade and investment to improved public services in education, to environmental protection with less air pollution and efficient energy consumption, Shandong has demonstrated its commitment to dynamic yet sustainable urban development. Nevertheless, as mentioned in our study, Shandong has more room for improvement in terms of coordinated development across its cities to reduce the development inequalities between them.

Notably, there are two developments to focus on as they will affect the discourse in the upcoming years. They are the Belt and Road Initiative (BRI) and the Communist Party of China's 19th National Congress.

Belt and Road Initiative

The BRI was launched by China and encompasses the Silk Road Economic Belt and the 21st Century Maritime Silk Road, connecting the three continents of Asia, Africa and Europe via land, sea and air passages. It is a massive project, which covers approximately 65% of the world's population and roughly a third of the world's Gross Domestic Product. The BRI aims at achieving greater economic growth for all countries involved through an expansion of trade connectivity, financial links and infrastructure development through the construction of essential infrastructure-such as roads, railways and pipelines, in some of the largest continents in the world. For instance, infrastructure needs in Asia are projected to be US $1.7 trillion per year between 2016 and 2030, which is much higher than the estimated US $881 billion that is currently being invested by the region each year (Asian Development Bank 2017). With the BRI, such gaps can be eased as greater regional cooperation and investments will facilitate the growth of such infrastructural needs.

In anticipation of the BRI, China has expressed its five major goals, namely policy coordination, facilities connectivity, unimpeded trade, financial integration and people-to-people bonds (National Development and Reform Commission, Ministry of Foreign Affairs, and Ministry of Commerce 2015). In doing so, China is expected to gain a renewed engine for growth, motivated by the strengthened economic ties with neighbouring countries due to the BRI. As such, the sheer size and influence as well as the potential for immense benefit of the BRI makes it difficult for China and Shandong to ignore.

First, the BRI will provide tremendous opportunities for Shandong to access new markets and achieve stronger economic growth. In particular, Shandong is a coastal province where seaport infrastructure can be expanded to raise sea trade activities. By complementing the BRI with improved seaports, Shandong will be able to exploit the opportunities of trade and investment as it creates economic links with other countries and regions. In doing so, Shandong can support economic growth well into the long run.

Second, the BRI provides a significant boost to urbanization, especially due to increased domestic connectivity. The enhanced transport infrastructure that accrue from the BRI allows quicker and easier flows of goods, services and people between locations. Such improvements not only raise the efficiency of trade and services but also provide greater convenience to people living in those areas. In addition, Shandong stands to benefit economically as goods may flow through the province for exporting via their seaports. However, more important is the fact that increased access and connectivity to various geographical locations can stimulate the development of those locations as well. Investments can flow more easily to support the construction of other urban amenities, including schools, hospitals, public housing, amongst others.

It is worth noting that this strategy of the BRI is consistent with the principle of open development in the Five Development Concepts, where China aims to foster deeper connections with the world to play a bigger role as well as to manage the opportunities and risks of globalisation. In particular, it is a proactive approach to strengthen interactions and partnerships among the eastern, western and central regions, while opening up the Chinese economy in a comprehensive way (National Development and Reform Commission, Ministry of Foreign Affairs, and Ministry of Commerce 2015). As such, this initiative is a testament to the commitment China has toward the implementation of the Five Development Concepts, thereby lending support to the robustness of the framework used in this study.

Communist Party of China's 19th National Congress

At the 19th National Congress held in Beijing from 18 to 24 October 2017, President Xi Jinping laid out the broad development goals for China for the next few decades. In particular, he stressed on building a "moderately prosperous society" by 2020 (Xi 2017). Specifically, the aim for a moderately prosperous society directly relates to poverty reduction across the country, where basic household needs are met. In a speech at Davos on 27 June 2017, Premier Li Keqiang recognised the significant strides China has made at reducing poverty, including lifting 700 million Chinese citizens out of poverty since the 1990s and providing new housing for 800 million more since 2010. At the same time, Premier Li reaffirmed the country's dedication towards raising a further 40 million people out of poverty by 2020 (Li 2017).

Also at the 19th National Congress, President Xi Jinping shared his vision for China to move towards becoming a modern socialist country that is prosperous, strong, democratic, culturally advanced, harmonious and beautiful. Many of these concepts regarding a modern socialist country are enduring value goals outlined at the national level at the 18th National Congress in 2012. However, it is worth emphasising that the notion of a "beautiful" city is new priority since the 18th National Congress and refers specifically to environmental conservation. This is a meaningful breakthrough for China as it has been criticised for neglecting the environment at the expense of economic growth, such as through hazardous amounts of air pollution from industrial activity in Beijing. As such, it is clear that China will include the consideration of the environment moving forward. By acknowledging this in the UCDI framework with the environment of Resource

Conditions and Environmental Protection, the idea of a beautiful and environmentally friendly country is incorporated in the understanding and benchmark of urban development.

Given such a context, the national direction set out during the 19th National Congress is undeniably critical and relevant to the development strategies that Shandong adopts, as it has to align itself appropriately to leverage on synergies with the national government as well.

The implications for Shandong province are two-fold. First, it has to draft and communicate the provincial development strategy to each city to ensure that they clearly understand the specific provincial objectives they need in response to President Xi Jinping's vision of a prosperous and urbanised China. In particular, the strategy and goals defined must align to both the long- and short-term goals of the country, such as in poverty reduction and environmental conservation. Properly drafting and communicating these goals allow Shandong to dispel misunderstandings and address concerns that any city may have. Second, the provincial government must enforce the objectives outlined with strict rules, regulations and penalties. This ensures that the cities in Shandong maintain the discipline to follow through and successfully achieve the objectives laid out in a timely manner. Such a two-pronged approach will ensure that Shandong's development goals are realised, in line with that of China as described by President Xi Jinping.

With these two significant developments emerging, Shandong should prepare itself by taking necessary measures early to exploit the abundant opportunities that they present.

21.5 Future Research Agenda

Looking ahead, Asia Competitiveness Institute's (ACI) future research agenda will broaden and deepen the analysis by increasing its emphasis on smart cities, as well as the addition of other practical improvements to future studies.

Smart and Intelligent Cities

Currently, there is no universal definition of smart cities. However, there is significant enthusiasm surrounding this topic. Nevertheless, the most common elements of smart cities include a networked infrastructure that facilitates socio-cultural development, emphasis on business-led urban development for growth, fostering of social inclusion and social capital, as well as the protection of the natural environment to encourage sustainability (Albino, Berardi, and Dangelico 2015). The interest in smart cities is quickly gaining traction as policymakers attempt to develop, deploy and integrate innovations to manage rapid urbanisation in the country. There are many reports illustrating this. According to the Smart City Tracker Report published by Navigant Research, it is estimated that there are over 250 smart city projects across 178 cities worldwide as of 2017. Moreover, the global market for smart city services is expected to rise from US$40.1 billion in 2017 to US$97.9 billion in 2026 (Navigant Research 2017). In China, more than 500 cities are expected to initiate their smart city transformations in 2017, according to the Economic Information Daily (China Daily 2017). Therefore, as cities become progressively essential to the provision of public services and social life, it is important to ensure that nurturing intelligent and smart cities that are resilient and able to cope with challenges remains a priority.

One key aspect of smart cities is the use of technology. This implies the development of a digital economy that enables its urban residents. The digital city should create an environment where society may conduct seamless information sharing, collaboration and interoperability in the city (Albino, Berardi, and Dangelico 2015). As such, the technologies introduced in a smart city must be contextually aware and cognitive, including state-of-the-art machine learning and artificial intelligence. In this regard, two kinds of technologies are gaining popularity. First are the smart technologies that monitor. Examples of these devices include the variety of sensors that use information such as temperature and activity in the house to monitor and alert homeowners of recommended or necessary actions. Further, these technologies are also employed for surveillance in areas, such as security and traffic monitoring.

The second branch of smart technologies are those that empower its people. For instance, cashless payments, online income tax filing and online grocery shopping are some of the ways technology improve the lives of urban residents through greater convenience in daily activities. In another example, preliminary processes such as the filling up of forms during hospital visits may be completed via smart phones instead of physical paper forms to reduce waiting times. Therefore, a vision of a digital city must entail the active work of the government to integrate technologies such as WiFi accessibility and Internet access throughout each city they govern. The advent of technology in recent years is making way for significant opportunities in this aspect.

Yet, the idea behind smart cities must go beyond the embodiment of technological improvements alone. Specifically, a smart city may be regarded as an "organic whole" that is capable of learning and evolving (Kanter and Litow 2009). This gives rise to the term of an intelligent city. They are, on the one hand, constantly looking towards the future to anticipate disruptions and maintain sustainability. On the other hand, these cities have shorter-term goals such as the investment in and adaptation of technology and innovations that enable and facilitate daily lifestyle and commercial activities. As such, there is a compelling case for governments to expend efforts that grow the digital and knowledge economy through the promotion of research centres and knowledge clusters to address all facets of society, including public services, transport, education and business, amongst numerous others. In the face of digital disruptions in sectors such as retail and commerce, the urgency for policymakers to promote a robust knowledge economy that can foresee challenges and formulate solutions is more now than ever.

Another vital component of smart cities is their need to be deeply connected to fully exploit opportunities. The spatial divides within and across cities generate inefficiencies as they restrict the mobility of goods, services and people. Resource-rich areas are unable to export and reap the returns while resource-scarce areas struggle to find sufficient resources. Further, locations isolated from the rest of society have limited opportunities to benefit from public services and government welfare. As a result, it is clear that smart cities must be able to establish connections through infrastructure developments to overcome these problems and facilitate a vibrant and economically active city. The necessary developments include physical ones such as roads and railways, while other connections are virtual, such as via the Internet. The ability to effectively transcend these divides will not only promote economic prosperity through more efficient flows of goods and services, but also raise the ability for government bodies to administer policies that improve previously disconnected areas.

In addition to connections internally, international networks are equally important. This paves the way for cities to extend their influence abroad through comprehensive collaborations and investments with businesses and policymakers abroad. Furthermore, such connectivity has the potential to boost the economic vibrancy of the city into areas previously not available. For instance, land-scarce cities like Singapore may invest in agricultural land abroad to cultivate crops. In doing so, small cities like Singapore may engage in heavily land-intensive activities that would otherwise not be feasible due to their disadvantages.

Smart cities must be centred around its people. Incorporating technologies into society is meaningless if its residents are not equipped with the right knowledge, skills and attitudes to use them. As such, there is a need to ensure that smart cities begin from the human capital side, rather than believing the notion that infusing information communication technologies into them will naturally lead to smart cities (Hollands 2008; Shapiro 2006). To enable urban residents, a constant and extensive investment into good education and leadership should remain central to any initiative that aims to improve the smartness of cities. This includes systematic steps in place to prepare society with the relevant information and skills to execute. For instance, cashless payment systems need to be followed up with easily accessible tutorials on how to use them. Only through such efforts can cities advance from the superficial adoption of technologies to their comprehensive integration into daily urban activities.

Finally, smart cities must be sustainable. This means that these cities have systems built into the city infrastructure to promote environmentally friendly behaviour. Such activities include waste management and recycling, water and energy efficient technologies, as well as the conservation of the natural environment through green spaces, biodiversity and natural habitats. These positive actions have significant consequences on the future of the city as the environment is passed on to subsequent generations. The regard for sustainability is therefore a strategic priority crucial for smart cities as they safeguard their future.

In view of the emerging global interest on smart cities, it is imperative for ACI to incorporate such ideas into future iterations of the urban development framework. Specifically, ACI's urbanisation and liveability studies will aim to include and improve indicators that measure smart, intelligent and knowledge cities. Such indicators include the rate of adoption of new technologies, number of initiatives by the government to promote smart cities and the investment into relevant research that promotes smart technologies. As it currently stands, the UCDI framework includes indicators related to smart cities, such as the Index for the Quality of E-Government Systems for smart public systems, Satisfaction with the Innovation Environment for technological innovation, and the Green Coverage Ratio of Built-up Area to capture sustainability. While it is not yet clear what more and how they should be included in the framework, it does not deviate from the aim to closely examine and rethink urban spaces and cities in the context of smart cities. In doing so, our study will be better able to incorporate the robust assessment of cities of the future.

Other Improvements to Future Urban Development Studies

Apart from the conceptual improvements to the UCDI framework, this study may expand towards other important areas. First, as alluded to in Section 21.3, the UCDI framework can be expanded to assess the urban development performance of other provinces in China. This is a natural extension of the framework because the UCDI was constructed with a specific focus on China's urban development, based on the government's vision of dynamic and sustainable cities. Ranking of other provinces allows us to analyse the broader applicability of our framework to provide insights to all levels of the government for their useful application. Second, beyond an extension, we should aim to improve the data in terms of its quality and quantity. Improved quality can be achieved through better data-collection methods, which may include engaging survey respondents via online channels. Enhanced quantity can be achieved by expanding the number of indicators to include more ideal indicators to keep up with evolving developments.

While this raises the concern of comparability of the index across time, it is possible to overcome this problem with a re-estimation of past rankings with the updated framework. Nevertheless, this solution is limited to non-survey data as it is not possible to conduct and obtain survey data for past years. Third, the project for the UCDI for 17 Shandong Cities should seek to collaborate with Chinese institutions and governments as broader objectives for provincial- and regional-level works are outlined. Such institutions may include the China Academy of Social Sciences, the various provincial-level social science academies as well as the various Chinese universities. Drawing from the experience of the successful collaboration with Shandong Academy of Social Sciences for this study, we are confident that future project partnerships will be equally fruitful and beneficial.

With other publications focussing on urban development in ACI running in parallel to this book such as the Global Liveable Cities Index and the Greater China Liveable Cities Index, the future update of this ranking and framework may draw insights gathered from these books as well. Possible modifications include the substitution for more representative indicators and the expansion in the total number of indicators and sub-environments. As China continues to forge ahead with bold urban development initiatives such as the BRI, all facets of the government and its people should share the ideals outlined in the Five Development Concepts to support the effort towards a more prosperous, liveable and sustainable China.

References

Albino, Vito, Umberto Berardi, and Rosa Maria Dangelico. 2015. 'Smart Cities: Definitions, Dimensions, Performance, and Initiatives'. *Journal of Urban Technology* 22 (1): 3–21. https://doi.org/10.1080/10630732.2014.942092.

Asian Development Bank. 2017. *Meeting Asia's Infrastructure Needs*. Asian Development Bank. http://dx.doi.org/10.22617/FLS168388-2.

CBRE Research. 2016. 'The New Era of Green Buildings in China'. http://greeninitiatives.cn/img/white_papers/1441531986096China_Major_Report_-_The_New_Era_of_Green_Buildings_in_China_July_2015.pdf.

China Daily. 2017. 'China's "Smart Cities" to Number 500 Before End of 2017'. 21 April 2017. http://www.chinadaily.com.cn/china/2017-04/21/content_29024793.htm.

China Foreigners Guide. 2011. 'Heze Overview'. 23 July 2011. http://www.cfguide.com/Heze/article/art361.htm.

Clean Air Alliance of China. 2017. 'Coal Power and Privilege: China's Problem With Industry-Owned Generators'. 5 September 2017. http://en.cleanairchina.org/product/9018.html.

Dazhong Daily. 2018. '郭树清省长在省十二届人大六次会议上的政府工作报告 2016 Jinan Annual Government Work Report (in Chinese)'. 7 February 2018. http://paper.dzwww.com/dzrb/content/20170207/Articel02002MT.htm.

Deloitte. 2018. 'China E-Retail Market Report 2016'. https://www2.deloitte.com/content/dam/Deloitte/cn/Documents/cip/deloitte-cn-cip-china-online-retail-market-report-en-170123.pdf.

Hollands, Robert G. 2008. 'Will the Real Smart City Please Stand Up?' *City* 12 (3): 303–20. https://doi.org/10.1080/13604810802479126.

Hong Kong Trade Development Council. 2012. 'Heze (Shandong) City Information'. Hong Kong Means Business. 11 December 2012. http://hkmb.hktdc.com/en/1X09QZFO.

———. 2015. 'Jinan: Profile of a Consumer Market'. 9 October 2015. http://china-trade-research.hktdc.com/business-news/article/China-Consumer-Market/Jinan-Profile-of-a-Consumer-Market/ccm/en/1/1X000000/1X0A3YSE.htm.

Kanter, Rosabeth Moss, and Stanley S. Litow. 2009. 'Informed and Interconnected: A Manifesto for Smarter Cities'. SSRN Scholarly Paper ID 1420236. Rochester, NY: Social Science Research Network. https://papers.ssrn.com/abstract=1420236.

Li, Keqiang. 2017. '李克强在第十一届夏季达沃斯论坛开幕式上的致辞 Li Keqiang's Speech at the Opening Ceremony of the 11th Summer Davos Forum (in Chinese)'. 27 June 2017. http://www.gov.cn/xinwen/2017-06/28/content_5206164.htm.

Massachusetts Institute of Technology Senseable City Lab. 2018. 'Exploring the Green Canopy in Cities around the World'. Treepedia :: MIT Senseable City Lab. 26 January 2018. http://senseable.mit.edu/treepedia.

National Development and Reform Commission, Ministry of Foreign Affairs, and Ministry of Commerce. 2015. 'Action Plan on the Belt and Road Initiative'. http://english.gov.cn/archive/publications/2015/03/30/content_281475080249035.htm.

Navigant Research. 2017. 'More than 250 Smart City Projects Exist in 178 Cities Worldwide'. Navigant Research. 16 March 2017. https://www.navigantresearch.com/newsroom/more-than-250-smart-city-projects-exist-in-178-cities-worldwide.

Report on the Quality of Higher Education in China. 2016. '盘点中国在校生人数TOP10大学 The Top 10 China Universities of Bigger Number of Students (in Chinese)'. 16 December 2016. www.sohu.com/a/121779800_190832.

Shapiro, Jesse M. 2006. 'Smart Cities: Quality of Life, Productivity, and the Growth Effects of Human Capital'. *The Review of Economics and Statistics* 88 (2): 324–35. https://doi.org/10.1162/rest.88.2.324.

uniRank. 2018. '2018 China University Ranking'. 24 January 2018. https://www.4icu.org/cn/shandong/.

Xi, Jinping. 2017. 'Secure a Decisive Victory in Building a Moderately Prosperous Society in All Respects and Strive for the Great Success of Socialism with Chinese Characteristics for a New Era; Delivered at the 19th National Congress of the Communist Party of China'. http://www.xinhuanet.com/english/download/Xi_Jinping's_report_at_19th_CPC_National_Congress.pdf.

Appendix A
List of Ideal Indicators for the Urban Composite Development Index

1. Ideal Indicators of Scale and Quality of Economic Activities (55 Indicators)					
1.1	**Economic Capacity**	**1.2**	**Openness to Trade and Services**	**1.2**	**Openness to Trade and Services**
1.1.01	Profits of Industrial Enterprises Above Designated Size Reported	1.2.01	Tourists Income (from Other Provinces)	1.2.11	English Proficiency (Survey)
1.1.02	Gross Regional Domestic Product (GRDP)	1.2.02	FDI/GRDP	1.2.12	Proportion of Industrial Output from Foreign Enterprises and Enterprises from Hong Kong, Macao and Taiwan
1.1.03	GRDP Growth Rate	1.2.03	Contribution of Foreign Companies to the Economy	1.2.13	Number of Foreign Investment Contract Signed
1.1.04	GRDP Per Capita	1.2.04	Number of Foreign Enterprises	1.2.14	Total Trade Volumes
1.1.05	Per Capita Fixed Investment	1.2.05	Tax Contribution of Foreign Enterprises (Tax from Enterprises/Regional Total Tax Revenue)	1.2.15	Trade Surplus
1.1.06	Per Capita Volume of Retail Sales	1.2.06	Foreign Enterprise Trade as a Percentage of All Foreign Trade	1.2.16	Dependency on Foreign Trade (Foreign Trade as a Share of GRDP)
1.1.07	Manufacturing Sector as a Percentage of GRDP	1.2.07	Foreign Enterprises as a Percentage of Industrial Enterprises Above Designated Size	1.2.17	Trade Surplus as a Percentage of GRDP
1.1.08	Service Sector as a Percentage of GRDP	1.2.08	Number of Starred Hotels Per 10,000 Population	1.2.18	Trade of Services as a Percentage of Total Trade
1.1.09	Urbanisation Rate (%)	1.2.09	Hotel Occupancy Rate	1.2.19	Foreign Investment in Actual Use
1.1.10	Registered Urban Population as a Percentage of Total Population	1.2.10	Ease of Doing Business (Survey)	1.2.20	Investment Abroad

1. Ideal Indicators of Scale and Quality of Economic Activities (55 Indicators, continued)					
1.3	**Inflationary Pressure**	**1.4**	**Market Development**	**1.4**	**Market Development**
1.3.01	Consumer Price Index (CPI)	1.4.01	Number of Employees in Public Administration as a Share of Total Employment	1.4.10	Rate of Autonomy in Management of Enterprises (14 Rights Stipulated by the Country)
1.3.02	Producer Price Index (PPI)	1.4.02	Contribution of Non-State-Owned Enterprises in the Total Sales of Industrial Products	1.4.11	Degree of Legislation for Bankruptcy
1.3.03	Retail Price Index	1.4.03	Contribution of Non-State-Owned Enterprises as a Percentage of the Total Fixed Asset Investment	1.4.12	Number of Customer Complaints
1.3.04	Urban Residents' Disposable Income Growth Rate	1.4.04	Contribution of Non-State-Owned Enterprises as a Percentage of Total Urban Employment	1.4.13	Government Expenditures as a Percentage of GRDP
1.3.05	Urban Residents' Per Capita Expenditure Growth Rate	1.4.05	Credits of Non-State-Owned Enterprises as a Share of Loans of Financial Institutions	1.4.14	Government Expenditure as a Percentage of Total Expenditure
1.3.06	Ratio of Housing Price to Income	1.4.06	Rural Immigrant Workers as a Percentage of Total Urban Employment	1.4.15	Number of Publicly Listed Companies
1.3.07	Residents' Satisfaction with Price Levels (Survey)	1.4.07	Proportion of Asset of Non-Public Economy	1.4.16	Number of Small Enterprises Per 10,000 Population
		1.4.08	Lawyers to Population Ratio	1.4.17	Number of Newly Registered Enterprises
		1.4.09	Registered Accountants to Population Ratio	1.4.18	Satisfaction of Business Environment (Survey)

2. Ideal Indicators of Financial Capacity, Labour Market Flexibility and Economic Vibrancy (45 Indicators)							
2.1	**Financial Deepening and Business Efficiency**	**2.2**	**Productivity Performance**	**2.3**	**Labour Market Flexibility**	**2.3**	**Labour Market Flexibility**
2.1.01	Non-Performing Loan Ratio	2.2.01	Total Factor Productivity	2.3.01	Active Labour Force	2.3.11	Self-Employed as a Share of Total Employment
2.1.02	Capital Adequacy Ratio	2.2.02	Primary Industry Total Labour Productivity	2.3.02	Inter-Industry Wage Differentials (Measured as Dispersion)	2.3.12	Proportion of Workforce Employed in Agriculture Sector

(Continued)

(*Continued*)

2. Ideal Indicators of Financial Capacity, Labour Market Flexibility and Economic Vibrancy (45 Indicators)							
2.1.03	Number of Financial Institutions	2.2.03	Average Profit Margin of Companies	2.3.03	Unemployment Benefit Replacement Rate	2.3.13	Proportion of Workforce Employed in Service Sector
2.1.04	Financial Sector Value-Added	2.2.04	Secondary Industry Total Labour Productivity	2.3.04	Proportion of Non-Agriculture Employed Persons	2.3.14	Proportion of Urban Workers Employed in State Enterprises
2.1.05	Deposit Balance Per Capita	2.2.05	Tertiary Industry Total Labour Productivity	2.3.05	Number of Employees	2.3.15	Proportion of Urban Workers Employed in Private Enterprises
2.1.06	Loan Balance Per Capita	2.2.06	Growth Rate of Overall Labour Productivity	2.3.06	Newly Increased Number of Employees		
2.1.07	Annual Loan Growth Rate	2.2.07	Percentage of the Employed Population with Tertiary Education	2.3.07	Rate of Migration Flow		
2.1.08	Insurance Net Income	2.2.08	Profit Margin of Enterprises Above Designated Size	2.3.08	Workforce Participation Rate		
2.1.09	Deepness of Insurance (Insurance Income as a Share of GRDP)			2.3.09	Urban Registered Unemployment Rate		
2.1.10	Financed Amount in Stock Market			2.3.10	Average Salary of Urban Employees		

2. Ideal Indicators of Financial Capacity, Labour Market Flexibility and Economic Vibrancy (45 Indicators)			
2.4	**Economic Vibrancy and Tripartite Relationship (Government, Employee and Employer)**	**2.4**	**Economic Vibrancy and Tripartite Relationship (Government, Employee and Employer)**
2.4.01	Total Working Days Lost	2.4.07	Amount of Overdue Salary Payments
2.4.02	Number of Labour Arbitration	2.4.08	Workers' Satisfaction of the Unions (Survey)
2.4.03	Ratio of Workers Joined Labour Unions (Survey)	2.4.09	Occurrence of Public Events
2.4.04	Number of Labour Disputes	2.4.10	Growth in Consumption of Electricity
2.4.05	Minimum Salary Adjustment (%)	2.4.11	Growth in the Number of Passengers Transported
2.4.06	Discrimination Rate in Employment (Survey) (such as Gender, Age, Race, Language, Religion, Family Condition etc.)	2.4.12	Growth in the Volume of Cargo Transported

3. Ideal Indicators of Good Governance, Effective Leadership and Social Stability (49 Indicators)							
3.1	**Fiscal Sustainability**	**3.2**	**Transparency and Accountability**	**3.3**	**Public Governance**	**3.3**	**Public Governance**
3.1.01	Debt Ratio = Local Government Debt Balance / GRDP	3.2.01	Public Trust in Government (Survey)	3.3.01	Index for Government System Function (Survey)	3.3.08	Index for Quality of E-Government System (Survey)
3.1.02	Government Fiscal Revenue	3.2.02	Number of Gift Buy-Back Shops	3.3.02	Index for Opinion Expression and Accountability System (Survey)	3.3.09	Public Acceptance of Policy Implementation (Survey)
3.1.03	Government Fiscal Revenue Per Capita	3.2.03	Number of Government Officials Above Director's Level Convicted for Corruption	3.3.03	Ratio between Urban and Rural Per Capita Disposable Income	3.3.10	Number of Public Servants Per 10,000 Population
3.1.04	Government Fiscal Expenditure	3.2.04	Number of Releases of Government Information for Public Viewing	3.3.04	Gini Coefficient	3.3.11	Average Public Servant Salary
3.1.05	Government Fiscal Expenditure Per Capita	3.2.05	Number of Responses to Government Issues of Public Interest	3.3.05	Urban Children and Aged Dependency Ratio	3.3.12	Number of Listed Items Under Executive Authority of the Government
3.1.06	Tax Revenue as a Share of Fiscal Revenue	3.2.06	Public Perception of Government Conduct (Survey)	3.3.06	Ratio of Middle-Income Class	3.3.13	Number of Administration Action and Reconsideration Cases
3.1.07	Fiscal Revenue Growth Rate	3.2.07	Satisfaction of the Just of Judiciary	3.3.07	Difference in Urban and Rural Expenditure Per Capita		

3. Ideal Indicators of Good Governance, Effective Leadership and Social Stability (49 Indicators)					
3.4	**Public Security and Social Stability**	**3.4**	**Public Security and Social Stability**	**3.4**	**Public Security and Social Stability**
3.4.01	Criminal Case Occurrence Rate / Crime Rate	3.4.09	Success Rate of Social Dispute Conciliation	3.4.17	Number of Food Safety Accidents
3.4.02	Juvenile Delinquency Rate / Crime Rate	3.4.10	Degree of Religious Harmony (Survey)	3.4.18	Satisfaction with Urban Management Personnel (Survey)
3.4.03	Detection Rate / Crime Rate	3.4.11	Public Perception of Security (Survey)	3.4.19	Number Internet or Telecommunication Frauds
3.4.04	Satisfaction of Police Services (Survey)	3.4.12	Growth Rate of the Number of Police Cases	3.4.20	Number of Theft Cases

(*Continued*)

(*Continued*)

3. Ideal Indicators of Good Governance, Effective Leadership and Social Stability (49 Indicators)					
3.4.05	Number of Foreign Cases Occurred	3.4.13	Growth Rate of the Number of Police Cases Solved	3.4.21	Number of Murder Cases
3.4.06	Crime Committed by Women	3.4.14	Fire Fatality Per 10,000 Population	3.4.22	Number of Drug Trafficking Cases
3.4.07	Crime Committed by Senior Citizens	3.4.15	Traffic Accident Fatality Per 10,000 Population		
3.4.08	Degree of Social Harmony (Survey)	3.4.16	Number of Production Safety Accidents		

4. Ideal Indicators of Technological Advancement and Innovation Capability (36 Indicators)					
4.1	**Research and Development Input**	**4.2**	**Technological Innovation Capability**	**4.3**	**Research and Development Output**
4.1.01	Research & Development Expenditure as a Share of GRDP	4.2.01	Number of Engineering Technology Research Centers and Enterprise Technology Centers at City Level	4.3.01	Contribution of Technological Advances
4.1.02	Total Imports and Exports on High-Tech Products	4.2.02	Proportion of Enterprise with R&D Facilities	4.3.02	High-Tech Industry Value-Added as a Share of GRDP
4.1.03	Number of R&D Institutions (University, Research Centers, etc)	4.2.03	Number of Public Technology Service Platform	4.3.03	Number of University-Industry-Research Cooperation
4.1.04	Average Spending Per Patent	4.2.04	Number of Enterprise Incubator	4.3.04	Revenue of New Products of Industrial Enterprises as a Share of Total Revenue
4.1.05	Reward Amount for Scientific and Technological Achievements	4.2.05	Number of Provincial-Level Science Parks	4.3.05	Output of Products with Independent Intelligent Property Right as a Share of Industrial Output
4.1.06	Number of Employees Involved in Innovative Activities as a Share of all Employees	4.2.06	Number of Engineering Technology Research Centers and Enterprise Technology Centers at Provincial Level	4.3.06	Number of High-Tech Enterprise
4.1.07	Research & Development Expenditure as a Share of Government Expenditure	4.2.07	Number of Key Laboratory at Provincial Level	4.3.07	Number of Technology Achievement Award at Provincial and National Level
4.1.08	Per Capita R&D Expenditure	4.2.08	Number of Hi-Tech Enterprises	4.3.08	Number of Patents Granted
4.1.09	Total R&D Man-Hour	4.2.09	Total Number of Members of Chinese Academy of Sciences and Chinese Academy of Engineering	4.3.09	Number of Existing Patents Per 10,000 Population

(*Continued*)

(*Continued*)

4. Ideal Indicators of Technological Advancement and Innovation Capability (36 Indicators)					
4.1.10	Number of Science and Technology Personnel	4.2.10	Number of Technological Specialists Per 10,000 Population	4.3.10	Number of Famous Product at Provincial and National Level
4.1.11	Total R&D Expenditure of Enterprises Above Designated Size	4.2.11	Number of R&D Personnel Per 10,000 Population	4.3.11	Total Output Value of Hi-Tech Industries
4.1.12	Total R&D Expenditure of Enterprises Above Designated Size as a Percentage of Cash Flow	4.2.12	Satisfaction with Innovation Environment (Survey)	4.3.12	Value-Added by High-Tech Industry as a Share of Value-Added by Secondary Industry

5. Ideal Indicators of Public Service Standards and Quality of Life Improvement (50 Indicators)					
5.1	**Social Security and Standard of Living**	**5.1**	**Social Security and Standard of Living**	**5.2**	**Public Health Care System**
5.1.01	Satisfaction of Housing Price Regulation (Survey)	5.1.10	Per Capita Annual Disposable Income	5.2.01	Infant Mortality Rate
5.1.02	Social Endowment Insurance Coverage	5.1.11	Engel's Index	5.2.02	Public Health and Medical Service Expenses as a Share of GRDP
5.1.03	Social Medical Insurance Coverage	5.1.12	Per Capita Housing Area	5.2.03	Public Health and Medical Service Expenses Per Capita
5.1.04	Unemployment Insurance Coverage	5.1.13	Number of Private Cars Per 100 Households	5.2.04	Number of Doctors Per 1,000 Persons
5.1.05	Area of New Public Housing	5.1.14	Residents' Perception of Happiness (Survey)	5.2.05	Number of Beds of Health Care Per 1,000 Population
5.1.06	Implementation Rate of Monetary Housing: Benefits	5.1.15	Poverty Population (%)	5.2.06	Average Life Expectancy
5.1.07	Satisfaction of Housing Conditions (Survey)	5.1.16	Satisfaction of Income Disparity (Survey)	5.2.07	Satisfaction of Public Health Care Services (Survey)
5.1.08	Proportion of the Population Above 65 Years Old	5.1.17	Public Expenditures on Social Security and Employment	5.2.08	Cleanliness of Public Toilet (Survey)
5.1.09	Minimum Subsistence Levels				

5. Ideal Indicators of Public Service Standards and Quality of Life Improvement (50 Indicators)							
5.3	**Public Education**	**5.3**	**Public Education**	**5.4**	**Public Transport Infrastructure**	**5.5**	**Public Culture and Information Services**
5.3.01	Annual Average Education Expenses by Family	5.3.09	Number of Tertiary Education Attendees Per 10,000 Population	5.4.01	Intensity of Urban Public Transport Per km	5.5.01	Number of Theatres Per 1 Million Population

(*Continued*)

(*Continued*)

5. Ideal Indicators of Public Service Standards and Quality of Life Improvement (50 Indicators)							
5.3.02	Proportions of Students in Primary and Secondary Schools to Total Population	5.3.10	Satisfaction of Public Education System (Survey)	5.4.02	Number of Urban Public Transport Vehicles Per 10,000 Population (Standard Number)	5.5.02	Number of Public Libraries Per 100 Population
5.3.03	Ratio of Public Education Appropriation to GRDP			5.4.03	Number of Urban Taxis Per 10,000 Population	5.5.03	Percentage of Public Expenditure on Cultural Initiatives
5.3.04	Public Education Appropriation Per Capita			5.4.04	Number of Passengers Transported	5.5.04	Number of Books in Public Library Per Capita
5.3.05	Number of Primary and Secondary Schools Per 10,000 Population			5.4.05	Per Capita Road Area	5.5.05	Frequency of Using the Internet for Daily Convenience (Survey)
5.3.06	Ratio of Teacher to Student in Primary and Secondary Schools			5.4.06	Satisfaction of Traffic Condition (Survey)	5.5.06	Number of Museums Per 10,000 Population
5.3.07	Number of Vocational Education Institutions Per 10,000 Population			5.4.07	Satisfaction of Public Transport Services (Survey)	5.5.07	Mobile Phone Penetration Rate
5.3.08	Average Years of Education					5.5.08	Internet Penetration Rate

6. Ideal Indicators of Resource Conditions and Environmental Protection (34 Indicators)					
6.1	**Environmental Quality**	**6.2**	**Natural Resources**	**6.3**	**Environmental Management**
6.1.01	Satisfaction of Air Quality (Survey)	6.2.01	Energy Consumption Elasticity Coefficient	6.3.01	Number of Green / Energy-Saving Buildings
6.1.02	Soil Heavy Metal Content	6.2.02	Annual Residential Energy Consumption Per Capita	6.3.02	Treatment Rate of Industrial Waste Water
6.1.03	Percentage of Days with Air Quality Index Being 100 or Less	6.2.03	Domestic Water Consumption Per Capita	6.3.03	Satisfaction of Environmental Governance (Survey)

(*Continued*)

(*Continued*)

6. Ideal Indicators of Resource Conditions and Environmental Protection (34 Indicators)					
6.1.04	Percentage of Surface Water Kith Category 3 Quality and Above	6.2.04	Electricity Consumption Per Capita	6.3.04	Forest Land Growth
6.1.05	SO2 Emission Per RMB 10,000 GRDP	6.2.05	Energy Consumption Per RMB 10,000 GRDP	6.3.05	Environmental Expenditure as a Percentage of Total Fiscal Expenditure
6.1.06	COD (Chemical Oxygen Demand) Per RMB 10,000 GRDP	6.2.06	Water Consumption Per RMB 10,000 GRDP	6.3.06	Residential Disposal Hazard-Free Treatment Rate
6.1.07	Ammoniacal Nitrogen Discharge Per RMB 10,000 GRDP	6.2.07	Electricity Consumption Per RMB 10,000 GRDP	6.3.07	Green Coverage Ratio of Built-up Area
6.1.08	NO-X Emissions Per RMB 10,000 GRDP	6.2.08	Energy Consumption Per RMB 10,000 Output from Industries Above Designated Size	6.3.08	Wetland Cover
6.1.09	Greenhouse Gases Emissions Per RMB 10,000 GRDP	6.2.09	Forest Cover	6.3.09	Urban Area Waste Water Treatment Rate
		6.2.10	Built-up Area Population Density	6.310	Per Capita Park and Green Space Acreage
		6.2.11	Per Capita Arable Land	6.3.11	Area of Natural Reserves to Administrative Area (%)
		6.2.12	Per Capita Freshwater Resource		
		6.2.13	Share of Renewable Energy from Gross Energy Consumption		
		6.2.14	Share of Electricity from Renewable Sources in Gross Electricity Consumption		

Appendix B
List of Practical Indicators for the Urban Composite Development Index

1. Practical Indicators of Scale and Quality of Economic Activities (21 Indicators)							
1.1	**Economic Capacity**	**1.2**	**Openness to Trade and Services**	**1.3**	**Inflationary Pressure**	**1.4**	**Market Development**
1.1.01	Gross Regional Domestic Product (GRDP)	1.2.01	Total Trade Volumes	1.3.01	Consumer Price Index (CPI)	1.4.01	Government Expenditures as a Percentage of GRDP
1.1.02	GRDP Growth Rate	1.2.02	Trade Surplus	1.3.02	Producer Price Index (PPI)	1.4.02	Satisfaction of Business Environment (Survey)
1.1.03	GRDP Per Capita	1.2.03	Dependency on Foreign Trade (Foreign Trade as a Share of GRDP)	1.3.03	Retail Price Index		
1.1.04	Per Capita Fixed Investment	1.2.04	Foreign Investment in Actual Use	1.3.04	Urban Residents' Disposable Income Growth Rate		
1.1.05	Per Capita Volume of Retail Sales	1.2.05	Investment Abroad	1.3.05	Urban Residents' Per Capita Expenditure Growth Rate		
1.1.06	Manufacturing Sector as a Percentage of GRDP			1.3.06	Residents' Satisfaction with Price Levels (Survey)		
1.1.07	Service Sector as a Percentage of GRDP						
1.1.08	Urbanisation Rate (%)						

2. Practical Indicators of Financial Capacity, Labour Market Flexibility and Economic Vibrancy (26 Indicators)							
2.1	**Financial Deepening and Business Efficiency**	**2.2**	**Productivity Performance**	**2.3**	**Labour Market Flexibility**	**2.4**	**Economic Vibrancy and Tripartite Relationship (Government, Employee and Employer)**
2.1.01	Financial Sector Value-Added	2.2.01	Secondary Industry Total Labour Productivity	2.3.01	Number of Employees	2.4.01	Growth in Electricity Consumption
2.1.02	Deposit Balance Per Capita	2.2.02	Tertiary Industry Total Labour Productivity	2.3.02	Newly Increased Number of Employee	2.4.02	Growth in the Number of Passengers Transported
2.1.03	Loan Balance Per Capita	2.2.03	Growth Rate of Overall Labour Productivity	2.3.03	Rate of Migration Flow	2.4.03	Growth in the Volumes of Cargo Transported
2.1.04	Annual Loan Growth Rate	2.2.04	Percentage of the Employed Population with Tertiary Education	2.3.04	Workforce Participation Rate		
2.1.05	Insurance Net Income	2.2.05	Profit Margin of Enterprises Above Designated Size	2.3.05	Urban Registered Unemployment Rate		
2.1.06	Deepness of Insurance (Insurance Income as a Share of GRDP)			2.3.06	Average Salary of Urban Employees		
2.1.07	Financed Amount in Stock Market			2.3.07	Self-Employed as a Share of Total Employment		
				2.3.08	Proportion of Workforce Employed in Agriculture Sector		
				2.3.09	Proportion of Workforce Employed in Service Sector		
				2.3.10	Proportion of Urban Workers Employed in State Enterprises		
				2.3.11	Proportion of Urban Workers Employed in Private Enterprises		

3. Practical Indicators of Good Governance, Effective Leadership and Social Stability (23 Indicators)							
3.1	**Fiscal Sustainability**	**3.2**	**Transparency and Accountability**	**3.3**	**Public Governance**	**3.4**	**Public Security and Social Stability**
3.1.01	Government Fiscal Revenue	3.2.01	Number of Releases of Government Information for Public Viewing	3.3.01	Index for Quality of E-Government System (Survey)	3.4.01	Public Perception of Security (Survey)
3.1.02	Government Fiscal Revenue Per Capita	3.2.02	Number of Responses to Government Issues of Public Interest	3.3.02	Number of Public Servants Per 10,000 Population	3.4.02	Growth Rate of the Number of Police Cases
3.1.03	Government Fiscal Expenditure	3.2.03	Public Perception of Government Conduct (Survey)	3.3.03	Average Public Servant Salary	3.4.03	Growth Rate of the Number of Police Cases Solved
3.1.04	Government Fiscal Expenditure Per Capita	3.2.04	Satisfaction of the Just of Judiciary	3.3.04	Number of Listed Items Under Executive Authority of the Government	3.4,04	Fire Fatality Per 10,000 Population
3.1.05	Tax Revenue as a Share of Fiscal Revenue	3.2.05	Number of Investigations for Power Abuses Per 10,000 Population	3.3.05	Number of Administration Action and Reconsideration Cases	3.4.05	Traffic Accident Fatality Per 10,000 Population
3.1.06	Fiscal Revenue Growth Rate					3.4.06	Satisfaction with Urban Management Personnel (Survey)
						3.4.07	Satisfaction of Police Services (Survey)

4. Practical Indicators of Technological Advancement and Innovation Capability (11 Indicators)					
4.1	**Research and Development Input**	**4.2**	**Technological Innovation Capability**	**4.3**	**Research and Development Output**
4.1.01	Research & Development Expenditure as a Share of Government Expenditure	4.2.01	Number of Provincial-Level Science Parks	4.3.01	Number of Patents Granted
4.1.02	Per Capita R&D Expenditure	4.2.02	Number of R&D Personnel Per 10,000 Population	4.3.02	Number of Existing Patents Per 10,000 Population
4.1.03	Total R&D Man-Hour	4.2.03	Satisfaction with Innovation Environment (Survey)		

(Continued)

(*Continued*)

4. Practical Indicators of Technological Advancement and Innovation Capability (11 Indicators)					
4.1.04	Number of Science and Technology Personnel				
4.1.05	Total R&D Expenditure of Enterprises Above Designated Size				
4.1.06	Total R&D Expenditure of Enterprises Above Designated Size as a Percentage of Cash Flow				

5. Practical Indicators of Public Service Standards and Quality of Life Improvement (33 Indicators)									
5.1	**Social Security and Standard of Living**	**5.2**	**Public Health Care System**	**5.3**	**Public Education**	**5.4**	**Public Transport Infrastructure**	**5.5**	**Public Culture and Information Services**
5.1.01	Proportion of the Population Above 60 Years Old	5.2.01	Public Health and Medical Service Expenses as a Share of GRDP	5.3.01	Ratio of Public Education Appropriation to GRDP	5.4.01	Number of Urban Public Transport Vehicles Per 10,000 Population (Standard Number)	5.5.01	Percentage of Public Expenditure on Cultural Initiatives
5.1.02	Per Capita Annual Disposable Income	5.2.02	Public Health and Medical Service Expenses Per Capita	5.3.02	Public Education Appropriation Per Capita	5.4.02	Number of Urban Taxis Per 10,000 Population	5.5.02	Number of Books in Public Library Per Capita
5.1.03	Engel's Index	5.2.03	Number of Doctors Per 1,000 Persons	5.3.03	Number of Primary and Secondary Schools Per 10,000 Population	5.4.03	Number of Passengers Transported	5.5.03	Frequency of Using the Internet for Daily Convenience (Survey)
5.1.04	Number of Private Cars Per 100 Households	5.2.04	Number of Beds of Health Care Per 1,000 Population	5.3.04	Ratio of Teacher to Student in Primary and Secondary Schools	5.4.04	Per Capita Road Area	5.5.04	Number of Museums Per 10,000 Population
5.1.05	Residents' Perception of Happiness (Survey)	5.2.05	Average Life Expectancy	5.3.05	Number of Vocational Education Institutions Per 10,000 Population	5.4.05	Satisfaction of Traffic Condition (Survey)	5.5.05	Mobile Phone Penetration Rate
5.1.06	Satisfaction of Income Disparity (Survey)	5.2.06	Satisfaction of Public Health Care Services (Survey)	5.3.06	Average Years of Education Received	5.4.06	Satisfaction of Pubic Transport Services (Survey)	5.5.06	Internet Penetration Rate

(*Continued*)

(*Continued*)

5. Practical Indicators of Public Service Standards and Quality of Life Improvement (33 Indicators)									
		5.2.07	Cleanliness of Public Toilet (Survey)	5.3.07	Number of Tertiary Education Attendees Per 10,000 Population				
				5.3.08	Satisfaction of Public Education System (Survey)				

6. Practical Indicators of Resource Conditions and Environmental Protection (17 Indicators)					
6.1	**Environmental Quality**	**6.2**	**Natural Resources**	**6.3**	**Environmental Management**
6.1.01	SO2 Emission Per RMB 10,000 GRDP	6.2.01	Water Consumption Per RMB 10,000 GRDP	6.3.01	Forest Land Growth
6.1.02	COD (Chemical Oxygen Demand) Per RMB 10,000 GRDP	6.2.02	Electricity Consumption Per RMB 10,000 GRDP	6.3.02	Environmental Expenditure as a Percentage of Total Fiscal Expenditure
6.1.03	Ammoniacal Nitrogen Discharge Per RMB 10,000 GRDP	6.2.03	Forest Cover	6.3.03	Green Coverage Ratio of Built-up Area
6.1.04	NO-X Emissions Per RMB 10,000 GRDP	6.2.04	Built-up Area Population Density	6.3.04	Wetland Cover
		6.2.05	Per Capita Arable Land	6.3.05	Urban Area Waste Water Treatment Rate
		6.2.06	Per Capita Freshwater Resource	6.3.06	Per Capita Park and Green Space Acreage
				6.3.07	Area of Natural Reserves to Administrative Area (%)

Appendix C

Telephone Survey on "Urban Composite Development Index for 17 Shandong Cities: Ranking and Simulation Analysis Based on China's Five Development Concepts"

关于"山东 17 个城市城市综合发展指数：根据中国五大发展理念的排名和模拟分析"的电话调查

开始语：您好!我们正在进行一项山东省民生服务满意度调查，您的意见对提高当地政府的服务质量意义重大，我们将对您的回答严格保密，非常感谢您的配合。

Preamble: Hello! We are conducting a survey on the satisfaction of people's livelihood in Shandong Province. Your comments are extremely important to help us improve the quality of service of the local government. Please be assured that we will keep your answers strictly confidential. Thank you very much for your cooperation and participation.

开始语备注：本次调查共 17 个问题，大约需要耽误您 5–8 分钟的时间。

Preamble: There are 17 questions in this survey, which will require approximately 5 to 8 minutes of your time to complete.

配额已满结束语：非常抱歉，您的条件不在我们的调查范围之内，感谢您的参与，祝您生活愉快！

Closing Statement (when the quota is reached): Unfortunately, your details do not fulfil our survey criteria. We extend our sincerest apologies and thank you for your participation. Have a good day!

第一部分 背景信息
Part 1 Background Information

P1. 被访者的性别________（不读出，由访问员判断）：

P1. Respondent's gender (Judged by the interviewer)

1. 男　　2. 女
1. Male　　2. Female

P2. 您的周岁年龄是：__________若为 **18** 岁以下则判定不符合调查条件，跳至不符 合条件 **1** 结束语（非常抱歉，您的年龄不在我们的调查范围之内，感谢您的参与，祝您生活愉快！）

P2. What is your age? If the response is below 18 years old, then the respondent does not meet the survey criteria. Respond with the closing statement.

1. 18 周岁以下（终止访问）
1. Under 18 years old (terminate interview)

2. 18–29 周岁
2. 18–29 years old

3. 30–39 周岁
3. 30–39 years old

4. 40–49 周岁
4. 40–49 years old

5. 50–59 周岁
5. 50–59 years old

6. 60 周岁以上（样本量控制在 10-17% 左右）
6. Above 60 years old (control the sample size at 10-17%)

P3. 您现在居住在哪个城市？

P3. Which city do you currently live in?

1. 济南 2. 青岛 3. 淄博 4. 枣庄 5. 东营
6. 烟台 7. 潍坊 8. 济宁 9. 泰安 10. 威海
11. 日照 12. 莱芜 13. 临沂 14. 德州 15. 聊城
16. 滨州 17. 菏泽

1. Jinan 2. Qingdao 3. Zibo 4. Zaozhuang 5. Dongying
6. Yantai 7. Weifang 8. Jining 9. Tai'an 10. Weihai
11. Rizhao 12. Laiwu 13. Linyi 14. Dezhou 15. Liaocheng
16. Binzhou 17. Heze

P3-1:（针对济南市）您居住在济南市的哪个区县？

P3-1: (For Jinan) Which district or county of **Jinan** do you live in?

1. 市中区 2. 历下区 3. 天桥区 4. 槐荫区 5. 历城区
6. 长清区 7. 章丘市 8. 平阴县 9. 济阳县 10. 商河县
11. 高新区

1. Shizhong District 2. Lixia District 3. Tianqiao District
4. Huaiyin District 5. Licheng District 6. Changqing District
7. Zhangqiu District 8. Pingyin County 9. Jiyang County
10. Shanghe County 11. High-tech Industrial Development Zone

P3-2:（针对青岛市）您居住在青岛市的哪个区县？

P3-2: (For Qingdao) Which district or county of **Qingdao** do you live in?

1. 市南区 2. 市北区 3. 城阳区 4. 李沧区 5. 黄岛区
6. 崂山区 7. 胶州市 8. 平度市 9. 莱西市 10. 即墨市

1. Shinan District 2. Shibei District 3. Chengyang District
4. Licang District 5. Huangdao District 6. Laoshao District
7. Jiaozhou City 8. Pingdu City 9. Laixi City
10. Jimo District

P3-3:（针对淄博市）您居住在淄博市的哪个区县？

P3-3: (For Zibo) Which district or county of **Zibo** do you live in?

1. 张店区 2. 临淄区 3. 淄川区 4. 博山区 5. 周村区
6. 桓台县 7. 高青县 8. 沂源县

1. Zhangdian District 2. Linzi District 3. Zichuan District
4. Boshan District 5. Zhoucun District 6. Huantai District
7. Gaoqing District 8. Yiyuan District

P3-4:（针对枣庄市）您居住在枣庄市的哪个区县？

P3-4: (For Zaozhuang) Which district or county of **Zaozhuang** do you live in?

1. 市中区 2. 山亭区 3. 峄城区 4. 台儿庄区 5. 薛城区
6. 滕州市

1. Shizhong District 2. Shanting District 3. Yicheng District
4. Taierzhuang District 5. Xuecheng District 6. Tengzhou City

P3-5:（针对东营市）您居住在东营市的哪个区县？

P3-5: (For Dongying) Which district or county of **Dongying** do you live in?

1. 东营区 2. 河口区 3. 垦利县 4. 广饶县 5. 利津县
6. 经济开发区

1. Dongying District 2. Hekou District 3. Kenli County
4. Guangrao County 5. Lijin County 6. Economic Development Zone

P3-6:（针对烟台市）您居住在烟台市的哪个区县？

P3-6: (For Yantai) Which district or c county of **Yantai** do you live in?

1. 芝罘区 2. 福山区 3. 牟平区 4. 莱山区 5. 龙口市
6. 莱阳市 7. 莱州市 8. 招远市 9. 蓬莱市 10. 栖霞市
11. 海阳市 12. 长岛县 13. 经济开发区 14. 高新区

1. Zhifu District 2. Hanting District 3. Muping District
4. Laishan District 5. Longkou District 6. Laiyang District
7. Laizhou District 8. Zhaoyuan City 9. Penglai City
10. Qixia City 11. Haiyang City 12. Changdao County
13. Economic Development Zone 14. High-tech Industrial Development Zone

P3-7:（针对潍坊市）您居住在潍坊市的哪个区县？

P3-7: (For Weifang) Which district or county of **Weifang** do you live in?

1. 潍城区 2. 寒亭区 3. 坊子区 4. 奎文区 5. 青州市
6. 诸城市 7. 寿光市 8. 安丘市 9. 高密市 10. 昌邑市
11. 昌乐县 12. 临朐县 13. 经济开发区

1. Weicheng District 2. Hanting District 3. Fangzi District
4. Kuiwen District 5. Qingzhou City 6. Zhucheng City
7. Shouguang City 8. Anqiu City 9. Gaomi City
10. Changyi City 11. Changle County 12. Linqu County
13. Economic Development Zone

P3-8:（针对济宁市）您居住在济宁市的哪个区县？

P3-8: (For Jining)Which district or county of **Jining** do you live in?

1. 任城区 2. 曲阜市 3. 兖州市 4. 邹城市 5. 鱼台县
6. 金乡县 7. 嘉祥县 8. 微山县 9. 汶上县 10. 泗水县
11. 梁山县 12. 高新区

1. Rencheng County　2. Qufu City　3. Yanzhou District
4. Zoucheng City　5. Yutai County　6. Jinxiang County
7. Jiaxiang County　8. Weishan County　9. Wenshang County
10. Sishui County　11. Liangshan County
12. High-tech Industrial Development Zone

P3-9:（针对泰安市）您居住在泰安市的哪个区县？

P3-9: (For Tai'an) Which district or county of **Tai'an** do you live in?

1. 泰山区　2. 岱岳区　3. 新泰市　4. 肥城市　5. 宁阳县
6. 东平县　7. 高新区

1. Taishan District　2. Daiyue District　3. Xintai City
4. Feicheng City　5. Ningyang County　6. Dongping County
7. High-tech Industrial Development Zone

P3-10:（针对威海市）您居住在威海市的哪个区县？

P3-10: (For Weihai) Which district or county of **Weihai** do you live in?

1. 环翠区　2. 乳山市　3. 文登市　4. 荣成市　5. 高新区

1. Huaicui District　2. Rushan District　3. Wendeng District
4. Rongcheng City　5. High-tech Industrial Development Zone

P3-11:（针对日照市）您居住在日照市的哪个区县？

P3-11: (For Rizhao) Which district or county of Rizhao do you live in?

1. 东港区　2. 岚山区　3. 五莲县　4. 莒县　5. 经济开发区

1. Donggang District　2. Lanshan District　3. Wulian County
4. Ju County　5. Economic Development Zone

P3-12:（针对莱芜市）您居住在莱芜市的哪个区县？

P3-12: (For Laiwu) Which district or county of Laiwu do you live in?

1. 莱城区　2. 钢城区　3. 农业高新区

1. Laicheng District　2. Gangcheng District　3. Agricultural High-tech Zone

P3-13：（针对临沂市）您居住在临沂市的哪个区县？

P3-13: (For Linyi) Which district or county of Linyi do you live in?

1. 兰山区	2. 罗庄区	3. 河东区	4. 沂南县	5. 郯城县
6. 沂水县	7. 费县	8. 平邑县	9. 莒南县	10. 蒙阴县
11. 兰陵县	12. 临沭县	13. 经济开发区		14. 高新区

1. Lanshan District	2. Luozhuang District	3. Hedong District
4. Yinan County	5. Tancheng County	6. Yishui County
7. Fei County	8. Pingyi County	9. Junan County
10. Mengyin County	11. Lanling County	12. Linshu County
13. Economic Development Zone	14. High-tech Industrial Development Zone	

P3-14：（针对德州市）您居住在德州市的哪个区县？

P3-14: (For Dezhou) Which district or county of Dezhou do you live in?

1. 德城区	2. 乐陵市	3. 禹城市	4. 陵城区	5. 宁津县
6. 齐河县	7. 武城县	8. 庆云县	9. 平原县	10. 夏津县
11. 临邑县	12. 经济开发区			

1. Decheng District	2. Laoling City	3. Yucheng City
4. Lingcheng District	5. Ningjin County	6. Qihe County
7. Wucheng County	8. Qingyun County	9. Pingyuan County
10. Xiajin County	11. Linyi County	
12. Economic Development Zone		

P3-15：（针对聊城市）您居住在聊城市的哪个区县？

P3-15: (For Liaocheng) Which district or county of Liaocheng do you live in?

1. 东昌府区	2. 临清市	3. 高唐县	4. 阳谷县	5. 茌平县
6. 莘县	7. 东阿县	8. 冠县	9. 经济开发区	10. 高新区

1. Dongchangfu District	2. Linqing City	3. Gaotang County
4. Yanggu County	5. Chiping County	6. Shen County
7. Dong'e County	8. Guan County	9. Economic Development Zone
10. High-tech Industrial Development Zone		

P3-16：（针对滨州市）您居住在滨州市的哪个区县？

P3-16: (For Binzhou) Which district or county of Binzhou do you live in?

1. 滨城区　2. 邹平县　3. 沾化县　4. 惠民县　5. 博兴县
6. 阳信县　7. 无棣县　8. 经济开发区

1. Bincheng District　2. Zouping County　3. Zhanhua County
4. Huimin County　5. Boxing County　6. Yangxin County
7. Wudi County　8. Economic Development Zone

P3-17：（针对菏泽市）您居住在菏泽市的哪个区县？

P3-17: (For Heze) Which district or county of Heze do you live in?

1. 牡丹区　2. 鄄城县　3. 单县　4. 郓城县　5. 曹县
6. 定陶县　7. 巨野县　8. 东明县　9. 成武县　10. 经济开发区

1. Mudan District　2. Juancheng County　3. Shan County
4. Yuncheng County　5. Cao County　6. Dingtao County
7. Juye County　8. Dongming County　9. Chengwu County
10. Economic Development Zone

P4. 请问您是否在本市已经居住六个月以上？________若非本地常住居民则判定不符合调查条件，跳至不符合条件 2 结束语（非常抱歉，您不在我们的调查范围之内，非常感谢您的参与，祝您生活愉快！）

P4. Have you resided in this city for more than six months? If the response is no, then the respondent does not meet the survey criteria. Respond with the closing statement.

1. 是　2. 否（终止访问）
1. Yes　2. No (terminate interview)

P5. 您是城市居民还是农村居民？________

P5. Are you urban resident or rural resident?

1. 城市居民　2. 农村居民
1. Urban resident　2. Rural resident

第二部分 满意度评价

Part 2 Satisfaction Rating

请您根据自己的切身感受，对本地区民生服务的满意情况进行打分，最低分为1分，最高分为 10 分，所有回答都无对错之分, 请您无需顾虑。

Please rate your satisfaction with the livelihood services based on your personal feelings on a scale of 1 to 10, with 1 being the lowest score and 10 being the highest score. There is no right or wrong answer, please do not worry.

增加拒答选项。此部分不清楚或拒答超过三个，问卷作废，以不符合条件处理。

Include the option: “decline to respond”. If there are more than 3 responses marked with either “refuse to respond “or “not clear”, then the survey response is considered invalid and does not meet the survey criteria.

A1. 您对本地日常生活中的消费品，如柴、米、油、衣等的价格满意吗？

A1. How satisfied are you with the price of daily consumables, e.g. food and clothes?

1	2	3	4	5	6	7	8	9	10

A2a. 您正在做生意或者将来打算做生意吗？

A2a. Do you currently have or planning to start a business?

1. 是　　2. 否（跳答题 A3）
1. Yes　　2. No (Jump to A3)

A2b. 您对当地的经商创业环境满意吗？（若被访者对经商创业环境有疑问，可告知：比如证件审批、信贷、税收、合同执行、投资者保护等方面的营商环境）

A2b. How satisfied are you with the business environment? (If asked, the business environment includes elements such as the certificate of approval, bank credit, government tax, contract execution and investor protection, etc.)

1	2	3	4	5	6	7	8	9	10

A3. 您对当地政府的廉政建设和反腐败的效果满意吗？

A3. How satisfied are you with the government conduct?

1	2	3	4	5	6	7	8	9	10

A4. 您对当地司法机关的公正情况满意吗？

A4. Are you satisfied with the just of judiciary?

1	2	3	4	5	6	7	8	9	10

A5a. 您在本市政务服务网上办过业务吗？（比如上网咨询、在线投诉、支付费用、办理证件申请、项目许可等）

A5a. Have you used a government e-service system before? (For example, internet consulting, online complaints, e-payment, document application and project permission, etc.)

1. 是　2. 否（跳答题A6）
1. Yes　2. No (Jump to A6)

A5b. 您对本市政务服务网提供的服务满意吗？

A5b. How satisfied are you with the e-government system?

1	2	3	4	5	6	7	8	9	10

A6. 您对本地的社会治安状况满意吗？

A6. How satisfied are you with the current level of public security?

1	2	3	4	5	6	7	8	9	10

A7. 您对本地城管的执法服务质量满意吗？

A7. How satisfied are you with the urban management personnel?

1	2	3	4	5	6	7	8	9	10

A8. 您对本地公安民警的服务满意吗？

A8. How satisfied are you with the services provided by the police?

1	2	3	4	5	6	7	8	9	10

A9. 您对本地政府利用科技成果提高居民生活的便利程度满意吗？

A9. How satisfied are you with the government's efforts to improve the living environment by employing high-tech innovations?

1	2	3	4	5	6	7	8	9	10

A10. 您对本地医疗服务满意吗？（比如医疗收费、医疗水平、就医方便性、医务人员的服务态度等）

A10. How satisfied are you with the current level of public health care services? (For example, fee for health care, quality of health care, accessibility to health care, and service attitude in health care centres, etc.)

1	2	3	4	5	6	7	8	9	10

A11. 您对本地公共厕所的卫生状况满意吗？

A11. How satisfied are you with the hygiene standards in public toilets?

1	2	3	4	5	6	7	8	9	10

A12. 您对本地教育服务满意吗？（比如入学方便性、教育公平、教育收费、师资力量、教学设施等）

A12. How satisfied are you with the public education system? (For example, accessibility to public education, fairness in the public education system, costs of public education, faculty and teaching facilities, etc.)

1	2	3	4	5	6	7	8	9	10

A13. 您对本地的道路质量、交通堵塞程度等交通状况满意吗？

A13. How satisfied are you with traffic conditions (for example, the quality of roads and traffic congestion)?

1	2	3	4	5	6	7	8	9	10

A14. 您对本地公交车和出租车的价格、便利程度满意吗？

A14. How satisfied are you with public transportation services (for example, the price of taxi and buses, and the accessibility to public transport)?

1	2	3	4	5	6	7	8	9	10

A15-1.（只针对城市居民询问）您对通过网络获取生活信息的便利程度满意吗？ （如网络订餐、手机支付、滴滴打车等）

A15-1. (For Urban Residents) How satisfied are you with the acquisition of lifestyle information through the Internet? (For example, online food ordering, mobile phone payment and DiDi Taxi, etc.)

1	2	3	4	5	6	7	8	9	10

A15-2.（只针对农村居民询问）您对通过网络获取生活信息和生产资料信息的便利程度满意吗？（如网络订餐、手机支付、滴滴打车等）

A15-2. (For Rural Residents) How satisfied are you with the acquisition of lifestyle and production information through the Internet? (For example, online food ordering, mobile phone payment and DiDi Taxi, etc.)

1	2	3	4	5	6	7	8	9	10

A16. 您对本地城乡居民收入差距的公平性满意吗？（如最低生活保障水平、工资增长频率与幅度等）

A16. How satisfied are you with the current level of income inequality? (For example, minimum living standard, frequency and magnitude of salary adjustments, etc.)

1	2	3	4	5	6	7	8	9	10

A17. 假如一个人的幸福感最高为 **10** 分，您给自己打几分？

A17. On a scale of 1 to 10 (where 1 is the least), how happy are you?

1	2	3	4	5	6	7	8	9	10

第三部分 个人信息

Part 3 Personal Information

最后，我们想简单问一些您个人的情况。
Lastly, we would like to ask you for some personal information.

P6. 您现在的文化程度是：________

P6. What is your current education level?

1. 小学及以下　2. 初中　3. 高中（含中专）　4. 大学（含专科）
5. 研究生及以上　6. 文盲　7. 拒答

1. Primary School and below
2. Secondary School
3. High School (including Specialised Secondary School)
4. University (Including Diploma)
5. Masters and above
6. Illiterate
7. Refuse to respond

P7. 您的职业是：________

P7. What is your current occupation?

1. 在校大学生
1. Undergraduate Student

2. 企业/公司职工
2. Enterprise/Corporate employee

3. 党政机关/事业单位/国企/央企工作人员
3. Party and government organisation/Institution/State-Owned-Enterprise/Central enterprise employee

4. 专业技术人员，如医生、律师、教师、科研人员
4. Professional, i.e. Doctor, Lawyer, Scientific Researcher

5. 个体商户经营者
5. Individual Business Operator

6. 离退休人员
6. Retiree

7. 家庭主妇
7. Housewife

8. 自由职业者
8. Freelancer

9. 现役军人
9. Active soldier

10. 其它（请注明：______________________________________）
10. Others (Please specify:)

结束语：我们的调查到此结束。再次感谢您的支持和配合，谢谢您的积极参与！祝您生活愉快！

Concluding Remarks: Our survey ends here. Thank you once again for your support and cooperation. We are very grateful for your active participation! Have a nice day!

Appendix D
Algorithm for the Computation of Rankings

D.1 Equal Weight Method

The computation procedure to produce the UCDI is described below for a general case of N cities, M practical indicators and C environments, with each environment comprising S sub-environments.

(1) Compute the mean value of practical indicator j ($j = 1, \dots, M$),

$$\bar{X}_j = \frac{1}{N}\sum_{i=1}^{N} X_{ij},$$

where X_{ij} represents the value that city i ($i = 1, \dots, N$) takes for practical indicator j.

(2) For each practical indicator j ($j = 1, \dots, M$), calculate its standard deviation (SD),

$$SD_j = \sqrt{\frac{1}{N}\sum_{i=1}^{N}\left(X_{ij} - \bar{X}_j\right)^2}.$$

(3) Compute the standardised value of indicator (SVI) that each city i ($i = 1, \dots, N$) takes under each of the practical indicators j ($j = 1, \dots, M$),

$$SVI_{ij} = \frac{X_{ij} - \bar{X}_j}{SD_j}.$$

(4) Compute the "ranked" standardised value of indicator (RSVI) that each city i ($i = 1, \dots, N$) takes under each of the practical indicators j ($j = 1, \dots, M$):

$$RSVI_{ij} = \begin{cases} SVI_{ij}, & \textit{if a higher value is better} \\ -SVI_{ij}, & \textit{if a lower value is better.} \end{cases}$$

(5) For each of the practical indicators j ($j = 1, \dots, M$), a ranking can be obtained for cities: cities with a higher value of RSVI for indicator j are ranked ahead of those with a lower value.

(6) For each city i ($i = 1, \dots, N$), calculate the RSVI for each sub-environment k ($k = 1, \dots, S$) belonging to environment l ($l = 1, \dots, C$),

$$Raw\_RSVI_{i,lk} = \frac{1}{y_{lk}}\sum_{p=1}^{y_{lk}} RSVI_{i,j_{lk,p}},$$

$$Mean\_RSVI_{lk} = \frac{1}{N}\sum_{i=1}^{N} Raw\_RSVI_{i,lk},$$

$$SD\_RSVI_{lk} = \sqrt{\frac{1}{N}\sum_{i=1}^{N}\left(Raw\_RSVI_{i,lk} - Mean\_RSVI_{lk}\right)^2},$$

$$RSVI_{i,lk} = \frac{Raw\_RSVI_{i,lk} - Mean\_RSVI_{lk}}{SD\_RSVI_{lk}},$$

where y_{lk} is the total number of practical indicators under sub-environment k of environment l and $(RSVI_{i,j_{lk,1}}, \ldots, RSVI_{i,j_{lk,y_{lk}}})$ are the RSVIs for city i that make up sub-environment k of environment l.

(7) For each city i ($i = 1, \ldots, N$), calculate the RSVI for each environment l ($l = 1, \ldots, C$),

$$Raw\_RSVI_{i,l} = \frac{1}{S_l}\sum_{k=1}^{S_l} RSVI_{i,lk},$$

$$Mean\_RSVI_{l} = \frac{1}{N}\sum_{i=1}^{N} Raw\_RSVI_{i,l},$$

$$SD\_RSVI_{l} = \sqrt{\frac{1}{N}\sum_{i=1}^{N}\left(Raw\_RSVI_{i,l} - Mean\_RSVI_{l}\right)^2},$$

$$RSVI_{i,l} = \frac{Raw\_RSVI_{i,l} - Mean\_RSVI_{l}}{SD\_RSVI_{l}},$$

where $(RSVI_{i,l1}, \ldots, RSVI_{i,ls})$ are the RSVIs for the S sub-environments under each environment l.

(8) Overall rank score of city i ($i = 1, \ldots, N$),

$$Raw\_R_i = \frac{1}{C}\sum_{l=1}^{C} RSVI_{i,l},$$

$$Mean\_R = \frac{1}{N}\sum_{i=1}^{N} Raw\_R_i,$$

$$SD\_R = \sqrt{\frac{1}{N}\sum_{i=1}^{N}\left(Raw\_R_i - Mean\_R\right)^2},$$

$$R_i = \frac{Raw\_R_i - Mean\_R}{SD\_R}.$$

A city with a higher R_i is ranked ahead of one with a lower value of R_i, and the city with the highest R_i is the most liveable city.

Step 5 of the ranking algorithm provides the ranking of each city for each individual practical indicator. To achieve this ranking, Step 4 of the ranking algorithm adjusts the value of the SVIs so that a lower value will lead to a better ranking in terms of urban development. Depending on the nature of the indicator in question, a higher or lower value may reflect a more developed city. Take, for instance, the practical indicators "1.1.01 Gross Regional Domestic Product (GRDP)" and "1.3.01 Consumer Price Index (CPI)". A higher "GRDP" but a lower "CPI" suggest better economic performance. In most cases, a higher value is better (e.g., GRDP). However, for indicators where the inverse is true (e.g., CPI), the SVI itself is compared between cities and a lower SVI value will lead to a better ranking. Step 4 of the ranking algorithm thus seeks to make all standardised values of all practical indicators consistent for ranking purposes.

Step 6 of the ranking algorithm determines the sub-environment rankings of each city. The average RSVI of all the indicators in the sub-environment are calculated and compared to other cities. Cities with a higher average RSVI rank better in the sub-environment. To arrive at the city ranking for each environment, the RSVIs of the sub-environments are aggregated as detailed by Step 7 of the ranking algorithm.

Finally, Step 8 of the ranking algorithm requires the RSVI values of each environment to be totalled to determine the overall ranking of the city. Although the number of sub-environments and indicators varies for each environment, the aggregate score for each main environment is given an equivalent weighting — approximately 16.7% of the UCDI. Identical weights are assigned to each environment as they represent equivalent significance to the computation of the UCDI. This method is repeated and applied consistently across all the cities to ensure precision of the rankings.

D.2 Shapley Weight Method

We will present the "Bottom-Up" approach in this appendix. We start with indicator-level computation, then sub-environment- and environment-level computation, and finally the index construction.

D.2.1 Indicator Level

For each indicator $i \in I$ and each economy $e \in E$, the standardised value (or z-score) is

$$SV_{ei} = \frac{X_{ei} - \overline{X_I}}{SD_i}, \tag{1}$$

where X_{ei} is the data input for economy e in indicator i, $\overline{X_I} = \frac{1}{E}\Sigma_{e=1}^{E} X_{ei}$ is the mean value of the indicator i, and $SD_i = \sqrt{\frac{1}{E}\Sigma_{e=1}^{E}(X_{ei} - \overline{X_i})^2}$ is the standard deviation of the indicator i.

Now, let v^I be the characteristic function of the indicators, where v^I: $2^I \to \mathbb{R}$. Then for each indicator $i \in I$, $v^I(i)$: $\mathbb{R}^E \to \mathbb{R}$, which reflects that the value of indicator i is derived from X_{ei} for all $e \in E$. As we involve large number of indicators in our case studies, for the ease of numerical computation, we simply define that

$$v^I(i) = \sum_{e=1}^{E} |SV_{ei}|. \tag{2}$$

The absolute value is used, as (1) it guarantees the positiveness of $v(i)$ which is required by the definition of Shapley value, and (2) the simple sum of the z-scores is zero, i.e., $\Sigma_{e=1}^{E} SV_{ei} = 0$.

We further assume the Additivity of the characteristic function v^I, i.e.,

$$v^I(i \cup j) = v^I(i) + v^I(j) \text{ for any indicator } i, j \in I. \tag{3}$$

With all these defined, we are able to proceed with the computation of the Shapley value Φ_i^I of indicator $i \in I$.

$$\Phi_i^I = \sum_{\mathbb{I} \subseteq I \setminus \{i\}} \frac{|\mathbb{I}|!\,(I - |\mathbb{I}| - 1)!}{I!} \left(v^I(\mathbb{I} \cup i) - v^I(\mathbb{I})\right) \quad \text{for all } i \in I \tag{4}$$

With the assumption Additivity, equation (4) can be simplified as

$$\Phi_i^I = \sum_{\mathbb{I} \subseteq I \setminus \{i\}} \frac{|\mathbb{I}|!\,(I - |\mathbb{I}| - 1)!}{I!} \left(v^I\left(\mathbb{I} \cup i\right) - v^I(\mathbb{I})\right)$$

$$= \sum_{\mathbb{I} \subseteq I \setminus \{i\}} \frac{|\mathbb{I}|!\,(I - |\mathbb{I}| - 1)!}{I!} v^I(i) = v^I(i)\,. \tag{4*}$$

Then the indicator weight w_i^I based on Shapley value is simply

$$w_i^I = \frac{\Phi_i^I}{\sum_{j=1}^{I} \Phi_j^I} = \frac{v^I(i)}{\sum_{j=1}^{I} v^I(j)}. \tag{5}$$

Economically, the Shapley value of each indicator i, Φ_i^I, measures the inequality among all the economies. The higher the Φ_i^I of an indicator i, the more divergent the performance across different economies. More weight, w_i^I, will thus be assigned to i. If a government has the aim of reducing inequality, it should implement policies to improve the indicators with more weight.

D.2.2 Sub-Environment Level and Environment Level

For each economy $e \in E$, the computed data of any sub-environment $s \in S$ is determined by the indicators comprised, i.e., I_s. Equation (5) has determined the weight of each indicator, and let $w_i^{I_s}$ be the weight of indicator $i \in I_s$. Thus, formally, the computed data of any sub-environment $s \in S$ for any economy $e \in E$ is

$$X_{es} = \sum_{i=1}^{I_s} w_i^{I_s} SV_{ei}. \tag{6}$$

Similar to the indicator-level analysis, we have the standardised score for sub-environment $s \in S$ as SV_{es}.

Let v^S: $2^S \rightarrow \mathbb{R}$ be the characteristic function for the sub-environments. Then for each sub-environment $s \in S$, $v^s(s)$: $\mathbb{R}^s \rightarrow \mathbb{R}$ represents that the value of sub-environment s is derived from X_{es} for all $e \in E$. We have

$$v^S(s) = \sum_{e=1}^{E} |SV_{es}|. \tag{7}$$

By the Additivity assumption, the Shapley value of each sub-environment $s \in S$ is

$$\Phi_s^S = v^S(s), \tag{8}$$

and the weight of each sub-environment is

$$w_s^S = \frac{\Phi_s^S}{\sum_{j=1}^{S} \Phi_j^S} = \frac{v^S(s)}{\sum_{j=1}^{S} v^S(j)}. \tag{9}$$

The construction of Shapley value and the weight associated with each environment is similar to the analysis above and thus is omitted. Let v^N: $2^N \rightarrow \mathbb{R}$ be the characteristic function for the environments. The Shapley value of each environment $n \in N$ is

$$\Phi_n^N = v^N(n), \tag{10}$$

and the weight of each environment is

$$w_n^N = \frac{\Phi_n^N}{\sum_{j=1}^{N} \Phi_j^N} = \frac{v^N(n)}{\sum_{j=1}^{N} v^N(j)}. \tag{11}$$

The economic interpretation of Φ_s^S and Φ_n^N are the same as that of the indicators. They capture the inequality across all the economies at sub-environment level and environment level respectively. The higher the weight w_s^S and w_n^N, the more divergent the performance across different economies. Thus, government attention should be drawn to such sub-environment and environment.

D.2.3 Index Construction

In order for us to construct the final index to rank all the economies, first, we find the final computed score for each economy $e \in E$, i.e.

$$F_e = \sum_{n=1}^{N} w_n^N SV_{en}, \tag{12}$$

where SV_{en} is the standardised value for economy e under environment n.

Then, we standardised the final computed score,

$$R_e = \frac{F_e - \bar{F}}{SD_F}, \tag{13}$$

where $\bar{F} = \frac{1}{E}\Sigma_{e=1}^{E} F_e$ and $SD_F = \sqrt{\frac{1}{E}\Sigma_{e=1}^{E}(F_e - \bar{F})^2}$.

All the economies, $e \in E$, will be ranked according to the value R_e, which is also the index score for each economy.